Springer Studies in the History of Economic Thought

This series offers an outlet for research in the history of economic thought. It features scholarly studies on important theoretical developments and great economic thinkers that have contributed to the evolution of the economic discipline.

Springer Studies in the History of Economic Thought (SSHET) welcomes proposals for research monographs, edited volumes, textbooks and handbooks from a variety of disciplines that seek to study the history of economic thinking and help to arrive at a better understanding of modern economics. Relevant topics include, but are not limited to, various schools of thought, important pioneers and thinkers, ancient and medieval economic thought, mercantilism, cameralism and physiocracy, classical and neoclassical economics, historical, institutional and evolutionary economics, socialism and Marxism, Keynesian, Sraffian and Austrian economics, econometrics and mathematical studies as well as economic methodology and the link between economic history and history of economic thought.

All titles in this series are peer-reviewed.

For further information on the series and to submit a proposal for consideration, please contact Johannes Glaeser (Executive Editor Economics) Johannes.glaeser@springer.com.

Jean-Pierre Potier

Léon Walras, Economist and Liberal Socialist

Essays

Springer

Jean-Pierre Potier
Lumière University Lyon 2
Lyon, France

ISSN 2662-6098 ISSN 2662-6101 (electronic)
Springer Studies in the History of Economic Thought
ISBN 978-3-032-04669-7 ISBN 978-3-032-04670-3 (eBook)
https://doi.org/10.1007/978-3-032-04670-3

Translation from the French language edition: "Léon Walras, économiste et socialiste libéral" by Jean-Pierre Potier, © author 2019. Published by Classiques Garnier. All Rights Reserved.

Originally published by Classiques Garnier

This Springer imprint is published by the registered company Springer Nature Switzerland AG
The registered company address is: Gewerbestrasse 11, 6330 Cham, Switzerland

Léon Walras in 1883 (B.C.U. Vaudoise. Manuscripts Department)

For Colette

Introduction

> I am an idealist. I believe that ideas transform the world into their image and that the ideals conceived by a man, by a school of thought, impose themselves on human affairs. I believe that the world has taken eighteen centuries to try—without success—to realise the ideals of Jesus and the first Apostles. I believe that the world will take another eighteen or perhaps twenty centuries to try, without better success, to realise the ideals conceived by the men of 89—ideals seen more clearly by us and clarified by our successors. Happy to think that I myself might have perhaps shed the slightest light on this picture [...]. (2000, vol. XIII, p. 551).

> [...] let us remain socialists, that is to say, progressivists; and become economists, that is to say, scientists. Let us keep the faith and acquire science (1867–68, vol. IX, p. 67; English transl., 2010, p. 48).

> Those [*the youth*] of 1830 have saved literature and art from triteness and dreariness by rising up against the academies in a struggle that was the intellectual festival of the century; it would be good to see the young people of the present standing up likewise to wrest economics and social science away from its abject and miserable condition of servility to bourgeois conservatism and financial feudalism. (1896d, vol. IX, p. 424; English transl., 2010, p. 347).

This book is a collection of essays written over the course of about thirty years. These studies are the result of a long acquaintance with the writings of Léon Walras, in the context of preparation of several volumes of his *Œuvres économiques complètes*.

It is well known that the literature dedicated to the presentation of Léon Walras's thought, from his death in 1910 until the 1980s, particularly in the Anglo-Saxon world, focused on pure economics and the theory of general economic equilibrium.[1] This literature applied to his work an approach similar to that which the Italian philosopher Benedetto Croce used towards Hegel: to clearly distinguish "what is living" from "what is dead". "What is living" refers to the "great work", the *Éléments d'économie politique pure* and the theory of general economic equilibrium; here the author should be regarded as the "precursor" of K. Arrow and G. Debreu. In contrast,

[1] A few exceptions should be noted. For example, the presentation of Walras's entire work by T. W. Hutchison is very qualified (1953, pp. 197–215).

his other works, primarily those on social and applied economics, would fall under "what is dead".

Such reductive interpretations emerge already during the Jubilee ceremony at the University of Lausanne, on 10 June 1909. Although Walras intends to emphasise the unity of his work in his speech entitled "Ruchonnet et le socialisme scientifique", his colleagues wish to pay tribute exclusively to the creator of the theory of general equilibrium and the founder of the Lausanne School. Two examples of this can be given. In his speech, Pasquale Boninsegni, who replaced Vilfredo Pareto in the chair of economics at the faculty of law, recalls in Pareto's language Walras's contribution to pure economics and states that he has "established the general conditions that allow the entire economic circulation to be grasped under a regime of private property and absolute free competition".[2] Ernest Roguin, a former student of Walras between 1872 and 1874, and a professor of law, directs his speech on social economics and synthetic socialism. At the risk of deeply offending his former professor, he declares:

> Scientific frankness and probity [...] compel me to say that your theory of social economics, formed of two parts, one of absolute socialism, and the other of extreme individualism, has not received the same universal acceptance from those capable of judging it, as the main ideas of your admirable system of pure economics.[3] This is explained by the fact that your social theory is the combination of a few demonstrated economic laws with principles of a natural law that can be absolutely rejected or only admitted with reservations.[4]

These reductive readings will quickly increase. Here are a few more examples. Vilfredo Pareto had several opportunities to express himself shortly after the death of Walras in 1910. In his article "L'œuvre scientifique de Léon Walras", published in the *Gazette de Lausanne*, he writes:

> The main merit of this scientist, his greatest merit, was to study, for the first time, a general case of economic equilibrium. In this way, he has opened up a path to economic science that can only be compared to that which Lagrange opened up to rational mechanics [...]. Léon Walras wanted to apply his theories to practical problems. This generous impatience is easily explained; but, it must be said frankly, that these applications were premature; and it will take a long time, many studies, many works, before one can think of putting the results of the theory into practice [...]. He tried to achieve for social economics what he had accomplished for pure economics; but his efforts were not successful. This does not detract from his merit; just as the merit of the great Newton is in no way diminished by the fact that he did not achieve, with his theory of light emission, the same success that so brilliantly crowned his theory of universal attraction.[5]

---

[2] Speech by Mr. Boninsegni, in: *Université de Lausanne, Jubilé Walras*, 1909, p. 24. On P. Boninsegni, see F. Mornati, 1999a.

[3] E. Roguin will acknowledge having been influenced by Walras: "There is no doubt that, without us clearly realising it, the idea of constructing a pure science of law was due, for a part that it is naturally impossible for us to specify, to the existence of pure economics, and to our friendly relations with the main of its creators" (1923, vol. 1, p. 63).

[4] Speech by Mr. Roguin, in: *Université de Lausanne, Jubilé Walras*, 1909, pp. 14–15.

[5] V. Pareto, 1910a, p. 1, re-ed. in: L. Walras, "Notice autobiographique" (1909a), Appendix 6, vol. V, pp. 42–43. This article appeared in Italian in the *Giornale degli Economisti* (re-ed. in: V. Pareto, 1982, pp. 644–46).

Furthermore, in an obituary article written for the *Economic Journal*, Pareto observes:

The work of Walras is complex, and only becomes intelligible when we analyse its elements. He himself attached chief importance to it as the expression of a reformer. But this is not its leading feature from a scientific point of view.

Recalling that Walras focuses on the theory of the "general case" of free competition, he also notes: "The use of mathematics enabled him to study cases of mutually dependent phenomena. These are far nearer to reality than when they are considered only under the aspect of causes and effects—the only aspect accessible to ordinary logic" (1910b, pp. 138–39).

In his first book *Das Wesen und der Hauptinhalt der theoretischen Nationalökonomie* (*The Essence and Principles of Theoretical Economics*) (1908), Joseph A. Schumpeter states that in the case of Walras, "we must carefully separate the work of the politician and the social philosopher from that of the theorist", adding that he drew practical claims from theoretical considerations (from his theory of rent, the nationalisation of land), an example of an approach that removes much of his authority from economic science (1908, 3rd part, chap. 2, p. 336, Italian transl., 1982, p. 272).[6]

Schumpeter did not change his mind after his visit to Walras in Clarens, probably in January 1909, and after reading the Jubilee documents. In his obituary article, "Marie Esprit Léon Walras. 1834–1910", he estimates that the theory of general equilibrium allows its creator to achieve immortality; on the other hand, the ideas on land nationalisation and his monetary policy proposals are nothing compared to sections II to VI of the *Éléments* (1910, English transl., 1952, pp. 76–77). Here we see that he blithely omits sections I ("Object and divisions of political and social economy "), VII ("Conditions and consequences of economic progress"), and VIII ("Price fixing, monopoly and taxation") of the 4th edition of the book. The same judgement will be repeated much later by Schumpeter in the *History of Economic Analysis*. The general equilibrium defined by a system of simultaneous equations represents the "Magna Carta of economic theory" (1954, p. 242), which would become self-sufficient, an exact science. He also asserts:

> [...] so far as pure theory is concerned, Walras is in my opinion the greatest of all economists. His system of economic equilibrium, uniting, as it does, the quality of 'revolutionary' creativeness with the quality of classic synthesis, is the only work by an economist that will stand comparison with the achievements of theoretical physics [...]. Unfortunately, Walras himself attached as much importance to his questionable philosophies about social justice, his land-nationalization scheme, his projects of monetary management, and other things that have nothing to do with his superb achievement in pure theory" (*op. cit.*, p. 827–28).

On his part, John R. Hicks, in the article "Léon Walras" published in *Econometrica* in 1934 on the occasion of his birth's centenary, notes about the work of our author: [...] it was in pure economics that his real interest lay, and the discovery of the conditions of static equilibrium under perfect competition was his central achievement", specifying just before that he does not wish to discuss in the article neither monetary theory,

---

[6] After receiving the work, Walras will translate into French the passage in which he is implicated ("Schumpeter, p. 336", note kept in the Lausanne collection under the reference F. W. V c, box 28).

nor "his relatively uninteresting writings on applied economics" (1934, p. 347). The existence of social economics is not even mentioned.

Such judgements have historically resulted in several drastic reductions:

- Throughout the XXth century, the majority of essays on Léon Walras are limited to pure economics. The other facets of his work, applied and social economics, remain ignored[7] or are deemed uninteresting.[8] The unity of thought, the theoretical programme, the great reformist project are thus obscured.
- Standard theory and the post-Walrasian orthodoxy reduce, for example, the question of "free competition" in Walras to a mere market structure, "pure and perfect competition" (*cf.* Chap. 5, *The conception of free competition in the* Éléments d'économie politique pure).
- Economists have gradually accredited the idea that general equilibrium in Walras was reduced to purely mathematical problems. In this sense, Werner Hildenbrand asserted:

> The edifice of General Equilibrium Theory has been compared to the great gothic cathedrals. These cathedrals were designed by inspired architects and constructed by great master builders who quite often extended and improved on the original design. If Walras and Pareto are generally credited with being the architects of the General Equilibrium Theory, it becomes apparent [...] that Debreu is the great master builder of that edifice.[9]

Indeed, after the Second World War, the Arrow-Debreu model occupied a central place in theoretical research programmes and the neo-Walrasian influence could be felt even in macroeconomics.[10]

It should be recalled that as early as 1862, Léon Walras had a complete project of "political and social economy", in which pure, applied, and social economics would be articulated, the three domains he would later teach at the Faculty of Law in Lausanne. However, after his retirement, Walras abandoned his plan to publish his courses on applied and social economics (contrary to what he had envisaged as early as September 1872), and replaced them with two volumes: *Études d'économie sociale* (1896e) and *Études d'économie politique appliquée* (1898d).

The edition of the *Œuvres économiques complètes* of Auguste and Léon Walras, in fourteen volumes, carried out in Lyon by a team under the direction of Pierre Dockès, has not only brought back into circulation texts that were difficult to access, but also unearthed numerous unpublished manuscripts.[11] The significant expansion

[7] The absence of an English translation of the *Études d'économie politique appliquée* and the *Études d'économie sociale* contributed to this ignorance. This gap is now filled with the translations of these two works (2005 and 2010) by J. Van Daal and D. A. Walker.

[8] During the 1950s–60s, only the "New School of Lausanne" (F. Oulès, M. Boson) brought these two components of "political and social economy" back to light by considering Walras as the "founder of scientific economic policy".

[9] W. Hildenbrand, 1983, p. 29.

[10] See R. Guesnerie, 2011.

[11] *Œuvres économiques complètes* of Auguste and Léon Walras, Paris: Economica, 1987–2005, 14 vols. See on this subject G. Busino, 2005, P. Dockès, 2014b, P. Dockès and C. Mouchot, 2009, M. Herland, 1991, J. Van Daal and D. A. Walker, 2007.

of the corpus made available to the scientific community has led an entire intellectual community to revisit not only the works of Léon but also of Auguste Walras. These "Walrasian studies" in the history of economic thought have allowed for a re-evaluation of the strong theoretical influence of the father on his son. They have led to a re-examination of each of the components of political and social economy, their own history, and of course the interactions between them. The interweaving of the three fields of political and social economy, which was already visible in texts such as the "Esquisse d'une doctrine économique et sociale" (1898c) and "Ruchonnet et le socialisme scientifique" (1909c), also appears in the *Mélanges d'économie politique et sociale* (1987), a posthumous project of book discovered in the Antonelli collection in Montpellier, on which Léon Walras was working until his last days.[12]

This book is divided into five parts, the content of which is briefly described here:

Part I *Paternal Legacy and Formation of the Field of Political and Social Economy*

In his "Notice autobiographique", Léon Walras recounts that in summer 1858, during a night walk in the Gave de Pau valley, his father energetically asserted to him that two significant tasks remained to be accomplished in the XIXth century: "to complete the foundation of history" and above all "to begin to create social science". And upon reaching the door of a villa named "Les Roseaux", convinced by his father's arguments, he promised him he would continue his work ("Notice autobiographique", 1909a, vol. V, p. 12). More precisely, he promised "spontaneously to devote [himself] to political and social economy rather than literature proper" (letter to Adrienne Belhache, 12 April 1898, in: *Correspondence*, III, l. 1348, p. 16). Upon returning to Paris, he therefore abandoned literature and art criticism and turned towards economics. For his part, Auguste Walras provided him with a number of manuscripts, gave him some notes, sent him books, and offered him close advice in his early days as an economist (see P.–H. Goutte and J.-M. Servet, 1990a, p. LXXVII–XI).

Chapter 1 (*Auguste Walras as a Transmitter of Ideas: From Jean-Baptiste Say to Léon Walras*) illustrates the theoretical relationship between Jean-Baptiste Say and the two Walras. The transfer of ideas mainly concerns the theory of value, the distinction between capital and income, and the theory of property, three fields difficult to dissociate in the entirety of Léon Walras's work. Notably, on the question of capital and income, the classical English analysis of social classes is challenged in favour of functional categories.

Chapter 2 (*From the Theory of Five Stages to the "Industrial and Commercial Regime"*) reveals that Léon Walras literally adopts the stages of societal evolution's theory developed by his father. However, this theory does not enable him to understand the mechanisms at work during the XIXth century following the industrial revolution. He then focuses on the most advanced stage, which he calls the "industrial and commercial regime". One can thus examine his ideas related to "modern industry", examine how he conceives the industrial revolution, the role of machinery, and the relationships between science and industry, and discover his fear of the "Americanism".

[12] See C. Hébert and J.-P. Potier, 1987.

The intellectual debt to his father is also evident in his classification of sciences and his approach to economics. However, Léon Walras quickly emancipates himself, constructing his own taxonomy of sciences and tripartite division of "political and social economy", which will be present in the *Éléments d'économie politique pure.*

Chapter 3 (*Taxonomy of Sciences and Divisions of "Political and Social Economy": An Attempt at Reconstruction*) examines this "model" and its tripartition, attempts to reconstruct its origins since the writings of the years 1858–62, then it highlights a change of "model" around 1896–98 as well as some modifications introduced in the status of the components of "political and social economy".

Part II *Pure Economics and Its Reception*

At the foundation of Léon Walras's theoretical edifice lies the field of pure economics and general economic equilibrium theory, which represents his "masterpiece", the culmination of his intellectual efforts.

Chapter 4 (*Genesis of a Masterpiece: The Theory of General Economic Equilibrium*) traces Walras's theoretical journey from his initial forays into mathematical economics to the various editions of the *Éléments d'économie politique pure*, in order to identify the pivotal moments in the genesis of the general economic equilibrium theory. The influences of Isnard, Poinsot, and Cournot are discussed. The final section questions the "positive" or "normative" nature of pure economics; recalling the "real types" and "ideal types" methodology used by Walras under the influence of Vacherot, it shows that this field pertains neither to the positive nor to the normative.

Chapter 5 (*The Conception of Free Competition in the* Éléments d'économie politique pure) deals with free competition in this purely theoretical field. It provides an example of the transition from the "real type" to the "ideal type", and from the "market-type" to "absolute free competition". Walrasian "free competition" essentially consists of the natural behaviour of free and rational individuals, possessing specific institutions. It cannot be assimilated to "pure and perfect competition" as a market structure in use in the contemporary neo-classical vulgate.

The dissemination of pure economics on an international level is a long and complex process. Only in the years 1895–1900 did Walras's work gain some recognition from the international scientific community, although not yet in France. Several studies in the history of economic thought had shed light on the reception and international dissemination of Walrasian pure economics adopting different approaches for certain countries: the Anglo-Saxon world (W. Jaffé, 1960, R. E. Backhouse and S. Medema, 2014), Germany (A. Alcouffe, 2013), Spain (J. Astigarraga and J. Zabalza, 2008), France (Y. Breton, 1986, 1992, 1998b, A. Zylberberg, 1990 and 1994), Italy (P. Barucci, 1972), Japan (K. Misaki, 2006) and Russia (F. Allisson, 2008). In this part, we will focus on Italy and France, countries where the situation of economics is very contrasted.

Chapter 6 (*An Early Reception of Pure Economics in Italy: The Correspondence with the "Lombard-Venetians"*) illustrates the reception of pure economics in Italy between 1874 and 1886 among economists influenced by the young German historical school. Indeed, during this period, Walras was not yet in contact with the first marginalists (M. Pantaleoni, V. Pareto, E. Barone), but with the "socialists of the chair", who enabled him to establish a genuine network of correspondents (including

A. Errera, G. Boccardo, Italian translator of the *Théorie mathématique de la richesse sociale*, and V. Cusumano).

Finally, Chapter 7 (*The Reception of Pure Economics in France (1873–1926)*) examines the difficult reception of pure economics within the French context. Charles Gide often lamented the lack of teaching of mathematical economics in France. The study takes as its temporal starting point the presentation at the Académie des sciences morales et politiques in 1873 of the "Principe d'une théorie mathématique de l'échange" and as its endpoint the 5th and final edition of the *Éléments d'économie politique pure.* Three main representative groups of readers are examined:

- the critics of pure economics: the liberals (Émile Levasseur), the defenders of State interventionism (Paul Cauwès), the mathematicians (Joseph Bertrand, Hermann Laurent, and Henri Poincaré) and the engineers–economists (Claude Cheysson and Clément Colson);
- the second group comprises the allies (Charles Gide) and "sympathisers" of pure economics (Émile Bouvier and Charles Rist, but also... Paul Valéry and Charles Péguy);
- the viewpoint of Walras's disciples is also examined: Pareto and the "Paretian" (Georges-Henri Bousquet) and the disciples in the strict sense (Albert Aupetit and Étienne Antonelli).

Part III *Reforming the Teaching of Political Economy*

Throughout his life, Léon Walras was interested in the reforms of higher education in European countries, in the teaching of "moral and political sciences" and of economics.

Chapter 8 (*From Criticism to the Reform Plan for the Teaching of Political Economy in France in the XIX*th *Century*) sets out his criticisms of French academic institutions, such as special schools and the promotion systems, particularly for professors at the Collège de France whose selection belongs to the "orthodox school". However, his attacks also target the *agrégation* competition in law faculties. Walras proposes a reform of higher education in France, comprising two levels of teaching. The first level would be based on a common core, covering both natural sciences and moral and political sciences, as "pure sciences". The second level would comprise two "periods" for a progressive specialisation of students in so-called faculties of "applied science". Regarding the content of the teaching of economics, his proposal relies on his own division of "political and social economy": in the first year, courses in pure economics and in the second and third years, courses in social and applied economics.

Chapter 9 (*Teaching Social and Applied Economics in Lausanne*) focuses on the progressive construction and content of courses in social and applied economics at the Faculty of Law in Lausanne, as well as on his teaching method. Walras indeed intended to publish the *Éléments d'économie sociale* and the *Éléments d'économie politique appliquée*, to complement the *Éléments d'économie politique pure.* Even after retiring from the university, he hoped to publish the content of his courses. Given his state of health, he gave up and prepared two collections, the *Études d'économie sociale* (1896) and the *Études d'économie politique appliquée* (1898). The written lessons of the courses in social and applied economics were finally published only in 1996 in the *Œuvres économiques complètes* (vol. XII, *Cours*).

Chapter 10 (*Léon Walras and the Commission of the University Library of Lausanne: the Purchases of Books in Economics*) reveals that since his arrival in Lausanne, Walras was concerned with providing his students with a substantial collection of books in economics at the university library. Based on the catalogue of the Guillaumin publishing house, he submitted a purchase list that included not only textbooks but also the works of the classics of the science ("Collection des principaux économistes", "Économistes et publicistes contemporains"). This chapter traces the difficulties he encountered with the library officials and the appeals he had to make to the public education authorities in the Canton of Vaud to achieve his goal.

Part IV *Critique of "Orthodox" Liberalism and "Empirical" Socialism*

Throughout his life, Léon Walras's concern was always to fight both the "orthodox" liberals and the "empirical socialists", a battle fought on two fronts.

Chapter 11 (*Ideas and Men: Criticism of the French "Liberal School"*) details his vehement criticisms directed against the French liberal school, who believe that the basic principles of economics are already established and who monopolise academic positions and the few available teaching chairs. In the early 1860s, Walras had the opportunity to closely associate with these "orthodox" liberals at the Société d'économie politique de Paris and at the *Journal des économistes* where he was a member of the editorial staff. Regarding them, he questions the relevance of the notion of a "school", given the divergences that arise among the authors on crucial issues. In his writings, he focuses his attacks on five economists: Michel Chevalier, Henri Baudrillart, Paul Leroy-Beaulieu, Émile Levasseur, and finally Léon Say, whom he calls the "pope" of "official" political economy in France.

Since his youth, our author has relentlessly criticised what he calls "empirical socialism" in its various forms. His first book as an economist *L'économie politique et la justice* (1860a) is indeed dedicated to refuting Pierre-Joseph Proudhon's theories.

Chapter 12 (*Criticism of "Empirical Socialism": The Cases of Louis Blanc and the Saint-Simonians*) deals with lesser-known criticisms. While the refutation of Louis Blanc on the role of competition and his project of *ateliers sociaux* is relatively easy for Léon Walras (as early as 1859, in the "Introduction à l'étude de la question sociale"), the consideration of Saint-Simonianism is more complex. Indeed, Auguste Walras was a fellow traveller of the Saint-Simonians, albeit with a critical view of their doctrine. In 1859–60, his son had the opportunity to associate with some Saint-Simonians and ex-Saint-Simonians and he would retain a great deal of sympathy for them. In 1896, he asserted that he owed the idea of reconciling individualism and communism largely to the "old Saint-Simonians" he had associated with in his youth. Obviously, he disagrees with them on several economic questions, but shares their denunciation of the harmful idleness of landowners.

The critique of "fraternal (*fraternitaire*)" socialism is present in the polemics led by Walras at the direction of the journal *Le Travail* between 1866 and 1868. According to him, the cooperative association is a means of pooling modest savings and also a school of democracy. However it is incapable of achieving social reform since it relies solely on individual initiative.

Chapter 13 (*Léon Walras, Paul Voituron and Constant Leirens at the Editorial Team of* Le Travail: *The Polemics on Cooperation (1866–1867)*) shows that the function of the cooperative association is at the heart of the dispute engaged between Walras and the Belgian editorial board (Constant Leirens and Paul Voituron) shortly after the birth of the journal. Indeed, from the first issue, both theoretical and political divergences on the status of cooperatives and on the solution to the social question appear among the collaborators; they will quickly worsen to the point of resulting in a definitive break after three issues. Léon Walras, with the help of Léon Say, would continue the publication of the journal, not hesitating to reprint the first three issues after removing the articles that had been the subject of disputes.

Part V *Social Reforms for the Implementation of a Liberal Socialism*

This final part focuses on the economic and social reforms that Léon Walras wishes to promote, which justify his lifelong position in "liberal socialism".

First of all, Chap. 14 (*Organisation of the Labour Market, Labour Legislation, and Social Insurance*) shows that questions relating to the labour market in a competitive environment, social conflicts, and social legislation deeply concerned Walras from 1859 throughout his career. He engaged in extensive debates on these issues with economists and socialists, and his ideas evolved significantly over time. This chapter presents his views on the poor and good functioning of the labour market, the desirable role of the State in better organising it, and also his ideas on labour legislation and social insurance systems. However, true social reforms can only stem from collective initiative.

For Walras, two social questions had to be resolved: ensuring that the distribution of social wealth among people was "as equitable as possible" (a problem of social justice) and ensuring the production of this wealth was "as abundant as possible" by preventing entrepreneurs from making profits other than under conditions of free competition (a problem of interest or economic efficiency). Two obstacles arise here: private land property and the exceptions to free competition (notably natural monopolies and railways).

Chapter 15 (*Towards the Repurchase of Land by the State and the Abolition of Taxes*) revisits the social justice theory, based on the "good old" natural law, bequeathed by Auguste Walras to his son and summarised in the general formula "Equality of conditions in the State; inequality of positions for the individual". Equality of social conditions requires the repurchase of land by the State, and inequality of positions should only be a result of individual merit. Léon Walras presents the principles justifying the systematic repurchase of land and the practical modalities to be implemented, a project ultimately leading to the abolition of taxes. Such a project has attracted criticism, including his allies (such as Charles Gide) and his disciples.

Chapter 16 (*Public Services and Natural Monopolies: What Role for the State?*). The question of the free competition principle, which refers to its applications and exceptions, is discussed in the field of applied economics. In this chapter we show that from 1875 onwards, Walras became increasingly preoccupied by the "exceptions" to this principle, which concern not only public services in a strict sense but also "natural and necessary monopolies". Railways, which fall under both public services and natural monopolies, occupy an important place in his thinking. Regarding the management of these different monopolies, Walras reviews several modalities of State intervention to respect the social interest. His continued reflections on these questions led him, in the years 1895–98, to consider the possibility of a "sole entrepreneur" State that would ensure the production equilibrium by mimicking the competition mechanism. A more or less generalised collectivism would thus be conceivable, even if it is not Walras's preferred solution.

However, economic and social reforms must be concretely realised by politicians. The transition of ideal to reality lies within the realm of practice and politics. From the perspective of a "rational" and not "empirical" policy, starting from the indications provided by scientists, statesmen must gradually implement the reforms.

Chapter 17 (*Towards a Political Reform? Universal Suffrage and Professional Representation of Interests*) deals with Walras's judgements on the political system in France during the XIXth century. Impressed by the Revolution of 1848 and long attached to the defence of direct universal suffrage, he was disappointed by the Third Republic's instability; from the 1880s onwards, he considered the possibility of a political reform to remedy the defects of direct universal suffrage through a system of professional representation of interests.

The studies gathered here seem to us to have a certain unity, insofar as they aim to shed light, without claiming to be exhaustive, to many unknown and overlooked aspects of Léon Walras's work, as well as the origins and genesis of the theoretical framework. They can be read in the order desired by the reader.[13] Preparing the *Œuvres économiques complètes* and writing of our essays required research in various archives (Walras collections in Lausanne and Lyon, Antonelli collection in Montpellier, William Jaffé collection, York University in Downsview, Canada), research facilitated thanks to the competence of the staff responsible for the conservation of these archives. At the University of Lausanne, we were fortunate to receive encouragement and logistical support of our colleagues and friends at the Centre d'études interdisciplinaires Walras-Pareto, and we would particularly like to thank the directors of this centre, Pascal Bridel and Roberto Baranzini. The first versions of several chapters were presented in seminars or at international conferences, including those of the International Walras Association, the Association Charles Gide pour l'étude de la pensée économique, and the European Society for the History of Economic Thought. During these conferences or friendly meetings, we benefited from remarks and comments of many colleagues, among whom we mention Roberto Baranzini, Pascal Bridel, Jérôme Lallement, Jan Van Daal, and Donald A. Walker. We would finally like to express our gratitude to Pierre Dockès for the numerous suggestions and encouragement he has given us over the years.

[13] In this book, we have sought to limit the inevitable repetitions as much as possible. We wished to propose the most faithful translations possible of Walras's quotations. For the *Éléments d'économie politique pure*, we used the two available English translations: *Elements of Pure Economics* (1954), prepared by W. Jaffé, and *Elements of Theoretical Economics* (2014), prepared by D. A. Walker and J. van Daal (2014). For the *Études d'économie politique appliquée*, we used the translation by Jan van Daal, *Studies in Applied Economics* (2005). Finally, for the translation of the *Études d'économie sociale*, we used D. A. Walker and Jan van Daal's translation, *Studies in Social Economics* (2010). Sometimes, we have slightly corrected the text, or preferred our own translation.

Contents

Part I
Paternal Legacy and Formation of the Field of Political and Social Economy

Chapter 1
Auguste Walras as a Transmitter of Ideas: From Jean-Baptiste Say to Léon Walras

1.1 Introduction

Auguste Walras's role as an "initiator in political economy" has often been recalled by his son[1] and both their blood and theoretical lineage[2] has been the subject of discussion since the end of the XIXth century. Already, in the preface of volume III of the *Dictionary of Political Economy* published under his direction, Robert Henry Inglis Palgrave noted:

> The biographical articles have been confined to notices of writers no longer living with the single exception of Prof. Léon Walras, who so closely carried on the work of his father Prof. Antoine Walras that it was not possible to mention the latter without also describing the works of his son. (1899, p. VIII)

In the eyes of Joseph A. Schumpeter, this lineage is not without interest, but it does not seem to be of primary importance to him from the point of view of economic analysis. Indeed, in his *History of Economic Analysis*, he observes regarding Léon Walras:

> He emphasized himself the influence of his father Auguste Walras and of Cournot. But, as has been pointed out before, we must add that of Say, his *true predecessor*. And, behind the figure of Say there looms the whole French tradition—Condillac, Turgot, Quesnay, Boisguilbert—however much or little he may have consciously absorbed from it. (emphasis by us, 1954, p. 828)[3]

---

[1] See "Un initiateur en économie politique, A. A. Walras" (1908b). One day, L. Walras would say:

> [...] I believe I have renewed the theory by the mathematical form I have given to it, which makes it of a truly scientific rigour. In short, it is a bit like an oil painting for which my father would have provided the pencil sketch. (letter to his mother, 18 June 1883, in: Correspondence, I, l. 560, p. 761).

[2] Blood relations do not necessarily induce scientific relations. See on this subject J.-P. Potier and P.-H. Goutte, 1992, pp. 174–76.

[3] J. A. Schumpeter also adds: "Say's work is the most important of the links in the chain that leads from Cantillon and Turgot to Walras" and further: "In the high heavens, Say's true successor was indeed the great Walras." (1954, pp. 492 and 497). These judgements do not please Alain

J.-P. Potier, *Léon Walras, Economist and Liberal Socialist*, Springer Studies in the History of Economic Thought, https://doi.org/10.1007/978-3-032-04670-3_1

For his part, in a text published at that time, the preface to Jean-Baptiste Say's *Textes choisis*, Pierre-Louis Reynaud notes:

> L. Walras also, if he only partially paid justice to Say, took up in broad terms his thesis of the productive services' association in production, he also used his notion of the entrepreneur and his general scheme of equilibrium. However, he paradoxically declares at least that "J.-B. Say did not conceive of the distinctive role of the entrepreneur: this personage is lacking in his theory". By presenting himself as closer to Smith than to Say, Walras did not show much fairness to the latter. It is true that Say, in his time, had treated with disdainful severity the theory of Auguste Walras on *rareté,* considered as the basis of value. (1953, p. 54)

These judgements therefore invite us to reflect on Auguste Walras's role as a transmitter of ideas from Jean-Baptiste Say to Léon Walras. Indeed, Say's works were an important source of reflection and theoretical inspiration for Walras, father and son, despite their limitations.[4]

In his first book, *De la nature de la richesse, et de l'origine de la valeur*, while addressing severe criticisms, Auguste Walras openly acknowledges his intellectual debt to Jean-Baptiste Say:

> I owe so much to Mr. Say, I have benefited so much by reading his excellent works, that if the zeal for truth forces me to fight and refute the erroneous opinions that have escaped him, I at least want to compensate for this painful obligation by bringing to light the true merit he has shown in his various writings. Now, I say it with conviction: his doctrine, imperfect as it is, still seems to me preferable to that of his predecessors. It presents an undeniable advantage over that of Smith and Ricardo. (1831b, vol. I, pp. 157–58)[5]

Let us also recall that after Say's death in 1832, he addressed a "petition" to the Minister of Public Instruction to present his candidacy for his succession to the chair of "Économie industrielle" at the Conservatoire des Arts et Métiers,[6] an unsuccessful attempt, since Adolphe Blanqui was preferred to him. And, according to Auguste Walras, Say would not have had eminent disciples in France.[7]

The emphatic tributes of Léon Walras to Jean-Baptiste Say are just as frequent in his work. In the *Cours d'économie politique appliquée*, the professor gets in the habit

---

Wolfelsperger who reacts thus: "Let us frankly say that it needs Schumpeter's francophile partiality to see Jean-Baptiste Say as the precursor of Walras." (1972, p. 17).

[4] Auguste Walras proposed to his son to write under his direction a treatise on political economy in 4 or 5 volumes intended to replace that of J.-B. Say, "which has only been followed by pale imitations" (letters of 4 and 16 December 1860, in: *Correspondence*, vol. IV, pp. 468–69 and 471). The 5-volume plan of this project, which did not come to fruition, is published by P.-H. Goutte and J.-M. Servet, 1990a, pp. LXXII–III.

[5] In the catalogue of printed works preserved by Léon Walras, one finds the *Lettres à Mr. Malthus* (1820), the *Catéchisme d'économie politique* (3rd ed., 1826), the *Traité d'économie politique* (5th ed., 1826) and the *Cours complet d'économie politique pratique* in a Belgian counterfeit in four volumes (Brussels: J.-P. Meline, 1832). See *Tables and Index*, vol. XIV, p. 289.

[6] A. Walras, letter to his father, 7 March 1833, in: *Correspondence*, vol. IV, p. 126.

[7] He pointed out to his son on this subject:

Since J.-B. Say, no renowned economist has emerged in France who has shown any originality, any breadth of mind. Blanqui and Garnier have sucked J.-B. Say to the marrow of his bones, and they have been careful not to correct and perfect his doctrine. (letter of 7 April 1864, in: Correspondence, vol. IV, p. 633).

of reading to his students long quotations from economists. Thus, for example, when he explains the "theory of markets", he provides very long excerpts from Chap. 15 of the *Traité d'économie politique* (5th ed., 1826) and declares that the author has rightly perceived the fact that this theory "will change the politics of the world". But he then adds about it:

> It is extremely ingenious and remarkable; but it would be, in our opinion, much better if it were based on a more scientific analysis of the fact of exchange because it would then provide much more precise indications concerning the effects of trade from the point of view, on the one hand, of the satisfaction of wants (or of utility) and, on the other hand, the price of commodities. (or value) (31st lesson, vol. XII, p. 595)

In this chapter, we will attempt to highlight the role of Auguste Walras as a transmitter of ideas through a few crucial themes, the theory of value, the analysis of capital and income, to which it is possible to associate the problem of property. Before examining these topics, it seems useful to very briefly present beforehand the question of the definition of economic science, an important issue, both for Say and for the two Walras's.

It is known that according to Jean-Baptiste Say, the object of political economy consists in knowing the means by which social wealth is formed, distributed, and consumed ([1803–26] 2006, vol. 1, pp. 2–3). As for property, understood as approved possession, "political economy assumes its existence as a matter of fact, and only considers its foundation and consequences incidentally" (*Epitome*, in: *op. cit.*, vol. 2, p. 1143).

Auguste Walras rejects this approach of political economy; Say's tripartition seems to him very questionable, despite its undeniable success.[8] Indeed, for him, it is necessary to distinguish:

- political economy, or "science of wealth". Political economy mainly includes, on the one hand, the theory of value, exchange, money and, on the other hand, the theory of capital and income, production and consumption (*Cours d'économie politique*, 1832–33, vol. III, pp. 170 and 173). It "belongs to arithmetic" and must leave the "moral sciences" and join the "natural sciences".
- The theory of property and distribution of wealth refers to the question of justice. This "moral science" belongs to "natural law".

Political economy benefits from "logical priority" over the theory of property, and its principles must enlighten those of natural law. Indeed, value is the cause of appropriation and constitutes "a natural and necessary fact that cannot be corrected, distorted, in its essential aspect, by the intervention of free fact, human fact, moral fact".[9]

[8] A. Walras, *Théorie de la richesse sociale* (1849c) and "Examen critique et réfutation du Livre de Mr. Thiers sur la Propriété" (1849a), vol. II, respectively, pp. 169 and 224. In a letter to his son Léon of 7 January 1860, Auguste Walras further observes concerning Say's tripartition: "This division has had its day." (*Correspondence*, vol. IV, p. 384). On political economy in A. Walras, see A. Diemer, 2010, pp. 505–22.

[9] A. Walras, letter to his son, 12 June 1860, in: vol. IV, p. 421.

Auguste Walras believes that one day political economy will become a mathematical science (1831b, vol. I, pp. 207–08), but he himself wrote nothing in mathematical economics, nor played any role in the birth of the theory of general equilibrium.[10]

From *L'Économie politique et la justice*, on the occasion of his analysis of P.-J. Proudhon's economic ideas, the young Léon Walras in turn criticises Say's definition of political economy, which he considers "inaccurate and dangerous" (1860a, vol. V, p. 147) and opposes it with a bipartite division strongly inspired by that of his father (*op. cit.*, pp. 153 and 157–58).[11] Subsequently, in the 1st lesson of the *Éléments d'économie politique pure*, before presenting his own conception of "political and social economy", he engages in the critique of previous definitions, those of the Physiocrats, Adam Smith and Jean-Baptiste Say. The Smithian definition allows for the integration of considerations of interest and justice, but it ignores the properly scientific part of political economy. In contrast, Say's definition reduces political economy to a "*natural* science". Indeed, for him, "the *production*, *distribution*, and *consumption* of wealth take place, if not completely independently, at least in a *manner* in some way independent of the human will" (emphasis by L. W., vol. VIII, 1st lesson, p. 30; English transl., 2014, p. 7).[12] This "naturalist" viewpoint leads to a production theory in which the motto "laissez-faire, laissez-passer" predominates. In reality, man possesses reason and liberty in matters of production and distribution of wealth, and he chooses the systems that seem to him most in conformity with interest and justice. And Léon Walras concludes, "inferior to Adam Smith's definition, which was only incomplete, J.-B. Say's is therefore incorrect" (vol. VIII, 1st lesson, p. 31; English transl., 2014, p. 8).[13]

Let us now examine the question of value, then those of capital, income, and property.

---

[10] The manuscript of A. Walras commenting in 1838 on the *Recherches sur les principes mathématiques de la théorie des richesses* by Cournot has not been found until now (see vol. XIV, p. 26).

[11] *Cf. infra* Chap. 3, *Taxonomy of Sciences and Divisions of "Political and Social Economy": An Attempt at Reconstruction.*

[12] See also "Une branche nouvelle de la mathématique" (1876b), vol. VII, p. 304.

[13] L. Walras continues by criticising the "empirical" divisions of the *Traité*. Two examples can be cited in this regard. Firstly, the property question is placed in the theory of production and that of taxation in the theory of consumption. Such a separation is untenable for our author, because there would only be a single theory of distribution, relating to property and taxation (*cf.* "social economics"). Furthermore, the issue of exchange value is placed in the theory of distribution, an absurd classification, because it is a matter of "pure economics", which must be resolved beforehand. In fact, according to L. Walras, Say's disciples will integrate the theory of value into that of production and the theory of property into that of distribution.

1.2 The Theory of Value

In *De la nature de la richesse, et de l'origine de la valeur* (1831b), Auguste Walras examines the theories of the value of commodities. He first notes that there are two completely opposed "opinions" on this subject. The first approach, mainly French, places the cause of value in utility. The second approach, mainly British, places the cause of value in labour or production costs. Curiously, Auguste Walras will take up[14] Say's thesis, expressed in the "Discours préliminaire" of the *Traité*, according to which Ferdinando Galiani would have brought the "seed" of the second approach.[15]

We will limit ourselves here to the discussion related to the first approach. First of all, for our author, it is possible to differentiate between utility according to ethics (here, objects that satisfy the wants recognised by reason are called useful) and utility according to political economy (here, all objects that man can desire, either in the interest of his existence or by the effect of his passions and whims, are called useful) (1831b, vol. I, pp. 67–68). Concerning utility in the sense of economics, Auguste Walras accepts Say's definition in the *Epitome* of the *Traité d'économie politique* ([1814–26] 2006, vol. 2, p. 1162), because "it is, in political economy, the faculty that things have to be able to serve man, in whatever way" (1831b, vol. I, p. 67).[16] Utility is the quality by which an object satisfies a want and provides enjoyment. But Auguste Walras intends to specify that "utility is a natural and necessary relationship between man's constitution and the conformation of external things. Utility derives, it is true, from the form that these things have, and this form is often given to them by man". By giving form to things through production and labour, man creates a greater or lesser utility, but he is not the creator of all useful things.[17] For men, being subject to wants and capable of experiencing enjoyments, pleasures, things that respond to them, become useful. Not sharing Say's distinction between material and immaterial products, Auguste Walras does not retain the distinction between material utility and immaterial utility: the fact that utility is fixed or not in a material object does not alter its characteristics (1831b, vol. I, p. 68).

Auguste Walras asserts that Say and his disciples make utility the cause of value. It should be noted here that he does not take into account the evolution of Say's ideas on the question of value between 1803 and 1826, particularly through his polemic with

---

[14] A. Walras, "Mémoire sur l'origine de la valeur d'échange" (1849b), vol. II, p. 508.

[15] In the "Discours préliminaire", from the 2nd edition, Say declares regarding Galiani's *Della Moneta*:

[…] what is singular in this work is that it contains some of the foundations of Smith's doctrine, and amongst others that labour is the sole creator of the value of things, that is to say, of wealth; a principle that is not rigorously true, as we will see in this book, but that taken as far as possible, could have put Galiani on the path to discovering and fully explaining the phenomenon of production. ([1803–26] 2006, vol. 1, p. 26).

[16] A. Walras also cites (1831b, p. 135) a passage of the *Catéchisme d'économie politique*: "one must understand by this word everything that is suited to satisfy the needs, the desires of man as he is. Now his vanity and passions sometimes give rise to needs as imperative as hunger". (*Catéchisme d'économie politique et opuscules divers*, vol. III, 2020, p. 91).

[17] A. Walras, "Mémoire sur l'origine de la valeur d'échange" (1849b), vol. II, p. 515.

Ricardo[18] and he relies exclusively on the 5th edition (1826) of the *Traité d'économie politique*, the 3rd edition (1826) of the *Catéchisme d'économie politique*, and the notes to the French translation (1819) of the 1st edition of Ricardo's *Principles*. For him, in order that Say's thesis be founded, two conditions should be met.[19] First, it would be necessary for the value to be the inevitable result of utility (1831b, vol. I, p. 75). However, it is easy to show that air or sunlight are extremely useful, but without value. Annotating Ricardo's *Principles* in 1819, Say attempted to answer, "that these objects are of immense, infinite utility, and that they consequently have, so to speak, a value equally without bounds" (1831b, vol. I, p. 75).[20] However, what characterises air or sun "in terms of immensity, is not their *utility*, it is their *quantity*" (1831b, vol. I, p. 76): their quantity is infinite and they are even indestructible. Secondly, in Say's perspective, if utility were the cause of value, value would have to be proportionate to utility (1831b, vol. I, p. 135). But this is not the case, since very useful things can have very little value.

Auguste Walras also notes

> […] that it is quite difficult to establish different degrees of utility among the countless number of things we use. Among the objects that are useful to us, we generally distinguish those that are absolutely *necessary* for our preservation, and those that are purely *pleasant* to us. It is a very old distinction between the *necessary* and the *superfluous*. […]. But however difficult it may be to rigorously assess the various kinds of utilities, and although it seems impossible to me to establish a classification free from arbitrariness, it is always quite easy to see that, among all these utilities, there are some that are less real, or, if you will, less reasonable, less well-founded than others. Bread is certainly more useful than this or that jewel, and meat serves us better than fireworks. (emphasis by A. W., 1831b, vol. I, p. 136)[21]

In fact, what leads men to make sacrifices to possess things is limitation or scarcity. Certainly, utility is a necessary condition of value, "but utility alone is not enough to produce this latter quality: it must be combined with the limitation or scarcity (*rareté*) of the useful thing" (1831b, vol. I, p. 79). The possession and enjoyment of values, or "rare utilities", constitute appreciable wealth (1831b, vol. I, p. 83).

---

[18] After presenting in the 2nd and 3rd editions (1814 and 1817) of the *Traité* a "symmetrical" theory of value (utility and production costs understood as the "two foundations" of value), in the 4th edition (1819), J.-B. Say defends the thesis that utility alone establishes the value of products, seeks productive services and establishes a value for them, the total of which forms the production costs. See on this point J.-P. Potier, 2002.

[19] See also A. Walras, "Mémoire sur l'origine de la valeur d'échange" (1849b), vol. II, p. 518 *et seq.*

[20] A. Walras refers here to a note by Say in Chap. XX of Ricardo's *Principles of Political Economy and Taxation*:

[…] the portions of this fund that do not need to be solicited, the sun, for example, which provides us with light and heat so necessary for the development of organised beings, are productive funds belonging to each of us, of infinite value, in terms of utility derived from them, since this utility is infinite, inexhaustible. (Notes et pièces diverses, vol. VII, tome 2, Marginalia, 2024, p. 198).

[21] Let us note in this regard that Auguste Walras reproaches the lack of rigour in the use of the notions of necessary, pleasant, and superfluous in Louis Say [*Études sur la richesse des nations et réfutations des principales erreurs en économie politique*, Paris: Renard, 1836] ("Études sur la richesse des nations, par M. Louis Say", vol. III, pp. 707–08).

Furthermore, Auguste Walras criticises Say's conception regarding non-appropriable natural agents (air, sunlight…) and appropriable natural resources (land), which does not permit the linking of the theory of wealth (political economy) with the theory of property (natural law) (*cf. supra*). He indeed observes:

> I think, for my part, that it is the role of political economy to highlight the relationship between property and wealth, and to note that it is precisely the same things that are the subject of property, which are also the subject of political economy; that the goods that one appropriates are the same that have value, and that the origin of value and appropriability lies in the same fact, which is the scarcity of certain goods, or the limitation of certain useful things. (1831b, vol. I, p. 88)

Auguste Walras continues with the critique of the distinction between natural and social wealth. Say would forget that natural products of the earth are indeed produced, distributed, and consumed and that unlimited goods (air…) are distributed equally among men (1831b, vol. I, p. 95). In the *Catéchisme d'économie politique*, he himself acknowledges that land and industrial faculties constitute "free gifts" from nature, either to humanity or to individuals, but which are also productive funds susceptible to value and therefore relevant to political economy (1831b, vol. I, p. 97).

Concerning the source of his theory of value, Auguste Walras (1831b, vol. I, pp. 169–70) claims Jean-Jacques Burlamaqui (1694–1748), a theorist of natural law, disciple of Pufendorf (1633–94), author of the *Éléments de droit naturel*, whose first Latin edition dates back to 1734.[22] For Auguste Walras, value is proportionate solely to scarcity (*rareté*), which is expressed by the relationship between the "sum of needs" experienced and the quantity of useful goods capable of satisfying them.[23] Scarcity is directly proportional to needs and inversely proportional to the quantity of goods. If the sum of needs increases for the same quantity of goods, or if the sum of goods decreases for the same sum of needs, scarcity increases, and vice versa (1831b, vol. I, pp. 78, 134, 205–07, 219, 228).[24] Let us note that here Auguste Walras establishes an equivalence between the sum of needs and the "number of men in whom these needs exist" (1831b, vol. I, pp. 137, 206, 219 and 221–22). The relationship between the sum of needs and the sum of goods is also likened to the relationship between "absolute" demand and "absolute" supply. The "general and

---

[22] According to Burlamaqui, the "proper and intrinsic price" of things has two "foundations", which intervene jointly: the first foundation is utility, or "the aptitude that things have to serve the needs, conveniences, or pleasures of life". This should be understood as not only "real utility" (water…), but also "arbitrary or fanciful utility" (precious stones…); the second foundation is scarcity (*rareté*), that is to say, "the difficulty one has in procuring these things" (the difficulty of a work, its delicacy, the reputation of the worker…) (*Éléments de droit naturel*, 1820, pp. 156–57). J.-J. Burlamaqui simplifies the analysis developed by Samuel Pufendorf in *De officio hominis et civis* (*The Duties of Man and Citizen*) (1675), republished jointly with his own. See also on this subject W. Jaffé, 1972, pp. 298–99. In fact, Burlamaqui's position is not identical to that of Auguste Walras.

[23] On A. Walras's theory of *rareté*, see A. Diemer, 2006.

[24] A. Walras rejects the Ricardian conception, which denies the characteristic of *rareté* to goods that human industry can multiply (1831b, vol. I, pp. 152–54). During his study, he suggests an analogy between *rareté* and speed. Speed is the ratio between the space covered by a mobile and the time taken to cover it. It is directly proportional to the space covered and inversely proportional to the time (1831b, vol. I, pp. 153, 206–07, 227–28).

absolute" demand indeed expresses all the combined needs, regardless of the means available for men to satisfy them, while the "general and absolute" supply expresses the quantity of scarce and available goods, knowing that the absolute supply is always less than the absolute demand.[25]

Under these conditions, "political economy is not so much the science of wealth as the science of *poverty*" (emphasis by A. W., 1831b, vol. I, p. 99). Men's efforts to reduce scarcity contributes to diminishing exchangeable values and thus social wealth. In his critical notes on Auguste Walras's book, Jean-Baptiste Say will see this paradox very well (*cf. infra*). Ultimately, Auguste Walras believes that Say "exaggerates the scope of utility" and ignores scarcity (1831b, vol. I, p. 167). To be honest, this judgement is somewhat excessive. Indeed, in a note added to the French translation of Chap. XXVII of Ricardo's *Principles of Political Economy*, Say takes scarcity into account in his own way and considers that

> […] the basis of each value is not the quantity of labour necessary to get a commodity, but the need for it, balanced by its scarcity. Labour, or in general the costs of production, are a difficulty to overcome which limits the quantity of a commodity that can be brought to the market, and it is in this sense that they are one of the elements of the value of things. But when this scarcity is voluntary, the effect is the same. (*Notes et pièces diverses*, vol. VII, tome 2, *Marginalia*, 2024, p. 204)

However, Auguste Walras will introduce some subtleties in his own theory of value. Indeed, he declares:

> But does utility have no influence on value? No. All that can be said in favour of utility is that it sometimes influences scarcity, and thereby the value that follows from it. It is possible, and indeed it happens, that a thing becomes all the rarer the more useful it is: then it becomes more expensive; but the value that seems to be proportionate to utility is actually proportionate to scarcity and scarcity alone. (1831b, vol. I, p. 136)

How then to explain this apparent paradox? Here, it is necessary to distinguish the variations of utility "in its intensity" and those "in its extension".

The variations of utility "in its intensity" are expressed in terms of the greater or lesser urgency of needs, while the variations of utility "in its extension" are expressed in relation to the number of needs, the number of men who experience them; indeed, some goods have a "general and universal utility", while others have utility only in certain cases, as J.-B. Say has indeed noted (1831b, vol. I, p. 137). The influence of utility on value operates only through its extension, one of the constitutive terms of the scarcity ratio (*cf. supra*).

But Auguste Walras immediately recognises that "the extension of utility is closely linked to its intensity" (1831b, vol. I, p. 138). Indeed, the more useful a good is ("the more its utility is real"), the more numerous will be the men willing to accept a sacrifice to obtain it. Under these conditions, "the quantity of useful things not varying, their scarcity will be in direct proportion to the extension of utility, and this extension will itself be in direct proportion to its intensity. Value will be proportionate

[25] The notions of absolute demand and supply must be distinguished from those of real or effective demand and supply.

to scarcity, and thereby to utility considered in its intensity". This is the sense in which utility can serve as a measure of value (1831b, vol. I, p. 138).

In his 1836–37 course at the Athénée Royal, Auguste Walras will revisit the definition he had given to scarcity in 1831. The difficulty lies, according to him, in the assimilation between the sum of needs and the number of men who express these needs. Indeed,

> [...] the same need does not make itself felt in each of us with the same energy, with the same intensity and the great difficulty that presents itself here is to find for each type of need a unit of measure (*unité de compte*). (vol. III, p. 380)

He illustrates his point with examples:

> I suppose a man who uses a pair of shoes per year. [...]. Next to this man, I suppose another one who uses a pair of shoes every six months [...]. I can still suppose a third who uses three pairs of shoes per year. [...]. Now when we want to assess the scarcity of shoes [...], if we take as a unit of measure the need of the first individual who uses a pair of shoes per year, it is evident that the three individuals that we have considered will give us for the expression of this sum, a number of needs expressed by 6. From which you can see at first that the sum of needs cannot be expressed by the sum of individuals who experience them. (*op. cit.*, pp. 380–81)

Later, relying on a similar example, Auguste Walras would confide to his son that the determination of the unit of need constitutes "the obstacle that prevents mathematics from taking hold of political economy [...]".[26]

In a note included in Chap. V of Book II of the *Traité d'économie politique* ([1803–26] 2006, vol. 2, p. 687), Say admitted to having long hesitated to discuss the question of value before that of production. For Auguste Walras, Say unfortunately opted, following A. Smith and his disciples, for the wrong solution and considered that value was a "produced thing", that wealth was the "fruit of production" and therefore that produced utility was the only one to have value (1831b, vol. I, p. 125). This would be a contradiction with the thesis that value would come from utility.[27]

However, Auguste Walras also highlights a particularly instructive passage of the 3rd edition of Say's *Catéchisme d'économie politique* (1826):

> A glass of fresh water can have a very high price during a sea voyage, when the water stock is exhausted, and although it cost nothing to the one who happens to have it in his possession. This extraordinary circumstance, which greatly increases the value of a thing without adding new utility to it, is the effect of a kind of *monopoly*[28]; it is not an increase, but a displacement of wealth. It transfers the price of the glass of water from the pocket of the passenger who desires it ardently to that of the passenger who agrees to do without it. There has been no creation of new wealth. (*Catéchisme d'économie politique et opuscules divers*, vol. III, 2020, p. 190, note 6 for p. 92)

[26] A. Walras, letter to his son of 18 May 1861, in: *Correspondence*, vol. IV, p. 491.

[27] According to A. Walras, this contradiction will lead Say in a passage of *Catéchisme d'économie politique* [*op. cit.*, 2020, p. 92] to inadvertently approach the theory of value of Smith and his disciples (1831b, p. 164). Léon Walras will support the same view in "Système des phénomènes économiques" (1872b, vol. XI, p. 450) and in the *Éléments d'économie politique pure* (vol. VIII, 16th lesson, pp. 247–48, English transl., 2014, pp. 180–81).

[28] In this note introduced in the 2nd edition of the *Catéchisme d'économie politique* (1821), the words "is the effect of a kind of monopoly" were added in the 3rd edition.

In fact, the resort to the monopoly is a very good explanation, unbeknownst to its author, provided it is generalised: indeed, all the values come from monopoly (defined as an exclusive sale), which is the effect of property, which is precisely the effect of limitation in quantity, or scarcity (1831b, vol. I, pp. 131–32).

In summary, Auguste Walras is convinced to have completely refuted Say's error of making utility the cause of the value of products and of productive services. He goes so far as to assert in his book: "Perhaps if the learned economist casts his eyes on this work, he will recognise the superiority of my principle over his own" (1831b, vol. I, p. 161).

Jean-Baptiste Say indeed read *De la nature de la richesse, et de l'origine de la valeur*, but he was hardly convinced. On his own copy, he annotates regarding his supposed contradictions on the cause of value, which would have led him to suspect the existence of a principle other than utility: "By Jove! I do believe it; do I not include the costs of production as one of the foundations of value? This is *the limitation* of which Mr. Walras boasts" (emphasis by J.-B. S., *Notes et pièces diverses*, vol. VII, tome 2, *Marginalia*, 2024, p. 362).

At the end of his reading of the book, he writes with rage:

> Summary: Mr. Say is wrong; Adam Smith is wrong; Ricardo is wrong; given that these fools said that wealth was something. Wealth is the scarcity of things, that is to say, it is nothing, and I open a new field to political economy by showing how to multiply wealth, that is to say, nothingness. (*op. cit.*, p. 365)

Moreover, in Say's manuscripts, there is a note in which he asserts:

> Extravagance of certain doctrines—That of Mr. Walras on production—The scarcity (*rareté*) of things is the sole source of their value. Scarcity pushed to the extreme is nothingness. It is therefore nothingness that produces the wealth of nations. Labour and industry reduce scarcity; consequently, they reduce wealth, and *wage an open war to the value.* Page 184. *De la nature de la richesse* by Mr. Walras.[29]

The young Léon Walras, initially, will adopt his father's theory of scarcity, in the "Introduction à l'étude de la question sociale" (1859b, vol. V, pp. 135–37), and in *L'Économie politique et la justice* (1860a, *op. cit.*, pp. 149–151). He will, of course, inherit the problem of measuring need. Later, in the 16th lesson of the *Éléments d'économie politique pure*, he will summarise the debate on the question of the value of commodities as follows:

> There are, in the science, three principal solutions to the problem of the origin of value. The first is that of A. Smith, Ricardo, and McCulloch; it is the English solution: it finds the origin of value in *labour*. This solution is too narrow and it denies that there is value in things that, in fact, do have it. The second is that of Condillac and J.-B. Say; it is the French solution: it finds the origin of value in *utility*. This solution is too broad and it finds value in things that do not, in fact, have it. Finally, the third, which is the right one, is the one espoused by Burlamaqui and my father, A.-A. Walras: it finds the origin of value in *rareté*. (emphasis by L. W., vol. VIII, p. 245; English transl., 2014, p. 179)

[29] Emphasis by J.-B. S., *Notes et pièces diverses*, vol. VII, tome 1, *Manuscrits*, 2024, p. 20. Let us note that later, P.-J. Proudhon will also engage in a critical reading of Auguste Walras's book (see E. Castleton, 2014).

Table 1.1 J.-B. Say's classification

Economic agents (producers)	Productive funds	Productive services	Incomes
Landowners	Land	Land services	Rent (*fermage*)
Capitalists	Capital	Capital services	Interest
Industrious (*industrieux*)[30]:			
Entrepreneurs (farmers, manufacturers, tradesmen, etc.)	Industriousness (*Industrie*) or industrial faculties	Industrial services of entrepreneurs	Profit: - wage of superintendence - residual profit
Workers (and other agents of entrepreneurs)	Industriousness (industrial faculties)	Industrial services of workers	Wages

1.3 Capital, Income, and Property

We must now consider Auguste Walras's role as a transmitter of Jean-Baptiste Say's ideas to his son about the distinction between capital and income and the question of property. It is worth noting here that in his philosophical writings, Auguste Walras attaches great importance to the notion of limitation. In the study "De la nature de la loi" (1833c), he argues that space and time are the two components of the being and the existence is limited in extent and duration. It follows that "science, considered as a whole, is nothing other than a picture of all the limits which, by a kind of successive superposition, produce this immense variety of beings and phenomena that constitute the universe" (vol. I, p. 312). The purpose of science is to gain knowledge of these limits, which concern either the quantity (case of scarcity, *cf. supra*), or the duration (question of capital and income).

Regarding the question of capital and income, the two Walras (or Walras father and son), following Say, criticise the approach of the classical English economists (Smith and Ricardo), in terms of social classes, which does not allow for the separation of the capitalist from the entrepreneur. Their analysis takes as its starting point Say's functional categories, whose roles can be combined in the same individual, and they introduce some modifications to them.

First of all, let us recall how Say envisaged the agents, the productive funds and services, and their remuneration. Table 1.1 outlines the main categories:

Inside the productive funds, the author distinguishes the industrial funds (industrial faculties or "industriousness (*industrie*)", that is to say, the action of the physical and moral forces of man applied to production) and the funds of industriousness instruments. The funds of industriousness instruments are composed firstly of capital and "appropriated natural instruments" (among which are land, but also mines and watercourses), and then of "unappropriated natural instruments" (sun's heat,

[30] The "scientists" (*savants*) constitute the third category of "industrious" in Say's work.

wind force…), which also contribute to production but are not paid. For Say, all the economic agents are "producers": landowners and capitalists are passive producers (through their lands and capital), while the "industrious (*industrieux*)" are active, direct producers. Among these, the entrepreneur deserves very careful examination, being the "main agent of production". He is an intermediary between the scientist and the worker, but also between the landowners and the capitalists (he buys their productive services) and more broadly between producers and consumers. He gathers knowledge about his activity from the "scientists", brings together the different "productive services" and organises the production. Among the moral qualities he must possess, "judgement" must be mentioned, indispensable in particular for assessing the needs of his products, for estimating the production costs. He must also show fertile imagination, as he introduces innovations. Moreover, he "is responsible for all the risks of production".[31] A capitalist can make his capital grow himself, but if he lends it to the entrepreneur, the latter will pay him interest. The interest includes two parts: firstly, a premium to cover the risk of capital loss and then the payment of the "productive service" for the advanced capital. Concerning the entrepreneur's "profits of industriousness", as considered by Say, two elements should be distinguished. Firstly, the main remuneration consists of a wage of superintendence, or an income from a specific production factor, included in the production costs, but paid after the payment of the other factors. Then, the entrepreneur can receive a residual profit (a "pure" profit) when the price of commodities is temporarily higher than the production costs incurred. Conversely, if the price is lower than the production costs, he will incur losses.

Say emphasises that the entrepreneur is simultaneously a buyer in the markets of "productive services" and a seller in the markets of goods:

> In developing the production of wealth's mechanism, I told you that a production entrepreneur buys the productive services rendered by industriousness, capital, land funds, and that he consumes them; which led me to represent production in general, as a kind of exchange, in which one *gives* the productive services (or what they cost) to *receive* in return the products (or what they can be sold for).[32]

Production is therefore merely a "great exchange".

What is Auguste Walras's position about this representation proposed by Say? In his early writings in economics, he quite faithfully follows the typology of the author of the *Traité*. In particular, he specifies that the "industrials (*industriels*)"[33] refer to the scientists, the entrepreneurs of industry and the workers.[34] In the *Théorie de la richesse sociale*, Auguste Walras presents his own typology of capital and income. He explains that social wealth includes capital and income, a set of scarce,

---

[31] J.-B. Say, [1828–29-1840] 2010, vol. II, tome 2, 5th part, Chap. VIII, p. 725; see also [1803–26] 2006, Book II, Chap. VII, vol I, tome 2, pp. 733–34.

[32] Emphasis by J.-B. S., [1828–29-1840] 2010, vol. II, tome 1, 3rd part, Chap. V, p. 377.

[33] A. Walras does not take up Say's term "industrious" but that of "industrial" from the Saint-Simonians.

[34] A. Walras, "De l'abolition de l'impôt, et de l'établissement de la Loi agraire" (1831a) and *De la nature de la richesse, et de l'origine de la valeur* (1831b), in: vol. I, respectively, pp. 14 and 144.

Table 1.2 Auguste Walras's classification

Economic agents	Capital	Services or income	Price of services or of income
Landowners	Land	Land services: *Rente*	Ground rent (*fermages*)
Capitalists	Artificial or proper capital	Services of capital: *Profit*	Interest
Workers - Labourers - Entrepreneurs	Personal faculties	Personal Services: *Travail* (Labour)	Wage

material or immaterial things. He first names the "*capital value* or *capital* all the social wealth that is not consumed or only consumed in the long run, all limited utility that survives the first service it renders us, that lends itself more than once to the same use" (land, machine, but also pleasure gardens, dwelling house…). He then names "*income* all the social wealth or exchangeable value that serves only once, that is consumed immediately, that does not survive the first service one derives from it" (food, everyday objects…) (emphasis by A. W., 1849c, vol. II, p. 140). He also specifies that the distinction between capital and income does not depend solely on the nature of things, but also on the use of social wealth. A tree that bears fruit is a capital, but if one decides to cut it down to get wood, it becomes an income. As is well known, Léon Walras draws heavily on this analysis in the *Éléments d'économie politique pure* (vol. VIII, 17th lesson, p. 265, English transl., 2014, p. 193).

Auguste Walras also enumerates numerous distinctions: those between "natural" capital (land, human faculties) and "artificial" capital (machines…), "inconsumable" capital (land) and "consumable" capital, "fixed or engaged" capital and "circulating or available" capital. According to him, income (consumable fund), in its relation to capital (productive fund), is composed of three elements: the service of capital or its "true income", depreciation, and insurance premium. Léon Walras will again take up and refine his father's analysis, notably in the 20th lesson of the *Éléments.* Table 1.2 provides Auguste Walras's classification:

In the *Théorie de la richesse sociale*, Auguste Walras indicates that he considers labour "in the most general and abstract manner", without denying the existence of inequalities between the different personal faculties, the different types of labour, and differences in wages. He therefore does not engage in any specific examination of the status of the entrepreneur and his remuneration. Referring to this personage in his writings, he merely regularly recalls that

> Mr. Say was right to say that *production* is a great *exchange* in which productive services are given to obtain products in return, and that the value of the products represents the value of the productive services consumed to obtain them.[35]

[35] Emphasis by A. W., *Théorie de la richesse sociale* (1849c), vol. II, p. 161; see also "Examen critique et réfutation du Livre de Mr. Thiers sur la Propriété" (1849a), *op. cit.*, pp. 216–17; "Mémoire sur l'origine de la valeur d'échange" (1849b), *op. cit.*, pp. 511 and 513; *Cours d'économie politique*

In his correspondence, Léon Walras will downplay this absence in his father's *Théorie de la richesse sociale*, by indicating that he, for his part, produced "a more complete analysis of the role of the entrepreneur!"[36] Except for the status of the entrepreneur, the great continuity existing between the *Théorie de la richesse sociale* (Chaps. IV and V) and the *Éléments d'économie politique pure* (17th lesson) is striking.[37] But on his side, Léon Walras specifically positions himself in relation to Jean-Baptiste Say.

In a youthful text, Léon Walras notes that unlike the Physiocrats, Smith and Ricardo, J.-B. Say, in his *Traité d'économie politique*,

> […] is the first economist who discerned the capital and declared it *productive*, who classified it among social wealth and made it intervene in the general system of production on the same level and rank as the land and the labour of human faculties.[38]

Certainly, for him, this analysis deserves some corrections. Later, in the *Éléments d'économie politique pure*, after citing a passage in Chap. 5, Book I of the *Traité d'économie politique* which deals with the payment of industriousness (wages), capital (interest), and land (ground rent—*fermages*), he states:

> That is a sufficiently clear and exact conception of the combination of the three productive services in the production process. The wording used is good so we have adopted it ourselves. But there remain important gaps to be filled in. In the first place, J.-B. Say did not conceive of the distinctive role of the entrepreneur: this personage is lacking in his theory. Furthermore, Say gave an imperfect explanation of what services wages, interest, and rent are the price; and his theory does not indicate, any more than did the Physiocrats' theory, how the price is determined. Here, it would be necessary to introduce a valid theory of value, of the mechanism of exchange, of capital and income, of the mechanism of production, the concept of entrepreneur, and of the markets for products and services […]. (vol. VIII, 40th lesson, pp. 64–649; English transl., 2014, lesson 32, pp. 370–71)[39]

Léon Walras's appreciation of the entrepreneur in Say ("this personage is lacking in his theory") is obviously very surprising when one knows the developments dedicated to him, not only in the *Traité*, but also in the *Cours complet* (*cf. supra*). But in another passage of the *Éléments*, Léon Walras criticises the error "of a certain number of French economists that make the entrepreneur a worker by considering him as specially charged with the work of direction of the firm" (vol. VIII, 18th lesson, p. 281; English transl., 2014, p. 207).[40] In this critique of the attribution to the entrepreneur

(1832–33), 7th lesson, Course of 1835 in Evreux, Course of 1863–64, vol. III, respectively, pp. 159, 327 and 400.

[36] L. Walras, letter to A.-H. Deschamps, 29 June 1904, in: *Correspondence*, III, l. 1575, p. 251.

[37] One can also refer to the manuscript, "Capital et revenu" (1870b), vol. XI, pp. 361–84.

[38] Emphasis by L. W., "L'industrie moderne et l'économie politique" (1861d), vol. VII, p. 140.

[39] Already, in his "Inaugural Speech" at Lausanne University, L. Walras stated: "I borrow […] from J.-B. Say, his conception of the three productive services, by rectifying it with the theory of exchange value and with the theory of capital and income given by my father" (1872a, vol. VII, p. 373).

[40] See also "De l'influence de la communication des marchés sur la situation des populations agricoles" (1874b), vol. X, p. 222; English transl., 2005, p. 198.

of a specific permanent remuneration (wage of superintendence), he undoubtedly also makes an implicit allusion to Say… but also to his father!

In the "theory of production", in the 18th lesson of the *Éléments* (vol. VIII, pp. 281–82, English transl., 2014, pp. 207–08), Léon Walras considers the market for products (raw materials and consumer goods) and the market for services (land services (*rente*), capital goods services (*profit*), and labour, with consumers' and productive services) in interconnection and he states the conditions of equilibrium of production, which includes that of exchange:

- the equality between the supply and effective demand of "productive services" and the setting of the price of each of them;
- the equality between the supply and effective demand of products and the setting of the selling price of each of them;
- the equality between the selling price of the products and the cost of productive services, this third condition being characteristic of the equilibrium of production.

The conclusion of the author's analysis is well known:

> […] in the state of equilibrium in production, the entrepreneurs make neither profit nor loss and it is possible to disregard their interventions to consider not only the productive services as being exchanged for products and products as being exchanged for productive services, but, when all is said and done, even consider the productive services as being exchanged for each other. (vol. VIII, p. 284, English transl., 2014, p. 210)

Thus, we find the idea of Jean-Baptiste Say that production is a "great exchange".

But what are the functions of the entrepreneur and what is his remuneration? He is "the person (an individual or a corporate entity)"[41] (vol. VIII, 19th lesson, p. 287, English transl., 2014, p. 211), whose role consists in the leasing of the three categories of capital (land, capital proper, personal faculties), that is to say, the purchase of the three productive services (land services or *rente*, capital services or *profit*, labour) and their combination in the various economic activities: agriculture, industry, commerce, etc. The place of intervention of the entrepreneur is more the market than the enterprise itself.[42] The entrepreneur can combine his function with those of landowner, capitalist, worker, thus ensuring up to four roles, "in real life", says Walras (vol. VIII, pp. 280–81, English transl., 2014, p. 207). He then credits himself with ground rent, interest, and a wage. These incomes constitute his only normal sources of subsistence, as he does not have a specific permanent income. However, it is indicated that entrepreneurs "make their living not as entrepreneurs, but as landowners, workers, or capitalists in their own firm or in others" (vol. VIII, p. 284; English transl., 2014, p. 210). The precision "or in others" generates even more ambiguities.

[41] In "L'économique appliquée et la défense des salaires" L. Walras specifies: "an individual or an association of individuals", or "a municipality or the State" (1897c, vol. X, p. 246, English transl., 2005, p. 217).

[42] We will not return here to the criticisms addressed to L. Walras (see D. A. Walker, 1986 and 1996, Chap. 13 and C. Mouchot, 2004).

In a letter addressed to the American economist Francis Amasa Walker, Walras provides us with an interesting clarification regarding the definition of the entrepreneur:

> For me, I consider him exclusively as the personage who buys the productive services on the market for services and sells the products on the market for products, thus forming a profit (*bénéfice*), as well as a loss. If he owns part of the land or capital involved in his enterprise or if he participates as a director or otherwise in the operation of transforming services into products, he is therefore by this fact a landowner, capitalist, or worker, and combines with his own function distinct functions. Practically, this combination is frequent and perhaps even generally necessary; but I believe that theoretically it should be excluded by analysis.[43]

Léon Walras distinguishes here the activity of the director in charge of the routine management ("service of labour") and the activity of the entrepreneur. He will moreover take the example of individuals united in a limited liability company who "become entrepreneurs" and who nominate "one or several managers" to carry out the enterprise's operations.[44]

Finally, it seems useful to very briefly present the question of property in order to attempt to highlight once again the role of Auguste Walras as a transmitter of ideas between Say and Léon Walras. First of all, let us recall Say's positions on the question of property.[45] A great continuity appears in him on this subject between the 2nd edition of the *Traité* and the *Cours complet*.

In a note in Chap. XIV of Book I of the *Traité d'économie politique*, from the 2nd edition (1814), Say notably indicates:

> Industrial talents are the most indisputable of properties, since they are derived directly from nature or through one's own efforts. They establish a right superior to that of landowners, which dates back to a spoliation (because it cannot be supposed that land has always been legitimately transmitted from the first occupant to our days); a right superior to that of capitalists: for even assuming that capital is not the result of any spoliation, but of a slow accumulation over several generations, it still requires, as for land, the help of legislation to secure its inheritance, a help that it may have granted only under certain conditions. ([1803–26] 2006, vol I, tome 1, p. 235)

In the *Epitome* of the *Traité d'économie politique*, from the 4th edition (1819), Say observes:

> The most indisputable property is that of personal faculties, for it has been given to no one else. The next most indisputable property is that of capital; as it was originally acquired by savings, and the one who saves a product could, by consuming it, destroy any other right than his own over that same product. The least honourable of all is landed property, for it is rare that it does not date back to a spoliation by fraud or violence.[46]

---

[43] L. Walras, letter to F. A. Walker, 12 June 1887, in: *Correspondence*, II, l. 800, p. 212.

[44] "L'économique appliquée et la défense des salaires" (1897c), vol. X, pp. 246–47, English transl., 2005, p. 217.

[45] See on this subject F. Laget, 2003.

[46] J.-B. Say, [1803–26] 2006, vol I, tome 2, p. 1143. See also [1828–29-1840] 2010, vol. II, tome 2, 9th part, "General picture of the economy of societies", p. 1225.

Finally, in the *Cours complet d'économie politique pratique*, after recalling this hierarchy, Say remarks:

> But even if a suspect origin would establish different degrees of legitimacy among the various properties; even if landed property were the least honourable of all, the interest of society requires that it be guaranteed equally with all others, and even that the laws relating to it be simplified so as to make each owner as secure in his enjoyment as possible while respecting the rights of others. ([1828-29-1840] 2010, vol. II, tome 1, 4th part, Chap. V, p. 546)

The idea that personal faculties would constitute the "most sacred" property is clearly inspired by John Locke. The judgement on landed property is in line with the industrialist ideas spreading in the journal *Le Censeur européen* (1817–19) and also in Saint-Simon's writings. The future indeed belongs to the "industrious" and not to the landowners.[47]

The passage cited above of the *Epitome* included in the *Traité* caught the attention of Auguste Walras. He remarks in this regard:

> By pronouncing the word spoliation, J.-B. Say certainly did not realise the strength and truth of this expression. He intended to speak, and he says so himself, of the spoliation that occurs through fraud and violence. He did not mean to speak of this spoliation by ignorance that occurs every day, unbeknownst to the owner and the worker, by the natural effect of economic laws, in a society that prospers [...]. ("La vérité sociale par un travailleur", 1848, vol. II, p. 72)

Auguste Walras indeed had the opportunity to explain himself on several occasions concerning this spoliation. In the supplementary chapters of the *Théorie de la richesse sociale*, dedicated to the "Théorie de la propriété", he observes that.

> [...] the *land belongs to the State*, the cultivable soil forms the common property of all citizens. The income from the soil or the rent (*fermage*) constitutes the *public income*. [...]. *Labour belongs to the individual*; in other words, the individual belongs to himself. [...]. The daily exercise of our personal faculties and the *wage* that results from it, constitute our *private income*, our personal fortune.[48]

As for artificial capital, the fruits of labour and savings, they belong, as well as the profit, legitimately to the individual. While personal faculties and artificial capital cannot be the subject of common property, unless by free consent, the same is not true for land. Indeed, land private property constitutes a "usurpation" of the public domain depriving the State of its legitimate income and forcing it to resort to taxation to cover public expenses, thus infringing on individual rights. His son would develop, from his early writings, the same perspective on property in the field of "social economics". We will return in detail to this question in Chap. 15 (*Towards the Repurchase of Land by the State and the Abolition of Taxes*). Just like his father, Léon Walras criticises the conception of land property presented by the author of the *Traité*. For him, the approach of Say and of the "utilitarians" (*utilitaires*) base property solely

[47] On this point, see E. Allix, 1910, pp. 341–63.

[48] Emphasis by A. W., "Théorie de la propriété" (1849d), vol. II, p. 184; see also "Un Chapitre de Mr Guizot…" (1849e), vol. II, pp. 541–44.

on considerations of interest, related to the production of social wealth, and Jean-Baptiste Say "does not know how to explain why the land was appropriated" (*Cours d'économie sociale*, vol. XII, p. 240).

1.4 Conclusion

Having examined these few crucial topics, what conclusions can we draw? Auguste Walras brings forth a new theory of value based on scarcity offering a critical analysis that involves several authors (notably Condillac, Smith, Ricardo), but remains strongly focused on Jean-Baptiste Say, of whom he provides a very biased reading of the value theory. On the question of capital and income, Auguste Walras indeed plays the role of a transmitter of ideas from Say to his son, by questioning the classical English analysis of social classes and favouring simple functional categories. However, he refuses to consider all economic agents as "producers", distinguishing the legitimate idleness of capitalists and the dangerous idleness of landowners. We will return to this point later in Chap. 12 (*Criticism of "Empirical Socialism": The Cases of Louis Blanc and the Saint-Simonians*), because it is one of his disagreements with the Saint-Simonians. On the other hand, apart from the idea of the interconnection between the markets for services and for products, Auguste Walras does not play a role as a transmitter about the role of the entrepreneur, with his son taking a critical stance in relation to Say. Finally, on the property question, he goes beyond the hierarchy in legitimacy proposed by Say and defends a much more radical position that will be developed by his son.

Chapter 2
From the Theory of Five Stages to the "Industrial and Commercial Regime"

2.1 Introduction

In this chapter, we will examine how Léon Walras considers the progress of humanity, during the xixth century, towards the most advanced stage of economic history, which he calls the "industrial and commercial regime". We will thus discover his ideas related to "modern industry" at this stage and examine his understanding of the industrial revolution, the role of " machinery, and the relationship between science and industry. This aspect of the work of the founder of the Lausanne School, which reveals the existence of a theory of stages of societies' evolution and a particular use of history, is little known and has hardly been examined so far in the secondary literature. The intellectual debt to his father is evident here. Our author presents his theory, on the one hand, in the field ofapplied economics", which deals with "industrial human facts" and determines rules of efficiency in terms of agricultural, industrial, commercial, and financial production of social wealth, and on the other hand, in the field of "social economics", which deals with "moral human facts" and determines principles of social justice.

Our study will include two sections. The first section will present the Walrasian theory of the different stages of economic evolution of society. The second section will focus on the characteristics of the "industrial and commercial regime" that emerged during the xixth century and its future prospects.

2.2 Economic History as a Theory of Stages

For Léon Walras, history intervenes at several levels: "pure moral science" upstream of the applied aspect of social economics, dealing with the effects of human free will and leading him towards the social ideal, then concrete science or empirical

J.-P. Potier, *Léon Walras, Economist and Liberal Socialist*, Springer Studies in the History of Economic Thought, https://doi.org/10.1007/978-3-032-04670-3_2

history providing "real types", and finally the domain of practice or politics.[1] The link between these different levels is notably achieved through a theory of stages of economic evolution of humanity. Indeed, in many of his writings in applied and social economics, from the 1860s onwards, our author refers to a "scientific" history of the human species on an economic perspective. This history is described through a succession of five "stages" or "economic regimes",[2] whose common feature is the division of labour. Economic history would consist of an in-depth study of these different stages. In fact, Léon Walras simply and almost verbatim adopts the theory of stages that his father had presented in several writings from 1832[3] and which saw there a true historical march towards "perfection". The sequence, as it appears with him, is as follows:

- The "savage stage", or "stage of hunting and fishing": here, men rely little on themselves and much on nature; lacking capital (except for bows, arrows, and nets), they engage in hunting, fishing, and gathering, without resorting to agriculture. What about land property in this first stage? For Walras, the liberals, defenders of private property, assert that in this stage, land property does not exist, which is "a complete error: it exists in the state of community" (*Cours d'économie sociale*, 44th lesson, vol. XII, p. 296). Indeed, it belongs to each tribe. A "certain equality of conditions" coexists with a "certain inequality of positions". This stage corresponds to the situation of the American savage tribes and would still be, in the XIXth century, the situation of Africa and Oceania.
- The "pastoral stage": nomadic (in Asia) or sedentary (in Europe), men now live from the product of livestock. In this stage, agriculture, industry, and commerce are practically non-existent, but the capital appears in the form of herds. Within this stage, art and science gradually emerge. The "inequality of positions" increases compared to the previous stage but is still reconciled with the "equality of conditions", since land property still belongs to the community.
- The "agricultural stage": within this third stage, men's subsistence is more assured and more varied than in the previous regimes. Capital, still rare, exists in the form of buildings, of agricultural instruments and livestock, and it is lent in exchange for the payment of interest at usurious rates.[4] At this stage, according to Walras, a

---

[1] See on this subject P. Dockès, 1996 (Chap. III, "Léon Walras et l'histoire"), 2014a; see also *infra* in this work.

[2] For the description of these stages, see notably "Exposition et conciliation des doctrines sociales" (1872c), vol. XIII; *Cours d'économie sociale*, 44th lesson ("Appearance of the Problem of Social Organisation in the Agricultural State"), vol. XII; *Cours d'économie politique appliquée*, 2nd lesson ("The Five Economic Regimes") and 2nd lesson [end] ("Causes and Consequences of the Five Economic Regimes"), vol. XII; "Théorie de la propriété" (1896c), vol. IX; "Esquisse d'une doctrine économique et sociale" (1898c), vol. X.

[3] See A. Walras, "Course of 1832–1833 in Evreux, 4th and 5th lessons", in: vol. III; "Examen critique et réfutation du Livre de Mr. Thiers sur la Propriété" (1849a), vol. II. A. Walras had proposed to his son to deepen within him the study of the history of the five economic regimes of societies (16 December 1860, in: *Correspondence*, vol. IV, pp. 471–72).

[4] L. Walras recalls that "the virtuous Cato the Elder lent at 40%" (*Cours d'économie politique appliquée*, 2nd lesson [end], vol. XII, p. 455).

"terrible question" arises, which remains unresolved in the XIXth century: alongside the increased "inequality of positions", but legitimate and in accordance with distributive justice, the "inequality of conditions" emerges, a violation of commutative justice (*Cours d'économie sociale*, 44th lesson, vol. XII, p. 298). Indeed, private land property appears with division among families and, within a few generations, the community itself gives away its legitimate resources intended to finance the growing burden of public services.[5] The division of land property gives rise to the civil society with its laws and opposing classes, initially citizens and slaves, and later landowners and proletarians (*Cours d'économie sociale*, 37th lesson, vol. XII, p. 264). Landowners will cease to cultivate the land by entrusting it to farmers, in exchange for the payment of ground rent. The proletarians, possessing only their personal faculties, must pay taxes on their wages to finance public expenditures ("Exposition et conciliation des doctrines sociales", 1872c, pp. 254–55; "Théorie de la propriété" 1896c, p. 190, English transl., 2010, pp. 145–46). Here, we can observe Walras's original position, that the proletariat does not originate in the "industrial stage" (*cf. infra*), but in the "agricultural stage". Within this stage, which occupies a large part of humanity's space and time,[6] three different "social states" will succeed one another: the theocracy and the castes of the East (Egypt, India, China…), then the slavery of Greek and Roman Antiquity, and finally feudalism and serfdom in Europe.

Léon Walras observes that these first three stages have been "noted by several authors", but he does not cite any names here. However, among the possible names, Turgot and Smith could have been mentioned.[7] The nomenclature being incomplete, two additional stages must be added to this sequence:

- The "industrial stage": if men only wanted food, humanity would never have surpassed the agricultural stage. Once clothed and housed, men "chase after pleasures whose number is infinite" (*Cours d'économie politique appliquée*, 2nd lesson, vol. XII, p. 450). This pursuit explains the birth and progress of the "industrial stage". In this fourth stage, a new class of men, more or less numerous, forms that of the industrials who devote themselves to manufacturing products such as dwellings, furniture, clothing, etc. Capital becomes more abundant and trade develops between agricultural and industrial products.
- The "commercial stage": this regime begins with the development of foreign trade. Indeed, men no longer content themselves with products of the land and of their countries; they exchange part of their own products (raw or manufactured) for foreign products. Thus, alongside farmers and industrials, a new class

[5] This question of social justice is discussed in Chap. 15, *Towards the Repurchase of Land by the State and the Abolition of Taxes*.

[6] Walras gives 3,000 years as an order of magnitude.

[7] L. Walras could cite, for example, the four stages theory (hunters, herders, farmers, modern society) by A. R. J. Turgot, presented in the "Plan du premier Discours sur la formation des gouvernements et le mélange des nations" (circa 1751), published in the *Oeuvres de Turgot* (Paris: Guillaumin, 1844, pp. 628–42), now in: G. Schelle (ed.), 1913, vol. 1, pp. 277–98.

of men emerges, merchants, whose function will be foreign exchange. Historically, the profits of commerce have made the power of cities like Tyre, Carthage, Venice, and also the Netherlands. The "commercial stage", in which the three varieties of industry (agricultural, manufacturing, and commercial) are found, is the most advanced of humanity. It contains all the others, fertilises them, and would therefore be the definitive stage of society.[8]

At first glance, the historical schema of Walras (father and son) presents obvious similarities with Friedrich List's five stages, set out in the *National System of Political Economy* (1841), which unfolds the following sequence: savage, pastoral, agricultural, agricultural-manufacturing, and agricultural-manufacturing-commercial stages.[9] And, just like Léon Walras, Friedrich List was particularly interested in the transition from the agricultural stage to the two subsequent stages. However, our author will never confront his theory of stages with those proposed by List and by the representatives of the German historical schools from the mid-XIXth century. In fact, he cannot accept the approach of the German economists, which consists in seeking the laws of the different stages by relying on factual data. In his view, "one must study history after the economic principles because economics illuminates history (and not history economics)".[10] History allows, in certain cases, the confirmation of economic theories.

Furthermore, Walras pre-emptively rejects any simplistic reading of his own theory of stages setting out several arguments (*Cours d'économie politique appliquée*, 2nd lesson, vol. XII, pp. 451–52). Firstly, there is no "clear and distinct difference" between these regimes: in each stage, one can find a bit of all the others. Secondly, the stages do not develop on the ruins of one another, but they overlap: for example, agricultural production is mostly flourishing in the industrial stage and, as shown by the case of England, agriculture and industry are most prosperous in the commercial stage. Finally, the five stages do not necessarily follow one another in a linear manner in all societies. The indigenous people of America remained at the first stage being unable to move to the pastoral and agricultural stages. Some peoples were able to begin with the pastoral or the agricultural stage. The latter case would be that of Mexico, due to the lack of animals to domesticate. Conversely, cities like Tyre or Venice were exclusively commercial cities.

How does one move from one stage to another? In fact, the transition from one stage to another results from a "revolution", whose aspects are at once technical, economical, and institutional. According to Walras, techno-economical changes require institutional adaptations, and humanity must therefore find solutions in terms

[8] On this point, Auguste Walras's position seems less rigid: "the *commercial* regime will add new developments to the agricultural regime and the industrial regime, and one cannot say today where the human species will stop" ("Examen critique et réfutation du Livre de Mr. Thiers sur la Propriété" (1849a), vol. II, p. 391).

[9] See F. List [1841] 1856, p. 72 *et seq*. Curiously, Émile Levasseur will also use a theory of five stages (savage, pastoral, agricultural, industrial, and commercial stages) in relation to degrees of increasing population density (1892, vol. 3, pp. 473–76).

[10] "Exposition et conciliation des doctrines sociales" (1872c), vol. XIII, p. 668, note 251.

of social organisation throughout history, bearing in mind that liberty is a driving force for progress. The transition to the agricultural stage was achieved through an "agricultural revolution" and the transition to the higher stage will occur through an "industrial and commercial revolution", which we will examine in the following section.

2.3 The "Industrial and Commercial Regime": Characteristics and Future Prospects

Very early, Léon Walras implicitly (never openly) admits that the paternal distinction between the "industrial stage" and the "commercial stage" is fragile, given that the commercial stage "follows very closely" the industrial stage. In fact, he understands that the typology in five stages is hardly suitable for understanding the economical transformations at work during the XIXth century. From his early writings, and then in the *Éléments d'économie politique pure* (vol. VIII, p. 598, English transl., 2014, p. 329) as well as in numerous later writings, it will mainly be a question of the emergence of a "stage" or of an "industrial and commercial regime".[11] Walras considers that during the XIXth century, we have barely emerged from the "agricultural stage" and peoples are "seriously" entering the "industrial and commercial stage" (*Cours d'économie sociale*, 44th lesson, vol. XII, p. 295). Certainly, industry and commerce have existed until now, but not yet under the conditions and on a scale suitable to constitute this new regime. In "Esquisse d'une doctrine économique et sociale", Walras adds an interesting compliment on this stage by observing that the "industrial and commercial stage […] is also a *financial* stage because the creation of capital by means of savings and speculation plays a role on a par with agriculture, industry, and commerce" (emphasis by L. W., 1898c, p. 420, English transl., 2005, p. 368).

The transition from the "agricultural stage" to the "industrial and commercial stage" occurred through an "industrial and commercial revolution", which began at the end of the XVIIIth century and developed throughout the XIXth century. England was the first country to adopt the new regime.[12] Agriculture must now shift from an extensive mode to an intensive, large-scale mode, using increasingly more capital.

---

[11] See notably "Paradoxes économiques, I" (1860c, vol. VII, p. 46); *Recherche de l'idéal social* (1867–68, vol. IX, p. 172, English transl., 2010, p. 131); "Exposition et conciliation des doctrines sociales" (1872c, vol. XIII, p. 252); *Cours d'économie sociale*, 44th lesson ("Appearance of the Problem of Social Organisation in the agricultural Stage"), vol. XII, pp. 295–96; *Cours d'économie politique appliquée*, 26th lesson ("History and Operations of Industry"), vol. XII, p. 573; "Un économiste inconnu: Hermann-Henri Gossen" (1885a), "Théorie de la propriété" (1896c), vol. IX, pp. 325 and 191, English transl., 2010, pp. 261 and 146; "Esquisse d'une doctrine économique et sociale" (1898c), vol. X, pp. 420–21, English transl., 2005, pp. 367–68.

[12] Walras observes that "the inauguration of the industrial and commercial regime" occurred in France "during the course of the second and third quarter of this century" (*Cours d'économie sociale*, 47th lesson, "Rising Cost of Living", vol. XII, p. 308).

Léon Walras frequently emphasises that industry is now very different from what prevailed before.[13] This difference appears in three key points[14]:

- The industry, which was "empirical", becomes "scientific": the discoveries and improvements are no longer the result of chance, but "are now demanded and borrowed from the progress of science itself, realised on its indications". The mathematical, physical, chemical and natural sciences are thus enlisted to serve the industry.[15]
- In the production process, "free natural agents" are now used through machines (an implicit reference to Jean-Baptiste Say's theory of the "natural agents of production"). Walras thus adopts Say's idea that industry uses the unappropriated forces of nature thanks to the mastery of laws provided by science. He indicates in this regard steam, electricity, and light and mentions the contributions of applied sciences and the emergence of the steam engine (James Watt) and the power looms (Richard Arkwright). According to him, "of all the machines, the steam engine is the most important for the development of modern industry. It has contributed with the mechanical loom to revolutionise the spinning and weaving industry, and it has revolutionised, on its own, the water and land transport industry".[16]
- In accordance with the "most rational rules of economics", industry and commerce rid themselves of their constraints and adopt the regime of freedom of work and free competition. In this regard, Walras mentions the birth of political economy with François Quesnay and the Physiocrats and also mentions Turgot. The lowering of customs barriers and free trade, which results in the division of labour and free competition applied on an international scale, marks "the entry of humanity into the industrial and commercial regime" (1897a, vol. X, p. 278). For Walras, England achieved a historical victory over landowners with the establishment of the freedom to import cereals and maintained the free trade regime from the 1880s ("Le problème fiscal", 1896d, vol. IX, p. 418, English transl., 2010, p. 342).

In "modern industry", with the arrival of machines, the "capital proper" or "artificial capital",[17] sees its importance become comparable to that of land capital and personal capital (human faculties). It will be noted that in his lessons at Lausanne University, to illustrate the industrial effects of machines and the productivity of labour, Walras uses only old examples. In the *Cours d'économie politique appliquée* (27th lesson, vol. XII, p. 577), he takes up various examples provided in 1841 by

---

[13] L. Walras is inspired here by the work of the physician François Verdeil, *De l'industrie moderne* (Paris: Victor Masson, 1861).

[14] "L'industrie moderne et l'économie politique" (1861d), vol. VII, pp. 135–36; "Exposition et conciliation des doctrines sociales" (1872c), vol. XIII, p. 253; *Cours d'économie sociale*, 44th lesson, vol. XII, pp. 295–96.

[15] L. Walras highlights the role played by Lavoisier in the field of chemistry. The role of chemists, physicists, and mathematicians in the establishment of new industrial processes had already been highlighted by J.-B. Say in the *Traité d'économie politique* ([1803–26] 2006, vol. I, tome 2, p. 728).

[16] *Cours d'économie politique appliquée*, 27th lesson ("On Machines"), vol. XII, p. 576.

[17] Capital artificially produced by the application of labour to raw materials.

Michel Chevalier, in his *Cours d'économie politique fait au Collège de France* (1842). Thus, with the railways, the productive power of man in America between the time of the Aztec emperor Montezuma and the present time would have increased in a proportion of 1 to 11 500. And in the *Cours d'économie sociale*, he re-uses a scientific chronicle by Louis Figuier published in the Parisian newspaper *La Presse* (6 April 1861) commenting on a book on steam engines by the Scottish engineer William Fairbairn,[18] which he had already quoted in an article, rejected at the time by the *Journal des économistes* ("L'industrie moderne et l'économie politique", 1861d, vol. VII, p. 145). Walras indicates that this engineer estimated

> [...] at 11 million horsepower the total mechanical force developed by all the machines operating in England in the mines, in manufacturing, for navigation and locomotion. Assuming these machines operated all year round, 10 hours a day, as the work of one horsepower is equivalent to that of 7 strong men, they would have replaced 77 million slaves [...]. Thus our modern industry would already offer us the equivalent of slavery. Could we not take advantage of it to do justice to our proletarians? (22nd lesson, "On Slavery, Serfdom and the Proletariat", vol. XII, pp. 203–04)

Certainly, one can question the reduction of employment caused by the development of machinery. According to Walras, machinery reduces the price of manufactured products, increases the demand for all other products and thus increases the demand for the service of labour; the conclusion of our author can only be optimistic:

> The reasoning thus establishes that after a momentary displacement, which constitutes in truth a more or less painful crisis for the workers and which must be softened as much as possible, the use of machines increases, far from diminishes it, the demand for labour. The facts confirm this reasoning in a striking manner. By comparing the number of workers employed a century ago in spinning, weaving, transport and those employed today in the same industries and in the industries in solidarity with each other, there is a difference ranging from a few thousand to several million.[19]

The question of crises in the "industrial and commercial regime" scarcely concerns Walras. According to him, industrial and commercial crises would be caused by speculation on the prices of certain products, helped by the abuse of credit.[20] Faithfulness to Jean-Baptiste Say's law of markets is complete. The Great Depression of 1873–95 does not shake his confidence. Referring to the "current crisis" in 1880, Walras argues that "to the overabundance of industrial products corresponds [...] to a shortage of agricultural products, except for wheat which has become for us a commercial and not an agricultural product". The remedy consists in diverting the "productive services" from industry to agriculture, which the State could promote

---

[18] Numerous mechanical processes are owed to William Fairbairn (1789–1874), particularly for the transmission of motive power in looms, the construction of water wheels, and, more generally, the substitution of iron for wood in mechanics.

[19] *Cours d'économie politique appliquée*, 27th lesson, "On Machines", vol. XII, p. 578. Later, Walras reaffirms: "after all, only a transfer of the demand for labour has occurred and not a reduction. All that is needed is to provide for a transition" ("Esquisse d'une doctrine économique et sociale" (1898c), vol. X, p. 429, English transl., 2005, p. 375).

[20] See the 57th lesson of the *Cours d'économie politique appliquée* (section X, "On Crises"), vol. XII, pp. 683–87.

by various means such as the creation of agronomical schools, the development of agricultural credit, the encouragement of the formation of joint-stock companies in agriculture and, of course, by rationally solving the question of land property.[21]

For Walras, the rapid and unprecedented development of "modern industry" impacts not only the facts of exchange value and property but also the ideas related to these facts, thus influencing the development of economics, on its laws and its rules for industry. As we saw in the previous chapter, he regards Say as the first economist who understood the importance and role of capital and who "made it intervene in the general system of production on the same level and rank as land and labour of human faculties" ("L'industrie moderne et l'économie politique", 1861d, vol. VII, p. 140). According to him, Say's analysis represents a step towards the taxonomy of the social wealth of his father and himself, the only one that would be "in accordance with the nature of things and justified by the comparative history of economics and modern industry" (*op. cit.*, p. 142).

During the transition to the "industrial and commercial stage", that is to say, to the "definitive social stage" (*Cours d'économie politique appliquée*, 23rd lesson, vol. XII, p. 569), a state that would allow reaching the "fulfilment of the economic life" ("Exposition et conciliation des doctrines sociales" 1872c, vol. XIII, p. 253; *Cours d'économie sociale*, 44th lesson, vol. XII, p. 296), a new social and institutional organisation must be established, through social reforms. And Walras insists on the fact that "the very establishment of the industrial and commercial regime requires the solution of the social question" ("Le problème fiscal", 1896d, p. 417, English transl., 2010, p. 342).

From the *Recherche de l'idéal social* (1867–68), Walras always insists on the fact that the "physiological and economical" destiny of man is expressed through industry (in the traditional sense, equated with labour), while the "psychological and moral" destiny of man is expressed through art, science, and customs (mores). This results in a necessary reconciliation between the following different principles: the Beautiful, the True, the Useful (or Interest), and the Just. Consequently, every society should normally allow for a balanced place for art, science, industry, and customs, which constitute the entirety of human destiny,[22] as observed through the detailed study of different economic regimes. However, in the "industrial and commercial stage", a threat coming from the United States looms over Europe. Walras's attention here is drawn to a lecture by the German physiologist Emil Du Bois-Reymond.[23] According to the latter, the United States has become the "main stronghold of utilitarianism". In this country, "the industrial side of scientific activity always insensibly comes to the forefront. The successive generations find themselves increasingly directed towards material interests" (1878, p. 681) and realism prevails over idealism and the

[21] *Cours d'économie sociale*, 50th lesson ("Insufficiency of Agricultural Production"), vol. XII, pp. 325–26.

[22] On these questions, see the following chapter.

[23] Emil Du Bois-Reymond (1818–1896), German physiologist, one of the founders of electro-physics. He was also interested in the limits of scientific knowledge ("ignoramus et ignorabimus") and especially published *Untersuchungen über thierische Elektricität* (1848–60) and *Gesammelte Abhandlungen zur allegemeinen Muskel -und Nervenphysik* (1875–77).

life of ideas. "Americanisation" thus constitutes a threat for German and European civilisation. Walras, for his part, observes that art and science are in a poor state in the United States, while mores are degraded there. His personal description of the picture of "Americanism" is therefore very alarming:

> [...] imagine a civilisation for which poetry and fine arts are superfluities, where the science of man and society is neglected and where, consequently, customs resolve into the financial and political exploitation of a coarse and brutal crowd by greedy and corrupted makers, where the science of nature itself is cultivated only for its applications, among whom the industry, in a word, claims to be everything, that is Americanism; a narrow and false conception that breaks the chain of humanity's traditions and imposes upon it an abnormal and monstrous development, treating it like a fattened ox and attempting to reduce it entirely to flesh through exclusive nourishment, forgetting that it is not destined for the slaughterhouse and that it consequently needs its bones, muscles, and nerves; an artificial and unhealthy regime from which inevitably arises a society rotten before it is ripe." (1878a, vol. XIII, p. 494)

In the *Cours d'économie sociale* (28th lesson, vol. XII, p. 226), Walras considers that for "serious people", the word "Americanism" serves to designate "a return to barbarism". Probably around the same time, he copies into an agenda the opening lines of a "Chronicle" published on 24 March 1878 in *Le XIXe siècle. Journal républicain conservateur* and signed by Henry Fouquier: "Charles Baudelaire liked to repeat this phrase, written by him in the preface of one of his books, 'that America was nothing but a great barbarism lit by gas and travelling on fast trains'".[24]

The spread of "Americanism" in European countries thus constitutes a real threat to come. While approving only partially the proposals for reforming German secondary education formulated by Du Bois-Reymond to counter this danger, Walras believes that one way to avoid it in France would be to redesign the secondary education system to provide both scientific (mathematics) and literary (the humanities) education necessary for the learning of various liberal professions as well as for the preparation of public functions (1878a, vol. XIII, pp. 495–96). In the subsequent years, our author's reflections on "Americanism" do not seem to change. In a "Note d'humeur" (jotting) dated 10 August 1898, he considers that American economists who do not understand his "Note on the Theory of Quantity"[25] are "incapable of understanding anything about mathematical economics, due to their narrow utilitarian mind and their insufficient scientific knowledge" ("Notes d'humeur", 2000, vol. XIII, p. 551).

---

[24] Agenda preserved in the Lausanne collection under the reference F. W. V/16/6. The words attributed to Baudelaire partly appear in "Edgar Poe, sa vie et ses œuvres", a text placed at the beginning of his translation of *Extraordinary Stories* by Edgar Allan Poe.

[25] On 25 October 1897, Walras sent this note to Henry Carter Adams, president of the American Economic Association for its presentation to the Tenth annual meeting and he also asked Irving Fisher to have it translated into English. F. W. Taussig accepted to orally present Walras's paper during the meeting. Unfortunately, the text is considered too short to be accepted for publication in the *Economic Studies* of the A. E. A. (see *Studies in Applied Economics*, 2005, p. 128, note VIII).

2.4 Conclusion

"Historicism", characterised by a specific theory of stages, is one of the lesser-known aspects of Léon Walras's thought. In his writings, we discover a duality between a theory of the five stages of human evolution inherited from his father, which concerns history in the long run, and another approach focused on the notion of "stage" or "industrial and commercial regime" intended to understand the economic transformations occurring in the XIXth century. However, the reader is struck by Walras's lack of interest in updating information on the characteristics of the ongoing industrial and commercial revolution in European countries. This lack of interest in economic history, even recent, is undoubtedly related to his aversion to the approach of the economists of his time who were disciples of the Historical School. Walras wishes that the establishment of the "industrial and commercial regime" would be the occasion to finally resolve, on a practical level, the social question(s), but he acknowledges that here there is no historical inevitability, especially as the threat of "Americanism" becomes increasingly apparent in Europe.

On "Americanism", we are far from the future reflections of Antonio Gramsci (1934), according to whom

> [...] whether we are undergoing a transformation of the material bases of European civilisation, which in the long run (though not all that long, since in the contemporary period everything happens much faster than in the past ages) will bring about the overthrow of the existing forms of civilisation and the forced birth of a new.

Gramsci will even add that

> [...] what is today called "Americanism" is to a large extent an advance criticism of old strata which will in fact be crushed by any eventual new order and which are already in the grips of a wave of social panic, dissolution and despair. (*Prison Notebook* 22, "Americanism and Fordism" [1934] 1971, p. 317)

Chapter 3
Taxonomy of Sciences and Divisions of "Political and Social Economy": An Attempt at Reconstruction

3.1 Introduction

Throughout the XIXth century, attempts to classify the sciences multiplied, particularly in France, a field of research that fascinated many thinkers. Léon Walras, for his part, remained interested in it throughout his life.[1] The present chapter does not aim to exhaustively discuss the methodological questions raised by his work. Instead, it primarily seeks to trace the genesis of the taxonomy of sciences and the divisions of "political and social economy" throughout his writings, attempting to identify the breakpoints, and question their significance and consequences.

The first section of this chapter presents the taxonomy of sciences used in the *Éléments d'économie politique pure* and the modifications it underwent between the first and second edition. This "model" presupposes the existence of a "foundation" (a "base"), that is to say, a set of general principles originating from an investigation of a metaphysical nature; this "foundation" appears in writings from the period 1863–68. The second section attempts to reconstruct the history of the *Éléments*' "model", of the "foundation", and of the tripartite division of "political and social economy", based on Walrasian texts, written between 1858 and 1862. The third section demonstrates that around 1896–98, while retaining the "foundation", Léon Walras attempts to construct a new model of taxonomy of sciences, as evidenced not only by the writings published at that time but also by a number of unpublished notes discovered in the Lausanne archives. This results in interesting modifications concerning the status of the components of "political and social economy".

[1] About Léon Walras's classification of sciences, see notably M. Boson, 1951 and 1963; A. Jolink and J. Van Daal, 1989, pp. 351–59; A. Jolink, 1991, revisited in 1996; P. Dockès, 1996; J. Lallement, 2000, pp. 449–97; M. Herland, 2000, pp. 471–84; R. Baranzini, 2001a and 2005; J. Van Daal, 2005 and 2006; M. Bee, 2013.

J.-P. Potier, *Léon Walras, Economist and Liberal Socialist*, Springer Studies in the History of Economic Thought, https://doi.org/10.1007/978-3-032-04670-3_3

3.2 The "Model" Presented in the *Éléments d'économie Politique Pure*

In the first section, entitled "Object and divisions of political and social economy", of the *Éléments d'économie politique pure*, the author distinguishes "science", "art", and "ethics", which leads him to present a sketch of "the general philosophy of science in order to arrive at the particular philosophy of political and social economy" (vol. VIII, 2nd lesson, p. 39; English transl., 1954, pp. 60–61). In these pages, we find what we will refer to as the model of taxonomy of sciences of the *Éléments*. It can be noted that already in the "Programme d'un cours d'économie politique", prepared at St-Aubin-sur-Mer during the summer of 1870, Walras planned, before dealing with "pure economics", "applied economics", and "social economics", to devote a number of introductory lessons on the theme of the "Philosophy of political and social economy".[2]

Before examining the *Éléments*' "model", it is necessary to present what we will call the "foundation", which it presupposes. The existence of this "foundation" is explained by the fact that, for Walras, science must always be enlightened by metaphysical critique, lest it stray from its role; we are dealing here with a solution that could be described as anti-positivist. Our author will one day confess to Antoine-Augustin Cournot that he inherited from his father "an interest in metaphysics almost as strong as his interest in political economy".[3]

3.2.1 *The "Foundation"*

The "foundation" groups together theses on the larger spheres of knowledge, natural, human (*humanitaires*), and metaphysical facts, as well as the four categories of human facts, with their respective criteria. The exposition of these theses already appears in the studies "Du matérialisme et du spiritualisme en économie politique et sociale", and "Recherche de l'idéal social en matière de propriété et d'impôt", both written in 1863. Their content is taken up in the *Recherche de l'idéal social*, and in the essay "Méthode de conciliation ou de synthèse" (1868c). These developments reappear later in the *Cours d'économie sociale*. In the *Éléments*, the author does not take them up in their entirety because, he says, he "thought it appropriate to maintain the absolutely calm tone that suits to science".[4]

---

[2] Here is the list: "1- Absence of philosophy; 2- Distinction between art and science; 3- Distinction between moral and natural science; 4- Analysis of the fact of the social wealth: *Exchange value - Industry - Property*; 5- Of the theory of exchange value - natural science; 6- Of the theory of industry - art; 7- Of the theory of property - moral science; 8- Conclusion - Programme" ("Programme d'un cours d'économie politique", 1870c, published following the General Introduction to vol. XII, p. 32).

[3] L. Walras, letter to A.-A. Cournot, 14 February 1875, in: *Correspondence,* vol. I, 1. 327, p. 469. At the time, Cournot is preparing to send him his book *Matérialisme, vitalisme, rationalisme.*

[4] L. Walras, letter to C. Renouvier, 25 September 1874, in: *Correspondence*, I, 1. 303, p. 435.

At the beginning of the 3rd lesson of the *Recherche de l'idéal social*, Walras recalls that there are three objects of each knowledge, belonging in reality to a single trunk: the "physical being" or "physical world", corresponding to nature, the "moral being" or "moral world", that is to say, man, and the "metaphysical being", or God. We are thus dealing with three series of facts: natural, human, and metaphysical. To know these three spheres, man has three specific instruments:

- the senses, or the "external experience";
- the conscience, or the "inner experience";
- the reason, or the "rational abstraction".[5]

Léon Walras, for whom "experience nourishes and supports reason, reason illuminates and guides experience" (*op. cit.*, 3rd lesson, p. 85 English transl., 2010, p. 61), will focus on the first two domains of knowledge. It seems absolutely fundamental to him to grasp the distinction between "natural facts" and "human facts".

The "natural" or "necessary" facts must be referred to the domain of natural forces, that is to say, "ineluctable" and "blind" (*op. cit.*, 5th lesson, p. 115 English transl., 2010, p. 86). It is specified in this regard "natural facts in the sense of being and remaining superior to social conventions and that of imposing themselves on human will".[6] The nature or the world of "things" includes minerals, plants, and animals; the latter, although endowed with a "soul", are "things" because they are subject to the domination of instinct. Furthermore, in nature, we also find the "animal man" or the "physical man". Indeed, two "natural facts" constitute the "double principle" of all "human facts", or "two doors" that lead from nature to humanity, that is to say, to the "man properly speaking", or "moral man":

- from a physiological point of view, man is capable of the division of labour and manifests it socially in the "Industry";
- from a psychological point of view, man possesses a "moral personality". This is revealed at three levels: sensitivity (with the "sympathetic love" and the "aesthetic sense"), intelligence (with understanding and reasoning), and finally, free will.[7] Man socially manifests these faculties, respectively in "Art", "Science", and "Customs (Mores)". Society thus appears as a "natural and necessary fact", and not a conventional or free one (*op. cit.*, 6th lesson, pp. 129 and 138; English transl., 2010, pp. 96 and 103).

While external experience (or physiological observation) allows the identification, by abstraction, of man as a being who divides labour, on the other hand, the intimate experience (or psychological observation) allows the identification, by abstraction, of man as a being endowed with sensitivity, intelligence, and free will.

---

[5] *Recherche de l'idéal social* (1867–68), 3rd lesson, vol. IX, pp. 70–73 and 85; see also the 4th lesson, p. 89 *et seq.*, English transl., 2010, pp. 49–52, 61, 67 et sq.

[6] L. Walras, letter to Louis Ruchonnet, 6 September 1870, in: *Correspondence* I, 1. 148, p. 210.

[7] *Recherche de l'idéal social*, 4th lesson, pp. 91–93 and 104–05; 5th lesson, pp. 113–14; "Méthode de conciliation ou de synthèse" (1868c), vol. IX, pp. 162–63, English transl., 2010, pp. 68–70, 78–79, 84–85, 122–23.

The "human facts", which concern the "man properly speaking", a free and responsible being, are thus divided into four "independent provinces": Art, Science, Labour (or Industry), and Customs. These categories are presented by Walras in the 4th lesson of the *Recherche de l'idéal social.*

Art and Science encompass the relationships of man's sensitivity and intelligence with the world and correspond to "receptive or internal" relationships.

- *Art.* It is defined as the "totality of man's sympathetic and aesthetic emotions". Walras includes here both "passions and natural poetry" as well as the Fine Arts and even "religion, as far as it concerns faith and sentiment, myth and worship" (*op. cit.*, 4th lesson, p. 105 English transl., 2010, pp. 79–80). The "principle" of Art is "Beauty".
- *Science.* It is defined as the "totality of notions and conceptions of human's judgements and reasonings formed through the understanding and reasoning power". Walras designates here both the "language" and three groups of sciences, pure and applied: physical or natural sciences, moral or human sciences,[8] and metaphysical science. He adds "religion as far as it concerns of ethics and theodicy" (*op. cit.*, 4th lesson, p. 105 English transl., 2010, p. 80). The "principle" of the Science is "True". Science, which represents the domain of perfection, of absolute, of ideal, is even defined as "the idealisation of reality". This domain contrasts with that "of practice and art", or the "achievement of the ideal".[9] Such an approach to science is directly inspired by the book of Étienne Vacherot, *La métaphysique et la science* (*cf. infra*).

Art and science representing "passive relations", Walras specifies in this regard that "we experience sympathetic and aesthetic emotions, we have our notions and conception, our ideas ("Méthode de conciliation ou de synthèse", 1868c, vol. IX, p. 163, English transl., 2010, p. 123).

Conversely, there are other human facts that do not present this characteristic, the "social facts". Translating the will and the real accomplishment of human destiny, these facts possess "active and external" features. Walras indicates here that "we exert our moral and industrial efforts" (*ibid.*). Industry and Customs are these "active relations".

- *Labour or Industry.* The industry is defined as the "entirety of men's efforts within the framework of division of labour, to prepare the achievement of their destiny". In the 4th lesson, Walras refers to the "economic or industrial society" and he considers the operations related to the multiplication of wealth, that is to say, "general industry": agriculture, industry, commerce, speculation, credit. However, in the 5th lesson, then in "Méthode de conciliation ou de synthèse", he indicates that "industry" also refers to "the making and using tools and machines

[8] The moral sciences are considered here in the broad sense and concern art, science, industry, and customs (see *Recherche de l'idéal social*, 4th lesson, vol. IX, pp. 89–90, English transl., 2010, pp. 67–68). They can be taken as synonyms for moral and political sciences.

[9] "Socialisme et libéralisme. Lettres à M. Éd. Schérer" (1863a), vol. IX, p. 15, English transl., 2010, pp. 7–8.

of all sorts", that is to say, "industry properly speaking".[10] In this perspective, the theory of "general industry" will be "applied economics" while the theory of "industry properly speaking" will be formed by the "technical arts". Finally, the study "Méthode de conciliation ou de synthèse" specifies that these social facts concern the "relations between things and persons introduced to subordinate the purpose of the things to the purpose of persons" (1868c, vol. IX, pp. 154 and 164–65, English transl., 2010, pp. 116 and 124). The "principle" of Labour (or Industry) is "Useful" or "Interest".

– *Customs (Mores).* Relating to "moral society", customs are defined as the "entirety of the voluntary decisions and free actions of men in the field of law and duty, to achieve their destiny". Under this heading, we find the questions of property and taxation, family and government. These three questions are the subject of the "social science properly speaking", or theory of customs, relating to the "rights of individuals in society". "Social economics", which focuses on the first of these questions, therefore possesses a "mixed character", as can be verified in the following[11] scheme:

Political and social economy	Pure economics	
	Applied economics	
	Social economics	Social science proper
	Theory of family	
	Theory of government	

The social facts called "customs (*moeurs*)" concern the "relations between persons and persons with a view to the coordination of people's interrelated destinies" (1868c, vol. IX, pp. 154 and 164–65, English transl., 2010, pp. 117 and 124). The "principle" of Customs is "Good" or "Just".

The "physiological and economical" destiny of man expressed through industry and his "psychological and moral" destiny expressed through art, science, and customs, results in a necessary concordance between the different "principles": Beauty, True, Useful (or Interest), and Good (or Just).[12]

Léon Walras will never later question this "foundation", constructed well before his installation at Lausanne; in the "Esquisse d'une doctrine économique et sociale"

[10] *Recherche de l'idéal social*, 5th lesson, vol. IX, p. 114; "Méthode de conciliation ou de synthèse" (1868c), vol. IX, pp. 164–65, English transl., 2010, pp. 85 and 124–25. In the *Cours d'économie sociale* (9th lesson, "The Social Categories"), L. Walras speaks here of "*technical industry*" to reserve the term of "*industry* proper", within the different economic activities (vol. XII, p. 146).

[11] *Recherche de l'idéal social* (1867–68), 2nd lesson, vol. IX, pp. 49–50, 5th lesson, p. 111, English transl., 2010, pp. 34–35 and 83; for the *Éléments d'économie politique pure*, see *infra*. This approach will be found in the 1st lesson of the *Cours d'économie sociale*, vol. XII, p. 116.

[12] *Recherche de l'idéal social*, 4th lesson, p. 90, and 5th lesson, vol. IX, pp. 111–14 and 123–24; see also "Méthode de conciliation ou de synthèse" (1868c), vol. IX, p. 166, English transl., 2010, pp. 68, 83–85, 92–93.

(1898c), he still refers to it, despite the changes made regarding the taxonomy of sciences and the divisions of "political and social economy" (*cf. infra*).

Examining the "foundation" reveals an ambiguity related to the concept of "social science". First of all, Walras considers the theory of customs as the "social science proper". Furthermore, in two lessons of the *Recherche de l'idéal social*, belonging to the section dedicated to the theme "Of Man and Society",[13] he discusses the question of the concordance between the principle of interest and that of justice (5th lesson) and the "general formula for the constitution of the social science" (6th lesson), aiming to allocate respective roles to the individual and the State. In this regard, he draws an analogy with astronomy. Just as astronomy defines, classifies, and determines the relationships of gravitation (natural facts) to derive "objective and real laws", the "social science" must define, classify, and determine the relationships of society (social facts, stemming from human will, that is to say, industry and customs) to derive "subjective and ideal laws".[14] Moreover, Walras specifies on various occasions, between 1868 and 1880, that before tackling "applied economics" and "social economics", it is necessary to answer two questions: What is social wealth? What is man in society? While "pure economics" provides the "economic foundations" of "applied economics" and "social economics", "social science" or the "general theory of society", for its part, provides the "moral foundations".[15] Thus, "pure economics" and "social science" are placed at the same level of abstraction. From this perspective, is not the "general theory of society" a "pure moral science"? This is all the more so since "society" is considered a "natural and necessary fact" (*cf. supra*). It will be seen that the "revision" of 1879 does not resolve the ambiguity and that our doubts will be dispelled in 1897–98, when Walras introduces the concept of "general cœnonics". It is now time to present the "model" of the *Éléments.*

3.2.2 *The Classification of Sciences in the Éléments*

In the first part of the book published in 1874, the exposition of the "model" appeared, in general terms, in the 3rd and 4th lessons and for the application to "political and social economy", in the 5th, 6th, 7th, and 8th lessons. From the 2nd edition of the *Éléments d'économie politique pure* (1889c), these lessons are grouped in pairs to form the 2nd, 3rd, and 4th lessons.

---

[13] This programme is announced in the 4th lesson, p. 107, English transl., 2010, p. 81.

[14] *Recherche de l'idéal social*, 6th lesson, vol. IX, pp. 129–31 and 145–46, English transl., 2010, pp. 96–97 and 108–09. The first case refers to problems of "physical truth" and the second to problems of "moral truth". Subsequently, L. Walras will claim the notion of law from Montesquieu ("the necessary relations deriving from the nature of things"). See "De la culture et de l'enseignement des sciences morales et politiques" (1879c) and "Des fonctions et de leur représentation géométrique. Théorie mathématique de la chute des corps" (1889b), vol. VII, resp. pp. 404 and 248–49.

[15] "Méthode de conciliation ou de synthèse" (1868c), vol. IX, pp. 151 and 162, English transl., 2010, p. 114 and 123; see also "Discours d'installation" (1872a), vol. VII, pp. 367 and 373; see also a note written in 1879–80, *in:* vol. IX, p. 441 note 1.

In the 2nd lesson, from the 2nd edition, Walras presents his distinction between "science", "art", and "ethics". First of all, he understands "science" in a narrower sense than between 1863 and 1868, retaining here only the physical or natural sciences and the moral or human sciences, both pure and applied. Science concerns a set of facts, their relationships, and their laws. While reiterating the distinction between "natural" facts and "human" facts, Walras considers, unfortunately without specifying, only the *social human facts*, those that refer to human will, the industrial facts, and the moral facts, or Industry and Customs (vol. VIII, pp. 39–42, English transl., 2014, pp. 15–18).

Which sciences correspond to natural and human (industrial and moral) facts? To answer this question, Léon Walras focuses on the distinction between science and art. He does not refer to the definitions proposed by J. S. Mill (*Essays on Some Unsettled Questions of Political Economy*, 1844) or by other British authors, but to those of Charles Coquelin presented in the article "Économie politique" in the *Dictionnaire de l'économie politique* (1852–53). According to Charles Coquelin,

> [...] art advises, prescribes, directs; science observes, describes, explains. When an astronomer observes and describes the course of the stars, he is practicing science; but when, after making his observations, he deduces from them rules applicable to navigation, he is practicing art [...]. Thus, to observe and describe real phenomena is science; to lay down precepts, prescribe rules, that is art.[16]

This separation does not equate to the distinction between theory and practice. Science lends its insights to art, while the latter highlights science's truths. In the logical order, science precedes art, but in the historical order, it is often the reverse (1852b, pp. 646–48); on this theme, Charles Coquelin very explicitly draws inspiration from the Idéologues' theorist, Destutt de Tracy[17]. In Walras's view, the author of the article "Économie politique" fails in his attempt to apply the distinction between science and art to economic science and he omits the one that should be made between art and ethics. He even ends up characterising political economy as "a branch of the natural history of man".[18]

According to our author, "natural" facts can only be recognised, observed, and explained, thus they are the subject of "*pure science*" or "science proper". The criterion is the truth, in the sense of "pure truth"; "pure economics" belongs to this field (*cf. infra*). Conversely, human (social) facts, arising from human will, "clear-sighted and free force", must be governed, and are the subject either of art or of ethics (vol. VIII, pp. 39–42, English transl., 2014, pp. 15–18).

The theory of "industry" is the "applied science" or the "art", understood not in the sense of "practice", but of "theory of art".[19] The human industrial facts, as

[16] C. Coquelin, 1852b, p. 646, cited in the 2nd lesson of *Éléments d'économie politique pure*, vol. VIII, pp. 36 and 40, English transl., 2014, pp. 12 and 16; see also the letter of L. Walras to Louis Ruchonnet, dated 6 September 1870, in: *Correspondence*, I, 1. 148, pp. 207–08.

[17] He quotes a passage from *Éléments d'idéologie* (second part, *Grammar*), by Destutt de Tracy ([1817] 1970, pp. 12–13).

[18] C. Coquelin, 1852b, pp. 660–663; vol. VIII, pp. 37–38, English transl., 2014, pp. 13–14.

[19] See on this subject, L. Walras, letter to Eduard Pfeiffer, 2 April 1874, in: *Correspondence*, I, 1. 256, p. 371; letter to Charles Renouvier, 6 September 1877, in: *op. cit.*, I, 1. 385, p. 542; letter to

(1874 - 1879)

Pure science	**Moral and applied science**
"Natural Science" Object: natural facts	"Applied science" ("art") Object: human industrial facts (Theory of industry).
	"Moral Science" ("ethics") Object: human moral fact (Theory of customs).

Diagram 3.1 Léon Walras's nomenclature

we have seen, consist of relationships between persons and things, the purpose of things being subordinated to that of persons. Here, we distinguish the industry proper or "technical operations", which are the subject of the "technical arts" (theory of machine construction…) and the operations related to the *economic* organisation of industry, which will be dealt with by "applied economics" (vol. VIII, pp. 42 and 58–61, English transl., 2014, pp. 18 and 30–33). Applied science subjects these facts to *rules* of interest.

The theory of "customs (*moeurs*)" is "moral science" or "ethics". The human moral facts, as we have seen, consist of relationships from person to person; their goals having to be coordinated, it results in rights and duties. Moral science subjects these facts to *principles* of justice. This "social science proper" encompasses, as we have seen, "social economics", the theory of family and that of government.

Diagram 3.1 summarises the Walrasian nomenclature, which is not illustrated by a list of disciplines:

In fact, Léon Walras will not be fully satisfied with this taxonomy. In the first version (prior to 1879) of the 9th lesson of the *Cours d'économie sociale*, he adds the "*historical* sciences, or history of social categories" to the three previous groups. History would relate to all categories of art, science, industry, and customs (vol. XII, p. 147).

In 1879, five years after drafting the first part of the *Éléments*, Walras publishes the study "De la culture et de l'enseignement des sciences morales et politiques". It is an opportunity for him to revise his classification of sciences:

> There is a *pure* science that observes facts and relationships, and an *applied* science that prescribes rules of conduct. There is a *pure natural* science that observes facts and relationships having their origin in the play of the fatal forces of the nature, and a *pure moral* science that observes facts and relationships originating in the exercise of man's free will. The former includes, starting from the simplest manifestations to the most complex manifestations of the being, mathematics, physics, chemistry, natural history, anthropology; the latter includes the history of human activity in all its forms: languages and literatures, religions, art, science, industry, customs, law, war, politics. There is a *natural applied* science

Vilfredo Pareto, 14 September 1891, in: *op. cit.*, II, 1. 1025, p. 464; see also "Une branche nouvelle de la mathématique" (1876b), vol. VII, p. 305, "De la culture et de l'enseignement des sciences morales et politiques" (1879c), vol. VII, p. 390.

> providing rules for the conduct of persons towards impersonal things, and a *moral applied* science providing rules for the conduct of persons towards one another. The former mainly includes agricultural and industrial technology, medicine; the latter includes individual and social ethics. (emphasis by L. W., 1879c, vol. VII, p. 414; see also p. 386)

The history "in all its forms" (preceded notably by a "metaphysical and moral philosophy") (*op. cit*, pp. 385–86 and 390), which concerns all social categories, human facts (and not only social ones), that is to say, the "individual and collective destiny of people", is now integrated into the "model" of the *Éléments*, under the heading of "pure moral science".

Léon Walras reproduces the revision of his classification in the 9th lesson of the *Cours d'économie sociale* ("Social Categories").[20] In 1889, he will integrate into the 2nd edition of the *Éléments* the "pure moral science" or "history", in the 2nd lesson:

> [...] as to the effects of human will, on the contrary, it is necessary <first to recognize them, to observe them, to explain them, then> to govern them [..]. The effects of human will be the subject <first> of a study which will be called <*pure moral science* or *history*, then of a study which will be called> of another name, either art or ethics [...].[21]

How to explain the reappearance of history in the Walrasian taxonomy? Indeed, we will see in the second section that the historical sciences, related to "progressive" or "providential" facts, appear in the classification of the very young Walras (1858–60), then disappear around 1862. This reintegration is undoubtedly explained by the fact that our author becomes very sensitive to the *renaissance* of historical studies in France. In the *Cours d'économie sociale*, and in the article "De l'enseignement de l'économie politique en France", he refers to the revival, from the late 1860s, of the "historical and philological sciences", in the 4th section of the École Pratique des Hautes Études (Paris), and he alludes to the work of Gabriel Monod. He also notes the publication of the prestigious *Revue historique*. For him, this vigour of the historical studies is an example to be imitated in economics (1880d, vol. VII, pp. 433 and 441–42). This historical school, called "methodical", claims a "strictly scientific" approach, free from political, philosophical, or religious opinions.[22]

However, we must note the great ambiguity of this return to history. Indeed, this "pure moral science" is also presented as relating to the effects of the "free will of man", thus referring to customs and industry, which was the field of "social science" as a "general theory of society", in the *Recherche de l'idéal social*, but... was not identified with history. Diagram 3.2 presents the new Walrasian nomenclature:

Walras specifies that just as the "pure natural science" is insufficient for "applied natural science", the "pure moral science" is insufficient for "applied moral science". A pure science serves several applied sciences (natural or moral) and an applied

---

[20] He even specifies in a note: "(to be developed in accordance with paragraph VI of the article on the Culture and Teaching of Moral and Political Sciences)". See *Cours d'économie sociale*, 9th lesson, vol. XII, note 98, p. 805.

[21] Emphasis by L. W. The words in brackets are inserted in the text for the 2nd edition, *Éléments d'économie politique pure*, vol. VIII, p. 40, English transl., 2014, p. 16; see also the "Terminologie des *Éléments d'économie politique pure* (4e éd.)", *op. cit*, p. 724.

[22] On this school, see C.-O. Carbonell, 1976, pp. 409–50.

(1879 - 1896)

Pure science (natural and moral)	**Applied science (natural and moral)**
"Pure natural science" ("science")	
Object : natural facts	
Disciplines : Mathematics, Mechanics, Astronomy, Physics, Chemistry, Physiology, Anthropology, Pure economics as "physico-mathematical science"	
- *"Pure moral science"*	- *"Applied natural science"* ("applied science" or "art")
Object : human facts, relating to the exercise of free will	Object : human industrial facts (Theory of the relations between persons and things)
Discipline : "History", in all its forms	Disciplines : Technical arts, Applied economics
	- *"Applied moral science"* ("moral science" or "ethics")
	Object : Moral human facts (Theory of the relations between persons)
	Disciplines: Theory of family, Theory of government, Social economics

Diagram 3.2 Léon Walras's new classification[23]

science borrows from several pure sciences (natural or moral).[24] This idea underpins the projects for reforming higher education that our author hopes to promote at the time.[25]

[23] See the unpublished diagrams constructed by L Walras preserved in the Lausanne collection: diagram on the back of a draft letter to MM. Guillaumin et Cie, 31 September 1877 (F. W. V b, box 19), diagram entitled "Classification des Éléments", written on the back of an envelope with postal mark "2 III 1898" (F. W. V b, box 22); diagram on the back of an envelope with postal mark "18 III 1898" (F. W. V b, box 22). See also "De la culture et de l'enseignement des sciences morales et politiques" (1879c), vol. VII, p. 414; Cours d'économie sociale, 9th lesson, vol. XII, p. 147.

[24] "De la culture et de l'enseignement des sciences morales et politiques" (1879c), vol. VII, p. 415.

[25] *Cf.* Chap. 8, *From Criticism to the Reform Plan for the Teaching of Political Economy in France in the XIXth century.*

	Branches	**Sub-branches**	**First-order sciences**
A) Cosmological sciences proper	1) Mathematical sciences	Mathematics proper	Arithmology Geometry
		Physico-mathematical	Mechanics (kinematics, statics, dynamics…) Uranology (astronomy, celestial mechanics …)
	2) Physical sciences	Physics proper	General physics (experimental physics, chemistry…) Technology
		Geological	
B) Physiological sciences	1)Natural sciences	Phytological (agriculture, botany)	
		Zoological proper	
	2) Medical sciences		

Diagram 3.3 A.-M. Ampère’s nomenclature

In terms of nomenclature, in the *Éléments*, there is no reference to the classifications of A.-A. Cournot, Auguste Comte, or Herbert Spencer.[26] However, in the field of “pure natural science”, Léon Walras implicitly and partly uses the classification of the “cosmological sciences” (related to the natural world), proposed by André-Marie Ampère in his famous *Essai sur la philosophie des sciences* (1834).[27] In Ampère’s book, the “cosmological sciences” are divided as follows (Diagram 3.3):

In this scheme, “arithmology” corresponds to arithmography, algebra, function theory, and probability calculus (“third-order sciences”). Ampère justified his “natural classification” by stating that a “man who would like to go through the entire series […] should never need […] to resort, for the study of a science, to other knowledge than that which he would have acquired by studying the preceding sciences” (1834, pp. 13–14).

In the 3rd lesson of the *Éléments d’économie politique pure*, the author clearly distinguishes the branch of “natural sciences properly” and the two sub-branches of mathematical sciences, on the one hand the “mathematical sciences properly” and on the other hand the “physico-mathematical sciences” (mechanics, hydraulics, astronomy). Concerning the first category of sciences, Walras noted in the first edition

[26] In a letter of thanks dated 20 December 1875, to Gerolamo Boccardo, who sent him his Preface to the *Nuova Enciclopedia Italiana* (6th ed., Torino: U.T.E.T., 1875), L. Walras states: “the table of the classification of sciences and arts particularly struck me because I have myself thought a lot about this subject” (*Correspondence*, I, l. 342, p. 490).

[27] It should be noted that the only reference to Ampère’s book in Walrasian writings is found in “Esquisse d’une doctrine économique et sociale” (vol. X, p. 407, note 1, English transl., 2005, p. 356, note 1). However, Ampère’s name sometimes appears in various notes preserved in the Lausanne archives (F. W. V b, box 22), and his book belongs to Walras’s personal library.

of the *Éléments* that they "purely and simply describe nature, they do not go beyond experience"; from the 2nd edition, he becomes more cautious on this subject: "I leave it to the natural scientists the task of answering this question" (vol. VIII, p. 53, English transl., 2014, p. 27).

The "physical sciences", placed in Ampère's nomenclature between the "mathematical sciences" and the "natural sciences", are not mentioned in the *Éléments*. However, in the "Application des mathématiques à l'économie politique" (2nd attempt, 1869–70, vol. XI, p. 343), Walras stated that "physical, chemical and natural sciences describe nature: they do not go beyond experience". Conversely, for mathematical sciences, the judgement is unequivocal:

> The mathematical method is not an *experimental* method; it is the *rational* method. [...] the physico-mathematical sciences, like the mathematical sciences properly speaking, do go beyond experience as soon as they have borrowed their type concepts from it. They abstract from these real types ideal types that they define, and on the basis of these definitions they construct *a priori* the whole framework of their theorems and proofs. They re-enter after into experience not to confirm but to apply their conclusions.[28]

Thus, in an abstract and ideal circle, the radii are equal and in an abstract and ideal triangle, the sum of the angles is equal to that of two right angles.[29] Here we have the exposition of the approach in terms of "ideal types". The criterion of truth is not situated in the reality, although experience or observation of reality is the starting point of the research (on this question, *cf. infra* the following chapter).

The young Vilfredo Pareto will reject this approach, preferring to align himself with John Stuart Mill's inductive-deductive method (*A System of Logic Ratiocinative and Inductive*, 1843), characterised by three stages: direct induction, deductive reasoning and verification, applicable also to the so-called "deductive" sciences (for example, geometry).[30] From this perspective, the use of mathematics goes hand in hand with the "experimental method", both for physico-mathematical sciences and for economics.[31]

Léon Walras will prepare a short note for Pareto, in which we can read:

> Undoubtedly reasoning and science cannot be in contradiction with experience and facts. But who knows the facts? Science states truths that experience cannot confirm. (π the resultant by the base [*sic*], the proportionality of values to *raretés*). It is self-sufficient and can rectify the facts. (Newton's system was in contradiction with the facts as long as the perturbations of

[28] Emphasis by L. W., *Éléments, op. cit.*, p. 53, English transl., 2014, p. 27; see also "Application des mathématiques à l'économie politique" (2nd attempt, 1869–1970)", *op. cit.*, p. 343.

[29] In *La métaphysique et la science ou Principes de métaphysique positive*, Étienne Vacherot illustrates the "type", an "a priori" concept, although not "independent of experience", by referring to the "ideal triangle on which geometers base their definitions and demonstrations" (1863, vol. 2, pp. 22–23; see also particularly, pp. 30, 102, 141, 169–70 and 221–22).

[30] Since the first publication of this study, the literature on Pareto's methodology and its relation to that of J. S. Mill has expanded. See notably, R. Marchionatti, 1999, pp. 283–86; R. Baranzini and P. Bridel, 2005, pp. 351–53; F. Mornati, 2018 (vol. I), pp. 140–48 and 2019 (vol. II), pp. 96–100.

[31] V. Pareto, letter to L. Walras, 2 August 1893, in: *Correspondence*, II, 1. 1145, p. 572.

Uranus had not been explained. Who completed the facts by discovering the planet Neptune? Reasoning, not experience).[32]

In the introduction to the 2nd edition of the *Éléments*, Walras states that the ultimate goal of science is the "progressive transformation of the experimental into the rational" and that, in the future, the sciences thus constructed could merge "into a single science which would be metaphysics".[33]

3.2.3 The Tripartite Notion of "Political and Social Economy"

In the first lesson of the *Éléments d'économie politique pure*, Walras critiques the definitions of political economy that have succeeded one another. In François Quesnay and his disciples' works, the theory of the "natural government of society" merges with "social science". Adam Smith, although having contributed to pure science, defines the discipline both as "applied" and "social economics", without succeeding to distinguish them clearly. In contrast, Jean-Baptiste Say brings an "exclusive colour of natural science" (as we saw in Chap. 1, *Auguste Walras as a Transmitter of Ideas: From Jean-Baptiste Say to Léon Walras*). Adolphe Blanqui and Joseph Garnier attempted unsuccessfully to remedy these defects by considering political economy both as a "natural science" (what is) and a "moral science" (what ought to be), but without succeeding to reveal the content of the "true natural science".

Pure Economics

Léon Walras defines pure economics as "in essence, the theory of the determination of prices under a hypothetical regime of absolute free competition (*libre concurrence absolue*)".[34] It is therefore a "theory of exchange value and exchange". The general fact of exchange value is "natural", from the point of view in both its origins

[32] Note written on the back of an envelope with post mark "16 II 92", Lausanne collection, block V b, box 21, published with some errors, in: *Correspondence*, II, note 8, p. 573; re-ed. in: "Notes d'humeur" (2000), vol. XIII, p. 567.

[33] "Des fonctions et de leur représentation géométrique. Théorie mathématique de la chute des corps" (1889b), vol. VII, p. 257 and note 11, p. 529. Vilfredo Pareto finds here the opportunity to reproach the author for leading economic science "into a metaphysical path, where reasoning prevails over experience" ("Considerazioni sui principii fondamentali dell'economia politica pura", *Giornale degli economisti*, vol. IV, series 2, May 1892, p. 395, re-ed. in: V. Pareto, 1982, p. 65). It should be noted that L. Walras will modify his text for its inclusion in the *Mélanges*, undoubtedly taking into account the new reflections presented in the "Esquisse d'une doctrine économique et sociale" (*cf. infra*). He removes "which would be the metaphysics" and adds regarding the unique science: "there are reasons to believe that we will never get there".

[34] Preface (from the 2nd edition) of the *Éléments d'économie politique pure*, vol. VIII, p. 11, English transl., 1954 revised, p. 40.

and its manifestations. Indeed, it does not stem from the will of the traders but is imposed upon them, in the market where "free competition" reigns, just like the law of gravity.[35] On this occasion, Walras will note:

> We are as free to direct, in applied and social economics, the natural tendencies inherent to the social wealth, as we are free to direct, in applied mechanics, the natural property inherent to matter. But just as, to build good machines, one must know the natural properties of matter, so too, to properly organise the economic society, one must know the natural tendencies of social wealth. We can only command the exchange value, as with gravity, by obeying it. Hence the necessity of pure economics as of pure mechanics.[36]

Thus, we see in what sense he understands one of his favourite maxims, borrowed from Francis Bacon, "man commands nature only by obeying it".[37] Léon Walras's intention is to establish, through algebra and geometry, "pure economics" as an exact science, a new "first-order science" (Ampère), which would join mechanics and "uranology" within the "physico-mathematical sciences".[38] Like other mathematical sciences, this discipline is based on an approach in terms of "ideal types", constructed from "real types". Certainly, the implementation of this approach is very delicate here, and one might be tempted to apply to "political and social economy"this reflection related to the "theory of society":

> There is a difference between the theory of society and geometry: the real type in geometry is immediately provided by experience, and the ideal type can be developed by the understanding by means of an immediate *a posteriori* synthesis. However, in the theory of society, the real type is not immediately given by experience, and the ideal type can be extracted only by means of a synthesis *a posteriori* that is very long and very arduous.[39]

While the starting point is the "experimental method", the essential part of the theoretical work is carried out through the rational, mathematical method. Léon Walras debates with Carl Menger on this point.[40] For the Austrian economist, mathematics (formulas and graphs), is merely an auxiliary science of economics, and represents

---

[35] *Recherche de l'idéal social*, 1st lesson, vol. IX, pp. 31–32, English transl., 2010, pp. 22–23 (passage included in the letter to L. Ruchonnet, 6 September 1870, in: *Correspondence*, I, 1. 148, pp. 208–09); "Application des mathématiques à l'économie politique" (2nd attempt), 1870a, vol. XI, pp. 341–42, passage included in the 3rd lesson of the *Éléments*, vol. VIII, pp. 50–51, English transl., 2014, p. 25; "Une branche nouvelle de la mathématique" (1876b), vol. VII, p. 326. One should also refer to the introduction prepared for the 2nd edition of the *Éléments*, "Des fonctions et de leur représentation géométrique" (1889b), vol. VII, pp. 236–60.

[36] L. Walras, letter to Vito Cusumano, 20 October 1874, in: *Correspondence*, I, 1. 311, p. 443; see also *Éléments d'économie politique pure*, vol. VIII, 3rd lesson, pp. 50–51, English transl., 1954, p. 69 and note 3 by Willian Jaffé p. 497.

[37] F. Bacon, in *Redargutio Philosophiarum* declares: "*Homo naturae non nisi parendo imperat*". It is also found in *Novum Organum* (I, 129): "*Naturae enim non imperatur, nisi parendo*" ("In reality, he is not the master of nature except by obeying it").

[38] See, for example, "Une branche nouvelle de la mathématique" (1876b), vol. VII, notably pp. 304–11 and 328–29.

[39] "Socialisme et libéralisme. Lettres à M. Éd. Schérer" (1863a), vol. IX, p. 16, English transl., 2010, p. 9, passage included in the 13th lesson of the *Cours d'économie sociale*, vol. XII, p. 166.

[40] See, on this subject, P. Garrouste, 1994 and S. Gloria, 2018.

only a "method of exposition and demonstration and not of research". Our author retorts that he uses the mathematical method both for research and for the exposition of the results.[41] In the *Éléments*, he emphasises that the exposition of a theory in mathematical form is essential for purposes of "demonstration".[42]

Concerning the necessity of applying mathematics to economics, Walras can claim illustrious predecessors, such as Antoine-Augustin Cournot. In the *Principes de la théorie des richesses* (1863), Cournot nevertheless considered: "Finally, just as in mathematics, it [the theory of wealth, J.P.P.] admits, it provokes, in all parts susceptible to scientific construction, the control of reasoning by experience [...].[43] Reacting to this remark, Léon Walras notes the following on his copy of the book: "Pure economics does not wait for confirmation from experience".[44]

Following in Cournot's footsteps, he misses no opportunity to highlight the analogy between "pure economics" and mechanics. The market of "absolute free competition" would play a role similar to that of "frictionless machines" in pure mechanics.[45] In this field, he refers to classical mechanics represented, in particular, by Newton's *Mathematical Principles of Natural Philosophy* (1687), Lagrange's *Mécanique analytique* (1788), and Laplace's *Mécanique céleste* (1799). Louis Poinsot's book, the *Éléments de statique* (see the following chapter), will be useful to him in his quest for analogies. In the Walrasian perspective, the analogy, far from representing a mere metaphor, assumes a function of delimiting the field of study and seeking scientific legitimacy. In this regard, one can speak of a "theoretical" analogy, rather than a "methodological" one with heuristic value.[46]

In various texts written from 1867 onwards, up to the 3rd lesson of the *Éléments*, Walras specifies that "pure economics" must precede "applied economics" just as "pure mechanics" must precede "applied mechanics".[47] Eduard Pfeiffer, interested

---

[41] Emphasis by C. M., letter to L. Walras, 28 June 1883 and reply from the latter on 2 July 1883, in: É. Antonelli, 1953, pp. 271 and 275–276, or *Correspondence,* I, l. 566 and 569, pp. 768 and 771–772.

[42] Preface from the 2nd edition of *Éléments d'économie politique pure*, vol. VIII, p. 15, English transl., 2014, p. XI.

[43] A.-A. Cournot, 1863, p. 16. See also the article "Mathématiques" written by Cournot for the *Dictionnaire des sciences philosophiques, par une société de professeurs et de savants*, Adolphe Franck (ed), Paris: Hachette, 2nd ed., 1875, pp. 1051–55. On the role of mathematics in Cournot, see L. Ragni 2011 and 2018.

[44] *Op. cit.*, annotation by L. Walras at the bottom of page 17 on his personal copy, kept at the Centre d'études interdisciplinaires Walras-Pareto de l'Université de Lausanne (ZAB 2350). Note here that he published a review of this work in *L'indépendant de la Moselle* (1863b).

[45] *Éléments d'économie politique pure*, 5th lesson, vol. VIII, p. 71, English transl., 2014, p. 43. Cournot mentioned the skillful engineer "diminishing friction through polished bearings and accurate gearing". See A.-A. Cournot, [1838] 2001, p. 8, English transl., 1897, p. 9; see also Cournot, 1863, p. 3.

[46] According to Michel de Coster's typology, 1978, pp. 26–31.

[47] *Recherche de l'idéal social*, 1st lesson, vol. IX, p. 32, English transl., 2010, p. 23; "Principe d'une théorie mathématique de l'échange" (1874a), vol. VII, p. 281, or vol. XI, p. 46, passage repeated in the letter to Paul Piccard, 25 October 1873, "Sur la théorie mathématique de l'échange", 1873a, vol. XI, p. 481; "Application des mathématiques à l'économie politique" (2nd attempt, 1869–70),

by this thesis, will point out to the author that while it is easy to apply the laws of pure mechanics to matter, on the other hand, the application of the laws of pure economics is more delicate because "man is not a matter of a determined quality that does not vary".[48] Walras admits the difficulty of the task to be accomplished and acknowledges that "perhaps one should not push the analogy between mechanics and economics too far".[49]

"Pure economics" must be carefully distinguished from "applied economics" and "social economics", which originally were supposed to be the subjects of the 2nd and 3rd volumes of a *Traité d'économie politique et sociale.*

Applied Economics

"Applied economics" is the theory of the production of social wealth, or the organisation of industry in the division of labour. Firstly, it must seek the rules of utility for an "abundant" and "well-proportioned" production of social wealth, or the "general and superior rule of agricultural, industrial, commercial, and financial production of wealth" (emphasis by L. W., *Cours d'économie politique appliquée*, 1th lesson, vol. XII, p. 446), namely "free competition". This rule is then applied to a long series of domains: agriculture, industry, commerce, credit, speculation, crises, insurance, association, and colonisation. The question of monopolies (railways, for example) is examined under the heading of "exceptions to the principle of free competition".

Léon Walras notes that in "applied economics", just as in "social economics", two instruments of investigation are necessary: reasoning and experience. One must start from experience, that is to say, from "geographical, ethnographical, and historical observation to obtain the definition of man from a physiologico-economical point of view" (*ibid*). From this definition of man, one can rationally deduce the rules for the "most suitable possible" production of social wealth.

Social Economics

"Social economics" is the theory of the distribution of social wealth among people in society. It seeks the principles of social justice in matters of property and taxation. For the distribution of wealth to be "as equitable as possible", the State must become the owner of all lands, by virtue of natural law. In this sphere as well, one must start from experience to obtain the definition of man from a "psychological and moral" point of view.

If the affirmed starting point is indeed pure economics, the "first science", should "political and social economy" be concluded with applied economics or with social

1870a, vol. XI, p. 343, passage repeated in the 3rd lesson of *Éléments d'économie politique pure*, vol. VIII, p. 52, English transl., 2014, p. 27.

48 Eduard Pfeiffer, letter to L. Walras, 17 March 1874, in: *Correspondence*, I, l. 252, p. 362.

49 L. Walras, letter to E. Pfeiffer, 2 April 1874, in: *op. cit.*, l. 256, p. 371.

economics? Regarding the last two disciplines, Walras frequently indicates that "the order can be reversed without any inconvenience".[50] This alternation was, moreover, his own practice as a professor at the Faculty of Law in Lausanne from 1871 to 1892. However, in a passage added in margin of the 5th lesson of the *Cours d'économie politique appliquée*, he reveals his preference: "[…] as after all justice should come before interest, and consequently, the problem of distribution should be solved before that of production […]" (vol. XII, pp. 471–72).

On a note kept with the manuscript of this lesson, he specifies that distribution "precedes" production, as its primary purpose is to establish the conditions "of a legitimate appropriation of productive services".[51] It can be noted that this sequence corresponds to the order of publication of the *Études d'économie sociale* (1896e) and the *Études d'économie politique appliquée* (1898d) and that it remains affirmed in the jubilee speech "Ruchonnet et le socialisme scientifique" (1909c, vol. VII, p. 509).

Léon Walras does not neglect a final field, somewhat overlooked, that of "practical economics (*économie politique pratique*)". Situated downstream of social and applied economics, it concerns not the theory of art, but the practice of art, or the "field of politics and business"; questions of governmental economic policy fall, for example, within this field.[52]

Walras would reproach the young German Historical School (the *Katheder-Sozialismus*) for producing under the name of "theoretical political economy" a "confused mixture of pure economics and applied economics" and for indulging in the field of "practical economics", first by drafting government law projects, then by entering parliament.[53] In 1876, he wished "sooner or later to write a substantive article on German political economy", in which he could have deepened his criticisms.[54]

---

50 "Note sur l'organisation de l'enseignement de l'économie politique et sociale à l'École pratique des Hautes Études" (1879d), vol. VII, p. 423.

51 Note on the back of an envelope with postal mark "21-VII-1886", published in: *Cours d'économie politique appliquée*, 5th lesson, vol. XII, note 113, p. 853.

52 On the notion of "practical economics", see L. Walras, letter to Eduard Pfeiffer, 2 April 1874, in: *Correspondence*, I, 1. 256, p. 371; letter to Émile Cheysson, 6 May 1886, in: *op. cit.*, II, l. 712, p. 119; "Une branche nouvelle de la mathématique" (1876b), vol. VII, pp. 305, 315 and 327; *Éléments d'économie politique pure*, vol. VIII, p. 651; "Théorie mathématique du bimétallisme" (1881a), vol. XI, p. 166. It should be noted that L. Walras used the term "practical economics" in a completely different sense, to designate the whole formed by applied and social economics, in his application letter addressed to L. Ruchonnet, 6 September 1870, in: *Correspondence*, I, 1. 148, p. 212.

53 "De la culture et de l'enseignement des sciences morales et politiques" (1879c), vol. VII, pp. 401–402.

54 L. Walras, letter to Vito Cusumano, 11 January 1876, Archivio Cusumano (Mazara, Sicily), published by Roberto Salvo, 1979, pp. 233–34; see also the letter to Alberto Errera of 19 November 1874, in: *Correspondence,* I, l. 318, p. 452.

3.3 At the Origins of the "Model" of the *Éléments*

It is now necessary to look into the early writings of Léon Walras in order to detect some constitutive materials of the "model" of the *Éléments* as well as the "foundation". The study of the writings from 1858–59 indeed allows for an understanding of the genesis of the "foundation", and reveals the first Walrasian approach to the taxonomy of sciences. Furthermore, the examination of works from the years 1859–62 shows how our author transitioned from a bipartite to a tripartite approach of economics.

3.3.1 *Formation of the "Foundation" and First Approach to the Classification of Sciences*

It is known that Walras, after his failures at the École des Mines, was attempting to pursue a literary career. In 1858, he worked on a book dealing with the *Philosophie de l'art.*[55] He would not manage to give it a definitive form, but the material would serve for the drafting of the study, "Du sens esthétique; de l'art; et des opinions en matière d'art".[56] In the *Philosophie de l'art*, the obligatory starting point of our investigation,[57] the question of the classification of sciences is far from being central. The author clarifies: "I did not intend to establish a complete and reasoned classification of the general facts and their theories, which could not fit within the limits of my work."[58] However, in the middle of the manuscript, a surprise awaits the reader. Léon Walras takes up pages from his father, dealing with the taxonomy of sciences, but whose original is probably lost today.[59] Although the source is not mentioned, it can be asserted that the content of these pages is extremely close to Auguste Walras's lessons on the theme of the idea of space and the idea of extent, undated, but probably written after 1846.[60]

---

[55] The original manuscript is kept in the Lausanne collection (F. W. Vb, box 17).

[56] This manuscript is published in vol. XIII, pp. 19–46.

[57] One of the first uses of this text for understanding Walrasian methodology is found in A. Jolink, 1991, Chap. 3, pp. 43–49; 1996, Chap. 3, pp. 37–42.

[58] *Philosophie de l'art* (1858a), 1st part, *Ontology*, 2nd chapter, "Physical and Moral Phenomena", folio 5.

[59] It consists of ten unnumbered sheets, inserted into the manuscript. Besides Auguste Walras's style, passages such as this one are noted: "in my time it was called *moral philosophy* a '*science of the human mind*' [...]".

[60] "One must not confuse the idea of space with the idea of extent." The manuscript of these lessons is kept in the Walras collection in Lyon under the reference F A III A 13: 01: 01 (19 f° + f° A and B). The classification of sciences is presented in folios 13–18. See also the "Philosophy Programme. Analytical summary of all the lessons of the school year 1840–1841", in the Royal College of Caen, lessons 3 to 6, f°s 5–14, kept in the Walras collection in Lyon under the reference F A III A: 09: 03. See also the manuscript "Object of Philosophy" (1840), (f°s 5–10), kept in the same collection, under the reference F A III A: 09: 02. Auguste Walras would later, presumably in 1863, revisit

Before examining the ideas of the author of the *Philosophie de l'art*, it seems necessary to outline the principle of his father's classification of the sciences. The latter was trained in spiritualist and eclectic philosophy, following the teachings of Victor Cousin (1792–1867) at the École normale.[61] Quite naturally, we find in his writings a strong influence of this movement. According to Auguste Walras, "matter" (a principle that extends in space) and "force" (a principle that extends in time) constitute the substance of the material world, of reality. From the union of the two, "bodies" and "phenomena" (or "beings" and "facts") are born. There are "non-organised" bodies (minerals) and "organised" bodies (plants and animals). Man, a "moral being", possesses three faculties: voluntary and free activity, sensitivity, and intelligence; the first is the most fundamental, for man is a "free force", according to Victor Cousin.[62] Science does not relate to "beings", but to the general facts or phenomena that occur within beings. Here, we find an idea belonging to Greek philosophy (Plato, for example). Science must be considered as "the theory of a general, universal, and permanent fact". Such a theory always consists of providing answers: (1) on the nature of the fact; (2) its cause, its origins; (3) its division into species (main and secondary); (4) its laws; and finally, (5) its effects, its consequences. Searching for causes requires observation and hypothesis, and searching for laws, requires observation and experimentation.[63] Auguste Walras intends to propose his own nomenclature of facts and sciences.[64] General facts are divided into three categories[65]:

- The "natural" or "necessary" facts. They occur in the universe or within man, independently of his will; human will can only exert an indirect influence on them.
- The "human" or "moral" facts. They are the expression of humans' free will and free choice. These facts relate either to the relationships between people (example: family) or to the relationships between people and impersonal nature (example: property).[66]

---

these ideas in the lessons dedicated to the theme, "On the True, the Beautiful, the Good", 5th lesson "Classification of Scientific Facts", the manuscript of which is kept in the same collection, under the reference F A III A: 13: 01: 03.

61 On the philosophy of Auguste Walras, see P.-H. Goutte, 2013.

62 A. Walras, "De la nature de la loi" (1833c), vol. I, 1990, p. 313; *Réfutation de la doctrine de Hobbes, sur le droit naturel de l'individu* (1835), *op. cit.*, pp. 298 and 323. See also Victor Cousin, 1853, pp. 31–33.

63 On the study of the general fact, see also A. Walras, "Vérité, science & art", undated lesson, preserved in the Walras collection in Lyon, under the reference F A III, 13 09, numbered folio 152 (3).

64 On A. Walras's classification of sciences, see A. Diemer and H. Guillemin, 2011, pp. 21–42 and A. Diemer, 2013, pp. 59–85 can be mentioned.

65 See also A. Walras, "Vérité, science & art", F A III A: 13: 09, numbered folios 152 (5) and (6).

66 Auguste Walras already indicates this division in the lessons on "extent" and "space" and emphasises it further in the 5th lesson of "On the True, the Beautiful, the Good" (Walras collection in Lyon, folio 22).

- The "historical" or "progressive" facts, such as the development of civilisation or of human knowledge. They succeed one another over time, with the contribution of free will, under the impulse of a divine Providence, and in this sense, one can say that "progress" is "inevitable".

To these three categories of facts correspond three groups of sciences.

- The natural sciences. The classification here is the most advanced. Insofar as the most general fact is the "very fact of existence", Auguste Walras believes that the first of the natural sciences must be "first philosophy, metaphysics, ontology". We then understand the remarks he will send to his son about metaphysics as the "queen of sciences".[67] Then come disciplines such as arithmetic or arithmology, geometry, mechanics, crystallography, botany, zoology, physiology, nosology or pathology, then the theory of sensitivity (aesthesiology[68]), the theory of instinct (not yet named), the theory of intelligence, studied by philosophers (which can be designated, at choice, by ideology, phrenology, or noology),[69] and finally the theory of free will (thelesiology).[70]
- The moral sciences, or the "science of free forces" or "of right and duty". They are based on natural law and encompass the theories of family, property, government (politics), jurisprudence.[71]
- The historical sciences. Here one finds "history proper", and the histories of sciences, arts, civilisation.

Finally, alongside the different sciences, there exist "arts" intended to realise in practice the theoretical discoveries. Thus, the natural sciences find applications in the mechanical arts, industrial arts, etc. This is also true for the moral sciences, which allow for the establishment of rules and prescriptions (administration, for example).

How does Léon Walras position himself in relation to his father's approach? The *Philosophie de l'art* reveals the influence of Victor Cousin's philosophy and of one of his disciples, Théodore Jouffroy (1796–1842). After having established two "articles of faith" concerning the existence and certainty of "Reason", Walras claims to be

[67] See the letter of Auguste Walras to his son dated 18 May 1861, in: vol. IV, p. 490. In his letter of 25 July 1863, he states: "I have always regarded metaphysics, or first philosophy, as Aristotle called it, as the most universal science, that is to say, as the theory of the most general fact there is in the world. Now, that fact is none other than existence itself [...]." (vol. IV, p. 592).

[68] "Aesthesiology" is a term in physiology denoting the study of the sensory organs.

[69] "Ideology" refers to the school of thought represented notably by Destutt de Tracy; "noology" denotes psychology.

[70] In Ampère, thelesiology forms a "first-order" science in the branch of "philosophical sciences", within the "noological sciences" (1843, pp. 40–41 and 46–47).

[71] In the manuscript "Object of Philosophy" (1840) which summarises his classification of sciences, A. Walras adds here the "Social, Public or Political Economy", relating to the facts of "labour" and "industry" (Walras collection in Lyon, F A III A: 09: 02, folio 8; see also the Philosophy Programme (1840–41), Royal College of Caen, F A III A: 09: 03, folio 11). See *infra* on the place of "political economy".

"eclectic with Jouffroy whose authority decides me".[72] However, from the drafting of the study "Du sens esthétique; de l'art; et des opinions en matière d'art", some distance is taken from this thinker.[73]

Following his father's footsteps, Léon Walras revisits the metaphysical conceptions of "matter", "force", "bodies" (both organised and unorganised), and "phenomena". He emphasises the distinction between man "from a physiological point of view", or "animal", which belongs to the "natural" world, and the "immaterial man" or "properly speaking", which belongs to the "moral" world. In the tradition of Victor Cousin, he recalls the three faculties of man: "free will", "sensitivity", and "intelligence". "Free will" is the principal faculty of man who deliberates, determines, and freely executes his actions. Intelligence and sensitivity share common organs, the senses (external perceptions) and consciousness (internal perceptions). While intelligence allows for "rational conceptions", sensitivity allows for emotions and feelings.[74]

In *Philosophie de l'art* and in the aforementioned study, Walras considers three categories of social facts, which find their origin in human faculties[75]:

- Art, stemming from sensitivity, whose criterion is the "Beautiful";
- Science, stemming from reason, whose criterion is the "True" and the "possible";
- Industry, stemming from free will and expression of the "principle of progress", whose criterion is "Useful" and "Good".[76]

For the young Walras, "Thus science and art precede, accompany, or follow industry. Thus industry, science, and art grasp reality, work on it, and transform it for the progressive fulfilment of humanity's destinies" ("Du sens esthétique...", 1859a, vol. XIII, pp. 33–34). Here we see that the social category of "Customs" is not yet clearly established and that the criteria of "Good" (Just) and "Useful" are not distinguished.

The author of the *Philosophie de l'art* asserts that science studies "general, universal, and permanent facts", of which "bodies" and "phenomena" are merely individual manifestations, and he very precisely follows the paternal methodological

72 *Philosophie de l'art* (1858a), 1st part, *Ontology*, Chap. 1, "Synthesis of the Ontological Fact", folio 13.

73 See also the Walrasian critique of "common sense" in T. Jouffroy in the first of the series of "Paradoxes économiques" (1860c), vol. VII, pp. 42–62.

74 *Philosophie de l'art* (1858a), 1st part, *Ontology*, Chap. 1, pp. 10–11. See also "Du sens esthétique; de l'art; et des opinions en matière d'art" (1859a), vol. XIII, pp. 26–27. Regarding this latter faculty, L. Walras discusses "sympathetic love" for the relationships between persons and the "aesthetic sense" for the relationships between persons and things. The concept of "sympathy" originates from T. Jouffroy's *Cours d'esthétique* (1843) (see "Du sens esthétique; de l'art; et des opinions en matière d'art", vol. XIII, pp. 30–32).

75 *Philosophie de l'art* (1858a), project of table of contents and "Du sens esthétique..." (1859a), vol. XIII, pp. 33–35.

76 The author also notes that "the Good contains the Useful" (Philosophie de l'art, "On the Good", 2 folio). Later, he will criticise Victor Cousin for completely separating "Useful" and "Good" and for ignoring the division of labour and Industry ("Méthode de conciliation ou de synthèse", 1868c, vol. IX, p. 166, English transl., 2010, p. 126).

programme (in particular, the five responses). However, he distinguishes not three, but four categories of general facts: "natural" or "physical", "moral", "social", and "progressive".[77]

Unfortunately, Léon Walras does not clearly state his position regarding his father's taxonomy of sciences. He only alludes to the division into three groups: natural (physical), moral, and historical sciences.[78] Perhaps he largely accepts it. Concerning natural sciences, he also places "ontology" at the forefront, which, in his view, should be established as a true "science of existence".[79] However, he refuses to include in this group of sciences, aesthesiology, noology, and thelesiology, which correspond, in reality, to "psychology" or "science of the soul". Indeed, the facts they account for are not "physical", but "moral".[80]

Writing of the *Philosophie de l'art* concludes in December 1858. The *Roseaux*'s promise during the summer of the same year leads Léon Walras to radically change his interests and turn towards economics. Furthermore, reading Étienne Vacherot's book leads him to reconsider his philosophical conceptions and to distance himself from his father. The discovery of *La métaphysique et la science* (1858) indeed represents a true revelation for him, and this work remained throughout his life "a bedside reading".[81] A disciple of Victor Cousin, Maine de Biran, and Jean-Philibert Damiron, Étienne Vacherot[82] follows Emmanuel Kant in his critique of the traditional metaphysics. A critic of materialism and spiritualism, he is not satisfied with "eclecticism", which relies on "common sense" as the criterion of true and false, and he attempts to rigorously reconcile metaphysics and science. Under the influence of this philosopher,

---

77 *Philosophie de l'art* (1858a), project of table of contents; see also a diagram inserted in the manuscript.

78 *Philosophie de l'art*, 1st part, Ontology, Chap. 1, folio 1.

79 *Op. cit.*, folios 6 and 7. L. Walras himself intends to start from "ontology" to reach "aesthetics".

80 This place within "moral facts" is confirmed, for example, in a diagram inserted in the manuscript of the *Philosophie de l'art*. L. Walras follows T. Jouffroy who radically separated physiology and psychology in the *Nouveaux mélanges philosophiques* (1842).

81 "Esquisse d'une doctrine économique et sociale" (1898c), vol. X, p. 413, English transl., 2005, p. 362. It is not the same for his father, who will only be able to read the work in the second edition. The critical aspect of the doctrines interests him, but the treatment of metaphysics leaves him unsatisfied because the author never defines "existence", that is to say, the most general fact it must address (see A. Walras, letters to his son, 9 May and 25 July 1863, in: vol. IV, pp. 585 and 592–593).

82 Étienne Vacherot (1809–97) first defended a Ph.D. thesis on Aristotle (1836), then becomes director of studies at the École Normale in 1837. In 1839, he succeeds Victor Cousin at the Sorbonne. He will be dismissed from his duties for refusing to take the oath to Emperor Napoléon III. Among his works, one can mention: *Histoire critique de l'école d'Alexandrie* (3 vols., 1846–51); *La métaphysique et la science—Principes de métaphysique positive* (2 vols, 1858, 2nd revised, corrected, and augmented edition, 3 vols., 1863); *La démocratie* (1859), for which he was given a short stay in prison; *Essais de philosophie critique* (1864); *La science et la conscience* (1870); *Le nouveau spiritualisme* (1884). On Vacherot's work, one can consult D. Parodi, 1930, pp. 38–103 and the study by E. Tatti (2000a). Hippolyte Taine portrays Vacherot under the name "M. Paul" in the 14th chapter ("On Method") of his book, *Les philosophes classiques du* XIXe *siècle en France*, Paris: Hachette, 3rd ed. 1868, pp. 345–50. The pseudonym "Paul" adopted by L. Walras to sign his "Chroniques de la quinzaine" in the *Gazette de Lausanne* in 1878, does it not come from there?

Léon Walras modified his theory of knowledge.[83] In spring 1859, he tells Adolphe Guéroult that he is preparing a work on the *Philosophie de la science* and that it would be possible to extract from Vacherot's work a "theory of reality that could serve as a basis for a theory of science in general", an essential starting point for the establishment of the "social science" and the theory of political economy.[84] In diagrams that seem to have been constructed at this time, dealing with the "search for the ideal", he first distinguishes the "metaphysical ideal" (or theological) and the "World ideal" (or cosmological). The "World ideal" is subdivided into a "physical ideal" (nature) and a "human ideal" (the "moral man"). The "human ideal", in turn, comprises several spheres, corresponding to four faculties, the first three pertaining to the "psychological" man and the last to the "physiological" man:

- to sensitivity, to the aesthetic sense, corresponds the "artistic ideal";
- to understanding and reason, corresponds the "scientific ideal", itself broken down into "physical", "moral" ("social"), and "historical" ideals;
- to free will, corresponds the "social ideal" (or "moral") which includes the "economic ideal" (property and taxation), "civil" (family), and "political" (government);
- to activity, corresponds the "industrial ideal".[85]

Here the term "industry" receives a new meaning. It is linked to the activity of the "physiological" man and the division of labour. "Customs" (and no longer "industry") are the expression of man's "free will".[86] Thus, the following four social categories are distinguished: Art with the Beautiful, Science with the True, Customs (property and taxation, family and government) with the Good, and Industry with the Useful.[87]

Given these elements, what will be the new perspective of the young Walras on the taxonomy of sciences, in the "Introduction à l'étude de la question sociale" (1859b) and in *L'économie politique et la justice* (1860a)? In his early economic writings, he maintains the division into three groups: "natural", "moral" (or "social"), and "historical" sciences.

Concerning the "natural sciences", which deal with "natural" and "fatal" facts, under Vacherot's influence, he no longer considers metaphysics in mind; it no longer belongs to these groups of sciences. Walras considers the "natural sciences" in two subsets, the "a priori sciences", which start from definitions and axioms, identities (algebra, geometry, mechanics…) and the "experimental sciences", inductive, based on the observation of facts (physical, medical sciences…) (1859b, vol. V, p. 97).

---

[83] On the relations between É. Vacherot and L. Walras, see V. Lhuillier, 1992; R. Koppl, 1995, pp. 43–55; E. Tatti, 2000a, pp. 417–28; R. Baranzini and E. Tatti, 2002, pp. 65–89.

[84] L. Walras, letter to Adolphe Guéroult, undated, in: *Correspondence*, I, 1. 16, p. 36.

[85] See three diagrams preserved in the Lausanne collection, under the reference F. W. V b, box 19.

[86] It should be noted that in Vacherot the ideal proposed to the "human will" is the "just" (1863, vol. 2, p. 157).

[87] See the diagrams mentioned above.

For the "moral sciences", Walras retains the distinction between "moral facts", relating to the individual, and "social facts", relating to the whole of individuals. "Moral facts" fall under "psychology", a field that hardly interests the author.[88] The "social facts" correspond to "the totality of the free activity of man living in society" (1859b, vol. V, p. 93), and refer both to customs and industry. They are the subject of the "general and complete theory of society" (*op. cit.*, p. 100), which includes "social science" and "social art".

"Social science" is subdivided into a theoretical part and an application part. The theoretical part is developed on a priori criteria, as it seeks a "rational ideal"; it is based on the "supreme social law", corresponding to the principle of "liberty" and "equality". The experimental part consists of applying the "supreme law" to questions of property, family, and government. It thus leads to the formulation of "special social laws". "Social science" therefore possesses a mixed character in terms of method.[89]

Then, we have "social art", whose criterion is the "useful", consisting in the establishment, not of theoretical laws, but of "practical rules" to increase the well-being of society. Here we find technical arts (theory of machine construction...), therapeutics, and the "theory of wealth production" (*cf. infra*).[90]

Finally, the "progressive facts", fatal or providential, related to the civilisation, are the subject of "historical sciences".[91] This third group of sciences will be quickly abandoned, undoubtedly under the influence of Étienne Vacherot's ideas.[92] In Walras's "Notes d'humeur", we find this note, probably written around 1862:

> As much as anyone, we know how much more perilous the historical theories are compared to physical and natural theories. To erroneous hypotheses, physical and natural experience opposes the denial of daily and simple facts. How much more painful is the recourse to reality against science in matters of history! Here, what are the facts tortured by false hypotheses? They are facts forever buried in distant times, or they are facts that develop before our eyes always with singular complexity; and it is generally admitted that, if the history of the past is difficult to do, the history of the present is impossible. (2000, vol. XIII, p. 590)

---

[88] *Op. cit.*, pp. 93–94 and 96. Later, L. Walras will say:

General psychology is a science that does not exist or whose elements, at least, are scattered and have never been brought together into a body of doctrine. Properly human psychology, more advanced, is itself far from being completed and perfected ("Recherche de l'idéal social en matière de propriété et d'impôt, 1863d, vol. XIII, p. 225).

[89] *Op. cit.*, p. 98. This division of science into a "rational part" and an "experimental part" seems to be borrowed from Étienne Vacherot (see 1863, vol. 3, p. 217).

[90] "Introduction à l'étude de la question sociale", vol. V, pp. 100–01.

[91] *Op. cit.*, p. 100. *L'économie politique et la justice,* vol. V, pp. 148 and 152.

[92] For É. Vacherot, "Providence is just a fine word" (1863, vol. 1, p. 158).

3.3.2 A First Bipartite Notion of Political Economy Under the Influence of Auguste Walras

From 1859 to 1860, Léon Walras began by adopting a bipartite approach of political economy strongly inspired by his father's works. We have already seen in Chap. 1 (*Auguste Walras as a Transmitter of Ideas: From Jean-Baptiste Say to Léon Walras*) that according to Auguste Walras, the fact of scarcity possessed a dual character (value and appropriation) and that two sciences could be distinguished:

1. "Political economy" or the "theory of social wealth", which is studied in itself. Focusing on the measurement of wealth, it "belongs to arithmetic" and must leave the "moral sciences" to rise to the rank of "exact sciences", becoming part of the "natural sciences". Indeed, the phenomenon of *rareté* is analogous to that of heat, movement, light, and gravity (*De la nature de la richesse, et de l'origine de la valeur*, 1831b, vol. I, pp. 207–08). "Political economy" will thus join geometry, mechanics, physics, chemistry, physiology, psychology.[93]

Even if he did not "understand well", he says, the content of Cournot's *Recherches sur les principes mathématiques de la théorie des richesses,*[94] Auguste Walras has some notions of mathematics. He favours the application of this discipline to "political economy", but on the condition of scrupulous observation of facts.[95] He refuses to elevate mathematics to the status of "master science", in place of "metaphysics", noting that the main obstacle making "slower and more difficult" its application to "political economy" is the difficulty determining the "unit of need" in the phenomenon of *rareté*.[96]

2. The "theory of property" and of the distribution of wealth. This "moral science" belongs to the vast field of "natural law". The distribution of wealth must be equitable and just. "Political economy" benefits of a "logical priority" over the theory of property, and its principles must enlighten those of natural law. Indeed, value is the *cause* of appropriation (1831b, vol. I, pp. 50–51 and 90), and it represents "a natural and necessary fact that cannot be corrected, distorted, in its essential nature, by the intervention of the free fact, the human fact, the moral fact".[97]

---

93 A. Walras, "Esquisse d'une théorie de la richesse" (1844), vol. I, pp. 429 and 439; letter to his son, 6 February 1859, in: vol. IV, p. 326.

94 Auguste Walras declares:

I have never really understood this work; but what I have been able to grasp, made me suppose that Mr. Cournot had translated Ricardo's metaphysics into algebra. I can say nothing about the translation; but the text not being to my taste, I care very little about the translator's fidelity (letter to his son, 18 May 1861, in: Correspondence, vol. IV, p. 490).

95 This point of divergence between A. Walras and the author of the *Éléments* is indicated by Gaëtan Pirou, [1934] 1946, pp. 75–77.

96 A Walras, letter to his son, 18 May 1861, in: vol. IV, pp. 491–92.

97 Walras, letter to his son, 12 June 1860, in: vol. IV, p. 421.

It should be noted that this approach to economic science seems to leave no room for the field of "applied economics", which is that of "art".

How does Léon Walras position himself in relation to his father's ideas in his early economic works? He explains this particularly in developments devoted to the theme of the "philosophy of economic sciences".[98] He admits that the value (exchange) and the appropriation form the two great general facts in economics, the first being "natural" and the second "moral and free", and he divides the "economic sciences" into two branches.

1. The "theory of exchange value, exchange, and production".[99] Here, two parts must be distinguished:

   - the "political economy proper" or the "theory of social wealth" considered as a "natural science". Indeed,

> [...] the utility relationship that exists between us and things is a natural fact in the sense that it depends on nature that our needs are of such or such a kind, and that things can or cannot satisfy them more or less. The scarcity of things is likewise a fatal fact in the sense that it does not depend on us that certain things are found in the world in limited quantity instead of being in indefinite quantity, or vice versa.[100]

Walras views "political economy proper" as the field of a fruitful application of mathematics, in the footsteps of A.-A. Cournot[101] and he highlights its analogies with geometry, "physics", and astronomy. But, undoubtedly under paternal influence, he still defines it as an "experimental science", that is to say, a science of rigorous observation of natural facts, of which "it determines the order and relationships".[102]

- The "theory of the production of wealth". An "economic" category of "social art",[103] it is based on the fact of "liberty" and the principle of the division of labour. It establishes the "set of rules of social work". Production must be "abundant" and "proportioned". The criterion here is the "useful". To designate this field, Léon Walras refers, in *L'Économie politique et la justice*, to Chap. VI of his father's *Théorie de la richesse sociale*, which deals with "*industry* or *production*" (1860a, vol. V, p. 157).

The "economic sciences" include a second branch:

---

[98] Two extracts of *L'économie politique et la justice* are published under the title "Philosophie des sciences économiques" in *Journal des économistes*, 2nd series, 6th year, vol. 25, no. 2, 15 February 1860, pp. 196–206.

[99] "Introduction à l'étude de la question sociale" (1859b), vol. V, p. 115; *L'économie politique et la justice, op. cit*, p. 153.

[100] *Op. cit.*, p. 99.

[101] As early as 1860, he drafted his first attempt of "Application des mathématiques à l'économie politique" (vol. XI, pp. 329–39).

[102] *Théorie critique de l'impôt, précédée de Souvenirs du congrès de Lausanne* (1861e), vol. V, p. 401.

[103] "Introduction à l'étude de la question sociale" (1859b), vol. V, pp. 100 and 114–16. In "L'industrie moderne et l'économie politique" (1861d, vol. VII, p. 137), L. Walras indicates that this theory is "less a science than an art".

2) The "theory of property, distribution, and consumption" (*op. cit.*, pp. 153 and 158). This branch, subordinate to the first, is also subdivided into two parts:
   - The "theory of property and distribution". This particular "moral science" belongs, like the theories of family and of government, to the "social science". Its criterion is the "just". This sphere will attract particular interest from the young author, starting in the summer of 1860, with some contributions on taxation.
   - The "theory of consumption". Just like the "theory of the production of wealth", it forms a part of "social art".

But Léon Walras will quickly revise his approach to political economy and move towards a tripartite conception.

3.3.3 *The Transition to the Tripartite Notion: "Political and Social Economy"*

The term "political and social economy" seems to appear for the first time in an article from the series "Paradoxes économiques" (February–March 1861).[104] At the end of the following year, in his letter to Jules du Mesnil-Marigny, Walras presents a project for a "Traité complet d'économie politique et sociale", whose first three volumes would respectively deal with "pure economics", "applied economics", and "social economics", in accordance with the three criteria of the "true", the "useful", and the "just".[105] (*cf.* the following chapter).

Firstly, what is the origin of the term "pure political economy (*économie politique pure*)"? Walras uses it for the first time in the first article of the series "Paradoxes économiques", written in May 1860 (vol. VII, p. 45), but he was undoubtedly comforted in the choice of this expression by a text by Jules Dupuit, relating to a review of his book *La liberté commerciale, son principe et ses conséquences* (1860), by Charles Dunoyer, published in the *Journal des économistes*. Jules Dupuit observes:

> I have [...] an opinion diametrically opposed to that of Mr. Dunoyer; I believe that the exact sciences are an excellent preparation for political economy; I go further and say that *pure* political economy is an exact science, that is to say, a science whose principles are capable of rigorous demonstration.[106]

According to him, to establish "pure political economy", one must borrow from the exact sciences, such as geometry, their methods of demonstration. Conversely,

---

[104] "Paradoxes économiques. II. De la richesse naturelle ou gratuite. – De la richesse sociale ou économique. – De la richesse intellectuelle" (1861c), vol. XIII, p. 53.

[105] L. Walras, letter to Jules du Mesnil-Marigny, 23 December 1862, in: *Correspondence,* I, 1. 81, pp. 119–20.

[106] Emphasis by J. D., J. Dupuit, 1861, p. 111, reproduced in: J. Dupuit, 2009, vol. II, p. 540. On his personal copy of the journal, kept at the Centre d'études interdisciplinaires Walras-Pareto de l'Université de Lausanne (B 1446), L. Walras drew a vertical line next to this quotation.

"applied political economy", whose questions are related "to ethics, politics, a host of diverse sciences", does not require this demand.[107]

In a letter to W. S. Jevons, after criticising Dupuit for the confusion of the utility curve and the demand curve and refusing to grant him any priority, Walras will point out this "good article of him whose subject is the character of pure economics".[108] But it should be noted that he himself, as well as Dupuit, are aware of the distinction between pure political economy and applied political economy, presented by Pellegrino Rossi in the 2nd and 3rd lessons of his *Cours d'économie politique* taught at the Collège de France).[109] From 1862–63, Léon Walras will conceive "pure economics" as a "physico-mathematical science".[110]

What is the origin of the polysemic term "social economics (*économie sociale*)"? This term, which appeared in the XVIIIth century, is used by several schools of thought during the XIXth century with very different contents. Between 1830 and 1860, we find it first in the liberal school with Jean-Baptiste Say (*Cours complet d'économie politique pratique*, 1828–29) and with Charles Dunoyer (*Nouveau traité d'économie sociale*, 1830). We also find it in the Christian-socialist tradition, with Constantin Pecqueur (*Économie sociale. Des intérêts du commerce* [...], 1839; *Théorie nouvelle de l'économie sociale et politique*, 1842) and with Auguste Ott (*Traité d'économie sociale*, 1851). We finally find it with social reformers such as Frédéric Le Play, founder in 1856 of the "Société d'économie sociale".[111] Furthermore, we must not forget its uses by Ampère *(Essai sur la philosophie des sciences)*, taken up by A.-A. Cournot *(Principes de la théorie des richesses)*.

Walras does not adopt these perspectives. During the ceremony of his jubilee, he recalls that he did not come to Lausanne "to seek and propose palliatives of philanthropy, insurance or association to social injustice, but to work to establish the social question on its true ground and, if possible, to resolve it scientifically" (1909c, vol. VII, p. 507). In the Preface to the novel *Francis Sauveur* (dated March 1858), he meant by "social economics" the "science of well-being" or of wealth.[112] But in 1862,

---

107 *Op. cit.*, pp. 112–13.

108 L. Walras, letter to W. S. Jevons, 25 May 1877, in: *Correspondence*, I, l. 379, p. 535. A note kept in the Lausanne collection indicates: "very important article by M. Dupuit on Pure political economy. *Journal des économistes*, July 1861" (note with mention on the back "Monsieur Walras, professor of law at the Academy of Lausanne", kept under reference F. W. V b, box 18).

109 See on this subject A. Diemer, 2004, pp. 69–76.

110 It is astonishing that this qualification of economics first appears under the pen of Pierre-Joseph Proudhon. After providing a list of works on the theme of the "agreement of political economy and ethics" (notably those of Henri Baudrillart, Henri Dameth and *L'économie politique et la justice* by L. Walras), Proudhon asserts: "political economy, a science to be constructed, a science both juridical and physico-mathematical, should unite all kinds of certainties [...]." (*De la Justice dans la Révolution et dans l'Église* [1868] 1931, vol. II, note for p. 145).

111 On the uses of the term and the different currents in the 19th century, see H. Desroche, 1984, pp. 43–52 and 1991.

112 *Francis Sauveur*, 1858b, pp. XVII–XVIII. It has already been noted that Auguste Walras used the term "social economics" (see also, "On the connectivity of human knowledge and scientific progress in general, and in particular, the influence that the study of political economy is called

he no longer gives it the same meaning. Later, in his "Notice autobiographique", he will provide an interesting clarification regarding this new content:

> I call social economics, as J. S. Mill does, the part of the science of the social wealth that deals with the distribution of this wealth among individuals and the State and which resorts to the principle of justice, and not, as the school of Le Play and our law faculties do, the study of employer and philanthropic institutions, cooperation, and insurance, all very interesting subjects of applied economics depending on the principle of charity, fraternity, free association, at most of social utility [...]. (1909a, vol. V, p. 17)

On the notion of "social economics", Léon Walras thus aligns himself with J. S. Mill who, in the *Principles of Political Economy with Some of Their Applications to Social Philosophy*, drew a line of demarcation within "political economy" between:

- the laws of the "production" of wealth, natural and invariable laws;
- the laws of the "distribution" of wealth, related to institutions, which depend, under certain conditions, on human will.

The "distribution" depends on the "laws and customs of society"[113] and the theory of property is a question of "social philosophy". The literal translation of the word is ambiguous, because in reality, J. S. Mill rather envisages "social science". Moreover, the French translation of the book's title (*Principes d'économie politique avec quelques-unes de leurs applications à l'économie sociale*) renders "social philosophy" as "*économie sociale*", which can confirm the origin of the expression used by Walras.[114]

However, Walras does not seem to make immediate systematic use of the new concept. In "Recherche de l'idéal social en matière de propriété et d'impôt" (1863d), he speaks of the "science of social ethics". In "Du matérialisme et du spiritualisme en économie politique et sociale" (1863c), the new concept appears in the title and in the text, which provokes a negative reaction from his father. According to the latter, the phrase "political and social economy" is redundant because "*political* and *social* are two adjectives that mean roughly the same thing, *politics* being only the organisation of *society*". It would be more appropriate to speak of "political economy" (science of wealth) on the one hand, and "social ethics" (theory of property) on the other.[115]

to exert on the advancement of moral and historical sciences", opening of the Cours d'économie politique, 9 December 1832, in: vol. III, p. 82).

[113] J. S. Mill, [1848] 1965, vol. 1, "Preliminary remarks", p. 21, book 2, Chap. 1, pp. 199–200; see also *Autobiography*, [1873] 1960, pp. 174–75.

[114] L. Walras owned in his library the second edition (1861) of the translation of J. S. Mill's book by H. Dussard and J.-G. Courcelle-Seneuil (2 vol. kept at the Centre d'études interdisciplinaires Walras-Pareto de l'Université de Lausanne, ZAB 3189). A.-A. Cournot, a critical reader of Ampère, claims that the theory of wealth or "chrematistics" (relating to the production and distribution of wealth) is subordinate ("daughter to mother relationship") to "social economics" (physiology, hygiene and "pathology of the social body"). L. Walras's reaction is obviously negative, as seen from the marginal annotations in *Principes de la théorie des richesses,* 1863, pp. 20–21 and 30–31 (kept at the Centre d'études interdisciplinaires Walras-Pareto under the reference ZAB 2350).

[115] Emphasis by A. W., letter to his son, 25 March 1864, in: vol. IV, pp. 623–25.

Nevertheless, despite paternal criticisms, Léon Walras will maintain the new concept and use it systematically.[116]

From 1863 onwards, a coherence appear in Walras's work between the tripartite division of "political and social economy", the "foundation" with a metaphysical character, and the classification of sciences, which gave rise to the "model" of the *Éléments.*

After this return to the sources, it is now necessary to examine the subsequent changes decided by Walras concerning the taxonomy of sciences and the division of "political and social economy".

3.4 Reconsideration of the Classification of the *Éléments* and Search for a "New Model"

Shortly after his retirement, Walras abandoned the idea of publishing his *Cours d'économie sociale et d'économie politique appliquée*, and prepared the edition of two collections dedicated to these fields. This work gave him the opportunity to reflect anew on the problems of classification of sciences and division of "political and social economy". Around 1893–94, he wrote a "Résumé d'une doctrine économique et sociale", in which he remains very close to the model of classification of sciences of the *Éléments.*[117] However, from 1896, he began to question this model, while retaining the "foundation"; this attempt is evidenced not only by published writings but also by unpublished documents, which we discovered in the Lausanne archives. These changes can only be understood by examining Walras's interest in the works of American sociology at the end of the XIXth century, more precisely those of Giddings.

American sociology, notably founded by William Graham Sumner and Lester Frank Ward, is profoundly marked by social Darwinism and Herbert Spencer's evolutionism. Franklin Henry Giddings[118] occupies a specific place within this discipline, as he seeks to reconcile Herbert Spencer, Auguste Comte (from whom he adopts the idea of a fundamental social science), and Gabriel Tarde (his social psychology). Furthermore, he is in favour of using statistics in sociological analysis, following the perspective opened by Quételet, Galton, etc. According to Giddings, society must be studied simultaneously from two inseparable and coordinated viewpoints, and thus be subject to both an objective interpretation by a physical principle (the struggle for existence) and a subjective interpretation by facts of consciousness. Now, the

[116] This is already evident in the study "De l'enseignement de l'économie politique dans les facultés de droit" (1864), vol. VII, p. 352.

[117] See the first pages of the manuscript, kept in the Lausanne collection, under the reference F. W. V b, box 22.

[118] After training as an engineer, Franklin Henry Giddings (1855–1931) began a career as a journalist in Springfield (Mass.). From 1888 to 1894, he taught political science at Bryn Mawr College (Pennsylvania) and from 1894 to 1928, sociology at Columbia University, New York. A member of the board of the Institut international de sociologie (founded in 1893), he contributed to the *Revue internationale de sociologie.*

elementary subjective fact of society is the "*consciousness of kind*", that is to say, a state of consciousness in which a living being recognises its kind and makes choices. This "consciousness of kind" is the basis of all association and all distinction or differentiation.[119]

F. H. Giddings also played a role in American economic thought, within the group of the American Economic Association, founded in 1885, of which he was vice-president. From 1886, he collaborated with John Bates Clark on the theory of distribution,[120] and then he contributed to the theory of capital and interest.[121] Walras noted certain works of Giddings and sent the author the 2nd edition of the *Éléments d'économie politique pure*[122]; on two occasions, he placed him alongside John Bates Clark and Irving Fisher in his list of contemporary mathematical economists.[123] In 1895, F. H. Giddings published the article, "Sociology and the Abstract Sciences", which deals with questions of the classification of sciences[124], and the following year, the book *The Principles of Sociology*,[125] which he sent to Walras. In his letter of thanks (March 1896), the latter particularly noted:

> […] it was with pleasure that I found on page 49 a small table of the *concrete sciences* and the *pure sciences* on which I was already working last year when I found it in the March

---

119 On Giddings' place in the American sociology, one can particularly consult the study by Clarence H. Northcott, 1948, pp. 744–65. See also the 2nd and 3rd parts of the book by Dorothy Ross, 1991.

120 See notably F. H. Giddings, "The Theory of Profit-sharing", *Quarterly Journal of Economics*, vol. I, April 1887, pp. 367–76; John Bates Clark and F. H. Giddings, *The Modern Distributive Process—Studies of Competition and its Limits, of the Nature and Amount of Profits, and of the Determination of Wages, in the Industrial Society of Today*, Boston: Ginn and Co, 1888.

121 F. H. Giddings, "The Theory of Capital", *Quarterly Journal of Economics*, vol. IV, 1889–90, pp. 172–206. After the reactions of James Bonar and Eugen Von Böhm-Bawerk, he published "The Growth of Capital and the Cause of Interest", *Quarterly Journal of Economics,* vol. V, 1890–91, pp. 242–48.

122 F. H. Giddings, letter to L. Walras, 26 August 1889, unpublished, kept in the Walras collection in Lausanne, block II, box 9.

123 See the note prepared at the request of Louis Gauthier in 1894, in: *Correspondence*, II, 1. 1195, note 5, pp. 624–25, and the "Prospectus of the *Éléments d'économie politique pure*" (February 1896), distributed by the publisher F. Pichon, on the occasion of the publication of the 3rd edition of the book, vol. VII, p. 289.

124 F. H. Giddings, "Sociology and the Abstract Sciences. The Origin of the Social Feelings", *Annals of the American Academy of Political and Social Science*, vol. V, no. 5, March 1895, pp. 94–101 [746–753]. L. Walras had this article in his library, kept at the Centre d'études interdisciplinaires Walras-Pareto de l'Université de Lausanne (ZAG 23).

125 F. H. Giddings, *The Principles of Sociology: An Analysis of the Phenomena of Association and of Social Organization*, New York: Macmillan, 1896. The work had three editions in the same year and there is a French translation made and prefaced by Viscount Gaëtan-Guillaume Combes de Lestrade, for the "International Sociological Library", directed by René Worms: *Principes de sociologie*, Paris: V. Giard & E. Brière, 1897. This book and its French translation are also part of L. Walras's library under the references ZAB 14,008 and 14,002. Giddings had also published *The Theory of Sociology* (Supplement to the *Annals of the American Academy of Political and Social Science*, vol. V, no. 1, July 1894), which included earlier studies.

issue of the *Annals*. I will use the opportunity to revisit this problem which interests me greatly.[126]

Moreover, in the same letter, Walras believes he detects a kinship of views on sociological questions between Giddings' work and his own *Recherche de l'idéal social*, which constitutes an exposition of the "principles of sociology", even if the word is absent.

During the summer of 1896, F. H. Giddings undertook a trip in Europe and during the first week of July, he visited Lausanne to meet Léon Walras, as well as Vilfredo Pareto.[127] The American sociologist, who undoubtedly discussed with his interlocutor the questions of the classification of sciences, promised to write a review or an article on the *Études d'économie sociale*, still in the process of being printed, probably for the *Annals of the American Academy of Political and Social Science*,[128] a promise that was never honoured.

3.4.1 F. H. Giddings' Classification of Sciences: A Source of Inspiration

To understand Giddings' nomenclature, it is necessary to first refer to *The Classification of the Sciences* by one of his mentors, Herbert Spencer. In this book, the latter, criticising the taxonomy of Auguste Comte (abstract sciences, which discover laws, and concrete sciences, which apply laws), argues that sciences cannot be arranged in a serial order, neither from a logical point of view nor a historical point of view. Rejecting any scale of complexity or generality, Spencer establishes a fundamental separation between the sciences related to "relations", to the "forms" under which the phenomena appear to us, or the "abstract sciences" (logic and mathematics), and the sciences related to the phenomena themselves. Among the latter, one must distinguish the "abstract-concrete sciences", which study the phenomena in their elements (mechanics, physics, chemistry...) and the "concrete sciences", which study phenomena as a whole (astronomy, geology, biology, psychology, sociology...). The "abstract sciences" serve as instruments to the other two, and these serve as material to the former. In his "Replying to criticisms", Spencer explains that the "concrete sciences" have as their subject-matters "aggregates", the "abstract-concrete

[126] Emphasis by L. W., letter to F. H. Giddings, 29 March 1896, in: *Correspondence*, II, 1. 1238, p. 674.

[127] F. H. Giddings, letter to L. Walras, 20 September 1896, in: *op. cit.*, II, l. 1258, p. 692. See also V. Pareto, letter to Maffeo Pantaleoni, 8 July 1896, in: V. Pareto, 1984, vol. XXVIII, 1, letter 215, p. 459. Pareto does not particularly appreciate Giddings' thought. He writes to Maffeo Pantaleoni on 9 April 1897: "Now I have read Giddings's *Principles of Sociology*, translated by your C. de Lestrade. It is a poor thing. Like the eagle, Spencer flies above these people". (our translation from Italian, 1984, vol. XXVIII, 2, letter 274, p. 61).

[128] L. Walras, letter to F. H. Giddings, 25 July 1896, in: *Correspondence*, II, l. 1253, p. 688; letter to F.H. Giddings, 26 November 1896, unpublished, kept in the Walras collection in Lausanne, F. W. I, 221.

sciences", the various kinds of "properties" possessed by these aggregates, and the "abstract sciences", the "relations" among aggregates and properties, and among the properties themselves.[129]

According to Giddings, in the scientific process, the "concrete description and abstract formulation play back and forth, one upon the other" (*The Principles of Sociology,* New York: Macmillan, 1896, p. 47). Thus, Herbert Spencer's classification between abstract sciences (exposition of relations), abstract-concrete sciences (exposition of properties), and concrete sciences (exposition of aggregates) must be questioned in turn. There are two categories of sciences: the "concrete sciences" which analyse the aggregates and the "abstract sciences" which analyse a group of relations and properties in all the aggregates where it appears; the former are interrelated with the latter.

To illustrate his approach, Giddings constructs a double-entry table, which articulates the "concrete sciences" (carried on the oy axis), descriptive, historical, and inductive with the "abstract sciences" (carried on the ox axis), hypothetical and deductive (*op. cit.,* p. 49).

According to the author,

> […] the concrete become explanatory only because they are traversed, or crossed, by the abstract sciences; that is to say, in so far as they get beyond mere description and history they do so by appealing to the hypothetical principles of the 'pure' or deductive sciences. On the other hand, the abstract sciences are not abstractions from nothing. They are abstractions from concrete phenomena. That is to say, they presuppose and take for granted the descriptive and historical matter of the concrete sciences (*op. cit.,* pp. 49–50). See Diagram 3.4:

The field of the "physical sciences" covers the area *opqr*; their "descriptive side" is represented by chemistry, astronomy, geology, biology, while their "explanatory side" is represented by mathematics and physics. On the other hand, the field of the "sociology" covers the area *svwu*; its "descriptive side" (which presupposes the "concrete physical sciences") is represented by the concrete sociology and its "explanatory side" is represented by the five "abstract" sciences. The squares *s'v'w'u'*, *u'w'w"u"* and *u"w"wu* indicate the existing interrelations between "sociology" and respectively, "pure economics", "pure ethics", and "pure politics" (*op. cit.,* pp. 50–51).[130]

How would Walras react to this table? The principle of this classification "seems enlightening" to him, even if one can discuss the details. In a letter, he points out to the author regarding his own *Recherche de l'idéal social*: "[…] it is a very deliberate attempt at 'pure ethics' exactly as you define it. The *geometrical* method is clearly stated and faithfully followed. The definitions, once carefully abstracted from reality, that is to say, borrowed from the 'descriptive sciences,' the reasoning is entirely

[129] H. Spencer, 1871, p. 14 *et seq* and 26 *et seq*; see also Patrick Tort, 1989, p. 346 *et seq.*

[130] On his personal copy of Giddings' book, Walras placed crosses in the first two squares.

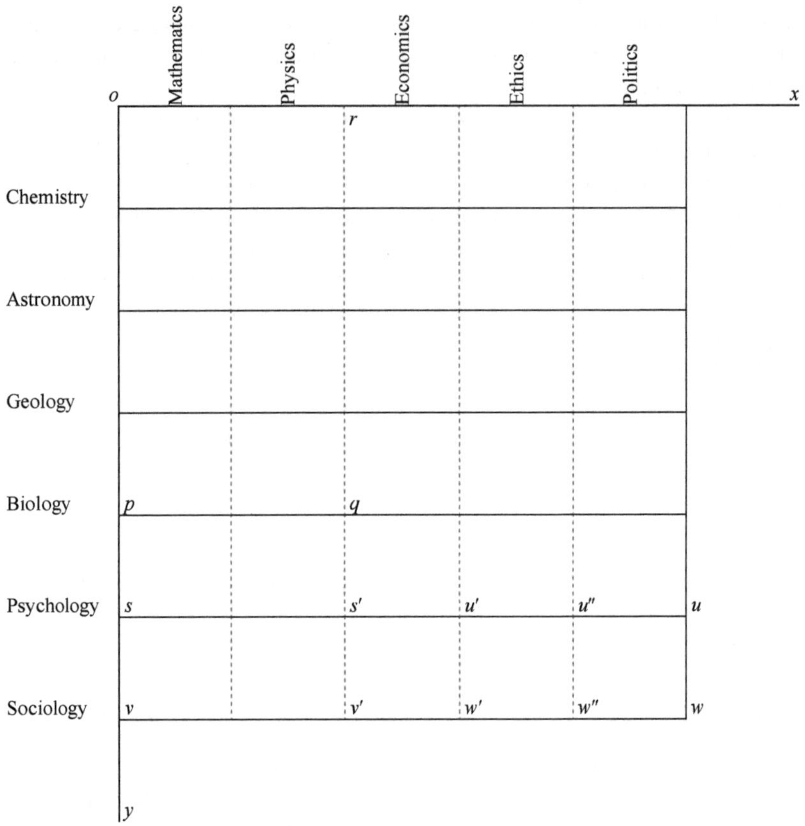

Diagram 3.4 *(Giddings, The Principles of Sociology, New York: Macmillan, 1896, p. 49)*

deductive. In short, I place myself and remain rigorously in the section *u'w'w"u"* of your *Principles of Sociology*'s table (p. 49)."[131]

Walras again points out this location in a note of the Preface (dated September 1896) to the *Études d'économie sociale* (vol. IX, p. 5, note c1). In this text, he observes that his own "rational social science", relating to facts arising from human will,

> appears to be, at least in part, the mechanics of moral forces, that is to say, an abstract and deductive science as much as and more than is the mechanics of physical forces. Experience, by the intermediation of concrete and inductive sciences, such as physiology, psychology and history, will first provide social science with its definition, from which it can derive its fundamental formula by the use of reasoning, and then the date for the great problems to which it will apply this formula logically. (*op. cit.*, pp. 4–5, English transl., 2010, p. LII)

[131] Emphasis by L. W., letter to F. H. Giddings, 25 July 1896, in: *Correspondence*, II, l. 1253, p. 688. We correct the reading errors with the original manuscript kept in the Lausanne collection (F. W.I., 221); notably, we read "descriptive sciences" and not "descriptive roots".

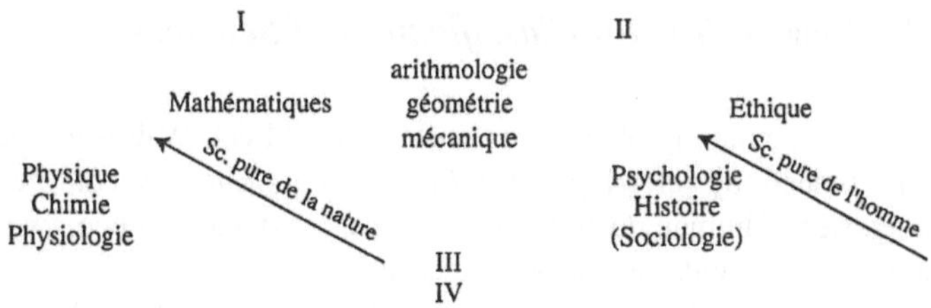

Diagram 3.5 Towards a new classification

Here we have the starting point of a new reflection on the problems of classification of sciences. Diagram 3.5 shows this.[132]

In June 1897, F. H. Giddings sent Léon Walras three brochures, and in particular a study entitled *The Theory of Socialization*,[133] which introduces the famous concept of "cœnonics". In this book, F. H. Giddings writes:

> Sociology includes more, however, than the abstract theory of socialization, as psychology includes more than the theory of appreciation. Sociology is a concrete, descriptive, and historical science of societies and of social evolution. It is traversed by certain abstract sciences which formulate its theoretical or explanatory propositions. These are economics, ethics, and cœnonics (κοινωνικός, social), or abstract politics. Cœnonics is the theory of socialization.[134]

Presented in *The Principles of Sociology,* the "cœnonics" studies the effects of the association and the formation of social groups; it follows that on the ox axis of the table, "politics" should be replaced by "cœnonics".

Walras finds "excellent these denominations" and takes advantage of this conceptual innovation to continue the reconstruction of his taxonomy of sciences. The results appear in "L'économique appliquée et la défense des salaires" and "Esquisse d'une doctrine économique et sociale" (new title of the "Résumé"), articles integrated into the *Études d'économie politique appliquée*, but also in diagrams and notes preserved in the Lausanne archives.

---

[132] On this note kept in the Lausanne collection (F. W. V b, box 22), L. Walras reproduces on the left Giddings' classification, then on the right his own, indicated by the mention: "*Moi*": Later additions appear next to "Ethics": "Economics, general cœnonics".

[133] F. H. Giddings, *The Theory of Socialization: A Syllabus of Sociological Principles for the Use of College and University Classes, With References to the Third Edition of "The Principles of Sociology"*, New York: Macmillan, 1897. See the letter of thanks from L. Walras to F. H. Giddings, 23 June 1897, unpublished, kept in the Lausanne collection, F. W. I., 221. The book is kept at the Centre d'études interdisciplinaires Walras-Pareto de l'Université de Lausanne under the reference ZAE 2945.

[134] *Op. cit.*, p. 6. The author immediately refers the reader to the previous table.

3.4.2 The New Walrasian Classification of Sciences

The change in the taxonomy of sciences does not lead Léon Walras to question the "foundation". Indeed, by referring to the *Recherche de l'idéal social*, he reaffirms the four categories of human destiny, two "passive", Art and Science, two "active", Industry and Customs, and their respective criteria.[135]

After recalling the "brilliant" principle of Giddings' classification, Walras presents his own, which brings modifications regarding the status of "pure science":

> I believe there exists *pure science*, studying all facts as such to which the world provides a theatre in order to formulate their laws, which could be called pure *natural* science or pure *moral* science according to whether facts owing their origin to the working of forces of nature are concerned or those stemming from the phenomenon of humanity as such, on the one hand, or originating in the working of the human will, on the other. Pure natural science results from the application of *mathematics* to *physics*, *chemistry* and the *physiology* of plants and animals. Pure moral science results from the application of *cœnonics*, of *economics* to *psychology*, *history*, *sociology*, *geography* and *statistics*. Next to pure natural and moral science, *metaphysics* may be placed here, if one should so wish, i.e. the science of the *universe* and mankind as a whole, which, according to Vacherot, also results from the application of an abstract and deductive science, *theology*, to a concrete and inductive science, *cosmology*. All pure science is composed of a view of *pure*, rational and experimental *truth*. I believe there exist, on the other hand, *applied science*, which conduct[s] the exercise of man's free will and may be called applied *moral* science and applied *natural* science, according to whether they set forth principles of the relations of persons to one another, or rules regarding relations between persons and things. Applied moral science has a starting point from the *truth of justice*, exclusively rational, and applied natural science from the *truth of usefulness* (*utilité*) rational and experimental. (emphasis by L. W., "Esquisse d'une doctrine économique et sociale", 1898c, vol. X, p. 408, English transl., 2005, pp. 357–58)

A page of notes preserved in the Walras collection in Lausanne,[136] which seems to have been used for the drafting of the "Esquisse", provides some additional details. It includes the following schema (Diagram 3.6), relating to pure science (natural and moral) and metaphysics:

"Pure natural science" relates to "physical, chemical facts, facts about vegetation and facts about life" which are studied "experimentally"; the world of nature is thus scrutinised by the exercise of the "senses" (1898c, vol. X, pp. 438–39, English transl., 2005, pp. 382–83). The concept of "experience" should not be understood here in the usual Walrasian sense (observation) but in the strong sense of "experimentation". In this perspective, "mechanics, physics, chemistry, physiology experiment" and develop laws by induction, as they relate to "impersonal facts", which can be isolated ("L'économique appliquée et la défense des salaires", 1897c, vol. X, p. 249, English transl., 2005, p. 219).

---

[135] "Esquisse d'une doctrine économique et sociale" (1898c), vol. X, pp. 408–409, 412 and 441, English transl., 2005, pp. 358, 361 and 385; see also the reprint of a passage in "La paix par la justice sociale et le libre-échange" (1907a), vol. VII, p. 472.

[136] This document, probably written around the beginning of January 1898, is kept under the reference F. W. V b, box 22.

[*Pure natural science* :]	[*Pure moral science*:]	[*Metaphysics* :]
Mathematics	Cœnonics, Economics	Theology
Physics Chemistry Plant and animal physiology	Psychology History Sociology Geography Statistics	Cosmology

Diagram 3.6 Pure science and metaphysics

"Pure moral science" relates to humans living in society, "dividing labour, endowed with sympathy and aesthetic sense, understanding and reason and with a conscious free will". The world of humanity is explored by "conscience"[137] and deduction must assist induction.

On the question of "experimentation", Walras disagreed with the principle of the classification of sciences by Claude Bernard. The latter, in *Le problème de la physiologie générale* (1878), distinguishes two degrees in human knowledge. The first degree is represented by the "natural sciences", "sciences of observation or descriptive". These sciences, such as astronomy, are passive, contemplative. On this basis, there is a second degree represented by the "experimental sciences", "sciences of experimentation or explanatory". Among these, one can mention physics, chemistry, physiology, medicine. Active and conquering, they must also invest in the "historical and moral sciences".[138] Upon reading these remarks, Léon Walras notes:

> Two observations to formulate. The physical and natural sciences properly speaking are as experimental as the physiology. The physiology will also be rational as well as experimental. Social science, *id*. The distinction of sciences into observational sciences: physical and natural sciences and experimental sciences: physiology, social science is bad. ("Notes d'humeur", 2000, vol. XIII, p. 558)

For Walras, the "scientific belief will live, both in ethics and physics, side by side with the metaphysical doubts" (1898c, vol. X, p. 408, English transl., 2005, revised p. 357). At the time of developing the aforementioned schema, he reflects on metaphysical questions and rereads La *métaphysique et la science* by Étienne Vacherot. He even conducts a careful comparison between the two editions of the book, that of 1858 and that of 1863,[139] with a view to drafting the sixth part of the "Esquisse", the pages on a "freethinker's prayer", which contain, according to him, "a sort of metaphysical profession of faith". He noticed that in the second edition of his book, Étienne Vacherot emphasised the separation in the metaphysical science (science of the infinite, of the absolute, of the universal), between a rational part, represented

---

[137] Document cited from the Lausanne collection and "Esquisse d'une doctrine économique et sociale" (1898c), vol. X, p. 439, English transl., 2005, p. 383.

[138] C. Bernard, 1878, pp. 101–10; see also *Introduction à l'étude de la méthode expérimentale,* [1865] 1984, pp. 44–49.

[139] See L. Walras, letter to R.F.A. Sully Prudhomme, 5 January 1898, in: *Correspondence*, III, 1. 1335, p. 3.

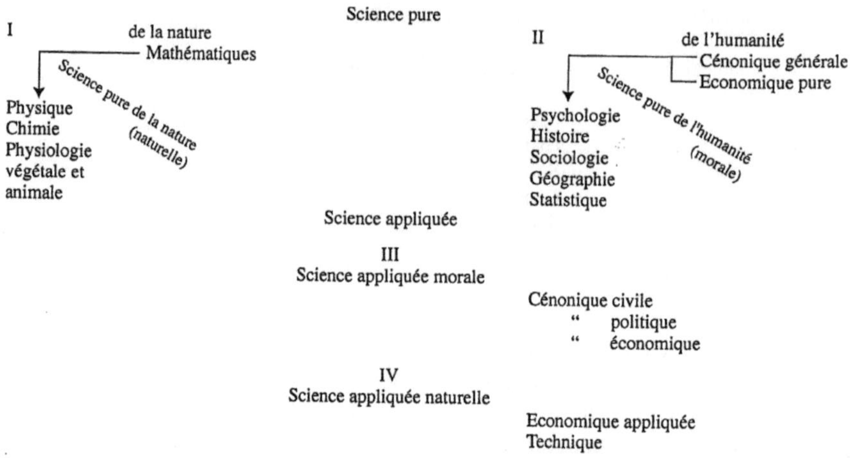

Diagram 3.7 Léon Walras's last nomenclature

by "theology" (science of the perfect being, of the ideal world) and a positive part, represented by "cosmology" (science of the real world, of the universe) and taking as its basis the "physical and moral sciences".[140]

In Walras's view, pure natural science and pure moral science, even if they were completed (or even if they achieved unification), could never do better than approach the "*how* of the differentiation between the being within myself and the 'non-I'"; only metaphysics would allow us to penetrate the "*why* of it".[141] In a discussion with the poet and philosopher R. F. A. Sully Prudhomme, who also declares himself a disciple of Vacherot, Walras notes that science "does not give me the *absolute*, but it gives me *some of the absolute*"; consequently, it possesses a "metaphysical value".[142] Thus, one can rise to metaphysics, conceived as the "crowning" (and not as the "base") of science, without needing to construct it a priori.[143]

A diagram preserved in the Lausanne collection[144] allows us to visualise the new Walrasian approach to the sciences (Diagram 3.7):

---

[140] É. Vacherot, 1863, volume 1, Preface, pp. VII and L–LI; vol. 3, 15th and 16th interviews.

[141] Emphasis by L. W., "Esquisse d'une doctrine économique et sociale" (1898c), vol. X, p. 440 and note 89, p. 510, English transl., 2005, p. 384.

[142] Emphasis by L. W., letter to R.F.A. Sully Prudhomme, 15 April 1898, in: *Correspondence*, III, 1. 1351, p. 19; see also the letter to Auguste Penjon, 27 July 1898, in: *op. cit.*, 1. 1360, p. 26.

[143] On the rejection of "dogmatic" metaphysics a priori, besides the letter to Sully Prudhomme of 15 April 1898, see the first manuscript of the "Esquisse", vol. X, p. 503, note 22.

[144] Document of the Walras collection in Lausanne, F. W. V b, box 22. In part II, we have added "sociology", in accordance with the previous scheme. Above "General cœnonics", one reads: "Ethics". At the bottom left, one reads: "Me, Vacherot, Giddings, to be reconciled" and on the right: "9 January 1898". A note in the same collection, probably dating from the time of writing the "Esquisse", bears the following mentions: "Pure natural science (of matter): Physics. Pure human science: Psychics. Applied industrial science: Technique. Applied moral science: Ethics" (F. W. V b, box 22).

In this diagram, one will note the new place granted to history, understood here in the sense of "narrative history".[145]

3.4.3 The Place of Cœnonics

Léon Walras adopts and transforms the term "cœnonics". For him, the "pure science of man and society" in the *Recherche de l'idéal social* (lessons 3 to 6) corresponds to the "general cœnonics".[146] Insofar as it refers to the four social categories, this "abstract and rational" moral science at first glance includes "pure ethics" and "pure economics", because the relationship of the social or cœnonics to ethics and economics is that of the general to the particular.[147] However, "pure economics" cannot be included into "general cœnonics", because it is not exclusively the rational science of the "physiological-economic man dividing labour": it is also a mathematical science.[148] The "general cœnonics" and "pure economics" consider the "will", the "need", the "desire", as the causes of human activity, just as mathematics (mechanics) considers the "force" as a cause of movement.[149]

Just as "pure economics" precedes "applied economics", "general cœnonics" precedes "civil cœnonics" (theory of family), "political cœnonics" (theory of government) and "economic cœnonics" (theory of property and taxation) which Walras agrees to still designate by the name of "social economics" to "facilitate the transition".[150] It is interesting to note in this regard that initially, Walras did not envisage "cœnonics" in this way. In the primitive version of the first three points of "L'économique appliquée et la défense des salaires", one reads:

---

145 As attested by a note (on the back of an advertising leaflet dated March 1898) written for the "Esquisse d'une doctrine économique et sociale", preserved in the Lausanne collection (F. W. V b, box 22).

146 "L'économique appliquée et la défense des salaires" (1897c), vol. X, pp. 245–246; "Esquisse d'une doctrine économique et sociale" (1898c), *op. cit.*, pp. 411–13, English transl., 2005, pp. 216–17 and 360–61. On the first manuscript of the "Esquisse" ("Résumé d'une doctrine économique et sociale", p. 5), L. Walras first notes "pure cœnonics" (F. W. V b, box 22).

147 "Esquisse d'une doctrine économique et sociale", vol. X, p. 406 and see note 8, p. 502, English transl., 2005, p. 356.

148 *Op. cit.*, p. 406 and see note 9, p. 502.

149 *Op. cit.*, p. 407. In a note, L. Walras points out here the analogy observed by A.-M. Ampère between "ethics" and "mechanics". In his "Notes d'humeur", he remarks, probably around 1898:

> [...] there is a singular, striking, decisive analogy between mathematics (geometry, algebra, mechanics) and abstract moral sciences (cœnonics, economics). Both have frankly as their object representations of the imagination: extent, duration, movement—moral person, workers dividing labour—ideal types, perfect, absolute, precisely because they are creations of the mind not without relation to reality, but without a correlative object in reality. Perfect circle, free will, two representations of the imagination. Same relation between theology and cosmology. (see Vacherot). (Emphasis by L. W., vol. XIII, p. 557).

150 "L'économique appliquée et la défense des salaires" (1897c), vol. X, p. 246, English transl., 2005, p. 217.

> [...] I will divide the *general cœnonics* into a *civil and political cœnonics* including the theory of *Family* and the theory of *Government*, and an *economic cœnonics* including the theory of *Property* or the distribution of wealth and the theory of *Industry* or the production of wealth. The elements of the old political economy would thus be included in the *economics* (*économique*) and in the *economic cœnonics*.[151]

Moreover, in certain notes drafted for the "Esquisse", one finds the indication "Create immediatly the *Association cénonique et économique française*".[152] This association would be composed of a "civil and political section", dedicated to family and government issues, and an "economic section", devoted to property and industry questions; the office would include a president, two vice-presidents, etc.[153]

What changes does the new nomenclature bring to the status of "political and social economy"? In the "Esquisse d'une doctrine économique et sociale", economic science no longer comprises three branches, but four[154]: two pertaining to "pure moral science", namely, "general cœnonics" and "pure economics", and two pertaining to "applied science", namely, "applied economics" and "economic cœnonics" (or "social economics").[155] Each branch refers exclusively to "human facts". Léon Walras argues against the proponents of the Historical School who define economics as an "experimental science". This discipline is indeed "a science of observation without being an experimental science", and unlike natural sciences,

> [...] it observes humanitarian facts that are always combined with each other and of which it can never certainly be said that they took place *because of or in spite of* something. From this it follows that deduction always has to assist induction.[156]

It is true that if "pure economics" is a rational science, "social economics is more rational and applied economics more experimental", given their respective criteria.

---

[151] Emphasis by L. W. See the first page of the manuscript, preserved in the Lausanne collection (4 pages), under the reference F. W. V b, box 20; also see under the same reference the draft of these pages: "[...] divide the general cœnonics into four branches. The *civil and political cœnonics* includes the theory of family [...] and the theory of government [...] and an *economic cœnonics* includes the theory of property [...] and the theory of industry [...]."

[152] Document in the Lausanne collection, F. W. V b, box 22, cited in: vol. X, note 78, p. 509.

[153] See two notes preserved in the same collection and under the same reference. In the "Esquisse d'une doctrine économique et sociale", the author calls for the formation of an "*Association française de science sociale*" (vol. X, p. 436, English transl., 2005, p. 381).

[154] Marcel Boson is one of the first authors to present this new approach, based on a reading of the "Esquisse" (1963, p. 37 and Chaps. V, VI, VII, and IX).

[155] In his letter to Arthur-Joseph Girault dated 9 October 1898, L. Walras announces the division of.

[...] the so-called political and social economy into four sciences, namely: pure science of man and society, pure science of social wealth, moral theory of distribution and applied theory of the production of social wealth, each with its own point of view. Shall I succeed in bringing out this revolution? I do not know. (Walras collection of Lausanne, F. W. I, 225, published in: Correspondence, III, 1. 1370, p. 36).

[156] Emphasis by L. W., "L'économique appliquée et la défense des salaires" (1897c), vol. X, p. 249. See also note 9, p. 480, English transl., 2005, p. 219.

Indeed, if the principle of "justice" is "almost exclusively rational", that of "interest" is subject to "experimental confirmation".[157]

3.4.4 Towards a "Denaturalisation" of Pure Economics

Léon Walras now links "pure economics" to "pure moral science"[158]; furthermore, belatedly, on the printing proofs of the *Études d'économie politique appliquée*, he decides to define it no longer as a "physico-mathematical" science, but "psychico-mathematical".[159] Where does this transformation come from? Reading the "Esquisse" does not provide a clear answer. To understand this modification, it seems necessary to refer to a study by Sidney Sherwood,[160] a proponent of American social Darwinism, dedicated to "The Philosophical Basis of Economics" and published in 1897.[161] The Lausanne archives reveal Walras's interest in S. Sherwood's article. A note contains the words, "Quote Sherwood, p. 73 (*Annals*, September 97) at the Baudrillart episode. Esquisse Doctrine", with an addition above, "this is the whole distinction, *physical, psychical* facts".[162]

For S. Sherwood, science must not only recognise the reality of "physical facts", but also that of "psychical facts", thus of the "Ego" (individual subject), that is to say, actions that find their origin in individual minds. Human actions, individual or social, are by nature "psychical". S. Sherwood notes that the distinction between the

[157] *Op. cit.,* note 6, p. 480. On justice, see also the draft Preface to the *Études d'économie sociale,* vol. IX, p. 427, note 6 and the letter to Charles Gide dated 25 July 1896, in: *Correspondence,* III, l. 1254, p. 689.

[158] "Esquisse d'une doctrine économique et sociale" (1898c), vol. X, p. 437, English transl., 2005, p. 381. See a note preserved in the Lausanne collection (F. W. V b, box 22) published in: *op. cit.,* p. 502, note 9: "struck by the *pure* character of economics, I had placed it in the *Éléments* among the *natural* sciences. However, if there are *pure moral* sciences, it is one of them" (emphasis by L. W.). See also another note preserved in the same collection and under the same reference, cited in: *op. cit.,* p. 502, note 9, which reprises a passage from the "Esquisse".

[159] "Esquisse d'une doctrine économique et sociale" (1898c), vol. X, p. 417 and see note 31, p. 504, English transl., 2005, p. 365. This passage is repeated in "La paix par la justice sociale et le libre-échange" (1907a), vol. VII, p. 475. See also a passage from the *Théorie de la monnaie* (1886a), vol. X, p. 460 (note 3 for p. 79). See too a note of the Lausanne collection from the time of the drafting of the "Esquisse": "Mechanics. Physico-mathematical science (Ampère); Economics. Psychico-mathematical science; Cœnonics. Not mathematical" (F. W. V b, box 23).

[160] Sidney Sherwood, professor of political economy at Johns Hopkins University, Baltimore, is the author of *Tendencies in American Economic Thought,* Johns Hopkins University Studies in Historical and Political Science, Fifteenth Series, no. XII, December 1897, 42 p.

[161] S. Sherwood, "The Philosophical Basis of Economics: A Word to the Sociologists", *Annals of the American Academy of Political and Social Science*, vol. X, September 1897, pp. 58–92 [206–40].

[162] Emphasis by L. W. Note kept in the Lausanne collection, F. W. V b, box 23. Another note in the same collection under the reference F. W. V c, box 27, mentions three passages in S. Sherwood's article: the *Ego* (p. 60) with the remark "T[rès] B[ien]", the distinction between the psychical and the physical in W. James's work (note on p. 63) and Sherwood's sentence: "Mind is no more elusive a fact for science than 'matter' or 'force'" (p. 64).

psychical and the physical is well presented in *The Principles of Psychology* (1890) by William James, with these words: "The pursuance of future ends and the choice of means for their attainment are thus the mark and criterion of the presence of [mind]" (*op. cit.*, p. 63, note).[163]

One can distinguish between "physical" sciences (physics, chemistry, biology) and "psychical" sciences (psychology, economics, sociology). Unlike F. H. Giddings, S. Sherwood believes that sociology is not a fundamental social science, whereas economics constitutes the "queen" of the "psychical sciences", as it studies "the interaction of all the motives that lead to choices and actions" (*op. cit.*, p. 77). The "principle of utility" (the greatest utility with the least sacrifice) represents the "psychical form of the physical law of evolution—the survival of the fittest" (*op. cit.*, p. 71). Thus, economics (and not sociology) represents the "general science of man in society" (*op. cit.*, p. 91).[164]

Naturally, Walras is far from subscribing to all aspects of Sherwood's analysis. In the volume of his collection of the *Annals*, he has made annotations on the pages of this study. He particularly notes that "he is an individualist" and that "he is also too utilitarian (*utilitaire*)".[165]

In 1909, the French translator of Alfred Marshall's *Principles of Economics*, F. Sauvaire-Jourdan, would point out to Walras that "pure economics" could be considered a "physico-mathematical science" insofar as "satisfaction is a measurable quantity, thanks to the use of money", thus an external, physical fact.[166] The latter would reply:

> This fact of the decrease in satisfaction, or in utility, with consumption remains (until further notice) a *subjective* fact. And it is because of this circumstance that I, for my part, agree to declare it *psychical* and not *physical*; all the more so because with this special character it has already rendered me very great services.[167]

Furthermore, in the study "Économique et mécanique" (1909b), Léon Walras distinguishes two kinds of "mathematical facts":

- the "external" mathematical facts, which are physical facts, perceived in the same way by everyone and objectively measurable. They are the subject of "physico-mathematical sciences", such as mechanics and astronomy;

---

[163] See William James, 1890, vol. 1, Chap. 1 ("The Scope of Psychology"), p. 8. In fact, W. James wrote, instead of "mind": "mentality in a phenomenon". Further on, he declares accepting "the principle that no action but such as are done for an end, and show a choice of means, can be called indubitable expressions of Mind" (p. 11). Thus, we understand the substitution made by S. Sherwood.

[164] Economics *lato* sensu contains three fields: "aesthetics", which studies the laws of "motive sensations", "economics" in a narrow sense, which studies the mind as seeking to adapt its environment to itself to produce the greatest harmony, and "ethics", which studies the adjustment of the subject to the environment for reaching harmony (pp. 80–83).

[165] Annotations on pages 65 and 71 (collection kept at the Centre d'études interdisciplinaires Walras-Pareto de l'Université de Lausanne under the reference ZAG 23).

[166] F. Sauvaire-Jourdan, letter to L. Walras, 26 June 1909, in: *Correspondence*, III, 1. 1766, p. 429.

[167] Emphasis by L. W., letter to F. Sauvaire-Jourdan, 30 June 1909, in: *op. cit.*, 1. 1767, p. 430.

– the "intimate" mathematical facts, which are psychic facts, insofar as they are not perceived in the same way by everyone and can only be appreciated subjectively and individually. They are the subject of the "psychico-mathematical science", or "pure economics". The "*rareté*", "need", or "utility" of things for the consumer represent "intimate" facts, appreciable in terms of "intensity".[168] Here we see the outcome of the discussion on the use of "arbitrary functions" that took place in 1901 between Walras and the mathematician Henri Poincaré (*cf infra* Chap. 7, *The Reception of Pure Economics in France (1873–1926)*).

We thus witness a complete reversal of perspective compared to the argumentation put forward in the youthful writings and presented in the *Éléments*. This "denaturalisation" of "pure economics"[169] does not lead Walras to question the method of "ideal types", but to re-examine the question of analogies. The version of the "Esquisse" published in the 1st edition of the *Études d'économie politique appliquée* (1898d) considered "pure economics" not as a science "analogous" to mechanics, but as "mechanics itself applied to the equilibrium and movement of social wealth". On the proof prepared around 1900–02, in view of a second edition of the *Études*, Léon Walras takes exactly the opposite stance to this assertion (vol. X, p. 406). Later, in "Économique et mécanique" (1909b), he presents a double analogy: between the theory of maximum satisfaction of the exchanger and that of maximum energy of the Roman balance, and between the theory of general economic equilibrium and that of the equilibrium of celestial bodies.

3.5 Conclusion

What was, ultimately, the scope and consequences of the transformations introduced between 1896 and 1898? It must be admitted that the changes in the taxonomy of sciences and the divisions of economics had rather limited consequences in later Walrasian works. The concept of "cœnonics" was not adopted in writings beyond 1898.[170] Moreover, Walras seems to have quickly distanced himself from Franklin Henry Giddings's ideas.[171] The latter, from 1898 onwards, substantially modified his methodological conceptions; under the influence of Karl Pearson and Ernst Mach,

---

[168] "Notes sur 'Masse et rareté'" (1907–08), vol. XI, p. 628; "Économique et mécanique" (1909b), vol. VII, pp. 330–32; see also the letter to Pasquale Boninsegni, 10 September 1908, in: *Correspondence,* III, 1. 1705, p. 374, and the letter to Maffeo Pantaleoni, 3 March 1909, in: *op. cit.,* 1. 1727, p. 394.

[169] For a different point of view, see P. Dockès, 1996, p. 46.

[170] Except on the occasion of the reprint of extracts from the "Esquisse" in "La paix par la justice sociale et le libre-échange" (1907a), vol. VII, p. 476.

[171] In the proofs prepared, around 1900–02, for a 2nd edition of the *Études d'économie sociale,* a note in the Preface that referred the reader to the *Principles of Sociology* and highlighted the similarities with his method was removed (vol. IX, p. 5, note c 1). One can also suppose Walras's irritation related to the fact that Giddings did not keep his promise to write a review of the *Études d'économie sociale.*

he now conceives science as descriptions of concomitant facts.[172] In the 4th edition of the *Éléments d'économie politique pure* which appeared in 1900, the author was unable or did not wish to completely revisit the question of the classification of sciences, as presented in the first section.[173] He merely corrected a passage of the 3rd lesson which designated "pure economics" as a "physico-mathematical science" and now indicates that it is a "science quite similar to physico-mathematical sciences".[174] Furthermore, in "Ruchonnet et le socialisme scientifique" (1909c), which does not constitute new research but a summary of his intellectual journey on the occasion of his jubilee, he merely recalls, in the "economic part of social science", the three components of "political and social economy".

[172] In this new perspective, Giddings publishes, in 1901, *Inductive Sociology* (See D. Ross, 1991, pp. 227–28).

[173] The "Terminologie des *Éléments* (4e édition)" only takes into account the modifications introduced in the 2nd edition (vol. VIII, pp. 724–25).

[174] *Op. cit.*, p. 52. He does not reproduce this correction in the following lines (p. 53).

Part II
Pure Economics and Its Reception

Chapter 4
Genesis of a Masterpiece: The Theory of General Economic Equilibrium

4.1 Introduction

After examining the taxonomy of sciences used by Léon Walras, it is necessary to consider the genesis of the general economic equilibrium theory, widely considered as his "masterpiece". On this topic, we will recall, as essential references, the collection of essays by William Jaffé (Donald A. Walker, ed., 1983) and Bruna Ingrao and Giorgio Israel's book, *The Invisible Hand. Economic Equilibrium in the History of Science.*[1] We must also mention the collection of reviews of Walras's *Éléments d'économie politique pure* gathered by Pascal Bridel (in collaboration with Roberto Baranzini), *Le chêne et l'architecte. Un siècle de comptes rendus bibliographiques des* Éléments d'économie politique pure *de Léon Walras. Textes et commentaires* (1996). We also have two working tools: on the one hand, the scientific correspondence of Léon Walras edited by William Jaffé in 1965 and, on the other hand, the *Œuvres économiques complètes* (1987–2005). Our approach here will not involve a precise analysis of the content of the different general equilibrium models throughout the editions of the *Éléments d'économie politique pure.* Much more modestly, our approach will follow Walras's theoretical itinery before and after the period 1871–77, from his early writings to the construction of the successive editions of the *Éléments,* in order to identify the essential moments in the genesis of the general economic equilibrium theory. Our study comprises three sections. The first section focuses on the French years and the initial research leading to mathematical economics. The second section deals with the Vaud years and the main stages of the construction of general economic equilibrium. The third section questions the status of pure economics: is it a "positive" or a "normative" project?

[1] B. Ingrao and G. Israel, 1987, American transl., 1990. This book offers a retrospective reading of the origins of the general equilibrium theory. For a critique, see A. Jolink, 1993, pp. 1303–11.

J.-P. Potier, *Léon Walras, Economist and Liberal Socialist*, Springer Studies in the History of Economic Thought, https://doi.org/10.1007/978-3-032-04670-3_4

4.2 The French Years: Early Research in the Direction of Mathematical Economics

4.2.1 Léon Walras's Education and Intellectual Heritage

Born in 1834, Léon Walras had a good secondary education.[2] After obtaining a *baccalauréat ès lettres* in August 1851, he specialised in mathematics as preparation to enter a Parisian *grande école*. In 1851–52, he was enrolled in an elementary mathematics class,[3] then in 1852–53, in a special mathematics class. In 1853, he obtained a *baccalauréat ès sciences*, but failed the entrance exam to the École Polytechnique. In 1853–54, he repeated the special mathematics class, but failed again to enter Polytechnique. However, in November 1854, Walras was finally admitted as an external student at the École des Mines. At this school, he failed the preparatory year in 1854–55 and again in 1855–56. In the autumn of 1856, he tried once more to pass the admission exam for vacant places for external students, but this time he was not even admitted as an external student. Why such failures? Léon Walras did not work diligently at the École des Mines; he dreamed of a literary career and had, in fact, written a novel, *Francis Sauveur*, which would be published in 1858.

What readings did Léon Walras engage in while preparing for the exams? In his "Notice autobiographique", he mentions that in 1853, he read the works of Descartes, Newton, Joseph-Louis Lagrange's *Mécanique analytique* (1788), and Jean-Marie-Constant Duhamel's *Cours d'analyse de l'École Polytechnique* (1841) and *Cours de mécanique* (1845–46).[4] He adds that he also read in the same year Cournot's *Recherches sur les principes mathématiques de la théorie des richesses*, although at the time, he was not yet interested in economics (1909a, vol. V, pp. 11–12). It is known by a letter that in 1853, he is reading Louis Poinsot's *Éléments de statique* (*cf. infra*).

As we saw in the first part, his father was his initiator in economics, passing on an intellectual heritage, particularly from Jean-Baptiste Say and Saint-Simonianism. But Léon Walras is also the heir of a French tradition dating back to the XVIIIth century. He indeed inherits a theoretical legacy from François Quesnay and Turgot. According to him, economic science was born not with Adam Smith's *Wealth of Nations* but with Quesnay's *Tableau économique*,[5] which highlights the interdependence between economic activities and the circulation of income. In Turgot, he found the notion of economic equilibrium, but also the principle of free competition (*cf.* the Edicts

---

[2] On the biography of Walras, see P. Dockès and J.-P. Potier, 2001.

[3] His programme includes five hours of mathematics per week, but also pure mechanics, physics-chemistry, and probably natural sciences.

[4] Later, Walras will read J.-M.-C. Duhamel's book, *Des méthodes dans les sciences de raisonnement* (Paris: Gauthier-Villard, 1868, 3 vols.). This work is cited in "Une branche nouvelle de la hématique" (1876b, vol. VII, p. 308) and the manuscript of his reading notes is preserved in the Lausanne collection under the reference F. W. V b 23, 17 f°

[5] See C. Salvat, 2004, pp. 29–45.

of 1776). This movement, which begins with the Physiocrats, culminates in Jean-Baptiste Say with the idea that at equilibrium, production constitutes only a "great exchange" (*cf. supra* Chap. 1, *Auguste Walras as a Transmitter of Ideas: From Jean-Baptiste Say to Léon Walras*). But one must also go back to Condorcet and the *Idéologues* to follow the trend of the mathematisation of social issues.

4.2.2 Outline of the Walrasian System

From 1860, Léon Walras attempts a first endeavour of "Application des mathématiques à l'économie politique", but which does not yet provide a path towards general equilibrium. At the time, he is interested in "absolute value", or "*valorie*" and he states that "the absolute value [...] of the unit of a type of social wealth is directly proportional to the sum of needs or economic desires and inversely proportional [...] to the provisions or the sum of quantities supplied".[6] The adoption of his father's theory of *rareté* remains an obstacle to progress: indeed, unlike the quantity supplied or sum of provisions, the quantity demanded or sum of needs is not susceptible to measurement. The search for the "unit of demand or need" is an open question. And Léon Walras still remains within a partial equilibrium problem.

In 1860, after the Lausanne congress on taxation, Walras is contacted by Jules Du Mesnil-Marigny (1810–85), probably with a view to co-authoring a work. The latter is a polytechnic and marine engineer, a member of the Société d'économie politique de Paris. Having become an advocate of a moderate protectionism, he published *L'Économie politique devenue science exacte, ou les Libres échangistes et les protectionnistes conciliés, ou Solution analytique des questions économiques restées jusqu'à l'état de problèmes* (Paris: Guillaumin, 1860).[7] Both particularly discuss the application of mathematics to economics. In 1862, Du Mesnil-Marigny proposes to the young Walras to write a book together. Walras takes the initiative by preparing a project for a *Traité complet d'économie politique et sociale* in four volumes, which he submits in a letter dated 23 December 1862. Here is this project:

"Volume I.—*Theory of Social Wealth* (Pure economics).

Section I.—On social wealth and exchange value.—On exchange, on supply and demand, on market.—On Money.

Sections II and III.—On capital and income.—On three types of capital and on three types of income: *land, personal faculties, produced or artificial capital. Land services, labour, profit, rents (*fermages*), wages, interest.*—The laws of wealth.

---

[6] "Application des mathématiques à l'économie politique (1st attempt 1860)", 1860d, vol. XI, p. 337.

[7] Previously, J. Du Mesnil-Marigny published a brochure with the aim of authorising the sale of new commodities by the auctioneers of Paris (*Débouchés nouveaux à ouvrir dans Paris pour les marchandises de toutes espèces au bénéfice des producteurs et consommateurs. Projet de loi sur les ventes aux enchères*, Paris: Dentu, 1852). He also published *Aperçus nouveaux en faveur du libre-échange* (Paris: Guillaumin, 1857).

Section IV.—On economic production and on consumption of incomes.

Volume II.—*On Production, Circulation and Consumption of Social Wealth* (Applied economics).

Section I.—On division of labour or on specialisation of occupations.—*On laissez-faire, laissez-passer,* or on free competition and free trade.

Section II.—On agricultural industry; on manufacturing industry and commercial industry.

Section III.—On credit and on credit institutions. On agricultural credit. On industrial credit. On commercial credit.

Section IV.—On speculation.

Volume III.—*On Property and Taxation* (Social economics).

Section I.—On the individual and the State, on individual interest and general interest, on private services and public services.

Sections II and III.—On property and taxation from the dual perspective of equity and of convenience.

Section IV.—Reasoned analysis of the French budget.

Volume IV.—*History of Ideas and of Economic and Social Theories.*

Section I.—The Physiocrats.

Section II.—The English School.

Section III.—Modern economists.[8]

Section IV.—Empirical socialism."[9]

Du Mesnil-Marigny and Walras will not succeed in reaching an agreement, undoubtedly due to disagreements on the content of pure economics and also on the issue of property and taxation. However, it should be noted that Du Mesnil-Marigny considers the application of mathematics to economics on the condition that the variables are quantifiable, and he is particularly interested in questions of national accounting and statistics.[10]

For his part, between 1863 and 1868, Léon Walras cannot engage in this book project and research in mathematical economics, as he is completely absorbed by his professional activities: indeed, from 1862 to 1865, he works at the secretariat of the Northern Railway Company and from 1865 to 1868, in the Parisian cooperative

[8] In this section, the thought of J.-B. Say and his disciples would be addressed.

[9] L. Walras, letter to J. Du Mesnil-Marigny, 23 December 1862, in: *Correspondence*, I, l. 81, p. 119.

[10] Shortly after, J. Du Mesnil-Marigny will publish a *Catéchisme de l'économie politique basée sur des principes rationnels* (Paris: Guillaumin, 1863) and later new editions of his 1860 book under the title, *L'Économie politique devenue science exacte, ou les Libres échangistes et les protectionnistes conciliés* (3rd ed., 1878, 4th ed., 1883). On Du Mesnil-Marigny, see A. Zylberberg, 1990, pp. 133–142 and R. D. Theocharis, 1993, pp. 69–73.

movement. However, between January 1869 and July 1870, when he holds a position as an employee at the bank "Trivulzi, Hollander and Co", he prepares a second "attempt" of an "Application des mathématiques à l'économie politique". It contains in particular some pages that will later be included in the *Éléments d'économie politique pure*:

- the natural character of the fact of exchange value;
- the prices or value ratios are equal to the inverse ratios of the quantities of commodities exchanged: the famous exchange equation in the absence of money; supply is reciprocal to demand: mVa = nVb thus Va/Vb = m/n and Vb/Va = n/m,[11] but the concepts of supply and effective demand do not yet appear;
- the problem of arbitrages.

We also find only a brief allusion to the possibility of expressing by equations a situation of "[general] market equilibrium".[12]

According to Walras, the *rareté* (scarcity) expressed as the ratio of the utility of a commodity to the quantity that exists is "just as speed is the ratio of the distance travelled by a moving object to the time taken for that journey—just as density is the ratio of the mass of a body to its volume".[13]

4.2.3 Are There "Precursors" of General Economic Equilibrium?

The literature devoted to Léon Walras has been interested in the question of the so-called "precursors" of general economic equilibrium. First of all, two names frequently recur, those of Isnard and Poinsot.

Achylle-Nicolas Isnard (1749–1803), an engineer of Ponts et Chaussées, anonymously published in 1781 a *Traité des richesses. Contenant l'analyse de l'usage des richesses en général & de leurs valeurs; les principes & les lois naturelles de la circulation des richesses, de leur distribution, du commerce, de la circulation des monnoies & de l'impôt* […] (Lausanne: François Grasset). In this book, Isnard develops a theoretical approach partly based on a critical analysis of the physiocratic conceptions.[14] Joseph A. Schumpeter unhesitatingly considers the author of the *Traité des richesses* "a precursor of Léon Walras" for having attempted, in a primitive form, to propose a mathematical definition of economic equilibrium and for having demonstrated it mathematically (1954, p. 217). William Jaffé goes further by considering Isnard as "a direct progenitor of the Walrasian general equilibrium

[11] A probable influence of Isnard (*cf. infra*).

[12] "Application des mathématiques à l'économie politique" (2nd attempt 1869–70)" (1870a), vol. XI, p. 346.

[13] *Op. cit.*, p. 354. On the 2nd attempt, see also W. Jaffé, 1972, pp. 300–301.

[14] Isnard's work is not limited to this book. The only study covering his entire work is that of Richard van den Berg, 2006.

model" (1969, p. 56). The *Traité des richesses* would offer a direct source of inspiration for the general equilibrium of exchange, but also for the theories of production and capitalisation.

At his turn, Robert F. Hebert does not hesitate to assert:

> Isnard [...] was the first writer to attempt a mathematical definition and a mathematical proof of an economic equilibrium. Furthermore, he gave specific form to the general equilibrium concept by constructing a set of simultaneous equations which, in general form and content, anticipated the major elements of the Walrasian system, including the general interdependence of markets and quantities, the technical specifications of the exchange ratios, and the mathematical determination of the *numéraire.* It remained for Walras to add the engine of utility maximization and to adapt Isnard's model to his own purposes, something which, according to Jaffé (1969), he did with persistence, if not with ease. Isnard's pioneer efforts do not in any way denigrate Walras's monumental achievement, but they do lend force to the conviction that the development of economics was, and remains, a cumulative process. (1987, p. 1004)

Gérard Klotz takes up and completes Jaffé's analysis concerning the Isnard-Walras lineage. According to him, "everything is there, the vocabulary, the main statements, the embryonic formalisation and above all the general order of exposition" (1994, p. 48). If Isnard can be considered a "precursor" of Walras, on the other hand, he cannot be regarded as the "first theorist of general equilibrium" (*op. cit.*, p. 48).

In reality, one finds in Isnard first what Walras recognises in him,[15] the fact that the ratios of values are equal to the inverse ratios of the quantities of commodities exchanged.[16] In Chap. 2 ("Of the relation between different kinds of wealth") of book I, the author uses the "theory of proportions"[17] and indicates that if a and b are the quantities offered of the units of two goods M and M', the relative values will be in inverse proportion to the quantities supplied: M/M' = b/a. He moves on to three goods, then to n goods. But he goes further by saying that one can express all the ratios a/b, a/c, of the quantities offered of goods in any commodity that will be chosen as "*numéraire*" (term used by Isnard).[18] He also suggests the necessity of equalising the number of equations and the number of unknowns (B. Ingrao and G. Israel, 1987, pp. 58 and 98). The influence on our author is evident, but one should not exaggerate

[15] Auguste Walras never cites Isnard in his writings, but it is highly probable that the copy of the *Traité des richesses*, preserved at the Centre d'études interdisciplinaires Walras-Pareto de l'Université de Lausanne (ZAB 2015/1 and 2), belonged to his collection. On 13 July 1878 (*Correspondence*, I, l. 410, p. 570) Léon Walras mentions the *Traité des richesses* to W. S. Jevons for his Bibliography of Mathematical Economics which will be published in an appendix of the 2nd edition of the *Theory of Political Economy* (1879). See the following note.

[16] The only explicit reference to Isnard in Léon Walras's published work is found in the introduction to the "Bibliographie des ouvrages relatifs à l'application des mathématiques à l'économie politique" (1878b). He asserts that "from the very first pages" of the *Traité des richesses,*

> the relationships of values are very correctly expressed in algebraic symbols as equal to the inverse relationships of the quantities of goods exchanged. This equation of exchange is neither delved into nor deepened by the author; but it is nonetheless the starting point of the scientific theory of social wealth, and it is sufficient to make, despite everything, within certain limits, pure economics a mathematical science. (vol. XI, p. 614).

[17] See G. Klotz, 1994, pp. 34–39.

[18] See W. Jaffé, 1969, pp. 64 and 75–76 and P. Bridel, 1997, pp. 4–5.

this lineage: the birth of general economic equilibrium cannot be reduced to a strong influence of Isnard on Walras. The concept of equilibrium is practically absent in Isnard's book and it is difficult to see in it an anticipation of the general equilibrium of production (*op. cit.*, p. 59).

Richard Van den Berg rightly invites us to be cautious:

> One does not find a *general* equilibrium of a Walrasian type in the *Traité* where relative prices are determined in a moment where all producers and consumers trade equilibrium quantities *simultaneously*. Instead [...], in his analysis of exchange the engineer assumes *given* marketed quantities, while in his analysis of production he considers *given* relative prices. Perhaps it is fair to say that this is not only due to shortcomings in Isnard's formal approach, but also reflects the fact that in contrast to Walras' static conception of the market economy, the engineer acknowledges the sequential nature of reproduction. (emphasis by R. v. d. B., 2006, p. 38)

Similarly, one should be circumspect about the role of Louis Poinsot in the birth of general economic equilibrium. A former student of P. S. Laplace and professor of analysis and mechanics at the École Polytechnique until 1817,[19] Louis Poinsot (1774–1859) succeeded Joseph-Louis Lagrange in 1813 in the geometry section of the Académie des sciences. In 1803, he published the *Éléments de statique*, intended for secondary teaching; this book was praised for its didactic qualities and went through 12 editions until 1877.[20] In 1834, he published a "Théorie nouvelle de la rotation des corps", which would make him famous. In a letter to Miss Dick May (1859–1925),[21] a friend of Georges Renard, Walras reveals that one evening in 1853, when he was preparing his *baccalauréat ès sciences*, he opened Poinsot's *Éléments de statique* and specifies: "this theory of equilibrium by the composition and decomposition of forces and couples seemed so clear and easy to me that I read the first half in one go; the next day, I dispatched the second".[22] In fact, he read the 8th corrected and augmented edition: *Éléments de statique, suivis de quatre mémoires sur la composition des moments et des aires; sur le plan invariable du système du monde; sur la nouvelle théorie générale de l'équilibre et du mouvement des systèmes; et sur la théorie nouvelle de la rotation des corps* (Paris: Bachelier, 1842).[23] Indeed (unlike Isnard's book), Walras took notes on Poinsot's book, which are preserved in the Lausanne archives (1853). He was particularly interested in Chap. 2, "On

---

[19] Among his students at the École Polytechnique, one must mention Auguste Comte. A correspondence between Poinsot and Comte is published by P. Laffitte, 1886, pp. 145–57.

[20] J. Bertrand will publish a review of the 11th edition of this book in *Journal des Savants* (July 1872, pp. 405–20).

[21] Known under this pen name, this woman of letters is actually named Jeanne Weill and she is a sister of the historian Georges Weill (1865–1944). Her mother is a cousin of K. Marx. Dreaming of creating a "young Sorbonne" to train a new democratic elite, she was the general secretary of the Collège libre des sciences sociales founded in 1895; in 1900, she founded the École des Hautes Études Sociales (see *infra* Chap. 7, *The Reception of Pure Economics in France (1873–1926)*).

[22] L. Walras, letter to Miss Dick May, 23 May 1901, in: *Correspondence*, III, l. 1483, p. 148. However, one can express some doubts about the speed of reading of this work by the young Walras!

[23] Walras's personal copy has not been found.

the conditions of equilibrium, expressed by equations", where one finds systems of simultaneous equations related to the equilibrium of a group of parallel forces. He also focused on the memoir "General Theory of Equilibrium and Movement of Systems". This is corroborated by a note that Walras had considered placing at the beginning of the first part of the "Esquisse d'une doctrine économique et sociale" (1898c), but which he ultimately decided not to publish. What does he say in this note?

> Poinsot developed statics rationally, that is to say, through the definition of force and a single [axiom] postulate resulting from this definition, and thus established the principle of virtual velocities as the basis of all [mechanics] dynamics (*Statics—General Theory of Equilibrium and Movement of Systems.* Note III. *Demonstration of the Principle of Virtual Velocities*).[24] I followed, in economics, Poinsot's approach in mechanics, especially since, in this case, all pure science consisted above all in knowing under what conditions and within what limits the economic system tends by itself towards equilibrium.[25]

William Jaffé considers that Poinsot's book constitutes "the *fons et origo* of his conception of general equilibrium within the framework of which he later evolved his characteristic economic theory". He mentions Chap. 2 and the third memoir.

> [...] where the equilibrium among physical forces is described, bristle with systems of simultaneous equations which are clear prototypes of L. W.'s multi-equational systems of the general equilibrium of market forces. [...] so L. W., after him, set up his system of general equilibrium equations by combining specified equilibrium equations with other equations imposing given constraints (e.g. the budget constraint), and then assumed that the system had a solution, provided that the number of independent equations equaled the number of unknowns.[26]

And it seems "evident" for him that this work remained a "bedside book" for Walras. But, in reality, Jaffé does not provide any tangible proof of this.[27]

If Isnard and Poinsot's books were true "sources", one might reasonably think that Walras could have developed the perspective of general economic equilibrium well before his arrival in Lausanne. Moreover, Walras does not cite either Isnard or Poinsot in the *Éléments d'économie politique pure*. In fact, these two authors cannot be considered "precursors" of the theory of general equilibrium.

Another lead would be Augustin Cournot (1811–77), the second "master" of Walras. We already know that he had read Augustin Cournot's *Recherches sur les principes mathématiques de la théorie des richesses* as early as 1853–54.[28] In Chap. 3,

---

[24] This is Note III attached to the third memoir "General theory of equilibrium and movement of systems", placed after the *Éléments de statique* (1842, pp. 475–83).

[25] Manuscript preserved in the Lausanne collection under the reference F. W. V b box 23, p. 1. Note published in the *Études d'économie politique appliquée*, vol. X, p. 501.

[26] W. Jaffé, note 7 to letter 1483 to D. May, in: *Correspondence*, III, pp. 149–50. See also W. Jaffé, 1965, p. 229 and 1968, p. 132. However, W. Jaffé would later soften his position by stating: "for the translation of the vision of general market equilibrium thus obtained into mathematical equations he found models in the works of A. N. Isnard, Augustin Cournot and Louis Poinsot" (1976, pp. 313–14).

[27] See J. Van Daal and A. Jolink, 1993, p. 11.

[28] When he was repeating his special mathematics class. See the "Notice autobiographique" (1909a), vol. V, pp. 11–12; see also "Cournot et l'économique mathématique" (1905), vol. VII, p. 462.

On the Exchanges (Du change), the author discusses a global economy in which exchange rates ("*coefficients du change*") are perfectly flexible. There are r places in communication (countries) and the number of unknown exchange rates must be r (r—1), but this number reduces to (r—1). And he specifies at the end of the analysis that "there are only just as many distinct equations as there are independent variables" (§ 15, 2001, p. 27, English transl., 1897, p. 34). This approach could indeed have helped Walras in his reflections on general economic equilibrium.[29] And furthermore, Cournot questions himself in the last three chapters of the *Recherches sur les principes mathématiques de la théorie des richesses* on the "communication of markets" (see Chap. X). However, in Chap. XI, the consideration of the interdependence of markets leaves Cournot sceptical:

> So far we have studied how, for each commodity by itself, the law of demand in connection with the conditions of production of that commodity, determines the price of it and regulates the incomes of its producers. We considered as given and invariable the prices of other commodities and the incomes of other producers; but in reality the economic system is a whole of which all the parts are connected and react on each other. An increase in the income of the producers of commodity A will affect the demand for commodities B, C, etc., and the incomes of their producers, and, by its reaction, will involve a change in the demand for commodity A. It seems, therefore, as if, for a complete and rigorous solution of the problems relative to some parts of the economic system, it were indispensable to take the entire system into consideration. But this would surpass the powers of mathematical analysis and of our practical methods of calculation, even if the values of all the constants could be assigned to them numerically. (§ 74, Chap. XI, p. 99, English transl., 1897, p. 127)[30]

In this passage, Cournot clearly understands the difference between partial equilibrium and general equilibrium, but he seeks to "evade this difficulty" of general equilibrium.

Léon Walras acknowledges Cournot's merits firstly about the use of the mathematical method in economics, particularly the programme stated in the Preface:

> I propose to show in this essay that the solution of the general questions which arise from the theory of wealth, depends essentially not on elementary algebra, but on that branch of analysis which comprises arbitrary functions, which are merely restricted to satisfying certain conditions. (Preface, 2001, p. 5, English transl., 1897, p. 4)

Walras then acknowledges Cournot's merits for the development of the "*courbe de débit*" and also regarding the use of analogies between economics and mechanics

---

[29] As observed by T. Negishi, Introduction to the *Recherches sur les principes mathématiques de la théorie des richesses*, 2001, pp. XI–XII, R. Dos Santos Ferreira, 2011, p. 72 *et seq*, R. Dos Santos Ferreira and R. Ege, 2013, pp. 631–34.

[30] Vilfredo Pareto would later insist on the difficulties of a numerical calculation of prices. In the *Manuel d'économie politique*, he observes:

[…] we have seen that in the case of 100 individuals and 700 commodities there would be 70 699 conditions […]; we would therefore have to solve a system of 70 699 equations. This practically exceeds the power of algebraic analysis, and it would exceed it even more if one considered the fabulous number of equations that a population of forty million individuals, and a few thousand commodities would give […]. In other words, if one could really know all these equations, the only means accessible to human forces to solve them would be to observe the practical solution given by the market. (1909, pp. 233–34).

(abstraction of all friction, polish of surfaces). However, he mentions the limits of his approach, which would not have remained faithful to the "indications of his own preface". The "*courbe de débit*" is posited a priori without taking into account the interdependence between markets. The author has not "rigorously solved" the determination of current equilibrium prices ("Une branche nouvelle de la mathématique", 1876b, vol. VII, pp. 321–23). In fact, Walras's theoretical approach will be different from that of Cournot. In Chaps. V to VIII of the *Recherches*, the author describes several states of competition according to the criterion of the structure of supply (monopoly, duopoly, unlimited (*indéfinie*) competition). Walras, on the other hand, in the *Éléments d'économie politique pure*, will focus on the "markets that are best organized in regard to competition" in order to rigorously determine the exchange value (vol. VIII, p. 70, English transl., 2014, p. 42). It is therefore difficult to consider Cournot as a mere "precursor" of Walras for general equilibrium.[31]

Léon Walras will not be able to carry out his research programme in his native country. Without a university degree, he cannot teach in French institutions. The move to Lausanne in 1870 will allow him to write the bulk of his work and to construct the theory of general economic equilibrium.

4.3 The Vaud Years: Main Stages of the Construction of the General Economic Equilibrium Theory

In June 1870, Louis Ruchonnet, head of the Department of Public Instruction of the Canton of Vaud,[32] offers Léon Walras the chair of political economy at the Faculty of Law in Lausanne. He agrees to enter the competition, open in July, having received certain assurances that his candidacy would be retained. Given the Franco-Prussian war, it was impossible to have the French candidates undergo the test of a public lecture and only the works were considered. Despite the reluctance of some jury members, particularly due to his ideas on the collective property of land, he was appointed (by four votes to three) on 12 November 1870 and would teach until 1892.

4.3.1 Preparation of the Eléments d'économie politique pure

At the Faculty of Law in Lausanne, Léon Walras gave an annual course on "pure economics (*Économie politique pure*)" in the first year. Unfortunately, he did not keep the manuscripts of his early lectures, because from 1874, he taught directly using the *Éléments d'économie politique pure*. The first course, hastily constructed

[31] J. A. Schumpeter moreover declares: "I do not think it historically correct to attribute to him more than a vague and non-operational idea of *general* equilibrium" (emphasis by J. A. S., 1954, p. 960).

[32] On Louis Ruchonnet, see O. Meuwly, 2006.

between December 1870 and June 1871, developed a few concepts, but it did not yet constitute a teaching of mathematical economics. The "box" is sparsely filled, as can be seen in the "Programme d'un cours d'économie politique" (Saint-Aubin-sur-Mer, 1870).[33]

The discovery in 1991 in the Lausanne archives by Albert Jolink of a third attempt at "Application des mathématiques à l'économie politique"[34] is significant. This attempt, probably written in the spring of 1871, although unfinished like the previous ones, is mentioned by Walras as "the good one". In fact, it is more of a series of essays, both graphical and algebraical, which allow him to eventually reach the notions of supply and effective demand at certain prices. But the concept of marginal utility is not yet present. If one refers to the exam questions posed to students in July 1871, the following themes are discovered:

> Law of supply and effective demand; General market equilibrium; Price curves; Origin of value—Smith—Say; Qualities of precious metals; On *numéraire.* On metallic money; On fiduciary money and crises; On exchange (*Du change*); Types of social wealth (capital and income); Elements of production; Mechanism of production; Capitalisation; Association of capital and land; Increase in the quantity of subsistence. Conditions of progress; Variations in the value of land, of personal faculties and of capital; Decrease in the rate of income.[35]

From July 1871, Léon Walras is dealing with the preparation of a second course in pure economics for the academic year 1871–72, more developed in the field of exchange and production.[36] Having the opportunity to give, in January 1872, ten public lectures at the Town Hall of Geneva on social doctrines, he decided to change the subject and present the "Système des phénomènes économiques", that is to say, pure economics and general equilibrium. He thus used the pure economics course he was teaching at the time at the Faculty of Law in Lausanne. Some notes on these lectures have been preserved. Walras used the notion of "*utilité d'extension*" as the quantity demanded at price 0, that is to say the quantity of goods that satisfies all the individual's needs. But he also used the notion of "*utilité d'intensité*" of the individual as the slope of the market demand curve and the notion of "*utilité effective*", to actually designate the consumer surplus in the manner of Jules Dupuit.

Then, around October 1872, Léon Walras consulted Antoine-Paul Piccard (1844–1929), an engineer and professor of industrial mechanics, from 1869 to 1881, at the Academy of Lausanne. These discussions would allow him to complete the mathematical apparatus necessary for the theory of exchange. Walras would acknowledge that Piccard provided him with a simple method to solve the problem of

---

[33] This programme is published in the "General Introduction" to the volume of *Cours*, vol. XII, pp. 30–34.

[34] A. Jolink, 1991, pp. 92–93 and 1996, pp. 83–84. The 3rd attempt (1871b) is published by Claude Mouchot in 1993 in vol. XI, pp. 385–409. On these attempts, see A. Rebeyrol, 1999, p. 101–06 and V. Lhuillier, 2002. p. 30–46.

[35] P. Bridel, "Presentation" of the *Matériaux sur le Cours d'économie politique pure*, vol XII, p. 720, note 10.

[36] During the summer of 1871, he had the solution to the problem of exchange which he introduced in the course of 1871–72 and in his lectures of January 1872; during 1872, he completed his theory of exchange and production and began writing his *Traité* (*Correspondence*, I, l. 275, p. 398).

utility maximisation under constraint,[37] to express the maximum satisfaction of the exchangers and to deduce the demand curves from the marginal utility curves, or "intensity of the last want satisfied", or *rareté* (scarcity) to pay homage to his father. The pure economics course of the year 1872–73 is thus now constructed on foundational bases that will remain unchanged thereafter.

4.3.2 Publication of the Eléments d'économie politique pure[38]

In September 1872, Léon Walras proposed to the Parisian publishing house Guillaumin a *Traité d'économie politique et sociale* in three volumes, the first of which would be the *Éléments d'économie politique pure*. But the project was rejected because the work was deemed unsellable due to its mathematical content. Thanks to Louis Ruchonnet, Walras found a publisher in Lausanne, Louis Corbaz, responsible for the publication of the *Nouvelliste vaudois*, with whom Guillaumin in Paris and H. Georg in Basel would be associated. From January 1873, the *Éléments d'économie politique pure* were in the process of composition and in July, 104 pages were already printed. Finally, on 27 July 1874, Walras announced the completion of the printing of the book's first part to the director of Guillaumin publishing house.[39]

Before the publication of the *Éléments*, as a preview, Léon Walras presents a communication, "Principe d'une théorie mathématique de l'échange", on 16 and 23 August 1873, before the Académie des sciences morales et politiques in Paris. The content of this text is centred on the theory of the exchange of two commodities for each other and is found in section II of the *Éléments d'économie politique pure*, "Mathematical Theory of Exchange". During this presentation, Émile Levasseur opposes him with the impossibility of an "exact measure" of the "intensity of need" of buyers; the fluctuations of needs have multiple causes and cannot be determined with mathematical precision and, in summary, human liberty cannot be put into an "algebraic formula"[40] (for more details on this question, *cf.* Chap. 7, *The Reception of Pure Economics in France (1873–1926)*).

Let us note that on his side, Jules Du Mesnil-Marigny in the Preface of the 3rd edition of his book, *L'Économie politique devenue science exacte*, delivers an implicit attack on Walras: "Thus, some, carried away by a feverish ardour, have they not wanted to subject to mathematical evaluations the things most refractory to such treatment, for example utility, scarcity, abundance?" [1859] 1878, pp. 4–5).

---

[37] The main piece of the file concerning Piccard's contribution consists of his undated note, discovered by William Jaffé. See L. Walras, letter to Henri Brocher de la Fléchère, 19 October 1872, in: *Correspondence*, I, l. 211, note 4, pp. 308–11. On the debate concerning the relative importance of Piccard, see the contributions of W. Jaffé (1964, pp. 206–07; 1972, pp. 303–04; 1976, pp. 314–15).

[38] See on this question C. Mouchot, 1988, in: vol. VIII, Annex I, pp. 795–819.

[39] L. Walras, letter to Miss Guillaumin, 27 July 1874, in: *Correspondence*, I, l. 284, p. 410.

[40] See the "Observations" of Levasseur, Valette and Wolowski, in: vol. VII, pp. 529–32.

Walras will reply to these attacks in the 2nd edition of the *Éléments*:

> We are told in the first place: - '*One of the elements of price determination under free competition is human freedom, the decisions of which cannot be calculated*'. Well, we have never attempted to calculate the decisions of human liberty; we have only attempted to express its effects by means of mathematics. In our theory, each exchanger can be assumed to establish his utility or want curves as he pleases. These curves once determined, we show how the prices result from them under a hypothetical regime of absolute free competition." (*Éléments*, 2nd ed., 1889c, vol. VIII, p. 334, English transl., 2014, p. 248)[41]

However, after his presentation at the Academy, Walras reports another criticism which, according to him, reveals ignorance of algebraic and infinitesimal analysis and functions and the assimilation to calculation of the application of mathematics to economics. He says thus to Joseph Garnier: "All these gentlemen imagine that the application of mathematics to economics has for its object exclusively the substitution, in certain given cases, of calculation for the mechanism of competition in the market. That is not it at all."[42]

The first part of the *Éléments d'économie politique pure* comprises three sections:

- section I, "Object and method of political and social economy";
- section II, "Mathematical theory of exchange", which includes the exchange of two commodities for each other and the exchange of several commodities for each other (general equilibrium).[43] It also includes the critique of the value theories of Smith and Say.
- section III, "On currency and money".

In 1874, the theory of money thus appears just after the theory of exchange and contains an equation that anticipates that of Irving Fisher with the notion of "*circulation à desservir*" ("circulation to be cleared").[44] The following year, Walras begins to develop the "Equations of Production" and in 1876 the "Equations of Capitalisation and Credit", which will form the 2nd and 3rd models of general equilibrium.[45] The second part of the *Éléments* only appears in September 1877. It includes the following three sections:

---

[41] Numerous passages regarding this episode can also be found in the "Notes d'humeur".

[42] L. Walras, letter to J. Garnier, 4 September 1873, in: *Correspondence*, I, l. 232, p. 333. Walras returns again to this critique in "Une branche nouvelle de la mathématique" (1876b), vol. VII, pp. 306–07.

[43] The case of the exchange of two commodities for each other is a particular case, an entry point to general equilibrium. In the 11th lesson, Walras will assert (2nd ed.): "The perfect or *general market equilibrium occurs only if the prices of any two commodities in terms of each other are equal to the ratio of the price of each one in terms of any third commodity*". (emphasis by L. W., vol. VIII, pp. 161–63, English transl., 2014, p. 124) and he demonstrates this by taking into account three commodities. See on this subject the letter of Walras to Cournot, 20 March 1874, in: *Correspondence*, I, l. 253, p. 363. See also A. Jolink and J. Van Daal, 1993, p. 11 and T. Negishi, 1989, Chap. 7, re-ed. in: D. A. Walker, ed. by, 2001, vol. 1, Chap. 20, p. 373.

[44] See on this question P. Bridel, 1997, Chap. 1.

[45] Three models of general economic equilibrium are found from the 1st to the 3rd edition of the *Éléments*: exchange, production, capitalisation.

- section IV. "Natural theory of the production and the consumption of wealth";
- section V. "Conditions and consequences of economic progress";
- section VI. "Natural and necessary effects of the various modes of the economic organisation of society".

In section IV, Walras places the theory of production,[46] which contains a theory of distribution under static conditions.[47] Concerning this model, in January 1877, unsatisfied with the hypothesis of "fixed coefficients of production,[48] Walras consulted Hermann Amstein (1840–1922), professor of analysis and mechanics at the Faculty of Sciences in Lausanne, on the problem of their variability. However, he does not seem to have understood Amstein's solution, which is based on the technique of Lagrange multipliers, and he will retain fixed coefficients of production in all editions of the *Éléments.*[49]

In section V, whose content is very heterogeneous, Walras places the theory of capitalisation and credit. In this model, a market for new capital proper is introduced. However, by claiming to no longer ignore the "accessory phenomena", Walras was taking a step towards the integration of time:

> [...] we pass from the hypothesis of a market that is held continuously, to that of a market that is held periodically, we could say once per day, we will say rather once per year to take better account of the renewal of the seasons. (vol VIII, p. 576; English transl., 2014, p. 315)

But we must go even further: "in order to approach closer and closer to the reality of things, we must still pass from the hypothesis of a periodic annual market to the hypothesis of a permanent market" (*op. cit.*, p. 579; p. 317). He would later clarify that this was the transition from "the static to the dynamic state". This "permanent market" always tends to equilibrium, but never reaches it, just like a "lake agitated by the wind; the water is always seeking its equilibrium without ever attaining it" (vol. VIII, p. 580; English transl., 2014, p. 318). But it is necessary to place ourselves within the framework of a "progressive society", that is to say a society in which capital and population increase. In this perspective, Walras introduces the important distinction between "economic progress" (when the value of the coefficients of production varies through the substitution of capital proper for land) and "technical progress" (when

---

[46] In the 2nd model, the "theory of production", Walras introduces a market for "productive services" (to complement that of "consumers' services") and a market for raw materials (to complement that of consumers' goods). Thus, there are two complete markets for *services* and *products*. Landowners, capitalists, workers, as well as entrepreneurs, appear. The capital of different kind is given and not produced.

[47] On the question of distribution, Walras remains quite discreet. Let us note that in the "Système des phénomènes économiques" (1872b), he advances: "it is a problem to be studied in these data that of price differences in an aristocratic or democratic society". (vol. XI, p. 433).

[48] A coefficient of production is the quantity of a productive service that enters the production of one unit of a specified commodity.

[49] That year, F. Y. Edgeworth used the Lagrange multipliers in his book, *New and Old Methods of Ethics*, 1877, p. 38 (see J. Creedy, 1980, pp. 371–76 and 1986, pp. 34–35). In France, Albert Aupetit in his Ph.D. thesis (*Essai sur la théorie générale de la monnaie*, Paris: Guillaumin, 1901) would use them for the first time.

the coefficients of production change because of the withdrawal and arrival of certain productive services) (vol. VIII, p. 585; English transl., 2014, p. 321). Furthermore, in this section, the author presents his criticism of the Physiocrats (lack of price theory for commodities and productive services) and of the Ricardian school on rent (Ricardo and John Stuart Mill's theories).

Finally, in section VI, Walras mainly deals with monopoly theory (Cournot and Dupuit) and also that of taxation's modes.

The models of general economic equilibrium with production represent extensions of the theory of pure exchange. Why begin general equilibrium with exchange rather than production? In his "Notes d'humeur", Walras notes in this regard: "The economists generally think that since things are produced *before* they are traded, production must be studied before exchange. Mistake. Things are exchanged *during* production or *before* as productive services" (emphasis by L. W., 2000, vol. XIII, p. 564). Here we find the idea that in a state of equilibrium, production is merely a "great exchange", leaving aside the role of the entrepreneur.

We have seen that in the *Éléments*, Léon Walras defines pure economics as "in essence, the theory of the determination of prices under a hypothetical regime of absolute free competition" (vol. VIII, p. 11, English transl., 1954 revised, p. 40). In this theory, perfectly organised markets are analogous to "frictionless machines" in pure mechanics. The author believes that "the world can be considered as a vast general market composed of various special markets", whose laws governing self-conducted buying and selling must be known (vol. VIII, 5th lesson, p. 71, English transl., 2014, p. 43). Exchange in free competition is not one hypothesis among others: it is a realistic hypothesis for Walras because it is the natural and general case from which one must begin (to construct the "real type" of the market, then its "ideal type") (*cf.* the following chapter).

Walras declares that just after the publication of his book directed against Pierre-Joseph Proudhon, *L'Économie politique et la justice* (1860a), he sought to mathematically prove that the general principle of free competition would provide the maximum utility.[50] In fact, while constructing the *Éléments d'économie politique pure* during the first half of the 1870s, he simultaneously considered the question of the exceptions to the principle of free competition. And about the consequences of the hypothesis of free competition, he would then say that they "come down to

[50] Following a discussion on *L'économie politique et la justice* with the Saint-Simonian polytechnician Charles Lambert, during the year 1860, Walras supposedly had this idea according to which: "It must be proved that *free competition yields the maximum utility.*" (emphasis by L. W., "Esquisse d'une doctrine économique et sociale", 1898c, vol. X, p. 419, English transl., 2005, p. 366) (*cf infra* Chap. 12, *Criticism of "Empirical Socialism": the Cases of Louis Blanc and the Saint-Simonians*). In his "Notice autobiographique", referring to this book, he explained:

> It was partly while writing it and partly immediately after publishing it that I recognised the fact of the increase of value of ground rent and of land as the population and wealth developed, and that of the maximum utility to be obtained by adopting the regime of free competition in agricultural, industrial, and commercial production, as being two facts to be demonstrated mathematically, and that I had the intuition of a pure and applied economics to be created in mathematical form. (1909a, vol. V, p. 12)

obtaining, *within certain limits*, the maximum of utility" (emphasis by us, vol. VIII, 22nd lesson, p. 334, English transl., 2014, p. 248).

Léon Walras feared that readers of the *Éléments d'économie politique pure* would take him for an unconditional supporter of "laissez-faire, laissez-passer". Already A. Cournot remarked to him on 3 September 1873 "but I fear that your curves of 'intensive and extensive utility' will lead you to pure laissez-faire [...]." Thus, in 1883, he wrote to Wilhelm Lexis:

> [...] it seemed to me that you considered me as a supporter of absolute free competition (on grounds of the fact that I study very closely and very meticulously the effects of free competition). Be that as it may, I insist in telling you that, on the contrary, it is rather the desire to reject unfounded and unintelligible applications of free competition made by orthodox economists who led me to the study of free competition in exchange and in production.[51]

Walras has a strategy for disseminating his theory in France and in other countries. During his lifetime, the *Éléments* will not be translated abroad. However, to make the theory of general equilibrium known, he prepares the *Théorie mathématique de la richesse sociale*, initially in the form of a brochure in 1877 (in four papers) which will be translated into Italian in 1878, and into German in 1881. A more complete edition, in seven essays, will appear in 1883. It should be noted that this book will have a few attentive readers, for example, Joseph Bertrand in France (*cf.* on this point Chap. 7, *The Reception of Pure Economics in France (1873–1926)*) and Wilhelm Lexis in Germany.

In Germany, in 1881, Walras's pure economics finds an attentive reader, Wilhelm Lexis (1837–1914), statistician and economist, close to the Historical School. A professor at the University of Freiburg im Breisgau, he publishes a joint review of the *Théorie mathématique de la richesse sociale* (in four papers) and the "Théorie mathématique du prix des terres et de leur rachat par l'État" (1881b).[52] This review is one of the most remarkable dedicated to Walrasian pure economics. Besides the question of the use of mathematics in economics, Lexis anticipates the main technical problems related to the modern theory of general equilibrium: existence, uniqueness, stability of equilibrium, and even the survival hypothesis of the consumer. As Pascal Bridel rightly indicates,

> Lexis perfectly understands that it is not enough to have an equal number of equations and unknowns to guarantee the existence of an equilibrium price vector. In a passage almost completely ignored by all historians of the general equilibrium theory,[53] he demonstrates that the Walrasian system of equations may very well not have a unique solution, nor even positive real solutions, nor even a solution at all. Even if he does not suggest a precise answer to this question, Lexis perfectly grasps the necessity of placing additional constraints on the Walrasian system in order that the solution of the system of equations gets economically a sense.[54]

---

[51] L. Walras, letter to W. Lexis, 17 March 1883, in: *Correspondence,* I, l. 548, p. 746.

[52] W. Lexis, 1881, pp. 427–34, in: P. Bridel, 1996, pp. 175–81.

[53] W. Jaffé is an exception (see notably W. Jaffé, 1977c, p. 89.

[54] P. Bridel, 1996, pp. 160–61. See also A.-L. Cot and J. Lallement, 2006, p. 1713 and A. Alcouffe, 2013, pp. 181–82.

Only in 1886, is the 1st edition of the *Éléments d'économie politique pure* exhausted. Léon Walras begins to work on the 2nd edition in November 1887, which will be published in Lausanne, in July 1889, by F. Rouge publishing house. The author reorganises the order and number of sections "to mark better the order of the four problems of which [he has] spoken" (vol. VIII, Preface, p. 8, English transl., 2014, p. VII): exchange, production, capitalisation and credit, and money. He introduces improvements in the theories of exchange, production, capitalisation and credit. In the last theory, he develops the "théorème de l'utilité maxima des capitaux neufs" (1889a), once again seeking the help of Hermann Amstein[55]; furthermore, he benefits from the critical comments of the young Bortkiewicz (*cf. infra*). He also modifies the theory of money by taking up the substance of the *Théorie de la monnaie* (1886a). In the 2nd edition of the *Éléments*, the theory of money appears in section V, which follows that of the capitalisation and credit theory, and it is now based on the notion of individual demand for "desired cash balance (*encaisses désirées*)", using an equation close to that of Cambridge.[56] Money is considered as a circulating capital that provides consumers and producers with a "service of availability (*service d'approvisionnement*)" whose price is the interest rate.

Furthermore, Walras adds a mathematical introduction, "Des fonctions et de leur representation géométrique". He has this text read by several mathematicians, particularly his friend Eugène Catalan (in 1889) and Maurice d'Ocagne (in 1891) whom he met at the Society of civil engineers. These mathematicians criticise him for his incorrect differential notations, and he responds that he taught himself differential and integral calculus.[57] Eugène Catalan returns the document with his annotations.[58] Maurice d'Ocagne takes the liberty of giving Walras "a little advice as a mathematician": to get the *Cours d'analyse de l'École polytechnique* by Charles Sturm, published (posthumously) in 1857–63 (Paris: Gauthier-Villars, 9th ed., 1888), which he considers the best French reference.[59]

Here is the table of contents of the 2nd edition of the *Éléments*:

Introduction. On functions and their geometric representation

Section I. Object and divisions of political and social economy

Section II. Theory of exchange

Section III. Theory of production

---

[55] L. Walras also sought the help of Hermann Amstein to translate pages from *Recherches sur la théorie du prix* by Auspitz and Lieben (1889), in order to critique it, which appeared in *Revue d'économie politique* (1890) and was later included in Appendix II of the *Éléments.*

[56] See P. Bridel, 1997, p. 87 *et seq.*

[57] It is true that Walras had "skipped" the courses at the École des Mines. Among the few references mentioned in his correspondence, one can note the work of Julien-Napoléon Haton de la Goupillière, *Éléments de calcul infinitésimal* (Paris: Mallet-Bachelier, 1860), professor of analysis at the École des Mines.

[58] L. Walras annotates on the cover page: "Corrections by M. Catalan—Many foolishnesses! L. W." (vol. VII, p. 527, note 1).

[59] Charles Sturm (1803–55) was professor of analysis and mechanics at the École Polytechnique from 1840 and the successor of Siméon-Denis Poisson to the chair of mechanics in the Faculty of Sciences.

Section IV. Theory of capitalisation and credit
Section V. Theory of money
Section VI. On price fixing, monopoly, taxation

4.3.3 Questions of Priority

Even before the publication of the first part of the *Éléments*, on 1 May 1874 Léon Walras sends to William Stanley Jevons the paper "Principe d'une théorie mathématique de l'échange". Jevons had already read it in the *Journal des économistes* and replies by asking if Walras has read his own book, *The Theory of Political Economy*, published in 1871. In his letter of 23 May 1874, Walras acknowledges W. S. Jevons's precedence in the theory of exchange of two commodities, and more specifically the "equation of maximum utility in exchange".[60] However, he thinks that Jevons did not derive the "equation of effective demand" from the maximisation of utility and therefore did not solve the problem of determining equilibrium prices. He made the mistake of "taking the quantities exchanged as the unknowns of the problem instead of the prices" (vol. VIII, p. 253, English transl., 2014, p.186).

In 1878, through Jevons, Walras learns of Hermann Heinrich Gossen's book, *Entwickelung der Gesetze des menschlichen Verkehrs und der daraus fliessenden Regeln für menschliches Handeln* (1854).[61] He accepts Gossen's priority only concerning the marginal utility curve (vol. VIII, Preface to 4th edit., p. 5, English transl., 1954, p. 37) and is greatly interested in his plan for nationalisation of land, which leads him to write the essay "Théorie mathématique du prix des terres et de leur rachat par l'État" in social economics. He even translates Gossen's book into French in 1879 with the help of Charles Secrétan.[62]

However, Walras refuses to grant priority to Jules Dupuit for the mathematical expression of utility. Let us briefly recall the origin of this refusal. After the publication of the *Éléments'* review by Auguste Langel in the newspaper *Le Temps* (14 October 1874), a supplementary note by A. Vernier in the same newspaper (10 November 1874) mentions a letter of a chief engineer of the Ponts et Chaussées indicating that a mathematical application to the question of utility had been attempted before those of Jevons and Walras by the engineer Jules Dupuit, in an essay on the measurement of public works's utility (1844).[63] Walras, who claims to know Dupuit's articles,[64] considers that this author indeed considered the mathematical expression of utility, but without solving it satisfactorily. He is keen to make

---

[60] See also the Preface of *Éléments d'économie politique pure*, from the 4th edition, vol. VIII, p. 5, English transl., 1954, p. 37.

[61] *The Laws of Human Relations and the Rules of Human Action Derived Therefrom.*

[62] L. Walras, 1879a [1995]. See also J. Van Daal and J.-P. Potier, 1992, pp. 131–43.

[63] J. Dupuit [1844] 2009, vol. I, pp. 203–41. Vernier's note is reissued in: P. Bridel, 1996, p. 65, note a.

[64] L. Walras undoubtedly knows both articles (1844 and 1849) by J. Dupuit since the 1860s.

this known, not only to his French and foreign correspondents,[65] but also in an article announcing the publication in Italy of the collection "Biblioteca dell'economista" (3rd series), under Gerolamo Boccardo's direction, which he submits to the *Journal des économistes*. Walras devotes half of this article to the "Dupuit case". His demand curve was highlighted before him by Cournot under the name of "*courbe de débit*" and he was wrong to seek the measure of utility in the area of the demand curve. Walras even admits to having "darkened some sheets of paper with figures following this path" before looking elsewhere. And he gratuitously claims that Dupuit "acknowledged his error" and that for this reason he did not publish the book he announced (1875b, vol. XI, pp. 604–06). Joseph Garnier (professor at the École des Ponts et Chaussées) refuses to publish in the *Journal des économistes* such a criticism addressed to the theory of an engineer from this *grande école*.[66] In the 2nd part of the *Éléments d'économie politique pure* (1877), only in the 61st lesson ("On Monopoly. Multiple price"), Walras presents Dupuit's utility theory by quoting the commentary on the first figure of the "Note" of the article and he renews his criticism (vol. VIII, pp. 668–71, English transl., 2014, pp. 451–54),[67] this time publicly, while having previously paid tribute to his theory of monopoly and price differentiation. We have here a very paradoxical criticism, insofar as Walras himself, in the 5th lesson of the "Système des phénomènes économiques" (1872b), before his discovery of the notion of marginal utility and maximisation under constraint, confused, in the manner of Dupuit but without citing him, demand function ("price curve") and utility function (vol XI, pp. 447–51).[68]

It is also out of the question for Walras to recognise any priority to Carl Menger, whose *Grundsätze der Volkswirtschaftslehre* (*Principles of Political Economy*) (1871) he discovers in 1883.[69] Walras will say to Bortkiewicz:

> The efforts of Menger and Böhm-Bawerk to establish the theory of *Grenznutzen* in ordinary language are both laborious and unsuccessful. And what will it be when it comes to establishing the general theory of the determination of prices of products and services by

[65] Let us note that W. S. Jevons will never be convinced by Walras's arguments. In the Preface to the 2nd edition of *The Theory of Political Economy*, he notes that Dupuit

> […] establishes, in fact, a theory of the gradation of utility, beautifully and perfectly expounded by means of geometrical diagrams, and this theory is undoubtedly coincident in essence with that contained in this book. He does not, however, follow his ideas out in an algebraic form. (underlined by W. S. J., 1879, p. XXXI)

[66] Finally, the *Journal des économistes* will publish in October 1875 a shortened version of Walras's article containing no reference to Dupuit.

[67] The Lausanne collection preserves a copy by L. Walras of Dupuit's Note placed at the end of his article (1844) with the four figures (F. W. V a 16). This document, attached to the handwritten copy of Vernier's note published in *Le Temps*, can be dated probably to 1874.

[68] On this point, see W. Jaffé, 1972, pp. 301–03 and 1977 b, pp. 82–83; P. Bridel, "Presentation" of the *Matériaux sur le Cours d'économie politique pure*, vol. XII, p. 722. On the differences between the utility theories of Dupuit and Walras, see F. Etner, 2011.

[69] See above Chap. 3, *Taxonomy of sciences and divisions of "political and social economy: an attempt at reconstruction.*

> the mechanism of free competition in terms of production and capitalisation and through the conception of the product market and the service market, of the entrepreneur?[70]

Léon Walras is very aware of the originality of his general economic equilibrium. Thus, he never places *The Theory of Political Economy* by W. S. Jevons (which he will nevertheless translate into French—1880a) on the same level as his *Éléments d'économie politique pure*. In the Preface to the 2nd edition of *The Theory of Political Economy*, Jevons remarked:

> Looking now to the eventual results of the theory, I must beg the reader to bear in mind that this book was never put forward as containing a systematic view of Economics. It treats only of the theory, and is but an elementary sketch of elementary principles. The working out of a complete system based on these lines must be a matter of time and labour, and I know not when, if ever, I shall be able to attempt it. (1879, p. XLVIII)

At this point, on his own copy of this edition, Walras notes in the margin in pencil, without hesitation, "*c'est fait! mon garçon* (It's done! my boy)".[71] In reality, he is very annoyed by the fact that Jevons does not mention his theory of the determination of prices and productive services. He will indicate in a letter to J. L. Laughlin on 12 June 1887 (thus after the Jevons' death):

> And, yet, already then, I had myself provided a general theory of the simultaneous determination of the prices of products and of productive services in my *Éléments* published in 1874 and 1877; and it seems to me that this theory was at least worth mentioning and discussing.[72]

Two years later, in a letter to Maffeo Pantaleoni, he goes even further, accusing Jevons of giving the impression, in the last ten pages of the Preface to the 2nd edition of his book, "of having discovered by himself the principle of determining the prices of productive services based on the prices of products, when he had simply found it in the 1st edition of my *Éléments d'économie politique pure*". This allegation of plagiarism obviously has no basis.[73] In the 2nd edition of the *Éléments*, this allegation is not found openly, the author merely indicating that Jevons, in ten "very curious" pages of his preface, declared that "he had to reverse completely the English school's formula, or at least that of the Ricardo-Mill school, and determine the price of productive services by the price of the products [...]" (vol. VIII, p. 17, English transl., 2014, p. XIII).[74]

---

70 L. Walras, letter to L. Von Bortkiewicz, 11 November 1887, in: *Correspondence*, II, l. 819, p. 232.

71 The copy is kept at the Centre d'études interdisciplinaires Walras-Pareto de l'Université de Lausanne (ZAB 14,088).

72 L. Walras, letter to J. L. Laughlin on 12 June 1887, in: *Correspondence*, II, l. 799, p. 211.

73 L. Walras, letter to M. Pantaleoni, 17 August 1889, in: *op. cit.*, II, l. 909, pp. 337–38. On this question, see R. D. Collinson Black, 1992, p. 119.

74 Walras dislikes Jevons's attack on Ricardo, a "wrong-headed man", who "shunted the car of economic science on to a wrong line" (1879, p. LVII). He defends Ricardo in a "note d'humeur" found in the Lausanne collection and published in the "Introduction des éditeurs", in: L. Walras ([1880a] 2022, p. 22).

4.3.4 *Completion of the Eléments d'économie politique pure*

Retirement in 1893, far from encouraging Léon Walras to reduce his scientific activities, pushed him to attempt new publications. In 1896, the 3rd edition of the *Éléments d'économie politique pure* was published. This edition is not truly new, as it is produced by the F. Rouge publishing house with the remaining copies of the second. The author removes four lessons on the applied theory of money (lessons 37 to 40), which will be re-used in the *Études d'économie politique appliquée* and adds three appendixes: "Théorie géométrique de la détermination des prix" (1891–92), "Observations sur le principe de la théorie du prix de MM. Auspitz et Lieben" (1890) and "Note sur la réfutation de la théorie anglaise du fermage de M. Wicksteed" (1896b). In particular, in the 3rd appendix, following a correspondence with Enrico Barone, Walras acknowledges the importance of the marginal productivity theory, hence the variability of production coefficients. At the time, he still feels some apprehension after the reading of the *Éléments* by someone competent in mathematics. Thus, he points out to the engineer Charles-Émile Wickersheimer: "I was able to develop this entire theory, although a minor (*très petit*) mathematician, and in my capacity as a good economist, because the mathematical difficulties are nil and only the economic difficulties are serious."[75]

In 1898–99, Walras tackles "a gap and a last problem to solve". In March 1899, he then announces:

> In a few weeks, I will have redone the 33rd lesson of my *Éléments d'économie politique pure* for the 4th edition by introducing the rigorous equations of the desired cash balance and circulating capital in the system of general equilibrium equations. I will thus have completely finished economic statics [...].[76]

He thus drafts the "Équations de la circulation" and now derives the demand for cash balances from the utility theory. This 4th general equilibrium model will be integrated into the last edition of the *Éléments d'économie politique pure* during the author's lifetime, which appears in September 1900. In truth, before 1898, we do not find traces of this project in Walras's writings or correspondence.[77]

Given the criticism he had received from E. Catalan and M. d'Ocagne (*cf. supra*), Walras will remove the mathematical introduction in the 4th edition, as he now prefers Irving Fisher's elementary course (*A Brief Introduction to the Infinitesimal Calculus*, New York: Macmillan, 1897), which he would have liked to translate into French.[78] He removes Appendix III, as he revisits the question in section VII, in the 36th lesson "The Marginal Productivity Theorem", a lesson that will be further modified for a subsequent edition (that of 1926). While considering the theory of marginal productivity as a "cardinal theory" in pure economics, he said he preferred

---

[75] L. Walras, letter to C.-E. Wickersheimer, 11 February 1897, in: *Correspondence*, II, l. 1297, p. 728.

[76] L. Walras, letter to H. Laurent, 24 March 1899, *in: op. cit.*, III, l. 1396, p. 66.

[77] On this question, see P. Bridel, 1997, Chap. 3, pp. 99–105 and Chap. 4.

[78] See vol. VII, p. 236, note 1.

not to introduce it into his "general theory of economic equilibrium, for fear that the general theory, which was already complicated enough, might then be too difficult to grasp in its entirety" (36th lesson, vol. VIII, p. 588, English transl., 1954, p. 385). For the 4th edition, Walras modifies the sections. He splits the theory of exchange: two commodities, then several commodities. But he also revises the *tâtonnement* procedure in general equilibrium models with production. Indeed, unlike the pure exchange model in which disequilibrium transactions had always been excluded, in models with production, the possibility of disequilibrium transactions existed. Léon Walras questions the *tâtonnement* mechanism he had maintained and now introduces a *tâtonnement* on tickets, or written pledges "(*tâtonnement sur bons*)" in order to achieve the instantaneous market equilibrium before the production process[79]:

> After certain prices for services have been cried and certain quantities of products have been manufactured, if these prices and quantities are not the equilibrium prices and quantities, it will be necessary not only to cry new prices but also to manufacture revised quantities of products. In order to work out a rigorous *tâtonnement* [...] we have only to imagine, on the one hand, that entrepreneurs use *pledges* (*bons*) to represent the successive quantities of *products* which are first determined at random and then increased or decreased according as there is an excess of selling price over the cost of production or vice versa, until selling price and cost are equal; and, on the other hand, that landowners, workers and capitalists also use *pledges* to represent the successive quantities of *services* [which they offer] at prices first cried at random and then raised or lowered according as there is an excess of demand over offer or vice versa, until the two become equal. (vol. VIII, 20th lesson, p. 309, English transl., 1954, p. 242, revised translation)

Here is the new table of contents of the *Éléments*:

Section I. Object and divisions of political and social economy.

Section II. Theory of exchange of two commodities for each other.

Section III. Theory of exchange of several commodities for one another.

Section IV. Theory of production.

Section V. Theory of capitalisation (formation of capital) and credit.

Section VI. Theory of circulation and money

Section VII. Conditions and consequences of economic progress. Critique of systems of pure economics.

Section VIII. Price fixing, monopoly, taxation.

Léon Walras notes in this regard that "all the dynamics" (present in sections VII and VIII) is now "relegated after the statics".[80]

Later, in 1925, Aline Walras obtained from the publishing house Pichon and Durand-Auzias a republication of the *Éléments d'économie politique pure*[81]; it would be realised in 1926. Although the 4th edition (1900) had been considered "definitive",

[79] In fact, the *tâtonnement sur bons* appears for the first time in "Équations de la circulation". This kind of *tâtonnement* has been the subject of numerous criticisms by D. A. Walker, 1996, D. A. Walker and J. Van Daal, 2014.

[80] L. Walras, letter to Léon Winiarski, 28 September 1899, *in: Correspondence*, III, l. 1423, p. 89.

[81] Aline Walras, letter to H. S. Foxwell dated 10 January 1926 and kept at Kress Library, Harvard (Cambridge, Mass).

Léon Walras introduced a series of modifications in 1902 for a subsequent publication. The 1926 edition is therefore the fifth and presented as the "definitive edition, revised and augmented by the author".

4.4 Pure Economics: A Positive or Normative Project?

The question of the "positive" and the "normative" in Léon Walras's pure economics has given rise to an extensive literature since the second half of the 1970s.[82] The debate on this subject began during the author's lifetime, as Vilfredo Pareto reproached him for not having followed the "experimental method". In a letter to Maffeo Pantaleoni, the latter states:

> I do not accept that there is, as he says [Walras], a rational method superior to the experimental method [...] I do not accept that pure economics *demonstrates* how the facts should follow, while it is the inverse; [...] I do not accept to study what must be, but [...] instead I study what is.[83]

On several occasions between 1974 and 1981, William Jaffé opposed the interpretation of Walras's commentators in the XXth century (particularly J. R. Hicks, J. A. Schumpeter, and M. Morishima), who argue that the *Éléments d'économie politique pure* would fall under what is now called "positive economics", insofar as the author sought to describe in a stylised manner the functioning of the capitalist economy of his time. According to Jaffé, Walras's real aim in pure economics was "prescriptive or normative rather than positive or descriptive". (1977b, p. 334). A breach would thus have occurred by an effect of "osmosis" in the partition erected by the author between pure and social economics (*op. cit.*, p. 340). If Walras's approach in the *Éléments d'économie politique pure* appears "wert-frei" (without value judgment) on the surface,

> […] his latent purpose in contriving his general equilibrium model was not to describe or analyse the workings of the economic system as it existed, nor was it primarily to portray the purely economic relations within a network of markets under the assumption of a theoretically perfect regime of free competition. It was rather to demonstrate the possibility of formulating axiomatically a rationally consistent economic system that would satisfy the demands of

---

[82] We will mention here only the main contributions to this debate: R. Baranzini, 1993, 2001a, 2005 (Chaps. 1 and 4), 2006, 2007, 2011 and 2014; R. Baranzini and E. Tatti, 2002; A. Berthoud, 1988; P. Bridel, 1987, 1988, 1996, 1997 (Chap. 4), 1999 and 2011; G. De Caro, 1980, 1989, 1991 and 1992; A. Debs, 2004; P. Dockès, 1996 (Chap. 1), 1999, 2005 and 2006; É. Huck, 1999; B. Ingrao and G. Israel, [1987] 1980; W. Jaffé, 1976, 1977a, 1977d, 1978, 1980 and 1981; A. Jolink, 1993 and 1996; R. Koppl, 1992 and 1995; J. Lallement, 1997 and 2004; E. Lendjel, 1997; C. Ménard, 1990; M. Morishima, 1977 and 1980; K. Nakakubo, 1999; D. Pokorný, 1978; A. Rebeyrol, 1999; E. Tatti, 2000a and 2000b; J. Van Daal, 1999 and 2006; J. Van Daal and A. Jolink 1993 (Chap. 17); D. A. Walker, 1984, 1996 (Chap. 2), 1999a, 2004 and 2006 (Chap. 4).

[83] Emphasis by V. P., letter to M. Pantaleoni, 19 December 1908, in: V. Pareto, 1984, vol. 3, p. 121. Our translation from Italian. On the differences between Pareto and Walras on pure economics, see F. Mornati, 1999b and P. Steiner, 2000.

social justice without overstepping the bounds imposed by the natural exigencies of the real world." (1977a, p. 105)

One would be dealing with a "theoretical representation of a just economy from the standpoint of 'commutative justice'; 'distributive justice' called for separate treatment in the *Études d'économie sociale*" (1980, p. 348). Thus, the *Éléments*'s world would correspond to a "realistic Utopia", a perfect ideal nevertheless developed from realistic ingredients (*op. cit.*, p. 345).

This stance has been the subject of detailed critiques from 1984 by Donald A. Walker, who intends to demonstrate the exclusively "positive" nature of Walrasian pure economics; according to him, in the *Éléments*, Walras would attempt to conduct an abstract and simplified analysis of the functioning of the real economy of his time, of its real markets. Walker's writings have sparked numerous critical reactions and reasoned responses. We will not delve into the details of this controversy here.

Let us first recall that in his application letter for the chair of political economy at the Faculty of Law in Lausanne sent to Louis Ruchonnet and in the *Éléments d'économie politique pure*, Walras refers to the distinction between "what is" and "what ought to be".[84] On this point, he pays tribute to Adolphe Blanqui's article, "Économie politique", published in the *Dictionnaire de l'économie politique,* C. Coquelin and G.-U. Guillaumin (ed.) (1852–53).

Here is how he expresses himself on this subject in his letter to Louis Ruchonnet dated 6 September 1870:

> [*Charles Coquelin*] very judiciously indicates a distinction neglected by economists and which should serve as the foundation for a new and better taxonomy of economic matters today confused, without order or method, under the common name of political economy: it is the one to be made between *science* and *art*, between science consisting "in the knowledge of certain phenomena or certain observed and revealed relationships", which "observes, exposes, explains", and art consisting "in a series of precepts or rules to follow" and which "advises, prescribes, directs".[85] Coquelin does not, however, attempt to make this fruitful distinction himself [...]. Mr. John Stuart Mill, in England,[86] and Mr. Courcelle-Seneuil, in France,[87] have also taken some steps in this direction, but without achieving definitive success.[88]

In the 2nd lesson of the *Éléments d'économie politique pure* (vol. VIII, p. 36, English transl., 2014, p. 12), Walras revisits Coquelin's distinction between science and art and he reproduces a note of this author which seems very important to him:

---

[84] This distinction appears in early writings. In "L'industrie moderne et l'économie politique", Walras explains that the human mind determines "in the order of natural facts, what is, and, in the order of moral facts, what should be" (1861d, vol. VII, p. 143). The distinction reappears in the 6th lesson of the *Recherche de l'idéal social* (1867–68, vol. IX, p. 130, English transl., 2010, p. 97).

[85] See C. Coquelin, 1852b, p. 646.

[86] See J. S. Mill, 1844, 5th essay, p. 123 *et seq.*

[87] See J.-G. Courcelle-Seneuil, 1867, vol. 1, pp. 4–12.

[88] Emphasis by L. W., letter to L. Ruchonnet, 6 September 1870, in: *Correspondence*, I, l. 148, pp. 207–08.

> The very real distinction which we have made between science and art has nothing to do with the distinction which, rightly or wrongly, is made between theory and practice. There are theories of art just as there are theories of science [...]. The rules that an art prescribes are general rules [...]. (1852b, p. 646, note 1)

Moreover, a science can enlighten different arts and reciprocally an art can rely on different sciences (*op. cit.*, p. 647). After lamenting that Coquelin did not succeed in applying the distinction between science and art "to the definition of political economy and to the classification of economic subject matter" (vol. VIII, pp. 37–38, English transl., 2014, pp. 13–14), Walras proposes his own distinction between pure science (relative to natural facts), then art and ethics (relative to human facts), which leads him to define pure, applied, and social economics, with their respective criteria: truth, interest, and justice. The normative character of applied economics and the applied aspect of social economics ("Realisation of the social ideal") raises no problem.[89] Thus, *in appearance*, at this stage, the triptych seems to coincide with the distinction between positive science and normative science, and one could compare the Walrasian distinctions to those of John Neville Keynes. Indeed, in *The Scope and Method of Political Economy*, the latter distinguishes three fields in political economy, the first two pertaining to "social science":

- "positive science", or a set of systematised knowledge concerning what is, highlighting "uniformities" and determining economic laws;
- "normative or regulatory science", or a set of systematised knowledge relating to what ought to be, which determines "ideals" ("a branch of ethics");
- "art of political economy" (expression preferred by the author to "applied economics" due to its polysemy), or a system of rules to achieve a given end, which formulates "precepts" (1890, 4th ed., 1917, pp. 34–36).

However, such a comparison between J. N. Keynes and Walras is misleading. Indeed, to understand the epistemological status of pure economics in Walras, it is necessary to refer to the sources of his conception of science and his scientific method. Let us recall that he is strongly inspired by Étienne Vacherot's book, *La métaphysique et la science* (1st ed., 1858), in which the author, a critical reader of Kant, aims for a synthesis between idealism and empiricism and within empiricism, between spiritualism and materialism.

Based on his reading of Vacherot, Léon Walras wishes to develop a "theory of reality that could serve as a basis for a theory of science in general".[90] In the study "Socialisme et libéralisme. Lettres à M. Éd. Schérer" (1863a, vol. IX, p. 15, English transl., 2010, pp. 7–8), the content of which will be taken up in the 13th lesson of the *Cours d'économie sociale* (vol. XII, p. 165), he distinguishes between the "world of facts and reality" (object and field of practice and politics), and the "world of

[89] Conversely, the "general theory of society" ("Recherche de l'idéal social"), "moral science" (which Walras would later call "*cénonique*—cœnonics"), corresponds to "pure moral science" and is placed by Walras at the same scientific level as "pure natural science" (distinction introduced from the 2nd edition of the *Éléments*).

[90] L. Walras, letter to A. Guéroult, probably March–April 1859, in: *Correspondence*, I, l. 16, p. 36.

ideas and the ideal" (object and field of theory and science). Furthermore, in the "Recherche de l'idéal social en matière de propriété et d'impôt" (1863d, vol. XIII, pp. 230–34), then in the 4th lesson of the *Recherche de l'idéal social* (vol. IX, pp. 97–101, English transl., 2010, pp. 74–76) whose content is taken up in the 5th and 6th lessons of the *Cours d'économie sociale* (vol. XII, pp. 129–137), Walras explains the path that leads from the first to the second world. Three degrees of knowledge corresponding to three intellectual faculties (imagination, understanding, reason) are distinguished. The influence of Vacherot is direct here (9th conversation, "Analysis of intelligence" and 10th conversation, "Critique of intelligence"),[91] knowing that he himself is inspired by the faculties of knowledge presented by Emmanuel Kant in the *Critique of Pure Reason.* The scientific approach requires the exercise of understanding (*entendement*), then of reason (*raison*).

The "notions" of understanding synthesise the "perceptions", which come from external experience (through the senses) and intimate experience (through consciousness). These "notions" are first concrete, then abstract. At the level of this a posteriori synthesis, the matter of scientific knowledge, appear ideas, essences, numbers, types. According to Walras, at the level of understanding, one first identifies "real types". Thus, from the more or less circular figures of reality, one arrives at the real type "circle". In a second phase, from these "real types", one derives "ideal types",[92] such as, for example, the ideal forms in pure geometry (see *infra*).

Then, reason intervenes, which is the faculty of judging, of grasping the relationships of things and ideas. Thus, through abstraction and generalisation, one reaches the metaphysical conceptions of the universal, the absolute, the perfect, the ideal.[93] Physical and moral laws can be discerned at this level.

In summary, science encompasses the totality of "notions and conceptions, judgements and reasonings of the understanding and of reason".[94] If reality (the relative) is imperfect, the ideal (the absolute) is "necessarily perfect". Science must therefore be conceived as "the idealisation of reality", and "art" (understood here as the practice of art), is the "achievement of the ideal" (1863a, vol. IX, p. 15, English transl., 2010, p. 8). Through this approach and by referring to "modern philosophy",[95] Walras

[91] The Lausanne collection preserves reading notes by Walras containing only quotations from the 9th and 10th conversations, probably written between 1859 and 1861 ("Critique of Intelligence", F. W. Vb, box 19).

[92] In *La démocratie*, Vacherot speaks of an "ideal type" concerning society, State, and government (1859, p. 2). In *La métaphysique et la science*, he most often speaks of "types", sometimes of "real type" (1863, vol. 2, p. 28) and "entirely ideal types" (1863, vol. 2, p. 157), without establishing a relationship between these two categories. It is Walras who establishes a relationship between the real type and the ideal type.

[93] This ideal, Walras describes it as "platonician" ("Notes d'humeur", 2000, vol. XIII, p. 560).

[94] *Recherche de l'idéal social*, 4th lesson, vol. IX, p. 105, English transl., 2010, p. 80.

[95] É. Vacherot is obviously part of it.

claims to reconcile "realism and nominalism, that is to say, idealism and empiricism, Plato and Aristotle".[96] In fact, his explicit position places him on the side of philosophical "realism".[97]

Such a conceptual framework applies not only to mathematics and astronomy, but also to the theory of society (moral science) and to pure economics. However, Walras notes an important difference between social science and geometry:

> [...] the real type in geometry is immediately provided by experience,[98] and the ideal type can be developed by the understanding by means of an immediate *a posteriori* synthesis. However, in the theory of society, the real type is not immediately given by experience, and the ideal type can be extracted only by means of a synthesis *a posteriori* that is very long and very arduous. (1863a, vol. IX, p. 16, English transl., 2010, p. 9; *Cours d'économie sociale*, 13th lesson, vol. XII, p. 166)[99]

The "ideal types" therefore do not correspond to mere scientific abstractions allowing for the development of deductive reasoning. Moreover, they must be the subject of careful selection in the case of pure economics. Such is the case with the mechanism of "absolute free competition",[100] as we shall see in the following chapter.

Walras's "ideal type" can hardly be equated with Max Weber's "ideal-type", which is a principle of knowledge for empirical sciences. However, it could be compared to the notion of "type" used by the Neapolitan Hegelian philosopher Benedetto Croce, in his interpretation of the labour theory of value in Marx: a "concept thought and taken as type", used as a "term of comparison" ([1899] 1973, pp. 58–59). Walras specifies in the *Éléments* that.

> [...] the mathematical method is not an *experimental* method; it is the *rational* method. [...] the physico-mathematical sciences, like the mathematical sciences properly speaking, do go beyond experience as soon as they have borrowed their type [of] concepts from it. They abstract from these real types ideal types that they define, and on the basis of these definitions they construct *a priori* the whole framework of their theorems and proofs. They re-enter after into experience not to confirm but to apply their conclusions [...]. Reality only approximately confirms[101] these definitions and proofs; it permits only a fruitful application of them. (emphasis by L. W., 3rd lesson, vol. VIII, p. 53, English transl., 2014, pp. 27–28)

[96] He adds: "Idealism rightly asserts the objectivity of the notions of understanding or ideas; but it is wrong when it attributes to the objects of these notions and ideas a substantial existence. Empiricism is right when it denies the second proposition; but it wrongly denies the first." (*Cours d'économie sociale*, 6th lesson, p. 135).

[97] On the two meanings of the word "realism" applicable to Walras, see P. Dockès, 1999, pp. 14–18 and 2011, pp. 9–10 and R. Baranzini, 2005, pp. 128–31, 2006, pp. 1672–73, 2011, pp. 154–57, 2014, pp. 290–91.

[98] Walras's viewpoint on geometry can be contested (see on this subject, D. A. Walker, 1996, p. 48).

[99] See also "Exposition et conciliation des doctrines sociales" (1872c, p. 303).

[100] Sometimes, Walras indicates that "absolute free competition" is a "pure and simple concept", a "concept of the mind" (letter to the Minister of Public Instruction, Jules Ferry, dated 3 July 1879, in: *Correspondence*, I, l. 444, p. 616).

[101] In the first three editions of the *Éléments*, it reads at this point: "does not confirm" and in the 4th edition, Walras corrects: "only approximately confirms".

The construction of pure theory therefore does not require empirical verification.[102] The return to imperfect reality pertains solely to the application of the theory. Here again, the influence of Étienne Vacherot is evident.[103]

Given this method, the theory corresponds to a perfect ideal and not to what is usually understood by hypothetical construction: it is rather a "true blueprint (*épure vraie*)", both mental and ideal. More precisely, as Pierre Dockès indicates,

> the economy of the *Éléments* is not conceived as an abstract model, an economy among other possibilities, it aims to be the blueprint of the real world, a blueprint that becomes more complex as it seeks to take into account the greatest number of essential elements, not concrete data, but *idealised* elements. (2006, p. 1784)

For Walras, just like Vacherot, the blueprint will allow the world to be made intelligible, just as geometrical figures make reality "geometrical" up to a certain point, and in this perspective, things will be the "images of ideas".[104] In such an approach, "it is no longer just the mathematical model that is an image of the market, it is also the real market that tends to function in the image of the mode of resolution of the equations' system" (P. Dockès, 1999, p. 22; see also 2006, p. 1787).

However, the *Éléments d'économie politique pure* do not correspond to a fiction, to a "realistic Utopia" (W. Jaffé), because the "pure economic truth" is supposed to be constructed from the concrete reality. Indeed, there is a "realism" at this level. Moreover, the *Éléments* do not contain any "normative bias", neither in terms of interest nor in terms of justice.[105] The "normative bias" in terms of interest does not exist, because the book does not aim to demonstrate the superiority of absolute free competition in terms of interest, economic efficiency, and does not advocate its widespread implementation in practice[106]; indeed, it is in the field of applied economics that the domains where the free competition principle can be practised and the domains of its exceptions are distinguished. The "normative bias" in terms of justice does not exist either in the *Éléments*. Indeed, pure economic truth coincides with commutative justice in exchange (fair equilibrium price), and furthermore, it

---

[102] We have previously seen that on his copy of the *Principes de la théorie des richesses* (1863, p. 17) by A.-A. Cournot, Walras had annotated: "Pure economics does not wait confirmations from experience", and that furthermore in his "Notes d'humeur" (2000), he remarked: "undoubtedly reasoning and science cannot stand in contradiction to experience and facts. But who knows the facts? Science tells truths that experience cannot confirm […]. It is self-sufficient and can rectify the facts"—subsequently, Walras cites the case of the discovery of the planet Neptune (vol. XIII, p. 567).

[103] See E. Tatti, 2000b, p. 26; R. Baranzini and E. Tatti, 2002, pp. 81–82; R. Baranzini, 2005, p. 119.

[104] É. Vacherot observes: "far from geometric figures being merely abstractions of reality, this reality itself only becomes an intelligible figure, and to a certain extent geometrical, through its relation to the types conceived by intelligence […] *things are only images of ideas*" (emphasis by É. V., 1863, vol. 2, p. 23; see also pp. 169–70).

[105] See on this subject P. Dockès, 1999, pp. 25–30.

[106] See on this subject the letter of Walras to W. Lexis dated 17 March 1883 (*Correspondence*, I, l. 548, p. 746), cited above.

is neutral with respect to commutative justice relating to the "equality of social conditions".[107]

4.5 Conclusion

In summary, Walrasian pure economics is neither "positive" nor "normative" in the usual sense of this distinction.[108] This characteristic is not inconsistent with the sporadic presence in the *Éléments* of normative statements, for example, in terms of justice, when the author notes that the rejection of slavery precludes the purchase and sale of persons as personal capital (vol. VIII, 17th lesson, pp. 270–71 and 28th lesson, p. 435, English transl., 1954, pp. 216–17 and 311) and in terms of interest, when the author mentions the question of the "principle" of free competition (*op. cit.,* 22nd lesson, pp. 335–36, English transl., *cit.*, pp. 256–57). Finally, let us note that when in his "Notes d'humeur" Walras considers his overall scientific project, and not the stage of pure economics, he compares his approach with that of Vilfredo Pareto:

> Mr. P[areto] believes that the goal of science is to get closer and closer to reality by successive approximations. And I believe that the ultimate goal of science is to bring reality closer to a certain ideal; that is why I express this ideal. (vol. XIII, p. 567)[109]

---

[107] Conversely, it can be noted that the "general general equilibrium model" constructed by J. Van Daal and A. Jolink (1993, Chap. 19), incorporating exceptions to free competition and State property of land, contains a "normative bias", both in terms of interest and justice (see also J. Van Daal, 1999, pp. 96–98).

[108] On the impossibility of applying the distinction positive *versus* normative economics to Walrasian pure economics, see R. Baranzini, 1993 and especially 2005, Chap. 4, J. Lallement, 1997, pp. 75–85 and 2004, pp. 84–86 and É. Huck, 1999, pp. 247–48 and 266.

[109] Walras also says, regarding science that "its ultimate aim is not to purely and simply express reality, but to bring reality closer to the ideal. It is therefore justified in expressing this ideal" ("Notes d'humeur", vol. XIII, p. 567). He also asserts:
[...] science [pure], whether cœnonics or economics, has been created in order to formulate the ideal conditions of a society that would be perfect in all respects, leaving it to the course of events to invent compromises and measure the degree of realisation [...]" ("L'économique appliquée et la défense des salaires", 1897c, vol. X, p. 253, English transl., 2005, p. 222).

4.5 Conclusion

Chapter 5
The Conception of Free Competition in the Éléments D'Économie Politique Pure

5.1 Introduction

Very often, contemporary economists equate the Walrasian "free competition" with "pure and perfect competition" as a market structure of the neo-classical canon. In this chapter, we will seek to show that for Walras, free competition is essentially a natural behaviour of rational and free individuals, having specific institutions that allow them to fully exercise these liberties. In the pure theory of exchange, there are two liberties: the liberty to quote prices upwards (*à l'enchère*) or downwards (*au rabais*) and the liberty to enter or leave the market. In the pure theory of production, to these two liberties is added the liberty to vary production according to profit (*bénéfice*) or loss situations. These liberties must be fully exercised thanks to a perfect organisation that guarantees an ideal functioning, the attainment of the equilibrium price, hence the existence of the following two rules:

- the exchangers must make their proposals public by crying them;
- the processes of outbidding and underbidding the price (*enchère et rabais*) must be completed and the equilibrium price reached before effective transactions take place.

Thus, the liberty of each will not be exercised to the detriment of others, the price being unique and each maximising its relative satisfaction.

In the manuscript, "Une branche nouvelle de la mathématique", published in Italy in 1876, there is a useful typology for understanding Walras's ideas on competition. He distinguishes the "fact", the "idea", and the "principle" of competition which correspond to three successive stages of the scientific approach. The "fact" refers to competition as it exists "under more or less imperfect conditions"; the "idea" refers to "absolute free competition" which could function without reference to criteria of interest and justice; the "principle" refers to free competition "as it should exist

J.-P. Potier, *Léon Walras, Economist and Liberal Socialist*, Springer Studies in the History of Economic Thought, https://doi.org/10.1007/978-3-032-04670-3_5

to satisfy these notions"[1] (1876b, vol. VII, p. 298). And our author will use these different notions in the 44th lesson of the *Éléments d'économie politique pure* (vol. VIII, 22nd lesson, pp. 334–36, English transl., 2014, pp. 248–50).[2] The distinction between "fact", "idea", and "principle" is not obvious, hence some divergent interpretations.[3] It must be related to a certain conception of the world and of the science (*cf.* the previous chapter).

Concerning the "fact", Walras recalls that in concrete reality, production and exchange, "since the world is world", operate under the sway of three factors (1876b, vol. VII, p. 298):

a. "under the dominance of competition", a historically increasing part; "assuredly competition is a natural tendency, like the sun is a physical fact" (*op. cit.*, p. 303);
b. "under the rule of legal restrictions": industry regulations, commercial tariffs, fiscal or protective taxes. This part historically declines in favour of competition; and
c. under the rule of "custom (*coutume*)", which "always has a considerable influence".[4]

The "fact" of competition is therefore associated with other phenomena, which makes it indecipherable; the first scientific step is therefore its identification. Let us recall that when Walras uses the term "fact", he sometimes means particular events, singular occurrences. However, he frequently uses the term in the sense of a *universal statement* like many scientists.[5] He thus speaks of the "fact of gravitation" or the "fact of exchange value". The "fact", in this sense, is the law before it has been *defined* by the scientist, such as it appears in objective reality, at the same level as the "real type", empirically drawn from the concrete world. On the other hand, the scientific law *defined* by the scientist is in the world of ideas, like the "ideal type" from which he will construct the theory.

Léon Walras therefore believes he must begin from the concrete forms of competition in more or less well-organised markets and, through an empirical synthesis, derive the "fact" of free competition because, under its dominance, "the exchange value left to itself arises naturally". Making free competition the general case and the necessary starting point seems to him a realistic "hypothesis", going to the heart of the matter (*cf. infra*).

---

[1] On the exceptions to the free competition principle, see Chap. 16, *Public Services and Natural Monopolies: What Role for the State?*

[2] This distinction also appears in the framework of the conference "Défense des salaires" (1879b, vol. X, p. 483). In the *Cours d'économie politique appliquée* (4th lesson, "Definition of Economic Competition"), the author adds a note in margin: "On the fact—hypothesis—principle (see the Italian article)." (vol. XII, p. 863).

[3] For interpretations different from ours, see R. Arena and L. Ragni, 1994 and R. Baranzini, 2011.

[4] On this point, L. Walras is inspired by J. S. Mill, who remarked that if competition governed wholesale trade and also retail trade in large industrial centres, it encountered established customs elsewhere.

[5] See R. Carnap, 1973, pp. 13–14.

In moving from the "real type" to the "ideal type", competition becomes "absolute free competition" insofar as it is here "entirely left to itself" to allow the study of the "natural and necessary effects" in terms of production and exchange; it is an analytical "*laissez-faire, laissez-passer*" in which the "ideal type" market is without "frictions", as in pure mechanics.

Regarding absolute free competition, Walras is aware of having discovered the existence of equilibrium, revealed its properties, and unveiled the process of convergence towards this price. This equilibrium (generally unique and stable) exists objectively. This does not mean that it is concretely realised. On the contrary, in dynamics, the "permanent market" continuously tends towards this equilibrium without reaching it, but its level nonetheless exists objectively: it is *the* objective exchange value. Similarly, the theoretical *tâtonnements*, these ideal processes of convergence towards equilibrium, have an objective existence for Walras. The solution by iteration of a system of simultaneous equations is not just one method among others, but the ideal of the *tâtonnements* practised in reality. Certainly, the author does not confuse both, but the solution is the same. In other words, the "ideal type" and the laws obtained, Walras reconstructs the real, idealises it. Thus, in reality, from the street to the Paris Stock Exchange and other well-organised markets, there exist only imperfect solutions that are classified according to *the* perfect solution, all "tending" towards the omega point that is *the* exchange value.

Our study will include two sections. The first section, "Free competition on concrete markets and on the market as 'real type'", examines how Walras takes into account concrete markets, constructs his real type market. The second section, "Free competition on the 'ideal type' market", examines the transition from the real type market to the ideal type market. Thus, Walrasian competition can be characterised in opposition to modern conceptions.

5.2 Free Competition on Concrete Markets and on the Market as "Real Type"

Léon Walras studies concrete markets, observable in practice. From the best organised, he will draw a sketch of "real type" and use the Stock exchange (or the wheat market) to operate a "type market" before our eyes.

5.2.1 Concrete Markets and Behaviours

In the 5th lesson of the *Éléments*, the author explains that the phenomenon of exchange value occurs on the market. He goes there, almost physically, since he defines the market as "a place where commodities are exchanged". How does the exchange value take place there? "left to itself, [it] occurs naturally in the market under the regime of *competition*" (vol. VIII, p. 70, English transl., 2014, p. 42). Competition, a natural phenomenon, produces a *certain* exchange value. And this phenomenon somehow allows the liberty of exchangers to express themselves and

> [...] as buyers, the traders make *offers to buy at higher prices* (*demandent à l'enchère*); as sellers, they make *offers to sell at lower prices* (*offrent au rabais*), and their competition thus leads to a certain value in exchange that is sometimes rising, sometimes falling, sometimes stationary. (emphasis by L. W., p. 70, English transl., 2014, p. 42)

We are dealing here with a key definition: from the outset, competition constitutes a natural behaviour and it is precisely:

- the ability of exchangers to make price proposals upwards or downwards to succeed in obtaining or disposing of a commodity;
- however, these price proposals are intended both to decide the co-contractor and to overbid potential other buyers and sellers;
- but Walras mentions: "and their coming together (*et leur concours*)", which implies a certain number of buyers and sellers capable of outbidding or underbidding.

We immediately see that the exchange value will manifest itself more or less rigorously according to the more or less efficient operation of competition. There exists an exchange value not only "rigorous", but which literally "pre-exists" and which can only be reached if the functioning of competition is perfect. The link is established between the good functioning of the competitive mechanism and the "true" character of the exchange value, a "natural price" as Adam Smith would say.

What is good functioning? Walras immediately refers to the organisation. He classifies markets into three categories from the best to the least organised. If we begin with the latter, those whose organisation proves to be "a little more flawed", we find the streets with their retail stores of all kinds: bakers, butchers, grocers, etc. And "it is similarly incontestable that competition presides in the determination of the value of doctors' and lawyers' consultations, of musicians' and singers' recitals, etc." (vol. VIII, p. 71, English transl., 2014, p. 43).[6] As better organised, Walras cites the fruit and vegetable markets, and those for poultry: these are markets where competition functions quite well, even if it is "less well regulated" than in the best organised markets. Regarding the latter, the author provides some particularly enlightening examples: Stock exchange, commercial bourses, grain bourse, fish markets. Obviously, this is not an exhaustive list. The organisation of markets is an essential task. While the less well-organised markets can be spontaneous and stem from individual or professional initiatives, on the other hand, the best organised markets must be organised by the State[7] to prevent the formation of "artificial monopolies".

[6] It can be noted that the labour market is not mentioned in the *Éléments*. On the other hand, in the *Études d'économie politique appliquée*, the author will tell us that this market is not organised at all, as evidenced by the existence of strikes and conflicts. On this point, see Chap. 14, *Organisation of the Labour Market, Labour Legislation and Social Insurance*.

[7] In the field of applied economics, Walras indicates "that introducing and maintaining free economic competition in a society is an undertaking of very complicated legislation, which is the responsability

This well-functioning competition takes place "by crying". Not by a single crier (*cf. infra*), but by the intermediation of agents such as "stockbrokers, commercial brokers or criers" who centralise the purchase and sale orders of their clients and who *cry* their price propositions either raising or lowering the bids (*à l'enchère ou au rabais*), making them *public*. It is the function of "*la criée*" that the exchanges are made under conditions known by all, that all could raise or lower the price before the effective transactions. The presence of brokers, stockbrokers, and various agents is, however, not indispensable. Indeed, Walras indicates that

> [...] it can be seen, on big markets that function even without agents and criers, that the current equilibrium price is determined in a few minutes, and considerable quantities of merchandise are exchanged at that price in half or three quarters of an hour. (vol. VIII, 6th lesson, p. 93, English transl., 2014, p. 67)

but he does not provide concrete examples in this regard.[8] No doubt he has in mind markets where the real buyers and sellers are present (D. A. Walker, 1996, p. 265). Ultimately, the whole world forms a market, "a vast general market composed of various special markets in which social wealth is sold and bought", with highly diverse levels of organisation. Note that so far, Walras has not yet spoken of "free competition", nor of "absolute free competition".

Walras aims to discover the natural laws of the exchange value's formation. It is therefore not a matter of empirically studying the formation of equilibrium prices in concrete markets. But, between practical markets and the ideal type market, one must go through the "real type" of the best organised markets in terms of competition.

5.2.2 *The Best Organised Markets as "Real Types" and the Stock Exchange as "Type Market"*

As we have seen, the synthesis that should allow the construction of a "real type" risks being long and difficult in social sciences. This is not the case here! It is summarised as follows: defining the "real type" of the best organised markets in regard to competition,

> [...] those in which purchases and sales are made by the crying out of prices, through the intermediation of agents, such as floor traders (*agents de change*), commercial agents, criers, who centralise transactions in such a way that no transaction takes place without the conditions being announced and know and without the sellers being able to lower their prices and buyers to raise them. (vol. VIII, p. 70, English transl., 2014, p. 42)

These characteristics of the "real type" are obviously not very precise and, when it is necessary to explain its functioning, Walras takes one of the best organised markets

---

of the State" ("Esquisse d'une doctrine économique et sociale", 1898c, vol. X, p. 427, English transl., 2005, modified, p. 373).

[8] In the *Cours d'économie politique appliquée*, he similarly declares: "the cried outbidding is not absolutely necessary, although it certainly constitutes the most perfect degree of the mechanism". (vol. XII, 4th lesson, p. 465).

and strips it of its specific characteristics to make it the "market type"[9] which, literally, represents the "real type".

In the "Principe d'une théorie mathématique de l'échange " (1874a), Walras refers to the "wheat market", with its commercial brokers or criers (vol. VII, pp. 266–67). But in the *Éléments d'économie politique pure* (§ 42, 5th lesson), he invites us to a session of the Paris Stock Exchange, at the cash market for the 3% French government bonds (*rente à 3%*). The real purchasers and sellers are not physically present at the market; they are represented by a limited number of stockbrokers who *centralise* their clients' orders and will conduct the crying out of prices. Here, the centralisation is achieved by the agent who collects the orders of his clients.[10] The 3% French government bonds has an opening price of 60 francs (previous session's closing price). The stockbrokers, on the one hand, have sale orders at best possible and at limited price (60 F, 59 F, 58 F and so on), so they offer a certain quantity of bonds at this price (effective supply) and, on the other hand, have purchase orders at best possible and at a limited price (60 F, 61 F, 62 F and so on), so they demand a certain quantity of bonds (effective demand). One of three things will happen:

1. If there is an exact counterpart: equality of supply and demand at this price of 60 francs, "the exchange takes place", the price remains steady, and there is a "stationary state or equilibrium". Otherwise, the initiative will come from the long side of the market.
2. If the Effective Demand is Higher Than the Effective Supply, the Initiative Will Come from the Demand Side:
   - the agents who have purchase orders at best price will outbid;
   - the purchasers at 60 F, 61 F, etc. will gradually withdraw (limited price purchase orders);
   - sellers attracted by the price increase will offer bonds during the session.

   This will result in a gradual reduction of the spread between the quantities supplied and demanded and the establishment of an equilibrium at a higher price than at the opening.
3. If the Effective Supply is Higher Than the Effective Demand, the Initiative Will Come from the Supply Side:
   - the agents who have sale orders at best price will underbid;
   - the sellers at 60 F, 59 F, etc. will gradually withdraw (limited price sale orders);
   - purchasers attracted by the price fall will demand bonds during the session.

This will result in a gradual reduction of the spread between the quantities supplied and demanded and the establishment of an equilibrium at a lower price than at the opening.

---

9 "La Bourse, la spéculation et l'agiotage" (1880b), vol. X, pp. 389–90, English transl., 2005, p. 341.

10 Already in his notes for the English translation of the *Éléments*, W. Jaffé already wrote: "Surely Walras never supposed for a moment that there was any one person or corporate entity that raised or lowered prices under perfect competition." (1954, p. 520, note 11). It remains that it is unfortunately he who sometimes translated "crieur" as "auctioneer" (*cf. infra*).

Why do active proposals express themselves *from the long side* of the market? In fact, the outbidding and underbidding behaviours of agents are motivated by the absence of a counterpart, that is to say, partners accepting the transaction and they wish to continue the negotiation.[11]

Walras believes that if agents do not find their counterpart in the market, "theoretically, trading must be suspended" (vol. VIII, p. 72, English transl., 2014, p. 44), a clarification added to the 2nd edition of the *Éléments*—1889c—(on this point and the observations of J. Bertrand (1883), *cf.* Chap. 7, *The Reception of Pure Economics in France (1873–1926)*). This suspension is consistent with the requirement that "no transaction takes place without the conditions being announced and known and without the sellers being able to lower their prices and buyers to raise them" (*op. cit.*, p. 70, English transl., 2014, p. 42): this process must be naturally extinguished with the cancellation of the net demand. The word "theoretically" (in the proposition "theoretically, trading must be suspended") poses a problem for those who imagine themselves on a concrete market, the Paris or London stock exchanges. But, let us not forget, this Paris Bourse is the "real type" of the best organised markets.

Léon Walras believes that the closer one gets to a perfectly organised market, the closer one will approach *the true* exchange value, and reasoning on a real type market is a step towards this determination that will only be perfect in the ideal. Walras's presentation of a "crying" session related to a "flagship" value of the time, therefore, does not constitute a rigorous description of the functioning of the Paris Stock Exchange. At the Bourse de Paris in the XIXth century,[12] on the "*parquet*", for the cash market, the "crying" mechanism is reserved for government bonds, other securities generally being subject to a "*par oppositions*" quotation.[13] In the "crying" system for government bonds, approximately sixty stockbrokers or their clerks are busy around the *corbeille* accompanied by a clerk or quoting agent (the *coteur*)[14] who, placed in the middle of the *corbeille*, follows the discussions, facilitates the negotiations, and records the price bids on a board. The session begins with the search of appropriate counterparts for at best orders, the limit orders being slower of execution. The discussion begins with an indicative price, nearly equivalent to the previous closing price. After agreement on the equilibrium price, this one will be registered on the board. For the government bonds of the "*groupe de la rente*", an official "*crieur*" must cry the equilibrium price.[15] The majority of orders is therefore

[11] See E. Lendjel, 1999, pp. 297–98.

[12] See P.-C. Hautcoeur, 2007, pp. 126–27.

[13] In the system of quotation "*par oppositions*", for a given security, the stockbrokers transcribe the prices corresponding to the limit orders on opposition sheets centralised then by a marking clerk in the form of scale of the extreme limits. A clerk will then collect all necessary information (quantities supplied and demanded) from the brokers' offices to proceed with an examination of the orders and propose an equilibrium price allowing the maximum exchange of securities to the quoting clerk, who must check before publication.

[14] The quoting agent is appointed by the Chambre syndicale des agents de change (the governing body of the company of the stockbrokers).

[15] The police regulation of the 1st Thermidor IX (July 20th, 1801) makes in theory obligatory for the "*rente*" the presence of a public "crier", appointed by the Chambre syndicale des agents de change.

executed at this fixing. However, contrary to the Walrasian presentation, successive fixings are carried out because of the arrival of new orders during the session.[16] Do there exist or have there existed concrete markets close to the real Walrasian type market, with a fixing mechanism? In a translation's note of the *Éléments* (1954, pp. 501–02, note 13), William Jaffé mentions a study by H. M. Bratter published in the *Journal of Political Economy* (1931) describing the London silver market. In this market, the representatives (brokers) of four "bullion firms" set up a daily fixing.[17] Curiously, John Maynard Keynes will give the same example in a letter to John R. Hicks,[18] after the reading of his article "Léon Walras", published in 1934 in *Econometrica.*[19]

In "Principe d'une théorie mathématique de l'échange" (1874a) and "Une branche nouvelle de la mathématique" (1876b), Walras had, however, envisaged another solution for the "market type". The stockbrokers (at the stock exchange) or the brokers or *crieurs* (at the commercial bourse or wheat market) have transcribed their clients' orders in order-books. Without making a public crying, they give their order-books to a "computing agent (*calculateur*)" who determines the equilibrium price. In this case, the physical presence of stockbrokers on the market is no longer even necessary. According to Walras, this "computing agent" will obtain the equilibrium price at the end of a time longer than that corresponding to the crying mechanism, but the calculation would be more rigorous (1874a and 1876b, vol. VII, pp. 270 and 316). Let us emphasise that this procedure will never be taken up again in the *Éléments* or in other articles. The solution of the "computing agent" resembles the French system of quotation "by locker (*par casier*)" at the Paris Stock Exchange in use in the 1990s; for low-liquidity securities, the purchase and sale orders are placed in lockers and the specialist of the security will transfer the orders onto a sheet in order to calculate the equilibrium price. More recently, the Walrasian "calculator" can be compared to the "box (*par boîte*)" quotation system (computerised), used exceptionally for securities that are volatile in the Nouveau système de cotation (N. S. C.).[20]

Out of the "group of French *rentes*", for the securities not traded "*par oppositions*", in absence of a crier, the quoting clerk twice underlined the equilibrium quotation.

[16] For a different perspective on the functioning of the Paris Stock Exchange in the XIXth century, see D. A. Walker, 2000 and 2001.

[17] H. M. Bratter, 1931, pp. 362–63. In the entry "Auctions" of the *New Palgrave Dictionary of Economics*, Vernon L. Smith thinks that the concrete markets closest to the Walrasian mechanism are the London markets of gold and silver, on which a chairman gives an opening price and the agents transmit the selling and buying orders coming from the whole world (1987, vol. 1, p. 139).

[18] J. M. Keynes, letter of 9 December 1934 to J. R. Hicks, quoted in "Some questions of time in Economics" (1976), re-ed. in: J. R. Hicks 1982, p. 296 note 16.

[19] In citing this letter (1996, p. 98), D. A. Walker considers that this case should be related to the "*calculateur*" mentioned by Walras, but not in the *Éléments* (*cf. infra*).

[20] This system was replaced in 2007 by the Universal Trading Platform system (U. T. P).

5.3 Free Competition on the "Ideal Type" Market

Let us now see how Walras moves from the "real type" or type market to the "ideal type" of market, and then how he complicates the analysis to extend it to situations with production.

5.3.1 *Transition to the Ideal*

One cannot reason analytically on the real type market (public government bonds). If it is a synthesis, it remains empirical and, therefore, the phenomena that play out there, the relationships that intertwine there, have both the extreme complexity of concrete reality and its necessary imperfection. It is therefore necessary to analyse the real, that is to say, to decompose it into simple ideal elements, define them, then to reason on them deductively, logically, through mathematical formalisation, and step by step reconstruct through successive complication in order to arrive in the world of ideas at finding the equivalent of the complex real type, but ideal, perfect. Theorisation assumes that the researcher somewhat retraces his steps, abandons the real type of competitive market, to lose in complexity in order to gain in perfection, to return at the end of the process to the same complex object, but reconstructed in the ideal, thus mathematically formalised. Here is Walras's explanation:

> To give a preliminary idea of the fact of exchange and the mechanism of competition, I have taken the example of buying and selling securities for gold and silver on the Bourse. But those securities are a very special kind of commodity, and the intervention of money in trading is also a special fact, the study of which will be postponed until later, and not interwoven, at the outset, with the general fact of value in exchange. Let us, therefore, retrace our steps [...]. (vol. VIII, 5th lesson, § 44, pp. 73–74, English transl., 2014, p. 46)

This retracing of steps is the recourse to analysis, the transition from the real type of market to the ideal type of market. Let us follow the author's reasoning:

> [...] to give our observations a scientific character", he writes, "let us take any two commodities, say oats and wheat, or, designate them even more abstractly as (A) and (B). I put the letters A and B in parentheses in order not to lose sight of the fact that they represent not *quantities*, which are the only category of things susceptible of being used in equations, but instead represent kinds, species, or, as would be said in philosophical terms, *essences*." (emphasise by L. W., *op. cit*., p. 74, English transl., 2014, p. 46)

We have already seen that Walras defined "pure economics" as "in essence, the theory of the determination of prices under a hypothetical regime of absolute free competition" (vol. VIII, Preface, p. 11, English transl., 1954 revised, p. 40). The author emphasises the nature of this "realistic" hypothesis in the sense that, far from being a hypothesis among the other possible ones, it is extracted from reality and, as an idea, it is also real, and perfect as an ideal. He has moved from the *fact* of competition to the *idea* of competition, thus to the scientific laws of exchange, and his concern is "to recognize the *laws* according to which these sales and purchases tend to be made of their own accord" (emphasis ours, vol. VIII, p. 71, English transl., 2014, p. 43). The "absolute free competition" is "the general case" from which one must always begin. Regarding his dispute with Edgeworth (*cf. infra*), Walras indicates to L. Von Bortkiewicz: "In the *tâtonnement*'s question, for example, I take the quasi-universal case of free competition in exchange, the one described by John Stuart Mill, and consisting in rising prices when demand exceeds supply and lowering prices when supply exceeds demand […]."[21]

It is therefore not appropriate for Walras (vol. VIII, p. 73, English transl., 2014, p. 45) to start from particular cases, such as diamonds or masters' paintings, like the case cited by J. S. Mill, quoting Thomas de Quincey, where two individuals exchange, in an isolated steam boat on Lake Superior, a music box, seemingly at auction, one buying when the last bell tolls ([1848] 1965, book III, Chap. 2, § 1, vol. 1, pp. 463–64). It is only in a second phase that it will become possible to analyse more complex particular situations that the theory will then manage to integrate and study the exceptions.

But why and in what way is competition the general case? Alongside the real type of the best organised markets in terms of competition, there are other conceivable real types, for example, the monopoly which seems more immediate. Why not start from a situation of bilateral monopoly, and then complicate by moving to n traders, to an indefinite number *à la Cournot*? The answer is that, for Walras, absolute and perfectly organised free competition is a situation in which traders, fully exercising their natural liberties, bring forth not *a price* of equilibrium, but the *true price*.

The controversy with Edgeworth is revealing in this regard.[22] We will limit ourselves here to recalling a few points. In his review of the 2nd edition of the *Éléments* ("The Mathematical Theory of Political Economy", *Nature*, 5 September 1889), F. Y. Edgeworth claims that the *tâtonnement* process is "not a very good idea". According to him,

> […] as Jevons points out, the equations of exchange are of statical, not a dynamical, *character*. They define a position of equilibrium, but they afford no information as to the path by which that point is reached. Prof. Walras's laboured lessons indicate *a* way, not *the way*, of descent to equilibrium. (emphasis by F. Y. E., 1889, reprinted in: P. Bridel, 1996, p. 268)

Very angry, Walras asks L. von Bortkiewicz to write a review of the *Éléments* containing some criticism of Edgeworth's point of view, which appears in January–February 1890 in the *Revue d'économie politique*. Bortkiewicz defends the static

[21] L. Walras, letter to L. Von Bortkiewicz, 27 February 1891, in: *Correspondence*, II, l. 999, p. 434. See also the note addressed to V. Pareto on 9 January 1895, in: *op. cit.*, II, l. 1200, p. 630. Indeed, J. S. Mill indicated in *Principles of Political Economy*: if the demand exceeds the supply, buyers compete among themselves, which raises the price; if the supply exceeds the demand, sellers compete among themselves, which lowers the price ([1848] 1965, book III, Chap. 2, § 4, vol. 2, pp. 466–67). In reality, Adam Smith already mentioned this active behaviour on the long side of the market to explain the discrepancies between the market price and the natural price of goods (1976, vol. I, pp. 73–74). On Walras's revival of the old tradition of competition, see A. Rebeyrol, 1999, pp. 249–50.

[22] On this controversy, see notably D. A. Walker, 1987 and 1996, pp. 302–15, A. Rebeyrol, 1999, pp. 87–100, P. Bridel, 1996, pp. 251–59 and 2008, P. Bridel and É. Huck, 2002, pp. 525–32, N. Berta, 2001, R. Marchionatti, 2007.

procedure of solving equilibrium equations and the "realism" of Walrasian *tâtonnement*.[23] Edgeworth then reacts in the *Revue d'économie politique* (January 1891) by maintaining that "the entire bargaining process whereby the market price is determined, the direction followed by the system to arrive at the position of equilibrium, lies outside the scope of science" (1891, p. 12, English transl., in P. Newman, 2003, pp. 312–13). The mutual misunderstanding arises from the fact that Edgeworth reasons, without specifying it, on the basis of his own theory presented in *Mathematical Psychics* (1881), an alternative approach which he considers more general than that of Walras. Edgeworth begins with the formation of a contract between two exchangers and in such a barter, there is not a single solution to the determination of the quantities exchanged, but a range of "final settlements" located along the "contract curve", the precise exchange rate being the result of the bargaining power of the exchangers. When the number of exchangers increases, the possibility of recontracting makes the solution "more or less indeterminate", and finally, with an infinity of agents, the "contract with *perfect* competition is perfectly determinate" (emphasis by F. Y. E., 1881, p. 20): the theory of Walras corresponds to this *particular case*. Even if Walras had read *Mathematical Psychics*, how could he accept Edgeworth's system where free competition is a particular case, where liberties are in conflict, where power of bargaining, higgling, and coalitions are inherent to recontracting and therefore in the walk towards equilibrium. Hence Walras's irritation when Edgeworth opposes him in other systems (the English government bonds market, the English auction system, the Dutch auction system),[24] whereas for him, absolute free competition is the natural, therefore general case, corresponding to the ideal, and the equilibrium price the true and just price.[25]

5.3.2 Specificities of "Absolute Free Competition"

Let us now return to the analysis of the *Éléments*. The characteristics of absolute free competition remain those that have been determined on the typical market. We find the two natural liberties:

- the liberty of outbidding and underbidding the price (*enchère et rabais*);
- the liberty of entry and exit of the market.

[23] The best study on the Walras-Bortkiewicz relations is that of P. Bridel, 2008, pp. 711–42.

[24] See F. Y. Edgeworth, "The Mathematical Theory of Supply and Demand and the Cost of Production", *Revue d'économie politique*, vol. 5, no. 1, 1891, p. 13 and L. Walras, letter to L. Von Bortkiewicz, 27 February 1891, in: *Correspondence*, II, l. 999, pp. 434–35.

[25] After Edgeworth's reaction, Bortkiewicz refused to pursue the controversy and finally Walras wrote to him:

> [...] it is not likely that I decide to intervene myself. [...]. If necessary, I shall wait until I find men who know that the secret of science is to keep the general case to the fore and to relegate particular cases and exceptions to the background; because fundamentally that is the crux of my quarrel with Edgeworth." (letter to Bortkiewicz, 27 February 1891, in: Correspondence, II, l. 999, p. 434).

There is also an obligation for the success of the coordination between agents: to make public one's proposals.

Walras insists on the specific behaviour of outbidding and underbidding: free and rational exchangers, informed by "the crying" of prices, will raise the price if there is an excess of demand or lower the price if there is an excess of supply. The equilibrium price must be made objective and the transactions take place at this price.

Let us first observe the absence in Walras's text of a market authority, a central "crier" or an "auctioneer" in charge of crying out the prices (and quantities in the case of models with production) and of eliminating the total net demands. This absence led R. Goodwin (1951, p. 5) to observe that unfortunately for the theory, there is *nobody* to change the prices. It is not true. In fact, Walras uses an ambiguous expression: "one causes the raise [...] the fall [...] (*on fait la hausse* [...], *la baisse* [...])".[26] If reality is the image of the theory, who or what is this "*one*"? The neutral "one" indicates a perfect, ideal mechanism; and in theory, this "one" can only be the mathematical economist. Thus, hovers on this reconstructed reality the shadow of a mechanism, an abstract being changing the price, which makes it possible us to understand the error of those who introduced this central crier who does not exist in Walras's presentation (as W. Jaffé had already noted)[27] it being understood that, for him, on a concrete market, including on the best organised markets, this "one" can be any exchanger.[28]

How did the "auctioneer" appear in relation to the bidding mechanism in Walras? Paul A. Samuelson offers his testimony to Donald A. Walker:

> Around 1935 Schumpeter's lectures at Harvard used to speak of 'an angel of the marketplace' or 'a Walrasian angel' or 'a Walrasian auctioneer', who lowered price systematically in some proportion to the excess of supply over demand. In my 1941 MIT lectures, I continued the rhetoric (26 September, 1991) (D. A. Walker, 2019, p. 152).

But in the literature devoted to the Walrasian general equilibrium, the figure of the "auctioneer" does not appear before the Second World War (except perhaps in the form of the "Central planning office" of O. Lange's market socialism model).[29] Why then did it emerge from the 1950s onwards? One can mention the impact of the English translation of the *Éléments,* carried out by William Jaffé, published only in

---

[26] For example: "if it is demand that exceeds supply, the price is raised [...]; if it is supply that exceeds demand, the price is lowered." (vol. VIII, 12th lesson, p. 189), and earlier: "[...] one cries m(m - 1) prices of the m goods into each other. These prices can be cried at random; to put it better, they can only be cried at random." (*id.*, Preface, pp. 12–13); see also "Esquisse d'une doctrine économique et sociale" (1898c), vol. X, p. 417, English transl., 2005, p. 365.

[27] W. Jaffé is clear on its absence in the *Éléments.* Within the framework of a mathematical determination of the equilibrium prices, on a purely theoretical level, therefore, its shadow appears in the 12th lesson with the "one" that raises the price and Jaffé notes that at this level, and only at this level, Walras "seems to be imagining a theorist operating a mathematical machine and moving price levers upwards or downwards until demand equals offer" (1954, p. 520, note 11). He *seems* (for W. Jaffé), but obviously, he does not do it. See also W. Jaffé, 1980, p. 355, note 27.

[28] For a different perspective on the auctioneer in Walras, see M. De Vroey, 1998, pp. 206–10, 1999, pp. 416 and 426–27 and 2003, pp. 466–67.

[29] See O. Lange, "On the Economic Theory of Socialism", *Review of Economic Studies*, vol. 4, n°1 and 2, October 1936 and February 1937.

1954, in which Walras's "*crieurs*" are sometimes translated as "criers", sometimes as "*auctioneers*" and in which the expression "*à la criée*" is translated as "*by auction*" (D. A. Walker, 1996, pp. 82 and 84–85; Tranlators' Introduction, in Walras 2014, pp. XXXV–VI).[30] Of course, following the article by Paul A. Samuelson (1941), re-used in the *Foundations of Economic Analysis* (1947), general equilibrium models have incorporated a central "auctioneer" who announces price vectors to which agents respond by submitting their offers and demands for all commodities.

Secondly, it is well known that the standard theory and post-Walrasian vulgate reduce the question of competition in Walras to a *market structure*, namely "pure and perfect competition". This is traditionally characterised by a series of conditions. Although in microeconomics textbooks there is no consensus on its conditions and definition, one can recall the list that is generally found[31]:

1. A very large number of agents participating in the market (atomicity);
2. Free entry and exit in the market;
3. "Price taker" agents;
4. Homogeneous goods;
5. Perfect information.

We have highlighted the difference in nature between Walras's free competition (a behaviour of free individuals with rules) and the vulgate's pure and perfect competition (market characteristics). However, even by playing the game of this vulgate, thus by taking up the list of conditions that define pure and perfect competition, one will observe fundamental divergences with Walras's position.

1. A very large number of agents participating in the market (atomicity). In fact, "absolute free competition" is not linked to a very high number of operators in the market, and a few participants at the exchange are sufficient. Walras represents purchasers and sellers by a limited number of agents; too many operators would be incompatible with the mechanism described, which consists of their direct interaction in the market and would come to oppose the process of "crying" (D. A. Walker, 1990, p. 656 and 658; 1996, pp. 82 and 84–85; 1997, p. 72).
2. Free entry and exit: indefinite competition.

[30] To our knowledge, the earliest use of the term "auctioneer" in the Anglo-Saxon literature on the Walrasian general equilibrium appears in the microeconomics textbook by J. M. Henderson and R. E. Quandt, 1958, p. 95 and 113). It concerns an "auctioneer" in each market. Henderson and Quandt worked on the *Éléments,* both in the French edition and in Jaffé's translation. According to R. Clower and P. Howit (1995, p. 31 note 1), the notion of "auctioneer" may have been invented by Richard Quandt in the United States; it was used at Northwestern University in 1959 and 1960. H. Uzawa, for his part, coined the expression "secretary of market" ("Walras' *Tâtonnement* in the theory of exchange", *Review of Economic Studies*, vol. 27, June 1960, p. 184).

[31] This list is obviously not exhaustive and depends on the configuration of each perfect competition model. Other conditions are sometimes added: perfect mobility of productive factors, absence of transaction costs... Contemporary textbooks often retain only one or two conditions (for examples 1 and 3). For the different definitions of perfect competition, see D. A. Walker, 1997, Chap. III.

This is a fundamental condition for Walras, the only one clearly found in him. It allows for the clarification of the expression "indefinite competition (*concurrence indéfinie*)" that Walras sometimes uses, an expression borrowed from Augustin Cournot,[32] but in a very different sense.[33] For Walras, it is opposed to the monopoly (natural or not) and is used to indicate a situation in which there is an "indefinite number" of firms.[34] When in the "Principe d'une théorie mathématique de l'échange" (1874a), Walras asserts that Cournot "starts from the monopoly to arrive at indefinite competition, and I believe preferable to start from indefinite competition, which is the general case, to arrive at the monopoly, which is the particular case" (vol. VII, p. 264; vol. XI, p. 29), or when similar remarks are found in the *Éléments* from the 2nd edition (vol. VIII, p. 665, English transl., 2014, p. 448) and in the *Abrégé des Éléments* (vol. VIII, p. 787),[35] one can estimate that, for the author, it is the number of participants that is indefinite and that is made such by free entry and free exit of the market.

3. "Price taker" behaviour of the agents

The Walrasian market is generally presented as formed of "price taker" agents with a crier or an auctioneer: the crier announces the price, the exchangers "take it" and, according to this one, they assess their effective offers and demands. In reality, the agents present in small numbers in well-organised markets that determine the prices themselves. As long as the equilibrium is not reached, the traders outbid or underbid in order to find their counterparts. The Walrasian approach is therefore not reduced to a "price taker" behaviour of agents at the equilibrium price.

4. Homogeneous goods

Walras accepts this condition, but only in an implicit way.

5. Perfect Information

If Walras (unlike W. S. Jevons) does not explicitly emphasise this aspect in his approach to competition (D. A. Walker, 1990, p. 654; 1996, p. 79 and M. De Vroey,

---

[32] In his *Recherches sur les principes mathématiques de la théorie des richesses* (1838), it is the title of Chap. VIII: "On Unlimited Competition (*De la concurrence indéfinie*)". Cournot defines this very rigorously: it is the case when "the effects of competition have reached their limit, when each partial production Dk is *inappreciable*, not only with reference to the total production D = F(*p*), but also with reference to the derivative F'(*p*), so that the partial production Dk could be subtracted from D without any appreciable variation resulting in the price of the commodity." (2001, p. 69, English transl., 1897, p. 90).

[33] See on this question, R. Dos Santos Ferreira and R. Ege, 2013, pp. 637–638.

[34] See notably "L'État et les chemins de fer" (1875a, vol. X, pp. 188–189 and 197), "Théorie mathématique du billet de banque" (1880e, vol. X, p. 311), English transl., 2005, pp. 165–166 and 273; *Théorie mathématique de la richesse sociale* (1883, vol. XI, p. 167); *Cours d'économie politique appliquée* (vol. XII, p. 636); "L'économique appliquée et la défense des salaires" (1897c, vol. X, pp. 248 and 250); "Esquisse d'une doctrine économique et sociale" (1998b, vol. X, p. 427), English transl., 2005, pp. 219–220 and 373–374 (here, the translation omits the words "*concurrence indéfinie*").

[35] See also L. Walras, letter to A.-A. Cournot, 26 August 1873, in: *Correspondence*, I, l. 230, p. 330.

2003, p. 469), it is nevertheless essential in his analysis through the "crying" which renders public the proposals made by outbidding and underbidding and finally the equilibrium price.

The theorisation, this reconstruction in the ideal of a complex reality, leads Walras successively to a model of exchange with two commodities, without money nor *numéraire*, to a model with three, then to n commodities, to arrive at the general model of exchange with *numéraire*. He can then discuss the pure theory of production.

At the beginning, there is the pure barter of two commodities: oats and wheat. The reasoning is initially geometrical, with Walras building the curves of effective demand and supply (6th lesson of the *Éléments*) which aim to be a generalisation, an "abstraction" of what generally happens in the real type market. To assess a partial effective demand curve (of an individual) as a function of price, our author posits that everyone has virtual or effective dispositions to buy or sell (vol. VIII, p. 82, English transl., 2014, p. 53), meaning that he wishes to increase the quantities of commodity A for increasingly lower prices. If, therefore, the individual does not go to the market and gets through an agent, *theoretically* he must have to give him a *written order* anticipating all the possible prices and his demands for all these prices. The demand curve or the demand equation is thus only the mathematical expression of each individual's virtual bidding intentions.

With the *total* demand curves for wheat and oats (since each demand curve for one commodity is a supply curve for the other), the *total* supply and demand curves for a commodity can be asserted, but this time in their purity and geometric precision: at a given price, if the net demand is negative, there will be a price decrease, if it is positive, there will be a price increase.

Walras will then move to algebraic reasoning, from curves to demand and supply equations, and seek the equilibrium solution. He will show that a solution exists, that it is generally unique and stable, but not necessarily. Note that when he reasons at general equilibrium, he will show that the equilibrium is practically always unique and stable. The algebraic solution assumes an algebraic *tâtonnement* corresponding to outbid and underbid. *The solution by iteration of a system of simultaneous equations becomes the ideal of the* tâtonnements *that occur in reality.* The "mechanism of competition in the market" is nothing other than "the practical solution, reached through the raising and lowering of prices, of the problem of exchange for which we have furnished the theoretical and mathematical solution" (vol. VIII, p. 93, English transl., 2014, p. 66).

Walras can then give us (in the 10th lesson) the analytical definition of free competition, relative to the exchange of two commodities for each other (this *analytical* definition being the criterion for the passage from real type to ideal type). It analytically corresponds to the behavioural definition founded on the exhaustion of the outbidding and underbidding process within the framework of what he will later call the "jevonian barter (*troc jevonien*" ("Théorie de la propriété", 1896c, vol. IX, pp. 179–80, English transl., 2010, pp. 136–38):

> *The exchange of two commodities for each other in a freely competitive market is an operation by which all holders of either one, or of both, of the two commodities can obtain the greatest satisfaction of their wants consistent with the condition of giving the commodity that they sell*

> *and receiving the commodity that they buy in a common and identical proportion.* (emphasis by L. W., vol. VIII, p. 142, English transl., 2014, pp. 110–11)

Walras specifies (*op. cit.*, p. 137, English transl., p. 108) that if this solution is mathematical, it reaches the solution on the market place that would be effectuated in the following manner: the prices being called out, the quantities supplied and demanded would be determined without calculation, but in accordance with the condition of maximum satisfaction. Finally, the concrete market is only an approximation of the mathematical solution.

From then on, could one not substitute the mathematical solution for the market solution? Walras therefore feels obliged to specify that "it must furthermore be understood that we have no intention of substituting one solution for the other".. The practical solution, indeed, "has a rapidity and reliability that leaves nothing to be desired" and the theoretical solution would be "in almost all cases, completely impractical", the substitution would generally be absurd (*op. cit.*, p. 93, English transl., p. 67). This precaution is there to answer to the liberal school who saw collectivism looming behind this mathematisation of exchange. But the devil lies in the details. Does Walras not add: "The advantage there may be, in certain cases, of constructing, totally or partially, the demand curve or the supply curve of a given commodity, and the possibility or impossibility of doing so, *is a question that we defer entirely*" (our emphasis, *op. cit.*). Let us now address the pure theory of production.

5.3.3 From Pure Theory of Exchange to Pure Theory of Production

Unlike the pure exchange model, in the production model, the purchasers and sellers are specified. The landowners, capitalists, and workers are purchasers of products and sellers of productive services, while entrepreneurs are sellers of products and purchasers of productive services. Walras will tirelessly repeat that the mathematical solution and the practical solution are basically identical, except for imperfections, and that practical *tâtonnement* through outbidding and underbidding approximates the theoretical, mathematical *tâtonnement* through the iterative method of search for the solution.

The analytical definition of free competition in production brings us back to the behaviour of outbidding and underbidding extended to the development or restriction of production, which is nothing other than a twofold liberty: it is

> [...] that is to say, the freedom of entrepreneurs to increase their output in the case of making profits and to restrict it in the case of making losses, combined with free competition in exchange; that is to say, the freedom of landowners, workers, capitalists and entrepreneurs to buy and to sell services and products, by bidding up and lowering prices [...]. (vol. VIII, p. 333, English transl., 2014, p. 247)

It must be understood that the analytical definition always rests on the (relative) maximum of satisfaction, but now with a twofold condition: that of the unique equilibrium price and the absence of profit and loss.

The equilibrium of production includes the equilibrium of exchange and assumes equality between:

- supply and effective demand of "productive services" and the setting of the price of each of them (ground rent, wage, interest);
- supply and effective demand of products and the setting of the selling price of each of them;
- the selling price of the products and the cost of productive services.

It is "an ideal and not a real state", but it is nonetheless the "normal state" or the natural state because in free competition, things tend by themselves towards this equilibrium. Since "in the state of equilibrium of production, entrepreneurs make neither profit nor loss" (vol. VIII, p. 284, English transl., 2014, p. 210), the function of the entrepreneur vanishes. One can, one must, disregard it and "consider not only the productive services as being exchanged for products and products as being exchanged for productive services, but, when all is said and done, even consider the productive services as being exchanged for each other" (*ibid.*).

Naturally, if equilibrium is not reached, one finds oneself in one or the other case:

- If for some entrepreneurs, the selling price of the products is higher than the cost of productive services, there is a "profit (*bénéfice*)". The entrepreneurs in the branch will then increase their production and there will be a surge of entrepreneurs in this activity, which will lead to a reduction in the initial gap.
- If for some entrepreneurs, the selling price of the products is lower than the cost of productive services, there is a "loss". The entrepreneurs in the branch will decrease their production or even leave it, which will lead to a reduction in the initial gap.

Ultimately, one is faced with a triple level of exercise of competition in production, corresponding to the same type of behaviour of free and clear-sighted, rational individuals:

- the entrepreneurs are free to change the level of production, according to profits and losses, and they do so if they are not constrained;
- the sellers and buyers of productive services are free to outbid and underbid, and they do so if they are not constrained;
- but to this is added the third liberty, the free entry and exit of the market: by entering the entrepreneurs increase production and by leaving it they decrease it.

5.4 Conclusion

Finally, for Walras, free competition, whatever the level at which it is apprehended (concrete markets, market type, ideal market, theories of exchange and of production), is essentially a natural behaviour for free men with institutions allowing them to fully exercise these liberties.[36] It stems from three related liberties: that of proposing prices by outbidding and underbidding; that of varying one's production "at profit and loss"; that of entering or leaving the market. These three liberties produce a natural behaviour, but must be able to be fully exercised, hence the two rules:

- the exchangers must make their proposals public by crying them;
- the processes of outbidding and underbidding must be extinguished and the equilibrium price reached before there are effective transactions.[37]

One could continue the demonstration ad nauseam with the *tâtonnement* on "*bons*" (tickets, written pledges), the theory of capitalisation, then that of money, but our knowledge of the Walrasian conception of competition would not be improved.

[36] This aspect is examined in particular by J. Lallement, 2000b, pp. 481–483.

[37] It should be added that all potential entrants and exits have done so.

Chapter 6
An Early Reception of Pure Economics in Italy: The Correspondence with the "Lombard-Venetians"

6.1 Introduction

"The correspondence of an author is always a valuable source of knowledge about his personality, the development of his work, and the society in which he lives and acts." With these words, Henri Bartoli (1990, p. 1088) began a review of a collection prepared by Giovanni Busino, *L'Italia di Vilfredo Pareto: Economia e società in un carteggio del 1879–1924*. On the Italian side of the Walrasian correspondence, William Jaffé's selection comprises 280 letters, which is far from negligible (on certain aspects, see G. Busino, 1968 and P. Barucci, 1972). Within this selection, a particular attention is given to the relationship with Vilfredo Pareto, comprising 126 letters, and attention has often focused on this theme. Conversely, the epistolary exchanges with lesser-known authors, who played a certain role in Italian economic thought, have received very little attention.

In this chapter, we will focus on the epistolary relations of Léon Walras with economists described as "socialists of the chair" and members of the "Lombard-Venetian school" between 1874 and 1886: Alberto Errera, Gerolamo Boccardo, Vito Cusumano, Luigi Bodio, and a few other representatives of the school or on its fringes. During this period, these economists were, in fact, the almost exclusive Italian correspondents of Léon Walras. From 1886 onwards, relations with this group became less frequent, and exchanges with the adherents of marginalism gradually increased, reaching their peak during the 1890s.

For the study of this subset of the Walrasian correspondence, William Jaffé's selection offers us a very comprehensive source from a scientific point of view containing around sixty letters. However, in the Lausanne archives, there are some letters from Walras (drafts) and from Italian economists not included in this edition, mostly because William Jaffé had excluded them due to their limited interest, or in some cases because they seem to have escaped his attention. In the same archives, there are also some notes and documents relating to the Italian correspondence as well as offprints of articles. Furthermore, the Léon Walras Library, which has been largely

J.-P. Potier, *Léon Walras, Economist and Liberal Socialist*, Springer Studies in the History of Economic Thought, https://doi.org/10.1007/978-3-032-04670-3_6

reconstructed, contains works by "Lombard-Venetian" economists. We will consider all these materials to provide a better appreciation of the extent of the exchanges, particularly in the second half of the 1870s. Additionally, in the appendix we publish three unpublished documents discovered in the Lausanne archives: a letter of Vito Cusumano to Léon Walras dated 24 October 1874, some notes by Walras concerning Vito Cusumano's letter dated 3 January 1875, and a table from Walras, relating to the first dissemination of pure economics in Italy.

Given that the letters received were written either in French or Italian, one might initially question Léon Walras's knowledge of Italian. At the beginning of his correspondence with Alberto Errera, he does not hesitate to assert: "I know enough Italian to understand it more or less when reading" (1st April 1874, *Correspondence,* I, l. 255, p. 368). However, in the following months, encountering difficulties in reading the works he had to review, he expressed the desire to become more familiar with Italian, "so as not only to read it but to speak it a little, to enter and remain in regular and constant communication".[1]

Before examining the Walrasian correspondence, it is necessary to provide some clarifications regarding the "Lombard-Venetian school". This term was coined by Francesco Ferrara (1810–1900), in a famous review, "Il germanismo economico in Italia" (F. Ferrara, 1874). The Sicilian economist laments the fact that in the former Lombard-Venetian Kingdom, intellectuals could appreciate "Germanic works", which are not very compatible with the principles of liberalism. He accuses these economists of advocating authoritarian, statist, and socialist measures, labelling them as "vincolisti" and "autoritari". He identifies two centres of diffusion of their ideas, on the one hand, the University of Pavia, with Luigi Cossa (and disciples such as Vito Cusumano) and on the other hand, the University of Padua, around Angelo Messedaglia (with Fedele Lampertico, Augusto Montanari, and Giuseppe Toniolo). In reality, this designation of a "provincial" nature is somewhat reductive, as the "school" attracted a movement of adherence in many cities of the peninsula, where local committees were very active (for example, in Naples, under Antonio Scialoja's influence). The official constitution of the "school" takes place between 1874 and 1875. The "circolare di Padova", dated 11 September 1874, signed by Antonio Scialoja, Luigi Cossa, Luigi Luzzatti, and Fedele Lampertico (reproduced in: R. Faucci, 1975, p. 663 note 136, and Parisi Acquaviva, 1978, pp. 339–40), announces the forthcoming organisation of a congress in Milan to debate the economic functions of the State, positioning themselves in opposition to the "fatalism of the optimists". The following questions will be submitted for consideration: factory laws, savings and workers' pensions, protective law for emigrants, forestry legislation, and mining legislation. The movement's promoters, who describe themselves as "reformists", intend to establish a rival association to the "Società Adamo Smith", emerging in Florence under the auspices of uncompromising liberals associated with the weekly *L'Economista* (F. Ferrara, A. Magliani, U. Peruzzi...). The Milan Congress held from 4 to 6 January 1875, attracted up to 190 participants from across Italy and

[1] L. Walras, unpublished letter to A. Errera, 19 August 1874, kept in the Lausanne collection under the reference F. W. I, box 2.

resulted in the "Associazione per il progresso degli studi economici". The "Lombard-Venetians" will have two platforms to promote their ideas. Firstly, they disseminate their concepts in the Roman weekly (founded in 1869), *L'Economista d'Italia*, whose editor-in-chief is Antonino Basile. Additionally, the *Rassegna di agricoltura, industria e commercio*, directed by Eugenio Forti, published from 1873 in Padua, becomes the *Giornale degli economisti* two years later. The first series of this journal (April 1875–December 1878), led by Eugenio Forti, will be the official organ of the new association.

Immersed in an intellectual climate imbued with positivism, the ideas of the "Lombard-Venetian school" draw from two main sources of inspiration that are barely distinguished in the literature of that time. The first is the "old" German Historical School (Wilhelm Roscher, Bruno Hildebrand, and Karl Knies), which advocates the historical method and recommends the application of statistics to social sciences. The second source is the "Kathedersozialismus", embodied by the "Verein für Sozialpolitik", an association born at the Eisenach Congress in October 1872, with, on one hand, the "young" Historical School (Gustav Schmoller, Ludwig-Josef Brentano, Ernst Engel), and on the other hand, the "State socialism" (Albert Schäffle, Adolf Wagner). Labelled by their opponents as adherents of "economic Germanism", the "Lombard-Venetians" do not, in reality, constitute a very unified movement on a theoretical and doctrinal level.

The closest disciples of the German "socialism of the chair are, without a doubt, Vito Cusumano (R. Salvo, 1979, Cassani, 1985, and P. Travagliante, 2003) and Carlo-Francesco Ferraris (G. Gozzi, 1983), both former students of Adolf Wagner and Ernst Engel in Berlin and belonging to the younger generation. In contrast, the spokespersons of the "school", such as Luigi Cossa, Luigi Luzzatti, Fedele Lampertico, regularly denounce certain excesses of the German "socialism of the chair" and refuse to align with Gustav Schmoller's conception of the State as an "ethical institution". These authors also reject the absolute relativism of German economists. They acknowledge the existence of natural laws in political economy but, as expressed by Fedele Lampertico, in the sense of "limit laws", which are verified only when all the factual conditions that form their presupposition are met (F. Lampertico, 1875, pp. 117–20; R. Romani, 1988, p. 139). Far from accepting the radical opposition between the "socialism of the chair" and the "Manchester school", they consider the "exceptions" to free competition formulated by John Stuart Mill. The reference to the classical English economist is important because, contrary to popular belief, the "Lombard-Venetians" are probably more "Anglophile" than "Germanophile". Indeed, in their view, England has already largely translated into action the ideas of German economists regarding State intervention (Factory Act, for example) (R. Scaldaferri, 1992; R. Romani, 1994).

Within the "school", there are many historians and statisticians whose work will allow for a better understanding of Italian reality; parliamentary inquiries will be conducted, for example, in the industry. The Statistics of the Kingdom, in Rome, will be an important centre of influence thanks to the energy of Luigi Bodio, with the publication of the *Annali di statistica* of the Ministry of Agriculture, Industry and Commerce and the *Archivio di statistica*, founded in 1876.

In the political life of the 1870s–80s, the "Lombard-Venetians" form an important pressure group, particularly within the Ministry of Agriculture, Industry and Commerce (notably with Marco Minghetti, Luigi Luzzatti, and Emilio Morpurgo). They succeed in promoting reforms and having a number of laws adopted. Thus, the Minghetti law, promulgated in April 1874, which sets a ceiling for the issuance of banknotes with forced circulation by six institutes, was developed by Luigi Luzzatti. The "Lombard-Venetians" are also behind the moderate increases in customs duties in 1878 and the strongly protectionist tariff of 1887, known as "V. Ellena—L. Luzzatti".

At the fringes of the "school", there are a few authors, much more eclectic, deeply imbued with positivism, such as Boccardo and Loria. Gerolamo Boccardo, a former liberal, will play a significant role in the dissemination of Walrasian thought in Italy through his translations. He will show openness towards "mathematical economists", but without understanding the profound significance of marginalism, and *a fortiori* of the general economic equilibrium. Achille Loria, for his part, promoter of an original "agrarian socialism", plays the role of "introducer" of Marx in Italy, on the academic level, since 1883.

6.2 Alberto Errera, "Representative of Walras in Italy"

In March 1874, Léon Walras wanted to publicise abroad his "Principe d'une théorie mathématique de l'échange" (read on 16 and 23 August 1873 before the members of the Académie des sciences morales et politiques). Realising that he was unlikely to receive favourable responses in his native country, where economics remained firmly controlled by the "orthodox" liberal school, he turned to England, Germany, and Italy. To obtain addresses in the peninsula, he contacted Marc Monnier, a poet and writer, professor of literature at the Academy of Geneva, and author of regular chronicles on Italy for the *Bibliothèque universelle et Revue suisse.* He wanted to contact professors of political economy and directors or collaborators of scientific journals, who might then be interested in the *Éléments d'économie politique pure.* Walras also hoped to benefit in this country from a translation of the "Principle", or some other text. Marc Monnier suggested two of his acquaintances, Antonio Scialoja and Alberto Errera, but recommended especially the latter.[2] Through Alberto Errera (1842–94),[3] Léon Walras thus came into contact with the "Lombard-Venetian school".[4]

Within a few months, Alberto Errera, a member of the staff of the *Rivista europea* (Florence), became the "representative of Walras in Italy" (P. Barucci, 1980, p. 76), enabling him to quickly establish a genuine network of correspondents. At the beginning of their relations, he observed:

> For a long time, your fame has been widespread also in Italy [...]. The trend of your studies is now attractive in Italy, but few people are involved in associating mathematical studies with economic researches [...]. In the Italian schools, prevails the idea that the deductive mathematical method is almost inapplicable to economics, while mathematical induction is preferred. The use of this induction, the processes, criteria, graphical representations that you adopt are now favored by us too. And there is a widespread conviction that mathematical induction is very useful and that starting from significant facts in their numerical elements until number can legitimately arrive, combines them, shows their relationships, draws laws from them and from laws, allows to rise to causes." (*Correspondence*, I, l. 254, 23 March 1874, pp. 367–68; our translation from Italian)

The letter's tone is extremely obsequious and, to be honest, regarding the knowledge of Walras's writings and their potential impact in Italy at the time, one can have serious doubts! Alberto Errera advised sending the "Principe d'une théorie mathématique de l'échange" to the statisticians, Angelo Messedaglia and Luigi Bodio. He then added the names of Augusto Montanari, Luigi Cossa, and Fedele Lampertico (8 April 1874, *Correspondence,* I, l. 259, p. 376). The list, which lengthens over the weeks, includes Gerolamo Boccardo, Marco Minghetti, Antonio Scialoja, and even non-economist mathematicians such as Andrea Zambelli and Giovanni-Antonio Zanon. In the correspondence, the names of seventeen recipients will gradually appear. Alberto Errera took charge of writing or arranging reviews of the "Principe d'une théorie mathématique de l'échange". To facilitate matters, he requested permission to translate the summary contained in the letter to Paul Piccard of 25 October 1873 (published in the *Bulletin de la Société vaudoise des sciences naturelles*) that Léon Walras had sent him.[5] The latter agreed, subject to a few formal

[2] L. Walras, letter to Marc Monnier, 12 March 1874, in: *Correspondence*, I, l. 251, pp. 360–61, and the unpublished response from Marc Monnier, dated 13 March 1874, kept in the Lausanne collection under the reference F. W. II, box 11.

[3] A law student at the University of Padua, Alberto Errera was imprisoned by the Austrian authorities for having participated in the drafting of an anonymous pamphlet published in Paris, entitled *La Vénétie en 1864*. After his release, he defended a Ph.D. thesis in law in 1867, then taught economics and commercial law at the Technical Institute of Venice. From 1874, he taught at the Technical Institute of Milan, then from 1877, at the Technical Institute of Naples; Only in 1880 did he obtain a teaching position at Naples University. He mainly published in the field of economic history. See Polsi, 1993. It can also be mentioned that Errera translated into Italian the 2nd edition of *Éléments d'économie politique* (1884) by Émile de Laveleye, modifying and completing the text, with the author's agreement.

[4] In the Lausanne collection, the following note is found, from L. Walras's pen: "Missing the first letter to A. Errera (21 March 74). V. Hodgson Pratt, 12 March 1874" (F. W. block Vc, box 27).

[5] "Sur la théorie mathématique de l'échange. Lettre à M. Paul Piccard, 25 October 1873" (1873a), vol. XI, pp. 477–81.

modifications (25 April 1874, *Correspondence,* I, l. 265, pp. 385–86). An announcement of the publication and a review of the "Principle" appeared as early as July 1874.[6] The review was prepared by Giovanni-Antonio Zanon in the form of a letter to Errera. Our author had in his hands a first version of the text, dated 27 April 1874, on which he made modifications before publication (5 May 1874, *Correspondence,* l. 268, pp. 388–89).[7] As we have already seen, the first part of the *Éléments d'économie politique pure* was released by the printer on 27 July 1874. Alberto Errera then helped Léon Walras to compile lists of recipients, and by mid-August, 43 dispatches to Italy could already be counted (ten of which were yet to be made).[8] In addition to the previously mentioned names, the following are noted: Salvatore Cognetti de Martiis, Vito Cusumano, Francesco Ferrara, Luigi Luzzatti, Marco Minghetti, Emilio Morpurgo, Emilio Nazzani, Francesco Protonotari, Pietro Rota, and Antonio Scialoja. It should be noted that the recipients could also be economists of the liberal school, such as Francesco Protonotari (director in Rome of the *Nuova Antologia*), and Francesco Ferrara (included on the list at Luigi Bodio's suggestion). The first favourable responses were conveyed through Alberto Errera, who also worked to obtain reviews of the book in the following months.[9] On 5 August, Walras sent the manuscript "Analyse des *Éléments d'économie politique pure*" (vol. XI, pp. 487–94) which he had just completed. This text was simply translated by Alberto Errera in a review published during the month.[10] In exchange for these valuable services, Léon Walras promised to write articles on his Italian friend's books for the *Bibliothèque universelle et Revue suisse* and the *Journal des économistes.* He thus prepared a review of two works, intended for the *Journal des économistes,* which he communicated in October to Alberto Errera for examination and revision before sending it to Paris. In this work, Walras criticised the "socialism of the chair for engaging

[6] A. Errera, "Rassegna bibliografica di opere di economia politica e di diritto industriale", *Rivista europea* (Florence), vol. 3, no. 2, July 1874, pp. 333–34, § 10 and 11; G.-A. Zanon, "Sulla teoria matematica dello scambio del professore L. Walras—Lettera del professore Giovanni-Antonio Zanon al professore Alberto Errera", dated 6 June 1874, *Rassegna di agricoltura, industria e commercio* (Padua), vol. 2, July 1874, pp. 217–23.

[7] The Lausanne collection (F. W. block Vc, box 27) preserves two versions, one Italian, the other French, of the original text written by G.-A. Zanon, from the pen of L. Walras, with corrections made in red: "Esame e parere del Prof. Zanon sulla memoria del Prof. Walras" (4 p.) and "Examen et avis du Prof. Zanon sur le mémoire du Prof. Walras" (4 p.).

[8] L. Walras, unpublished letter to A. Errera dated 19 August 1874, preserved in the Lausanne collection, under the reference F. W. I, box 2. For the dispatches, L. Walras draws from the stock of 100 copies of the first part of the *Éléments* subscribed by the Council of State of the Canton of Vaud.

[9] Antonino Basile, "Il metodo matematico nell'economia politica—*Éléments d'économie politique pure* by Léon Walras", *L'Economista d'Italia*, 6th year, no. 40 and 42, 4 and 18 October 1874, pp. 518–20 and 543–45; A. Zambelli, "La teoria matematica dello scambio del Signor Leone Walras—Lettera diretta al Prof. Errera dott Alberto", Padua: Premiata tipografia alla Minerva, 1876, 28 p. The first review is hostile to the application of mathematics to economics and reveals a misunderstanding of Walrasian thought. The second review was revised by L. Walras before its publication.

[10] A. Errera, "Appunto bibliografico, *Éléments d'économie politique pure* by Léon Walras", *La Perseveranza* (Milan), 17th year, no. 5678, 18 August 1875, pp. 2–3.

in statistics and history while believing they were practising economics, and for confusing science with politics. However, very cleverly, at the end of the study, he attempted to spare Errera. The latter had enlisted in the ranks of the "socialists of the chair" probably due to his practical activities as a promoter of workers' and cooperative societies; "historian" and "statistician", he was also an "economist" and "one of ours" (Walras, 1874e, vol. XIII, p. 488). Errera was quite satisfied with the review.[11] In 1877, offering to publicise the second part of the *Éléments* which had just been published, Alberto Errera would have greatly appreciated a review of his two recent works (*Le grandi e le piccole industrie* and *Storia dell'economia politica negli Stati della Repubblica Veneta*) in the *Journal des économistes* or in another journal (10 September 1877, *Correspondence,* l. 387, p. 544). However, these books never reached Léon Walras.[12] Regarding the second part of the *Éléments,* which was published the same year, Alberto Errera seemed to have been less successful in seeking reviews. Despite solicitations, including from economists hostile to the application of mathematics to economics, such as Antonino Basile,[13] this second part received little attention in Italian journals and newspapers. In the following years, the Errera-Walras correspondence became increasingly sparse. In November 1882, Alberto Errera sent Walras his book *Le finanze dei grandi comuni: Riforme ai prestiti e ai dazi di consumo in Italia* and asked him "to write a bibliography for the *Journal des économistes* or another periodical", offering, for his part, to publish a summary of the paper on the "fixity of value of the monetary standard" (the 3rd part of the "Théorie mathématique du bimétallisme").[14] Walras was not tempted to write this review, but he took the opportunity to obtain from Alberto Errera a list of the "main Italian scientists or politicians" to whom it would be useful to send the "Théorie mathématique du bimétallisme" (25 November 1882, *Correspondence,* I, l. 539, pp. 731–32) (*cf. infra*). However, from 1874, he had a second support in Italy for the dissemination of his writings, Gerolamo Boccardo.

---

[11] One of Errera's two works will be used by L. Walras in the 26th lesson of the *Cours d'économie politique appliquée*, entitled "History and operations of industry" (vol. XII, pp. 573–74). Furthermore, L. Walras annotated the offprint of Errera's article "Il nuovo indirizzo degli studj industriali-Lezioni", published in the *Rassegna di agricoltura, industria e commercio* (no. 8, December 1873); this document is preserved in the Walras collection in Lausanne under the reference F. W. XI, E1.

[12] L. Walras, unpublished letter to A. Errera, 17 February 1879, preserved in the Lausanne collection under the reference F. W. I, box 2. In this document, Walras seeks his assistance for the publication in Italy of the "Bibliographie des ouvrages relatifs à l'application des mathématiques à l'économie politique", developed in collaboration with W. S. Jevons (1878b, vol. XI, Annex II, pp. 609–22).

[13] See the unpublished letter of L. Walras to A. Basile, 6 September 1877, in which he asks him to "criticise like the first" the half-volume in *L'Economista d'Italia* (letter preserved in the Lausanne collection under the reference F. W. I, box 1).

[14] A. Errera, letter to L. Walras, 21 November 1882, unpublished, preserved in the Lausanne collection under the reference F. W. II, box 8 bis.

6.3 Gerolamo Boccardo, Editor of the "Biblioteca dell'Economista"

Gerolamo Boccardo (1829–1904)[15] succeeded Francesco Ferrara as a director of the third series of the "Biblioteca dell'Economista", giving it a rather eclectic orientation, also open to statistics and sociology. The series he compiled will welcome the German "socialists of the chair" and even the "heretics of political economy", such as Owen, Proudhon, Lassalle, and Marx. In December 1874, sending him the "General Introduction" to the first volume of the "Biblioteca dell'Economista"'s new series, Gerolamo Boccardo offered our author to publish the *Éléments d'économie politique pure* in the second volume, alongside William Whewell's *Mathematical Exposition of some Doctrines of Political Economy*, Antoine-Augustin Cournot's *Recherches sur les principes mathématiques de la théorie des richesses*, and William Stanley Jevons's *The Theory of Political Economy* (30 December 1874, *Correspondence*, I, l. 322, p. 460). Walras confesses to being very "flattered and touched" by this proposal, but two difficulties arise. Firstly, the decision regarding the publication of the second part of the *Éléments* belongs to the publishers Corbaz & Co, and it hardly seems possible to get its printing completed before the middle of 1876. Furthermore, Walras wishes to promote the book's dissemination abroad, and any translation project will probably be considered premature (3 January 1875, *Correspondence*, I, l. 324, pp. 465–66). Matters remained as such until the end of 1875. Walras then proposed to publish in the "Biblioteca dell'Economista" a collection of four papers: "Principe d'une théorie mathématique de l'échange", "Équations de l'échange", "Équations de la production", and "Équations de la capitalisation et du crédit" (20 December 1875, *Correspondence*, I, l. 342, p. 490). Gerolamo Boccardo immediately accepted this project and offered to translate these texts himself,[16] which form together a *Théorie mathématique de la richesse sociale.* In an unpublished response, Léon Walras specified his conditions:

> Moreover, you will see, I think, no difficulty in granting me the following three small conditions: – that the proofs will be communicated to me, not to make corrections, but simply to verify the translation's accuracy – that a small note will indicate, at the beginning, that these papers form a summary of my *Éléments d'économie politique pure* - finally, that an another note will reproduce, translated into Italian, at the end of the 1st paper, the two letters

[15] In March 1848, G. Boccardo participated in the Milan uprising. The following year, he obtained a doctorate in law at the University of Genoa, then he turned towards economics. In 1860, he was awarded the chair of political economy at the University of Genoa. He published numerous works, among which can be cited: *Trattato teorico-pratico di economia politica* (1853), *Dizionario della economia politica e del commercio* (1857–63), *Le banche e il corso forzato* (1863), *L'economia politica e la sociologia* (1883). See A. Benvenuto Vialetto and G. Ancona, 1969.

[16] G. Boccardo, letters to L. Walras, 22 December 1875, in: *Correspondence*, I, l. 343, p. 492, and 29 December 1875, unpublished, preserved in the Lausanne collection under the reference F. W. II, box 7.

exchanged between Mr. Jevons and me on the priority's question concerning the condition of maximum satisfaction.[17]

In February 1877, Gerolamo Boccardo indicated that he had begun the translation of the first paper, and on 31 May, he announced the completion of the translations and their submission to the publisher.[18] While reading the proofs, Léon Walras discussed with Boccardo the Italian equivalent of certain concepts, such as land services, capital services, personal services, and their respective prices. The *Teoria matematica della richezza sociale* was published the following year in the volume dealing with "Dell'applicazione dei metodi quantitativi alle scienze economiche, statistiche e sociali" (including the works of Whewell, Cournot, Jevons, Quételet, Herschell, and Walras). From the beginning of 1875, to advertise the Italian series, Léon Walras had drafted two publication announcements, one in the organ of the Vaudois Radical Party *La Revue*, and the other in the *Journal des économistes* (vol. XI, Annex I, pp. 599–608).

Between October 1875 and February 1876, Walras wrote the essay "Une branche nouvelle de la mathématique". Having failed to publish it in France, he turned again to Italy and consulted Gerolamo Boccardo. The latter succeeded in obtaining the publication of the article in the *Giornale degli economisti* and offered to translate it into Italian; it appeared in the April 1876 issue, under the title "Un nuovo ramo della matematica—Dell'applicazione delle matematiche all'economia politica". In this text, Walras refrained from discussing in detail methodological questions with the director of the "Biblioteca dell'Economista". Indeed, from the publication of Gerolamo Boccardo's article "Del metodo in economia politica", in the *Giornale degli economisti*, in May 1875, he had received an offprint. He annotates this document, but he cannot share, for example, the following assertions: "Economics is an experimental science, like physics, like physiology. History and statistics are its great laboratories, its vast museums, in which we must draw from the living source of facts the elements of our laws and theorems".[19] However, the acceptance of analogies between economics and mechanics, the interest in the applications of mathematics to economics reassures him somewhat (see his letter to Boccardo, 21 June 1875, *Correspondence,* I, l. 320, p. 477). In "Une branche nouvelle de la mathématique", he confines himself to highlighting "the remarkable *Preface*" by Boccardo to the second volume of the "Biblioteca dell'Economista", entitled "Dell'applicazione dei metodi quantitativi alle scienze economiche, statistiche e sociali—Saggio di logica economica", available in October 1875 (1876b, vol. VII, pp. 292 and 324).

[17] L. Walras, letter to G. Boccardo, 2 January 1876, unpublished, preserved in the Lausanne collection under the reference F. W. I, box 1. Walras refers to the "Correspondance entre M. Jevons, Professeur à Manchester et M. Walras, Professeur à Lausanne" (1874c).

[18] G. Boccardo, letters to L. Walras, 14 February 1877, in: *Correspondence*, I, l. 371, p. 527, and 31 May 1877, unpublished, preserved in the Lausanne collection under the reference F. W. II, box 7.

[19] G. Boccardo, "Del metodo in economia politica", *Giornale degli economisti*, vol. I, no. 2, May 1875, p. 18 of the offprint; on the dedicated copy, preserved in the Lausanne collection under the reference F. W. XI, B2. L. Walras noted two question marks in the margin of this passage.

Léon Walras will then send Gerolamo Boccardo the papers "Théorie mathématique du billet de banque" (1880e), "Théorie mathématique du prix des terres et de leur rachat par l'État" (1881b) and "Théorie mathématique du bimétallisme" (1881a), perhaps in the hope of obtaining new translations or reviews, but these texts do not seem to have aroused a real interest in the Genoese professor.

In December 1882, Walras asks Gerolamo Boccardo to provide him with a "small list" of "professors, journalists, politicians or businessmen" likely to be interested in the "Théorie mathématique du bimétallisme" (23 December 1882, *Correspondence,* I, l. 542, p. 735). A senator of the Kingdom, the latter is in contact with a very large number of personalities; he immediately sends him a dozen names, among which are Domenico Berti, Minister of Agriculture, Industry and Commerce, Vittorio Ellena, Director General of the "Gabelles",[20] Agostino Magliani, Minister of Finance, Marco Minghetti, Luigi Luzzatti, Quintino Sella.[21] Léon Walras will have the opportunity to meet them during his stay in Rome (*cf. infra*).

6.4 Vito Cusumano, "Socialist of the Chair"

Alberto Errera allowed Vito Cusumano to read the manuscript of the review of his works, and it is the occasion for a brief exchange of letters with Walras, between October 1874 and January 1876. While staying in Germany, Vito Cusumano (1843–1908)[22] had the opportunity, thanks to Adolf Wagner, to participate in the Eisenach Congress in October 1872 (see V. Cusumano, 1872). He openly declares himself a disciple of the German "socialism of the chair and writes a series of articles for the *Archivio giuridico* of Pisa, in 1873–74, immediately afterwards gathered into a brochure (dedicated to Ernst Engel and Adolf Wagner) entitled *Sulla condizione attuale degli studi economici in Germania.* This collection plays an important role in the debate between the "Lombard-Venetians" and the economists of the liberal school grouped around Francesco Ferrara. Having read the review of Errera's books as well as the first lessons of the *Éléments d'économie politique pure*, Vito Cusumano does not grasp the Walrasian point of view in the conflict opposing the "socialism of the chair" and the "Manchester school". He observes that if one concedes that the

20 "Gabelle" are taxes on some consumer goods.

21 G. Boccardo, unpublished letter to L. Walras, 25 December 1882, preserved in the Lausanne collection under the reference F. W. II, box 7.

22 After defending a Ph.D. thesis in law at the University of Palermo, Vito Cusumano won a competition in 1869 allowing him to further his studies for two years in the history of economic thought, at the University of Pavia, under Luigi Cossa. Having subsequently obtained a scholarship for a stay in Germany, he attended the courses of Adolf Wagner and the seminar of Ernst Engel in Berlin (1871–73). After working for some time with Luigi Bodio at the Ministry of Agriculture, Industry and Commerce, he was appointed, in October 1874, lecturer in political economy at the Technical Institute of Palermo. His difficult relations with the liberal Giovanni Bruno (president of the Sicilian Society of Political Economy, local branch of the "Società Adamo Smith") would long prevent him from obtaining a chair of financial science at the University of Palermo (he would only obtain it in 1893). His main work is *Storia dei banchi della Sicilia* (1887 and 1892).

> [...] current economic order" is "artificial" rather than "*natural* and *divine*", "one must also accept that economic laws are not *natural*, one must also accept that the *current economic order* is not *the only possible one*, one must also accept *a priori* the intervention of the State .(emphasis by V. C., 15 October 1874, *Correspondence*, I, l. 309, pp. 440–41, revised from the French original, F. W., II, 8)

Finally, he communicates to his interlocutor some references on Italian economic literature related to these questions. Léon Walras attempts to provide him with some answers:

> The economic and social order, in other words, the system of organisation of industry and property is certainly artificial in the sense that it depends on us to modify it, to transform it. We are as free to direct, in applied economics and social economics, the natural tendencies inherent in social wealth, as we are free to direct, in applied mechanics, the natural properties inherent in matter. But just as, to build good machines, one must know these natural properties of matter, so too, to properly organise the economic society, one must understand the natural tendencies of social wealth. We can only command the exchange value, as with gravity, by obeying them. (20 October 1874, *Correspondence*, I, l. 311, p. 443)

Thus, Léon Walras recalls the distinction made in the *Éléments* between "pure science", related to natural facts, which includes "pure economics", and "moral and applied science", related to human, moral, and industrial facts, which encompasses "social economics" and "applied economics". He adds that the contributions of the "old political economy" from the Physiocrats to Say and the two Mill, father and son, should not be dismissed. He certainly does not favour the "Manchester school" nor the "official French school", whose only claim is "*laissez-faire, laissez-passer*", and it is "a political economy that could be taught to a parrot in a morning with a few pieces of sugar". He is also not satisfied with the "contemporary German school". The main criticism of the latter lies in the lack of elucidation of the major questions of "pure economics", such as the status of the entrepreneur, theories of ground rent, and wages. This school merely records numbers and facts through statistics and history, whereas "it is time to stop tuning the piano and start playing some music". To better explain to the young Italian his differences with the "socialism of the chair regarding method, Léon Walras sends him his lessons of 1867–68, *Recherche de l'idéal social*. Finally, he expresses the desire to learn about Italian works on the "socialism of the chair" and considers travelling to Milan and Florence to attend the congresses of the two opposing schools, if the dates are convenient for him (*op. cit.*, pp. 443–44). In a first unpublished answer, hastily written on 24 October, Vito Cusumano optimistically suggests the possibility of reconciling the viewpoints. He informs Walras of the forthcoming dispatch of the book *Sulla condizione attuale degli studi economici in Germania*[23] and some other documents (for example, the issues of the *Nuova antologia* in which the articles by Francesco Ferrara and Luigi Luzzatti were published). For now, he simply sends him the text of a lengthy letter, recently published in *L'Economista d'Italia* (Cusumano, 1874), which is more nuanced than his previous articles, particularly on the impact in Italy of the "socialism of the chair".

[23] V. Cusumano, letter to L. Walras, 24 October 1874, published for the first time hereafter, Appendix 1.

The study cites a passage from § 7 of the 2nd lesson of the *Éléments d'économie politique pure* relating to the production and distribution of social wealth, which follows a critique of the conception of political economy as exclusively a "natural science" in Jean-Baptiste Say. Vito Cusumano finds there arguments in favour of his thesis that "economic laws are neither *natural* nor *immutable*, but *historical, ethical, social* laws" (1874, pp. 555–56).[24] Walras considered this article "extremely powerful, both very moderate and very skilful" (letter to Errera, 19 November 1874, *Correspondence,* I, l. 318, p. 452).

On 3 January 1875, Vito Cusumano sends Walras a second, very well-argued response, after reading his works. He states:

> Although the *present industrial order* is artificial, it is nevertheless necessary to study its trends, in the same way that, to build good machines, we must understand the natural properties of the material. From these very reasonable economic observations supported by [Your Illustrious Lordship] and, I believe, also by the historical school of Political Economy, I draw only two consequences, namely: 1° to admit *a priori* State intervention and to justify it *a priori*; 2° not to admit *absolute* and *natural* economic *laws* in the sense of the Manchester school, but to admit some *natural laws* in the same sense in which [Your Illustrious Lordship] admit them, namely natural laws of an artificial system. (emphasis by V. C., 3 January 1875, *Correspondence,* I, l. 323, p. 461; our translation from Italian)

Thus, it is possible to find a common ground. Cusumano, who finds Walras poorly informed about recent developments in German political economy, continues in the same letter:

> German economists do not want to create a new system of Political economy, nor to develop to new theories on *profit*, on *ground rent*: they do not deny the progress that political economy has made through the British and French's works [...], they blindly follow John Stuart Mill and are somewhat admirers of *Sismondi* and of the *social school* that is *entirely French.* The dispute between the Socialists of the chair and the Manchesterians is therefore not a matter of system. Pure political economy, that of the Physiocrats and Smith remains unchanged, and the Germans have never considered destroying it. The question that divides them and others is the question of State intervention [...]. German economists want *laissez-faire* as a *rule* [...] when discussing social issues, they rejected the *absolute principle of self-help*, and opted for the intervention of the *State itself* and society in social matters [...]. While they make too much use of *figures* and *history*, it cannot be denied that figures and history are necessary in the field of applications just as no one can deny the progress achieved by statistics in this century. The best Germans support the *deductive method* in Theoretical political economy: they appreciate the value of theory, but at the same time they want to study social *facts.* Germans are idealists, like. [Your Illustrious Lordship], in *science*, and *realists* in *economic policy*

While defending himself from apologism, Vito Cusumano acknowledges that it is possible sometimes to find some exaggerations in the German economists' writings. In his view, the only way to effectively fight socialism is through "economic and legislative reforms". He specifies in this regard:

> We want the so-called *factory laws* to be introduced in Italy, which regulate the labour of children and women [...]. We want a good forestry law [...]. We want a good mining law [...].

---

[24] This issue of *L'Economista d'Italia* (1874) is preserved in the Lausanne collection under the reference F. W. XI/REV/E.

> We want [...] the State to introduce *postal savings banks* among us [...] we want the State to promote the formation of funds for the disabled, for illnesses, and old age, and to grant *legal personality* to the workers' societies in Italy. (emphasis by V. C., *op. cit.*, pp. 461–63; our translation from Italian)

Rather unusually, Walras took care to summarise the main theses of the author on a sheet.[25] It can be noted that he interprets the second consequence drawn by Vito Cusumano as "to admit only *natural* laws in *pure* economics and not in *applied* economics and *social* economics. While he is undoubtedly not convinced by all the arguments of his correspondent, he replies in a letter that

> [...] it is now quite certain that we are in perfect agreement on some of the most essential points, for example, on the fact that there are, properly speaking, *natural* laws only in *pure economics* and also on the nature and role of the State, and on the necessity of its intervention for social progress.

He also observes:

> I also adhere to all your claims in favour of laws on *manufactures*, on *forests*, on *mines*, etc. However, there remains one of the most serious questions on which I must express my reservation: the respective limits of the rational method and the historical method in political and social economy, until I have gained an exact and complete knowledge of your book. You will find, in this regard, my agreement or, if necessary, my response in my article. (emphasis by L. W., 10 February 1875, *Correspondence,* I, l. 326, p. 469)

In the same letter, Walras indeed promises to write "not just a simple bibliographical notice, but an extensive and in-depth article" on the questions raised by Cusumano's book. Such a project is considered as early as November 1874; it would be "a substantial article on the socialism of the chair that would succeed in rallying some men from both parties around a synthetic doctrine".[26]

As revealed by the dedication, Vito Cusumano will send to Walras his book *Sulla condizione attuale degli studi economici in Germania* only in the course of January 1875, requesting a review in the *Journal des économistes.* The work contains annotations on the first twenty pages, which most often serve as signposts and translations of a few words. Examining the objections raised against the first German historical school, the author states:

> In fact, its erroneous part is the tendency to limit Political Economy to the description of economic phenomena and factual conditions, and to the examination of what it is; because in this way we remove the best part of science, namely, that can be based on deductive theories, we are prevented from giving a judgment on the greater or lesser absolute rightfulness of systems, because for this purpose a higher criterion is lacking. This makes Political Economy as a kind of Statistics in the sense of Achenwall. (1873, p. 17)[27]

[25] This unpublished document, entitled "Note correspondance Cusumano", preserved in the Lausanne collection, under the reference F. W. bloc Vc, box 27 (new reference V/16/2), is published in Appendix 2.

[26] L. Walras, letter to A. Errera, 19 November 1874, in: *Correspondence*, I, l. 318, p. 452; see also the unpublished letter to A. Errera, 11 January 1875, preserved in the Lausanne collection under the reference F. W. II, box 2, and the letter to V. Cusumano, 11 January 1876, published by R. Salvo, 1979, p. 233.

[27] Our translation from Italian. Gottfried Achenwall (1719–72), professor at the University of Göttingen, is considered the inventor of the word "statistics".

In the margin of this passage, Walras humorously notes: "very well, Cusumano...". In December 1875, Vito Cusumano sends him the second entirely revised edition of this book, entitled *Le scuole economiche della Germania in rapporto alla questione sociale* (dedicated to Fedele Lampertico), asking him to kindly review it in the *Journal des économistes* and also to present it at the Société d'économie politique de Paris.[28] The work contains new developments, particularly on socialism and *Capital* by Karl Marx (Cusumano, 1875; Filippi, 1984; Spoto, 1984). The copy received by Léon Walras contains no annotations.[29] In a letter to Vito Cusumano (11 January 1876), he attempts to justify the postponement of writing a "substantial article" on the "socialism of the chair":

> I am completely absorbed, for the time being, by the preparation of my second volume of pure economics and by writing four papers I promised to Mr. Boccardo for the second volume of his *Biblioteca dell'Economista*, as well as a substantial article I wanted to dedicate to this second volume, all without prejudice to my professorial and rectoral duties.

Indeed, besides the second part of the *Éléments* and the papers of the *Théorie mathématique de la richesse sociale*, Walras is in the process of writing the study "Une branche nouvelle de la mathématique" (*cf. supra*). Moreover, the publication of a simple bibliographical notice on Cusumano's books in the *Journal des économistes* seems out of reach to him, as "the editorial team of this *Journal*, dissatisfied with the liberty of my heterodox opinions, only accepts my communications with the utmost reluctance". He cites as evidence the delay of more than six months for the insertion concerning the publication of the "Biblioteca dell'Economista". The solution would be to find another, more welcoming journal (letter to Cusumano, 11 January 1876, in: Salvo, 1979, pp. 233–34). In fact, Walras will not write the promised article on the "socialism of the chair" and the exchanges with Cusumano will never resume.

6.5 Luigi Bodio, Statistician of the Kingdom of Italy

As early as 1874, Luigi Bodio (1840–1920),[30] a statistician of international reputation, corresponds with our author. Concerning the difficulties he experiences in reading the first part of the *Éléments*, Walras indicates to him:

---

[28] V. Cusumano, letter to L. Walras, 27 December 1875, unpublished, preserved in the Lausanne collection under the reference F. W. II, box 8.

[29] The copy is preserved at the Centre d'études interdisciplinaires Walras-Pareto de l'Université de Lausanne (ZAB 14011).

[30] A stay in France in 1862 enabled L. Bodio to be in contact with Adolphe Bertillon, Frédéric Le Play and Émile Levasseur. From 1864, he taught statistics in Livorno, Milan, and Venice. Secretary of the "giunta centrale di statistica" of the Ministry of Agriculture, Industry and Commerce in 1872, he was appointed director in 1878. In 1883, he became Director General of Statistics of the Kingdom. Among his works, one can mention: *Della statistica nei suoi rapporti colla economia politica e colle altre scienze affini* (1869), *Del movimento della popolazione in Italia* (1876), *Sul movimento dell' emigrazione italiana* (1886). See notably F. Bonelli, 1969 and M. Soresina, 2001.

> In the volume that you received I have succeeded in dispensing with any recourse to infinitesimal calculus, using only the elementary formulas of function calculus and analytical geometry. To follow me, it is sufficient to know what $y = F(x)$ means. Do not be intimidated by the off-putting appearance of double indices and skip over all the paragraphs of *discussions*, focusing especially on the theorems of *maximum satisfaction* and of *general equilibrium*. In this way, you will grasp, without difficulty, the very essence of the new theory. (emphasis by L. W., 26 September 1874, *Correspondence*, I, l. 304, p. 436)

Luigi Bodio remains somewhat sceptical about his correspondent's use of mathematics; three years later, he observes:

> I do not believe, in truth, that social phenomena always lend themselves to mathematical analysis because they are excessively complex, and it is not easy to isolate their determining causes. Nevertheless, the mathematical method has this particular advantage, that it sometimes reveals the falsity of certain deductions, which, in common language, remain concealed under phrases. (16 May 1877, *Correspondence*, I, l. 378, p. 534)

Upon receiving the "Théorie mathématique du billet de banque", he writes to Walras:

> Your works are always the products of a high intelligence, but your studies would have even greater interest if you would step out of the realm of abstraction and apply your formulas to the rich material provided by the bank statistics, etc.[31]

Our author replies a few months later, thanking him for sending statistical studies on banks related to different countries: "I found that you were perfectly right; and consequently, I promised my friend Mr. Tallichet, Director of the *Bibliothèque universelle* an article on *the regime of issuing banks in the main countries of Europe and the United States*".[32]

This project will never be realised. Suffering from a cerebral fatigue he calls, at the time, "cerebro-cardiac neurosis", Walras is forced to request a leave from the Academy of Lausanne for the winter semester of 1882–83. He decides to undertake a trip to Rome with his daughter Aline, in the first quarter of the following year. This stay is intended to enable him to meet his Italian correspondents and friends, as well as to "prepare a good reception" in Italy for his *Théorie mathématique de la richesse sociale* (letter to G.-A. Zanon, 25 December 1882, *Correspondence*, I, l. 543, p. 736). The Roman stay takes place in February and March 1883. While there, Walras negotiates the distribution in Italy of the *Théorie mathématique de la richesse sociale* (which will be released in June 1883), with the bookseller-publisher Ermanno Loecher. After his return to Lausanne, he will be able to send him a list of 46 names for a free distribution of the book (30 May 1883, *Correspondence*, I, l. 551, p. 751). Walras entrusts the young Achille Sinigaglia (a mathematician introduced to him by Luigi Perozzo, inspector at the Direction of Statistics) with seeking potential

---

[31] L. Bodio, unpublished letter to L. Walras, 6 July 1880, preserved in the Lausanne collection under the reference F. W. II, box 7.

[32] Emphasis by L. W., unpublished letter to L. Bodio, 9 February 1881, preserved in the Lausanne collection under the reference F. W. I, box 1. The table of contents of the *Cours d'économie politique appliquée* includes lessons on these themes: 45th ("History of the Bank of England"), 46th ("History of the Banks of Scotland"), 47th ("History of Banks on the European Continent") and 48th ("History of Banks in the United States"). Only the 45th lesson was drafted (vol. XII, pp. 652–60).

reviewers. However, several review projects will not come to fruition, including those of Carlo-Francesco Ferraris in *Il Diritto*, of Luigi Perozzo in the *Archivio di statistica*, of Giuseppe Ricca-Salerno in the *Rivista critica*, and of Bonaldo Stringher in the *Nuova antologia*. These difficulties can partly be explained by the fact that the *Théorie mathématique de la richesse sociale* is already known in its version in four memoirs by Boccardo's translation, and the presence in the French edition of three additional studies (on banknotes, bimetallism, and the repurchase of land by the State) hardly rekindles interest in our author's research. In Rome, Walras multiplies contacts and meetings: Luigi Bodio, Luigi Perozzo, Alessandro Messedaglia, but also Francesco Ferrara and Agostino Magliani, Minister of Finance. He is also invited by the Minister of Agriculture, Industry and Commerce, Domenico Berti.[33] Finally, Luigi Bodio, Luigi Perozzo and Ranieri Simonelli (Secretary General of the Ministry of Agriculture, Industry and Commerce) decide to offer Léon Walras a banquet in his honour, with politicians and economists.[34] The latter discusses with the Italian statisticians the possibilities of applying his system of "gold money with regulating silver token (*monnaie d'or avec billon d'argent régulateur*)", already outlined at the end of the "Théorie mathématique du bimétallisme". Luigi Bodio and Luigi Perozzo will provide him for this purpose with "unpublished price statistics" (1884, vol. X, p. 15, English transl., 2005, p. 11). In 1885–86, Léon Walras will attempt to interest his statistician friends in the development of price indices, but without tangible success.

In June 1885, at the initiative of the British "Statistical Society", the International Statistical Institute was founded, presided over by Rawson William Rawson; Luigi Bodio is the secretary general. This association is composed of "honorary members", "members", and finally "associates", whose initial lists are established during the founding assembly in London. Among the "honorary members", we find the following names: Gerolamo Boccardo, Ernst Engel, Francesco Ferrara, H. G. J. Goschen, Paul Leroy-Beaulieu, Agostino Magliani, Wilhelm Roscher, and Léon Say. Among the ordinary "members", the presence of Luigi Bodio, Émile Cheysson, Alfred de Foville, Robert Giffen, Georg-Friedrich Knapp, Émile Levasseur, Wilhelm Lexis, Luigi Luzzatti and Angelo Messedaglia is noted. Finally, among the "associates", the following names are found: Richard T. Ely, Clément Juglar (promoted to member in 1886), Étienne Laspeyres, James L. Laughlin, Gustave de Molinari, Luigi Perozzo, Nicolaas G. Pierson, Gustav Schmoller, and Adolf Wagner. In the spring of 1886, Walras learns that his name will be proposed on the list of "associates" at the first session of the Institute, which is to be held in September, in Rome (R. W. Rawson to L. Walras, 19 May 1886, *Correspondence*, I, l. 714, p. 121). The latter,

[33] L. Walras had sent him the "Théorie mathématique du bimétallisme" (see the letter of Minister Berti to L. Walras, 30 December 1882, unpublished, preserved in the Lausanne collection under the reference F. W. II, box 7).

[34] This banquet took place on 9 March 1883 at the "Caffè di Roma". It brought together, around L. Walras notably, Marco Minghetti, Quintino Sella (former ministers), Alessandro Messedaglia, Achille Sinigaglia, Bonaldo Stringher. At the end of the dinner, L. Walras had to make a "quick presentation of the essentials of [his] economic and social doctrine" (letter to G. Maugin, 16 March 1883, in: *Correspondence*, I, l. 547, p. 744).

"very honoured and very happy" with the proposal, considers participating in the Roman meeting and possibly presenting a communication on questions "related to the determination of the formula for the average price of social wealth in currency, the construction of the curve of variation of this average price, the determination of the modes of action to be exerted on this curve" (letter to L. Bodio, 17 June 1886, *Correspondence*, I, l. 725, p. 134), themes discussed in the third part of the *Théorie de la monnaie* ("Statistical Desiderata"). Initially, Luigi Bodio sees no objection to this project and invites Walras to submit "twenty pages to be printed in the next issue of the Bulletin" of the Institute, which is to appear before the Rome Congress. Walras accepts the proposal, but encounters reluctance from the president of the institute. Indeed, R. W. Rawson fears that the article and the public presentation would remain at the level of mathematical economics and would not be supported by statistical data (L. Bodio to Walras, 27 June 1886, *Correspondence*, I, l. 729, pp. 136–37). Very displeased, Walras then decides to withdraw his communication proposal and refrains from sending the twenty pages; he points out to his Italian friend that the president's position towards him is in blatant contradiction with the statutes of the Institute and he recalls that his work would have been situated in the field of "theoretical statistics", just like a recent work by Émile Cheysson, published in the same *Bulletin* (29 June 1886, *Correspondence*, I, l. 730, pp. 137–38). Luigi Bodio thanks him for his candour and observes that, in fact, not yet being elected as an "associate", he cannot present a communication in Rome: "therefore, only the publication of your proposals in the Bulletin remains", in a form accessible to non-mathematicians and using "official statistics on money, prices, productions, etc". (2 July 1886, *Correspondence*, I, l. 732, pp. 140–41). However, Walras considers that, not being able to present a communication, any publication in the *Bulletin* is now useless. He sees in this episode a sneaky action by the orthodox French liberal school, "narrower, more intolerant, more tyrannical than the Inquisition of the Holy Office", after the publication of the first two parts of the *Théorie de la monnaie* (5 July 1886, *Correspondence*, I, l. 733, pp. 141–42). On the substance of the matter, he notes that his Italian friend is "completely aligned with this view of your President according to which the importance of a curve can only be pointed out to the Institute when it has been constructed on real data"; he adds:

> I do not want to be difficult with you. Therefore, although an economist and not a statistician, although proposed as an *associate* and not as a *member* of the Institute, I will try to conform to this programme. However [...] I do not give up on theoretically posing, before undertaking to solve it practically, the problem of the statistical regulation of the value of money in a short work such as the one you had asked me for. (emphasis by L. W., 9 July 1886, *Correspondence*, I, l. 735, p. 143)

Due to a cholera epidemic, the first session of the International Statistical Institute will be postponed to April 1887. In the meantime, the association's board proceeds with the vote of the new "associates". Thus, the following names are noted: Ludwig-Josef Brentano, Hector Denis, Arthur T. Hadley, Maffeo Pantaleoni and Léon Walras. Informed of his election, Walras initially considers presenting the content of the third part of the *Théorie de la monnaie* at the Rome session, in front of a few colleagues. He decides shortly after to also communicate a work entitled "Étude de deux courbes réelles de variation du prix moyen d'un certain nombre de marchandises" (vol. X, Appendix II, pp. 519–27). On 5 April 1887, he leaves Lausanne to travel to Rome, but at the Turin stage, suffering from nervous troubles, he decides to abandon the journey (letter to L. Bodio, 19 April 1887, *Correspondence,* l. 796, p. 207).

6.6 Other Episodic Relations

Two prominent members of the "Lombard-Venetian school" did not enter into regular correspondence with Walras: Fedele Lampertico[35] and Alessandro Messedaglia.[36] The near absence of epistolary exchanges with Lampertico is all the more curious as he is one of the few theorists of the school, particularly through the series published between 1874 and 1884, under the title *Economia dei popoli e degli stati,* in five volumes (*Introduzione, Il lavoro, La proprietà, Il commercio, Il credito*), some of which he had sent to Léon Walras. The first volume, *Introduzione,* published in 1874, gives in particular an overview of the "school"'s methodological conceptions (see S. Chiecchi, 1976 and R. Camurri, 1992).

From 1874, Walras established contact with Alessandro Messedaglia, but the latter does not appear to react to his invitation (A. Borghini, 1999, p. 246). Later, during his stay in Rome in March 1883, Messedaglia promises to present a report on his work at the prestigious "Accademia Reale dei Lincei", of which he is an associate member. In this perspective, Walras sends him a copy of the *Théorie mathématique de la richesse sociale* in seven memoirs.[37] In reality, the promised communication never takes place (A. Borghini, 1999, p. 249). Undoubtedly, Messedaglia is reticent towards the Walrasian theoretical approach. Indeed, in a letter to his friend Luigi Bodio, dated 12 March 1890, he observes that the use of mathematics in economics can be useful provided that the data, hypotheses, and laws are based beforehand on experience. He adds:

> It is important, in my opinion, to have first of all an Economy of observation or experimental economy as we like to say, and it is only on this basis that a mathematical economy can be built. So much the better if we make progress jointly and at the same time, with the necessary precautions, but never the second without the first, a mathematical economy that stands in a certain way its own. (G. Pietra, 1936–37, p. 345, our translation from Italian)

---

[35] Fedele Lampertico (1833–1906), professor at the University of Padua, was a deputy from 1866 to 1870 and a senator from 1873.

[36] Alessandro Messedaglia (1820–1901). He taught political economy and statistics at the University of Padua from 1858, then at that of Rome from 1870. In particular, he trained the staff in the Direction of Statistics. Furthermore, he was a deputy (1866–83), then a senator from 1884. See notably A. Pellanda, 1984 and V. Gioia and S. Noto, 2011.

[37] L. Walras, unpublished letters to L. Bodio of 17 April, to G. Boccardo of 3 July, and to A. Messedaglia of 3 July 1883, preserved in the Lausanne collection under the reference F. W. I, boxes 1 and 4.

By implicitly referring to the "Théorie mathématique du bimétallisme" (included in the *Théorie mathématique de la richesse sociale*), he reproaches Walras for postulating that gold or silver metal passes indifferently from the currency to industry and vice versa, which is contrary to the observation of facts (*op. cit.*, p. 345).

Luigi Cossa (1831–96),[38] a professor at the University of Pavia, was introduced to Léon Walras by Alberto Errera. In February 1877, upon receiving the memoir on the "Équations de la capitalisation", he writes to Walras:

> Although unfortunately in no way involved in differential and integral calculus, and thereby inclined to believe that mathematics serve more to express in a brief and elegant language truths that can be reached by other means, than to discover new truths, I try to benefit as much as possible from your excellent works which I have always read with profit, even with the publication of your *Éléments.*

Luigi Cossa sends in return the very recent 3rd edition of his *Primi elementi di economia politica* (which he also intends to send to Jevons), in the hope of obtaining a favourable echo in the Walrasian writings (20 February 1877, *Correspondence,* I, l. 374, pp. 529–530). Walras gives him a courteous reply, advising him to read the article "Un nuovo ramo della matematica".[39] Following the reception of the 5th edition (1881) and then the 6th edition (1883) of *Primi elementi di economia politica,* Walras finally promised a review in the *Journal des économistes* or in the *Bibliothèque universelle et Revue suisse.*[40] He would honour his promise only in 1885, with a very diplomatic review of two books by Cossa, *Primi elementi di scienza delle finanze* (3rd ed., 1882), and *Primi elementi di economia politica* (1885b). Tasked by Charles Gide with recruiting collaborators or correspondents abroad for the *Revue d'économie politique*, Walras would approach Luigi Cossa.[41]

Léon Walras also establishes a relationship with Achille Loria (1857–1943). Trained in the positivism of Roberto Ardigò, this economist is a student, in Pavia, of Luigi Cossa, Carlo-Francesco Ferraris, and Giuseppe Ricca-Salerno. He also attends Adolf Wagner's lectures in Berlin. In 1882, he makes contact in London with William Stanley Jevons and Friedrich Engels. In 1883, he writes the famous obituary article "Karl Marx" for the *Nuova antologia,* which would introduce the author of *Capital* to Italian intellectuals (see R. Faucci, 1976–77, J.-P. Potier, 1986, M. Varejão, 1997 and A. d'Orsi, 2000).

---

[38] A student of L. Von Stein in Vienna and Wilhelm Roscher in Leipzig, L. Cossa obtained a doctorate in law at the University of Pavia in 1853. He taught at this university since 1858. Among his works, one can cite *Guida allo studio dell' economia politica,* Milan: Hoepli, 1876, 3rd ed., 1892, under the title, *Introduzione allo studio dell' economia politica,* English translation by Louis Dyer, *Introduction to the Study of Political Economy*, London: Macmillan, 1893. See notably L. Dal Pane, 1963, S. Chiecchi, 1971 and R. Faucci, 1984.

[39] L. Walras, letter to L. Cossa, 25 February 1877, unpublished, preserved in the Lausanne collection under the reference F. W. I, box 2.

[40] L. Walras, letter to L. Cossa, 4 July 1883, unpublished, preserved in the Lausanne collection under the reference F. W. I, box 2.

[41] L. Walras, letter to L. Cossa, 25 December 1886, unpublished, preserved in the Lausanne collection under the reference F. W. I, box 2.

The same year, Achille Sinigaglia advises Walras to propose a review of the *Théorie mathématique de la richesse sociale* to Loria, author of *La rendita fondiaria e la sua elisione naturale* (1880). So Walras sends a letter to the economist of Mantua (4 July 1883, *Correspondence,* l. 571, pp. 775–76). In his book, Achille Loria was captivated by the "theory of multiple prices" of the author of the *Éléments,* provided it was applied not only to the case of pure monopoly but also to situations of market imperfection and even to "free competition". Moreover, he criticised the theories of land nationalisation, defending, for his part, an original form of agrarian socialism, based on a kind of sharecropping, called "mixed association". In his acceptance letter, Achille Loria announces the sending of his work (It will be dedicated "to my eminent colleague Léon Walras"), and recalls his interest in the "theory of multiple prices", and his disagreement on the repurchase of land by the State. He also declares himself a disciple of Jevons and supports without hesitation: "I hope you will find that I have completely aligned myself with the economists of the mathematical school, of which you, Sir, are the leader and theorist" (12 August 1883, *Correspondence,* I, l. 584, p. 784).

Faced with such claims, Walras's surprise is not insignificant. He immediately retorts to Achille Loria : "You claim to be a student of Jevons and you refer, for your conclusions, to theories (notably that of the cost of production) that this great mind thought he had completely demolished, as indeed, in my opinion, he had done." However, he promises to write "a few lines" on *La rendita fondiaria e la sua elisione naturale* (27 September 1883, *Correspondence,* I, l. 585, p. 785).

In the passage of the review of the *Théorie mathématique de la richesse sociale,* dedicated to the "Théorie mathématique du prix des terres et de leur rachat par l'État", Achille Loria laments the rejection of the Ricardian theory of rent and, quoting the Walrasian statement according to which "the pure and applied moral and political sciences, as they stand now, are only meaningless babble" (1881b, vol. IX, p. 306, English transl., 2010, p. 244 or *Théorie mathématique de la richesse sociale*, vol. XI, p. 277), he concludes: "I agree: but it could not possibly be also by chance a *mathematical babble* (*bavardage mathématique*)?"[42]

6.7 Conclusion

Thanks to Alberto Errera and Gerolamo Boccardo's efforts, Léon Walras was able to establish a very dense network of correspondents in Italy and even extend it over the years 1870–80. Consequently, he found himself in direct contact with the leading economists of the peninsula. The penetration of writings on pure economics was a success, compared to attempts made towards England and Germany during the same period. The document reproduced in Appendix 2, in Walras's own hand,

---

[42] Emphasis by A. L., "L. Walras—*Théorie mathématique de la richesse sociale*", *Rivista critica delle scienze giuridiche e sociali,* no.10, October 1883, pp. 311–13, reissued in: P. Bridel, 1996, pp. 213–14.

reconstructs the stages of the initial dissemination of pure economics in Italy through correspondence; although it mainly concerns the year 1874, it is very significant in this regard. However, such a strategy encountered some limits. Firstly, it can be noted that the dissemination of Walrasian thought is confined to this field. Contributions in the areas of "applied economics" (for example, the monetary question) and "social economics" (the repurchase of land by the State) received little attention in the peninsula. Furthermore, the dissemination of "pure economics" was the task of eclectic economists rather than true disciples. While they show an interest in the application of mathematics to economics, they never perceive the theoretical significance of marginalism and of general economic equilibrium. Moreover, Walras, harbours few illusions about the analytical capabilities of correspondents such as Alberto Errera and Gerolamo Boccardo. However, it should also be noted that as early as 1874, Léon Walras did not hesitate to let William Stanley Jevons benefit from his Italian network, whose promotion of writings would be ensured by Gerolamo Boccardo and Luigi Cossa. The first great theorist of Italian marginalism, Maffeo Pantaleoni, would follow in the footsteps of Jevons rather than those of Walras (P. Barucci, 1980, p. 80).

Appendix 1: Letter from Vito Cusumano to Léon Walras

Rome, 24 October 1874[43]

Dearest Professor,

You, most kind Professor, in responding so promptly to my letter and to the observations I had made to you regarding the *current economic order*, have shown yourself to be a noble-minded and most kind gentleman. Since I must leave today for Palermo, where I have been appointed Professor of Political Economy, I refrain from responding to your learned letter in *a forthcoming from me*, although I already recognise that we could easily reconcile our economic opinions.

I hope to send you my work *Sulla condizione attuale degli studi economici in Germania* (which was already published in articles in the journal, *Archivio giuridico*, July, August, September–October 1873 and February 1874). In it, there is an extensive account of the principles of the *socialists of the chair*, regarding State intervention in economic matters, the *realism* in science (method), the *ethical element* in Political Economy, *property* and *liberty*, and, finally, the principle of *income* (seeing Hermann) in Science of Finance. My work was considered *faithful* and *impartial* by the Germans themselves.[44] I studied Political Economy in Berlin with *Wagner* and *Engel*, and I was a member of the 1st Congress of German economists in Eisenach.

[43] Unpublished letter preserved in the Lausanne collection under the reference F. W. II, box 8. Emphasis by V. C. Our translation from Italian.

[44] The work will be translated into German under the title: *Ueber die gegenwärtige Lage der volkswirtschaftlichen Studien in Deutschland*, with preface and appendix by S. Emele, Sigmaringen, 1881.

I also hope to send you the issues of the *Nuova Antologia*, where the articles of *Ferrara* and *Luzzatti*[45] are found because this morning the Director[46] of this journal promised them to me. In the twenty-first issue of the aforementioned journal, an article by *Boccardo*, against my economic opinions, will be published.

The Congress of Milan will take place in November as Senator Lampertico writes to me: but the day has not yet been set.[47] If you wish to write about the current economic movement in Italy, I can provide you with books and publications, asking you to return them to me as soon as you have read them, because I have only one *copy*.

Along with this letter of mine, you will receive an issue of the *Economista d'Italia*, in which one of my articles is found.[48] *L'Economista* of Florence, the organ of the *A. Smith* Society, which is opposed to us, has been publishing last month articles against us: You could obtain it; for the *Economista d'Italia* I will always send it myself.

The Italian Reformers are Cossa, Lampertico, Scialoja, Montanari, Errera, Toniolo, Lo Savio[49] and a few others. There are also other professors of *related* sciences who have joined our society and who will write on such topics.

In my article inserted in the *Econ[omista] d'Italia*, I cite your work:[50] the article, however, was not yet published when your letter reached me. In any case, I will have the honour of making your learned work known to the Italians, from the reading of which they will derive great benefit. In the book on *Socialism*, that is to say on the *question of the individual and the State* (for which I thank you so much),[51] I will certainly find a mine of beautiful and learned observations, which are all the more dear to me, as they will greatly facilitate the part of my work (2nd edition) that deals with *modern Socialism* in Germany. From the 2nd edition of my work speaks 1° of the exchanged books; 2° of the academic socialists; 3° of the conservatives; 4° of the socialists of Germany. The title of the book (a volume of 350 pages) will be *Le scuole economiche della Germania in rapporto alla questione sociale.*

My address is in *Palermo* (Sicily). Meanwhile, accept, learned Professor, the sentiments of devotion and profound esteem.

Of the most devoted friend

Vito Cusumano

P.S. I will keep Your Most Illustrious Lordship informed of the day on which the Congress of Milan will be held.[52] I have been informed that Wolowski intends to

---

[45] F. Ferrara, 1874 and L. Luzzatti, 1874.

[46] Francesco Protonotari.

[47] In fact, it will take place from 4 to 6 January 1875.

[48] See V. Cusumano, 1874.

[49] Nicolò Lo Savio, statistician, professor of political economy at the University of Bari, collaborator of the *Giornale degli economisti.*

[50] See L. Walras, letter to V. Cusumano, 10 February 1875, in: *Correspondence*, I, l. 326, pp. 468–69 and note 7.

[51] *Recherche de l'idéal social. Leçons publiques faites à Paris. Première série (1867–68),* Paris: Guillaumin/Agence générale de librairie des auteurs et compositeurs, 1868 (vol. IX).

[52] A. Errera will convey information to L. Walras regarding the Milan Congress.

write on the current economic issues raised in Italy.[53] My friend *Bodio* has sent him materials in this regard. However, you will be able to receive many from me and from my friend *Errera*, who sends his regards to you.

Appendix 2: "Note correspondence Cusumano"[54]

Owed me a letter.

Have I received the Nuova Antologia ?[55]

Sent me the *Economista d'Italia.*[56] Will send me his book, *Le scuole economiche della Germania in rapporto alla questione sociale.*[57]

Read me. Draws 2 conclusions:

1° to admit and justify a priori the intervention of the State.
2° to admit only *natural* laws in pure economics and not in *applied* economics and *social* economics.

Applied economics, facts and conditions divided by places and times. *If* and *when* should intervene the State.

I am poorly informed about the current trends and aspirations of German economists.

They do not wish to create a new system of political economy. They follow Sismondi more than Mill.

The question between the socialists of the chair and the Manchesterians is not a question of system.

Pure economics remains the same, and the Germans have not undertaken to destroy it.

The question is that of State intervention, one of the main scientific questions, but not a questioning of the entire system. They want *laissez-faire* as a rule.

The origin of this struggle born in Germany and spreading across Europe proves that it concerns *questions of science*, but not the *entirety of science*. The German economists, in discussing social questions, reject the *absolute principle of self-help*, decide on intervention of the State and of society in the social question. Figures, history, necessary on the ground of application. Progress achieved through statistics.

---

[53] See "Le questioni economiche in Italia giudicate dal Wolowsky", *L'Economista d'Italia*, 24 November 1874.

[54] This note titled thus by L. Walras is written after receiving V. Cusumano's letter dated 3 January 1875 (*Correspondence*, I, l. 323, pp. 460–64). Emphasis by L. W.

[55] In his letter, V. Cusumano wonders if Walras has indeed received the issues of the *Nuova Antologia* which contain the articles by F. Ferrara and L. Luzzatti on the "economic Germanism in Italy".

[56] See V. Cusumano, "Lo Smithianismo, i riformisti, e i socialisti cattedratici", *L'Economista d'Italia*, vol. 6, no. 43, 25 October 1874, pp. 554–56.

[57] V. Cusumano, *Le scuole economiche della Germania in rapporto alla questione sociale—Studii*, Naples: G. Marghieri, 1875.

They support the *deductive method* in theoretical political economy, but also wish to study the facts.

Idealists in science and *realists* in politics.

He[58] does not make an apology for the Germans. But just as in philosophy of law he cannot support Rousseau and Kant's individualism—nor *economic individualism.* What is being discussed between the German and French economists is a question of philosophy of law. France. Sismondi.

French socialism, to make reforms! England, Cairnes, Fawcett, Newmarch.

Italy, exclusively agricultural. Congress of Milan. To introduce the *factory laws*, child and women labour, compulsory education. Laws on *forests*, floods. Laws on *mines*, property above and below. Property and labour. *Savings* bank, *retirement* fund. Legal personality for workers' associations.

According to Ferrara, Italy is ruined.

He has read me. He will send me his work shortly. He deals with:

1° The German school of free trade.
2° The so-called [school of the] *socialists of the chair*.
3° The social conservatives.
4° The socialists. Socialism in Germany from Fichte to the present day.

He will send me *On the Current Condition of Economic Studies in Germany.*

P.S. The Congress will take place on 4th, 5th, 6th January.[59]

Appendix 3: Stages of the First Diffusion of Pure Economics in Italy Through the Correspondence, Summarised by Léon Walras[60]

[*Letters sent*]	1874	[*Letters received*]
	March	
12: Marc Monnier		13: Marc Monnier
		23: A. Errera
25: A. Errera		
	April	

(continued)

[58] V. Cusumano.

[59] The Milan Congress is held from 4 to 6 January 1875.

[60] This sheet is preserved in the Lausanne collection, under the reference F. W. V, II 18. L. Walras noted on the left and right, respectively, the letters he sent and those he received. He retained here only the correspondence relating to the strategy of disseminating his writings. Seven letters are not published in the collection of W. Jaffé. Among these, we have found in the Lausanne collection the letters of L. Walras to A. Errera dated 19 August and 10 October 1874 as well as the letter of L. Walras to A. Basile dated 26 October and the reply from the latter dated 2 November 1874.

(continued)

[*Letters sent*]	1874	[*Letters received*]
1: A. Errera		8: A. Errera
13: A. Errera		
14: (Montanari, Cossa, Lampertico)		21: A. Errera (sends me a testimony from Boccardo, Cossa, Cassani, Zambelli)
25: A. Errera		27: A. Errera (Ex. Zanon)[a] sends me a testimony from Bodio [a] See note 6.
	May	
		4: d'Aulnis de Bourouill
5: A. Errera		
9: d'Aulnis de Bourouill		12: W. Stanley Jevons
23:W. Stanley Jevons		
	June	
2: A. Errera (I send him the correspondence with Jevons		17: A. Errera
	July	
29: A. Errera (I acknowledge receipt of the *Rivista europea*; I send him 2 copies of the *Éléments*, one for Zanon		31: A. Errera (indicates to me V. Cusumano)
	August	
5: A. Errera (I send him a summary of the *Éléments*		9: A. Errera
		11: Bodio (recommends to me Messedaglia and Ferrara
19: A. Errera		
	September	
26: Bodio		
	October	
10: A. Errera (I acknowledge him receipt of *L'Economista d'Italia*; I communicate to him my Bibliography for the *Journal des économistes*)		15: A. Errera—V. Cusumano
20: V. Cusumano		
26: A. Basile		
	November	
		2: A. Basile

(continued)

(continued)

[Letters sent]	1874	*[Letters received]*
19: A. Errera (the Bibliography appeared in the *Journal deséconomistes*; I acknowledge receipt of 2 issues of *L'Economista d'Italia*)		
	December	
		4: A. Errera
		30: Boccardo (sends me the General Introduction to the *Biblioteca dell'Economista*; asks me for authorisation to reproduce the *Éléments*)
	1875	
	January	
3: Boccardo		
	October	
4: A. Errera. I return to him the manuscript of the work of Zambelli		

Chapter 7
The Reception of Pure Economics in France (1873–1926)

7.1 Introduction

A few months before Léon Walras's death, on 10 June 1909, a ceremony of his *Jubilée cinquantenaire d'économiste* took place at Lausanne University. On this occasion, a group of French economists paid homage to him at this university. In this text, one can notably read:

> Mr. Walras became yours indeed, with such signs that in much of treaties on political economy he is called the Swiss economist[1] and that this monument has been erected in honour of the founder of the Lausanne School [...]. Perhaps, however, Mr. Walras left France too early to have had time to establish a school there. Mr. Walras' predecessor, Cournot, who had been forgotten, returned to the limelight. It is true that he was only recognised after his death! However, Mr. Walras would have already found disciples and a more favourable public opinion whose his presence would have accentuated the value. How would it be possible that the French mind, so enthusiast of clearness, unity and logic, had not been attracted—from the day when it would have understood it—by the beautiful arrangement of Walras's economic system, this system which embraces the whole economic world and in which the same formula combines the price of all products and the value of all services? It has been compared to Kepler's system, but is it not Kepler who said that, since God had waited 6000 years for a man to understand him, he himself could well wait a few centuries to be understood? Mr. Walras will not have to wait so long. Here already is the day when posterity crowns him, living, with the laurel that it usually only bestows upon the dead.[2]

[1] Note that F. Y. Edgeworth names Walras "the Swiss Jevons" (1891, p. 23).

[2] University of Lausanne. Walras Jubilee, 1909, pp. 43–44 and *Correspondence*, III, l. 1745, Annex, p. 410. The signatories of this tribute are not all economists. Here is the list: Émile Levasseur, Alfred de Foville, Clément Colson, André Liesse, Charles Andler, Georges Renard, Charles Gide, Auguste Souchon, Alfred Bonnet, François Simiand, Adolphe Landry, Albert Aupetit, Auguste Dubois, François Sauvaire-Jourdan, Paul Pic, Charles Brouilhet, Émile Bouvier, Charles Rist, and Émile Chatelain.

J.-P. Potier, *Léon Walras, Economist and Liberal Socialist*, Springer Studies in the History of Economic Thought, https://doi.org/10.1007/978-3-032-04670-3_7

This astonishing text is the result of a compromise between the signatories. Indeed, Charles Gide had drafted a first version which had to be expurgated of several passages to secure the agreement of the economists of the liberal school.[3]

Charles Gide spared no effort to make Walras's work known in France, as we shall see later. Our author will even receive the support of his close friend, the socialist Georges Renard (1847–1930), with an article entitled "Un économiste socialiste", which summarises the different facets of his work and describes the author as the "French Karl Marx", encountering a wall of silence from the "appointed guardians of the official science", from the "optimistic, immobilist school, the school of *nothing to be done*".[4]

Therefore, this chapter examines the reception in France of Walrasian pure economics. Our study of the main representative authors will cover the period 1873–1926, from the reactions to the presentation at the Académie des sciences morales et politiques in Paris of the "Principe d'une théorie mathématique de l'échange" to the publication of the 5th (definitive) edition of the *Éléments.* Our approach will not be strictly chronological. It seems, indeed, more interesting to study the different groups and sub-groups of Walras's readers by taking into account their institutional situation. We will classify the emblematic authors into three distinct groups: first the critics, then the allies and the "sympathisers" of pure economics, and finally the disciples of Walras.

7.2 Criticism of the Walrasian Pure Economics

Within this first group of Walras's readers, we will distinguish several categories of critics: those of the liberal school, those of law's professors, in favour of State interventionism, those of the mathematicians, and finally those of the engineers–economists.

7.2.1 Criticism of the Liberal School: Émile Levasseur and the Others

The hostility of the French liberal school towards Walrasian pure economics remained very sharp during the last quarter of the XIXth century.[5] Even before the publication

[3] As C. Gide explains to Walras in his letter of 20 June 1909 (*Correspondence*, III, l. 1764, pp. 427–28). In his letter, Gide attaches, confidentially, the original text with the indication of the deleted passages. Unfortunately, this document has never been found in the Walras collection in Lausanne.

[4] Emphasis by G. R., "Un économiste socialiste", *La petite République française*, 18th year, n°6416, 7 November 1893, re-ed. in: P. Bridel, 1996, pp. 379–82. This text will be completely approved by Walras.

[5] See Y. Breton, 1986 and 1992; A. Zylberberg, 1990, Chap. III.

of the first part of the *Éléments d'économie politique pure* (1874d), Léon Walras presents a communication, "Principe d'une théorie mathématique de l'échange", on 16 and 23 August 1873, before the Académie des sciences morales et politiques in Paris. The content of the text is centred on the theory of exchange of two commodities for each other and will find its place in section II of the *Éléments d'économie politique pure* ("Mathematical Theory of exchange"). Contrary to usual belief, the economists of the liberal school who will respond to Walras's presentation are not the most orthodox. Indeed, Émile Levasseur (1828–1911)[6] and Louis Wolowski (1810–76),[7] both of whom are proponents of the historical method in economics, view the State as a regulator and promoter of economic and social progress (see C. Silvant, 2010). The reactions to Walras's performance come almost exclusively from Levasseur.[8] Indeed, the latter presents several objections to which Walras responds in his own way and freely in his "Notes d'humeur". First of all, Levasseur indicates that the author has used geometry to present his mathematical theory of exchange. However, the intensity of the buyer's desire for a given commodity is not susceptible to an "exact measure":

> Mr. Walras is the first to acknowledge that, in mathematical operations, the results are only as good as the data. However, his data are, so to speak, incommensurable; hence it follows that his curves are unfounded, I add, not very solid, are false, dangerous, because they make one believe that one possesses the precise and mathematical expression of a fact [...]. (vol. VII, p. 530)

In his "Notes d'humeur", Walras reacts at this point: "Mr. L[evasseur] should be asked to study mathematics. He would learn to distinguish between *incommensurable* quantities and *non-appreciable* quantities. Mr. L[evasseur] means that non-appreciable quantities escape calculation, which is inaccurate [...]." (emphasis by L. W., vol. XIII, p. 534)

Levasseur continues by stating:

> The fluctuations of need, whether rising or falling, depend on circumstances, and one gets a much more accurate idea by thought than by the author's mathematical formulas. The intensity of need is a contingent fact, eminently variable like the multiple causes that produce it. (vol. VII, p. 530)

Here, Walras finds that his critic "is not very demanding in terms of accuracy of ideas". Levasseur also recalls that Auguste Walras had published a book on the theory of value, basing it solely on *rareté* (scarcity) and that his son supports the same thesis (in fact, he confuses the father's theory with that of his son). However, the *rareté* ("a defect that human industry precisely aims to correct by creating abundance") is not the only cause of value. To this, "two other elements must be added, which are utility and labour" (vol. VII, p. 531). Walras reacts to these statements as follows:

> The question of labour, of cost price, of production costs is naturally reserved for the second of the two problems of pure economics. As for utility, if Mr. L[evasseur] would kindly peruse

[6] On É. Levasseur, see *infra* Chap. 11, *Ideas and Men: Criticism of the French "Liberal School"*.

[7] On L. Wolowski, see M. Lutfalla, 1991, P. Markiewicz, 1994 and J.-P. Potier, 2016, pp. 25–26.

[8] Levasseur's objections to the Walrasian approach are studied by T. M. Mueller, 2017, pp. 450–55.

> my father's book, which he has obviously never opened, he would know that for my father, utility is contained by definition in *rareté* (scarcity). And if Mr. L[evasseur] would kindly examine my paper, which he has obviously not opened, he would see that one of the main points in this paper is the study of utility, its mathematical expression, the investigation of its influence on price [...]. It is to engage in a vicious circle to explain oneself with people who judge and refute you without even knowing what you have said. (vol. XIII, p. 534)[9]

Finally, in his intervention, Levasseur insists on the danger of reducing complex things to unity and applying mathematics to economics, an order of.

> [...] phenomena whose causes are so variable, so complex and in which intervenes above all this eminently variable and irreducible cause in algebraic formula: human liberty. In most cases where the moral sciences can employ it, the geometrical method or rather the graphical method is useful as a means of demonstration much more than as a research instrument." (vol. VII, pp. 531–32)

On this point, Walras's reaction is even harder:

> What a type! The cretin of the Institute. The gentleman with the *rosette* of the *Légion d'honneur* holding fourteen positions, knowing not a word of psychology or mathematics, who tells you that '*human liberty cannot be put into an equation!*'. (emphasis by L. W., vol. XIII, p. 533)

He also observes that Levasseur admitted earlier in his intervention the construction of curves of birth and mortality statistics, areas where human liberty indeed exerts its influence (*op. cit.*, pp. 534–35).[10]

For his part, at the end of the session, Louis Wolowski approves Levasseur's remarks and finds that Walras claims to make political economy an "exact science" and thus to misunderstand its true character, "a moral science, which has as its starting point and aim man" (vol. VII, p. 532). In his "Notes d'humeur", Walras responds here with humour: "Well, well! Here are some truths. Would Mr. W[olowski] tell us what a moral science is? *The one which has man as its starting point and aim.* And medicine?" (emphasis by L. W., vol. XIII, p. 533).

Joseph Garnier,[11] very reluctant at first, agrees to publish in the *Journal des économistes* the communication to the Academy as well as the Walras-Jevons correspondence on questions of priority. However, the first (1874d) and second (1877) parts of the *Éléments d'économie politique pure* are ignored by the *Journal des économistes*. This is not the case for the *Théorie mathématique de la richesse sociale* (1883) which is the subject of a favourable review by Charles Gide (*cf. infra*). However, the journal commissions a very critical review of the 2nd edition of the *Éléments* (1889c) by Auguste Ott (1814–1903). Ott, who declares himself an

[9] Very similar remarks on scarcity and utility are found in the letter of L. Walras to J. Garnier dated 12 February 1874, in which he states: "I will make no response, neither direct nor indirect, to Messrs. W[olowski] and L[evasseur]. The paper pre-emptively answers all their objections and it would be quite unnecessary to add anything to it" (*Correspondence*, I, l. 248, p. 357).

[10] Walras implicitly responds to Levasseur's objections at the end of the study "Une branche nouvelle de la mathématique" (1876b), vol. VII, pp. 325–329. He returns to it again in the 2nd edition of the *Éléments*. See *supra* Cha. 4, *Genesis of a Masterpiece: the Theory of General Economic Equilibrium*.

[11] On J. Garnier, see R. Arena, 1991.

"*amateur*" in mathematics, wrote a devastating criticism of Walras's work, whose economic theory "appears to him absolutely false". He explains that

> [...] the study of a treatise on algebra or analytical geometry, or even differential and integral calculus, seems less painful to him than the reading of these endless pages of equations, arriving at banal conclusions that by the ordinary method could have been demonstrated in a few lines or to the development of hypotheses devoid of any certainty." (1890, p. 100)

In Walras's book, "it is the economic order overturned" in which man is stuck between land and capital while labour is no longer the means of transformation and distribution of products for common prosperity. Economic science is focused on exchange and determination of prices (p. 112).[12] This review makes Walras very angry,[13] and several of his Italian correspondents are astonished (Maffeo Pantaleoni and Luigi Perozzo, notably).

The following year, in his book *Les progrès de la science économique depuis Adam Smith*, Maurice Block fights the "ardent advocates" of the mathematical method such as "Jevons, Mr. Walras and a few others". Algebraic formulas can be useful as a "means of exposition", but mathematical analysis cannot be an "instrument of discovery". Thus, "we have seen ingenious works, which proved nothing, or which proved, over 10 pages, that 2 and 2 make 4, which could have been stated in one line as an axiom" (1890, vol. 1, pp. 34–35).

Later, the 3rd edition of the *Éléments d'économie politique pure* is subjected to a devastating criticism by Yves Guyot, (1843–1928) in the daily newspaper *Le Siècle*, he is managing. After a paraphrase of the prospectus of the book, the author states:

> It should be remembered that economic science is an observation science and that mathematics are satisfied with very few observations and are very daring in their deduction. There is here a danger to which the excess exposes the economic science and for which it is necessary to take good care. (1896, p. 414)

The same year, in his *Traité théorique et pratique d'économie politique*, Paul Leroy-Beaulieu relies on the "law of substitution"[14] to reject the application of mathematics to economics. He even adds:

> It is a pure chimera, a true dupery [...]. This is why the so-called mathematical school has no scientific basis, nor any practical application; it is a pure mental exercise, a set of fictions outside of all reality and contrary to all reality. This mental exercise looks like the search for martingales at the roulette of Monaco. (1896, vol. III, p. 62)[15]

[12] He also says that in Walras's theory of production, the individual is unfortunately forced to find a place between land and capital proper.

[13] See his letter to Luigi Perozzo dated 18 March 1890, in: *Correspondence*, II, l. 969, p. 403.

[14] When a good becomes scarce, its price does not increase proportionally, because consumers turn to another good; so that it is impossible to determine the price reaction to the variation in demand.

[15] L. Walras will note these remarks in an unpublished variant of the first version of "Économique et mécanique" (1909b), vol. VII, p. 535, note 2.

As can be seen, the consideration of Walras's pure economics does not evolve much among the French liberal economists during the last quarter of the XIXth century.[16]

7.2.2 *Criticisms of Interventionist Law's Professors: The Case of Paul Cauwès*

Among the professors of law faculties who have been teaching economics from the implementation of the May 1877 decree, ignorance or scorn for the Walrasian theory is also very present. This is the case, for example, with Paul Cauwès (1843–1917), a professor at Paris Law Faculty from 1873, an adherent of the "young" German Historical School and of the historical method, and a defender of State interventionism on social issues.[17] In his *Précis du cours d'économie politique*, he claims that Walras adopts in the *Éléments* the theory of value "the most specious", that of scarcity presented by Nassau Senior[18] (1878, vol. 1, p. 431). He maintains his viewpoint in the 3rd edition of his *Cours d'économie politique* (1893, vol. 1, p. 314). Not only will Cauwès be unfavourable to mathematical economics, but he will see in the perspective of general equilibrium a means of justifying economic liberalism, hence his strong hostility later to Aupetit and Antonelli (*cf. infra).*[19]

7.2.3 *Criticisms of the Mathematicians: Joseph Bertrand, Hermann Laurent, and Henri Poincaré*

We will present now the reactions of the mathematicians J. Bertrand, Hermann Laurent and Henri Poincaré.

As early as 1877, Walras sent the *Théorie mathématique de la richesse sociale*, in four essays to the mathematician Joseph Bertrand (1822–1900), a professor at the Collège de France and a member of the Academy of Sciences; he even met him in Paris, by chance, at the beginning of December of the same year. Bertrand, sceptical

[16] Walras's pure economics is ignored in the *Nouveau Dictionnaire de l'économie politique*, published under the direction of Léon Say and Joseph Chailley-Bert (1891–92); his name is mentioned there twice, just in passing (vol. 2, pp. 49 and 591).

[17] See J.-P. Potier, 2016, pp. 29 and 31–32.

[18] N Senior, *An Outline of the Science of Political Economy* (1838). See Y. Breton, 1998b, p. 409.

[19] In 1887, after reading the *Théorie de la monnaie*, Cauwès nevertheless affirmed to the author that he established "with more scientific rigour" the correct monetary theory (*Correspondence*, II, l. 768, p. 179).

about the use of mathematics in economics, seems hardly to appreciate his work.[20] On 6 December 1877, Walras reported to J.-N. Haton de la Goupillière:

> He told me, speaking about my attempt, that it was as if I was studying the hydraulics of muddy liquids. I answered that it really was so, but that I would not be considering the mud, i.e. all the disturbing circumstances of exchange and production. I do not know if after this answer he will be more receptive. (*Correspondence*, I, l. 396, p. 552)

Later, in September 1883, Joseph Bertrand published a joint review of *Recherches sur les principes mathématiques de la théorie des richesses* (1838) by A.-A. Cournot and *Théorie mathématique de la richesse sociale* (1883) in the *Journal des savants*. Among several topics, he intervenes on the question of the realism of the *tâtonnement* for the exchange of two commodities for each other based on the first memoir. He replaces the commodities A and B with wheat sold by farmers and money held by buyers, the market agents able to be represented (or even replaced by a "calculator"). His main objection is this: the equilibrium to which the market converges depends on the order in which the transactions take place and the endowments of the agents change during this process. The curves of the purchasers will become deformed during the *tâtonnement*. Thus, according to him:

> One must note that the curves representing the orders of the purchasers at different prices must necessarily, without any change of intention, vary for each one of them throughout the market. The resulting curves, whose intersection solves the problem, are continually deformed, and it can easily be demonstrated the necessary variation of the abscissa of the point where they intersect [...]. For each price a similar problem arises, and the curve representing the orders must, after each transaction, must be calculated and drawn anew. Does one have to use the new curve to obtain the equilibrium price? If the answer is yes, Mr. Walras's theorem loses its geometrical character, and the final result depends on the accidental circumstances that we had the conceit to eliminate.[21]

Léon Walras first reacted to this essential objection in a note of the article "Un économiste inconnu: Hermann-Henri Gossen", published in the *Journal des économistes*:

> With respect to the intersection of the demand and supply curves, which yields the current price, Mr. Bertrand objects that the problem of exchange has not been solved, because in case of an excess of demand over supply or supply over demand, certain buyers or sellers will be satisfied initially, after which the prices have to be increased or decreased further in order to satisfy the others. To this, I answer that on the theoretical market in the case of excess of demand over supply, nobody will be satisfied, and that trade will be suspended until raising or lowering of the prices results in the equality of supply and demand, after which everybody will be satisfied. (1885a, vol. IX, p. 312, note 1, English transl., 2010, pp. 250–51, note 2)

Concerning this objection, on the suspension of exchanges, Walras will specify in a note to Vilfredo Pareto that it is a "hypothesis that no scientific mind will hesitate

[20] Note that when Walras submitted the manuscript "Une branche nouvelle de la mathématique" to the *Revue des Deux Mondes*, J. Bertrand took it upon himself to inform him that it was not suitable for this type of journal (*Correspondence*, I, l. 345, p. 494).

[21] *Journal des savants*, September 1883, p. 506, reissued in: P. Bridel, 1996, p. 201.

to concede to the theorist".[22] However, this suspension of exchange is present in the study "La Bourse, la spéculation et l'agiotage", written between 1874 and 1879 for his *Cours d'économie politique appliquée*: "If the quantity demanded is equal to the quantity offered, the price is the *current price* and exchange takes place at that price [...]. Otherwise, there will be no exchange" (1880b, vol. X, p. 371, English transl., 2005, p. 325).

Walras therefore did not wait for the criticism of J. Bertrand.[23] In the 2nd edition of the *Éléments*, in the 5th lesson which describes the establishment of the equilibrium price of the "rente à 3%" in Paris Bourse, in the absence of a counterparty, either for buyers or for sellers, Walras adds that "theoretically, trading must be suspended" and further: "trading is suspended" (vol. VIII, p. 72, English transl., 2014, p. 44).[24] The introduction of preliminary *tâtonnements*, no longer actual, but on "written pledges (*bons*) in the fourth edition (1900) of the *Éléments* will constitute an attempt of an answer to Bertrand's criticism.

Hermann Laurent (1841–1908) is a polytechnician who defended a Ph.D. thesis in mathematics (1865).[25] From 1866, he became an actuary and specialist in insurance matters. Examiner at the École Polytechnique and professor at the Agronomic Institute, he is notably the author of a *Traité de mécanique rationnelle* (1870), a *Traité du calcul des probabilités* (1873), and a *Traité d'analyse* (1885–91). Having appreciated the "Principe d'une théorie mathématique de l'échange", he suggests to Hippolyte Charlon, secretary-treasurer of the French Actuaries' Circle, to contact Walras to offer him the hospitality of the *Journal des actuaires*.[26] But this opening will be short-lived, as Charlon becomes hostile to mathematical economics. Only from 1898, Hermann Laurent, vice-president (since 1890) of the French Institute of Actuaries,[27] wishes to arouse an interest among his colleagues for Walras's pure economics.[28] That year, he consults Walras on a question that concerns some actuaries, which would consist of choosing the kilogram-metre as a unit of value (*Correspondence*, III, l. 1374, 29 November 1898). This results in a correspondence between them, in which our author attempts to make his interlocutor understand that value is not an absolute, but a relative magnitude.

In 1900, Hermann Laurent presents a communication to the French Institute of Actuaries on the "Lausanne School"'s principles in which he criticises the Walrasian theory of utility. On 21 June, he indicates on this question:

---

22 L. Walras, letter to V. Pareto, 9 January 1895, in: *Correspondence*, II, l. 1200, p. 630.

23 See D. A. Walker, 1996, pp. 95–100 and A. Rebeyrol, 1999, pp. 72–73.

24 On the Bertrand-Walras debate, see P. Bridel, 1996, pp. 163–67; P. Bridel and É. Huck, 2002, pp. 519–20; R. Dos Santos Ferreira, 2014, pp. 31–37.

25 On H. Laurent, see Y. Breton, 1998a.

26 See the letter of H. Charlon to L. Walras dated 22 September 1873, in: *Correspondence*, I, l. 234, pp. 337–38.

27 Whose president is Paul Guieysse and honorary president is... Léon Say.

28 He publishes the "Note sur l'équation du taux de revenu net" by Walras in the *Bulletin trimestriel de l'Institut des actuaires français* (1900).

> Mr. Walras determines the prices by admitting that exchange is carried out according to a maximum of satisfaction which can be measured by a function of the quantity given. How to accept that a satisfaction can be measured? No mathematician would agree to it. It is the derivative of this measurement of satisfaction which the author calls the *rareté* and of which he determines the relationship to the satisfied needs. It is necessary to be able to admit in all this logic that the idea of pleasure, of desire, is measurable.[29]

Despite this criticism, he acknowledges the interest of this research and proposes to later present Walras and Pareto's works. Léon Walras is very displeased with the objection. He declares to Miss Dick May:

> At the Institute of the French actuaries, one opposes the objection drawn from the circumstance to me which the utility [...] is not an appreciable measure. They confuse the *mathematical expression* of this measure with the theoretical study that I continue, with its *numerical evaluation* for applications practice of which I do not concern myself.[30]

This type of confusion, which had not surprised him in 1873 during his presentation at the Académie des sciences morales et politiques, astonishes him coming from a mathematician. From this date, relations between Laurent and Walras deteriorate. The latter never considers Laurent as one of his disciples.[31] In 1902, Hermann Laurent publishes a *Petit traité d'économie politique mathématique, rédigé conformément aux préceptes de l'École de Lausanne* (Paris: Charles Schmid), in which he reaches the threshold of the ordinal utility theory.[32]

Annoyed by Hermann Laurent's objection, Walras decides to contact Henri Poincaré (1856–1912). The latter, a former student of the École des Mines and the École Polytechnique, is a famous mathematician, recently re-elected president of the French Mathematical Society. Why contact him? Walras discovered in the first part of Émile Bouvier's article (*cf. infra*) quotations taken from a study by Poincaré, "Les relations entre la physique expérimentale et la physique mathématique", published in the *Revue générale des sciences pures et appliquées* (vol. 11, no. 21, 15 November 1900, pp. 1163–75), which seem very applicable to his case. In September 1901, he sends to Poincaré the 4th edition of the *Éléments d'économie politique pure*, asking an opinion on the application of mathematics in economics.[33] Henri Poincaré quickly responds that he is not opposed to such an application "provided that one does not go beyond certain limits".[34] Walras then explains to him that his *rareté* (or intensity of the last want satisfied), a decreasing function of the quantity

[29] Note 2 to the letter of Walras to Léon Marie, *Correspondence*, III, l. 1448, p. 113; see also the exchange of letters with H. Laurent in May 1900.

[30] Emphasis by L. W. Note attached to the letter of 1st December 1900 to Dick May, in: *Correspondence*, III, l. 1469, p. 133.

[31] It seems difficult to consider H. Laurent as "the unloved disciple" of Walras, as A. Zylberberg does (1988, p. 50, 1990, pp. 79–81 and 1994, pp. 80–82).

[32] According to Schumpeter, the *Petit traité* is "a brief but very good abstract of the Walras-Pareto theory" (1954, p. 840, note 2). Later, H. Laurent publishes *Statistique mathématique* (Paris: Doin, 1908), in which he considers that the conclusions of economics must be verified by statistical observations.

[33] L. Walras, letter to H. Poincaré, 10 September 1901, in: *Correspondence*, III, l. 1492, pp. 158–59.

[34] H. Poincaré, letter to L. Walras, undated, in: *Correspondence*, III, l. 1494, pp. 160–61.

consumed of commodity, "was not an appreciable quantity, but that it was enough to conceive it" and demonstrate that commodities are exchanged for each other in inverse proportion to their *rareté*.[35] Poincaré responds shortly after. He considers that the Walrasian definition of *rareté* is legitimate and observes:

> Can satisfaction be measured? Then I could say that one sort of satisfaction is greater than another, since I prefer one to the other. And then I could say that one satisfaction is twice or three times larger than another. That does not have any sense in itself and could not acquire one other than by arbitrary convention. Satisfaction is thus a quantity, but not a measurable one [...], you can measure satisfaction by an arbitrary function provided that this function always grows at the same time as the satisfaction which it represents.

Poincaré also pointed out that utility was not comparable between two individuals. By introducing preferences, without realising it, he proposes to follow the path of the ordinal conception of utility.[36] Very happy, Walras responds to him immediately after,[37] but he does not seem to understand the full scope of the mathematician's remarks. Thus, he will remain a "cardinalist" in his last writings on pure economics. In "Économique et mécanique", he will assert that utility

> [...] is nonetheless a quantity and even [...] an appreciable quantity. Of two useful things that I need [...] I know very well which one is more useful to me or which one I have the greatest need for. It is the one I prefer to the other." (1909b, vol. VII, p. 332)[38]

And he will publish in the appendix of "Économique et mécanique" Poincaré's response with some modifications (accepted by his correspondent).[39]

7.2.4 *Criticisms of the Engineers–Economists: The Cases of Émile Cheysson and Clément Colson*

A graduate of the École Polytechnique, Émile Cheysson (1836-–910) managed the Creusot factories from 1871 to 1874. Later, from 1886, he served as General Inspector of the Ponts et Chaussées administration. From 1885 to 1905, he taught industrial economics at the École des Mines and from 1887 to 1905, he taught political economy and social economy at the École libre des sciences politiques. Deeply concerned with social questions, he declared himself a disciple of Frédéric Le Play and contributed to the theme of social economics. In 1901, he was elected to the Académie des

[35] L. Walras, letter to H. Poincaré, 26 September 1901, in: *Correspondence*, III, l. 1495, pp. 161–62.

[36] H. Poincaré, letter to L. Walras, undated, in: *Correspondence*, III, l. 1496, pp. 162–63. In 1902, in Chap. II ("Mathematical magnitude and experience") of his book, *Science and Hypothesis*, Poincaré observes: "the magnitudes we have studied so far are not *measurable*; we can indeed say whether a given one of these magnitudes is greater than another, but not whether it is twice or thrice as great" (emphasis by H. P., [1902] 1905, p. 23). This passage is rightly noted by M. H. Turk, 2012, p. 156.

[37] L. Walras, letter to H. Poincaré, 3 October 1901, in: *Correspondence*, III, l. 1498, p. 167.

[38] On this question, see W. Jaffé, 1977a, A. Zylberberg, 1990, pp. 42–45; P. Bridel, 1996, p. 445; M. H. Turk, 2012, pp. 154–58.

[39] "Letter from Mr. H. Poincaré to Mr. Léon Walras", in: 1909b, vol. VII, pp. 340–41.

sciences morales et politiques. Given his profile (communicated by J.-N. Haton de la Goupillière) as an engineer-economist and professor at the École des Mines, Léon Walras attempted in 1885 to interest him in his work by sending a series of papers dedicated to monetary issues, including notably "Monnaie d'or avec billon d'argent régulateur".[40] Even before responding to Walras, Cheysson remarked to Haton de la Goupillière regarding the application of mathematics to economics:

> In principle, I have little faith in the success of attempts aimed at encapsulating in algebraic formulas phenomena where human liberty is at stake. Equations necessarily overlook some data that distort the conclusions while giving them a dangerous appearance of rigour.[41]

One might think we are re-reading Émile Levasseur's observations at the Institute just after Walras's communication! In fact, as he was going to explain to Walras himself, Cheysson was interested in what he called "geometrical statistics". Starting from experimental statistical data, he constructed graphical methods to solve concrete industrial problems, such as remunerative tariffs, the quantity of labour required, etc. And in these researches, he dismissed "abstractions and purely mathematical speculations".[42] Walras then wanted to let him know that he too dismissed mathematical abstractions and speculations, being "much more an economist than a mathematician", adding that he had "never resorted to mathematics except to give their true expression to facts and economic relationships that are essentially quantitative, but always borrowed from the most rigorous observation or experience".[43] Cheysson, who expressed criticisms on the feasibility of the "gold money with regulating silver token" project for statistical reasons during a session at the Paris Statistical Society, seemed somewhat reassured about Walras's objectives. The latter then decided to send him the *Éléments d'économie politique pure.*[44] But he would not find in him a true ally. When he received the first version of Cheysson's article, "La statistique géométrique" (which would appear in *Le génie civil* in January and February 1887), he discovered with astonishment a "*courbe des débouchés*" without mention of Cournot's "*courbe de débit*" (1838), nor mention of its presentation in the *Éléments*; he was indignant and let him know.[45] Their correspondence would practically cease from that date.

Clément Colson (1853–1939)[46] successfully completed the École Polytechnique (classmate of Henri Poincaré) and the École Nationale des Ponts et Chaussées. He also held a law degree. He began a career as a senior civil servant by becoming an

[40] L. Walras to É. Cheysson, 6 July 1885, in: *Correspondence*, II, l. 660, pp. 58–59.

[41] É. Cheysson to J.-N. Haton de la Goupillière, 10 July 1885, in: *Correspondence*, II, l. 665, note 2, p. 62.

[42] É. Cheysson to L. Walras 19 July 1885, in: *op. cit.*, II, l. 666, p. 63.

[43] L. Walras to É. Cheysson, 21 July 1885, in: *op. cit.*, II, l. 667, p. 64.

[44] L. Walras to É. Cheysson, 20 January 1886, in: *Correspondence*, II, l. 694, p. 98.

[45] L. Walras to É. Cheysson, 24 May 1886, in: *op. cit.*, II, l. 719, p. 126. Cheysson will reply: "I was therefore wrong not to know what I was ignorant and to rediscover all by myself through my personal reflections what others had found before me in other forms and for other applications." (letter to L. Walras, 26 May 1886, in: *op. cit.*, II, l. 721, p. 129).

[46] On C. Colson, see C. Picory, 1989, M. Zouboulakis, 2000, J. De Paoli, 2018 and 2020.

auditor at the Conseil d'État. Seconded to the Ministry of Public Works, he would become chief of the minister's staff (1880–82). In 1894–95, he held the position of Director of Railways, Roads, and Navigation. Furthermore, he held teaching positions in some *grandes écoles*. From 1892 to 1932, he was professor of political economy at the École Nationale des Ponts et Chaussées; he also taught at the École Polytechnique (1918–28) and at the École libre des sciences politiques from 1905. He was also active in several statistical associations (International Statistical Institute, Paris Statistical Society...). His main contribution is the *Cours d'économie politique* (1st ed., 1901–10, in six books; definitive and augmented ed., 1924–33, in seven books). Member of the Académie des sciences morales et politiques in 1910 (in replacement of Cheysson), but close to Le Play's disciples, he does not base his liberalism on abstract principles, but on practice.[47] In his lessons, Clément Colson will have as students François Divisia (1889–1964), Jacques Rueff (1896–1978),[48] and René Roy (1894–1977).

What is his position concerning mathematical economics and Walras's works? Let us first note that in 1900, Léon Walras sent him the 4th edition of the *Éléments*[49] and that he would later receive in exchange the 2nd edition of Book I of the *Cours d'économie politique.*[50] According to Colson, mathematical analysis, constructed from observations, leads to conclusions that must be subject to verification by observing facts. Contrary to the hopes of some economists, economic science cannot become a primarily mathematical science. In Book I of his *Cours d'économie politique*, Colson argues that

> [...] the use of *mathematical formulas* could not be regarded as the current method, even in pure economics. It is not [...] *human liberty* which obstructs it. Whether the actions of an individual are subjected to an absolute *determinism* or whether they result from a really free choice, it is sufficient that they obey the *law of large numbers* so that their calculations are applicable to them [....]. (emphasis by C. C., 1924, p. 142)

The author completes his judgement by noting that

> [...] the economic phenomena lend themselves well, by their nature, to the setting of equations, because they are phenomena presenting relations of *interdependence*, rather than of *cause and effect*, relations easy to represent by formulas where one can indifferently consider one quantity or another as an independent variable. One could prove the existence of *general*

[47] See A. Zylberberg, 1990, p. 119.

[48] Jacques Rueff attended Colson's courses in 1920–21, at the École Polytechnique, when he is in the process of writing his book *Des sciences physiques aux sciences morales* (1922). Colson recommends him the reading of the *Éléments* by Walras. In the new introduction (1969) to the 2nd edition of his book, Rueff recounts concerning the *Éléments* by Walras that he "devoured them in a few days, in the enthusiasm of a discovery that was going to provide me with [...] a brilliant confirmation of the validity and fertility of my analysis" (1969, p. 24).

[49] C. Colson thanks L. Walras for this dispatch in a note dated 15 July 1900, published by C. Picory, 1989, p. 685.

[50] In December 1907, C. Colson sent Walras the 2nd edition of the first volume of his *Cours d'économie politique*; in a letter dated 19 December to Émile Borel, L. Walras regrets that C. Colson does not mention him in his work (*Correspondence*, III, l. 1673, p. 344), which is not accurate.

> *equations of economic equilibrium*, to show that, when a certain number of men are present, with a certain number of commodities, their relations are subjected to a sufficient number of conditions to determine all the operations carried out on the market. But it is quite difficult to draw from these general notions enough precise conclusions to really extend our knowledge of the phenomena." (emphasis by C.C., *Cours d'économie politique*, Book 1, 1924, p. 143)

And Colson continues by stating that

> [...] the mathematician economists have certainly rendered great services to science, by the new precision which they brought in the theory of value. Their studies led to some interesting results. They provide especially comparisons or analogies helping to seize the nature of certain phenomena and to specify the direction and the range of certain laws.[51] But they will not be able, for a long time and perhaps never, to constitute the normal form of science." (*op. cit.*, 1924, p. 143

Thus, it is clear that Colson, fearing the axiomatisation of economic science, cannot be considered a disciple of Walras. He is in favour of a limited use of mathematics through graphical representations and to verify the coherence of reasoning. Reasoning in partial equilibrium, he studies price setting in monopoly and competition regimes and highlights the consumer surplus (*rente des acheteurs*). It should be noted that in France, Colson is one of the first authors to use graphical representations, just like Alfred Marshall in England.

7.3 Allies and "Sympathisers" of Pure Economics

Let us now examine the viewpoint of the readers who can be considered the allies of Walras in the strategy of disseminating his writings and the viewpoint of those who are only "sympathisers" of pure economics.

7.3.1 Charles Gide, the Main Supporter

From 1880, Charles Gide (1847–1932) has been professor at Montpellier Faculty of Law. Later, from 1921 to 1930, he taught cooperation at the Collège de France. His book, *Principes d'économie politique* (1st ed., 1884), was one of the few textbooks including a presentation of the marginalist school with a summary of the theoretical contributions of Jevons, Walras, and Menger. Gide has always maintained a certain interest for pure economics.[52] However, one of the difficulties of which he was conscious was his weak knowledge of mathematics (M. Pénin, 1997, p. 116). We

[51] In a note added at the end of the work, Colson specifies that a better understanding of economic laws is possible "provided that one always verifies by observation the conclusions to which the particular ease given to the chain of reasoning by the mathematical form would have allowed to reach" (1924, p. 544).

[52] See C. Montet, 1982 and M. Pénin, 1997.

can recall the remarks he made in 1883, in his favourable review of the *Théorie mathématique de la richesse sociale*:

> We cannot help but think that, if Mr. Walras had presented his doctrines in ordinary language, not only would he have spared himself this 'cerebral neurosis' he complains about in his preface, but he would also have avoided it for some of his overly conscientious readers, and this without any harm to his doctrines. Quite the contrary, I believe that his ideas could only gain much by being stripped of the formulas that envelop them like a shell bristling with spikes. (1883, p. 302)[53]

In 1887, Gide was setting up the *Revue d'économie politique* which challenged the primacy of the *Journal des économistes.* At that time, Walras, who broke with the Société d'économie politique de Paris and with the *Journal des économistes*, wished that the new periodical would allow the expression of theoretical and mathematical research. The *Revue* would not take this direction, as it opened up to all French and foreign economic schools (particularly the Historical School) and to social sciences in general, placing great importance on industrial and social legislation issues.

When the 2nd edition of the *Éléments* appeared, Gide considered himself unable to write a review and he hardly knew who to ask in France. He then turned to the Dutch economist Antoine Beaujon (1853–90), who will re-use in the *Revue d'économie politique* the main points of his review recently published in *De Economist*. However, Gide accepted to publish Ladislaus von Bortkiewicz's review in reaction to Edgeworth and the latter's reply (January–February 1890 and January 1891). The difficulty in finding competent economists to review the subsequent editions of the *Éléments* will reappear. Gide briefly announced the publication of the 3rd edition while referring to the Bortkiewicz's review (*Revue d'économie politique*, vol. 10, 1896, p. 717) and that of the 4th edition by noticing that if it had only French readers, this work would not have surpassed the first edition! (*Revue d'économie politique*, vol. 15, 1901, p. 211).

In his Report to the International Congress on the Teaching of Social Sciences (Paris, 30 July–3 August 1900), Charles Gide regretted the lack of teaching in France of mathematical economics and in particular of Walrasian pure economics:

> Another major gap is the absence of any teaching on the method and more particularly on mathematical economics. It is really a shame to think that in France, in a country which holds a preeminent rank in mathematical sciences and which with Cournot inaugurated mathematical economics, one does not find anyone teaching this matter and probably not

[53] From January 1898, Gide had given a free course on the theme of "La Coopération (l'idéal et la pratique)" at the University of Lausanne, which gave him the opportunity to meet Léon Walras from time to time. The latter, who announced his course in the *Gazette de Lausanne*—(1898a), offers the following testimony:
Mr. Gide, who spent the winter in Lausanne, eventually let me try to explain to him mathematically certain points of economics; and, thanks to the fact that he had a bit of algebra at his disposal, I succeeded. But he has left, and this seed will undoubtedly be devoured by the birds of the sky. (letter to Auguste Penjon, 27 July 1898, in: Correspondence, III, l. 1360, p. 26).
A document written by L. Walras, "Observations to Mr. Gide (June 1898)", which does not seem to have been sent, testifies to the efforts made by Walras in this direction (manuscript kept in the Lausanne collection, new reference F. W. V/16/9/4), three sheets). The first lines of the first sheet are published and translated by J. Van Daal and A. Jolink, 1993, p. 19 and note 14, p. 169.

> one professor who is able to do it! And by a strange irony, this teaching has been brilliantly represented in Lausanne for twenty years by a French man, but who is known worldwide as a Swiss: Walras.[54]

Later, in the *Histoire des doctrines économiques depuis les physiocrates jusqu'à nos jours* (1909), written in collaboration with Charles Rist, Gide granted a place to pure economics.[55] In a chapter on the "Hedonists" (!), in a section devoted to the "mathematical school", he paid homage to Walras, because this economist "boldly embraces in his formulas every aspect of the economic world—something like Laplace's system of the universe" and he quotes in this regard a booklet written by V. Pareto (*L'Économie pure*, 1902) which compared the *Éléments* to Newton's *Principia* (1909, p. 693) (*cf. infra*). He then attempted to summarise the Walrasian theory of production starting from the famous session of the Paris Stock Exchange. The entrepreneur, placed at the centre of the "*corbeille*", on the one hand, buys from the landowners, capitalists, workers their productive services in exchange for "rent",[56] interest and wages, and on the other hand, sells the products to consumers. The subtleties of *tâtonnement* were obviously ignored. Gide noted that the selling price and the cost of production necessarily coincide in a regime of absolute free competition, and the result is that the entrepreneur makes no profit ("*bénéfice*"). However, in the real world, profit does exist like the oscillations around a fixed point, just like waves at the sea level.[57] Finally, Gide compared the Walrasian theory of production, which forms a closed circuit, with the "Tableau économique" of F. Quesnay, the latter being "only closer to reality" (1909, p. 604).

On 18 April 1909, Gide told Walras[58] about the forthcoming publication of the *Histoire des doctrines économiques* with a postscript: "We would be grateful if you would kindly indicate anything that might appear inaccurate or erroneous to you—we will try to correct it for another edition if necessary." We can see here that he spoke with much precaution! Walras had no illusion about Gide, but what was his reaction? On 15 May, he sends the following note to the authors:

> L. W., very absorbed in the preparation of his Jubilee Speech, can only briefly express to Mr. Gide, as he does to Mr. Rist, the admiration that the work of vast erudition and patient critique that constitutes their *Histoire des doctrines économiques* inspires in him at first glance, and the gratitude he owes them for the truly magnificent place they have given him in this work.[59]

---

[54] See C. Gide, 1900, p. 9; passage noted by L. Walras, in: *Correspondence*, III, l. 1479, of 1st March 1900, p. 145. See also C. Gide, 1907, pp. 202–03.

[55] On this episode, see J.-P. Potier, 2018.

[56] Gide was mistaken because "*rente*" is the productive service, while the "*fermage*" is its price.

[57] In the 1st edition (1909, p. 604, note 1), Gide declares: "will a day come when, equilibrium being perfectly achieved, there will be no more profit? … The day when perfect equilibrium is achieved in the physical and economic world, everything will stop and the world will end". In the 4th edition (1922, p. 637, note 1), he replaces this passage with the following: "A day may come when, with the balance perfectly achieved, there will really be no more profit? This is indeed what the cooperativists believe and what they strive to achieve from now on."

[58] C. Gide to L. Walras, 18 April 1909, in: *Correspondence*, III, l. 1739, p. 404.

[59] Note dated 15 May 1909, kept in the Lausanne collection under reference I, 220. However, in his "Notes d'humeur", Walras writes:

However, after delving into the reading of the *Histoire des doctrines*, Walras writes to Gide on 23 October 1909:

> In the six months that I am reading this work with the greatest care and fullest satisfaction, I have found only two points on which I have to present a serious observation to you: naturally they are two points of mathematics. I indicate them on the enclosed sheet. The second is a rather delicate point which I think I have established in Nos 3 and 4 of my *Appendix I* in the *Éléments*.[60] If you would accept this observation, I allowed myself to provide you with the text and the figures with which you would have to replace the note of p. 602 [...].[61] (*Correspondence*, III, l. 1775, pp. 436–37)

His article, "Doctrines économiques", published in the *Gazette de Lausanne* on 6 January 1910, the day after his death, contains a favourable overall appreciation of the *Histoire des doctrines économiques depuis les physiocrates jusqu'à nos jours.*

Later, Charles Gide engages, in the *Revue d'économie politique*, in a quick review of the 5th edition ("definitive, revised and augmented by the author") of the *Éléments d'économie politique pure* (1926). His assessment is disillusioned:

> To find 'the keys' is undoubtedly an important thing; when you have them, to open the doors seems easy. However, here the lock is a little bit complicated, and until now the work started with Walras has not been continued. (p. 485)

According to Gide's view, the theory of general equilibrium (here, "the lock") is undoubtedly a prospect that economists will find difficult to discern.

"We would be grateful if you would kindly indicate anything that might appear inaccurate or erroneous to you. We will try to correct it for another edition if necessary." Ch. Gide, letter 18 April 09. Hedonists (Gide), Rent (Rist). It would be long and difficult. They would need to be taught mathematics. (emphasis by L. W., vol. XIII, p. 541).

[60] See the "Théorie géométrique de la détermination des prix, I—De l'échange de plusieurs marchandises entre elles" (1892, vol. VIII, pp. 696–99, English transl., 1954, p. 466–71).

[61] The sheet attached to this letter (*op. cit.*, p. 437) is published by William Jaffé. Léon Walras first points out a lack of parentheses in Gide's equations. Then, he raises an objection to the supply and demand graph. Gide had represented convex supply and demand curves. Walras proposes a quasi-concave supply curve with a comment. Charles Gide replies to L. Walras on 3 November 1909: I thank you very much for your corrections. I will certainly take advantage of them for a 2nd edition when the time comes; but I do hope to see you before then and ask you for some explanations. In any case, I am reassured by the thought that you have not found any other serious error—nor has Mr Edgeworth. (Correspondence, III, l. 1776, p. 438).
In the 2nd edition (1913) of the *Histoire des doctrines économiques*, Gide will correct the omission of parentheses in the equations (p. 610, note 1). Based on Walras's indications, he will modify the graphical representation by constructing this time a concave supply curve, merely indicating that "it is possible that at a certain degree the supply becomes decreasing for the very simple reason that there is no longer any product available on the market" (p. 623, note 1). However, his comment regarding the place of prices and quantities remains contradictory (pp. 623–24, note 1); the contradiction will finally be resolved following the critical remarks of Jacques Moret (4th ed., 1922, pp. 634–35, note 1). The problem in this matter is that Walras reasons in pure exchange, while Gide considers from the 2nd edition a production process.

7.3.2 "Sympathisers" of Pure Economics at the Faculty of Law: Émile Bouvier and Charles Rist

Émile Bouvier (1862–1930) was a professor of public finance at Lyon Law Faculty from 1897 and a professor of colonial legislation and economics at the École supérieure de commerce of Lyon.[62] Not a mathematician, he nevertheless declared having used some "propositions" of Walras and Pareto in his courses at the École supérieure de commerce de Lyon (1901a, p. 1031). He decided to prepare a review of the 4th edition of the *Éléments d'économie politique pure* for the *Revue critique de législation et de jurisprudence* in 1901. In this text, after a short presentation of Walras's main arguments, he drew up a panorama of the objections made with the use of the mathematical method in economics. One can gather his reflections under four points. First of all, some affirm that mathematical method is not a method of research, but only of an exposition of results already well known. On this question, Léon Walras made the point that his method makes it possible to achieve new results, in particular the demonstration of the free competition principle. Second objection: the data and economic phenomena being so variable and complex, it is impossible to draw general laws and consequently to use systems of equations. However, according to Walras, it is necessary to admit the need for general laws and the possibility of discovering them and to express them by mathematics. And science leads to the display of rules and principles applicable to reality. Third objection: the algebraic and geometrical demonstrations would have a mysterious, obscure side. Unfortunately, this criticism comes from the mathematical gaps in the economist's training. Finally, Bouvier indicates another criticism: "the contradictions of mathematicians and uncertainty of their conclusions". According to him, this situation is inevitable, because science does not reach perfection immediately and must advance by trial and error.[63]

Furthermore, in 1901 Émile Bouvier published a paper, "La méthode mathématique en économie politique", in two parts in the *Revue d'économie politique.* The study was enlarged to form a volume which appeared the same year under the same title. This interesting study show that Bouvier understood very well Walras's methodology and the construction of ideal types from real types. It gave a report on the misadventures of mathematical economics in France during the XIXth century. Bouvier notes in connection with the mathematical method that

> [...] at this time, it is impossible, at the present stage of science, to decide formally for or against. One must thus avoid condemning *a priori,* as Mr. Paul Leroy-Beaulieu does, a method which after all could be invaluable, and at the same time being blindly enthusiastic about this reasoning which, though that Mr. Léon Walras says a lot, still contains some points not sufficiently clarified." (1901, p. 1085)

He addressed his message in particular "to the young economists and to the young mathematicians" and concluded by saying that "the new school has the merit of

[62] On É. Bouvier, see Y. Breton, 2000.

[63] On 21 December 1901, Walras immediately thanks the author for this "excellent and charming bibliographical notice" (*Correspondence*, III, l. 1509, p. 182).

testing a different way from the preceding ones" and that it "is necessary to get out of the current rut for a start" (1901a, p. 1086).[64] Walras thanks the author for sending the 2nd part of the article, "our two ways of seeing being identical," he says. He then provides him with a "statement of facts" concerning the objection of H. Laurent and the viewpoint of H. Poincaré, the Ph.D. thesis of A. Aupetit and V. Pareto's course at the École des Hautes Études sociales (*cf. infra*). He concludes his letter on their convergences of view regarding the organisation of the teaching of mathematical economics[65] (*cf.* Chap. 8, *From Criticism to the Reform Plan for the Teaching of Political Economy in France in the XIXth century*).

Charles Rist (1874–1955) was a student of Paul Cauwès at the Paris Faculty of Law. In 1899, he was successful in the *agrégation* competition in economics[66] and was appointed professor at the Faculty of Law of Montpellier. In his first article "Économie optimiste et économie scientifique", published in 1904 in the *Revue de Metaphysique et de Morale*, he tried to refute the ultraliberal interpretation that had been given to the Walrasian theory by the contributions of Pareto. Rist wished to show that in the Walrasian theory of exchange, free competition leads to the maximum satisfaction for each individual, only a relative maximum, taking into account the desires of the exchangers, while taking also as given the mode of private property, the distribution of wealth, and the type of market on which the exchange takes place. Therefore, no "optimistic" conclusion can be drawn from it, nor any judgement on the current organisation of exchange, the role of the State, the system of property or the distribution.[67] In particular, Rist tried to refute the idea supported by Cauwès according to which pure economics would be an instrument at the service of the liberal orthodoxy.

In a letter sent to Walras, who considers himself a "disciple", Charles Rist explains that French economists from the faculties of law are not opposed in principle to theoretical research, but they are not interested in it; Charles Gide represents an exception in this milieu. He also indicates:

> Unfortunately I do not know mathematics like my friend Aupetit. I had to learn it for four or five years, under very bad conditions, and I realise that it is an instrument which I will

---

[64] Charles Gide will write a favourable review of É. Bouvier's book in *Revue d'économie politique* (vol. 17, no. 1, 1903, pp. 94–95).

[65] L. Walras, letter to É. Bouvier, 11 January 1902, in: *Correspondence*, III, l. 1514, pp. 188–90. In his unpublished answer of 18 January 1902, É. Bouvier thanks Walras for his encouragement and adds:

> The article you read is indeed the end of my work. Only now I am going to make a[n] offprint of it, and spread it as much as I can. I hope to thus provoke a movement in France, and conduct an inquiry which I could publish more [of] later the results if they are interesting. I will address the men whose names you mention to me, and others too whom I am thinking of, notably certain mathematicians. Besides, if you think of anyone else who might be interested in the matter, you can let me know and I will send them my work. (Lausanne collection, F. W. II, 2317).

[66] The jury, presided over by Jules Léveillé a (professor of criminal law and comparative penal legislation), includes Émile Levasseur, Jules Garnier, Paul Beauregard, and Maurice Bourguin.

[67] C. Rist, 1904, p. 662. On the offprint of this article (kept in the Lausanne collection, XI/R2), L. Walras wrote question marks, some annotations in margin, and inserted a graph.

> be able to admire when employed by others, but in which I could never be useful myself without presumption. (*Correspondence*, III, l. 1630, 8 August 1906, pp. 308–09)

In fact, Rist trained himself by working on Irving Fisher's manual, *A Brief Introduction to the Infinitesimal Calculus* (1897), for which Walras desired a French translation. At the time, Rist is preparing with Charles Gide the *Histoire des doctrines économiques depuis les Physiocrates jusqu'à nos jours* (*cf. supra*). He would say about his collaboration with Gide:

> [...] I tried to maintain my own line, which tended to give Walras and Menger's work a central place in our book, while Gide, with touching obstinacy, kept returning to make the cooperative doctrine, of which he was the apostle, the culmination of economics. (1955, p. 983)

Unfortunately, Rist would not continue his efforts in the direction of mathematical economics. After the First World War, he specialised in monetary questions and in 1926 became Deputy Governor (*sous-gouverneur*) of the Banque de France. After Gide's death, he took on, with Gaëtan Pirou, the editorial management of the *Revue d'économie politique.*

7.3.3 Unexpected "Sympathisers": Paul Valéry and Charles Péguy

Paul Valéry (1871–1945), a famous poet and philosopher, studied at the Faculty of Law in Montpellier from 1888 to 1892. Charles Gide probably suggested him to read Walras.[68] In a review of the 3rd edition of the *Éléments* published in November–December 1896 in the *Revue générale de droit, de législation et de la jurisprudence*, Valéry praises Walras's courageous efforts to construct a "Mathematical Economics". However, he expresses some regrets about the first section of the book. First of all, he indicates:

> We regret finding many paragraphs there that lack rigour and criticism, and a whole chapter (2nd lesson) on the distinction between science, art and ethics that show us that Mr. Walras's analytical mind did not often deviate from the field of pure economics.

Valéry does not like Walras's taxonomy of facts and sciences and he immediately adds:

> We also regret not seeing a general idea of the physico-mathematical method, and especially an account of the theory of the *units* at the beginning of the volume, instead of a draft of the theory of functions which is insufficient both for the mathematician and the non-mathematician. (1896, pp. 419–20)

In short, Valéry questions the relevance of the Mathematical Introduction (which will be withdrawn in the 4th edition) and considers that the questions of measurement and units, although crucial, has not been discussed satisfactorily. Moreover, he

---

[68] Paul Valéry is a friend of André Gide, Charles Gide's nephew.

finds remarkable the budget equation according to which "the sum of the quantities supplied and demanded at various prices is zero".[69] We are thus dealing here with an intelligent reading.[70]

At the École Normale Supérieure in Paris, a group of non-Marxist socialists is interested in Walras's work, and among them we find the famous poet and writer Charles Péguy (1873–1914). In 1896, he discovers the *Éléments d'économie politique pure* and probably Georges Renard asks him to write a review of the *Études d'économie sociale*, which have just been published. In his first publication, "Un économiste socialiste, M. Léon Walras", which appears in February 1897 in the *Revue socialiste*, Péguy not only discusses the content of the *Études d'économie sociale*, but he also comments on the *Éléments d'économie politique pure*.[71] According to Péguy, in this work, Walras has "established a science" on par with mechanics and mathematical physics. From heterogeneous economic phenomena, it was first necessary to abstract the "homogeneous elements, still very complex", then to abstract and select the simplest principles (1897, p. 174). Thus, to starting from competition "very often distorted by constraints and consequently heterogeneous, exercised by individuals not only varied but unequal among themselves, it [the mathematical economics] abstracts a homogeneous competition exercised by equal individuals" (1897, pp. 174–75). This approach allows the author to establish relationships, calculate maxima, and draw curves. Charles Péguy then examines the issue of barter in Jevons and Gossen, discussed in the "Théorie de la propriété" (inserted in the *Études d'économie sociale*) and he explains why Walras aligned himself with Jevonian barter, which respects the individual property of the traders (1897, pp. 175–77).[72] He is undoubtedly the only commentator at the time to understand the stakes of the difference between these two types of barter. Nevertheless, Péguy engages in a critique of the author's approach in the *Éléments*. He believes that he should have begun with an analysis of "the use of mathematical methods in economics". Indeed, in mathematics, the number and the line are indefinite. In contrast,

> [...] the social, economic number of men, means, products, works, is a number at each moment defined. Hence, the units that constitute this number are not only interdependent like the units of the ordinary mathematical number or like the points of the ordinary mathematical line, but are linked together, so to speak, by a circular, closed solidarity. (1897, p. 184)

Péguy illustrates his point by indicating that

> [...] it is inaccurate to start by positing n men or n francs, but, assuming that the total number of men and the total number of francs, at the considered moment, are respectively Th and Tf, it is accurate to start by positing: n/Th men and n/Tf francs, expressions whose value will never exceed 1. (1897, p. 184)

Thus, one posits n men or n francs without separating them from the rest of humanity or the rest of the *numéraire*. Léon Walras finds Péguy's text excellent for

69 See vol. VIII, 12th lesson, p. 179.

70 See on this subject P. Dockès, 1996, pp. 259–61.

71 On this review, see P. Dockès, 1992, 1993 and 1996, pp. 252–58; M. Bee, 2011.

72 See "Théorie de la propriété" (1896c), vol. IX, pp. 179–184, English transl., 2010, pp. 136–140.

its presentation of mathematical economics. However, he disagrees with the last critique. He will observe:

> I do not believe, for my part, to have proceeded in this way. Mathematics allows us to take into account, with three points, all men and all francs. In pure economics, when I say: let the commodities be (A), (B), (C), (D)..., let the exchangers be (1), (2), (3)..., I consider all commodities and all exchangers *without exception.*[73]

After publication of the review, Péguy prepares a manuscript on the origins of mathematical economics dealing with Cournot, Gossen, Jevons, and Walras, which he used for a presentation at the École Normale. In February 1897, he sends his text to Léon Walras, who returns it to him with annotations. Unfortunately, this document has been lost until now. Although not feeling comfortable on philosophical grounds, Walras wishes to meet the author to engage in a fruitful dialogue in person.[74]

7.4 Disciples of Léon Walras

Of course, Vilfredo Pareto and the "Paretians" played a part in the diffusion of the Walrasian ideas in France, although they were not disciples, strictly speaking. On the other hand, Aupetit and Antonelli were, in France, direct disciples of Walras.

7.4.1 The Case of Vilfredo Pareto

Léon Walras expected very much of Vilfredo Pareto in the diffusion of pure economics, when he succeeded him at the University of Lausanne. Indeed, in 1893, to help him write his first course, he prepared a first version of what will later become the *Abrégé des Eléments*, which minimised the use of mathematics. Actually, Pareto's lessons, which will lead to the publication in 1896–97 of the *Cours d'économie politique*, differ in form and content from that of Walras,[75] but they contribute to the dissemination of the theory of general economic equilibrium.

In November 1900, Miss Dick May founded the École des Hautes Études Sociales in Paris.[76] She wished to establish a course in mathematical economics there. After searching in vain for a candidate, in February 1901, she proposes to Walras to take on this teaching himself. The latter, no longer feeling able to teach again, declines

---

[73] Emphasis by L. W., letter to C. Péguy, 31 March 1897, in: *Correspondence*, II, l. 1310, p. 742.

[74] *Op. cit.*, p. 742–43.

[75] See P. Bridel, "Introduction" to the *Matériaux sur le Cours d'économie politique pure*, vol. XII, p. 730 *et seq.*

[76] The École des Hautes Études Sociales is a private institution, founded from a split within the Collège libre des sciences sociales and the merging of an École de morale, an École de journalisme, and an École sociale. It is directed by the successor of Louis Pasteur, Émile Duclaux. C. Gide is president of its board of directors. On this school, see C. Prochasson, 1985.

the proposition. In the following months, Dick May offers Vilfredo Pareto to take charge of the course. Having learned of Pareto's choice, Walras indicates to her that he is "the most qualified man" since no Frenchman is up to the task, but adds, "it is precisely this circumstance that surprises and afflicts me as very unfortunate for my country".[77] In 1901–02, Pareto teaches the course in pure economics by presenting his own conceptions. In the booklet that contains a summary of this course, he addresses a number of criticisms to Walras without naming him, but he acknowledges:

> It is Mr. L. Walras who was the first to found one of these systems of equations that which refers to the case of free competition. This discovery is of the utmost importance and one could not praise the merit of this scientist too highly. Of course science has already developed and will continue to develop in the future, but that does not take away any of the importance of Mr. Walras' discovery, just as the progress of celestial mechanics did not decrease the importance of the *Principia* of Newton, quite the reverse. (1902, p. 132)[78]

Pareto sends the booklet to Walras, who thanks him for his comparison with Newton, but without sharing his irritation regarding the criticisms.[79] In the Lausanne archives, however, there is a handwritten note, dated 6 November 1901, on which Walras listed his points of disagreement with Pareto. Among these points, one finds, notably, pure economics as an approximation of economic phenomena and the question of practical applications, the *rareté* (scarcity) as an appreciable magnitude, the causes of exchange value, the theory of marginal productivity, etc.[80]

7.4.2 *The Paretians' Camp: Georges-Henri Bousquet*

Georges-Henri Bousquet (1900–78) studied at the Paris's Faculty of Law and at the École libre des sciences politiques, where he was a student of Clément Colson. He was deeply impressed by two meetings held during the year 1923: those of Vilfredo Pareto in Céligny and of Joseph Schumpeter in Vienna. In an article published in 1924, we find the general lines of his interpretation which he will regularly reassert in his writings.[81] According to him, Walras applies mathematics to economics to express "the relations of mutual dependence that bind the various parts of the whole economic world to each other". He solved the following question:

[77] L. Walras, letter to Dick May, 23 May 1901, in: *Correspondence*, III, l. 1483, 23 May 1901, p. 148.

[78] According to Louise Renard, during the first lesson, Pareto presented his own theory without mentioning Walras and the audience was "drowsy" (letter to L. Walras, 19 November 1901, in: *Correspondence*, III, l. 1504, p. 175). For precise information on Pareto's judgement on Walras's work, see P. Steiner 1994; A. Legris and L. Ragni, 1999; P. Bridel and F. Mornati, 2009.

[79] L. Walras, letter to V. Pareto, 3 November 1901, in: *Correspondence*, III, l. 1501, 3 November 1901, p. 169 and note 3, pp. 169–70.

[80] See note 11 to the letter of Walras to Léon Winiarski, 15 November 1901, in: *Correspondence*, III, l. 1502, pp. 171–72.

[81] On G.-H. Bousquet, see A. Alcouffe and B. Belloc, 2000.

> How to show the way to determine the prices and the quantities of commodities exchanged in a hypothetical regime of free competition, given the tastes and the endowments of the individuals involved [...] only mathematics can enable the exposure of this mechanism in all its generality, and the first, Walras, without external suggestion, succeeded in employing these in a brilliant way to achieve his goal [...] *all* the work of pure economics that Pareto produced stems directly from Walras's theory of economic equilibrium and would not exist without it. (emphasis by G.-H. B., 1924, 1st part, p. 229)

But unfortunately, according to Bousquet,

> [...] the purpose of the *Éléments* of Walras was to defend a practical doctrine and contain, along with the systems of equations for which the author is famous, sentimental and metaphysical proposals stripped of any value, but to which he attached great importance. On the contrary, the purpose of the whole of Pareto's works is the elimination of any proposal which is not rigorously scientific, the exclusion of sentiment in the development of the theory and constant research towards the very ideal of Science: absolute objectivity. (1924, 1st part, p. 230)[82]

So, for Bousquet, the books and articles in mathematical economics by Pareto thus leave far behind the *Éléments* of Walras.

7.4.3 Disciples Strictly Speaking: Albert Aupetit and Étienne Antonelli

Albert Aupetit (1876–1943) is neither a mathematician, nor an engineer-economist. He studied at the Faculty of Law in Paris and was self-taught in mathematics. In April 1901, he defended a Ph.D. thesis entitled *Essai sur la théorie générale de la monnaie* (Paris: Guillaumin), the first thesis on mathematical economics in France.[83] The first (and best) part of the work is devoted to "rational economics" (one of the first uses of the term). Aupetit presents here a general equilibrium model which used Lagrange multipliers. With functions of production with substitutable factors, he highlights the behaviour of maximisation of profit by the entrepreneurs in free competition, an approach that appears neither in Walras nor Pareto (A. Zylberberg, 1990, pp. 75–77).[84] In the second part devoted to "experimental economics", he examines the functions of money, drawing inspiration from the *Théorie de la monnaie* and the *Éléments d'économie politique pure*. According to Joseph A. Schumpeter, Aupetit's *Essai* is

> [...] a youthful work of striking quality that still deserves perusal, marks a non unimportant step in the theory of money but is mentioned here because of the still greater significance of

[82] In his *Cours d'économie pure* (1928, p. 5), Bousquet laments that Walras was "a 'social reformer', not a scientific mind".

[83] We do not know who his Ph.D. thesis supervisor was.

[84] G.-H. Bousquet will republish the first part ("Rational Economics") of Aupetit's thesis with a Foreword (Paris: Marcel Rivière, 1957).

the relatively early reformulation of Walrasian equilibrium theory it presents. (1954, p. 840, note 2)[85]

The thesis having been noticed (for its second part) by the Governor of the Banque de France, Georges Pallain, Aupetit obtained a position in the economic studies department of this institution.

Walras considers Aupetit as his "first French disciple", with a promising brilliant future[86] and he informs Miss Dick May that he would be an excellent candidate for the course at the École des Hautes Études Sociales.[87] However, Aupetit failed the first time in the 1901 *agrégation* competition in economics.[88] In 1903, Charles Gide offered him a lectureship at the École des Hautes Études Sociales dedicated to the principles and applications of the mathematical method in economics.[89] Aupetit accepted, while Walras, on his side, prepared what would become in November 1903 a new version of the *Abrégé des Éléments.* At the jury of the 1903 competition in which Aupetit participated, although Edmond Villey and Émile Levasseur, both of the liberal school, supported the candidate, Paul Cauwès was very hostile to him and secured his elimination.[90] Furious, Walras attributed this failure to Gide's refusal to participate in the jury, leaving his place to Camille Perreau who, along with the president Jules Léveillé, sided with Cauwès' opinion.[91]

After this new failure, Aupetit gave up the project of a course at the École des Hautes Études Sociales..[92] He remained at the Banque de France where he quickly became chief of the administrative service and of economic studies. A few years later, in August 1907, in Clarens, Aupetit met Walras, who gave him the *Abrégé des Éléments* in exchange for his commitment to teach mathematical economics in Paris and to write an "elementary treatise on pure economics" ("Notice autobiographique", 1909a, vol. V, pp. 25–26). In the autumn of 1907, Albert Aupetit

---

[85] On A. Aupetit, see also P. Bridel, 1997, pp. 139–41.

[86] L. Walras sent the 4th edition of the *Éléments* to Aupetit with the following dedication: "To Mr. Doctor Albert Aupetit, my first French disciple, with the assurance of my certainty of having lost nothing by waiting for him." (copy which later came into the possession of G.-H. Bousquet). See G.-H. Bousquet, 1948, p. 171.

[87] L. Walras, to A. Aupetit, 7 August 1903, in: *Correspondence*, III, l. 1491, p. 156.

[88] The jury, presided over by Jules Léveillé, includes É. Levasseur, C. Gide, A. Souchon and C. Turgeon. The subjects of Aupetit's lessons are very far from his concerns: "La culture maraîchère"; "Quel est le meilleur usage à faire du boni des sociétés coopératives" (see M. Pantaleoni, letter to V. Pareto, 10 November 1901, in: V. Pareto, 1984, vol. 2, pp. 384–85).

[89] A. Aupetit to L. Walras, 30 May 1903, in: *Correspondence*, III, l. 1546, p. 228.

[90] The subject of Aupetit's lesson is indicated in a letter of Georges Walras to his father, in: *Correspondence*, III, l. 1558, p. 235.

[91] According to M. Pénin (1997, p. 121, note 1), the presence among the candidates of Édouard Dolléans, close to Gide, and thus the obligation to choose between supporting Dolléans and supporting Aupetit constitutes a plausible explanation for Gide's refusal to participate in this jury.

[92] Curiously, Aupetit translated into French the *Theory of Political Economy* by W. S. Jevons (C. Gide to L. Walras, 10 August 1903, in: *Correspondence*, III, l. 1553, p. 232), but the manuscript remained unpublished. He publishes the article "L'oeuvre économique de Cournot" in *Revue de métaphysique et de morale* (May 1905, pp. 377–93), in which he defends the application of mathematics to economics.

submitted to Maurice d'Ocagne a book project entitled *Économique rationnelle*, for the *Bibliothèque de mathématiques appliquées* of the *Encyclopédie scientifique* of Doctor Édouard Toulouse, published by Doin.[93]

In 1906, Léon Walras hopes for the opening of an "elementary course in mathematical economics" at the Collège libre des sciences sociales[94] and he is counting on the support of Georges Renard for this purpose.[95] The attempt fails; it is difficult to find a professor and the director of the college, Ernest Delbet, does not seem very interested in the matter, especially since the holder of the chair of political economy in this private institution is none other than Yves Guyot, an orthodox liberal. In 1908, Léon Walras hopes that a course in pure economics will be established at the college during the winter of 1908–09 and entrusted to Albert Aupetit and Alfred Barriol, director of the Institut des finances et des assurances.[96] After the death of the director (E. Delbet), he hopes that this teaching will be carried out by Albert Aupetit.[97]

From 1912, Aupetit shared with François Simiand the course on the history of economic doctrines at the École Pratique des Hautes Études, previously taught by Adolphe Landry from 1907. He teaches mathematical economics until 1927, but his lessons do not seem very attractive for the students (with the exception, for example, of Gaëtan Pirou).[98] Furthermore, from 1921 to 1926, he taught political economy at the École libre des sciences politiques, where he seems to have presented the theory of general equilibrium in a simplified form (A. Zylberberg, 1990, p. 29).

A student at the Faculty of Law in Aix-en-Provence, Étienne Antonelli (1879–1971) defends two Ph.D. theses: *La protection de la viticulture par l'État* (Paris: Chevalier et Rivière, 1905) and *De la résiliation du louage de travail* (Paris: Arthur Rousseau, 1906).[99] He is then appointed lecturer at the law faculties of Montpellier (1906–10), Paris (1910–12), and Poitiers (in 1914). He had joined in 1906 the "Comité de démocratie sociale", a movement of young socialists and radicals led by Paul Boncour and Aristide Briand.[100] This committee aims to reflect on ways to achieve urgent social reforms, such as tax justice, workers' pensions, arbitration in social conflicts, mutuality, etc. After a first failure at the *agrégation* competition in economics in 1908,[101] he becomes interested in the work of Léon Walras,

---

[93] In fact, François Divisia will publish his own *Économique rationnelle* (with a preface by C. Colson) in this collection … in 1928.

[94] The Collège libre des sciences sociales, a private institution subsidised by the State from 1901, was founded in Paris in December 1895 by Dick May and Théophile Funck-Brentano. It was directed until 1908 by Ernest Delbet. On this institution, see C. Bruant, 2007.

[95] L. Walras, letter to Georges Renard, 14 September 1906, in: *Correspondence*, III, l. 1631, p. 310.

[96] L. Walras, letter to Henry Ludwell Moore, 12 March 1908, in: *Correspondence*, III, l. 1680, p. 351; letter to Joseph A. Schumpeter, 12 October 1908, in: *op. cit.*, III, l. 1710, p. 379.

[97] L. Walras, letter to Albert Aupetit, 11 January 1909, in: *Correspondence*, III, l. 1710, pp. 386–87.

[98] See G. Pirou, 1945.

[99] On É. Antonelli, see L. Frobert, 1997 and 2000; L. Le Van-Lemesle, 1992 and 1994a.

[100] É. Antonelli will draft the manifesto of the movement: *La Démocratie Sociale devant les idées présentes* (Paris: M. Rivière, 1910).

[101] The jury, presided over by C. Gide, notably includes A. de Foville and C. Rist.

probably on the advice of Georges Renard. Thanks to documents lent by Aline Walras, who considers him "the best disciple of [her] father", Antonelli was able to publish the study "Léon Walras" in 1910 in the *Revue d'histoire des doctrines économiques et sociales*. In the study that traces the career of the founder of the Lausanne School, Antonelli offers a praiseworthy presentation of the different facets of his work, without omitting to make some criticisms. Walras's main merit for him is the study of a general economic equilibrium and the clarification of the "principle of mutual dependence of all economic phenomena" (1910, p. 187). But his contributions to the applied and social economics seem premature. His applied economics lacks unity and the moral basis of his social economics is drastically reduced to the property's question for land and personal faculties (1910, p. 184).

At the *agrégation* competition of 1910, during his fourth (and last) lesson, Antonelli asserts his desire to contribute "to perpetuate the memory of the teaching of the great ignored economist Léon Walras" and he indicates to the jury members "that the time has come for you to decide if these theories must be represented in the French higher education of faculties, as they are in all the other countries". But the president of the jury, Paul Cauwès, does not accept this statement. He retorts that "as long as I am president of the jury, you will never be admitted at the *agrégation* competition". When Antonelli asks him the motive, he adds "because you want to lead the science in a way where I do not want it to go" (J. Morini-Comby, 1953, pp. 358–59 and cited by L. Le Van-Lemesle, 1994a, pp. 109–10). As we already saw, mathematical economics for Cauwès is allied with liberal orthodoxy. Therefore, Étienne Antonelli was not admitted.[102]

On a proposal by Georges Renard, Étienne Antonelli teaches at the Collège libre des sciences sociales, from November 1910 until 1913, a course entitled "Les théories d'économie politique mathématique. Léon Walras".[103] For his lessons, he used the *Abrégé des Éléments*, entrusted to him by Aline Walras.[104] From April 1912, Aline Walras decides to gather her father's scientific correspondence. As the drafts are very difficult to decipher, she contacts the numerous correspondents or their descendants to retrieve the originals of the letters. She is assisted in this task of deciphering and translation by Étienne Antonelli. She hopes for publication of the letters exchanged by Léon Walras with French and foreign scientists between 1871 and 1909, with the unpublished "Notice autobiographique" (1909a) as a preface. By October 1913,

[102] The jury includes A. de Foville, H. Truchy, C. Brouilhet and E. Allix.

[103] See the course programme of the Collège libre des sciences sociales which begins on 7 November 1910 (Walras collection of Lausanne—Leduc section, XII, box 138).

[104] At that time, a friend of Étienne Antonelli, the jurist Léopold Leseine (author of a Ph.D. thesis on *L'influence de Hegel sur Marx*, 1907) publishes with Louis Suret (author of a Ph.D. thesis on the *Théorie de l'impôt progressif*, 1909) an *Introduction mathématique à l'étude de l'économie politique* (Paris: Félix Alcan, 1911). The aim of the book is to enable the French reader to decipher the writings of Cournot, Jevons, Walras and Pareto. Louis Suret will also be the translator of several works including the *Recherches sur la théorie du prix* by Auspitz and Lieben (Paris: Giard & Brière, 1914) and with Georges Lutfalla, the *Elements of Statistics* by Arthur Bowley (Paris: Marcel Giard, 1929, translation of the 5th English edition).

120 files are ready.[105] Étienne Antonelli proposes the publication of the "dossier Bortkiewicz", composed of sixty-four letters, to the *Revue d'histoire des doctrines économiques et sociales*, but the journal's staff refuse due to their overly mathematical content.[106]

Following his teaching, Antonelli publishes in 1914 the *Principes d'économie pure. La théorie de l'échange sous le régime de la concurrence*, prefaced by Georges Renard (Paris: Marcel Rivière). In this book, he presents the theories of exchange, production, capitalisation, and circulation without deviation from his model, the *Abrégé des Éléments* and without any analytical contribution. Curiously, he distinguished within the "mathematical school" two "tendencies" which would apparently converge in the determination of the marginal utility. The first position is "Anglo-Germanic", with Gossen, Jevons, Edgeworth, and also Pareto (*Cours* and *Manuel*). This position considers exchange as a phenomenon based on hedonistic psychology. The second position, a French one, with Cournot and Walras, on the contrary, considers exchange as a natural and social, not psychological, phenomenon (1914, pp. 12–18 and 63). Antonelli criticises Émile Bouvier (1901a) for having confused mathematical economics and pure economics. For Walras, pure economics must be seen as the science of the general economic equilibrium, and the author considered "a determined market in relation to a given economic field, where absolute free competition exists" (*op. cit.*, p. 45) and it is in this market that he establishes the conditions for the determination of the exchange value of commodities.

After the First World War, in 1920,[107] Antonelli finally succeeds in the *agrégation* competition[108] and is appointed to the Faculty of Law in Lyon. The following year, Aline Walras entrusts him with the responsibility of the project to publish her father's scientific correspondence. With Aline's help, he establishes the "fonds Walras de Lyon" in December 1924. However, in May, he has been elected socialist deputy of the Haute-Savoie department on the "Cartel des Gauches" list, and his political responsibilities and action in favour of social insurance will lead him to forsake the project of publication.

7.5 Conclusion

The reception of the Walrasian general equilibrium theory was difficult in France and slow on an international level. Léon Walras remarked to Louise Renard:

[105] Aline Walras, letter to Ernst Duschinsky, 12 May 1912, kept in the Lausanne collection, Leduc section, block XII, box 129; see also Aline Walras, letter to Albert Aupetit, 23 October 1913, in: G.-H. Bousquet (ed.), 1951, p. 153–154.

[106] Aline Walras, letter to Albert Aupetit of 23 October 1913, in: G.-H. Bousquet (ed.), 1951, p. 155. É. Antonelli will publish some excerpts from this correspondence in his book of 1914.

[107] The *agrégation* competitions in economics will not be opened, neither in 1912 for budgetary reasons, nor in 1914 due to the world conflict.

[108] The jury, presided over by Fernand Faure, includes E. Allix, A. Dubois, A. Aftalion and J. Lescure.

> If one wants to harvest quickly, one must plant carrots and lettuces; and if one has the ambition to plant oaks, one must be wise enough to say to oneself: My great-grandnephews will owe me this shade. I have taken this course myself.[109]

At the end of the Preface to the 4th edition of the *Éléments* (1900), he insists on specifying:

> It took from a hundred to a hundred and fifty or two hundred years for the astronomy of Kepler to become the astronomy of Newton and Laplace, and for the mechanics of Galileo to become the mechanics of d'Alembert and Lagrange. On the other hand, less than a century has elapsed between the publication of Adam Smith's work and the contributions of Cournot, Gossen, Jevons, and myself. We were, therefore, at our post, and have performed our duty. (vol. VIII, p. 22, English transl., 1954, pp. 47–48)

According to him, justice will be done to him during the XXth century. He also often recalls towards the end of his life a remark by Pierre-Simon Laplace, expressed in the *Exposition du système du monde* (1796), according to which about fifty years passed since the discovery of the universal attraction by Newton, "without anything remarkable being added to it". Laplace noted subsequently that it "took all this time for this great truth to be generally understood and to overcome the obstacles posed by the accepted opinion on the continent [...]." ([1796] 1984, p. 530). And Walras noted ironically that he did not claim to surpass Newton and that he had to wait at least fifty years from... 1877—2nd part of the *Éléments* ("Notes d'humeur", 2000, vol. XIII, p. 518). Therefore, he should wait at least until 1927!

The influence of Walras on French economists of his time and subsequent generations remains weak. In the years 1910–26, a noticeable change is observed in the reception of pure economics, despite the break constituted by the First World War. Courses are established, and a number of works are published: those of Antonelli, then those of Bousquet. But the pure economics that is disseminated is often more that of Pareto than of Walras.

Beyond our period of examination, contributions will arrive, for example, from François Divisia (*Économique rationnelle*, Paris: Doin, 1928), from the *X Crises* group starting in 1931 (the Guillaume brothers) and from Gaëtan Pirou with his seminar at the École Pratique des Hautes Études from 1932 to 1934, which will lead to the book *Les théories de l'équilibre économique. Walras et Pareto* (Paris: Domat-Montchrestien, 1934). In fact, France does not participate in the international renewal of studies related to Walrasian general equilibrium that arises since 1930 in Europe and the United States.[110] It will be necessary to wait until the 1940s and 1950s with the contributions of Maurice Allais and Gérard Debreu.

---

[109] L. Walras, letter to Louise Renard, 13 April 1903, in: *Correspondence*, III, l. 1543, p. 225.

[110] Mention will be made here of the entry onto the scene in 1930 of Willam Jaffé (see J.-P. Potier and D. A. Walker, ed., 2004).

Part III
Reforming the Teaching of Political Economy

Chapter 8
From Criticism to the Reform Plan for the Teaching of Political Economy in France in the xixth Century

8.1 Introduction

How does the founder of the Lausanne School judge the development of the teaching of political economy in France during the XIXth century and what are his reform proposals? In the article dedicated to the taxation problem, published in 1896 in the *Revue socialiste*, Léon Walras presented a particularly virulent attack on the state of the teaching of economics in France:

> The class, in our country, that confiscated the Revolution to its benefit by ruining and debasing the State at the economic level, that has founded its wealth on the acquisition of the nation's assets (*biens nationaux*) at ridiculously low prices, that has increased it with coal mines, railways and other monopolies conceded without any serious care for the public interest, with industries protected at the expense of consumers this class formerly never permitted normal and regular education in economic and social science. First, they completely prohibited this education; then for a long time they tolerated it only on a scale and conditions that were laughable. Later they found a better solution: they succeeded in seizing all positions in that field and filled them with their own people, recruited and controlled by their own political leaders, this applying to science itself the clever and triumphant formula that they already were applying to the majority of agricultural, industrial, commercial and financial matters in which they could interfere: *exploitation by monopoly under the mask of liberty*. (emphasis by L. W., "Le problème fiscal", 1896d, vol. IX, p. 420, English transl., 2010, p. 344)

Walras thus explains the deplorable state of the teaching of economics by the deliberate behaviour of the dominant bourgeois class, which saw its fortune grow through the protection of the State and customs barriers. He distinguishes two stages in the attitude of this class. In the first phase, political economy has no place, then is barely tolerated; in the second phase, it becomes, on the contrary, a mere instrument in the hands of the bourgeois class, which controls all available chairs.

The discipline indeed experienced a difficult development in France in the XIXth century. Introduced under the Restoration and the July Monarchy, it was given a very limited space of liberty. The "optimistic" school was suspected, because it advocated free trade and more generally economic and political liberties. The Revolution of

J.-P. Potier, *Léon Walras, Economist and Liberal Socialist*, Springer Studies in the History of Economic Thought, https://doi.org/10.1007/978-3-032-04670-3_8

1848, its aftermath, and the early years of the Second Empire were hardly favourable to the economists of the liberal school. After the conclusion of a free trade treaty with England, the Empire became more tolerant towards this discipline, but the main teaching positions were occupied by the liberals of the *Journal des économistes* and the Société d'économie politique de Paris. It would take until the early years of the Third Republic to see a new impetus: in March 1877, political economy became a compulsory subject of the law degree and the liberal monopoly would be challenged.[1]

With the Republicans in power, on 16 May 1877, Walras hoped to return to his native country to teach his theoretical concepts. He counted on the support of an old friend, Jules Ferry, who would soon become Minister of Public Instruction and Worship (in February 1879). Initially, he hoped for the creation of a chair of political economy at the École des Mines de Paris, but did he have the right profile? His failures at this school did not argue in his favour. When a chair of economics was created at this school in 1885, it was entrusted to the polytechnician Émile Cheysson. Finally, Walras considered two other possibilities: either a chair at the École Pratique des Hautes Études, if the fifth section of "Sciences économiques" created in 1869 could be organised, or a chair in a faculty of law, for example, in Montpellier where he had very reliable friends,[2] since economic teaching was about to be generalised in universities. However, Jules Ferry lost interest in his career, especially from the summer of 1879. Léon Walras invoked, to explain his friend's indifference, the anti-clerical campaign that had completely absorbed him. In fact, he could not overcome major obstacles: he did not come from a *grande école*, he was not an *agrégé* in law and he was an opponent to the economists of the liberal school. In November 1879, Michel Chevalier, holder of the chair of political economy at the Collège de France, died. Upon hearing this news, Léon Walras inquired with the ministry about the application formalities for this position, without having any illusions about his chances. He did not receive the slightest response from the Director of Higher Education, Albert Dumont. In spring of 1880, he then wrote the study, "De l'enseignement de l'économie politique en France". In a note to the title, added for its posthumous publication in the *Mélanges d'économie politique et sociale*, he specified the context of its writing:

> In March–April 1880, having learned of Leroy-Beaulieu's presentation for Michel Chevalier's chair by the Collège de France, and at the moment when I decided to cease all efforts to be called from Lausanne to Paris, I composed this article by quickly jotting down what I wanted to say to Jules Ferry, Minister of Public Instruction, if I could have seen him. ("De l'enseignement de l'économie politique en France ", 1880d, vol. VII, p. 424)

Walras finally decided to stay in Lausanne, having obtained an increase in his salary.[3]

---

[1] The works on the institutionalisation of the teaching of economics in France are very numerous. In particular, we can mention the works of Lucette Le Van-Lemesle, 1980a, 1980b, 1983, 1991, and 2004.

[2] In particular, the prefect of the department of Hérault, Émile-Honoré Cazelles.

[3] The account of his attempts to obtain a position in France, then the negotiation of his salary in Lausanne are detailed in the correspondence published by W. Jaffé. On a note kept in the Lausanne collection, Walras briefly recounts how his salary increase was accepted in April 1880 (see the Appendix to this chapter).

In the first section, we will present the Walrasian critique of university institutions and promotion systems. In the second section, we will examine his reform project.

8.2 Criticism of Institutions and Promotion Systems

8.2.1 Criticism of Academic Institutions

Léon Walras formulates a whole series of grievances against the French special schools' system, which he himself had the opportunity to experience in his youth. In the study "De la culture et de l'enseignement des sciences morales et politiques", Léon Walras identifies three major defects in this system:

> [...] it breaks the unity of science by preventing communication between professors to professors and students to students, by confining both groups within narrow and limited specialisations; it reduces the education of the youth to a mnemonic and mechanical preparation, thus annihilating the spirit of curiosity and research; finally, it constitutes a combination through which, by means of an entrance exam and an exit exam, the civil servant is, if he wishes, excused from working for the rest of his career. Any other country than France would have been intellectually ruined by such a regime. (1879c, vol. VII, p. 413)

Léon Walras first criticises the system of special schools for breaking the unity of science; the teaching of moral and political sciences is fragmented and remains incomplete. This regime prohibits the dual scientific and literary education, which is indispensable for mastering the economic discipline.[4] The second criticism targets the "mnemonic and mechanical preparation". It is hardly original in itself and is found on numerous occasions throughout the XIXth century, even in the writings of orthodox liberal economists.[5] Thirdly, Walras views in the *grandes écoles*' system a "combination" that excuses the civil servant from "working for the rest of his career". He repeats this remark verbatim to define the École Polytechnique in his "Notes d'humeur" (2000, vol. XIII, p. 541). However, the attack is not very precise here; does he mean the military, given that 80% of polytechnicians throughout the XIXth century choose the army, and more specifically the artillery? He therefore proposes the outright abandonment of this system in favour of universities and faculties. However, the existing university system far from satisfies him, as it also does not allow for adequate teaching of moral and political sciences. Political economy has been introduced into law faculties while jurists are "detractors" of this discipline and economists are adversaries of law. The antagonism can only be reduced if a "political economy for law faculties" develops, "inoffensive", "conciliatory", in short, a "well-thinking, colourless as well as insipid science to please the Government and not to cast any shadow on well-established influences".[6] Finally, Léon Walras expresses a more

---

[4] See also L. Walras, letter to Charles Gide, 4 January 1891, in: *Correspondence*, II, l. 994, p. 426.

[5] See for example, J.-G. Courcelle-Seneuil, 1872, p. 336.

[6] "De l'enseignement de l'économie politique dans les facultés de droit" (1864), vol. VII, p. 357.

general criticism concerning the excessive concentration of scientific institutions and specialised schools in Paris, to the detriment of the provinces.[7]

Let us now turn to the Walrasian critique of promotion systems.

8.2.2 Criticism of Promotion Systems

Léon Walras condemns in violent terms the promotion systems in use in French higher education institutions. Describing the situation at the beginning of the 1860s, he states in his "Notice autobiographique":

> The positions to aspire to, consisting, for all of France, of three professorships and eight academician seats, were monopolised by the orthodox school, that is to say, by this school which, by virtue of varied, often contradictory, and always bad arguments, presents us with the current social regime as a *nec plus ultra* capable of sufficing humanity until the end of time. The holders, much more politicians and businessmen than scientists, accumulated them with one another and, under the pretext of cooptation, passed them on from father to son, from father-in-law to son-in-law, from uncle to nephew and nephew by marriage.[8]

Indeed, as Walras explains,

> [...] not only does the Minister no longer appoint the professors, but it is no longer even the Collège de France or the Institute, and it is ultimately the professor himself who appoints his successor. Here is how. When he has found the fortunate mortal to whom he wishes to leave his place, he establishes him as an economist by having him obtain some of these prizes that the Académie des sciences morales et politiques awards, by virtue of foundations and which are only obtained by addressing the subjects put forward to competition in accordance with the most hackneyed and academic opinions. Once he has had some crowned memoirs then published in volumes, the aspiring professor is appointed a member of the Académie des sciences morales et politiques, then he is proposed for the chair's substitute. On the day his patron dies, he already has his feet in his shoes. How, indeed, would he not be presented in the first line by his colleagues from the Collège de France and by his peers from the Institute who dine at his house and at whose house he dines; and therefore, how would he not be appointed? ("De l'enseignement de l'économie politique en France", 1880d, vol. VII, pp. 430–31)

A concrete illustration of this promotion system is provided by the Collège de France, where the chairs are "the prey of the most brazen and scandalous nepotism". As we will see later, Walras considers the career of Michel Chevalier as the most remarkable illustration of his thesis. After having made his chair "a springboard from which one launches into influential or lucrative positions in politics and industry" (*op. cit.*, p. 427), Chevalier organised his succession in favour of his son-in-law, Paul Leroy-Beaulieu, by having him obtain awards complacently granted by the Académie des sciences morales et politiques on hackneyed subjects and by proposing him as his substitute. After his death, the son-in-law was presented in the "first line" first

---

[7] In his "Notes d'humeur", he wishes the creation in the provinces (outside Paris) of "seven or eight university and intellectual centers" (vol. XIII, p. 528).

[8] "Notice autobiographique" (1909a), vol. V, p. 13; see also "Notes d'humeur", vol. XIII, p. 531.

by the assembly of professors of the Collège de France, on 14 March 1880, then by the Académie des sciences morales et politiques, on 20 April 1880. In the "second line", on both lists, was Frédéric Passy, "nephew" of Hippolyte Passy, but in this specific case, an "impossible candidate", according to Walras. The Minister of Public Instruction could only endorse the double choice of Paul Leroy-Beaulieu.[9]

Walras also has reservations about the promotion system in law faculties. He cannot accept the fact that the teaching of economics is entrusted to young law *agrégés* who have received no specific training. Furthermore, he deplores the great difficulties encountered in the *agrégation* competitions by candidates who have a genuine profile of economists. Thus, in 1903, the second failure in the competition of his "best French disciple", Albert Aupetit—*cf.* the previous chapter—will be for him the occasion to condemn this promotion system. Léon Walras finds it scandalous that such a small number of professors, the five members of the jury, can prevent access to all the French universities for a candidate specialising in mathematical economics. His relations with Émile Bouvier, professor at the Faculty of Law in Lyon, which were excellent, will deteriorate for this reason,[10] and he will have a quarrel with Charles Gide who, at the last moment, withdrew from the jury. In summary, according to him, "there is no free social science in France in universities with *agrégation* competitions where conservative politicians appoint professors".[11]

One understand Walras's indignation at promotion systems that do not take competence into account, and where the degree of kinship plays a role. However, it seems difficult to completely follow him on the question of the organisation of succession by the professor himself. Indeed, while he initially was reluctant to deal with the choice of his successor, he strongly contributed in 1892 to ensuring his succession to the chair of the Faculty of Law in Lausanne, the competition no longer existing at that time. He feared "that they might have given or promised [his] chair to some radical Tartempion",[12] perhaps to a disciple of Louis Ruchonnet! After unsuccessfully proposing the position to Ladislaus Von Bortkiewicz, in August 1892,[13] he

[9] The criticisms of Walras echo those of Charles Gide. The latter laments the fact that the chair of political economy at the Collège de France held by Leroy-Beaulieu does not attract regular students. In an article published in an American journal, he even adds:

> [...] it is a public course of lectures, where strangers in Paris come to listen as they would pass an afternoon at the Louvre or an evening at the Comédie Française, but whose regular attendants are a few young women who wish to add the finishing touches to their education, and some poor devils who come in winter to keep warm and in summer to keep cool, and at all times to sleep. (1890, p. 616)

[10] See, in this regard, the letters of L. Walras to É. Bouvier, 17 January and 2 February 1904, in: *Correspondence*, III, l. 1563 and 1565, pp. 241 and 242. Émile Bouvier, who is surprised by Walras's knowledge of the content of the jury's deliberations for the 1903 competition, retorts to him that "the competition is still the best mode of recruitment for professors" (É. Bouvier, letter to L. Walras, 1st February 1904, in: *Correspondence,* III, l. 1564, p. 241).

[11] L. Walras, letter to Louise Renard, 10 May 1907, in: *Correspondence*, III, l. 1653, p. 328.

[12] L. Walras, letter to Vilfredo Pareto, 3 December 1892, in: *Correspondence*, II, l. 1101, p. 525.

[13] L. Walras, letter to L. Von Bortkiewicz, 20 April 1893, in: *Correspondence*, II, l. 1127, p. 555. Bortkiewicz refuses because, at that time, he hopes to obtain a chair at the University of Strasbourg;

invited Vilfredo Pareto to offer his services to the Head of the Department of Public Instruction and Worship, Eugène Ruffy.[14]

8.3 The Reform Proposed by Léon Walras

8.3.1 The Project of Reform of Academic Institutions

Walras develops his ideas on a possible reform of French university institutions in the study "De la culture et de l'enseignement des sciences morales et politiques", on which he works intermittently from the end of 1877 until April 1879, that is to say, during the period when he hopes to obtain a teaching position in his native country. The reform proposals are not limited to the economic discipline but concern all "moral and political sciences", in a unified perspective of knowledge.

In order to understand the Walrasian project, which assumes a complete reorganisation of the faculty system and leaves no room for special schools, it is first necessary to recall the general conception of sciences that underpins it. At this time, as we saw in Chap. 3 (*Taxonomy of sciences and divisions of "political and social economy": an attempt at reconstruction*), the founder of the Lausanne School proposes the following decomposition:

- the "pure natural science", which includes mathematics, astronomy, mechanics, physics, chemistry, anthropology, and also pure economics;
- the "pure moral science", which includes history in all its forms;
- the "applied natural science", which includes agricultural and industrial technology, medicine, and also applied economics;
- the "applied moral science", which refers to individual and social ethics (theology, law, social economics).

Such a division is compatible with the organisation of universities into faculties of pure science (faculties of sciences, of letters) and faculties of applied sciences such as faculties of technology and medicine, faculties of theology and law ("De la culture et de l'enseignement des sciences morales et politiques" (1879c), vol. VII, p. 414). Naturally, for our author, this distribution is not as strict in practice. Indeed, pure sciences such as pathology and Roman law are taught respectively in the faculties of medicine and law (*op. cit.*, pp. 414–15). The institutional separation between pure and applied sciences is not desirable, as it ignores the complexity of relationships that actually develop between these two groups of sciences.

---

in April 1893, unaware that the decisions are already made, he consults Walras about the chair in Lausanne.

[14] See L. Walras, letter to Vilfredo Pareto, 17 December 1892 and the latter's response of 22 December 1892, in: *Correspondence*, II, l. 1107 and 1109, pp. 530–31 and 533. L. Walras goes so far as to write a laudatory "snippet" about Pareto, on 20 April 1893, intended for the *Gazette de Lausanne* (vol. XII, pp. 37–40).

Walras formulates the "a *priori* plan" for reforming higher education in France, carefully distinguishing two levels of education.

The first level of education would be based on a common core. It would necessarily take place within a faculty of sciences and a faculty of letters, or *better, within a single faculty of sciences and letters,* and it would cover all pure sciences, including natural and moral and political sciences. After obtaining the "first grade" diploma, students would have access to the second level of education.

The second level of education would be organised in the various faculties of applied science. For natural sciences, it would involve "technical faculties",[15] comprising different sections (mines, civil engineering, mechanics, industrial chemistry, military engineering...), faculties of medicine, comprising different sections (medicine, surgery, pharmacy). For the moral and political sciences, there would be the faculty of theology and the faculty of law. The latter would include at least two main sections: law and political sciences. Within the "political sciences" section, applied economics, finance, and statistics would be taught, and licences in political sciences would be awarded to young people preparing to enter central and departmental administration. Walras envisions, for the second level of education, two "periods": the first would not overly specialise students; the second would lead to final specialisation. The interest of this reform is to propose a dual literary and scientific education, which allows access to the true scientific methods of induction and deduction.[16]

The coexistence of economics with law not pleasing him much, Léon Walras proposes a more radical solution, immediately applicable. In his "offer of services" letter dated 9 February 1879, addressed to Minister Jules Ferry, he suggests the creation in France of a few "faculties of moral and political sciences", modelled on the German faculties of administrative sciences, or the Faculty of Social Sciences at the University of Geneva; the peculiarity of these establishments is to be independent from the faculty of law. The École libre des sciences politiques, founded by Émile Boutmy, would merge into these new faculties. The birth of such establishments would constitute an effective means to combat the "clique currently holding the concession for the exploitation of political economy".[17] Léon Walras's proposals actually align with those already formulated by former Minister Victor Duruy (1811–94) in 1870, and then by the deputy Paul Bert (1833–84) in 1872.[18] But, to successfully carry out such an overall reform of higher education, professors need to be trained. Walras placed a great deal of his hopes in the organisation of the fifth section

---

[15] This creation raises a problem for Walras, due to the existence of the École Polytechnique and the application schools attached to it! (*op. cit.*, p. 417).

[16] On the Walrasian "plan", see "De la culture et de l'enseignement des sciences morales et politiques", (1879c), vol. VII, pp. 415–17. On the question of dual training, also see the letter of L. Walras to Charles Gide, 4 January 1891, in: *Correspondence*, II, l. 994, p. 426.

[17] L. Walras, letter to Jules Ferry, 9 February 1879, in: *Correspondence*, I, l. 429, pp. 593–95.

[18] Senator Victor Duruy proposed on 4 July 1870 the creation of "faculties of economic and administrative sciences" based on a model inspired by German universities (H. Hauser, 1903, p. 133). In 1872, Paul Bert presented a more elaborate project for the creation of "faculties of economic and political sciences" (J. Chailley-Bert, 1892, p. 353).

of the École pratique des hautes études, intended for "economic sciences", created by Victor Duruy in January 1869.[19]

Having failed to obtain a chair in 1879–80, he would no longer take a close interest, during the following years, in the reform of higher education in France[20]; it would not be until 1900 that he returned to this theme. That year, there was much discussion in France about the problems of higher education, particularly in the social sciences. In Paris, in July 1900, an international congress on the teaching of social sciences is held, under the patronage of the Collège libre des sciences sociales; Walras's name appears among the members of its Honorary Committee. Our author envisions the possibility of improving the teaching of economics in French universities. He proposes that it should no longer be entrusted exclusively to the faculty of law, but should be shared with the faculty of sciences. The latter would be entrusted with a course in "mathematical statistics" and especially a course in "pure mathematical economics". The faculty of law would retain the teaching of economics in its literary form. Professors from faculties of law and sciences could jointly award "doctorates in economic and social sciences". In this perspective, it is essential to quickly train doctors in science who will teach economics at the faculty of sciences.

The idea of a dual teaching of economic science is shared by the dean of the Faculty of Law in Lyon, Émile Bouvier, very attracted by pure mathematical economics (*cf.* Chap. 7, *The Reception of Pure Economics in France (1873–1926)*). In the second part of his study "La méthode mathématique en économie politique", published in the *Revue d'économie politique*, in December 1901, Émile Bouvier emphasises that courses in political economy should not remain the exclusive domain of law faculties; in the future, this teaching must be partially transferred to the faculties of sciences. Courses in these latter faculties would deal with different areas of economics and propose a different teaching method, the mathematical one.[21] Walras is quite delighted with this convergence of views and he declares on 11 January 1902 to Émile Bouvier:

> In any case, I see you, in Lyon, in full possession of the solution to the problem of renewing economic and social science—teaching pure economics in mathematical form at the faculties of sciences and in non-mathematical forms at the faculties of law by doctors and *agrégés* who have attended the courses of the faculty of sciences.[22]

Émile Bouvier's response does not lack realism: "As for the division of Pol[itical] Econ[omy] between the faculties of law and sciences, do not believe that it is already

[19] See notably "Note sur l'organisation de l'enseignement de l'économie politique et sociale à l'École pratique des Hautes Études" (1879d), vol. VII, pp. 419–23. In reality, this project will not come to fruition. In 1886, a 5th section will be instituted, but focusing on "religious sciences". The 6th section devoted to "Economic and Social Sciences" will only be created in 1947 at the initiative of Fernand Braudel.

[20] Note that in 1895 a doctorate in "political and economic sciences" will be created and in 1896 the *agrégation* in law, option economic sciences (see L. Le Van-Lemesle, 2004, Chap. X).

[21] É. Bouvier, 1901a, pp. 1079–80, reproduced in the book with the same title, pp. 132–34.

[22] L. Walras, letter to É. Bouvier, 11 January 1902, in: *Correspondence*, III, l. 1514, p. 189; also see the letter to É. Bouvier of 21 December 1901, in: *op. cit.*, l. 1509, p. 182.

realised, even in Lyon, I proposed it in my article, and I believe that this is the future, but it is not yet done".[23]

8.3.2 *The Reform of the Content of the Teaching of Political Economy*

While countries such as England, Austria, Italy, and the Netherlands introduced the teaching of pure economics, France remained completely apart from this movement. Walras was deeply shocked by this. A good example of his proposals for reforming education in his native country can be found in the study prepared for the eventual organisation at the École Pratique des Hautes Études of the fifth section of "Sciences économiques" (1879d). The founder of the Lausanne School envisions a comprehensive education that spans three years, based on the division into three parts of "political and social economy".

The first year must be obligatorily devoted to "pure economics", which consists of the "study of the mechanism and effects of absolute free competition in exchange, production, and capitalisation". In the second year would focus on "applied economics", that is to say, the "search for interest rules according to which the production of wealth in agriculture, industry, commerce, credit, speculation, association, insurance, colonization must be carried out". Finally, in the third year, the field of "social economics" remains to be addressed, or the "search for principles of justice according to which the distribution of wealth between individuals and the State by property and taxation must be carried out".[24] The programmes of the second and third years can be interchanged without inconvenience. The annual hourly volume of each course can be 60 h, spread over thirty weeks, at a rate of two hours per week.

It is clear that Walras is proposing here the set of courses he has been teaching at the Faculty of Law in Lausanne from his appointment in 1870. However, at an institution like the École Pratique des Hautes Études, the course must be complemented by a "conference", dedicated to "practical exercises". These sessions allow for explanations of the course, commentaries on texts, and enable the enhancement of students' personal work, through presentations, for example. The hourly volume of the conference would be identical to that of the course.

---

[23] É. Bouvier, letter to L. Walras, 18 January 1902, unpublished, kept in the Lausanne collection under the reference F. W. II, 2317. L. Walras's enthusiasm at this time is such that he drafts a testamentary document in which he declares he will donate all his papers and books to the University of Lyon, if the faculty of sciences decides to offer a course in mathematical economics (document dated 8 October 1902, kept in the Lausanne collection under the reference F. W. IV a 4). He will abandon this idea on 27 December 1903, after A. Aupetit's failure at the *agrégation.*

[24] "Note sur l'organisation de l'enseignement de l'économie politique et sociale à l'École pratique des Hautes Études" (1879d), vol. VII, pp. 422–23.

With such teaching, it would become possible to quickly publish enough "*Annales de sciences économique et politique*, as they exist for mathematics, physics, chemistry, and natural sciences" (1880d, vol. VII, p. 441), which would be reserved exclusively for specialists in the discipline. After ten years, one could consider the publication of a "*Revue économique*", similar to the *Revue historique* founded in 1876 by Gabriel Monod, in charge of the 4th section in the school (*op. cit.*, p. 441).[25]

8.4 Conclusion

By the late 1870s, Léon Walras justified the necessity of such a reform in the teaching of his discipline with a hint of nationalism. According to him, at the end of the XVIIth century, France held an enviable position in the physical and natural sciences, which allowed the birth of modern industry. However, this field was now being dominated by Germany. In order to compete against this challenge, France must focus on the development of moral and political sciences, which would one day enable politicians to implement necessary reforms without resorting to the methods of "empirical socialism".

Appendix: Walras's Untitled Note (1880)[26]

I had here 4000 F at the Academy,[27] plus some casual income, and 600 F at *La Suisse*. Total, *4600 F*.

I was asking for 6000 [F] from the École des Hautes Études. I would have had to deduct 1000 (800 for rent over two years of lease, 200 for travel). Remaining *5000*, a move to do, and to live in Paris.

That was financially the deal.

Good Friday 26 March [1880], talked with Dr Recordon.[28]

[Friday] 2 April, saw the doctor again. Agreed that the matter of the increase would be submitted to Mr Ruchonnet at dinner on Monday. On Tuesday, I received a favourable response.[29]

---

[25] In Walras's view, this *Revue économique* would probably have had a strictly marginalist orientation, and not open to all currents as was the *Revue d'économie politique* by Charles Gide.

[26] This document is kept in the Walras collection in Lausanne under the reference F. W. IV 15.

[27] Annual salary of Walras since October 1872.

[28] Frédéric Recordon, doctor and Head of the Health Bureau, is one of the administrators of the insurance company *La Suisse*, where Walras is an actuary.

[29] Doctor Recordon, who had important Vaudois politicians to dinner at his home, successfully submitted Walras's request (see the letter of L. Walras to Louis La Cour de la Pijardière dated 18 May 1880, in: *Correspondence*, I, l. 479, p. 663).

[Friday] 9 [April], saw the doctor again. Communicated my note written in the morning. Saw Mr Boiceau.[30]

Saturday 10 [April], saw Mr Ruchonnet.

Thursday 15 [April], decision of the Council of State.[31]

In 15 days, the deal was settled.

[30] *Op. cit.*, p. 663. Charles Boiceau is Head of the Department of Public Instruction and Worship of the Canton of Vaud. The "Note submitted to Messrs. Boiceau and Ruchonnet" on 9 April 1880 is published in: *Correspondence*, I, l. 475, pp. 657–60.

[31] The Council of State grants Walras 5000 F, the maximum legal salary for a professor at the Academy of Lausanne (see C. Boiceau, letter to L. Walras, 15 April and the latter's response of 16 April 1880, in: *Correspondence*, I, l. 476 and 477, pp. 660–61 and 661–62).

Chapter 9
Teaching Social and Applied Economics in Lausanne

9.1 Introduction

On 12 November 1870, Léon Walras was appointed as an associate ("*extraordinaire*") professor of political economy to the Faculty of Law at the Academy of Lausanne. Although the appointment was initially for one year only, the following year (on 24 July 1871), he was promoted to full professor and officially installed in the chair by Louis Ruchonnet, on 20 October 1871. The faculty's programme provided for a course in "theoretical political economy" in the first year and a course in "applied economics" in the second year. Walras proposed giving a course in "pure economics" in the first year and, a course in "applied economics" and a course in "social economics" alternately to the second and third-year students combined.[1] This proposal was accepted.

Two months after his appointment, in a letter dated 11 January 1871 to the Dean of the Faculty of Law of Lausanne, Walras submitted, for approval by the Department of Public Instruction and Worship, his teaching programme, which included three components: pure, applied, and social economics. He specified:

> [...] the theory of social wealth or pure economics would be taught every year to first-year students. The theory of production and the theory of the distribution of wealth would be taught alternately every other year to second and third-year students, the theory of production, for example, in 1870-71 academic year, the theory of distribution the following year and so on.[2]

This cycle would remain unchanged throughout Walras's academic career. And the audience he addressed was rather modest: about twenty students per year.

This chapter will include three sections. The first section will trace the construction of the social economics course. The second section will trace the construction of the applied economics course. The third section will focus on Walras's teaching method.

[1] On the organisation of the courses, see the "General Introduction" to vol. XII.

[2] Letter to the Dean of the Faculty of Law of Lausanne, 11 January 1871, in: *Correspondence*, I, l. 171, pp. 260–61.

J.-P. Potier, *Léon Walras, Economist and Liberal Socialist*, Springer Studies in the History of Economic Thought, https://doi.org/10.1007/978-3-032-04670-3_9

Table 9.1 Cours d'économie sociale

Years	Number of actual lessons	Hours per week[3]
1871–72	56	2
1873–74	56	2
Summer 1876	56	5
Summer 1878	56	5
Summer 1880	56	5
Summer 1882	56	5
Summer 1884	56	5
Summer 1886	56	5
Summer 1888	48	5
Summer 1890	42	5
Summer 1892	38	5

9.2 Construction of the Cours d'économie sociale

During the 1871–72 academic year, Walras inaugurated the *Cours d'économie sociale* and during the summer of 1892, he delivered his last lectures. Table 9.1 is the schedule of the teaching years, with information on the number of actual lessons and the weekly hourly volume, reconstructed from the Lausanne archives, notably the attendance lists:

Thanks to the lesson manuscripts, the various course plans, certain notes inserted in the course or scattered in the archives, the exam subjects, and the student attendance lists,[4] one can approximately reconstruct the construction of the course over the period 1871–80 and assess its evolution from 1882 to 1892.[5]

9.2.1 Construction of the Cours d'économie sociale from 1871–72 to 1880

An indication of the content of the first lessons is provided by the course programme prepared during the summer and autumn of 1870 in Saint-Aubin-sur-Mer. The "second series" of this programme contains a fairly precise list of possible themes. Here is this list:

---

[3] From the academic year 1875–76 onwards, the course schedules vary according to the semesters.

[4] These archives are kept in the Walras collection in Lausanne, under the reference F. W. V d, box 29 (former reference).

[5] We here take up elements from the "Presentation" by P. Dockès of the *Cours d'économie sociale*, vol. XII, pp. 45–84. A summary table of the lessons and sections of this *Cours* appears in the edition of the *Cours*, vol. XII, pp. 79–84.

III. Theory of Property and Taxation, or of the Distribution of Social Wealth (Social economics).

1. Study of man and human destiny from the dual perspective *physiologico-economic* and *psychologico-moral.*
2. On the concordance of Interest and Justice.
3. Definition of the individual and the State—of individual interest and of the general interest—of private services and public services.
   Solution to the problem of order through the reconciliation of liberty and authority, and to the problem of justice through the reconciliation of equality and inequality.
   Demonstration of the principle of the *equality of conditions* and of the *inequality of positions.*
4. Organisation of property and taxation from the dual perspective of equity and convenience.
   Slavery—Serfdom—Proletariat.
5. Relations between the organisation of property and taxation with the organisation of industry and credit.
6. Critique of socialism.[6]

To prepare his first course, Walras already has substantial elements at his disposal. Indeed, the first three points of the programme correspond to the titles of the 4th, 5th, and 6th lessons of the *Recherche de l'idéal social* (1867–68). He can also use the manuscript "Méthode de conciliation ou de synthèse" (1868c). Finally, he has at his disposal *L'Économie politique et la justice* (1860a), the *Théorie critique de l'impôt, précédée de Souvenirs du Congrès de Lausanne* (1861e), and the memoir *De l'impôt dans le canton de Vaud* (1861f).

The preparation of the lessons leads our author to draft the manuscript "Exposition et conciliation des doctrines sociales" (1872c), which will be used from the 1873–74 course onwards. Section VI of this course will integrate into three lessons the material from the review of Gaston Le Couppey's book, "Le cadastre et l'impôt foncier" (1873b). In the official programme of the Faculty of Law of Lausanne for 1873–74, the following information is found:

Theory of the distribution of wealth:

- Of man and of human destiny
- Of the concordance of interest and justice
- Of the individual and the State
- Of the appropriation of wealth from the perspective of justice
- Of the appropriation of wealth from the perspective of interest
- Of taxation. (General introduction to vol. XII, p. 36).

A reconstruction of the 1873–74 course plan is given in Appendix 1 of this chapter. It comprises 52 lessons, and there is uncertainty about the four missing lessons. The courses of 1876 and 1878 do not involve substantial changes. In section V, Walras integrates lessons drawn from the study "De l'influence de la communication des marchés sur la situation des populations agricoles" (1874b), which will be published

[6] Emphasis by L. W. "Programme d'un cours d'économie politique. Saint-Aubin-sur-Mer, 1870" (1870c), vol. XII p. 34.

later in the *Études d'économie politique appliquée*. Probably in 1878, he introduces a lesson on "The Swiss Allmenden", the content of which dealing with municipal properties is drawn from two chapters of Émile de Laveleye's book, *De la propriété et de ses formes primitives* (Paris: Germer Baillière, 2nd ed., 1877) (see vol. XII, p. 851, note 1).

9.2.2 Plan of *Cours d'économie sociale* from 1880

Léon Walras introduces some modifications in the course taught in 1880. Indeed, in section IV, the 41st and 42nd lessons entitled "On Land Tax" and "Opinion of James Mill" become "On Intellectual Wealth" and "On Intellectual Property". This latter lesson reprises the first two parts of the study published under this title (1880c) in the *Gazette de Lausanne* of 10–12 June. In the 52nd lesson (section V), Walras integrates elements from the first part of the "Théorie mathématique du prix des terres et de leur rachat par l'État" (1881b), which he is in the process of drafting.

Here is the new section V of this course:

> On the appropriation of wealth from the perspective of interest. History of property and taxation
>
> 43rd lesson: Economic theory of property
>
> 44th lesson: Organisation of property in the savage stage and in the pastoral stage
>
> 45th lesson: Social systems of the Orientals and the Ancients
>
> 46th lesson: Social system of the Middle Ages
>
> 47th lesson: On the high cost of living
>
> 48th lesson: On living cheaply
>
> 49th lesson: Agricultural industry and market communication
>
> 50th lesson: Insufficiency of agricultural production
>
> 51th lesson: The Swiss Allmenden
>
> 52th lesson: Doctrines of J. Mill and H. H. Gossen"

In section VI, the lessons on indirect and direct taxation have disappeared.

From 1882 to 1892, the structure of the actual course is not fundamentally modified. Section I is split into two new sections entitled, respectively "Of man and human destiny. Social categories" (lessons 1 to 10) and "Distinctions between social science and politics. Method of social science" (lessons 11 to 14). In 1882 and 1884, Léon Walras introduces six lessons corresponding to parts II to VI of the "Théorie mathématique du prix des terres et de leur rachat par l'État". In 1888 and 1890, some lessons are not delivered to the students. For knowledge of the content of the summer semester 1890 lessons, we have the complete course notes of the student Georges Pellis, in eight sections of 42 lessons.[7]

Let us now focus on the construction of the applied economics course.

[7] Georges Pellis had his notes from the *Cours d'économie politique appliquée* (1889) bound with those from the *Cours d'économie sociale* (1890), in a single volume (18 × 21 cm). This volume is

Table 9.2 Cours d'économie politique appliquée

Years	Number of actual lessons	Hours per week
1871	65–67 (?)	3[8]
1872–73	56	2
1874–75	56	2
Summer 1877	56	5
Summer 1879	56	5
Summer 1881	52	5
Summer 1883	56	5
Summer 1885	56	5
Summer 1887	54	5
Summer 1889	54	5

9.3 Construction of the Cours d'économie politique appliquée

On 9 January 1871, Walras inaugurates the *Cours d'économie politique appliquée* and in early July 1889 he gives his last lessons.[9] Table 9.2 gives the teaching calendar, with indications on the number of actual lessons and the weekly hourly volume, obtained from the Lausanne archives, notably the attendance lists:

Thanks to the lesson manuscripts, course plans, certain notes inserted in the course or scattered in the archives, exam subjects, and student attendance lists,[10] one can approximately reconstruct the construction of the course over the period 1871–79 and assess its evolution from 1881 to 1889.[11]

---

kept at the Centre d'études interdisciplinaires Walras-Pareto de l'Université de Lausanne. A note in Léon Walras's handwriting contains an assessment regarding the student Georges Pellis: "mal suivi l'éc*[onomie]* pol*[itique]* appl*[iquée]*; bien *[suivi]* l'éc*[onomie]* soc*[iale]* " (note kept in the Lausanne collection, 7.5 × 23.5 cm, under the reference F. W. Vd, box 29). Georges Pellis (1867–1940) would become a lawyer and defend a Ph.D. thesis in law (*Du régime matrimonial des époux mariés sans contrat en droit international privé*, Lausanne: G. Bridel Printing, 1893).

[8] For seven weeks, in January and February 1871, Walras conducted four hours weekly, which allowed him to very partially make up for his delay. The number of actual lessons could have reached circa 65–67. It will be seen later that the plan found for 1871 only envisaged 45 lessons.

[9] He will be on leave during the summer semester of 1891.

[10] These archives are kept in the Lausanne collection, under the reference F. W. V d, box 29 (former reference).

[11] We here take up elements from our "Presentation" of the *Cours d'économie politique appliquée*, vol. XII, pp. 385–439. A summary table of the lessons and sections of this *Cours* appears pp. 435–39.

9.3.1 *Construction of the Cours d'économie politique appliquée from 1871 to 1879*

To get an idea of the content of the first lessons, one must go back to the course programme prepared during the summer and autumn of 1870 in Saint-Aubin-sur-Mer. The "second series" of this programme contains a fairly precise list of possible themes. Here is this list:

II. Theory of industry, or the production of social wealth (Applied economics).

1. Study of the principle of the division of labour or of the speciality of occupations.
2. Demonstration of the free competition principle and free trade. Formula of *laissez-faire, laissez-passer.*
3. Detailed study of organisation, based on the principle of division and liberty of labour:
    1. On agricultural industry;
    2. On manufacturing industry;
    3. On commercial industry.[12]
4. Theory of association and insurance.
5. Theory of colonisation. Examination of the *colonial* system.
6. Organisation of credit. Banks and credit institutions.
7. Agricultural credit;
8. Industrial credit;
9. Commercial credit.
10. Public credit.
11. Theory of speculation or of the capitalisation of savings.
12. Study of industrial and commercial crises.[13]

In fact, for the academic year 1870–871, only one draft plan has been found. It corresponds to the programme communicated to the Dean of the Faculty of Law of Lausanne.[14] The table of contents, which includes ten sections and 45 lessons, is given in Appendix 2 of this chapter. What are its characteristics? It is divided into ten sections: I Division of labour ; II Laissez-faire, laissez-passer; III Agriculture; IV Industry; V Commerce; VI Credit; VII Credit institutions; VIII Association and insurance; IX Speculation; X Colonisation.

Walras must have planned a preliminary lesson intended to establish the object and method of applied economics. Over the weeks, he selected more specific lesson titles and increased their number, in order to best ensure his service. What materials could he already have at his disposal on the eve of his first course? In fact, he had very few, unlike in the field of social economics. He seems to have delivered his courses in 1871 and probably also partially in 1872–73 without a complete drafting of the lessons, using as his main support some articles from the famous *Dictionnaire de*

[12] L. Walras inserts in margin of themes 4, 5, and 6, with a view to an insertion between themes 6 and 7: "Refutation of the *mercantile, exclusive* systems, etc."

[13] Emphasis by L. W., "Programme d'un cours d'Économie politique. Saint-Aubin-sur-Mer, 1870" (1870c), vol. XII, pp. 32–34.

[14] L. Walras, letter to the Dean of the Faculty of Law of Lausanne, 11 January 1871, in: *Correspondence,* I, l. 171, p. 260.

l'économie politique by Charles Coquelin and Gilbert-Urbain Guillaumin (*cf. infra* on this subject). In support of this hypothesis, we can note the presence within the manuscript of the "Programme d'un cours d'économie politique" of a distribution of this dictionary's entries into the three fields of "political and social economy". It can also be established that for section VIII, in the part dedicated to association, Walras uses the articles published in *Le Travail* and the book *Les Associations populaires de consummation, de production et de crédit* (1865) and that for section IX, he probably uses the study "De la spéculation—Étude d'économie financière" (1868b). Some developments devoted to banknotes may be found in the article "Des billets de banque en suisse", published in the *Bibliothèque universelle et Revue suisse* (1871a).[15] Finally, part X on colonisation will never be drafted, neither for the actual courses nor for the version intended for publication.

The course plan for 1872–73, comprising approximately 56 lessons, has not been preserved in the archives. One can only discover in the official programme of the Faculty of Law of Lausanne for 1872–73 (and also for 1874–75) the following information:

Theory of the production of wealth:

- On the superior principle of the industrial production of social wealth;
- Application of the principle of liberty of labour and of exchange to agricultural industry, manufacturing industry, commercial industry;
- On credit and credit institutions;
- On speculation. On association and insurance.[16]

At this time, Léon Walras probably had a first draft of the lessons on the following themes: the division of labour (advantages and disadvantages), the five economic stages (that is to say, the theory of stages inherited from his father): the free competition principle, agriculture, industry, commerce, credit and cooperative associations.

The course plan for 1874–75 (approximately 56 lessons) has not been found in the archives. It may have been based on an already significant drafted set. During the first two years of the *Cours d'économie politique appliquée* (1870–71 and 1872–73), Walras probably did not deal with the areas in which free competition could not function. However, in 1874–75, he introduced a lesson called "Exceptions to the Free Competition Principle".[17]

After this date, the course is no longer spread over the academic year, but is concentrated during the summer semester. Although the course plan for the summer

[15] Concerning the lectures on the issuance of banknotes given in 1871, 1872–73, 1874–75 and 1877, no manuscript seems to have been preserved except for a sheet of notes entitled, "On the banknote and the liberty of issuing banks", containing quotations and references to A. Smith, T. Tooke (quoted by J.-B. Say in his *Traité d'économie politique*), Lemaître (quoted by L. Wolowski in the Preface of his book, *La question des banques*), M. Chevalier, H. Cernuschi (sheet preserved under the reference F. W. V b box 18).

[16] "General Introduction", vol. XII, p. 36.

[17] *Cours d'économie politique appliquée*, Appendix to section II, vol XII, pp. 514–18.

of 1877 has not been preserved either, it is possible, to reconstruct with considerable precision, using several documents, the table of contents of the summer 1879 course in 56 lessons (*cf.* Appendix 3 of this chapter). What are the characteristics of this plan? It is constructed in twelve sections:

I. On the division of labour (probable title);
II. On laissez-faire, laissez-passer. Exceptions to the free competition principle (probable title);
III. On economic systems;
IV. On agriculture;
V. On industry;
VI. On commerce;
VII. On credit;
VIII. Short-term credit institutions. On the issuance of banknotes;
IX. Long-term credit institutions. On Stock Exchange operations;
X. On crises;
XI On association and insurance;
XII On colonisation.

In the 1st lesson of the *Cours d'économie politique appliquée*, Walras justifies his plan as follows:

> What does the fact of the *division of labour* consist of, in which man is summarised and by which he is defined from this point of view? This is therefore the first question we have to examine. Once this preliminary question is resolved […] we will be able to establish the *general and superior rule of agricultural, industrial, commercial, and financial production of wealth* and to refute the different and opposing *systems*. We will then do a detailed application of this rule to *Agriculture*, *Industry*, and *Commerce*. We will also do a detailed application to *Credit* and *Credit Institutions*, as well as to *Speculation* and to *Crises*. Crises are accidents or diseases of the economic body. We will investigate where they come from and how they could be ended or prevented. Lastly, we will study the fact of *Association* and *Insurance*, and that of *Colonisation*. (emphasis by L. W., vol XII, p. 446)

Compared to previous tables of contents, two new sections are noted. The new section III ("On economic systems") deals with the mercantile system, corporations, Colbertism, and the Navigation Act. The new section X ("On crises") includes two lessons (48 and 49). Walras actually places here the 28th and 29th lessons of the *Cours d'économie politique pure* of 1872–73, "Monetary crises, industrial and commercial crises, financial crises; On paper money". The first lesson disappeared from the *Cours d'économie politique pure* as early as 1873–74 and the second, as early as 1874–75. This suggests that the boundaries between pure and applied economics were not yet completely established at this time.

Section VII ("On credit") includes lessons 31 to 35 ("Nature of credit", "Long-term credit and short-term credit", "On credit securities: special securities", "On credit securities: general securities", "General principles of credit. On the liberty of interest rate"). These lessons will form the draft from which Walras will develop the "Théorie du crédit" (1898b), integrated into the *Études d'économie politique appliquée*.

In section VIII ("Short-term credit institutions. On the issuance of banknotes"), the manuscript of the 36th lesson ("Discount and issuing banks") has been found. However, this is not the case for lessons 37 to 40, covering the following themes: "Depreciation of money by issuance of banknotes"; "Increase of capital by issuance of banknotes"; "Impossibility of liquidating the issuance of banknotes"; "On the liberty of issuing banks". In fact, these lessons correspond to the substance of the paper "Théorie mathématique du billet de banque", written during the year 1879 and publicly read in November at the *Société vaudoise des sciences naturelles.*[18]

In section IX, the main lessons on the Stock Exchange form the raw material for the article "La Bourse, la spéculation et l'agiotage", which will appear in 1880 in the *Bibliothèque universelle et Revue suisse.* For a graphical representation of forward transactions on the Paris Stock Exchange, Walras uses the first two parts of the study by H. Lefèvre, "Physiologie et mécanique sociale. Fonctions de circulation. La Bourse", published in the *Journal des actuaires français*, in July and October 1873.

9.3.2 Plan of the Cours d'économie politique appliquée from 1881

The table of contents of the applied economics course for the summer 1881 includes 54 lessons. What are its characteristics? The plan is now reduced to ten sections: I—General and superior rule of wealth production; II—Exceptions to the free competition principle; III—On economic systems; IV—On agriculture; V—On industry; VI—On commerce; VII—On credit; VIII—On short-term credit institutions. The issuance of banknotes; IX—On long-term credit institutions. Stock Exchange operations; X—On association and insurance.

A new section I now groups the former sections I and II (except for the question of "exceptions"). Let us first examine the lessons removed compared to the 1879 course:

- a lesson on the causes and consequences of the five economic regimes;
- a lesson on the Navigation Act;
- three historically oriented lessons on agriculture, industry, and commerce;
- the two lessons from the "On Crises" section;
- two lessons on cooperative societies;
- the sole lesson of the "On Colonisation" section, concerning emigration.

From 1879 onwards, Walras wanted to remove the lesson on "Exceptions to Free Competition" and replace it with a new section entirely dedicated to this topic. The main material comes from the manuscript "L'État et les chemins de fer", which the

[18] For lessons 37 and 38, Walras uses the summary of the "Théorie mathématique du billet de banque" published under the title "De l'émission des billets de banque" in *Gazette de Lausanne* (1879e).

Journal des économistes refused to publish in 1876. However, our author lent the original manuscript to Jules Ferry without keeping a copy.[19] In February 1879, he wanted to retrieve it, at least "for a few weeks". Indeed, he wanted.

> [...] to extract two or three lessons for my [third-year Economics] course. I am indeed completing the writing of these courses and before the end of this year, I will have [in my possession] a set of 180 lessons in pure, applied and social economics [...].[20]

However, Jules Ferry kept the manuscript at least until March 1881. When he regained possession of his manuscript, Walras did not integrate "two or three lessons", but eight for the course actually delivered at the law faculty. Indeed, in the new section II ("Exceptions to the free competition principle"), lessons 9 to 16 are now found: "Public services"; "On economic monopolies"; "On railways as public services"; "On railways as economic monopolies"; "On railway tariffs. On price of maximum profit (*bénéfice*) on railways"; "On railway tariffs. On multiple price on railways"; "On State intervention in railway matters"; "Examination of objections to State intervention in railway matters".

This concern for "exceptions" to the free competition principle will grow in the following decade. As we will see in Chap. 16 (*Public Services and Natural Monopolies: What Role for the State?*), around the mid-1880s, Walras revises the text of the 29th lesson of the *Cours d'économie politique appliquée* ("On the relations of labour and capital"). In the new draft, the social question is partly placed on the field of social economics and partly on that of applied economics: to obtain the repurchase of land by the State and, on the other hand, put an end to the great monopolies of mines, railways, issuing banks, etc. (vol. XII, pp. 584–85 and note 35 pp. 883).

In section VIII, lessons 39 to 42 are now composed of excerpts from the paper "Théorie mathématique du billet de banque" (1880e), published in the *Bulletin de la Société vaudoise des sciences naturelles*. Finally, in section IX, Walras splits the lesson, "Legitimacy, utility, and limits of financial speculation".

The 1881 plan thus reveals a significant break with the previous courses and from this date, very few changes are to be noted. Two additional lessons will be incorporated, probably on the theme of association. It can also be noted that from 1885, Walras writes the 54th lesson, "On Insurance Companies". Finally, for knowledge of the content of the lessons of the summer semester of 1889, the last ones delivered in applied economics, we have the complete course notes of the student Georges Pellis, in ten sections of 54 lessons.

After his retirement, Walras considers a revision of his *Cours d'économie politique appliquée*. A document from the Lausanne archives provides us with some information on this subject:

> I want to transfer the applied theory of money from *Pure economics* to *Applied economics* in the following manner.

---

[19] L. Walras, letters to Jules Ferry of 23 February and 11 March 1878, in: *Correspondence*, I, l. 401 and 403, pp. 559 and 561.

[20] L. Walras to Jules Ferry of 9 February 1879, preserved in the Lausanne collection under the reference F. W. I, 191, published in: *op. cit.*, l. 429, p. 595.

Merge the current section III of the latter (*On economic systems*) into section I by placing the three lessons that compose it after the first five lessons.

Create a section II entitled: *On money* and composed of the following four lessons[21]:

9th lesson: Conditions of *numéraire* and of money. Qualities of precious metals;

10th lesson: Rational system of *numéraire* and of money;

11th lesson: Critical examination of Cournot and Jevons' doctrines on the measurement of the variations [of value] of money. Determination of the price of social wealth in money.

12th lesson: Regulation of the [variation of] value of money. The monetary quadriga. (Insert here the Solution to the Anglo-Indian monetary problem).[22]

Make the current section II a section III entitled: *Exceptions to the free competition principle* and comprising the 13th, 14th, 15th, 16th, 17th, 18th lessons.

The course would thus be extended to 52 lessons, of which some could be removed.

Lausanne, 28 May 1893. Léon Walras.[23]

9.4 Léon Walras's Teaching Method

The teaching method used by Walras would always remain very academic, based on a word-for-word dictation, in 45-min units, of the essential content of the written lessons. The *Cours d'économie sociale*, which from the outset relies on a substantial volume of previous publications, is a good example. However, it is possible that the very first lessons of the *Cours d'économie politique appliquée* of 1871, not written, were characterised by a certain improvisation.

In applied economics, the teaching refers to an economic literature almost exclusively published by Guillaumin in Paris. The professor makes extensive use, as a source of historical or technical information, of the *Dictionnaire de l'économie politique* by Charles Coquelin and Gilbert-Urbain Guillaumin (1852–53).[24] Here are some articles frequently used or cited in the course:

Charles de Brouckère: "Traité de commerce";

Michel Chevalier: "Chemins de fer";

Ambroise Clément: "Accaparement", "Associations", "Coalitions industrielles", "Règlements de fabrique";

Charles Coquelin: "Acte de navigation", "Banque", "Concurrence";

[21] These are the 37th, 38th, 39th and 40th lessons of the 2nd edition of the *Éléments d'économie politique pure* (1889c), removed from the 3rd edition (1896a).

[22] Likely reference to the "Note sur la solution du problème monétaire anglo-indien" (1887).

[23] Document preserved under the reference F. W. Vb, box 18. Walras refers here to a table of contents in 12 sections and 48 lessons created around 1881–82 by an aggregation procedure, in which section I comprises only 5 lesssons and section III, 3 lessons (vol. XII, p. 398 *et seq*).

[24] In his library, L. Walras annotates the 2nd edition of 1854 (copy preserved at the Centre d'études interdisciplinaires Walras-Pareto de l'Université de Lausanne under the reference ZAB 14,103/1 and 2).

Jules Dupuit: “Péages”, “Voies de communications”;

Léon Faucher: “Salaires”;

Gustave de Molinari: “Céréales”, “Liberté du commerce—Liberté des échanges”;

Hippolyte Passy: “Agriculture”;

Horace Say: “Assurances”;

Louis Wolowski: “Crédit foncier”.

Moreover, Walras has the habit of reading long quotations from economists to his students. For example, when discussing the benefits of the division of labour, he extensively quotes the French translation of *The Wealth of Nations* by Adam Smith.[25] When presenting the “theory of markets”, he provides lengthy excerpts from Chap. 15 of the *Traité d’économie politique* by J.-B. Say with laudatory remarks. When he addresses the issue of free competition, starting from the 4th lesson, he quotes long passages from the article “Concurrence” in the *Dictionnaire de l’économie politique*, written by Charles Coquelin (*cf.* Chap. 11, *Ideas and Men: Criticism of the French “Liberal School”*) in which the author claims not to defend the principle of industrial and commercial competition, being “too great, too elevated, too holy”, and confines himself to exposing its beneficial effects. Walras denounces here a strange “pretension to elevate laissez-faire, laissez-passer to the level of a sort of religious dogma”. If competition constitutes a “natural tendency” of social wealth, it depends on us to leave it free or to “confine it within certain limits” (vol. XII, p. 466). In the lessons devoted to “exceptions to free competition”, Walras is particularly keen to explain to his students the role the State must play in matters of natural monopolies and railways.

This teaching method, which offers no room for improvisation or digressions on current questions, will be maintained throughout the course. We do not have any testimonies from students regarding these two subjects. Nevertheless, we can cite, among others, two appreciations related to Walras’s teaching. In his speech at the Jubilee, Ernest Roguin mentions the difficulties of the audience: “we sometimes had trouble following you at the height of your abstractions”. He also relates that a delegation of students presented themselves before the professor to request (unsuccessfully) a modification in the programme, more specifically, “to discuss more particular and contemporary problems”.[26] For his part, in his last article, the Swiss writer Édouard Rod (1857–1910) testifies:

> I had the honour of attending his lessons: as he incorporated a lot of mathematics into them, I hardly understood them. But, if “pure economics” eluded me, the master who taught it left me with beautiful memories. He had the eloquence that gave strong convictions, a precise, refined, and pleasant language, and his whole person radiated benevolence.[27]

---

[25] On Walras’s annotations regarding the division of labour on his copy of the *Wealth of Nations*, see K. Misaki, 2021, and 2024, Chap. 1.

[26] Discours de M. Roguin, in: *Université de Lausanne, Jubilé Walras*, 1909, p. 12.

[27] É. Rod, 1910, pp. 141–42.

Throughout his career in Lausanne, Léon Walras conducted oral exams for his students in the faculty of law. In his archives, we found the lists of exam subjects in social economics from 1871–72 to 1878 and in applied economics from 1871 to 1881. The titles are broad and generally correspond to the titles of the lessons taught.

For the year 1871–72, the subjects of social economics follow the sequence of the course very faithfully:

1. Object and divisions of social economics. The theory of the distribution of wealth is not part of political economy, but of social ethics.
2. Social categories: definitions of art, science, customs, industry—Of good or justice as the principle of customs.
3. The division of labour and customs (property, family, government). The division of labour and science. The division of labour and art.
4. Method of social ethics. Reconciliation of socialism and liberalism.
5. General formula for the constitution of social science. Solution to the problem of order. Solution to the problem of justice.
6. Insufficiency of current theories of property.
7. Exposition and refutation of the socialist doctrine.[28]
8. Exposition and refutation of Mr. Thiers's theory of property.
9. History of the organisation of property.
10. On the single tax on ground rent considered as realising the ideal of justice and interest in the distribution of wealth. Opinion of James Mill.
11. On the land tax in the Canton of Vaud.
12. On a conversion of all existing taxes into a land tax in the Canton of Vaud.[29]

For summer 1878, the exam subjects of social economics are classified by sections of the course:

> I—Object and division of social economics; Social categories; Of good or justice, of the three principles; Synthesis of socialism and liberalism; II—Industry and customs; Industry and science—Industry and art; III—On liberty and authority. On equality and inequality; IV—Definition of property; Moral theory of property; Insufficiency of scientific doctrines; Doctrine of the Saint-Simonians; Doctrines of L. Blanc, Girardin, Proudhon; V—Organisation of distribution in the savage, pastoral and agricultural stages; Social systems of the Orientals and the Ancients; Social system of the Middle Ages; VI—Land cadaster and fiscal cadaster; On the basis of land tax; On the revision of cadastral taxes.[30]

Concerning now applied economics, the list of subjects proposed in 1871 is as follows:

> The five economic stages; The fact of the division of labour; General principle of laissez-faire, laissez-passer; [Liberty] of coalitions and strikes; Excess of production. Insufficiency of consumption; The three modes of association of labour, capital and land in agriculture; On

[28] Walras crossed out here: "the Saint-Simonians".

[29] P. Dockès, "Introduction" to the *Cours d'économie sociale*, vol. XII, pp. 59–60.

[30] *Op. cit.*, p. 66.

machines; The grain trade; Free trade; On long-term credit or fixed capital loan and short-term credit or circulating capital loan; Issuing banks—Deposits—Banknotes—Discount; Cooperative associations; On speculation.[31]

It is evident that the range of subjects quite broadly covers the programme treated in the Walras courses.

In 1874–75, the list is somewhat different:

Object and divisions of applied economics; Definition of economic competition; Exceptions to free competition principle; On the excess of production and the insufficiency of consumption; Condition of peasant-owners; Sharecropping. *Métayage*; On coalitions and strikes; Theory of markets; Nature of credit; Long-term credit and short-term credit; Mortage banks; Stock-Exchange operations; On limits of speculation; On the participation of workers in the profits (*bénéfices*) of enterprises.[32]

The subjects of 1877 remain very close, but also include discount and issuing banks and the question of crises; those of 1879 include the graphical representation of forward Stock Exchange operations.

9.5 Conclusion

From autumn 1872, Léon Walras hoped to publish his courses on social and applied economics, and from this date, a long drafting process was set in motion. Particularly in 1879 and 1880, Léon Walras redoubled his efforts to advance the finalisation of his lessons. In May 1879, he informs Louis de la Cour de la Pijardière that he "hopes to publish the *Éléments d'économie politique appliquée* the following year and the *Éléments d'économie sociale* in 1882".[33] Two months later, he repeated this information to Jules Ferry, adding that he is "currently completing the theories of agriculture, industry, commerce, credit, property, tax".[34] The death of his first wife in June, after a long illness, forced him to delay his projects. During 1880, he again advanced the preparation of vol. 2 and 3 of his *Traité d'économie politique et sociale.*[35] On 12 March 1881, he mentioned in a draft letter to Jules Ferry that he wants "to publish next year" the *Éléments d'économie politique appliquée.*[36] In October, he indicated that the volumes of *Éléments* "are well advanced" and that if his health improves, they could appear "by the end of the year".[37] In 1881, the structure of the

[31] J.-P. Potier, "Introduction" to the *Cours d'économie politique appliquée*, vol. XII, pp. 410–11.

[32] *Op. cit.*, p. 417.

[33] L. Walras, letter to Louis La Cour de la Pijardière, 22 May 1879, in: *op. cit.*, l. 438, p. 606.

[34] L. Walras, letter to Jules Ferry, 3 July 1879, in: *op. cit.*, l. 444, p. 616.

[35] L. Walras, letters to W. S. Jevons, March 1880 and to C. Boiceau, 16 April 1880, in: *op. cit.*, l. 465 and 477, pp. 646–47 and 661.

[36] Document from the Lausanne collection classified under the reference F. W. I, 191. The information does not appear in the version kept at the Bibliothèque de l'Arsenal, published in: *Correspondence*, I, l. 498, p. 686.

[37] L. Walras, letter to Ludwig Gebhard von Winterfeld, 14 October 1881, in: *op. cit.*, l. 519, p. 711.

Éléments d'économie politique appliquée included a table of 66 lessons, divided into twelve sections. In 1882, the structure of the *Éléments d'économie sociale* included a table of 64 lessons, divided into eight sections.

From 1883 to 1891, Léon Walras still hoped for the publication of the *Éléments d'économie sociale* and the *Éléments d'économie politique appliquée.* He specified to L. G. Von Winterfeld that these volumes "are both in my files in first draft or nearly so. But, if my health fully returns, I want to revise them both before publishing them alongside a second edition of my *Éléments d'économie politique pure*".[38] From 1885 onwards, the publication deadline faded[39] and five years later, Léon Walras confides to Maffeo Pantaleoni that he must reserve his strength for the publication of the two volumes.[40] But after 1893, he eventually gives up on publishing his courses. The lessons of social and applied economics will only appear in 1996, forming volume XII of the *Œuvres économiques complètes.*

Appendix 1: Plan of the Cours d'économie sociale of 1873–74

Section I—Of man and human destiny. Of the method of social economics
1st lesson: Object and divisions of social economics
2nd lesson: On the fact of the division of labour
3rd lesson: Analysis of human sensitivity. Interested emotions
4th lesson: Analysis of human sensitivity. Disinterested emotions
5th lesson: Analysis of human intelligence. Perceptions of the imagination
6th lesson: Analysis of human intelligence. Notions of understanding and conceptions of reason
7th lesson: Analysis of human will. Definition of moral personality
8th lesson: Analysis of human will. Critique of intimate experience
9th lesson: Social categories
10th lesson: Of good or of justice. Of the three principles of relations between men
11th lesson: Liberals and socialists
12th lesson: On synthetism
13th lesson: Synthesis of socialism and liberalism
14th lesson: Of the French, English and German genius

Section II—Of the concordance of interest and justice. Of the criterion in social economics
15th lesson: Of materialism and spiritualism in social ethics

[38] L. Walras, letter to L. G. Von Winterfeld, 17 December 1884, in: *op. cit.*, II, l. 628, p. 27.

[39] The "*Traité complet d'économie politique et sociale* in three volumes" will appear "in a few years" (L. Walras, Note attached to the letter to Redl, 9 November 1885, in: *op. cit.*, II, l. 684, p. 83).

[40] L. Walras to Maffeo Pantaleoni, 13 March 1890, in: *op. cit.*, II, l. 966, p. 401; see also the letter to H. Blabed, 7 February 1892, in: *op. cit.*, l. 1042, p. 478.

16th lesson: Utilitarians and moralists
17th lesson: Interest and justice are distinct and not identical
18th lesson: Are interest and justice concordant or contradictory?
19th lesson: Industry and customs
20th lesson: Industry and science. Industry and art
21th lesson: Synthesis of moralism and utilitarianism
22th lesson: Of slavery, serfdom and proletariat

Section III—Of the individual and the State. General formula of constitution of social economics
23rd lesson: Society is a natural and necessary fact and not conventional and free
24th lesson: General formula of constitution of social science
25th lesson: Of liberty and authority; of equality and inequality
26th lesson: Application to the problem of taxation
27th lesson: Synthesis of communism and individualism
28th lesson: Of antiquity, the Middle Ages and modern times

Section IV—On the appropriation of wealth from the perspective of justice. Doctrines of economists and of socialists
29th lesson: Definition of property
30th Lesson: Moral theory of property
31st lesson: Doctrines of economists
32nd lesson: Doctrine of Bastiat
33rd lesson: Doctrine of Mr. Thiers
34th lesson: On occupation
35th lesson: On prescription
36th lesson: Insufficiency of scientific doctrines
37th lesson: Doctrine of the Saint-Simonians
38th lesson: Doctrine of Mr. Victor Considérant
39th lesson: Doctrines of Cabet, of Mr. Louis Blanc and of Mr. Émile de Girardin
40th lesson: Doctrine of Proudhon
41st lesson: On land tax
42nd lesson: Opinion of James Mill

Section V—On the appropriation of wealth from the perspective of interest. History of property and taxation
43rd lesson: Economic theory of property
44th lesson: Organisation of property in the savage stage and in the pastoral stage
45th lesson: Social systems of the Orientals and the Ancients
46th lesson: Social system of the Middle Ages
Section VI—On the cadaster and land tax
47th lesson: On indirect tax [?]
48th lesson: On direct tax [?]
49th lesson: Current organisation of the cadaster
50th lesson: Land cadaster and fiscal cadaster
51st lesson: On the basis of land tax. Co-ownership of land by the State
52nd lesson: On the basis of land tax. Distinction of land from capital

Appendix 2: Plan of the Cours d'économie politique appliquée of 1871

Section I—Division of labour
Lessons 1 and 2: Five economic stages
Lessons 3 and 4: Fact of the division of labour

Section II—Laissez-faire, laissez-passer
Lessons 1 and 2: Demonstration of the free competition principle
L (3 and 4) 5 and 6: Liberty of enterprises
Lessons 7 and 8: Liberty of wages—*Id.* of interest
Lessons 9 and 10: Excess of production. Insufficiency of consumption

Section III—Agriculture
Lessons 1 and 2: Technical details. Three modes of association
Lesson 3: Peasant proprietors. Sharecropping
Lessons 4, 5, 6: Leasehold. English agriculture

Section IV—Industry
Lesson 1: Birth
Lessons 2 and 3: Machines
Lesson 4: Large industry. Industry by the State

Section V—Commerce
Lesson 1: Nature. Domestic. Foreign
Lesson 2: Domestic trade. *Id.* of grains
Lesson 3: Speculation and hoarding
Lessons 4 and 5: Foreign trade. Free trade

Section VI—Credit
Lessons 1 and 2: Defined as leasing of capital—short-term, long-term
Lesson 3: Credit on special securities
Lessons 4 and 5: *[Credit on]* general securities—General principles

Section VII—Credit institutions
Lessons 1 and 2: Banks
Lesson 3: Banknotes
Lesson 4: Mortage and industrial credits

Section VIII—Association and insurance
Lessons 1 and 2: Association. Cooperative associations
Lesson 3: Insurance

Section IX—Speculation
Lessons 1 and 2[41]
Lesson 3

[41] It is noted here the absence of titles for the three lessons of section IX and for that of section X.

Section X—Colonisation
Lesson 1

Appendix 3: Plan of the Cours d'économie politique appliquée of 1879

Section I—On the division of labour [*probable title*]
1st lesson: Object, divisions and method of applied economics
2nd lesson: The five economic regimes
3rd lesson: Causes and consequences of the five economic regimes
4th lesson: The division of labour; its advantages
5th lesson: True character of the division of labour; its disadvantages and its limits

Section II—On laissez-faire, laissez-passer. Exceptions to the free competition principle [*probable title*]
6th lesson: Definition of economic competition
7th lesson: Free competition determines the exchange relations of productive services among themselves
8th lesson: Free competition ensures abundance in the production of wealth
9th lesson: Free competition ensures proportion in the production of wealth
10th lesson: Exceptions to the free competition principle

Section III—On economic systems
11th lesson: Exclusive or mercantile system
12th lesson: System of regulations and tariffs. Corporations
13th lesson: System of regulations and tariffs. Colbertism
14th lesson: The Navigation Act
15th lesson: On the excess of production and the insufficiency of consumption

Section IV—On agriculture
16th lesson: History of agriculture
17th lesson: Agricultural operations
18th lesson: Cultivation systems
19th lesson: Condition of owner-farmers
20th lesson: Sharecropping; *métayage*
21st lesson: On the leasehold. Comparative rural economy of England and France
22nd lesson: On the leasehold. Causes of the superiority of English agriculture

Section V—On industry
23rd lesson: History and operations of industry
24th lesson: On machines
25th lesson: On coalitions and strikes
26th lesson: On the relations of labour and capital

Section VI—On commerce

27th lesson: History of commerce
28th lesson: Theory of markets
29th lesson: On the liberty of grain trade
30th lesson: On international free trade

Section VII—On credit
31st lesson: Nature of credit
32nd lesson: Long-term credit and short-term credit
33rd lesson: Credit securities: special securities
34th lesson: Credit securities: general securities
35th lesson: General principles of credit. On the liberty of interest rate

Section VIII—Short-term credit institutions. On the issuance of banknotes
36th lesson: Discount and issuing banks
37th lesson: Depreciation of money by the issuance of banknotes
38th lesson: Increase of capital by the issuance of banknotes
39th lesson: Impossibility of liquidating the issuance of banknotes
40th lesson: On the liberty of issuing banks

Section IX—Long-term credit institutions. On Stock Exchange operations
41st lesson: Mortage banks
42nd lesson: Industrial credit banks
43rd lesson: Definition of financial speculation
44th lesson: Nature of Stock Exchange operations
45th lesson: Graphical representation of Stock Exchange operations
46th lesson: Effects of Stock Exchange operations
47th lesson: Legitimacy, utility, and limits of financial speculation

Section X—On crises
48th lesson: On crises
49th lesson: On paper money

Section XI—On association and insurance
50th lesson: On the principle of association and insurance. On the liberty of companies
51st lesson: On the participation of workers in profits of enterprises
52nd lesson: On popular cooperative associations
53rd lesson: Cooperative consumer companies. Cooperative companies for the purchase of raw materials. Housing cooperative companies
54th lesson: Cooperative production companies. Credit cooperative companies. Exchange counters
55th lesson: On insurance companies

Section XII—On colonisation
56th lesson: Emigration

Chapter 10
Léon Walras and the Commission of the University Library of Lausanne: The Purchases of Books in Economics

10.1 Introduction

Shortly after his arrival in Lausanne, one of Léon Walras's priorities was to check the resources of the University Library about books in economics necessary for his teaching, and then to draw up purchase lists. He explained this on 13 June 1871 to Félicité Guillaumin:

> One of my first tasks upon arriving here was to inquire about the library's resources the field of economics. I found that they were almost non-existent and insisted on the need to fill this gap. I was authorised to make the necessary proposals and recently I submitted a first list of books selected from your catalogues which seemed to me the most essential. There are about F. 700 worth. It is a beginning and I certainly do not intend to stop there. I took care to indicate in a note to Mr. Wiener, Prof. of Greek literature,[1] who I believe will be in charge of this purchase, that all these books were available from you. I take the liberty of recommending this matter to you when it arises.[2]

In support of his request to the Library, Léon Walras wrote (probably) to the Head of the Department of Public Instruction and Worship, Louis Ruchonnet, in July 1871, in the following draft letter:

> [...] I handed Mr. Wiener a list of books in economics forming a good initial library collection amounting to about F. 700. I have tried to be as restrained as possible. I would be grateful if you could do what you can to ensure that this acquisition is made without reduction if possible and also without delay, as there are some books on the list that I will use myself

[1] Hermann Samuel Wiener (1813–897) had been a professor of Greek language and literature at the Academy of Lausanne from 1849 onwards. Between 1869 and 1872, he was the dean of the faculty of letters. He ended his career as an honorary professor for ancient languages, from 1878 to 1896. Between 1857 and 1873, he was a member of the commission of museums and the university library of Lausanne. He notably wrote the preface of the *Catalogue de la Bibliothèque cantonale vaudoise* (Lausanne, 1853–56). We would like to thank Olivier Robert, archivist at the University of Lausanne, for providing us with this information.

[2] L. Walras to Miss Guillaumin, 13 June 1871, kept in the Lausanne collection, under the reference F W I box 3, published in: *Correspondence,* I, l. 186, p. 279.

J.-P. Potier, *Léon Walras, Economist and Liberal Socialist*, Springer Studies in the History of Economic Thought, https://doi.org/10.1007/978-3-032-04670-3_10

> during my holidays to prepare my courses for next year. You are undoubtedly aware that there is practically only one publisher in economics. It is Guillaumin and Co on whose catalogue I have collected all the books in question. As I am on very good terms with Miss Guillaumin who currently runs this bookshop, I wrote her a note of recommendation without, however, positively asking to reduce the prices in your favour. She spontaneously replied 'that she will give you all possible advantages and facilities'.[3] I leave you to judge what should be done to take advantage of this good mood. It seems to me only, if my opinion seems good to you, that it would be appropriate to add this in the order letter, or to present yourself on my behalf, clearly asking for a certain discount. The one I enjoy as an author is 20 to 25%.
>
> Allow me, Sir, to repeat once again that I am pleased to see you taking this matter under your protection. After which I have only to apologise for bothering you in this way.[4]

What was the first list of books drawn up by Walras in June 1871? The document actually communicated to Hermann Wiener, a member of the university commission, has not been found in the Vaud cantonal archives (archives of the cantonal library and of the Department of Public Instruction and Worship). However, in the Lausanne collection, there is a summary copy of a list of 71 titles, which according to Walras's own calculations, amounts to 108 volumes. This list (three sheets) is attached to the draft of a letter addressed to Charles Estoppey (without mention of the recipient's name), dated 21 April 1872[5] (*see this letter below*). In this list, on which many titles are crossed out in red ink, it is specified after verification that two books are out of print (A. Smith in the *Collection des principaux économistes* and A. Blanqui, *Histoire de l'économie politique, see below*), reducing the order to 69 titles. However, the price of the last title on the list, *La liberté du travail* by C. Dunoyer is missing (was this title out of print at this time?), and the total order amounting to exactly 703 Francs 75 covers only 68 titles.

Furthermore, the Centre d'études interdisciplinaires Walras-Pareto de l'Université de Lausanne holds a collection of publishers' catalogues that Walras kept throughout his life. Among them is a *Répertoire général d'économie politique, statistiques, finances, commerce, comptabilité, administration, droit commercial, droit des gens,* etc. *Catalogue de la Librairie Guillaumin et Cie*, 1863, printed January 1868. On the copy of this catalogue, Walras ticked the books to be purchased by the library. It is thus possible to reconstruct his list by adding bibliographical details in brackets:

[3] In her letter to L. Walras dated 4 July 1871, Félicité Guillaumin states: "We have not yet received Mr. Wiener's list. You can be assured that we will give him all possible advantages and facilities." (unpublished letter kept in the Lausanne collection under the reference F. W. II, box 9).

[4] L. Walras, probably to L. Ruchonnet, July 1871, in: *Correspondence*, I, l. 188, p. 284.

[5] This list as well as the drafts of unpublished letters of L. Walras to C. Estoppey are kept in the Lausanne collection in a folder bearing the mention "I. To the State Councillors [typed] and to the Department of Public Instruction [in pencil]", under the reference II, box 10.

10.2 List of Books in Economics Proposed for Purchase in 1871 at the University Library

Folio 1:

Collection des principaux économistes:

[T I:] *Éc[onomistes] financiers du XVIIIe siècle,* 1 vol.

[T II:] *Physiocrates*, 1 vol.

[T. III et IV:] *Turgot*, 2 vol.

[T. V et VI:] *A. Smith*, 2 vol. (out of print).

[T. VII et VIII:] *Malthus*, 2 vol.

[T. IX à XII:] *J.-B. Say*, 4 vol.

[T. XIII:] *Ricardo,* 1 vol.

[T. XIV et XV:] *Mélanges*, 2 vol.

Économistes et publicistes contemporains:

[Adolphe-Jérôme] Blanqui: *Histoire de l'éc[onomie] pol[itique en Europe depuis les anciens jusqu'à nos jours, suivie d'une bibliographie raisonnée des principaux ouvrages d'économie politique*, Paris: Guillaumin, 4th rev. and annotated ed., 1860], 2 vol. (out of print).

[John Ramsay] McCulloch: *Principes d'éc[onomie] pol[itique, suivis de quelques recherches relatives à leur application et d'un tableau de l'origine et du progrès de la science*, translation from the 4th edition by Augustin Planche, Paris: Guillaumin, 1863], 2 vol.

J[ohn] St[uart] Mill: *Principes d'éc[onomie] pol[itique, avec quelques-unes de leurs applications à l'économie sociale*, translation by H. Dussard and Courcelle-Seneuil, Paris: Guillaumin, 2nd ed., 1861], 2 vol.

[Pellegrino] Rossi: *Cours d'éc[onomie] pol[itique,* taught at the Collège de France, 4th edition, revised and augmented with unpublished lessons collected by M. A. Porée [...] preceded by a bibliographical note on Rossi's works, by Joseph Garnier, Paris: Guillaumin, 1865], 4 vol.

[Pellegrino Rossi]: *Mélanges [d'économie politique, de politique, d'histoire et de philosophie, published by his sons*, Paris: Guillaumin, 1867], 2 vol.

[Frédéric] Bastiat: *Œuvres complètes,* [*arranged, revised, and annotated according to the author's manuscripts* (by P. Paillottet and R. de Fontenay), Paris: Guillaumin, 2nd ed., 1862–64], 7 vol.

Léon Faucher: *Études sur l'Angleterre*, [Paris: Guillaumin, 2nd ed. considerably augmented, 1856], 2 vol.

[Léon Faucher]: *Mélanges [d'économie politique et de finances*, with an introduction by L. Wolowski, Paris: Guillaumin, 1855–56], 2 vol.

[Thomas C.] Banfield: *Organi[sation] de l'industrie [...]ouvrage rédigé sur les leçons d'économie politique professées par l'auteur en 1844, à l'Université de Cambridge*, translated from the 2nd English edition and annotated by Émile Thomas, Paris: Guillaumin, 1851], 1 vol.

Mich[el] Chevalier: [*Examen du] système [commercial connu sous le nom de système] protecteur*, [Paris: Guillaumin, 2nd ed., 1853], 1 vol.

[Henry Charles] Carey: *Princ[ipes] de la sc[ience] sociale*, [translated by MM. Saint-Germain-Leduc and Augustin Planche, Paris: Guillaumin, 1861], 3 vol.

G[uillaume] Roscher: *Principes d'éc[onomie] pol[itique*, translated from the 2nd edition and annotated by M. L. Wolowski, Paris: Guillaumin, 1857], 2 vol.

L[uigi] Cibrario: *Éc[onomie] pol[itique] du Moyen Âge* [translated from the 4th edition by Mr. Barneaud and preceded by an introduction by M. Wolowski, Paris: Guillaumin, 1859], 2 vol.

[Marco] Minghetti: [*Des] R[apports] de l'éc[onomie] pub[lique] av[ec] la morale [et le droit*, translated by M. Saint-Germain-Leduc, preceded by an introduction by M. H. Passy, Paris: Guillaumin, 1863], 1 vol.

Bibliothèque des sciences morales et politiques:

L[éonce] de Lavergne:

Essai sur l'économie rurale de l'Angleterre, [de l'Écosse et de l'Irlande, Paris: Guillaumin, 4th ed., 1863], 1 vol.

Économie rurale de la France [depuis 1789, Paris: Guillaumin, 3rd ed., 1866], 1 vol.

L'agriculture et la population, [Paris: Guillaumin, 2nd augmented ed., 1865], 1 vol.

Folio 2:

[Alexandre] Moreau de Jonnès: *Éléments de statistique, [principes généraux de cette science, sa classification, sa méthode, ses opérations, ses divers degrés de certitude, ses erreurs et ses progrès, avec son application à la constatation des faits naturels sociaux et politiques, historiques contemporains*, Paris: Guillaumin, 2nd ed., 1856], 1 vol.

[Alexandre] Moreau de Jonnès: *Statistique de l'industrie de la France*, [Paris: Guillaumin, 1856], 1 vol.

[Alfred] Sudre: *Histoire du communisme, [ou Réfutation historique des utopies socialistes*, Paris: Guillaumin, 5th ed., 1856], 1 vol.

[Henri] Baudrillart: *Manuel d'éc[onomie] pol[itique*, Paris: Guillaumin, 2nd ed., 1865], 1 vol.

[Henri Baudrillart]: *Études de phil[osophie] mor[ale] et d'éc[onomie] pol[itique*, Paris: Guillaumin, 1858], 2 vol.

[Jean-Jacques] Rapet: *Manuel populaire [de morale et d'économie politique*, Paris: Guillaumin, 2nd ed., 1863], 1 vol.

Arthur Young: *Voyages en France [pendant les années 1787, 1788 et 1789*, new translation by M. Lesage, preceded by an introduction by M. Léonce de Lavergne, Paris: Guillaumin, 1860, 2 vol.].

[Arthur Young]: *Voyages en Italie et en Espagne [pendant les années 1787 et 1789*, translation by M. Lesage with an introduction by M. Léonce de Lavergne, Paris: Guillaumin, 1860], 1 vol.

Ch[arles] Coquelin: *Du crédit et des banques*, [2nd revised edition, annotated, augmented with an Introduction by J.-G. Courcelle-Seneuil and a Biographical Notice by G. de Molinari, Paris: Guillaumin, 1859], 1 vol.

[Patrick James] Stirling: *Philosophie du commerce, [ou Esquisse d'une théorie des profits et des prix, contenant un examen des principes qui déterminent la valeur relative du blé, du travail et du numéraire*, translated by Saint-Germain-Leduc, Paris: Guillaumin, 1861], 1 vol.

J[oseph] Garnier: *Traité d'éc[onomie] politique. [Exposé didactique des principes et des applications de cette science et de l'organisation économique de la société*, Paris: Garnier frères/Guillaumin, 5th considerably augmented ed., 1863], 1 vol.

[Charles Coquelin et Gilbert-Urbain Guillaumin:] *Dictionnaire de l'économie politique*, [Paris: Guillaumin, 1852–53, 3rd ed., 1864], 2 vol.

[Collective work:] *Dictionnaire [universel théorique et pratique] du commerce et de la navigation*, [Paris: Guillaumin, 1st ed. 1859–61, 2th ed., 1863], 2 vol.

[Adolphe-Jérôme] Blanqui: *Précis élémentaire [de l'économie politique, précédé d'une introduction historique et suivi d'une biographie des économistes, d'un catalogue et d'un vocabulaire analytique*, 3rd ed., Paris: Guillaumin, 1857], 1 vol.

[Charles] Le Hardy de Beaulieu: *Traité élémentaire [d'économie politique et de quelques unes de ses applications les plus usuelles*, Paris/Brussels: A. Lacroix, Verboeckhoven et Cie, 2nd ed., 1866], 1 vol.

[Antoine-Élysée] Cherbuliez: *Simples notions de l'ordre social, [à l'usage de tout le monde*, Paris: Guillaumin, 1848], 1 vol.

[Jean-Gustave] Courcelle-Seneuil: *Traité théorique et pratique [d'économie politique*, Paris: Guillaumin, 2nd ed., 1867], 2 vol.

[Antoine-Élysée] Cherbuliez: *Précis de la sc[ience] éc[onomique et de ses principales applications*, Paris: Guillaumin 1862], 2 vol.

[Gustave] de Molinari: *Cours d'éc[onomie] pol[itique*, Paris /Brussels: A. Lacroix, Verboeckhoven et Cie, 2nd ed., 1863], 2 vol.

[Antonio] Scialoja: *Les princ[ipes] de l'éc[onomie] soc[iale, exposés selon l'ordre logique des idées*, work considerably enlarged and entirely revised by the author, translated and annotated by H. Devillers, Paris: Guillaumin, 1844], 1 vol.

[Auguste] Ott: *Traité d'écon[omie] sociale, [ou l'Économie politique coordonnée au point de vue du progrès*, Paris: F. Renou, 1851], 1 vol.

R[oger] de Fontenay: *Du revenu foncier*, [Paris: Guillaumin, 1854], 1 vol.

Folio 3:

H[ippolyte-Philibert] Passy: *Des systèmes de culture en France [et de leur influence sur l'économie sociale*, Paris: Guillaumin, 2nd ed., 1853], 1 vol.

É[douard] Lecouteux: *Traité des entreprises de grande culture, [ou Principes généraux d'économie rurale*, Paris: Librairie agricole, 2nd ed., 1861], 2 vol.

[Émile] de Laveleye: *[Essai sur l']économie rurale de la Belgique*, [Paris: Guillaumin, 2nd ed. Revised and enlarged, 1863], 1 vol.

[Alexandre] Moreau de Jonnès: *Statistique de l'agriculture en France, [comprenant la statistique des céréales, de la vigne, des cultures diverses, des pâturages, des bois et forêts et des animaux domestiques*, Paris: Guillaumin, 1848], 1 vol.

[Charles] Le Hardy de Beaulieu: *Du salaire. [Exposé des lois économiques qui régissent la rémunération du travail et des causes qui modifient l'action de ces lois*, Paris: Guillaumin, 2nd ed., 1862], 1 vol.

J[ules] Duval: *Histoire de l'émigration [européenne, asiatique et africaine au* XIXe *siècle. Ses causes, ses caractères, ses effets*, Paris: Guillaumin, 1862], 1 vol.

[Félix Esquirou] de Parieu: *Histoire des impôts [généraux sur la propriété et le revenu*, Paris: Guillaumin, 1856], 1 vol.

[Félix Esquirou] de Parieu: *Traité des impôts [considérés sous le rapport historique, économique et politique en France et à l'étranger*, Paris: Cotillon/Guillaumin, 2nd ed., 1866–67], 4 vol.

É[douard] Vignes: *Traité élémentaire des impôts en France, [comprenant: 1° un aperçu économique et historique; 2° un exposé méthodique et raisonné de la législation; 3° l'indication, sur chaque point, des lois, ordonnances ou décrets; 4° l'organisation des administrations financières; 5° les tarifs en vigueur; 6° des renseignements statistiques sur tous les services financiers; 7° le tableau de toutes les taxes autorisées*; 2nd ed. Updated with legislation up to 1st January 1868, Paris: P. Dupont, 1868], 1 vol.

[Jean-Gustave] C[ourcelle]-Seneuil: *Traité [théorique et pratique] des op[érations] de banque*, [Paris: Guillaumin 5th ed. revised and enlarged, 1871], 1 vol.

A[ugust] Cieszkowski: *Du crédit et de la circulation*, [Paris: Guillaumin, 2nd ed., 1847], 1 vol.

[Alphonse F. M.] Léon: *Lettres sur la question des monnaies*, [Paris: Guillaumin, 2nd ed., 1860], 1 vol.

[Nicolas] Damaschino: *Traité des magasins généraux [(Docks) et des ventes publiques de marchandises en gros*, with an introduction by Maurice Block, Paris: Guillaumin, 1860], 1 vol.

[Augustin] Renouard: *Traité des brevets d'invention*, [Paris: Guillaumin, 3rd ed., 1865], 1 vol.

[Jean-Gustave] C[ourcelle]-Seneuil: *Traité [théorique et pratique] des entreprises industrielles, commerciales et agricoles [ou Manuel des affaires*, Paris: Guillaumin, 2nd ed., 1857], 1 vol.

[*added, but already mentioned above*: Ch. Coquelin: *Le crédit et les banques*].

Ch[arles] Le Touzé: *Traité [théorique et pratique] du change, [des arbitrages et des matières d'or et d'argent: contenant les changes et les monnaies des principales places du commerce du monde* […], Paris: Guillaumin, 1868], 1 vol.

[*crossed out*: Goschen]

[Henri] Cernuschi: *Mécanique de l'échange*, [Paris/Brussels: A. Lacroix, Verboeckhoven et Cie, 2nd ed., 1866], 1 vol.

[Pierre-Auguste] Boutron: *Théorie de la rente foncière*, [Paris: Guillaumin, 1867], 1 vol.

C[lément] Juglar: *Du change et de la liberté d'émission*, [Paris: Guillaumin, 1868], 1 vol.

[*crossed out:* Le Hardy]

[Charles] Le Hardy de Beaulieu: *La propriété et sa rente [dans leurs rapports avec l'économie politique et le droit public*, 2nd ed., Brussels: C. Muquardt, 1869], 1 vol.

[Charles Le Hardy de Beaulieu]: *Petit manuel [d'économie politique à l'usage spécial des Écoles et des Bibliothèques populaires, free translation from the German of Otto Hubner with numerous additions*, Mons: Manceaux, 3rd ed., 1869], 1 vol.

[Alphonse F. M.] Léon: *De l'uniformité des monnaies. [Notes présentées à l'Académie des sciences et suivies d'une lettre à M. le ministre des Finances*, Paris: Gauthier-Villars, 1868], 1 vol.

J[ules] Dupuit: *La liberté commerciale, [son principe et ses conséquences*, Paris: Guillaumin, 1861], 1 vol.

[Charles] Dunoyer: *[De] la liberté du travail, [ou simple exposé des conditions dans lesquelles les forces humaines s'exercent avec le plus de puissance*, Paris: Guillaumin, 1845], 3 vol.

10.3 Walras's Arguments to Overcome the Reluctance of the Library, and the Results Obtained in 1872

However, things are dragging on. The library commission does not seem willing to make such purchases. In spring the following year, Walras follows up on the matter with Charles Estoppey,[6] the successor of Louis Ruchonnet as the head of the Department of Public Instruction and Worship. The latter will ask the cantonal library about the reasons for not acquiring the books. On 12 April 1872, he receives a response on behalf of Ch.-Ph. Dumont, cantonal assistant librarian:

"Dear Councillor,

Having been unable to find any documents related to the purchase of the hundred works on political economy requested by Mr. Professor Walras, I turned to Mr. Professor Wiener, a member of the Cantonal Library Commission.

Mr. Wiener informed me that this proposal, submitted for the commission's examination, revealed that a very large proportion of the books indicated by Mr. Walras had already been part of the Cantonal Library for some time and were listed in the catalogues. For the other items on the list, a selection was required by the commission. This is how the number of books in political economy was reduced to fifteen; their acquisition was carried out immediately.

Please allow me to express the wish that Mr. Professor Walras be invited to specify the books whose acquisition he now deems necessary and which the Library does not already possess."[7]

Charles Estoppey noted on the back of this letter: "15 April [18]72. To transmit by copy to Mr. Professor Walras". Léon Walras then became aware of its content and addressed the following unpublished letter to Charles Estoppey:

Mr State Councillor, Head of the Department of Public Instruction and Worship.

Lausanne, 17 April 1872,

Mr Councillor,

Yesterday, I received the copy you kindly sent to me of a letter dated 12th of this month, in which the cantonal assistant librarian transmitted to you a response from Professor Wiener, a member of the Library Commission, concerning the books in political economy whose purchase I requested last year. This response prompts the following observations from me, which I hasten to address to you:

---

[6] Charles Estoppey (1820–88). Cantonal judge from 1862 to 1866, he was elected State Councillor in 1866 under the radical banner. Head of the Department of Public Instruction and Worship in 1872, he resigned in May 1873 to return to the Cantonal Court. Re-elected State Councillor in December 1874, he would lead the Department of the Interior, then that of Justice and Police (1875–88).

[7] The cantonal sub-librarian to the Department of Public Instruction and Worship, 12 April 1872, letter kept in the Vaud cantonal archives under the reference K XIII/52/4/700.

According to Mr. Wiener, "the purchase proposal in question, submitted for the Cantonal Library Commission's examination, demonstrated that a *very large number* of the books I indicated had already been part of the cantonal library for some time and are listed in its catalogues". Allow me to first examine this important point.

Upon verification, of the 70 books[8] mentioned on my list, I find 4 for which Mr. Wiener's assertion is accurate. I compiled this list after examining the *Catalogue of the Cantonal Library*, but undoubtedly not the supplements. However, I do indeed find in these the following books[9]:

In the 1st Supplement: Bastiat, *Oeuvres complètes*[10]; Rapet, *Manuel de morale et d'économie politique.*[11]

In the 2nd supplement: Blanqui, *Histoire de l'économie politique.*[12]

In the manuscript catalogue: De Parieu, *Traité des impôts.*[13]

However, I must point out that the library's copy of Bastiat's *Oeuvres* contains only 6 volumes instead of 7 and that Rapet's *Manuel*, an important work, is the first edition since which a second *entirely revised* edition has been published. Consequently, I am removing the last two books from my list; I only retain volume VII of Bastiat's *Oeuvres* and Rapet's *Manuel* for the 2nd edition.

With this correction made, I still find on my list 4 other books regarding which I can explain, but not to the same extent, Mr. Wiener's response. They are as follows:

Adam Smith, *Oeuvres complètes*

Malthus *id*

J.-B. Say *id*

Ricardo *id*

These books are part of the *Collection des principaux économistes* from the publisher Guillaumin. I confess that, although I had found in the Catalogue the main works of

---

8 On the draft of this letter, kept in the Walras collection in Lausanne, it reads: "68 works".

9 With the draft of this letter, there are two sheets with the letterhead of the "Caisse d'escompte des associations populaires" on which Walras noted references taken from the First, Second, Third Supplements of the catalogue of the Cantonal Library (1858, 1864, 1868), as well as from the Manuscript Catalogue.

10 According to the references noted by Walras: 1855, 6 vol., it concerns F. Bastiat, *Œuvres complètes, mises en ordre et précédées d'une notice biographique par R. de Fontenay*, Paris: Guillaumin, 1855, 6 vol.

11 According to the references noted by Walras: 1858, it concerns J.-J. Rapet, *Manuel de morale et d'économie politique à l'usage des classes ouvrières*, Paris: Guillaumin, 1858.

12 According to the references noted by Walras: 4th ed., 2 vol., it concerns A. Blanqui, *Histoire de l'économie politique en Europe*, 4th ed. revised and enlarged, Paris: Guillaumin, 1860, 2 vol.

13 According to the references noted by Walras: 2nd edition, 4 vol., it concerns F. Esquirou de Parieu, *Traité des impôts considérés sous le rapport historique, économique et politique en France et à l'étranger*, 2nd ed., Paris: Guillaumin, 1866–67, 4 vol.

these authors, I had thought I could refrain from excluding their complete works from the Collection. Here were my reasons in this regard. The editions of the Cantonal Library are old editions, sometimes preceding other editions given by the authors themselves. Those of the Guillaumin collection are editions published after the death of these authors, perfectly complete, enriched with biographical and bibliographical notices, Introductions, and especially explanatory notes that greatly facilitate reading for the beginners.[14] Among the theories of these classical writers, several have certainly remained in the science, but many have also been replaced. To place only these old editions in the hands of students is, for this reason, to risk confusing their ideas much more than clarifying them, and I do not hesitate to declare that, for my part, I would not advise them to read these masters, as long as they cannot do so in the new editions, with the accompaniment of remarks from modern science.

These new editions, very compact, are moreover extremely inexpensive. The dispositions revealed by the commission of the library, the slowness of its decisions as well as the nature and the form of its responses are not such as to make me hope that my reasons, however serious they may be, could prevail; but for the sake of my conscience, I nonetheless leave on my list the *Collection* as complete as possible of the *Principaux Économistes.*

Adding these 4 books to the previous 4, we reach the number of 8 which still seems quite far from the *very large number* indicated by Mr. Wiener. By searching carefully, I still notice two other works for which the commission of the library may have believed that my request was redundant. These are: Rossi, *Cours d'économie politique*; Ch. Dunoyer, *La liberté du travail.*

The library indeed possesses an old edition for two years of the Rossi's *Cours*[15] and an edition also very old of Dunoyer's book,[16] which has since been completely redone and whose title has even changed. Is it necessary to say that these old editions are, in such conditions, absolutely of no use? What would one say of a critic, for example, who would flatter himself to have studied the ideas of Dunoyer because he had examined the first edition, published in 1825, of a work that the author developed throughout his life and which he completely revised twice under two different names from the first? If such are the principles generally applied by the commission of the Library to its purchases, I declare them completely ridiculous. However, I am certain that it must proceed differently in the matter of editions of Greek and Latin authors; for if it did so in this case (which, all things considered, would still have fewer disadvantages than in the matter of economics), the professors responsible for teaching these subjects would have long since decided to consider the cantonal library as non-existent.

---

[14] On the draft of this letter, it reads at this point: "the reading of these classics, of which certainly some theories have remained in science, but of which some have also been refuted".

[15] According to the references noted by Walras: year 1836–37, Paris: 1840–41, 2 vol. The desired acquisition is the 4th edition, 1865, in 4 vol (*cf infra*).

[16] According to the references noted by Walras: *L'industrie et la morale considérées dans leurs rapports avec la liberté,* Paris: A. Sautelet et Cie, 1825.

Finally, I requested the French translations of the treatises of McCulloch, and of Carey.[17] The commission, relying on its Catalogue, apparently believes itself justified in refusing them to me on the pretext that it possesses these treatises in English.[18] However, if it is true that nine-tenths of our students are unable to read the original text, would it not be better, for the commission, to clearly state that reading these authors seems useless for them?

Perhaps at heart that is its idea? This is what one might surmise without being sure. Indeed, whatever the previous observations, and the 12 books above mentioned, if one wishes, completely set aside, there were still more than 50 on my list that the library did not possess. What are the reasons that have so far postponed and seem to indefinitely postpone the purchase of these latter ones?[19]

"On these other items, Mr. Wiener tells us, a selection *was required* by the commission". That being so, I have no choice, Mr. Councillor, but to wait for the commission to kindly share its reasons with us. I will hasten to discuss them.

"This is how, it is finally said, the number of these works in political economy has been reduced to *fifteen*; their acquisition was carried out immediately." There is here a final and quite notable inaccuracy. The works acquired are, in reality, not 15, but purely and simply 10. They are as follows:

Léon Faucher, *Études sur l'Angleterre*;

Id, *Mélanges*;

Courcelle-Seneuil, *Traité d'économie politique*;

Id, *[Traité] des opérations de banque*;

Id, *[Traité] des entreprises industrielles*;

Ch. Coquelin, *Du crédit et des banques*;

Boutron, *Théorie de la rente*;

Cernuschi, *Mécanique de l'échange*;

C. Juglar, *Du change et de la liberté d'émission*;

Dictionnaire de l'économie politique.[20]

After transmitting[21] this response, the assistant librarian expresses the desire "that I be invited to specify the books whose acquisition I now deem necessary". As a result of

[17] On the draft, it reads at this point: "and of Roscher".

[18] According to the references noted by Walras: J. R. McCulloch, *Principles of Political Economy*, 4th edition, Edinburgh, 1849; H. C. Carey, *Principles of Political Economy*, Philadelphia, 1837–40, 3 vol.

[19] On the draft, in place of the passage from "Perhaps at the bottom [....] these last ones?", it reads: "Be that as it may, and these 12 works aside, there remain 56 on the list."

[20] This list also appears on the back of the sheet on which L. Walras has noted references taken from the 2nd Supplement of the catalogue of the Cantonal Library (1864).

[21] On the draft, it reads at this point: "from Mr. Wiener".

the observations, I have just had the honour to submit to you, Mr. Councillor, I believe I can, stick to my original list, from which, however, the *Histoire de l'économie politique* by Blanqui and the *Traité des impôts* by Mr. de Parieu, as well as Volumes I to VI of Bastiat's *Œuvres* and the 10 books that have been acquired, must be removed. Moreover, I confidently rely on your judgement, well convinced that you will know how to ensure that the teaching of political economy finds in the cantonal library modest resources but not so meagre as those the commission would like to spare it."[22]

What is Charles Estoppey's reaction? On the back of the cantonal assistant librarian's letter, he drafts the following letter intended for Léon Walras:

"18 April [18]72

To Mr Walras, professor of political economy at the Academy.

Sir,

We have taken note of the letter you addressed to us in response to the explanations provided by the cantonal assistant librarian concerning the books you had requested for acquisition. We believe that the best course of action would be for you, without renouncing the list you have drawn up, to provide us with an indication of those books from this list whose purchase appears to you to be truly urgent. Given the limited nature of our resources, it would hardly be possible to purchase all the books you indicated in the same year. This acquisition will necessarily have to be spread over several years. The important thing is that each year, we acquire those whose necessity is most keenly felt."[23]

Léon Walras then sends the following response:

"Mr Estoppey, State Councillor, Head of the Department of Public Instruction and Worship.

Lausanne, 21 April 1872

Mr Councillor,

I hasten to acknowledge receipt of your letter of the 18th of this month and to thank you for the obliging promptness with which you have kindly responded to me regarding the books in political economy whose purchase I am requesting by the Cantonal Library.

It seems quite natural to me to spare the resources of the library, and I have always understood this necessity so well that I had indicated on my first list the books whose acquisition seemed to me the most urgent, assuming that it was not possible

[22] L. Walras to C. Estoppey, 17 April 1872, unpublished letter kept in the Vaud cantonal archives under the reference K XIII/52/4/700; the draft of the letter is kept in the Walras collection in Lausanne under the reference F W II, box 10.

[23] C. Estoppey to L. Walras, 18 April 1872, unpublished draft letter preserved in the Vaud cantonal archives under the reference K XIII/52/4/700.

to purchase all those listed at once. It was Mr Wiener himself, when I pointed out these indications to him, who assured me that the available funds[24] allowed for the purchase of the entire list. In any case, I only had to highlight the books I had thus noted on my first list to compile the one I have the honour of addressing you on the other hand.

I would be extremely grateful if you could do what depends on you, Mr. Councillor, to ensure that the order is fulfilled and the books catalogued for the next holidays; for I am currently reduced to lend my own books to those of my students preparing their *thèses de licence* or competition dissertations, which is extremely inconvenient for them and for me."[25]

Charles Estoppey annotates on the back of this letter: "25 April 72. Send the attached list to Mr. the Cantonal Librarian, and inform him that it is the indication of the books in political economy whose acquisition is requested by Mr. Walras as being most urgent. The department wishes this acquisition to take place without delay."[26]

On 1st May 1872, the cantonal librarian Ferdinand Lecomte then replies to the Head of the Department of Public Instruction and Worship:

"Mr. State Councillor,

In response to your honoured letter of the 26th of last month prescribing the purchase of 19 books in political economy requested by Mr. Professor Valras [*sic*], I have the honour to inform you that I have just ordered all these books, except for three which I take the liberty of suspending until further agreement with Mr. Valras [*sic*] or further orders from you, namely:

1st Turgot, *Économie politique*; given that we have the general works of Turgot (M 761), a good edition in 9 volumes also including political economy.

2nd Carey, *Principes de la science sociale*, which we have in the original edition, in English, S 257.

3rd Roscher, *Principes d'économie politique*, which we have in the original edition in German, S 294.

On this occasion, I will complete the explanations already provided to the Department in response to its letters of 22 March and 9 April, by stating that the previous lists from Mr. Professor Valras [*sic*] were transmitted to me as general indications and for perusal, not as definitive purchase lists. I kept them in this same capacity for

[24] On the draft of this letter, it reads at this point: "[…] amounted to 2800 or 3000 francs. I could boldly request the purchase of 6 or 700 F of books on economics. And that is why I was very surprised by his last response".

[25] L. Walras to C. Estoppey, 21 April 1872, unpublished letter preserved in the Vaud cantonal archives under the reference K XIII/52/4/730. The draft is preserved in the Walras collection in Lausanne under the reference F W II, box 10. On the reverse of the draft of the letter and on three attached sheets, L. Walras drafted the list of works deposited with the library, the total amount of which comes to 703 F, 75.

[26] The list of Walras is therefore not preserved with the letter.

the purchases of 1872. I will add that besides the books ordered and received last autumn, there are still two ordered and not received, namely:

1st Dunoyer, *Liberté du travail*, out of print edition, but which we are trying to obtain second-hand.

2nd *Dictionaire de commerce et navigation*, which is in the process of a new edition and which we should receive as soon as it is published.

Accept, Mr. State Councillor, the assurance of my respectful consideration.

F. Lecomte

P.S. Following your verbal order this morning, I have just also ordered Carey and Roscher, only still suspending Turgot."[27]

The matter is therefore on the right track, since Léon Walras addresses Félicité Guillaumin on 5 September 1872:

> […] Firstly it concerns book purchases for our cantonal library. I encountered some difficulties this year with the commission of this library which showed no eagerness to satisfy me. I had to complain to the State Council. Finally, everything was settled, the commission and I are currently on the best terms, and I am authorised, as are several of my colleagues, to purchase directly myself, within the limits of a reasonable credit, the books whose acquisition I deem necessary. It is a latitude that I will certainly use. I only ask you to tell me two things; 1° If you can grant me a certain credit, before reimbursing you by providing on me, so that I have time to browse the books and have the purchase made by the library before paying? If so, for what term and what amount? – 2° If, under these conditions, you can still grant me a discount from which I can myself benefit the library, and of what amount? – Furthermore, I would ask you to kindly prepare and send me a copy of your current catalogues on which you would have erased the out-of-print books. I add this request because of the inconvenience I had last year of designating for purchase by the library commission and some of my students books listed on your catalogues and which turned out to be out of stock. […]."[28]

10.4 Conclusion

The policy of purchasing books in economics from the cantonal library through Walras' efforts is not limited to this episode. The ordering of books will continue over the following years. One can first mention the existence of a list of books bearing at the bottom the note: "handed over on 8 July 1874 to the Department [of Public Instruction and Worship]", which was transmitted to Charles Boiceau.[29] This list includes the following authors:

---

[27] The Cantonal Librarian to the Department of Public Instruction and Worship, 1 May 1872, unpublished letter preserved in the Archives cantonales vaudoises under the reference K XIII/52/4/773 (2 folios).

[28] L. Walras to Miss Guillaumin, 5 September 1872, preserved in the Walras collection in Lausanne under the reference F W I, box 3, published in: *Correspondence*, I, l. 202, p. 298.

[29] Charles Boiceau (1841–1907). Head of the Department of Public Instruction and Worship from 1874 to 1885, he was a member of the boards of several companies and also a journalist at the *Nouvelliste Vaudois*.

Rossi, 4 vols.[30]

J. S. Mill, 2 vols.[31]

E. de Laveleye, 1 vol.

Levasseur, 1 vol.[32]

Mantellier, 1 vol.[33]

[*crossed out*: Du Puynode, 1 vol.]

Wolowski, *La liberté commerciale.*[34]

Id., L'or et l'argent.[35]

Girardot, 1 vol.[36]

Ferr-Herzog, 1 vol.[37]

Léon, 1 vol.

P.P., 1 vol.

Bochin, 1 vol.[38]

[*illegible*], 1 vol.

Schulze-Delitzsch, 2 vols.[39]

---

[30] P. Rossi: *Cours d'économie politique,* professé au Collège de France, 4th ed., revised and enlarged by unpublished lessons collected by M. A. Porée [...] preceded by a bibliographical note on the works of Rossi, by Joseph Garnier, Paris: Guillaumin, 1865, 4 vols.

[31] J. S. Mill: *Principes d'économie politique, avec quelques-unes de leurs applications à l'économie sociale,* translated by H. Dussard and Courcelle-Seneuil, Paris: Guillaumin, 3rd ed., 1873, 2 vols.

[32] Considering the acquisitions of the Cantonal Library, it may concern the following two books: Émile Levasseur, *La question de l'or*, Paris: Guillaumin, 1858 and Émile de Laveleye, *Le marché monétaire et ses crises depuis cinquante ans*, Paris: Guillaumin, 1865.

[33] It may concern Philippe Mantellier, *Mémoire sur la valeur des principales denrées et marchandises qui se vendaient ou se consommaient en la ville d'Orléans au cours des XIVe, XVe, XVIe, XVIIe et XVIIIe siècles,* Orléans: Imprimerie de G. Jacob, 1861.

[34] Louis Wolowski, *La liberté commerciale et les résultats du traité de commerce de 1860*, Paris: Guillaumin, 1869.

[35] Louis Wolowski, *L'Or et l'argent*, Paris: Guillaumin, 1870.

[36] It may concern Auguste-Théodore de Girardo, *Des subsistances de 1789 à 1795*, Paris: Librairie P. Dupont, 1854.

[37] May be Carl Feer-Herzog, *La France et ses alliés monétaires en présence de l'unification universelle des monnaies: déposition faite devant le Conseil supérieur du commerce, de l'agriculture et de l'industrie de France, accompagnée de notes et documents*, Paris: Guillaumin, 1870.

[38] May be J. Bochin, *Du cadastre dans ses rapports avec la propriété foncière. Rapport de M. Bochin [...] à l'assemblée générale des agriculteurs de France*, Paris: Guillaumin, 1873.

[39] Certainly, Hermann Schulze-Delitzsch, *Cours d'économie politique à l'usage des ouvriers et des artisans, traduction et précédé d'une esquisse biographique et d'un Aperçu sur les nouvelles doctrines économiques et leur application par Benjamin Rampal*, Paris: Guillaumin, 1874, 2 vols.

+Jevons.[40]

The total amount of the order adds up to 107 F, 25.[41] This list of books seems to have been acquired without difficulty, given the dates of entry of the books into the library.

In the summer of 1875, Léon Walras was elected (for two years) rector of the Academy of Lausanne and held this position from October 1875 to October 1877. From the time of the end of his mandate, there exists a draft letter of Walras to Charles Boiceau, unpublished, preserved in the Lausanne collection. This document reveals that difficulties with the library commission reappear:

"Ouchy sur Lausanne, 19 October 1877.

Sir, Head of the Department of Public Instruction and Worship,

I have the honour to request that you kindly decide the purchase by the Cantonal Library of the following two books.

W. Stanley Jevons. *La monnaie et le mécanisme de l'échange*,[42] 6 F.

W. Roscher. *Grundlagen der NationalOekonomie*,[43] 14 F, 70.

[…]. The first of these books is the most complete and the most original […] theory of money that has appeared. It contains in particular a study of the clearing house and the cheque that is absolutely new. […].

The second is an exposition of the state of pol[itical] ec[onomy] in Germany which is especially recommended by these economic bibliographies of the most comprehensive and valuable nature.

It has already been more than a year since I acquired these books and handed them over to Mr. Wiener, a member of the library commission. I would be particularly grateful to you, Sir, the Head of the Department […]".[44]

According to the supplements to the cantonal library's catalogue, it appears that these books were eventually purchased.

---

[40] It is likely to be W. S. Jevons, *Theory of Political Economy*, London, 1871. The mark of the cantonal library at the end of the work bears the handwritten note "7.8.74", which indicates the date of entry (shelfmark S. 219).

[41] A sheet preserved in the Walras collection in Lausanne under the reference F W V b 26. In the Vaud cantonal archives, the following entry is found in the registers of the Department of Public Instruction and Worship: "4 August 1874. authorises the attached list of books in political economy proposed by Mr Professor Walras and which are necessary for his treatise on Pure economics, cost 107 F, 25" (K XIII/13).

[42] Paris: Germer Baillière, 1876. French translation of *Money and the Mechanism of Exchange*, London: H. S. King and Co, 1875.

[43] 12th ed., Stuttgart, 1875.

[44] L. Walras to Mr the Head of the Department of Public Instruction and Worship [Charles Boiceau], 19 October 1877, unpublished letter preserved in the Lausanne collection under the reference F W I, box 10.

Part IV
Critique of "Orthodox" Liberalism and "Empirical" Socialism

Chapter 11
Ideas and Men: Criticism of the French "Liberal School"

11.1 Introduction

Throughout his life, Léon Walras fought against what he termed the "clique currently holding the concession for the exploitation of economics", a school that had managed to apply to economic science the formula "*exploitation by monopoly under the mask of liberty*".[1] He refers here to the group of economists of the liberal school that was formed during the 1840s and largely dominated French economic thought until the end of the Second Empire. This group would benefit from greater tolerance from the political power after the signing of the free trade treaty between France and England (January 1860). Institutionally, among its Parisian strongholds, one can cite the Académie des sciences morales et politiques, a class of the Institut, re-established in 1832; the Société d'économie politique de Paris, founded in 1842; the publishing house of Gilbert-Urbain Guillaumin, the *Journal des Économistes*, established in 1841; and the chairs of political economy at the Collège de France, the Conservatoire des arts et métiers, and the École des Ponts et Chaussées.

Léon Walras encountered hostility from economists who rejected his attempts to apply mathematics to economics,[2] who did not accept his ideas on State intervention (labour legislation, railways, monetary issuance, etc.) and abhorred his project of land nationalisation. He faced, as he stated in his "Notice autobiographique", "the exorbitant influence, the silent but relentless hostility of the hereditary mandarins tasked with preventing science from being made" (1909a, vol. V, p. 19). In his "Notes d'humeur", he even specifies:

> These gentlemen of the Academie des sciences morales et politiques, they too, prevent anyone *who knows what he is talking about*, who does not share their ideas on value or

[1] Emphasis by L. W., "Le problème fiscal" (1896d), vol. IX, p. 420, English transl., 2010, p. 344. Due to his intolerance towards opposing opinions and his sectarianism, Charles Gide refuses to call this school "liberal". He believes it is better designated under the name "optimistic school" (1890, p. 612).

[2] On this point, *cf. supra* chapter 7, *The Reception of Pure Economics in France (1873–1926)*.

J.-P. Potier, *Léon Walras, Economist and Liberal Socialist*, Springer Studies in the History of Economic Thought, https://doi.org/10.1007/978-3-032-04670-3_11

> property, not only from writing, but from being named in the *Revue des D[eux] M[ondes]* and the *J[ournal] des D[ébats]*, and they put up signs at their establishment in large letters: *Liberal School, Free School, School of Liberty*. It is nauseating. (I leave the reader to insert a more forceful expression) (emphasis by L. W., "Notes d'humeur" (2000), vol. XIII, p. 543).

These reproaches from the Lausanne School's founder are, no doubt, somewhat excessive. It can be noted, for example, that between 1874 and 1885, he managed to publish in the *Journal des économistes* (edited by Joseph Garnier) five articles, three book reviews, a correspondence with William-Stanley Jevons, and a bibliography.[3] As we have already seen, a part of the *Mélanges d'économie politique et sociale* is entirely devoted to the problems of teaching the economic discipline. Walras expresses there the accumulation of his grievances against the French "system". The violence of his remarks, sometimes insulting, against some economists explains why the author was reluctant to publish the *Mélanges* during his lifetime. Two levels of criticism can be identified in the attacks: a critique of the liberal economists' ideas and a critique of individuals.[4] Without claiming to be exhaustive, we will successively present each of these two aspects, focusing mainly on the second.

11.2 Criticism of the Ideas of the French Liberal School's Economists

What general approach of economic science do the French liberal economists propose? On this subject, one can refer to the "Introduction" by Ambroise Clément, written for the *Dictionnaire de l'économie politique* (1852) edited by Charles Coquelin and Gilbert-Urbain Guillaumin:

> Like all other branches of human knowledge, Political economy is indefinitely perfectible; however, we are convinced that it is today advanced enough to leave no legitimate doubt on its essential principles, and that the truths expressed by these principles will not be more shaken by future research or discoveries than the elements of geometry or the laws of universal gravitation have been by the works of Lagrange or Laplace.[5]

Once the "essential principles" of political economy have been established, no one can claim to refound or reconstruct it. This approach is defended, for example, by Joseph Garnier, in his commentary on the creation of the first chair of political economy at the Faculty of Law in Paris (1864, p. 12). It is also found in the report written by Minister Victor Duruy, which justifies the establishment of this chair.[6] It is reiterated during the 1870s–80 s by the leading economists associated with the

---

[3] It is true that the publication of six of these works is concentrated over the period 1874–76.

[4] The question of promotion systems was discussed in chapter 8, *From Criticism to the Reform Plan for the Teaching of Political Economy in France in the* XIX*th century.*

[5] Clément, 1852, p. XIV. One can also refer to the article "Économie politique", written by C. Coquelin (1852b, pp. 643–666).

[6] Report by Victor Duruy, *Le Moniteur*, 18 September 1864, reissued in Garnier's article, *op. cit.*, pp. 5–10.

Journal des économistes. The various textbooks in economics ultimately reveal a "simple science". As Hervé Dumez indicates,

> [...] it is indeed an invitation to travel, it follows the different phases of the commodity's existence, from its birth to its death. The commodity is first anticipated in the human need that creates value (in the treatises: introduction, general notions). Then it is born, it is produced by the combination of factors (First part: Production). It then circulates and is exchanged (Second part: Circulation; exchange). Once exchanged, the amount of its sale is shared among the various factors, direct such as land, labour, and capital, indirect such as the State (Third part: Distribution). The economic death finally occurs in the phenomenon of consumption (Fourth and last part: Consumption). This plan thus follows chronologically the commodity (in this respect, the distribution raises a problem because it does not exactly chronologically connect to the other phases. Consequently, its place varies from one treatise to another: second or third position) (1985, p. 56).

Léon Walras sees in the consideration of a completed economic science an absolutely coherent attitude for those who pass on academic chairs and positions from father-in-law to son-in-law or from uncle to nephew. If they admitted that new discoveries could still be made in economics, they would be forced to leave places for their authors ("Notes d'humeur", 2000, vol. XIII, p. 545). In reality, for Walras, economic science had deteriorated in France since Jean-Baptiste Say and Pellegrino Rossi's deaths; its teaching has been "completely misled" with the courses of Adolphe Blanqui, Louis Wolowski, and Michel Chevalier.[7] Most liberal economists abuse the formula "laissez-faire, laissez-passer". In short,

> [...] it is a political economy that could be taught in a morning to a parrot with a few pieces of sugar. [In fact, this is indeed how it is taught in France at present. The parrots are sons, nephews, or sons-in-law of academicians and the pieces of sugar are competition prizes distributed to them].[8]

Walras laments that "at the Société d'économie politique they continue to marvel at the 'petition of the candlemakers'" by Frédéric Bastiat.[9] Incapable of contributing to the development of theory, these economists declare it complete and they all deal

---

[7] Some liberal economists are very clear-sighted in this matter. Thus J.-G. Courcelle-Seneuil does not hesitate to assert in *Journal des économistes*:

> In fact, political economy in France now counts only a small number of adherents, much fewer than a hundred years ago. This small number does not even have the faith or the life that animated its predecessors; it receives the teaching second-hand, coldly, with distraction, without being convinced: it does not fertilise this teaching with its own thoughts, with ideas of application, so that if there is no positive decline, there is at least a complete absence of progress. (1875, p. 312).

Faced with such remarks, the editor-in-chief of the *Journal des économistes*, J. Garnier must react: "Our collaborator, as we can see, does not hold back. But it is up to us to say that his judgement is excessive [...]." (1875, p. 312, note 1).

[8] L. Walras, letter to Vito Cusumano, 20 October 1874, in: *Correspondence*, I, l. 311, pp. 443–44. The passage in brackets is crossed out on the original letter, kept in the Lausanne collection. On the theme of the parrot and sugar lumps, see also "Une branche nouvelle de la mathématique" (1876b), vol. VII, p. 302.

[9] L. Walras, letter to J. Garnier, 8 November 1874, in: *Correspondence*, I, l. 317, p. 450.

exclusively with practical questions, most often descending into poor journalism and political discourse.[10] Walras therefore denounces on numerous occasions "this moth-eaten (*rongée des mites*) science offered to us by the *Journal des économistes*".[11] However, in his writings from 1863, he distinguishes two schools: that of Say or the "utilitarians", and that of Bastiat or the "moralists".[12] For Walras, these two schools, whose philosophical principles would rest either on empirical materialism or on spiritualism, converge on the ground of "absolute individualism". They attribute all social wealth to the individual, without introducing any reservation regarding the community or the State; the latter, reduced to a collection of individuals, should do nothing.[13]

- "The school of J.-B. Say", heiress to the Physiocrats who supposedly invented the *laissez-faire, laissez-passer* formula (1859 b, p. 113),[14] defends a "naturalist" point of view on free competition, identified as "a natural law". Walras is not a priori opposed to such an approach, but he believes it merely makes pure and simple assertions and fails to "demonstrate" the principle.
- "The school of Bastiat", on the contrary, defends the "moralist" point of view. It considers free competition as "a liberty and a right analogous to civil and political liberties and to the rights of man in society". In this current, within which Walras includes, besides Bastiat, authors such as Henri Baudrillart,[15] the demonstration of the principle operates exclusively on the base of justice.

During the 1870s, Walras adopts an increasingly reserved attitude towards the first school. In the *Cours d'économie politique appliquée* and the study "Une branche nouvelle de la mathématique", he targets the best available "demonstration" of free competition, that of Charles Coquelin in the article "Concurrence" from the *Dictionnaire de l'économie politique* (1852–53). According to Coquelin, competition in industry does not differ "in principle" from other forms of competition, such as that which exists in the administrative career. It differs rather by its consequences. In fact, according to him:

[10] In his "Notes d'humeur", Walras declares that he would gladly exchange "three orthodox political economy professors for an intelligent grocer" (vol. XIII, p. 523).

[11] L. Walras, letter to C. Gide, 9 December 1886, in: *Correspondence*, II, l. 756, p. 168.

[12] See "Du matérialisme et du spiritualisme en économie politique et sociale" (1863c), vol. XIII, pp. 188–89 and 195–96; "De l'enseignement de l'économie politique dans les facultés de droit" (1864), vol. VII, pp. 352–53; *Recherche de l'idéal social* (1867–68), 2nd and 3rd lessons, vol. IX, pp. 55–56 and 77–78, English transl., 2010, pp. 39–40 and 55.

[13] On these two currents, see P. Dockès (1996), pp. 85–91.

[14] See also *L'économie politique et la justice* (1860a), in: vol. V, pp. 158 and 182; *Les associations populaires de consommation, de production et de crédit.* (1865), p. 28; *Recherche de l'idéal social*, vol. IX, 1st and 3rd lessons, pp. 45 and 77, English transl., 2010, pp. 33 and 35. F. Quesnay uses the maxim "laissez-faire, laissez-passer" once (curiously attributing it to Nicolas Baudeau), in the "Lettre de M. Alpha sur le langage de la science économique" (*Éphémérides du citoyen*, October 1767). Mirabeau and Le Mercier de la Rivière attribute this maxim to Vincent de Gournay.

[15] See F. Bastiat, *Harmonies économiques*, 1851, chap. I ("Natural Organisation. Artificial Organisation") and chap. X ("Competition"), pp. 15–33 and 293–326; H. Baudrillart, 1860, p. 210.

> It should not be believed that [...] we aim to defend industrial and commercial competition against the puerile attacks of which it has so often been the object. God forbid! He has always seemed somewhat unseemly to economists to pay attention for defending such a principle. It is too inherent to the primary conditions of social life; it is at the same time too great, too elevated, too holy and, in its general application, too high above the reach of the pygmies who threaten it, for it to be necessary to defend it. One does not defend the sun although it sometimes burns the earth when it should only provide light and heat: nor should one defend competition, which is to the industrial world what the sun is to the physical world. The task of the economist is only to explain its action in the industrial sphere and to expose its marvelous effects. This is the best defense that can be made of it and the only suitable one (1852a, p. 450).

Such a perspective notably influenced liberals such as Joseph Garnier (1863, pp. 146–49).

In the naturalistic approach, Walras discerns two serious faults: firstly, a "very confused and very nebulous conception" of competition, neither defined nor rigorously demonstrated; secondly, a confusion between the "conception" and the "principle", thus between the field of pure economics and that of applied economics. Concerning his own demonstration of the "principle", our author reminds Joseph Garnier, director of the *Journal des économistes*, of the key steps of his own approach:

> I demonstrates [*sic*] that the sale and purchase of products on the product market and of productive services on the market of these services in accordance with the law of supply and demand is an operation by which productive services combine into products of the nature and quantity suitable to provide the maximum effective utility within the limits determined by the condition that there is only one price for each product and for each productive service on the market. [...]. A rigorous demonstration of free competition must therefore firstly rest on an exact definition and analysis of this competition and the supply and demand mechanism. Yet none of your authors provides not only the analysis but the definitions in question. Coquelin, among others, begins with a deplorable confusion between economic competition and all sorts of other competitions that have no relation whatsoever with it. Then a rigorous demonstration of free competition also presupposes a study of effective utility as well as a distinction between individual needs or private utility that each consumer is able to appreciate and social needs or public utility which is assessed in a completely different manner.[16]

Furthermore, Walras laments the weakness of the arguments in favour of free trade proposed by the French liberal school. These economists place too much trust in Providence and "exaggerate a little too much the specialisation of industries from one nation to another" (*Cours d'économie politique appliquée*, 33rd lesson, 1996, p. 607). For our author, "complete" free trade, with beneficial consequences, presupposes a perfect "shift" of productive services (capital proper, personal faculties, and land) from import to export activities, which require a certain delay and the absence of obstacles. Unlike England, in French agriculture, "social institutions" (small property lacking capital and technical knowledge) and property transfer taxes (*droits de mutation*) have hindered the "shift" of productive services and the advent of intensive agriculture ("Théorie du libre-échange", 1897a, pp. 273–74, English transl., 2005, pp. 239–40). Walras is therefore very critical of the free trade motto of the economists

[16] L. Walras, letter to Joseph Garnier, 8 November 1874, in: *Correspondence*, I, l. 317, p. 450.

of the liberal school who enthusiastically welcomed the trade treaty between France and England (1860) prepared by Richard Cobden and Michel Chevalier. This treaty would have launched France "on the road to free trade, more or less as a dog is thrown into the river to teach it to swim" (*op. cit.*, p. 276, English transl., p. 242).[17]

However, very early on, Walras was forced to question the relevance of the notion of a "liberal school". As early as 1863, he noted that the economists, "unanimous in proclaiming the state of advancement and perfection of political economy, all profess, on the other hand, economic opinions and theories very different from one another and even very opposed to each other". They are divided on the nature of wealth, on the origin of exchange value, on the distribution of wealth.[18] Later, in 1896, Walras would observe:

> The *liberal school*, the High School of *liberty* and *liberalism*, may be recognized by this respectful tolerance of opinions opposed to their own. And yet, if this school only were a real school! If it had, about each fundamental issue of the science, a theory, no matter how poor it might be but nevertheless held by all its leaders! But no! It has several theories, which are all bad and, moreover, contradictory. These doctrinaires have no doctrine (emphasis by L. W., "Le problème fiscal", 1896d, vol. IX, p. 421, English transl., 2010, p. 345).

For example, Paul Leroy-Beaulieu and Léon Say disagree on the issue of land property; the same is true for Michel Chevalier and Louis Wolowski on money. These economists do not possess a genuine theory of prices and of distribution. Thus,

> [...] the author of a theory of ground rent[19] crowned by the Académie des sciences morales et politiques begins by deliberately asserting that the selling price of products is determined by their cost of production. After which, he defines rent (*fermage*) as the excess of the selling price of products over the wages and interest expanded on their production. If it had been a matter of providing the theory of wages, obviously he would have defined it as the excess of the selling price of products over the interest and rent expanded on their production. And if the Academy had put the theory of interest up for competition, there is no doubt that he would have won the prize by defining it as the excess of the selling price of products over the rent and wages expanded on their production.[20]

Consequently, when Walras, in numerous texts, speaks of these economists as belonging to the "liberal school", the "official and orthodox school",[21] he refers neither to theory nor to economic and social policy, but places himself on the ground of pure polemics. He is thus led to underestimate the real theoretical and doctrinal

[17] On free trade in Walras, see P. Dockès, 1996, pp. 122–24 and 199–202.

[18] "Du matérialisme et du spiritualisme en économie politique et sociale" (1863c), vol. XIII, pp. 186–87.

[19] Léon Walras refers here to the book of a philosophy professor in Auxerre, Pierre-Auguste Boutron, *Théorie de la rente foncière*, Paris: Guillaumin, 1867.

[20] "Une branche nouvelle de la mathématique" (1876b), vol. VII, p. 297. Walras re-uses here a passage from the *Éléments d'économie politique pure* (40th lesson), vol. VIII, p. 649, English transl., 1954, p. 426.

[21] Let us note that according to Joseph Garnier, the expressions "official school" and "liberal school" are disparaging, even insulting, qualifications coming from protectionists and socialists ("Société d'économie politique. Meeting of 6 May 1867", *Journal des économistes*, 3rd series, 2nd year, vol. 6, n°17, May 1867, pp. 293–94).

divergences that have always existed among liberal economists,[22] for example, on the social question which is so dear to him, on free trade, on the colonial question. Thus, it is difficult to classify in the same camp ultra-liberals such as Joseph Garnier and Gustave de Molinari, and moderate liberals such as Jérôme-Adolphe Blanqui, Louis Wolowski, Michel Chevalier, and Paul Leroy-Beaulieu.

11.3 Criticism of Men

We will now present the criticisms made by Léon Walras about five liberal economists who were particularly targeted in his writings: Michel Chevalier, Henri Baudrillart, Paul Leroy-Beaulieu, Émile Levasseur, and Léon Say.

11.3.1 Michel Chevalier (1806–1879)

Walras shows little indulgence towards Michel Chevalier, a polytechnician, chief engineer of Mines, and successor to Pellegrino Rossi, in 1840, to the chair of political economy at the Collège de France.[23] He begins by stating, indeed:

> An engineer on leave and a frenzied Saint-Simonian, Michel Chevalier, when appointed professor of political economy at the Collège de France in 1840, was neither an economist nor a professor; he could have become one, but the fact is that he remained something else entirely. Already involved in politics under Louis-Philippe, State Councillor in 1838, deputy in 1845,[24] he found it more convenient to successively discuss some specific issues, such as means of communication, money, free trade, than to scrutinise and establish the general theory of the production and distribution of social wealth (1880d, vol. VII, pp. 425–26).

The qualification of "frenzied Saint-Simonian" deserves a brief clarification. Michel Chevalier was converted to Saint-Simonianism in 1830 and he actively participated in the *Globe*'s editorial staff and took sides with Prosper Enfantin on the women question. Sentenced to a year in prison (at Sainte-Pélagie), he broke with the sect in 1833, but he remained thereafter a "realistic" Saint-Simonian, concerned with industrial development and the improvement of the situation of the working classes.[25] Walras criticises him for his lack of contribution to the development of economic theory, even ironically mentioning his creation of a company for the construction of a Channel tunnel. Michel Chevalier mainly devoted his lessons at the Collège de

[22] On the divisions of the liberal school, see Y. Breton and M. Lutfalla, 1991; L. Le Van-Lemesle, 2004; C. Silvant, 2010; F. Etner and C. Silvant, 2017, 2nd part.

[23] On M. Chevalier, see A. Vinokur, 1986, pp. 175–202; Y. Breton 1991 and 2010; P. Steiner, 1998; F. Taricone, 2015.

[24] Michel Chevalier is elected deputy of Aveyron for only one year.

[25] Auguste Walras does not seem to have had contact with him when he attended the sessions of doctrine exposition, and the same is true for his son when he associated with former Saint-Simonians in 1859–60 (see the following chapter).

France to political economy as a "science of application".[26] However, it should be noted that Joseph A. Schumpeter, in *History of Economic Analysis,* pays a nuanced tribute to Michel Chevalier, in his "review of the troops" of the "classical age": the French economist would leave a youthful work that is very descriptive but interesting, and his book on *La monnaie* (1850) "merits admiration rather than contempt".[27]

Walras completes this author's "biography" with the following passage:

> Michel Chevalier had found in the *Journal des Débats* the door to return from socialism to orthodoxy and from S[ain]te Pélagie to the *Conseil d'État*. He never ceased to belong intimately to this journal, which has always been the instrument of a clique much more than the organ of an opinion, even when, in the aftermath of the *coup d'État*, he actively engaged in the politics of the Second Empire (1880d, vol. VII, pp. 427–28).

The *Journal des Débats*, founded and directed by Louis-François Bertin known as "the Elder" (1766–1841), had put itself at the service of the July Monarchy. Michel Chevalier joined as an editor in 1833, that is to say, just after his break with P. Enfantin, and at the time of his study trip to the United States. Under the Second Empire, the *Journal des Débats*, directed by Édouard Bertin, was an organ of the liberal opposition.

Walras further adds about Chevalier:

> Charged under the Second Empire with preparing the conventions with the major railway companies (1857) and the trade treaty with England (1860), presiding over the Universal Exhibition (1867), becoming a senator,[28] administrator of the Crédit Mobilier, of the Forges and Fonderies of Aveyron, he had himself substituted from 1852 to 1866 (*op. cit.,* p. 426).

Having become a councillor of State in ordinary service in 1852, Chevalier indeed asked to be substituted at the Collège de France by Henri Baudrillart.[29] In short, here is a fine example where the professorial chair constitutes "a springboard from which one leaps to influential or lucrative positions in politics and industry", and Walras also recounts the episode of the quarrel, in 1866, between Michel Chevalier and Henri Baudrillart. At the time when the Crédit Mobilier was experiencing serious difficulties that would soon lead to its collapse, Michel Chevalier, who had financial needs, decided to reclaim his chair; but he would be willing to abandon it to his substitute under certain conditions that Walras knew about thanks to a memorandum that Henri Baudrillart distributed in France. The first draft of the study "De l'enseignement de l'économie politique en France" reveals the details of the negotiation: "Michel

[26] On Michel Chevalier's teaching at the Collège de France, one can refer to André Garrigou-Lagrange, 1946, pp. 137–47.

[27] J. A. Schumpeter, 1954, p. 497, note 15 and also see p. 711, note 15. Let us note that Auguste Walras, while drafting his study "De la réforme de la monnaie", declared himself "very pleased" with the article "Monnaie" by M. Chevalier published in *Dictionnaire de l'économie politique* edited by C. Coquelin and G.-U. Guillaumin (Paris: Guillaumin, vol. 2, 1853, pp. 200–19) and he advised his son to read it (letter of 14 July 1861, in: *Correspondence*, vol. IV, p. 501).

[28] He is appointed senator in 1860.

[29] Following the refusal of the Collège administrator who based it on the prohibition of combining the function of State Councillor with another public function, Minister Fortoul will decide in favour of M. Chevalier (J.-L. Chappey and J. Vincent, 2017, p. 380).

Chevalier proposed to leave them to him [*the 10 000 francs annual salary*] on the condition that M. de Sacy, still editor-in-chief of the *Débats* and very well in court, would intercede to have orders for cloth for the troops granted to the factories that he, Michel Chevalier, owned in Hérault department" (1880d, vol. VII, p. 541 note 16).[30]

The long letter in which Henri Baudrillart sets out his grievances to the holder of the chair, published in the Appendix to this chapter, confirms these details. The deal could not be concluded, and Michel Chevalier resumed his teaching on 18 December 1866.[31] Léon Walras declares in this regard:

> He returned to his chair from 1866 to 1878, and it would be impossible to say what he taught there, or if he taught anything at all. We see from the *Journal des économistes* that in 1874, he was telling to his listeners the life of Adam Smith (1880d, vol. VII, p. 426).

Walras here indulges in a somewhat easy attack. He refers, indeed, to the opening speech of Michel Chevalier's course, delivered on 9 December 1873, published the following year in the *Journal des économistes*. Yet this study far from offers a mere biography of the author of the *Wealth of Nations*. It actually contains some interesting developments on the personal and theoretical relationships between Adam Smith and François Quesnay.[32]

11.3.2 Henri Baudrillart (1821–1892)

Professor of legislation and of political economy at the Chaptal College, Henri Baudrillart was Michel Chevalier's substitute at the Collège de France from 1852 to 1866. Furthermore, from 1855 to 1866, he replaced Joseph Garnier as director of the *Journal des économistes*. In 1853, he published *Jean Bodin et son temps—Tableau des théories politiques et des idées économiques au XVIe siècle* (Paris: Guillaumin), a book, according to Joseph A. Schumpeter (1954, p. 164, note 4) "which the lapse of nearly a century has not deprived of its authoritative position". He subsequently

---

[30] In the margin of the manuscript, Walras adds: "episode of the jonquil cloth". Henri Baudrillart is the son-in-law of Samuel Sylvestre de Sacy (1801–79), editor-in-chief of the *Journal des Débats*. In the final text of his study, Walras removed the details of this incident. Having married in 1845 the daughter of a great industrialist in Hérault department, Chevalier was the owner of a drapery near Lodève.

[31] Here is how Joseph Garnier announces the event:

> M. Michel Chevalier will resume, on the 18th of this month, after several years of interval, his course at the Collège de France, which he had to interrupt due to his functions at the Council of State; this year, he will discuss the fundamentals of political economy. J.-B. Say and Rossi's successor return to his chair with knowledge and experience that will make the lessons of one of science's most illustrious and persistent apostles especially appealing (1866b, p. 508).

[32] Voir M. Chevalier, 1874, pp. 8–33.

published, also for Guillaumin, a *Manuel d'économie politique* (2 vol., 1858) and *Des rapports de la morale et de l'économie politique* (1860).

In October 1859, Léon Walras offered his services to Henri Baudrillart, then director of the *Journal des économistes*. Following a recommendation from Frédéric Passy, the young economist, who had just joined the Société d'économie politique de Paris, was offered by Baudrillart a regular collaboration with the journal. His project to publish a series of "Paradoxes économiques" was accepted. However, after the International Congress on Taxation in Lausanne, he was accused of "socialism" in the journal, and only the first of the "Paradoxes économiques" would appear in December 1860.[33] Baudrillart's refusal of the other works in the series, written in 1861 and 1862, ended the collaboration with the *Journal des économistes*. In May 1860, Walras had written for the liberal opposition newspaper *La Presse*, a brief review entitled, "Des rapports de la morale et de l'économie politique—Cours professé au Collège de France par M. H. Baudrillart". But the following month, the newspaper's editorial staff rejected the text.[34] This very cautious review defined Baudrillart as a "liberal economist philosopher, and we might even say, perhaps more liberal than economist".[35]

In the study "De l'enseignement de l'économie politique en France", Walras informs us that, during the years of replacing Michel Chevalier at the chair of the Collège de France,

> M. Baudrillart did not know a single word, he had not written a line of economics; he had only written a few articles on Vauvenargues and Mme de Staël. Not only did he never deliver a continuous course in political economy, but the isolated topics he tackled were somewhat beside and outside the science; they were, like that of the *Rapports de la morale et de l'économie politique*, rather subjects of moral philosophy or at most philosophy of political economy than subjects of political economy. He is currently a member of the Académie des sciences morales et politiques in the moral section. His substitution lasted 14 years. Besides substituting for Michel Chevalier at the Collège de France, he signed his articles in the *Journal des Débats*. It was common knowledge that the articles in this journal signed *Henri Baudrillart* were solely by M. Baudrillart and that the articles signed *Baudrillart* alone were by Michel Chevalier. This arrangement enabled an opposition newspaper to host the prose of a supporter of the Empire, as well as this friend of the Empire to collaborate with an opposition newspaper.[36]

After his disagreement with Michel Chevalier, Henri Baudrillart secured the opening of a new course at the Collège de France thanks to the intervention of his father-in-law, Samuel Sylvestre de Sacy, with the Minister of Public Instruction, Victor Duruy. It

---

[33] "Paradoxes économiques I—Que le sens commun n'est point le critérium de la science en général, ni en particulier celui de l'économie politique" (1860c), vol. VII, pp. 42–62.

[34] L. Walras, lettre à Gilbert-Urbain Guillaumin, 3 june 1860, in: *Correspondence*, I, l. 34, p. 61.

[35] "Des rapports de la morale et de l'économie politique" (1860b), vol. XIII, pp. 163–64. One finds also in the Lausanne collection (F. W. V a 16) a sheet of page references to Baudrillart's book. In particular, there are two points with exclamation marks by Léon Walras: "*Rossi*—Moral superiority of land property" (p. 441) and "The sacrosanct land property" (pp. 546–47).

[36] Emphasis by L. W., « De l'enseignement de l'économie politique en France» (1880d), vol. VII, p. 428.

was a complementary course on the history of political economy.[37] Baudrillart taught from December 1866 to spring 1868,[38] and not just for "a few months", as Walras claims. Subsequently, he became editor-in-chief of the pro-government newspaper *Le Constitutionnel*, a task in which "he completely failed", according to our author. To complete this "biography", it can be noted that Baudrillart became the holder, from 1881 until his death in 1892, of the chair of political economy at the École des Ponts et Chaussées, where he succeeded Joseph Garnier. He also served as the inspector general of public libraries. He published a monumental *Histoire du luxe privé et public depuis l'Antiquité jusqu'à nos jours* (Paris: Hachette, 1878–80, 4 vol.).

11.3.3 Paul Leroy-Beaulieu (1843–1916)

Paul Leroy-Beaulieu is substitute (1878–80), then successor to Michel Chevalier at the Collège de France, until his death, in 1916.[39] In the study "De l'enseignement de l'économie politique en France", Walras portrays him as follows:

> Wealthy by himself and married early to the daughter of Mr. Michel Chevalier, he easily obtained as many prizes as he wished from the Academie des sciences morales et politiques for papers on the *situation of the working classes, on emigration*, etc. A laureate of the Institute fifteen years ago, he became a member four or five years ago. He is an editor of the *Journal des Débats*, a member of the *Revue des deux Mondes* 's editorial staff, and editor-in-chief of *L'Économiste Français*. He applied to be a member of parliament for Algeria (1880d, vol. VII, p. 432).

This rather summary "biography" deserves to be corrected and completed. Paul Leroy-Beaulieu was initiated in cameral sciences at the universities of Bonn and Berlin (1864–65), which represents a somewhat original education. In 1870, he succeeded to win four prizes at once from the Institute, for various works such as, for example, a treatise on *La colonisation chez les peuples modernes*, published in 1874. Only in 1878 he was admitted as a member of the Académie des sciences morales et politiques. A contributor to the *Revue des deux Mondes*, from 1867, he

---

[37] According to Joseph Garnier,

> Mr. Henri Baudrillart, who, even as a young man, had been called upon to replace the learned professor in the chair of the Collège de France, and who had soon replaced him with great distinction, has just been appointed by the Minister of Public Education to a course on the history of political economy. The course, which will focus on the history of luxury and economic doctrines on the consumption of wealth, will be inaugurated on the 20. We can only applaud this innovation, while regretting that the Minister for Public Education did not give preference to the Sorbonne or the École Normale for this teaching, for which Mr. Baudrillart had better ability than any other (1866b, p. 508).

[38] His successor will be Émile Levasseur (*cf. infra*).

[39] Sur P. Leroy-Beaulieu, voir M. Baslé, 1991; G. Faccarello, 2010; Y.-A. Durelle-Marc, 2011.

became in 1872 both member of the editorial staff of the *Journal des Débats* and editor-in-chief of *L'Économiste français*. Before replacing Michel Chevalier at the Collège de France, he taught at the Chair of Finance at the École libre des sciences politiques. Furthermore, he was an administrator of several companies and owner of large agricultural estates in Normandy and especially in Tunisia, where he owned vineyards.[40]

On his work, Walras's judgement is unequivocal:

> Mr. Leroy-Beaulieu is an intelligent and industrious man whom nature and studies have made a prolific journalist and, if necessary, a politician,[41] but who has none of the qualities of a professor and a scientist. He multiplies newspaper and journal articles and special books with a facility that would be miraculous if he put his own ideas into them but is only remarkable since he confines himself to compiling figures and facts and following, in terms of opinions, the most probable among those that have been expressed before him. His *Traité de finances*[42] is a compilation of this kind which lacks any serious critique because it lacks any original doctrine (1880d, vol. VII, p. 431).

Léon Walras describes Paul Leroy-Beaulieu as a relentless compiler who lacks serious and original knowledge; he notes in this regard in his "Notes d'humeur": "One can understand the bitterness of people who do pol[itical] econ[omy] with scissors against those who spoil the trade by doing it with ideas" (2000, vol. XIII, p. 536).

Thus, *Le collectivisme* (1880) owes much to Adolphe Thiers's book, *De la propriété,* published in 1848 (*op. cit.,* pp. 536–37). Curiously, our author also reproaches "Mr. Leroy-Beaulieu for appropriating my theory of the entrepreneur and my theory of the decline in the rate of interest in a progressive society" (*op. cit.,* p. 536).[43] He also criticises him for his total misunderstanding of the objectives of mathematical economics, for example, in the third volume of the *Traité théorique et pratique d'économie politique* (1896) in which he writes that

> [...] the so-called mathematical school has no scientific basis, nor any practical application; it is a pure mental exercise, a set of fictions outside of all reality and contrary to all reality. This mental exercise looks like the search for martingales at the roulette of Monaco (1896, volume III, p. 62). (*Cf.* chapter 7, *The Reception of Pure Economics in France (1873–1926)*).

---

[40] Walras copies a significant passage, read in Charles Gide's review of Paul Leroy-Beaulieu's book, *L'Algérie et la Tunisie* (Paris: Guillaumin, 1887), in *Revue d'économie politique* (vol. I, 1887, p. 542): "[...] the details he [Leroy-Beaulieu] gives leave us the impression that he is himself one of the biggest vine growers in Tunisia." (handwritten note on a piece of stamped envelope of 1888, preserved in the fonds de Lausanne (F. W. V b 19).

[41] In the margin of the original manuscript, Walras angrily notes: "a mediocrity of the first order".

[42] *Traité de la science des finances*, Paris: Guillaumin, 1st ed., 1877 (2 vol.).

[43] Certainly, Walras refers here to P. Leroy-Beaulieu's book, *Essai sur la répartition des richesses et sur la tendance à une moindre inégalité des conditions,* Paris: Guillaumin 1880 (voir les chapitres VIII et IX). This book is based on the course given at the Collège de France, from 1878 to 1880, replacing Mr. Chevalier.

11.3.4 *Émile Levasseur (1828–1911)*

A former student at the École Normale Supérieure, Émile Levasseur began his career in 1852 as a history teacher at the Saint Louis and Henri IV *lycées* in Paris. In 1854, he published the *Recherches historiques sur le système de Law* (Paris: Guillaumin), a reference book for the XIXth century, and in 1857 he was admitted to the Société d'économie politique de Paris.[44] Influenced by the German Historical School, he conceived political economy as an observational science that can only obtain laws through the study of facts.[45] He was also the author of *Histoire des classes ouvrières en France depuis la conquête de Jules César jusqu'à la Révolution* (Paris: Guillaumin, 1859) and *Histoire des classes ouvrières en France depuis 1789 jusqu'à nos jours* (Paris: A. Rousseau, 1867). In 1868, he became a member of the Académie des sciences morales et politiques and succeeded Henri Baudrillart in the supplementary course on the history of political economy at the Collège de France, which was to be entitled "Histoire des faits et doctrines économiques". Concerning this course transfer, Walras states:

> [...] it was entrusted to Mr. Émile Levasseur, historian and geographer, not at all an economist, but nephew by marriage of Mr. Wolowski,[46] professor of political economy at the Conservatoire des Arts et Métiers, member of the Institute, the rival of Michel Chevalier, his antagonist on the question of money, on that of banks.[47]

But Walras further specifies:

> He had the supplementary course transformed into an ordinary course by having Mr. Jules Simon set up in 1872 a chair of *histoire des doctrines économiques* which would be a chair of political economy. But he indicates, on the Collège de France's posters, this official title with a subtitle in parentheses as follows: *histoire et géographie économiques*, which allows him to do history and geography or, to put it better, whatever he wants. At this moment (1879–1880), under the pretext of presenting the economic history of France and the organisation of labour before and after the Revolution of 1789, he simply delivers his very mediocre book on the *Histoire des classes ouvrières en France. Suppléant,* then *remplaçant* of his uncle at the Conservatoire, he holds two chairs of political economy and has barely published in terms of book no more than a small manual absolutely grotesque.[48]

Émile Levasseur is, indeed, holder of two chairs, the first at the Collège de France of "Histoire des doctrines économiques", obtained in December 1871 with the support of the Académie des sciences morales et politiques (a chair which was titled in

---

[44] On É. Levasseur, see L. Le Van-Lemesle, 1994 b; N. Commerçon and B. Boureille, 2000; J.-P. Potier, 2016, pp. 27–28 and 30.

[45] É. Levasseur uses this methodological approach in his book *La question de l'or* (Paris: Guillaumin, 1858).

[46] The niece of Louis Wolowski, Nathalie Wolowska, married Émile Levasseur.

[47] "De l'enseignement de l'économie politique en France" (1880d), vol. VII, p. 429. L. Wolowski is the author of *La question des banques*, Paris: Guillaumin, 1864.

[48] "De l'enseignement de l'économie politique en France" (1880d), vol. VII, p. 430. Concerning the "absolutely grotesque little manual", Walras is undoubtedly referring to the *Précis d'économie politique*, whose 4th edition will appear in 1883 (Paris: Hachette).

1885 "Géographie, histoire et statistique économiques"), the second of "Économie politique et de législation industrielle", obtained in 1876, at the Conservatoire des arts et métiers and previously held by Louis Wolowski. At the École libre des sciences politiques, he also provided from 1872 a course in statistics, which was titled, from 1892, "Géographie commerciale et statistique".

The scathing judgements we have just read seem a settling of scores. Indeed, following his presentation to the Académie des sciences morales et politiques of the paper "Principe d'une théorie mathématique de l'échange", during the summer of 1873, Walras had incurred the wrath of Émile Levasseur, the official report of the session indicating:

> Mr. Levasseur insists, in conclusion, on the danger of wanting to reduce to unity things which by essence are complex, as well as applying to political economy a method which is excellent for the physical sciences, but which cannot be applied without discernment to an order of phenomena whose causes are so variable, so complex and in which intervenes above all this eminently variable and irreducible cause in algebraic formula: human liberty.[49]

We have already seen in detail Walras's strong reaction to these remarks. Later, on 27 February 1903, he notes with a certain vanity:

> Lev[asseur] and I do not operate on the same ground. He is on the ground of official science, of academic chairs, of Academy seats, of decorations, where I have nothing to claim. I am on the ground of truth, of the future, of glory, where I do not fear his competition. It is pointless to fight there. (Let it suffice for me to insert his observations following my communication to the Institute in 1873) ("Notes d'humeur", 2000, vol. XIII, p. 535).

But in 1903–04, Émile Levasseur seems to have risen in his esteem if one judges by his correspondence. Indeed, Levasseur, colleague and friend of Georges Renard at the Conservatoire national des arts et métiers, defends Albert Aupetit at the agrégation competition of 1903, and the following year, he makes him his collaborator at the *Revue économique internationale* of Brussels which he manages.[50] Finally, it is amusing to note that after the death of Léon Walras in 1910, Émile Levasseur becomes the Honorary President[51] of the French section of the international committee that should have been responsible for the edition of his complete works!

11.3.5 Léon Say (1826–1896)

After his participation in the events of June 1848, the grandson of Jean-Baptiste Say publishes a *Histoire de la Caisse d'escompte de 1776 à 1793* (1848),[52] then

[49] *Compte-rendu des séances et travaux de l'Académie des sciences morales et politiques,* vol. 101, XXXIIIrd year, volume 1, January 1874, re-ed. in: vol. VII, pp. 531–32.

[50] See L. Walras, letter to Louise Renard, 30 October 1904, in: *Correspondence*, III, l. 255, p. 255; "Notes d'humeur" (2000), vol. XIII, p. 535.

[51] C. Gide effectively presides over it.

[52] This private establishment is considered a "model" of the future Banque de France.

collaborates on the *Dictionnaire de l'économie politique* edited by Charles Coquelin and Gilbert-Urbain Guillaumin. He marries Geneviève Bertin, daughter of Édouard Bertin (1797–1871), director of the *Journal des Débats*, which allows him to become an important collaborator of this very influential journal. In 1857, his friend Alphonse de Rothschild brings him into the administrative committee of the *Chemin de fer du Nord* company. As we will see in Chapter 13 (*Léon Walras, Paul Voituron and Constant Leirens at the Editorial Team of* Le Travail*: the Polemics on Cooperation (1866–67)*), he founds in 1865 with Léon Walras the Caisse d'escompte des associations populaires and takes over with him, the following year, the journal *Le Travail—Organe international des intérêts de la classe laborieuse—Revue du mouvement coopératif*. He seems to follow with interest his lessons on the "*Recherche de l'idéal social*".[53] This common experience in the cooperative movement ends in December 1868. After the Franco-Prussian War, Adolphe Thiers, who names Léon Say, "the grandson of free trade", allows him a rapid political ascent: he becomes deputy of the Seine department at the Bordeaux's National Assembly in February 1871, prefect of the Seine after the crushing of the Paris Commune in June 1871, Minister of Finance in 1872–73. He becomes Minister of Finance again from 1875 to 1879 and for a few months in 1882. Moreover, he sits in the Senate from 1876 to 1889. In 1882 only, the Académie des sciences morales et politiques admits him as a full member, while the Académie Française will open its doors to him in 1886 to occupy the seat of the novelist Edmond About. He multiplies speeches and conferences on monetary and financial questions.[54]

Léon Say's name does not appear on the list of economists against whom Walras rages in the study "De l'enseignement de l'économie politique en France" (1880d). This omission does not seem fortuitous. One might think that he avoids launching an attack on a very powerful and influential political figure who, on the one hand, is not primarily a professor, and on the other hand, has not yet published many works in economics.[55] But another type of argument must be invoked. In 1880, the relations between Léon Walras and Léon Say have not completely deteriorated, although they have become "insignificant" since 1870, as he himself indicates in his correspondence. In 1883, their ties will even tighten for a while to face an attack in the journal *Le Figaro* concerning the circumstances of the liquidation of the Caisse d'escompte des associations populaires.[56] On 11 June, Walras goes so far as to ask Léon Say for a recommendation to obtain a review of his *Théorie mathématique de la richesse sociale*, recently published by Guillaumin in the *Journal des Débats*! In the

---

53 After the 2nd lesson, Léon Say writes a favourable article in the *Journal des Débats* (13 November 1867, p. 3).

54 His lectures at the École Libre des Sciences Politiques are compiled under the title, *Les solutions démocratiques de la question des impôts* (Paris: Guillaumin, 1886, 2 vol.).

55 L. Say will publish *Le socialisme d'État* in 1884 and *Contre le socialisme* in 1896. Furthermore, he will ensure the coordination of two dictionaries: Léon Say and Joseph Chailley-Bert (ed), *Nouveau dictionnaire d'économie politique* (Paris: Guillaumin, 2 vol., 1891–92) and the *Dictionnaire des finances*, published under the direction of Léon Say by Louis Foyot and H. Lanjalley (Paris: Berger-Levrault et Cie, 2 vols, 1889 and 1894).

56 See the "Entrevue avec M. Léon Say en 1883", vol. VI, pp. 3–10.

same letter, he points out that the Société d'économie politique de Paris, instead of focusing on "science in the strict sense", confines itself to discussing questions such as the "drilling of the Simplon".[57] Léon Say's response on this matter is particularly interesting:

> You are right to say that science is hardly favoured in our Société d'économie politique. We are overrun by *reporters*. I have been making great efforts since I became president, but I am not achieving much. The only questions that interest the society are business or political current affairs.[58]

After their meeting on 23 July 1883 in Paris, as recounted by Walras, personal relations cease definitively. Eager to present in France the "applied theory of money" he has just developed, our author has the following question added to the permanent agenda of the Société d'économie politique de Paris in October 1884: "On a system of gold currency with regulating silver token." In April 1885, President Léon Say has this topic removed from the agenda, under the pretext of "not allowing the discussion of the value of the Bank of France's cash reserves".[59] Walras then decides to resign from the Société d'économie politique. From this date, according to him, Léon Say becomes his "persecutor". As an influential member of numerous journals and learned societies' direction, he would systematically prevent him from publishing works on mathematical economics in his native country. Walras claims to have "suffered the tyranny of Mr. Say in at least four scientific societies, besides that of the actuaries",[60] and he rages against the "pontiff of the official school", the "pope of the official political and social economy" ("Le problème fiscal", 1896d, vol. IX, p. 420, English transl., 2010, revised, p. 344).

In his "Notes d'humeur", he notably indicates: "I know well what political economy has done for Mr. Say, but I am completely ignorant of what Mr. Say has done for political economy" (2000, vol. XIII, p. 532). In another passage of these notes, he paints a particularly virulent caricature of his "tyrant":

> Develop this about the princes of contemporary affectedness: If Mr. Say really had a bit of wit and heart, one could come to an understanding with him, let him get a certain place that would be deserved, exert a certain influence that could be beneficial. But Mr. Say has always been, is, and will always be a fool, that is to say, a man who is nothing and wants to be everything. Whether Mr. Say has any value as a politician or not, I will not seek here; but his value as a scientist is absolutely nil. He has never clarified a point of economics. He only says stupid things (...). Moreover, what would he do with science? Senator, academician, president of

[57] See L. Walras, letter to Léon Say, 21 June 1883, in: *Correspondence,* I, l. 563, p. 765.

[58] Emphasis by L. S., letter to L. Walras, 25 May 1883, excerpt published by W. Jaffé, in: *op. cit.*, p. 765, note 9.

[59] Remarks by L. Say cited by L. Walras in his "Notice autobiographique" (1909a), vol. V, p. 19; see also the letter to C. Gide, 28 October 1887, in: *Correspondence,* II, l. 816, p. 227. Walras's monetary propositions will be criticised by Émile Cheysson and Léon Say during the session of 16 December 1885 of the Société de statistique de Paris (*Journal* of this Society, vol. 27, no. 1, January 1886, pp. 2–5). L. Walras will examine very seriously the objections of É. Cheysson, which will lead him to write in 1886 his *Théorie de la monnaie* (see the correspondence with É. Cheysson, *in: Correspondence*, II, and the "Introduction" of the *Théorie de la monnaie*).

[60] L. Walras, letter to H. Laurent, 9 July 1899, in: *Correspondence*, III, l. 1410, p. 81.

> 36 societies, associations, leagues, etc., etc., he spends his time rolling from platform to platform, from banquet to banquet (...), a true Tartarin of Tarascon[61] surrounded by his cap hunters. And despite everything, Mr. Say wants to be the pontiff of political economy, as Cousin was the pontiff of philosophy. In his inept presidential summaries (give samples), he lets fall on your head, without having understood or even read you, some excommunication, where bitterness competes with stupidity, obviously suffocated at the idea that one dares not to prostrate before a man like him, who walks around with two academician's coats on his back, consecrated as a great economist by the Academie des sciences morales et politiques, and a great writer by the Académie Française. He must be left.[62]

Yet despite this unequivocal condemnation, Walras will decide to include six studies by Léon Say of the years 1866–67 and the note entitled "Entrevue avec M. Léon Say en 1883", from the third project (1902) of *Les Associations populaires coopératives.* One must conclude that only Léon Say's cooperative texts held any interest for him!

11.4 Conclusion

What assessment can we draw from this overview of Walras's criticisms of the French liberal economists, which were deployed on two levels, the conceptions of the "school" and the men? In the sequence of these stages, one might have legitimately expected that the criticism of content would represent a very important, even central, aspect of Walras's approach, the second moment, for its part, focusing on the illustration, through the examination of some important works of the "orthodox" economists. However, neither the study "De l'enseignement de l'économie politique en France", mainly examined here, nor the "Notes d'humeur" engage in this path. In reality, Walras demonstrates a very imperfect knowledge of the works of the economists he criticises. When he happens to read them, he does so in a very superficial and incomplete manner. The purpose of his reading seems more to be the detection of possible borrowings (for example, in the case of Paul Leroy-Beaulieu) rather than a precise, even critical, analysis of the content. Essentially, he reviews a few exemplary "biographies", often erroneous on certain points. It is noteworthy that the four authors criticised in "De l'enseignement de l'économie politique en France" all held a position, at one time or another, at the Collège de France. Such an approach necessarily leads him to overlook the main theoretical differences existing among liberal economists. One might question the reasons for such an attitude. Firstly, there is a political hostility concerning the issue of "socialism". But there is also an "essential" hostility that was also bequeathed to him by his father. Léon Walras is convinced that French liberals harm economic science, hinder its development, while he himself contributes to its advancement. The "school" thus inspires in him the deepest contempt. Finally, there is a hostility that could be described

[61] Main character of three novels of Alphonse Daudet.

[62] Document on envelope of 4 May 1887, in: vol. XIII, pp. 530–31; see also "My Position vis-à-vis M. Say", *op. cit.*, pp. 531–32.

as "psychological". Walras wants to settle personal scores with certain representatives, such as Henri Baudrillart and Émile Levasseur. He had to endure refusals, suffer humiliations, and even give up teaching in France in the years 1877–79. These episodes explain his accumulation of resentment, even hatred. One of the clearest manifestations of this type of hostility appears in his attitude towards Léon Say, who becomes a veritable scapegoat from 1885 onwards, following his break with the Société d'économie politique de Paris.

Appendix: Letter from Henri Baudrillart to Michel Chevalier[63]

23 April 1866

To Sir Michel Chevalier, Senator

Sir and honoured master and colleague,

I have learned from my friend Mr. Monjean[64] that you are complaining about my silence. Please, attribute it only to the reluctance I feel to enter into explanations that are painful for me. Yet I must decide to break this silence which might otherwise establish my situation with you unclearly and leave you in doubt about my real thoughts. I have only to transcribe the letter I intended to send you in response to the one you honoured me with on 31 March, where you kindly justify your decision to resume your chair of political economy at the Collège de France:

I will tell you frankly, sir and honoured master and colleague, there could not be a more complete disagreement concerning the way we both appreciate the situation that has been made for me. You write to me that I *should have foreseen* the blow that strikes me. You add that I must understand that, if I wish to teach at the Collège de France, there is no reason for you to be insensitive yourself to the utility presented by the propagation of science through teaching. Let me tell you, on the contrary, that all this, far from being foreseen by me, throws me into the deepest astonishment. For about six months, there was no question between you and me, Mr. Léon Say, my father-in-law, and finally Mr. de Sacy, to whom you spoke about it, of this question of the Collège de France except in relation to your financial matters and your industrial difficulties in Lodève. You wanted to partly address them, you first told me, by resuming a portion of the salary, if the government did not grant your request for a merger with another military cloth factory located in another department, and if Mr. de Sacy and Mr. E. Bertin could not obtain anything from the Minister of the Interior. Then, two months later, in October, you told me that if I could arrange a retirement pension equivalent to half your salary, you were determined to retire from the Collège de France, and you asked me to make efforts to this effect with the administrator Mr.

[63] We wish to thank Arnold Heertje, professor at the University of Amsterdam (Naarden, Netherlands), who authorised us to publish this letter in our work.

[64] Maurice Monjean, director of the Collège Chaptal since 1859.

Stanislas Julien,[65] and with the Ministry of Public Instruction, with Mr. Jourdain, who was in charge of the pension service. The result of these efforts was that you did not have the necessary conditions for retirement. Consequently, last November, you modified your resolution to worsen it towards me, so foreign to all these matters, so far from believing that on the part of a man with such a high position, I could ever feel in my modest means of existence so necessary to my family the repercussions of a money question! Indeed, it was towards the end of last November that you wrote to Mr. de Sacy, in Compiègne, to ask him to discuss your request with the Empress. You declared in this letter that, if the government persisted in refusing your request, you would consider repairing your losses to some extent by resuming your chair, which, you added, *would be detrimental to your son-in-law Baudrillart*. And here, when I was told that these Lodève affairs have been settled, of which you no longer spoke to me, and of which I awaited with a very natural reserve that you would say a word to me, since you made me a party to them, here I learn from a letter from you in the last week of March that you had declared to the Minister of Public Instruction your intention to resume your chair for 1866–1867; you allege to me the desire to put your experience acquired in high public office at the service of science. Should I not be surprised that, having so many other means to defend and spread your ideas, such as speaking in the Senate, giving depositions in inquiries, presenting reports at the Universal Exhibition of Industry, writing books and articles for the most important newspapers, everything that serves as instruments to your great and just influence and your eminent talent, you wish to add public teaching to them, a heavy burden, to say the least, to add to the others, without fearing to cause me the most serious harm?

How could I be less astonished, sir and illustrious master and colleague, by the way you invoke what you call your ever-existing right to return to your chair? This right, which you did not have as a State Councillor but have as a senator, is not in question. But is it to you that I must ask if the legal right is everything in this world, and if there are not moral and equitable proprieties just as strong? You take the cruel decision for me, after fourteen years, to do this unprecedented thing of returning to a chair abandoned for such a long interval; for you, the interest involved is without any comparison with mine because for me, it is immense, it is my life, it is my career; there was every reason to believe that my future lay there. Who knows, I was told from all sides, if Mr. Michel Chevalier, blessed by fortune, honours, and a brilliant reputation, still having great occupations, and reaching an age where the most energetic activity rather thinks of reducing its commitments than multiplying them, will not have the good sense of crowning in you his own work, a long and persevering effort that earned you the distinguished honour of becoming his colleague at the Institute, if finally, as a friend of Mr. de Sacy, a witness to your marriage, having more than once shown you his friendship, he will not finish treating you as a friend. Far from it, sir and master, you have broken me. First you declare to the minister that you are taking

[65] Stanislas Julien (1799–1873), holder of the chair of Chinese language and literature at the Collège de France from 1832 and administrator of the Collège from 1854.

back your chair from me; then, the blow struck, you leave my fate to the randomness of subsequent steps, without even a precise goal known to you and me!

Ah! How much, sir and honoured master, an hour of benevolent, affectionate conversation, where you would have told me that if you resumed your course, you would only do so when I had been provided with a position, and where we could have amicably understood each other, would have spared me from perplexities!

You go, sir and eminent colleague, as far as to write to me on 31 March, that after all, I have never been a substitute for more than a year, the annual presentation being necessary, and that *you have shown excessive condescension* in presenting me thus year after year, instead of taking several substitutes on trial. Let us leave aside the harshness of such language, to speak only of the facts. Can it be that you have forgotten the starting point of our relations as they were regulated by the decree of 13 April 1852? This decree provides for a substitution not annual but indefinite and the abandonment of the entirety of the salary as conditions for combining the title and functions of State Councillor. All this is very explicitly stipulated. Certainly, I did not believe then, when you confirmed with friendly words what such an engagement seemed to assure me and when the minister showed me in such a substitution the basis of a certain future, I did not believe that fourteen years later, I would hear from you that I had maintained myself by an *excessive condescension*! It was only eight years after this decree that Mr. Rouland[66] created annual substitutions, a pure precaution, he kindly told me then, against substitutes unworthy of remaining in possession of high teaching for long time, and which could affect me all the less as my situation was exceptionally regulated. Can I see without astonishment that you make today a particular merit of not having used in dismissing me a faculty that none of the holders who were in the ordinary relations of holder to substitute used, that is to say, of not having exceptionally mistreated me?

Do I forget, then, sir and honoured master and colleague, that you opened the career of political economy to me in a brilliant manner? No, and those who know me are aware that I do not have a cold and ungrateful heart. For you personally, I have always professed towards my friends or publicly, as a writer, entirely different sentiments. But here again, please, I beg you, see things as they are. I would not want to diminish my former obligations by saying that if you chose me as a substitute, it is also because I was to your liking; but do you not admit that what is an advantage at 30 loses much of this character at nearly 45, that a 60-year-old substitute without rights has a hard time believing himself still obliged to the holder, and that there is nothing below the condition of a perpetual substitute than that of a substitute evicted without assured compensation and in too summary a manner? You cannot doubtless admit that a substitute who counts by himself, who has certain interests and a certain value, is exclusively the man of the holder, good only to keep his place, in exchange for certain more or less precarious advantages, until it is possible and pleasant for the latter to take it back, except to see afterwards what can be done for the substitute sent away after 15 or 20 years? What will it be if the substitute was appointed under exceptional conditions that seemed likely to protect him, and found

[66] Gustave Rouland (1806–78), Minister of Public Instruction and Worship from 1856 to 1863.

himself in particular relations with the holder such that they could appear to him as guarantees of security?

I have taken advantage, you add, of these fourteen years: I have reached the Institute. I fully acknowledge that the substitute position to which you honoured me by calling me has facilitated the means; but you might be wrong to believe that without it I would not have arrived through my books and another teaching. In 1852, I had achieved significant academic successes; the highest-ranking men in the University spoke of me as soon to be designated for higher education to which I indeed aspired; my contemporaries then, the Janet,[67] the Lévêque,[68] and others are today members of the Institute and holders. My titles will be counted, you say again; I hope so, but you will understand that I take it upon myself to assert them. Whether I succeed or fail, I carry with me the conscience that, during these long years of teaching, I have nothing to reproach myself, neither towards you, sir and honoured master, nor towards the science of which you honoured me by entrusting me with the deposit.

Accept, Sir and most eminent colleague, the assurance of my most distinguished sentiments.

H. Baudrillart

[67] Paul Janet (1823–99), holder of the chair of history of philosophy at the Sorbonne since 1864 and member of the Institute since 1866.

[68] Charles Lévêque (1818–1900), holder of the chair of Greek and Latin philosophy at the Collège de France and member of the Institute since 1861.

Chapter 12
Criticism of "Empirical Socialism": the Cases of Louis Blanc and the Saint-Simonians

12.1 Introduction

Throughout his career, Léon Walras had numerous opportunities, while presenting the facets of his own "liberal socialism", to refute the ideas of the socialists of his time. To refer to these authors, he uses the generic term "empirical socialism". What typology of currents will he apply in his writings? He always uses an evaluation scale from best to worst. Indeed, he begins with socialists who exhibit "a certain science and a certain critical strength" ("Exposition et conciliation des doctrines sociales", 1872c, vol. XIII, p. 281), here referring to Saint-Simon and his school, as well as Charles Fourier and his disciple Victor Considérant, the Fourierist school being, according to him, clearly inferior to the first (*Cours d'économie sociale*, vol. XII, p. 267). Next, he moves to the socialists possessing "a certain superiority of logic", referring to the "fraternal communism" of Louis Blanc and Étienne Cabet (*Cours d'économie sociale*, vol. XII, pp. 271 and 291). Finally, he turns to socialists whose doctrine remains confused and incoherent: this is the case of Pierre-Joseph Proudhon, to whom he dedicated a specific book (1860).

However, it is worth noting that Walras considers Jean-Jacques Rousseau as the "father of the contemporary socialism", citing a famous passage from the *Discours sur l'origine et les fondements de l'inégalité parmi les hommes*:

> The first man who, having enclosed a piece of land, be thought himself of saying: This is mine, and found people simple enough to believe him, was the real founder of civil society. From how many crimes, wars and murders, from how many horrors and misfortunes might not any one have saved mankind, by pulling up the stakes, or filling up the ditch, and crying to his fellows: "Beware of listening to this impostor; you are undone if you once forget *that the fruits of the earth belong to us all, and the earth itself to nobody.*[1]

[1] Emphasis by J.-J. R., [1754] 1959, vol. III, p. 164; *Cours d'économie sociale*, vol. XII, p. 264; « Exposition et conciliation des doctrines sociales» (1872c), vol. XIII, p. 273.

J.-P. Potier, *Léon Walras, Economist and Liberal Socialist*, Springer Studies in the History of Economic Thought, https://doi.org/10.1007/978-3-032-04670-3_12

In Walras's view, even if it points to the origin of the inequality of social conditions, this kind of declamatory phraseology is far removed from any scientific reasoning and can be found among the socialist authors of the XIXth century.

In this chapter, we will not engage in an exhaustive analysis of the criticism addressed by Walras to each socialist current or author. Many works have been devoted to his critique of Proudhon,[2] so we have preferred to focus on relatively lesser-known critiques, those of Louis Blanc and the Saint-Simonians. The critique of the former is harsh and excessive, while that of Saint-Simonianism is more measured.

12.2 Criticism of Louis Blanc

In the "Introduction à l'étude de la question sociale" (1859b), which precedes the refutation of P.-J. Proudhon's economic ideas in *L'Économie politique et la justice* (1860a), Walras already devotes several pages to the systematic critique of Louis Blanc's ideas.[3] On 23 November 1859, his father, who guided his early steps as an economist, wrote to him:

> It would not be bad either for you to demolish the theories of Louis Blanc on the organisation of labour, using the correct and reasonable political economy that I have inspired in you. As long as you target the unintelligent socialists with prudence and circumspection, *without revealing the bottom of your own bag*, which always seems easy to do to me, I do not think you will get into bad quarrels with the power that governs us (emphasis by us, vol. IV, p. 373).

In short, it would be an easy critique of "empirical communism" to conduct. It is worth noting that all liberal economists of the XIXth century detested Louis Blanc as a publicist and politician of the 1848 Revolution. They deliberately equate the *ateliers nationaux* with the project of "*ateliers sociaux*" and they express their hatred of the "right to work" claim. Walras too will mock Louis Blanc and his supporters who believe that "the Republic cannot dispense with providing a few thousand amateurs with the opportunity to move stones" (*L'Économie politique et la justice*, 1860a, p. 282). However, Auguste Walras's advice to his son to criticise this author "without revealing the bottom of [his] own bag", to avoid trouble, is important. Indeed, the Walras, father and son, are not aligned with the positions of the liberal economists of their time and, on a political level, they are republican opponents of the Empire.

The various criticisms can be grouped into three categories: philosophy, the rejection of competition, and the project of *ateliers sociaux*.

---

[2] See M. Boson, 1951; P. Dockès, 1996; M. Herland, 1996 and 2013b.

[3] Léon Walras will always use the 9th edition of the book *Organisation du travail*, published in 1850, which his father entrusted to him.

12.2.1 Philosophical Weaknesses

Léon Walras engages in an ironic critique of the "philosophy" of Louis Blanc, in "Exposition et conciliation des doctrines sociales" (1872c), a study whose substance he re-uses in the *Cours d'économie sociale*'s 39th lesson ("Doctrines of Mr. Louis Blanc and Mr. Émile de Girardin"). Interestingly, he deals in the same chapter with the "absolute communism" of Louis Blanc and the "absolute individualism" of the journalist Émile de Girardin, whose "individualist socialism" consists in the establishment of a single proportional tax on capital proper and land to enable the State to fulfil its functions as a social insurer.

For our author, "Mr. Louis Blanc is anything but a philosopher, anything but an economist. His philosophy does not go beyond Rousseau and his economics stops at Mably" (vol. XII, 39th lesson, p. 271). In his view, it is less interesting than the theories of the Saint-Simonians and of Charles Fourier. He argues that Blanc's theory is that "of pure and simple fraternal (*fraternitaire*) communism". He also notes that.

> [...] it is he who to the obscure Saint-Simonian formula: - to each according to his capacity, to each capacity according to its works, has substituted this other formula so clear and so distinct: - From each according to his capacity, to each according to his needs" (emphasis by L. W., op. cit., p. 271),

even adding that "it is he who spoiled for us the beautiful revolutionary motto: *Liberty, Equality* by the addition of the word: *Fraternity*, as if fraternity could be inscribed in the law" (*op. cit.*, pp. 271–72). He alludes here to the motto of the Constitution of the Second Republic and it is known that Louis Blanc's socialism is the natural development of this formula: Liberty, equality, fraternity (F. Démier, 2005, p. 145).

Walras considers, for his part, the principle of "fraternity", or of charity, or even of devotion, as a purely optional, voluntary, non-reciprocal principle. Fraternity is a duty but not a right, unlike justice which is a principle both reciprocal (duty/right) and obligatory ("Théorie de la propriété", 1896c, pp. 187–88, English transl., 2010, pp. 143–44).

In his writings, notably in the *Cours d'économie sociale* (vol. XII, 39th lesson, p. 272), Walras quotes a passage of Louis Blanc from the *Histoire de la Révolution française*, in which the author indicates that "three major principles govern the world and history: *authority, individualism, fraternity*". However, he omits to reproduce the following presentation of these three principles:

> The principle of authority bases the life of nations on blindly accepted beliefs, on a superstitious respect for tradition, on inequality, and which, as a means of government, employs constraint. The principle of individualism takes man outside of society, makes him the sole judge of what surrounds him and of himself, gives him an exalted sense of his rights without indicating his duties, abandons him to his own devices, and, for all government, proclaims the *laissez-faire*. The principle of fraternity considers the members of the great family as united, tends to one day organise societies, the work of man, on the model of the human body, the work of God, and bases the power to govern on persuasion, on the voluntary assent of hearts (1847, vol. 1, p. 9).

In reality, Walras contents himself to quote the following passage of Louis Blanc:

> *Authority* was wielded by Catholicism with a brilliance that astonishes; it prevailed until Luther. *Individualism*, inaugurated by Luther, developed with irresistible force; and, freed from the religious element, it triumphed in France through the publicists of the Constituent Assembly. It governs the present; it is the soul of things. *Fraternity*, announced by the thinkers of the Montagne, then disappeared in a storm, and still appears to us today only in the distant ideal; however, all great minds call for it, and already it occupies and illuminates the highest sphere of intelligences" (emphasis by L. B., 1847, vol. 1, pp. 9–10).

Let us recall here that Walras does not advocate individualism; according to him, the individual and society are equivalent "social ideal types" and it is not acceptable to conceive society as a collection of individuals (*cf.* chapter 15, *Towards the Repurchase of Land by the State and the Abolition of Taxes*). However, he does not wish to discuss this question in his commentary on Louis Blanc. He finds it very amusing to see this writer begin the world with authority and Catholicism. He argues that in the Athens republic, authority did not prevail. Consequently, Louis Blanc's communist philosophy would erase Ancient Greece from the history of humanity (1859b, vol. V, p. 103). Ultimately, according to him, the "philosophy of history of Mr. Louis Blanc […] is extremely narrow and superficial; but if all this is not profound, at least it is simple" (vol. XII, 39th lesson, p. 272).

Let us now address the question of competition.

12.2.2 Workers in Competition

In his book *Organisation du travail*, Louis Blanc denounces what he calls "*capitalism*", that is to say, "the appropriation of capital by some, to the exclusion of others". He disagrees with classical economists such as Adam Smith or Jean-Baptiste Say who extol the virtues of free competition. According to him, competition turns the market into "a trap", because sometimes the producer has to sell his commodities at a loss, sometimes the consumer finds himself extorted. Competition leads to bankruptcies, periodic crises, and unemployment. In summary, competition is "for the people a system of extermination" and "for the bourgeoisie a constantly active cause of impoverishment and ruin", to the benefit of "a few industrial oligarchs" (1850, Book 1, chap. I, p. 24 and chap. III, p. 58). In short, not only are the people (i. e. citizens deprived of capital) victims, but it is also the case for the bourgeoisie (i. e. citizens who work possessing tools and capital). The camp of the victors is that of the financial and industrial oligarchy which profits from monopoly situations. Paradoxically, on this point, Louis Blanc joins to some extent some liberal economists of the *Journal des économistes* who attack the financial aristocracy and monopolies (Adolphe Blanqui, for example).

Already, in the "Introduction à l'étude de la question sociale", Walras reacts to the question raised by Louis Blanc, in *Organisation du travail*: "*Is competition a means of assuring work to the poor?*" (1850, Book I, chap. II, p. 26). He responds at that time:

> [...] from the point of view of an ideal society, the word *poor* does not have any economic sense: because a man, in a such a society, is always rich at least in his personal faculties, which constitute a capital whose labour is the income. Only the sick, disabled persons, the lazy ones are poor; and all these people are under the jurisdiction of charity, outside the economic law. Society does not have to ensure them work more particularly than anybody else. Therefore, the right question is this: Is competition a means of preventing the worker from being in full possession of the income of his faculties? (emphasis by L. W., 1859b, vol. V, pp. 118–19).

Louis Blanc argues that competition is "labour put up for auction". For him:

> An entrepreneur requires a worker: three present themselves. How much for your work? - Three francs: I have a wife and children. – Good, and you? – Two francs and a half : I have no children, but I have a wife. – Excellent, and you? – Two francs will content me: I am single. - "You then is preferred." It is done: the bargain is concluded. But what becomes of the two rejected workers? They will die quietly of hunger, it is to be hoped. But suppose they turn robbers? Fear nothing, we have police. Or murderers? We have the executioner. As for the luckiest of the three, his victory is only temporary. Should a fourth worker arrive robust enough to fast one day out of two, the scale of reduction would descend to the lowest point; new pariah, perhaps another recruit for the galleys! (1850, Book I, chap. II, p. 26).

In the "Introduction à l'étude de la question sociale", the young Walras comments on this passage arguing that rather than engaging in a passionate discourse, one must examine the question of wage formation coldly and scientifically. His argument against Louis Blanc will be improved later in the *Cours d'économie sociale.* Regarding this passage, he now declares:

> Let us concede that at a given moment, in a given country, things happen this way. Would that be enough to reject the principle of free competition? No, not at all; because if workers offer work by underbidding (*au rabais*), entrepreneurs demand it by outbidding (*à l'enchère*). The competition of workers operates to the benefit of employers, the competition of employers is exercised for the benefit of workers (vol. XII, 39th lesson, p. 273).

We will return in more detail to this question in chapter 14 (*Organisation of the Labour Market, Labour Legislation and Social Insurance*). What now of the project of *ateliers sociaux* which is at the heart of the "Social Revolution" desired by this critic of competition?

12.2.3 The Ateliers Sociaux Project

For Louis Blanc, after repurchasing the railways, mines, insurance companies through borrowing and transforming the Banque de France into a State bank (but independent of Treasury), the State would allocate a special budget for the initial financing of *ateliers sociaux* in the main branches of industry and agriculture and would again resort to borrowing. In the "Exposition et conciliation des doctrines sociales" (1872c) and also in the 39th lesson of the *Cours d'économie sociale*, Walras argues that "Mr. Louis Blanc organises his *ateliers sociaux* of agriculture and industry under the direction of the State and of its *national State bank*". (emphasis by L. W., *op. cit.*, p. 272). He immediately adds:

> The State is thus the sole entrepreneur. That is not all: the State is also the sole landowner and the sole capitalist: it owns all the lands and capital. Does the individual at least own his personal faculties? As much as it can be when he can only work for the State alone, and that, in exchange for work provided according to his capacity, he receives a wage paid according to his needs, that is to say as much as in the theocracy or slavery's systems, that is to say not at all (*op. cit.*, p. 272).[4]

Walras concludes that Louis Blanc resolves the question of production by leaving it in the hands of the State as "sole entrepreneur", and that he resolves the question of distribution "by making the State the sole owner of land, of capital *and of personal faculties*" (emphasis by us, *op. cit.*, p. 272). Regarding the question of ownership of "personal faculties", this interpretation is ambiguous and debatable.[5]

Finally, concerning this system, Walras notes that to establish it scientifically, it must be founded not only "on philosophical bases", but also "on economic bases", which constitutes a problem of applied economics, whose criterion is economic efficiency. And "economically, it would be necessary to demonstrate that, with the State acting as the sole farmer, the sole manufacturer, the sole trader, goods of all kinds will always be in great abundance and in perfect proportion" (*op. cit.*, pp. 272–73). However, this project cannot ensure that. Indeed, Louis Blanc merely applies the "empirical method": he identifies the defects of the current society and suggests a practice diametrically opposed to competition by proposing monopoly (1859b, vol. V, p. 102).

Ultimately, Walras's attacks on Louis Blanc are violent and unjust. He forgets that for him, it is about "preparing the future, in a word, without violently breaking with all the past" (1850, "Responses to various objections", p. 211). Our author cannot accept a State "banker of the poor" (1850, "Introduction", p. 13) to finance the *ateliers sociaux*, while he himself envisages a large loan for the repurchase of land by the State (*cf. infra*).

Even the liberal economist Joseph Garnier took some precautions in 1845 when attacking Louis Blanc:

> According to the explanations of Mr. Louis Blanc, the State would only be a regulator, legislator, protector of industry, and not a universal manufacturer and producer. But as it exclusively protects the *ateliers sociaux* to destroy private industry, it inevitably leads to monopoly and falls back into the Saint-Simonian theory despite itself, at least as far as production is concerned (J. Garnier, 1845, p. 425).

In fact, Walras's attacks broadly align with those published in the newspaper *Le Commerce*, on 3 August 1841, which accused *Organisation du travail*'s author of making the State a (sole) industrial entrepreneur and responsible for providing for the needs of private consumption. Louis Blanc responded to the attacks of this newspaper. According to him, these attacks were rather aimed at Saint-Simonianism, and not at his own system. He even asserts:

---

[4] Instead of receiving a wage, the price of his labour, he receives an income according to the principle of fraternity. See on this subject P. Dockès, 1996, p. 190.

[5] Walras's interpretation is clearer on this point in "Exposition et conciliation des doctrines sociales" (1872c), vol. XIII, p. 282.

> We do not ask that the State become an industrial entrepreneur and concentrate all monopolies in its hands; we ask that it intervenes to provide working tools to some workers' companies, by imposing on these companies such legislation that it becomes impossible for them not to gradually extend across the whole kingdom (1850, "Responses to various objections", p. 200).

And there would be a new form of competition between socialism and liberal competition.[6]

However, for Louis Blanc, who was influenced by Fourier (F. Démier, 2005, p. 134), it is impossible to reconcile association and competition. Indeed, in *Organisation du travail*, he declares: "We cannot understand those who have imagined some mysterious coupling of the two opposing principles. Grafting association onto competition is a poor idea, it is like replacing eunuchs with hermaphrodites" (1850, Book I, chap. III, p. 60).

For his part, Walras also believes that association is a school of democracy, but he defends an approach diametrically opposed to that of Louis Blanc. According to him, production, consumption, or even credit cooperatives do not constitute a sector protected by the State; they operate in a competitive environment. However, cooperation does not stem from collective, but from individual initiative: it is an optional principle, just like fraternity. In his view, the different French socialist currents (Fourierists, Proudhonians…) were wrong to conceive association as a new "principle of labour organisation" and the practical solution to the entire "social question". Hence the attacks against the projects of French cooperativists in the 1860s as well as against the *ateliers sociaux*.

Furthermore, Louis Blanc thought that part of the profits (net of interest) of the *ateliers sociaux* could be allocated not only "to alleviate crises that would weigh on other industries", but also "to support the elderly, the sick, the disabled" (1850, Book I, chap. V, p. 72). This idea cannot be accepted by Walras, who believes that everything related to social protection (old age, illness, disability) must be covered by individual insurance (*cf.* chapter 14, *Organisation of the Labour Market, Labour Legislation and Social Insurance*).

The dialogue between the two authors is therefore impossible and our economist acknowledges it himself:

> Between Mr. Louis Blanc and us, any controversy would be impossible. Where we speak reason, he speaks sentiment, where we speak justice, right and duty, he speaks devotion and fraternity; these are two different grounds, and our arguments would not reach the sphere where his empiricism wanders ("L'industrie moderne et l'économie politique", 1861d, vol. VII, p. 147).

Much later, in the mid-1890s, Walras will have the opportunity to discuss a socialism that refuses free competition, Karl Marx's socialism. This leads him to reflect on the practical possibility of a "collectivism of production" with a "sole entrepreneur" State, a market socialism. This solution does not correspond to his liberal socialism, but he considers it seriously… without returning to Louis Blanc (*cf.* chapter 16,

[6] See on this point F. Démier, 2005, pp. 144 and 148.

Public Services and Natural Monopolies: What Role for the State?). Let us now consider Walras's attitude towards Saint-Simonianism.

12.3 Léon Walras and Saint-Simonianism

The relationship of Léon Walras with the Saint-Simonian movement is relatively unknown. It is hardly discussed by those who have taken an interest in his life and work, with the exception of the few pages devoted to it by Marcel Boson (1951, pp. 135–38), William Jaffé (1971, pp. 273 and 278–79), Albert Jolink (1996, pp. 50–52) and Pierre Dockès (1994, pp. 293–95; 1996, pp. 71 and 185–86). Yet, in a "note d'humeur" dated February 1862, Walras did not hesitate to declare: "I sincerely believe that Saint-Simon or some other reformer, with a less improvised philosophy and a less superficial science, could have been the Newton of social science" (2000, vol. XIII, p. 582). In fact, he owes to his father the attention he pays to Saint-Simonianism.[7]

12.3.1 Auguste Walras, Fellow Traveller and Critic of Saint-Simonianism

Working on theories of value and property, Auguste Walras took a strong interest in the ideas that the Saint-Simonians strove to spread through their public lectures and booklets.[8] According to his son's testimony, he attended in 1829 and 1830 the famous sessions presenting the doctrine at 12 rue Taranne in Paris.[9] He himself acknowledges having been an assiduous reader of the journal *Le Globe* at the café Momus.[10] He collected Saint-Simonian pamphlets and offprints.[11] Furthermore, he seemed to frequent the Saint-Simonian leaders.[12]

---

[7] For further developments on the relations between Auguste Walras, Léon Walras and the Saint-Simonian movement, see G. Jacoud and J.-P. Potier, 2020.

[8] P.-H. Goutte and J.-M. Servet, 1990b, p. CXXVIII.

[9] L. Walras, "Un initiateur en économie politique: A.-A. Walras" (1908a), vol. IV, p. 33.

[10] A. Walras, letter to his son dated 15 April 1857, in: *Correspondance*, vol. IV, p. 275. L. Walras indicates in a letter addressed on 16 April 1908 to Georges and Louise Renard that a complete collection of the *Globe* was in his father's library (unpublished letter kept in the Lausanne collection under the reference F. W. I, 474). Unfortunately, searches in the Bibliothèque cantonale et universitaire de Lausanne have not been able to locate this collection.

[11] Sixteen of the Saint-Simonian pamphlets from 1831 and 1832 collected by his father will be bound by Léon Walras under the title *Saint-Simonisme*, in two volumes, kept at the Centre d'études interdisciplinaires Walras-Pareto de l'Université de Lausanne (ZAB 180/1 and 2).

[12] For example, he personally knows Pierre-Paul Chéruel (a close associate of Olinde Rodrigues) and lends him books on economics (letter to Louis-Léon Gadebled dated 17 June 1832, in: *Correspondence*, vol. IV, *cit.*, p. 122).

Was it a mere "scientific curiosity"[13] or complete adherence to Saint-Simonianism as his political opponents tried to suggest?[14] Auguste Walras appears rather as a fellow traveller, because convergences of thought appear on certain points. In a very laudatory letter dated 12 December 1831 to an unknown correspondent, probably an editor at the *Globe*, he indicates: "Even before having received the Saint-Simonian revelation, I had reached the clear-cut, [*illegible*] and crucial distinction that you yourself have judiciously established between the idler (*oisif*) and the worker" (*Correspondence*, vol. IV, p. 112).

Here, the idler refers to the landowner. However, in November 1831, a schism occurred within the Saint-Simonian group between Saint-Amand Bazard and Prosper-Barthélemy Enfantin. This rupture, which leads to the resignation of many disciples, confounds Auguste Walras. He is clearly in disagreement with Enfantin on the question of women and of religion and he seems to have more sympathy for Bazard and Pierre Leroux.[15]

Retrospectively, Auguste Walras reveals in his "Examen critique et réfutation du Livre de Mr. Thiers sur la Propriété":

> I have known, I have frequented the Saint-Simonians; I have attended their teachings; I have read most of their publications, I have studied their works, I have been nourished as much as anyone else by reading the *Globe*. And yet I have never been a Saint-Simonian. I have never worn the garb. I have made no profession of faith in the Saint-Simonian Church; I have taken no commitment with it (1849a, vol. II, p. 289).

And he set out three points that separate him from the Saint-Simonians. Firstly, on the proposal to abolish inheritance, he notes:

> I have pointed out to them many times that it was necessary first to deal with the establishment of property, that the question of transmission would come afterwards. We could never agree. [...]. The Saint-Simonians kept their ideas, I kept mine, time will tell who is right or wrong (*op. cit.*, pp. 289–90).[16]

Concerning ground rent, Auguste Walras asserts:

> The Saint-Simonians, misinterpreting Ricardo's narrow and incomplete doctrine, had claimed that rent of the land and profit of capital were diminishing facts that would eventually disappear and that humanity would one day be freed from paying rent to the landowners and capital owners. As far as the profit of capital is concerned, the Saint-Simonians were right to a certain extent [...]. As for ground rent, the Saint-Simonians were completely wrong [...] (*op. cit.*, p. 290).

Finally, concerning idleness, Auguste Walras explains:

---

[13] É. Antonelli, 1923, pp. 517 and 535, note 28.

[14] The abbé Daniel, having become again the rector of the Academy of Caen thanks to the reaction, in a letter addressed on 22 March 1849 to the Minister of Public Instruction to overwhelm Auguste Walras, mentions "his Saint-Simonian past" (J.-M. Servet, 1997, p. 20).

[15] See P.-H. Goutte and J.-M. Servet, vol. I, p. 471, note 91.

[16] See already A. Walras, 1831a, vol. I, p. 16. A. Walras returns to this in the letter of 1 April 1860 to his son (vol. IV, pp. 399–400. In reality, the Saint-Simonians do not wish to abruptly abolish inheritance. They advocate measures such as the abolition of collateral successions and the increase of inheritance taxes (see on this issue G. Jacoud, 2014, pp. 310–11).

> The Saint-Simonians are the first who have raised the distinction between workers and idlers (*oisifs*). Once again I have never fully agreed with them [...]. There is a fruitful idleness or that can become so [...], it is the idleness of the capitalist, and it is perfectly respectable. There is a dangerous idleness which leads to the likelihood of laziness and [*illegible*], an idleness moreover which is more harmful, since it is only based on the labour of another, it is the idleness of the landowner; it has nothing to do with respectability and can be legitimately combated. The Saint-Simonians have always confused and fought under the name of idlers, the landowner and the capitalist, and that is yet another reason why I have never been able to be a Saint-Simonian (*op. cit.*, p. 291).[17]

Concluding his analysis, Auguste Walras indicates that he leaves aside "the religious and moral proper point of view", which implies more numerous and significant divergences with Saint-Simonianism. One thus understands why he warns his son against his Saint-Simonian acquaintances in Paris. In a letter dated 1 April 1860, he declares to him: "I hope you will not be swayed by their fine words. It is one of the sects I know best, for I have studied their doctrines at length [...]".[18]

12.3.2 Léon Walras's Critique of Saint-Simonianism

Indeed, in 1859–60, Léon Walras works on Saint-Simonianism, which he had become acquainted with in his early youth.[19] In June 1860, he informs the publisher Gilbert-Urbain Guillaumin that he was in the process of finishing a study on Saint-Simon for the *Journal des économistes*,[20] which unfortunately has not been found in his archives. He gets the *Œuvres choisies* of Saint-Simon (Brussels: F. Van Meenen et Cie, 1859, 3 vols.), whose introduction, "Essai sur les œuvres et la doctrine de Saint-Simon" (vol. I, pp. V–CV) by Léon Brothier[21] and Charles Lemonnier was criticising the interpretations of Saint-Simon's writings by Enfantin's disciples.[22] The first article in the "Paradoxes" series, the only one published in the *Journal des économistes*, contains an attack on the Saint-Simonian school without explicitly naming it, through the words of the "Scientist". This school "aims to eliminate idlers (*oisifs*) as much as possible, leaving only workers in the State" and to this end, it "abolishes inheritance in whole or in part. The share that the State collects

[17] See also the letter of 1 April 1860 to his son, in: *Correspondence*, vol. IV, p 400.

[18] A. Walras, letter to his son, 1 April 1860, in: *op. cit.*, p. 399.

[19] In his letter to Georges and Louise Renard of 16 April 1908, he reveals having read "at 15 or 16 years old" the *Globe* in his father's library (unpublished letter kept in the Lausanne collection under the reference F. W. I, 474).

[20] L. Walras, letter to G.-U. Guillaumin, 3 June 1860, in: *Correspondence*, II, l. 34, p. 61.

[21] The ex-Saint-Simonian of Toulouse Léon Brothier (1803–70) participated in several editorial initiatives of the philosopher Charles Lemonnier, including that of the *Revue philosophique et religieuse* (1855–58). L. Walras also has in his library the study by L. Brothier, *Saint-Simon et le Saint-Simonisme*, Paris: Librairie de Castel, 1859 [excerpt from *La libre recherche. Revue universelle*, vol. 4, January-March 1859] (Lausanne collection, XI/B4).

[22] The copy is kept at the Centre d'études interdisciplinaires Walras-Pareto de l'Université de Lausanne (ZAB 141/1 to 3).

from inheritances or their entirety constitutes the tax [...]. This is the triumph of common sense, I mean superficial empiricism".[23] At this time, some Saint-Simonians unsuccessfully attempt to convert Léon Walras to their doctrine.[24] The latter remains always clear-sighted, especially towards those who proposed "an exchange of good favours" to various monarchs up to Napoléon III[25] and towards those who have turned to finance and speculation. Indeed, in an article rejected by the *Journal des économistes*, "Paradoxes économiques. II. De la richesse naturelle ou gratuite. – De la richesse sociale ou économique. – De la richesse intellectuelle" (February–March 1861), Walras reports a probably imaginary dialogue between a prominent financier offering new ideas to a young economist in search of article topics. The financier explains that the goal of the Saint-Simonians "was to substitute work for idleness everywhere in society". However, this problem has been solved or is being solved by speculation. The young economist replies:

> I am quite disposed [...] to side with Saint-Simonianism, at least in terms of the end, if not in regards [*sic*] to the means. I am however quite unwilling to contest the morality and the economic advantages of speculation in situations where the limits are quite broad. But what I refuse to accept is the association of socialism at the helm of finance and philosophical humanitarian speeches in the language of the Stock exchange in the mouths of those who boast of having both made their fortune and our happiness.[26]

The financier then retorts that if, thirty years ago, a rentier was content to collect interest and was an idler, this is no longer the case today. Those who hold capital must think, calculate, inform themselves, speculate and thus become workers. And the young economist easily opposes him by pointing out the difference between capital and income and between the profit of a speculation and the wage of labour in the economic sense.[27]

In 1859–60, Léon Walras seeks to publish articles in the daily press. To this end, he contacts and meets in Paris a number of journalists, some of whom are former Saint-Simonians. As his letters addressed to his father have been lost, we cannot know precisely his Saint-Simonian contacts. However, it can be noted that Adolphe Guéroult, Louis Jourdan, and Charles-Joseph Lambert are among them.

Adolphe Guéroult (1810–72) was a Saint-Simonian (a member the *Globe*'s editorial staff) who did not follow the sect in its retreat of Ménilmontant. Won over to the liberal cause in economics, he became a journalist at the newspaper *Le Crédit*

---

[23] "Paradoxes économiques. I. Que le sens commun n'est point le criterium de la science en général, ni en particulier celui de l'économie politique" (1860c), vol. VII, p. 57.

[24] Around 1860 in Paris, during an evening at Georges Le Roy's home, a nephew of Maxime Du Camp, an attempt is made to convert Léon Walras and his friend Gustave Maugin to Saint-Simonianism (L. Walras, letters to Henri Fouquier, 9 June 1883 and to Gustave Maugin, 31 December 1901, in: *Correspondence*, I, l. 553, p. 753 and III, l. 1513, p. 187).

[25] "Méthode de conciliation ou de synthèse" (1868c), vol. IX, p. 158, English transl., 2010, p. 119; "Exposition et conciliation des doctrines sociales" (1872c), vol. XIII, p. 289; *Cours d'économie sociale*, 11th lesson "Liberals and Socialists", vol. XII, p. 157.

[26] "Paradoxes économiques. II. De la richesse naturelle ou gratuite. – De la richesse sociale ou économique. – De la richesse intellectuelle" (1861c), vol. XIII, pp. 48–49.

[27] *Op. cit.*, pp. 49–52.

(1848–50, whose editor-in-chief was Charles Duveyrier), after having directed the newspaper *La République* in 1848. Later, he was a journalist at the *Courrier de l'industrie. Journal du commerce, des opérations financières* (1853). In 1858, he became the political director of the newspaper *La Presse*, and then in September 1859, he obtained permission to found a new political newspaper *L'Opinion Nationale.*[28] He was part of the left wing of Bonapartism, democratic and anti-clerical, led by Prince Napoléon, cousin of the Emperor.[29] In 1859, Léon Walras contacted him and was very insistent in obtaining publication in *La Presse*, not hesitating to detail his work programme to him.[30]

Louis Jourdan (1810–81) was one of the editors of the newspaper *Le Siècle* from 1849 onwards. Close to Barthélemy-Prosper Enfantin, he contributed to the *Courrier français*, directed by the ex-Saint-Simonian Émile Barrault. Léon Walras, who knew his articles, gave him his book *L'Économie politique et la justice*, recently published, and met him in Paris. In a letter, he outlined his main ideas, hoping to obtain a favourable review.[31]

Charles-Joseph Lambert (1804–64), a former student of the École Polytechnique and of the École des Mines, was an even more important Saint-Simonian figure. Having rallied the doctrine in 1829, he participated in the teachings of rue Monsigny and contributed to the *Globe*. After the movement's split, he chose Enfantin's camp. Very devoted to the latter, he followed him to Egypt in September 1833. In this country, he founded and directed the École des Mines (1836–40), then created and directed the École Polytechnique of Boulac, near Cairo (1840–49), training numerous engineers. He prepared projects intended for the digging of a canal through the Isthmus of Suez. In 1847, for his services rendered, he was awarded the title of bey, hence his name "Lambert-Bey". In 1851, he returned to Paris where he worked in the administration as chief engineer. Always faithful to Enfantin's ideas, he initiated young people into the doctrine, such as Maxime Du Camp.[32] Léon Walras sent him *L'Économie politique et la justice* (1860a) after its publication, then visited him at his home to discuss the book's content. Charles Lambert, who saw in him "a disciple to recruit"[33] read the book carefully. He addressed a "vigourous criticism" of it, which will impress him in the long run and contributed to the evolution of his reflections. In a long paragraph, Walras describes their discussion on that day:

[28] Auguste Walras appreciates the content of this journal and Guéroult's articles (letter to his son dated 6 February 1860, in: *Correspondence*, vol. IV, p. 388).

[29] On Guéroult, see Bernard Coste, *Un journaliste saint-simonien sous le Second-Empire: Adolphe Guéroult et l'Opinion nationale*, Ph.D. thesis, University of Paris, 1968.

[30] L. Walras, letter to A. Guéroult undated, but written in March–April 1859, in: *Correspondence*, I, l. 16, pp. 35–39.

[31] L. Walras, letter to Louis Jourdan, 23 March 1860, in: *Correspondence*, I, l. 25, pp. 48–50.

[32] In 1860, with Enfantin, Arlès-Dufour, Chevalier, the Péreire brothers and a few others, C. Lambert participated in the founding of a mutual aid society intended to perpetuate the Saint-Simonian Family, which would be presided over by Fournel (S. Charléty, [1931] 1965, p. 261).

[33] In his own library, L. Walras possesses the offprint of C. Lambert's articles published in the *Revue philosophique et religieuse*, nos. 3 and 4, 1856 (kept in the Lausanne collection under the reference F. W. XI, L2).

> He was willing to admit that free competition was a means of determining the quantities and prices of products manufactured. He did not believe, or at least he did not accept as demonstrated by economists, or by me, that these quantities and prices would be the only ones or the best possible. I defended myself as best I could against this engineer of Mines, who is said to have entered the École polytechnique as first and left it in the same position. However, on leaving I had not yet reached the foot of the stairs before confessing to myself that he was right. I do not know how long I remained standing stock-still before Douniol's window, staring at a volume with a blue binding the title of which I never read. Finally, I went away saying, 'Obviously! It must be proved that *free competition yields the maximum utility*.' I had been led to mathematical economics. I embarked on it and told my father, who replied in a letter dated 18 May 1861, indicating that it would be not impossible but very difficult because with utility there is no way of measuring its magnitude. Indeed, that was just the heart of the question and it was solved by the function *intensity of the last want satisfied* by a *quantity consumed* of a commodity, already discovered by Gossen, which Jevons was seeking, and I myself found ten years later.[34]

As decisive as it may be, the meeting between Charles Lambert and Léon Walras has an impact that perhaps owes more to the former's status as a polytechnician than to that of a Saint-Simonian, insofar as it leads the latter to consider that pure economics can be constituted as a mathematical science.

As we will see later in chapter 15 (*Towards the Repurchase of Land by the State and the Abolition of Taxes*), he revealed in 1896 that he owed the idea of reconciling individualism and communism largely to the "old Saint-Simonians" he had associated with in his youth. Léon Walras will have the opportunity to express his views on the Saint-Simonians, in "Exposition et conciliation des doctrines sociales" (1872c) and in the 37th lesson ("Doctrine of the Saint-Simonians") of his *Cours d'économie sociale* at the Faculty of Law in Lausanne.

In these two texts, our author puts aside "the religious paraphernalia and the apocalyptic and prophetic style of the school" in order to focus on the "positive points of the doctrine". He explains that.

> […] the Saint-Simonians did not call for the establishment of absolute communism; they merely intended to limit individual property by absorbing inheritances through taxation for the benefit of the State, that is to say, instead of limiting individual property in terms of its object, by granting it certain types of wealth to deny others, they limited it in terms of its effects by allowing it to be exercised during life and prohibiting its transmission after death (vol. XII, p. 265; 1872c, vol. XIII, p. 274).

At this point, in the margin, Walras notes: "Apparent conformity with the equality of conditions" (vol. XII, note 153, p. 837). As P. Dockès indicates, this remark is important, because Walrasian equality of conditions has often been criticised for

[34] Emphasis by L. W., "Esquisse d'une doctrine économique et sociale" (1898c), vol. X, p. 419, English transl., 2005, pp. 366–67. This passage undoubtedly inspired the following statement by Pasquale Boninsegni, in his speech at the Jubilee of V. Pareto:

Léon Walras was moreover a passionate man, a man of faith. Saint-Simonian [*sic*], he had to demonstrate, with the help of mathematics, in accordance with the teachings of the master, that absolute free competition is the necessary and sufficient condition for the individual and society to achieve the maximum economic well-being which […] coincides and merges with the maximum social well-being. ("Speech by Dr. P. Boninsegni", in: *Université de Lausanne. Jubilé du Professeur V. Pareto. 1917*, p. 26).

not limiting the right of inheritance (P. Dockès, 1996, p. 185). Here, Walras follows his father in contesting the infringement on the right of property that constitutes the impossibility for a father to pass on his property to his children, both from the point of view of justice and from the point of view of interest.[35] Recalling the opposition between workers and idlers (*oisifs*), he criticises the Saint-Simonians for not distinguishing the legitimate and useful idleness of the capitalist, who risks losing his lent capital, and the illegitimate and harmful idleness of the landowner, whose land is imperishable. But above all, he claims, "the Saint-Simonians displayed a very mediocre knowledge in pure economics" (vol. XII, p. 266) by considering ground rent and interest as decreasing phenomena in a progressive society. Indeed, according to him, while interest decreases with the fall of its rate and the decrease in the value of capital (new capitals devalue the old ones), ground rent constantly increases due to the surplus value of land. It can therefore be said that the idleness of the capitalist is decreasing, while that of the landowner is increasing (vol. XII, p. 266; see also 1872c, vol. XIII, p. 275).

Léon Walras believes that he has thus identified the "major economic and moral errors of the Saint-Simonians, alongside which one could cite many sharp and insightful views" (vol. XII, p. 267). Although he does not inform us about this in his *Cours d'économie sociale*, he gives us an example in the "Exposition et conciliation des doctrines sociales". It is the famous Saint-Simon's parable according to which if France lost its fifty leading physicists, chemists, mechanicians, and other bankers or merchants, the country would collapse, whereas if it lost its politicians, marshals, or members of the high clergy, it would result in no harm to the country (1872c, vol. XIII, pp. 276–78). After reproducing the text, Walras exclaims: "What an insight into a society in transition where producers in possession of all social importance dispute political power with the remnants of an aristocracy that has only the benefits without any of the burdens of its former position!" (*op. cit.*, p. 278).

12.4 Conclusion

It can be noted that Léon Walras's positions on Louis Blanc and the Saint-Simonians become fixed over time, with the critical argumentation remaining always identical. Ultimately, according to him, "neither the Saint-Simonian abolition of inheritances [...] nor the ateliers sociaux of Mr. Louis Blanc", can lead to a solution to the social question (*Cours d'économie sociale*, 48th lesson, "Doctrine of Proudhon", vol. XII, p. 279). This solution involves the synthesis between individualism and communism, as we will see later.

[35] Such a position is reminiscent of that of P.-J. Proudhon, in his book *Système des contradictions économiques ou Philosophie de la misère* (1846).

Chapter 13
Léon Walras, Paul Voituron and Constant Leirens at the Editorial Team of *Le Travail*: the Polemics on Cooperation (1866–1867)

13.1 Introduction

During the liberal phase of the Second Empire, Léon Walras became involved in the cooperative movement in Paris, which was then booming and was encouraged by Napoléon III. Initially, he participated with his friend Louis La Cour de la Pijardière in an attempt to establish a credit association called the *Banque du Travail.* He then joined the project launched by Léon Say to establish the *Caisse d'escompte des associations populaires de consommation, de production et de crédit.* From April 1865, he served as the appointed administrator of this *Caisse.* Furthermore, on 5 December 1864, he obtained from the Minister of Public Instruction and Worship, Victor Duruy, the authorisation to deliver three public lectures at the "Cercle des sociétés savantes" on the theory and practice of popular credit, production, and consumption associations. Delivered in January and February 1865, they respectively presented the economic principle of associations, the financial and legal organisation, and the application of the principle in the French context.[1]

However, to consolidate his action and disseminate his ideas, Walras wished to create and direct a newspaper. In 1864, he developed a programme for publishing a bi-monthly newspaper entitled: *L'Association populaire—Organe des intérêts du travail, moniteur international des sociétés de coopération de France, de Belgique, d'Angleterre et d'Allemagne.* He planned a structuring of this periodical into ten sections.[2] The project seemed well advanced, as Walras had a proof of the first page of the newspaper made, which was to appear on 1 October 1864.[3] We do not know with what support he intended to embark on this experience, which did not come

[1] *Les associations populaires de consommation, de production et de crédit.* (1865), vol. VI, pp. 15–89.

[2] The summary type of *L'Association populaire*, initially published in J.-P. Potier, 1990 (Appendix I, p. 58) is included in the Appendix of this chapter.

[3] This proof, dated "Saturday 1st October", is preserved in the Lausanne collection (F.W., VI, box 30).

J.-P. Potier, *Léon Walras, Economist and Liberal Socialist*, Springer Studies in the History of Economic Thought, https://doi.org/10.1007/978-3-032-04670-3_13

to fruition. This attempt failed while at the same time, in November, a monthly with a rather similar title, *L'Association*,[4] printed in Belgium, appeared in Paris. This publication, to which Fourierists, Proudhonians, disciples or former disciples of Cabet (J.-P. Beluze) and Buchez contributed, exerted a great influence on Parisian workers. In 1865, Léon Walras considered applying for government authorisation to publish a weekly newspaper or to have a newspaper printed in Belgium. On 15 April 1865, his father remarked to him on this subject:

> I completely agree with your idea that it is not in a large political daily newspaper that your teachings should be buried. A special weekly newspaper, as you say, is the platform that suits you, and if you could find one already established and authorised, you could try to penetrate it, and to take the upper hand later. *L'Association* has a nice title; but it is weak, and it is monthly. Would it be authorised to become weekly? And would the current editors admit you *in illo docto corpore?* Would they understand all the benefit you could do for them? Would they even have the sense to make your lectures a fair report?[5]

In fact, Léon Walras did not listen to his father, who advised him to join *L'Association,* and then transform it from within once he had established his position. He preferred to create his own newspaper, but did not have the financial means to embark on this experience alone. At the end of 1865, he saw no immediate solution.[6] His project would finally materialise in spring 1866,[7] thanks to the support of two Belgian cooperativists. However, the first issues of the newspaper led to episodes still poorly known today.[8] Indeed, from the first issue, both theoretical and political divergences appeared between Walras and his Belgian collaborators; they quickly worsened to the point of resulting in a definitive break after three issues. In this chapter we try to revisit these debates on cooperation based on letters and documents preserved in the Walras collection at the Cantonal and University Library of Lausanne and the Voituron collection of the University Library of Ghent.[9] We will also rely on articles published in *Le Travail* and in *Le Travailleur associé.*[10]

---

[4] *L'Association—Bulletin des coopératives françaises et étrangères* (which became, in 1865, *Bulletin international des sociétés coopératives*), appears in two series. The first series is monthly from 1 November 1864 to 7 January 1866. The administrator of the journal is Edmond Potonié and its manager Jean-Baptiste Béraud. Among its contributors, one can cite Jean-Pierre Beluze, Paul Blanc, Abel Davaud, Ignace-Einhorn Horn, Élie Reclus. The second series is weekly from January 1866; Élie Reclus becomes manager. Due to four successive seizures, the journal's management decided to cease publication at the end of August 1866.

[5] A. Walras, letter to L. Walras, 15 April 1865, in: *Correspondence*, vol. IV, p. 699.

[6] See the letter of Auguste Walras to his son, 15 December 1865, in which he even offers to contribute to the journal! (*Correspondence*, vol. IV, p. 738).

[7] Auguste Walras died in April 1866 and therefore did not see the birth of *Le Travail.*

[8] William Jaffé was unable to reconstruct the history of the journal *Le Travail*: "I have not been able to trace any record or correspondence relating to the founding of this journal" (*Correspondence*, I, l. 108, note 2, p. 153).

[9] Concerning the resources of this library, we wish to thank Guido Erreygers (University of Antwerp) for the assistance he provided us.

[10] The Walras collection in Lausanne holds a copy of each of the first three issues of the journal *Le Travail* (from 31 July to 30 September 1866) at references F. W., VI 30 and XII 131. The University Library of Ghent holds a volume containing the first three issues of the journal *Le Travail* followed by

13.2 Birth of the Newspaper *Le Travail*

The cooperative newspaper *Le Travail* was established in July 1866. According to the opinion that still prevails today, this creation would be the result of a joint initiative by Léon Say and Léon Walras. Indeed, the latter accredits this thesis on several occasions. In his official letter of application for the chair at the Faculty of Law of Lausanne, he declares:

> I myself founded in 1866, with the assistance of Mr. Léon Say, administrator of the Chemin de fer du Nord and editor of the *Journal des débats,* grandson of J.-B. Say, a monthly review of political economy specially devoted to questions of cooperative association, *Le Travail,* and directed it for two years.[11]

Other correspondences, at different times, reaffirm this point of view.[12] However, in his "Notice autobiographique", Léon Walras seems to show some caution on this subject: "[…] I contributed to the publication and editing of the newspaper *Le Travail, revue du mouvement coopératif,* which appeared for two years in 1866–1867 and 1867–1868 […]".[13]

How were things seen at the time? In September 1866, in the *Journal deséconomistes*, Joseph Garnier reports on the new publication, not without a certain irony:

> We announce with pleasure the birth of a young monthly colleague, *Le Travail*, which seems to come into the world in the best conditions, and which aims to be the international organ for the interests of the working class and a special review of the cooperative movement, at the cost of 1 F 60 per year! It was founded and will be directed by two economists of very good reputation, Mr. Constant Leirens, for the Belgian part, and Mr. Léon Walras, for the French part (1866a, p. 475).

In the *Journal des Débats* of 20 September 1866, the journalist P. David provides us yet another version:

> A newspaper, or rather a monthly review, has just been founded in Ghent, with the aim of satisfying the ever-growing number of people interested in the cooperative movement. The founders of this review, Messrs. Voituron and Leirins [*sic*] […] have enlisted two Frenchmen, Mr. Léon Say, our collaborator, and Mr. Léon Walras, director of the Caisse d'escompte des associations populaires, in order to give *Le Travail* […] a serious and real character as an international organ.[14]

---

the complete collection of the journal, *Le travailleur associé*, and the *Bulletin belge du Travailleur associé* (from 15 November 1866 to 15 July 1867). On this copy, an anonymous hand has indicated the authors of the unsigned articles (Universiteit Gent, Centrale Bibliotheek, G. 005 941); it is digitised on Google Books.

[11] L. Walras, letter to Louis Ruchonnet, 6 September 1870, in: *Correspondence*, I, l. 148, p. 205.

[12] See L. Walras, letter to Alberto Errera, 13 April 1874, in: *Correspondence*, I, l. 261, p. 378; letter to the Minister of Public Instruction [Jules Ferry], 3 July 1879, in: *op. cit.*, I, l. 444, p. 613; note to the letter to Émile Bouvier of 3 January 1903, in: *op. cit.*, III, l. 1537, p. 218.

[13] "Notice autobiographique" (1909a), vol. V, p. 14.

[14] P. David, untitled article, *Journal des Débats*, 20 September 1866, p. 3.

In reality, in spring 1866, Léon Walras and Léon Say were looking for a Belgian partner for the publication of a newspaper. The publication of a periodical in Belgium, then its importation into France, was an interesting solution, given the laws in force on the press at this time.[15] We do not know who suggested the name of Leirens to them. Constant Leirens (1813–1886), residing in Brussels, doctor of law and publicist, is a wealthy lawyer with progressive democratic opinions, who has been advocating for workers' association since the Revolution of 1848. He has the material means to print a newspaper: he is, in fact, the owner of the P. Cagny printing house in Ghent. With the help of his friend Paul Voituron (see *infra*), he wishes to create and distribute a monthly newspaper in France to support the cooperative movement, but which does not harm the newspaper *L'Association* of which he was a shareholder.[16] We do not know if he had a precise knowledge of the ideas developed by Walras in his lectures on *Les Associations populaires de consummation, de production et de crédit*.

After having extensively discussed the details, Léon Walras and Constant Leirens signed a convention in Paris on 16 May 1866, in which they specified the publishing rules for a "French journal of political and social economy": *Le Travail—Organe international des intérêts de la classe laborieuse*. The archives of *Le Travail* reveal their hesitations concerning the choice of title: *Les Idées—Nouvelles philosophiques, économiques et politiques; La Démocratie libérale; La Défense du travail; Le Travail*.[17] In fact, the structure of the journal is largely inspired by the project developed by Léon Walras in 1864 for *L'Association populaire*.

According to the convention, Léon Walras is responsible for the editorial management of the journal,[18] while Constant Leirens commits to providing the material resources he possesses. Walras will have this printed monthly in Ghent and will distribute at least four thousand copies in France.[19] Constant Leirens will ensure its distribution in Belgium and the Netherlands. If Leirens covers the manufacturing

---

[15] After the *coup d'État* of 2 December 1851, the future Emperor Napoléon III attacked the liberty of the press, mainly by means of the organic decree of 17 February 1852, which would remain in force until 1868. This decree contains the following provisions: no newspaper "dealing with political or social economy matters" can be founded without the prior authorisation of government; the newspaper must be subject to a declaration concerning the names of the owners, administrators and editors-in-chief, to be renewed with every change; the owner of the newspaper must deposit a guarantee in cash to the public treasury, at a variable rate, to enable the execution of any potential financial penalties; the owner of the newspaper must pay a stamp duty on each printed sheet, regardless of the print run. The organic decree of 17 February 1852 and the decree of 1 March 1854 subject foreign newspapers "dealing with political or social economy matters" to prior governmental authorisation and the payment of a special stamp duty. Finally, press offences fall under the jurisdiction of the correctional courts and the repressive system includes several degrees: warning, suspension limited to two months after two warnings, suppression of the newspaper.

[16] In his letter of 20 August 1866 to L. Walras (a few days before the disappearance of *L'Association*), Constant Leirens would declare: "In what terms are you with the editorial team of *L'Association*? I would be delighted to learn that *Le Travail* does not overshadow these gentlemen." (F. W. II, box 10).

[17] A sheet from L. Walras's hand preserved in the Lausanne collection (F. W. VI, box 30).

[18] The headquarters of the Parisian editorial office are located at the Librairie ancienne et moderne of the Agence générale des auteurs et compositeurs, 10, rue de la Bourse.

[19] On the actual print runs of the first issues of *Le Travail*, see J.-P. Potier, 1990.

costs, Walras must bear the editorial expenses; for this purpose he will retain the proceeds from advertisements and sales in France, or possibly in countries other than those mentioned above. The convention stipulates

> that approximately one-third of the journal will be devoted to articles, correspondences, news, varieties, etc., on subjects of interest to Belgium, the subject or subjects indicated, chosen or treated by mutual agreement between Mr Walras and a person designated by Mr Leirens;

on the manuscript, just above this line, the name of this person is written: "Mr Voituron of Ghent". Constant Leirens and Léon Walras may cancel the contract at least three months before the end of the subscription year (which ends on 1 July) after which each party is free to continue the publication of the journal under the same title. Any dispute would be examined by "an arbitral tribunal composed of two persons, one designated by Mr Leirens, the other by Mr Walras" and in case of disagreement between them, these two persons would solicit a third. The convention also includes an "additional article" concerning potential legal actions: in the event of an issue being banned at the border, the issue's cost would be borne by Walras and in the event of a permanent ban, the convention is automatically terminated.[20]

The person designated to present the Belgian situation is therefore Paul-Eugène Voituron (1824–1891). A member of the municipal council of Ghent, this lawyer at the Court of Appeal of that city has been a friend of Constant Leirens since the Revolution of 1848 and both share the same progressive democratic views.[21] Constant Leirens and Paul Voituron are former members of the "Société Huet",[22] active in Ghent between 1846 and 1851, and they have collaborated on its press organs.[23]

But in the days following the signing of the convention, the French party does not seem to have received any news from Constant Leirens. Thus, Léon Say seeks to gather information about him. By a letter dated 9 June 1866 (not found), he instructs a certain Lambert[24] to contact Leirens at his home in Brussels. He succeeds in meeting him on 14 June and indicates to Say that "this gentleman seems very well, perfectly organised and moreover he has a rather pleasant manner".[25] In any case, Constant

---

[20] The draft of the publication agreement of *Le Travail* of 16 May 1866, in the handwriting of L. Walras, is preserved in the Lausanne collection (F. W. II, box 13, 2 sheets).

[21] Paul Voituron is the author of *Recherches philosophiques sur les principes d'une science du beau*, Brussels: Lacroix et Cie, 1861–62, 2 vols.

[22] On the "Société Huet", see J. Cunliffe and G. Erreygers, 1999, pp. 584 and 601.

[23] Constant Leirens and Paul Voituron published articles on cooperation in a Flemish newspaper (see letter of C. Leirens to L. Walras, 5 October 1866, F. W. II, box 13). It is undoubtedly the radical democrat daily, *De Broedermin* (*La Fraternité*), which appeared from 1848 to 1859.

[24] Our research in the Walras collections in Lyon and Lausanne did not allow us to identify this person.

[25] See Lambert, letters to Léon Say of 12 and 14 June 1866, kept in the Lausanne collection (F. W. II 12); see also on this meeting the letter of C. Leirens to L. Walras of 14 June 1866, kept in the same collection (F. W. II, box 10).

Leirens, who had been occupied notably by the electoral campaign in Belgium, resumes contact by letter with Walras from 14 June.[26]

13.3 Publication of the First Issue of *Le Travail* and the Beginning of Disagreements with the Belgian Editorial Team

For the first issue of *Le Travail*, Léon Walras submits an article entitled "Programme économique et politique", which curiously used with slight modifications the unpublished study, "Des réformes économiques", prepared in 1861 but rejected by the editors of the journal *La Presse*.[27] The second and third parts of "Programme économique et politique" deal extensively with taxation, summarising "the entire economic and social aspect of the development of the [1789] Revolution". In this text, the cooperative association is presented in a purely allusive manner. According to the author,

> [...] many writers, we know, see a social question in the question of association. These people and we, probably, do not agree on the terminology. Among the causes of pauperism, and setting aside those that originate in the inevitability of natural laws, there are some that stem from the defectiveness of certain particular arrangements, and there are others that, on the contrary, arise from the imperfection of social conventions. We call, for our part, questions of individual initiative the questions relating to the causes of the first order, among which we unhesitatingly include the question of association; and we reserve the term of questions of collective or common initiative or social questions for those that seek to eliminate the causes of the second order and of which the question of taxation is essentially a part (1866b, vol. VI, p. 135).

Let us not forget that at the time, among the Empire's opponents, the topic of democracy is important. In his book *Les Associations populaires de consummation, de production et de crédit,* Walras explained that democracy must prevail in France not only in political institutions but also in economic institutions and "two channels will lead it there: tax reform and the application of the principle of popular associations" (1865, vol. VI, p. 42). Our author is convinced that the rise of the cooperative movement can only come from individual initiative alone and that no help should be expected from the State, except for a reform of the legislation. He analyses cooperation in relation to the formation of savings and capital. According to him, the proletarians, especially insofar as they are subject to tax deductions on their wages, can hardly save. Cooperation enables them to pool their modest savings; it is therefore a means available to individuals to reduce the inequality of their positions. Moreover, it exerts an educational influence on workers, enabling them to raise their

---

[26] The first letter of C. Leirens to L. Walras, kept in the Lausanne collection, is dated 14 June 1866 (F. W. II, box 10).

[27] See the "Introduction" to vol. XIII, pp. 14–15. The text "Des réformes économiques" (1861a) is found in this volume, pp. 55–65. On the cover of this manuscript, Walras noted: "Used for the programme of *Travail*" (*op. cit.*, note 1, p. 654).

material and moral level, and it is also a school of democracy, thus in this respect a path towards social reform. In a cooperative production company, the member *as a worker* receives a wage at the market rate and *as a capitalist*, participates in the profits according to his share in the social capital (or he must contribute to the losses).[28] Only the capital, alienable in case of losses, is associated and consequently cooperative companies can only be capital companies (*sociétés de capitaux*) and not partnerships (*sociétés de personnes*). The administration of the cooperative must be entrusted to a council appointed and controlled by the members, a mechanism that can be referred to as "*self-administration*" (1865, vol. VI, pp. 72–73).[29] At the end of his work, Walras noted: "I know that we economists are accused of wanting to banish fraternity from this world." And to this, he replied:

> But if I believe that nothing great is conceived and undertaken except under the inspiration and influence of fraternity, I also believe that nothing sound is established and founded except with the idea and under the conditions of justice. That is why, while giving sympathy its due place, I only ask that it not take the place of right [...]. The distinctive and imposing sign of right is that it commands a correlative, obligatory and enforceable duty; it is therefore that it can thus appear in the law and in contracts. The particular and sacred character of fraternal sympathy is that it is a duty that commands no right; it is that if it is solicited, it is diminished; it is that imposing it is to annihilate it [...] (1865, vol. VI, p. 88).[30]

The content of the "Programme économique et politique" proposed for the *Le Travail*'s first issue will be the subject of an initial dispute. On 19 July 1866, with the support of Voituron, Leirens expressed his complete disagreement with "some economic ideas" of Walras's 'Programme'. He particularly targets the last paragraph of the first part of the manuscript, in which one can read:

> France does not exist exclusively for itself like England: it is in Europe the initiator of all revolutionary ideas; there lies its greatness for more than half a century [...]. While England, free at home, hardly scruples to ally with despotism outside, France on the contrary, in order to fight despotic excesses everywhere, does not hesitate to even suspend the exercise of its own liberties. Once again, these kinds of dictatorships that it imposes or accepts are only temporary [...].[31]

---

[28] *Op. cit.*, p. 68; see also "Des doctrines en matière d'association coopérative" (1866e), vol. VI, pp. 172–74.

[29] Serge-Christophe Kolm does not hesitate to assert in this regard that Walras is "one of the best defenders of self-management in enterprises" (1984, pp. 55–56).

[30] In the 2nd lesson of the *Recherche de l'idéal social*, Walras will observe:

> [...] looking for social reform in cooperative association is just like looking for it in charity or philanthropy, or like looking for it in mutual insurance. At one and the same time, this demeans, if not underrates, social reform—and exaggerates cooperative association and thereby compromises it (1867–68, vol. IX, p. 66, English transl., 2010, p. 47).

On Walras's ideas on cooperation, see notably C. Hébert, 1988; C. Hébert and J.-P. Potier, 1990, pp. X–XVII; K. Nakakubo, 2000; C. Ferraton, 2007.

[31] The full text of this paragraph is published in *Les Associations populaires coopératives*, vol. VI, p. 506, note 3.

Although an opponent of the Second Empire, here the author lets his pen flow with nationalist fervour. However, for the Belgian publicist, this passage "is getting on panegyric" and would produce "a deplorable effect" in his country, as Walras does not hesitate to "somehow amnesty the iron regime that weighs on France, presenting the situation as if this deplorable regime testified to the self-sacrifice, the devotion to the principles of '89".[32] Constant Leirens absolutely refuses to take responsibility for such a text too favourable to the Empire. This incident foreshadows a difficult collaboration, so he immediately proposes to Walras to print two separate editions, one French, the other Belgian, which would follow each other at a fortnight's interval. Each editorial team would freely choose its own articles and publish its programme in the first issue.[33]

Walras, for his part, seeks to downplay the incident and does not see the urgency of opting for a double editorial team. He does not wish to be seen as an admirer of the Empire while admitting that the expression may have betrayed his thoughts in the disputed article; to settle the matter, he proposes to replace the contested passage with another paragraph.[34] Should this solution appear insufficient in the eyes of the Belgian editorial team, he is ready to forgo the publication of the study.[35] Such a position clearly attests to his willingness to conciliate.

Constant Leirens and Paul Voituron accept the replacement of the contentious passage, but they remain very reserved about the ideas developed in the "Programme économique et politique"; in particular, Constant Leirens doubts that it adheres to the "true principles of French Democracy" and notes that the author shows an evident preference for the taxation question, relegating to the background that of cooperative association: in this regard, he rightly suggests adding a few lines on this latter question.[36]

The first issue of *Le Travail—Organe international des intérêts de la classe laborieuse—Revue du mouvement coopératif* appears on 31 July 1866. The issue opens with an editorial notice, titled "Notre but", in the summary, dated "Ghent, 30 July 1866", explaining the journal's objectives and signed "Constant Leirens (for the Belgian part) and Léon Walras (for the French part)".[37] After recalling the rallying of important personalities and notably economists, to the cooperative association's ideas, in England (J. S. Mill), in Belgium (G. de Molinari), in France (A.-P. Batbie, L. Say, I.-E. Horn, F. Passy, J. Duval…), the editorial notice specifies:

---

[32] C. Leirens, letter to L. Walras, 19 July 1866 (F. W. II, box 10).

[33] Constant Leirens even offers to bear the additional costs generated by this new combination (*ibid.*).

[34] See L. Walras, "Programme économique et politique" (1866b), vol VI, pp. 134 and note 3.

[35] See C. Leirens, letter to L. Walras, 25 July 1866 (F. W. II, box 10); see also L. Walras, letter to C. Leirens, 12 October 1866 (F. W., I, 327 bis).

[36] Emphasis by C. L., letters to L. Walras, 25 and 30 July 1866 (F. W. II, box 10).

[37] See C. Leirens, letter to L. Walras, 31 July 1866 (F. W. II, box 10). In the Lausanne collection, there are two versions of a draft, penned by L. Walras, which presents the publication of the *Travail* and bears the note at the bottom: "Constant Leirens, Léon Walras" (F. W. VI, box 30, two sheets).

> For a long time, we have shared this enthusiasm of hearts and minds for the cooperative system; firstly, because we are convinced that this system is strictly in accordance with *Justice* and that its implementation is likely to contribute in large proportions to the *moral* and *material* improvement of the working classes; secondly, because we are no less convinced that its foundations are irreproachable from the point of view of the most rigorous science, provided, of course, that one refrains from making an unconsidered application of the system.

And the notice also indicates:

> *Le Travail* will thus be an *international Journal.* It will not limit itself to discussing the principles of association and the practical application that each nation makes of these principles, according to the needs of its specific economic situation; but it will strive, as much as possible, to facilitate the need for reciprocal relations and external communications of existing companies.[38]

Just after this text, in *Le Travail* appears the "Programme" of Léon Walras, with a new paragraph proposed by the author, but without additions on the cooperation question. Then follows the study entitled "De la situation des partis et des progrès de la démocratie en Belgique", written by Paul Voituron. This text, presented as "the political and economic programme of the persons who contributed, in Belgium, to the foundation of this publication", harshly criticises the liberal party in power in Belgium. It discerns two factions within the "liberal bourgeoisie": one conservative, an enemy of equality, which defends its privileges and "confuses the general interest with its particular interest"; the other progressive, faithful to the principles of the 1848 Revolution, which "reaches out a hand to the underprivileged classes". The latter group, operating under the name of the "progressive liberal party", is particularly concerned with "the improvement of the condition of the working classes by granting facilities to workers' associations and studies that open all career paths to the children of the poor".[39] The first issue of *Travail* also contains an article by Léon Say entitled "La crise financière et les sociétés coopératives".[40]

[38] Emphasis in the text. *Les Associations populaires coopératives*, vol. VI, pp. 507–09.

[39] "De la situation des partis et des progrès de la démocratie en Belgique", unsigned article, *Le Travail*, 1st year, no. 1, 31 July 1866, col. 8–12. For his part, L. Walras will not show any hostility towards this text, since C. Leirens notes: "I am delighted with the way you judge the programme of the Belgian editorial team." (letter to L. Walras, undated, but from early August 1866, F. W. II, box 10).

[40] Vol. VI, Appendix no. I, pp. 299–304.

13.4 Deepening of the Theoretical Disagreement

The second issue of *Le Travail* appears on 31 August 1866. Constant Leirens and Léon Walras have decided to introduce a "political bulletin", placed on the first page, written by the journalist Clément Duvernois (1836–79).[41] The issue also includes an article by Léon Say, "La guerre et la paix en Allemagne",[42] a study by Constant Leirens on "Le mouvement coopératif belge" and the first part of an article by Léon Walras devoted to the "Société coopérative immobilière" (1866c). However, the differences in views between the two directors are far from being resolved. Thus, Constant Leirens remarks to Léon Walras on 3 September 1866: "I see, Sir, that we will have to opt later for the double edition's system, as we will never be able to rally to your way of seeing in matters of taxation and concerning the mission of the State." The "fraternity" question also constitutes a source of divergences.[43]

The third issue of *Travail* appears on 30 September 1866. After the political bulletin, this time written by Léon Say, this issue notably contains an article by Paul Voituron, "Caractère du mouvement démocratique et social en Europe", and the second part of Léon Walras's study on the "Société coopérative immobilière" (1866d). At the time of the release of this issue, the theoretical disagreements between Walras and the Belgian collaborators are set to intensify. Indeed, during the last week of September, Léon Walras contests the ideas developed by Paul Voituron in the article "Caractère du mouvement démocratique et social en Europe", as well as in a manuscript prepared for the fourth issue of *Travail,* on "Les conséquences morales et économiques du mouvement coopératif".[44]

In the text published in the September issue, Paul Voituron wrote:

> Popular education is the moral revolution; the extension of the right to vote, the political revolution, and the cooperative association, the social revolution [...]. The association, finally, is mutual trust, it is voluntary and free union; the more it extends, the more there is solidarity, peace, and *fraternity,* that is to say, true society, among men [...]. Finally, the association of workers is the essential characteristic of true *socialism* which only requires liberty and equality before the law to destroy pauperism and the proletariat. False socialism resorts to force, constraint, despotism of the State to realise fictitious theories, to temporarily level fortunes and dry up at their sources the individual activity and social wealth.[45]

[41] See C. Leirens, letter to L. Walras, undated, but certainly from early August 1866 (F. W. II, box 10). The articles by Clément Duvernois published in *La Presse*, at the beginning of 1866, led to two warnings to the newspaper and raised fears of its imminent suspension. But Duvernois will quickly rally to the Empire from 1867.

[42] Vol. VI, Appendix I, pp. 305–07.

[43] C. Leirens, letter to L. Walras, 3 September 1866 (F. W. II, box 10).

[44] The title of the manuscript appears in the letter of P. Voituron to L. Walras, 21 September 1866 (F. W. II, box 12 bis).

[45] Emphasis in the text, P. Voituron, 1866a, col. 68.

Furthermore, in the manuscript on "the moral and economic consequences of the cooperative movement",[46] Paul Voituron recalled that in terms of workers' association, State intervention should be limited to stimulating individual initiatives. According to him, in this domain,

> [...] mutual trust, devotedness, solidarity, and fraternity must complement, not exclude, the principle of individual interest and that of justice [...]. The principle of individual property is, in the economic order, the very foundation of justice, for it has as its formula: to each what belongs to him. The errors of 1848 have produced a new reaction, and today some exclusive schools, notably the individualist economists, absolutely reject any intervention by the State or the municipalities, at the risk of leaving the people or a large part of the people in misery for a long time yet. They claim that individual interest alone governs the cooperative movement, to the exclusion of devotedness, fraternity, and other purely moral incentives.

Paul Voituron thus tends to think that Walras (who, as an opportunist, still conceals the essence of his ideas) is part of these "individualist economists". For the Belgian author, cooperative associations of credit, consumption, and production enable the reconciliation of personal interest with fraternity, mutuality, solidarity, and ethics. The cooperative association constitutes an "association of people, by itself far superior to the association of capital and the restricted association of capital and labour", whose motive is personal interest alone. Although the "economists of the individualist school" consider this type of association to be impossible, it can be asserted that "the associated worker is an immense progress over the salaried worker". It should be noted here that by characterising the cooperative association as an association of people and not of capital, Voituron aligns with many French authors who discussed this subject in 1865, such as not only Émile Jay, Auguste Vavasseur, Jules Simon but also Gustave Chaudey (executor of Proudhon's will) or Élie Reclus, who wrote in the journal *L'Association.*[47] Finally, by relying on the British case, Paul Voituron offers a very optimistic view of the economic situation:

> In England, in localities where consumption and production associations have developed to a certain extent, small industry and isolated small commerce have not been able to withstand the competition; even the large industry with its immense resource of capital association can only very [*sic*] difficultly compete against the factories operated by associated workers. In these localities, the outcome of the struggle between cooperative association and capitalist association, between solidarised labour and isolated labour, between coordinated competition and anarchic competition, can no longer be in doubt. It is the cooperative movement that prevails.[48]

These theses on cooperation diverge strongly from those that Léon Walras strives to assert in *Le Travail.* We then understand the firm reaction of the latter. Firstly, in a letter to Voituron dated 25 September 1866, he particularly states:

---

[46] Until now, this manuscript has not been found, but it was published later in the first issue of the *Travailleur associé* (*cf infra*) under the title "Le mouvement coopératif".

[47] See "La discussion du Corps législatif sur les sociétés à capital variable" (1867c), vol. VI, notably pp. 219–23.

[48] P. Voituron, 1866b, col. 99–04 (*cf. infra* on this journal).

> […] as I have had every opportunity to inform my French readers that the question of association does not appear to me to be a social question, it is only fair that in turn, you can tell your Belgian subscribers that this question is the whole social question.[49]

However, Paul Voituron seeks to minimise the importance of the incident. According to him, while they are evident divergences on "some points of pure theory", there is agreement on the "practical consequences". Moreover, he declares himself ready to make any necessary concessions to avoid offending the principles defended by Walras.[50] However, in a letter dated 27 September 1866, Walras clearly disagrees. He contests Voituron's approach concerning the relationship between the principle of liberty and the principle of authority. He also points out to him:

> If you would kindly take the trouble to reread my article on the organisation of the *Société immobilière*,[51] you will see very well what cooperation means for us. It is an optional path for all, obligatory for none, from the position of non-capitalist salaried proletarian to the position of capitalist-owner. The individual property of capital remains for us an unassailable right, much more a persistent fact even within the association. For you, on the contrary, as for most French writers whose doctrines we are preparing to combat, the association, having become a *social question*, the advent of *true fraternal socialism*, must lead to a real transformation of the mode of *capital property*.[52]

Moreover, Léon Walras does not appreciate the tirades against the "capitalist bourgeois" and the "individualist economists", contained in the second article, and the text seems to him "not very consistent with the conclusions of economics regarding the role of capital".[53]

Paul Voituron reacts immediately to Walras's new attacks. In his letter dated 28 September 1866, he notes that the divergences relate "more to the meaning of words than to the things themselves". For example, on cooperation, he noted:

> You said in your program that the cooperative movement is not a social question, because it is not the result of collective action, of State action. But you recognize its importance; you believe, as I do, that cooperative associations must change the moral and material situation of the working class.

---

[49] Extract copied in a letter of C. Leirens to L. Walras, 15 October 1866 (F. W. II, box 13).

[50] P. Voituron, letter to L. Walras, 26 September 1866 (F. W. II, box 12 bis).

[51] In reality, Walras did not develop his ideas on the cooperation. He merely indicates that the status of a member of a cooperative housing company is that of a

> […] collective owner or tenant owner, an intermediary between that of a pure and simple tenant and that of an individual owner, perhaps inferior to the latter, but certainly far superior to the former, and which constitutes the most excellent transition from one to the other ("Société coopérative immobilière. Combinaison financière" [2nd part] (1866d), in: vol. VI, pp. 152–53).

[52] Emphasis in the text. L. Walras, letter to Paul Voituron, 27 September 1866, excerpt selected and copied by C. Leirens in his letter to L. Walras of 15 October 1866 (F. W. II, box 13).

[53] See notably the letter of L. Walras to C. Leirens, 19 October 1866, actually written by Léon Say (F. W. II, box 13).

On the question of fraternity, again, the differences are on the meaning of the words, not on the substance:

> You attach a meaning to the word that is not mine. I see nothing but the agreement of all, mutual trust, mutual benevolence, purely moral sentiment. You see communism, equal sharing of wages, community of capital, etc., *all things that I reject in the most formal way.* I am a very determined individualist in this regard. The partners, in my view, must have individual property of capital, be both capitalists and workers.

However, Voituron does acknowledge a real difference with Walras on the question of land property: "If I separate myself from you, it is on something that is not discussed in my article: land community or land property. I am for the property." Finally, on the subject of "individualist economists", Voituron now insists that he was targeting not the economists who admit private property, but those who are hostile to cooperative association, "those who have been screaming with Messrs. Thiers, Villermé, L. Reybaud, etc. that such associations are impossible".[54]

In this controversy, Paul Voituron will suffer from "accusations of communism regarding capital" made against him by Walras about his manuscript on "the moral and economic consequences of the cooperative movement". He clearly asserts himself as "a supporter of the individual property of capital and land", and he rejects the "authoritarian and communist doctrines regarding land", defended by Léon Walras.[55] He therefore declares himself very pessimistic about his relations with him and considers withdrawing his collaboration from the journal.

13.5 Towards the Break

The dispute takes on a new dimension, because in the meantime, Constant Leirens has intervened in the controversy. In a very stormy nine-page letter dated 5 October 1866, he reproaches Léon Walras for gravely distorting the doctrines professed by his friend, by attributing to him the position that the cooperative association would represent "the whole" social question and especially by accusing him of spreading "communist" ideas, hostile to the individual property of capital. He vouches for the ideas of Paul Voituron, with whom he once fought communism in Belgium. He also notes:

> [...] it is evident, despite your laudatory formulas, that you are convinced that you have the misfortune of having collaborators in us who are ignorant of the basics of social science in general and of cooperative association in particular. Fortunately, you are the star destined to guide these novices! You charitably refer Mr. V. to one of your oracle-articles in press so that he may learn the *true* principles!

[54] Emphasis in the text, P. Voituron, letter to L. Walras, 28 September 1866 (F. W. II, box 12 bis).

[55] P. Voituron, letter to L. Walras, 16 October 1866 (F. W. II, box 13). L. Walras, on his part, will assert never having "uttered the word communism" in the letter of 27 September (letter to C. Leirens, 19 October 1866, same reference).

In this dispute, Constant Leirens wishes for the arbitration of Léon Say who, according to him, probably does not defend the same point of view as Léon Walras.[56]

Walras transmits the main elements of the quarrel to Léon Say and on 12 October, he sends a dry and ironic letter to Constant Leirens, in which he recalls the accusations made against him in July concerning the "Programme économique et politique" and the flexibility of his attitude. Today, the situation is reversed and Paul Voituron would certainly have been ready to show similar flexibility, without the untimely intervention of Constant Leirens.[57] On the same day, Léon Say, who has not yet had knowledge of this letter, writes to Constant Leirens to try to calm the controversy:

> I must confess that I do not find *very practical* for us to make little professions of faith to each other. We know that we belong to the liberal party, and that should suffice for us to jointly produce a journal of facts much more than of doctrine [...]. For me, there are no more *good socialists* than *good reactionaries*, and when I hear the expression of good socialism being used, I am always afraid that one wants in this way to bridge, not the chasm that exists between doctrines, that is impossible, but the one that exists between men. I do not hope to bring them back, and I do not want to work with them. The disciples of Proudhon and Cabet will never be my friends in politics [...].[58]

However, even though he regrets the harsh tone adopted by Walras in his correspondence with the Belgian editorial team, Léon Say will agree to defend him in this conflict and will remind Leirens of his commitment alongside Walras since the journal's inception.

On 19 October, in a letter dictated by Say, Walras warns that he will never accept the "compulsory insertion" of articles from the Belgian editorial team, even those that would be signed "R[édaction] B[elge]." In the immediate term, he does not in any way admit the publication of Paul Voituron's article on the cooperative movement, prepared for the fourth issue.[59] Constant Leirens completely rejects these claims. If Walras is not replaced in his functions by "a man tolerant and enlightened enough" to respect the "reciprocity of rights", a break must be considered, which could take place from the fifth issue of *LeTravail.* Indeed, Leirens still agrees to print at his own expense the fourth issue, which would contain "a notice to announce the withdrawal of the Belgian Editorial team". Walras remains free to continue the publication of *Le Travail* under this title and will publish, for his part, in Belgium, a new journal.[60]

---

[56] C. Leirens, letter to L. Walras, 5 October 1866 (F. W. II, box 13).

[57] L. Walras, letter to C. Leirens, 12 October 1866 (F. W., I, 327 bis).

[58] Emphasis in the text. Letter of L. Say to C. Leirens, 12 October 1866, published without mention of the recipient by G. Michel, 1899, pp. 56–58. A copy of the postscript is made by Léon Say in a letter to L. Walras not dated, but probably on 12 October (F. W. II, box 13). In his answer of 18 October, C. Leirens observes that Say's position is more flexible than that of Walras. He states: "it is much less a matter of a conflict of principles between us than a *difference of dictionary*". According to him, the expression "good socialism" "is by no means the rehabilitation of the doctrines of Proudhon, Cabet, etc.; fundamentally, it simply means that one can find in the doctrines of this or that socialist writer some *true opinions*" (Emphasis in the text, F. W. II, box 13).

[59] A copy of this letter of L. Walras to C. Leirens of 19 October 1866 is kept in the Lausanne collection (F. W. II, box 13).

[60] C. Leirens, letter to L. Say, 21 October 1866 (F. W. II, box 13); C. Leirens, letter to L. Say, undated (same reference).

But Walras does not accept these proposals, which he considers to be in violation of the clauses of the convention signed in May, which provides for arbitration in case of conflict and a certain delay in case of rupture.[61] He then decides to immediately cease all relations with Constant Leirens. For the continuation of the journal *LeTravail,* Léon Say and Léon Walras will quickly find another printer in Belgium, "Veuve H. Parent et fils" in Brussels, who compose cooperative journals. On the first page of the fourth issue of *Le Travail,* there is a notice not signed, but from Walras's pen:

> Since our last issue appeared, Mr. C. Leirens and those of his friends who had contributed with him to the foundation of *Travail,* have ceased to have any part in the writing and publication of this journal. *Le Travail* remains nonetheless an international journal, published in Belgium, in which questions concerning Belgium will be studied with special care and always resolved from both a liberal and democratic point of view.[62]

What will happen on the Belgian side? On 3 November, François Huet (1834–69)[63] offers to Paul Voituron the report of a visit from Constant Leirens to his home in Paris. He notably indicates:

> We had our old friend Leirens here. He is rid of his Walras and came to replace him. He had gone astray. Independently of personal relations, with Say and Co, he was fully into economic doctrinairism. We could not go far together. I advised him to get in direct contact with the journal *La Coopération,*[64] successor of the *Association,* and even to try to make the two newpapers work together; which would increase the strength and useful effect. The thing seems done and well done. You are now in contact with the democratic part of French cooperation. Moreover, you will be the masters at home, there must be only one direction in a publication. You can do a lot of good by spreading the principles to the last layers, thanks to the extreme modesty of the price.[65]

In fact, Constant Leirens will undertake the publication at his own expense of a new monthly journal, *Le Travailleur associé—Propagateur international des doctrines coopératives.* He ensures the editorial team with the help of Paul Voituron; the first

---

[61] L. Walras, letter to C. Leirens, 24 October 1866, not sent (F. W., I, 327 bis and copy, F. W. II, box 13), published in *Correspondence*, I, l. 108, p. 154 note 2, with the date "28 October" and without mention of the recipient. It was replaced by a letter of L. Say to C. Leirens, undated (copy of L. Say, F. W. II, box 13).

[62] The original manuscript of this notice is kept in the Lausanne collection (F. W. V b, box 26, one sheet).

[63] François Huet taught philosophy in Ghent. He does identify with "liberal socialism", but from a different perspective to that of Walras (*cf. infra* chapter 15, *Towards the Repurchase of Lands by the State and the Abolition of Taxes*).

[64] *La Coopération—Journal du progrès social* is a bi-monthly every 15 days, from 9 September 1866 to 14 June 1868. Its editor-in-chief is Abel Davaud.

[65] F. Huet, letter to Paul Voituron, 3 November 1866, in: Paul Voituron: "Philosophical Correspondence (1845–1870)", Universiteit Gent, Centrale Bibliotheek, Hs G 11791. Virginie Loveling (1836–1923), who had translated for the *Travail* the "Lettres d'un ouvrier anglais" by M. Manley, reports a trip to Paris by Constant Leirens, his wife and herself, which would have taken place on 20 November 1866 with the aim of meeting François Huet (V. Loveling, "Milan van Servië", 1906, pp. 144 and 148).

issue is published on 15 November 1866.[66] The first article, "Aux lecteurs du *Travail*" indicates:

> The editorial team of the monthly journal *Le Travail* founded in Ghent, splits. The journal is continued, under the original title, by the French Editor, and under the one inscribed at the head of this issue, by the Belgian Editors, who are assured of the collaboration of several foreign writers (French, Germans, etc.) honourably known [...]. The new journal does not limit its programme to questions that are specifically within the domain of the association; it will discuss, according to the needs of the situation, all those that interest the working class.[67]

For its distribution in Belgium, the journal is supplemented by a monthly supplement entitled *Bulletin belge du Travailleur associé*, edited by Paul Voituron. However, *Le Travailleur associé* will have a shorter lifespan than *Le Travail* as it only appears until 15 July 1867.[68]

13.6 Epilogue

Were there any controversies between *Le Travail* and *Le Travailleur associé*? In fact, the two journals largely ignored each other during the first half of 1867. However, it can be noted that in a study on "La définition des sociétés coopératives", which was published on 15 July in the last issue of *Le Travailleurassocié*, Paul Voituron criticises Léon Walras's article, "La discussion du Corps législatif sur les sociétés à capital variable", which appeared on 30 June in *Le Travail*. According to him, the main characteristic of cooperative companies is the proportional sharing of profits, which destroys the wage system. But in terms of form, the controversy is now virulent, as he adds:

> This is what the *Revue du mouvement coopératif* [*Le Travail*], which is considered in France as the organ of the small group of doctrinaire economists, has perfectly grasped [...]. This review argues, in a special article on the discussions taking place in the Corps législatif, that cooperative associations are, like all others, associations of capital and not associations of persons; that only capital can be associated, and that *labour must be salaried*. This is the pure and simple negation of the object and purpose of cooperation, and it will, we believe, open the eyes to the peculiar friends of the cooperative movement who write this review. But what is perhaps most curious is the cutting, self-satisfied, and pedantic tone with which the

[66] *Le Travailleur associé* is printed in Ghent in a format identical to that of the *Travail*; it retains the same overall structure. The first issue is designated as "No. 4, 15 November 1866". After the release of the two "fourth issues", the newspaper *La Coopération* publishes a snippet on the "division of labour" and provides unwavering support to the new publication by Constant Leirens (*La Coopération*, 1st year, no. 7, 2 December 1866, p. 4).

[67] "To the readers of *Le Travail*", *Le travailleur associé*, 1st year, no. 4, 15 November 1866, col. 97.

[68] Given the failure of the newspaper's distribution, Leirens and Voituron wish to launch a new newspaper intended for the working class, but which would no longer be limited to the cooperative question, *L'instruction du peuple*. However, we have not found any tangible trace concerning the actual creation of this newspaper in Belgium. Later, Constant Leirens will settle in Vevey in Switzerland, where he will end his life.

> most incredible nonsense imaginable is delivered to defend an impossible thesis. All those who have been involved in cooperation know that cooperative companies are associations of persons. Messrs. Garnier-Pagès, Jules Simon, Ernest Picard, Émile Ollivier in the Corps Législatif, and Messrs. Reclus, Chaudey, Jay, etc., in numerous articles in the *L'Association* and *La Cooperation* have recognised it. Only the doctrinaire economists fail to see this obvious characteristic of cooperative associations, blinded as they are by their theory of the wage system.[69]

A second attack on the article "La discussion du Corps législatif sur les sociétés à capital variable", this time published in *La Cooperation*,[70] gives Walras the opportunity to answer to these two journals. For him, there are only three possible solutions:

> [...] to participate neither in losses nor in profits; to participate in profits without participating in losses; to participate in both losses and profits. When one is in the first situation, one is *salaried*; when one is in the second, one is simply *interested* or *participating*; when one is in the third, one is *associated* in the true sense of the word. Labour can accept the two situations, either as salaried or as interested or participating; only capital can expose itself to the situation of being associated, because only it can be alienated in case of losses.[71]

Probably around February 1867,[72] Léon Walras had decided, in agreement with Léon Say, to have the first three issues of *Le Travail* reprinted in Belgium, with a view to compiling a collection of the first year. However, he decides not to reproduce the issues identically. Indeed, he has *Le Travail* recomposed according to his views; he modifies not only the order of the arrival of some articles, but makes some disappear without informing the reader.[73] Notably, the removal in the July issue of the editorial notice signed by Léon Walras and Constant Leirens, along with the "programme" of the Belgian editorial team, written by Paul Voituron, is noteworthy. Also, in the September issue, the elimination of Paul Voituron's study, "Caractère du mouvement démocratique et social en Europe", which represented one of the pieces of the conflict between the two parties, is noted.

---

[69] Emphasis by the author. P. Voituron, 1867, col. 152–53.

[70] "La coopération négative", signed Capron, *La Coopération*, 2nd year, no.1, 8 September 1867, p. 6.

[71] Emphasis by L. W., untitled article, *Le Travail*, 2nd year, no.3, September 1867, in: vol. VI, Annex II, p. 383.

[72] This date can be established from the letter of H. Parent to L. Walras of 3 March 1867 (F. W. VI, box 31). In spring, Walras drafts a "Prospectus du journal *Le Travail*" (1867b).

[73] One reads, for example, in no.1, 31 July 1867 of the 2nd series of *Le Travail*, in the first column, after the announcement of the sale of the collection of the first year: "The three issues of July, August and September 1866, which were out of print, have been reprinted in the same type as the following ones. These issues are sold separately [...]."

13.7 Conclusion

The controversy engaged between Walras on one side and Leirens and Voituron on the other is very revealing of the differences in approach that were expressed during the years 1864–68 in France and Belgium regarding the function of cooperative associations and their potential role in solving the social question. Moreover, the journal *Le Travail*, after being taken over by Walras, intends to combat the representatives of positions very close to those of Leirens and Voituron. Referring to the Caisse d'escompte des associations populaires and the publication of the journal *Le Travail* in a letter to Jules Ferry, Minister of Public Instruction, dated 3 July 1879, Walras acknowledges:

> […] we could not prevent, despite everything, our customers from leaning towards the ideas of the opposing group. For my part, I remain convinced that the success would have been better if we had confined ourselves to seeking in the cooperative association an easy and quick means of saving and not 'a principle of labour organisation' and 'a social revolution'.[74]

Appendix: L'Association populaire—Organe des intérêts du travail, moniteur international des sociétés de coopération de France, de Belgique, d'Angleterre, et d'Allemagne[75]

I. Paris, 1st October 1864.[76]

II. *Theoretical part* (scientific articles).

On the relations of labour with land property and with capital in the fact of economic production—Interest rate—Wage rate—Coalitions—Women's work.

Theory of credit—Mechanisms of agricultural, industrial, and commercial credit institutions—Issuing, deposit banks—Banknotes, cheques.

On association and insurance—Principles of mutuality and solidarity—Cooperative associations.

Critique of legislation.

III. *Application part* (current affairs articles)

Study of official documents: laws (explanatory statements and projects); decrees, international treaties.

Monograph of cooperative companies: statutes, functioning, histories.

Various questions: workers' societies, savings banks, retirement funds.

Correspondences from England—from Germany.

IV. *Report* of the Legislative Chambers;

---

[74] L. Walras, letter to the Minister of Public Instruction [Jules Ferry], 3 July 1879, in: *Correspondence*, I, l. 444, p. 613.

[75] This document by Léon Walras is preserved in the Lausanne collection (F.W. VI, box 30, one sheet).

[76] It is undoubtedly the editorial.

[*Report*] of Academies and learned societies, - of congresses;

[*Report*] of the Courts.

V. *Varieties.*

On association at various periods of history.

On association in all its forms: scientific and artistic associations. Analysis and critique of important books concerning the improvement of the condition of the working classes and popular association.

Excerpts from books in press.

VI. *Financial bulletin.*

VII. *News.*

VIII. *Bibliography.*

IX. *Advertisements.*

X. *Stock exchange and markets*

Part V
Social Reforms for the Implementation of a Liberal Socialism

Chapter 14
Organisation of the Labour Market, Labour Legislation, and Social Insurance

A strike is an overturned bicycle and its rider in a ditch
("Notes sur 'Masse et rareté'", 1907–08, vol. XI, p. 631).

14.1 Introduction

At the end of his life, in the speech delivered for his fiftieth anniversary as an economist at the University of Lausanne, Léon Walras remarked:

> First, it is clear that wage determination by means of strikes and *lock-outs*, i.e., ultimately, by throwing stones against gunshots, is a barbarian behaviour. But it is also clear that for the purpose of replacing it by the determination of prices of various kinds of work with the mechanism of outbidding and underbidding (*enchères et rabais*), mathematical pure economics would be absolutely necessary (1909c, vol. VII, p. 510).

Here, as in other areas, recommendations in applied economics must be based on the theoretical results of pure economics.

The question of the working of the labour market and more broadly the "social question" deeply worried Walras during his entire career, leading him into some controversies with the French liberal school and the socialists of his time. Our author has the opportunity to express himself several times about the labour market, social conflicts, and social legislation. Indeed, he tackles the problem of wage determination and strikes from his first works (1859–60), then in several articles published in his cooperative newspaper, *Le Travail* (1866–68). He re-examines the question in the *Cours d'économie politique appliquée* in the Law Faculty of Lausanne, in the sections devoted to industry, association, and insurance.[1] More later, Walras reconsiders these questions, especially in the article "L'économique appliquée et la défense

[1] See our edition of the *Cours d'économie politique appliquée*, vol. XII, 1996.

J.-P. Potier, *Léon Walras, Economist and Liberal Socialist*, Springer Studies in the History of Economic Thought, https://doi.org/10.1007/978-3-032-04670-3_14

des salaires", published in the *Revue d'économie politique* in December 1897 and included in the *Études d'économie politique appliquée.*

In this chapter, we will recall the evolution of Léon Walras's ideas on the labour market, strikes, workers' coalitions, and the role of the State for the organisation of this market. We will examine also his ideas concerning labour legislation and social security. Lastly, we will present his viewpoint on the useful means to maintain and increase workers' income.

14.2 Is the Labour Market Spontaneously Organised?

In his first text as an economist, the "Introduction à l'étude de la question sociale" (1859), Léon Walras adopts an optimistic tone *à la Bastiat* in a polemic on free competition and the labour market which would be spontaneously organised. According to him,

> It is not enough, in fact, to prevent any intervention by the political authority in the matter of economy; it is also advisable to separate production from any kind of administrative action, or rather it is perfectly superfluous to subject the production to it. [....] here indeed private interest contributes naturally and by itself to the satisfaction of the general interest (1859b, vol. V, p. 117).

Therefore, any form of regulation would disturb the spontaneous harmony resulting from the absolute principle of the liberty of work and trade, or of *laissez-faire, laissez-passer*. Without weakness, the "providential fate of the natural laws" would ensure a production of wealth abundant and well proportioned at the same time. Consequently, the principle of free competition can be successfully protected against the attacks of the "empirical socialists", such as Louis Blanc and Pierre-Joseph Proudhon, who advise social reforms without supporting them with serious theoretical arguments.

In Chap. 12 (*Criticism of "Empirical Socialism": the Cases of Louis Blanc and the Saint-Simonians*), we saw that in this text an imaginary dialogue was engaged between Louis Blanc and the young Léon Walras. To the assertion that competition would be "labour put up for auction", Walras responds with a certain cynicism: "Obviously! That is to say, it is the assimilation of labour, income from a capital, to the other incomes of other capitals. Competition [...] is the regular uniformity in the setting of wages, rent, profit" (1859b, vol. V, p. 119). He is weary of Louis Blanc's discourse, which he considers purely emotional, and claims to approach the problem coldly and scientifically: competition pushes the entrepreneur to lower wages, but does it allow him to lower them indefinitely?

> That is the question. Now if superficial passion settles the problem affirmatively, in-depth reasoning resolves it negatively. Impartial science notes a tendency of workers to raise wages, a tendency favoured by the competition of entrepreneurs, and capable of balancing the first and maintaining the wage rate at the normal equilibrium of their natural value (1859b, vol. V, pp. 119–20).

In summary, for Walras,

> [...] it is the competition of workers that supports the entrepreneurs; it is the competition of entrepreneurs that protects the workers. Competition creates equilibrium. And to disturb this equilibrium in the direction accused by Mr. Louis Blanc, what would be needed? A coalition of entrepreneurs that the law can punish or make harmless by not prohibiting workers' coalitions (*op. cit.*, pp. 120–21).

And in *L'Économie politique et la Justice*, our author uses the same argument against P.-J. Proudhon's ideas (1860a, pp. 185–86).[2] The labour market would therefore be perfectly organised! In the words of the young Léon Walras, one does not find the reservations expressed by Adam Smith, and later renewed by Jean-Baptiste Say, albeit in a milder form, about the asymmetry of the labour market to the detriment of workers.

However, in the writings drafted during his cooperativist period (1866–68), Walras modifies his analysis and already uses the distinction between the "normal" working and the "abnormal" working of the labour market. His ideas further evolve after his move to Lausanne in 1870, particularly on the question of the organisation of this market.

14.3 "Normal" Working and "Abnormal" Working of the Labour Market: Questions of Strikes and Workers' Coalitions

As we saw at the beginning of this book, Léon Walras revisits and refines his father's analysis regarding the distinction between capital, "services", and their price on the market. In pure economics, the task of the entrepreneurs, who possess neither capital nor productive services, essentially consists in the hiring of land, capital proper, and personal faculties, i.e. the purchase on the markets of the three productive services (land services, capital goods services—*profit*, labour) and their combination in the various economic activities. In the "theory of production", in the 18th lesson of the *Eléments* (vol. VIII, pp. 281–82, English transl., 2014, pp. 207–08), Walras considers the market for products and the market for productive services (land services, profit, and labour) in relation to each other and he states the conditions of equilibrium: in addition to equality between supply and effective demand of productive services and products and the setting of their prices, it is necessary to obtain equality between the selling price of the products and the cost of productive services. Free competition designates a specific behaviour and not a market structure; in the case of the labour service as in that of any productive service, if at a given price the effective demand exceeds the effective supply, entrepreneurs will outbid, and the price of the labour service will rise; conversely, if at a given price the effective supply exceeds the effective demand, workers will underbid, and the price of the labour service will fall. But, as we will recall later, for Walras, every worker has an absolute right, not to

[2] Let us note that he aligns himself with the positions defended in the "Notes sur Proudhon" that his father, Auguste Walras, transmitted to him (1859, pp. 619–20).

an employment ("the right to work"), but to the *entirety* of the service of personal faculties and its price on the market, the wage. With these elements recalled, how does Walras consider the "normal" and "abnormal" working of the labour market?

14.3.1 "Normal" Working of the Labour Market

Concerning the "normal" working of the labour market, it is specified in the *Cours d'économie politique appliquée* that only when competition among the entrepreneurs acts to reduce the spread between the selling price and the cost in productive services, "the industry is doing well". And "it is the case, as Cobden said, where two employers seek a worker. In this case, there is no need to strike to get a rise of wages since it is done by itself" (vol. XII, 28th lesson, "On Coalitions and Strikes", p. 581).[3]

Admittedly, one could wonder about the reduction of employment caused by the development of machinery. According to Walras, machinery reduces the price of manufactured products, increases the demand of all other products and therefore increases the demand for labour services; so, the conclusion can only be optimistic:

> [...] the reasoning establishes that after a temporary transfer, which constitutes truly a more or less painful crisis for the workers and makes it necessary to soften it for them as much as possible, the use of the machines increases the demand for labour, far from decreasing it. The facts confirm this reasoning strikingly [...] (vol. XII, 27th lesson, "On Machines", p. 578).[4]

In addition, in the case of the introduction of free trade, the transfer of the various productive services from industries with importation to industries with exportation is needed; the State can help the entrepreneurs "in giving them some time" and in removing the indirect taxes. The transfer of personal faculties and the services of labour is not "as easy" as in the case of the fixed and circulating capital, but it can nevertheless take place if workers move towards industries which thrive. However, Walras affirms having understood the workers' point of view who complain about the competition of foreign workers: "In fact, workers who have raised, wrongly, such lively opposition to the use of machinery, and also, but less wrongly, to foreign workers, will not be so fiercely opposed to free trade" ("Théorie du libre échange", 1897a, vol. X, p. 273, English transl.,2005, p. 240).

Free trade extends to the whole world the free competition regime, which consists in the exchange of productive services between them according to the double condition of maximum satisfaction of the needs (relating to interest) and unique price for each service on the market (relating to justice). However, for Walras, the second condition, or "restriction", is just inside a country, but not from one country to another:

[3] Here Walras repeats the main argument of a part of an article published in *Le Travail*, "Discussion sur les coalitions et les grèves à la Société d'économie politique de Paris" (1867a), pp. 210–11.

[4] Later, Walras reasserts: "So, after all, only a transfer of the demand for labour has occurred and not a reduction. All that is needed is to provide for a transition" ("Esquisse d'une doctrine économique et sociale" (1898c), p. 429, English transl.,2010, p. 375).

> In other words, has the seller of a service a natural right to sell abroad if the service is more valuable there than in his own country ? Does the buyer of a service have a natural right to sell abroad if the service is less expensive there than in his own country? [....]. I am a European worker; I have done my military service, I pay heavy taxes. Does justice require me to sell my labour at the same price as a Hindu or Chinese who is not subject to such charges? Abolish taxes and perhaps the two cases will be nearer to equality (*op. cit.*, pp. 274–75, English transl.,2005, p. 241).

Therefore, Walras does not accept the co-called "social dumping". And his proposal for an abolition of taxes leads us to the social reform that will be discussed in the next chapter.

14.3.2 "Abnormal" Working of the Labour Market and Solutions for It

Unfortunately, according to Walras, there exist circumstances which prevent the labour market from normal working. This is the case when the reduction of the gap between cost in productive services and selling price no longer comes only from competition between the entrepreneurs. In this case, "industry goes badly" and our economist gives us some examples on this matter:

> It is what happens, for example, when a reduction in import duties or in transport costs produces a sudden and significant lowering of the selling price, by intervention of foreign competition. It is what still happens with changes in the surrounding economic conditions: works of demolition and rebuilding of cities, development of speculation and of luxury: all that brings about the rise in the value of various elements of the cost in productive services such as, inter alia, that of land on which the industrial settings up are made. It is then the case where one can see two workers seeking one employer (*Cours d'économie politique appliquée*, vol. XII, 28th lesson, pp. 581–82).[5]

According to Walras, in such a context, the strike turns out rather badly and will backfire on the interests of the workers, because the entrepreneurs will perhaps be constrained to close their workshops. Here, it is useful to mention that Walras was very much interested in the history concerning the prohibition of combinations and strikes in France. First of all, he has great praise for the Turgot *Edit* of 9 February 1776 which abolished the *jurandes* and the *maîtrises* and tried to establish "liberty of work" in France. If implicitly, he accepts D'Allarde law, adopted by the Assemblée Constituante on 2 and 17 March 1791, on the other hand, he disapproves of the vote of Le Chapelier law (14 June 1791). Le Chapelier law tried to harshly suppress the "meetings" which aim at compelling the entrepreneurs to increase the price of daily work and at fomenting workers' revolts. Article 2 of this law (quoted by Walras in the 28th lesson, p. 579), indicated:

---

[5] In fact, here Walras takes up entirely a part of his article published in *Le Travail* (1867a, p. 211), quoted above.

> The citizens in the same position or profession, the entrepreneurs, those who have a shop, the workers and apprentices of an unspecified art, when they are together, will be not able to appoint neither president, neither secretaries, nor syndics, to hold registers, to adopt decrees or deliberations, to establish rules concerning their so-called shared interests.[6]

In fact, the Le Chapelier law tackled the workers' combinations. Opportunely, Léon Walras also points out the reinforcement of the legal arsenal against the combinations with the 22 Germinal year XI [12 April 1803] law and then the *Code pénal* of 1810. Also, let us note that after the Revolution of 1848 in France, the repressive measures will be restored.

Throughout the XIXth century, the French liberal economists are very much divided on the question of combinations. Some were opponents to the right of combination (Charles Dunoyer, Jules Dupuit, for example), while others, faithful to the message of Adam Smith and Jean-Baptiste Say proclaimed the absolute freedom of combination (Frédéric Bastiat, Joseph Garnier, Gustave de Molinari, for example), wishing to repress only its abuses (intimidations and violence). Walras is supporting the last point of view, because he considers the prohibition of employers and workers' combinations as "useless and dangerous" from the point of view of economic efficiency:

> Undoubtedly, one can by the means of a combination, create the monopoly of a product or a productive service, and the monopoly is against the interest of society. But this result is […] almost impossible to obtain in a country where industry and trade would be truly subjected to a free competition regime […]. In such a country, there will be always competitors to be held apart from the combination, unless the special character of industry does not lend itself to monopoly, in which case it returns in the category of economic monopolies and must be acknowledged or conceded by the State. The only danger would be that by intimidation, threats or violence, the allied could retain in the combination those which would like to be kept out. […] the law should be restricted to prohibit and repress *intimidation, threats* and *violence* (emphasis by L. W., vol. XII, 28th lesson, pp. 579–80).

However, in the first half of the XIXth century, the agreements and combinations remained possible and they escaped from justice, in particular those of the employers. Moreover, there existed, without legal framework and especially in Paris, some "Chambres syndicales d'entrepreneurs", whose competence was recognised by the commercial courts in legal actions. During the liberal stage of the Second Empire, with the multiplication of social conflicts, the law of 25 May 1864 was promulgated. This law removed the offence of combination and legalised strikes, but punished by

> […] imprisonment from six days to three years and a fine of 16 F to 3000 F or either of these two sentences, for anyone using violence, assault, threats, or fraudulent conspiracy, would have brought or maintained, tried to bring about or maintain a concerted work stoppage, with the aim of forcing the rise or fall of wages, or attacking the free functioning of industry or work.

In his *Cours d'économie politique appliquée*, around the years 1879–1881, commenting on this law, Walras notes that it permits the workers to assemble, but

[6] See also J.-P. Potier, 1989.

still subject to prior approval for the organisation of their meetings. The experiment having been very positive, our author wishes French legislation to move in the direction of workers right to meet (vol. XII, 28th lesson, p. 580).

It is necessary to recall that during the period of his involvement in the cooperative movement (1866–68), Walras was also interested in the project of "Chambres syndicales de travailleurs".[7] These *Chambres* would have the task of negotiation on the rules of workshops, working conditions, the fixing of wages, but would also play a part in conciliation in the case of conflicts with the "Chambres syndicales d'entrepreneurs".[8] In the *Cours d'économie politique appliquée*, Walras again proposes the representation of workers in the "Chambres syndicales de travailleurs" in order to defend their moral and material interests (vol. XII, 28th lesson, p. 580). Finally, the law of 21 March 1884 ("Waldeck-Rousseau law"), brought the Le Chapelier law to an end in France by authorising the formation of trade unions, except for civil servants.

Taking into account the institutional context's evolution, how can one avoid or solve the social conflicts? To allow an efficient negotiation between entrepreneurs and workers, Walras begins to advocate the formation of "professional unions associations" like the British trade unions, encouraged by the State, and based on the condition that they constitute a similar united body and do not consider the employers as opponents ("L'économique appliquée et la défense des salaires", 1897c, vol. X, p. 257, English transl.,2005, p. 226).

On the question of which procedures to use in case of social conflicts, Walras recommends "arbitration". Here he refers mainly to the experiments in England, where courts of conciliation and boards of arbitration were born spontaneously in 1860, then became legal in 1867 and 1872.[9] However, according to him, the arbitration solution outside the context of England encounters several difficulties. On the one hand, the members of the boards of arbitration must be qualified in business, able to puzzle out the accounting of enterprises and, on the other hand, their impartiality must be unanimously acknowledged (vol. XII, 28th lesson, p. 582). Walras mentions also the "price scales" of products (1897c, p. 254; English transl., 2005, p. 223). Here, he implicitly refers to the system, from the 1870s–80 s, using sliding scales, which bind in the enterprises (for example, coal mines) the selling price of the product and wages (possibly comprising a floor and a ceiling for average wages). Such devices were frequently used by the conciliation courts in England and in the United States.

---

[7] Maurice Sabatier, a member of the staff of the newspaper *Le Travail*, prepared a study on this subject (M. Sabatier, 1868, pp. 355–63).

[8] During the 1870s, this solution will give rise to some experiments in Paris.

[9] In France, as regards conciliation, the system of the *conseils de prud'hommes* (appeared in Lyon in 1806) was extended by the imperial decree of 20 February 1810, then reformed by the laws of 4 June 1853 and 7 February 1880. But the most important law is that of 27 December 1892 on conciliation and optional arbitration between employers and workers; some *juges de paix* can form conciliation or arbitration committees.

14.4 Towards the Organisation of the Labour Market by the State

About the stopping of strikes by means of arbitration, Léon Walras hastens to add in a quite imprudent way:

> [...] it is an extra-scientific solution. The scientific and final solution is the outbidding and underbidding on the labour market, outbidding of the entrepreneurs when the demand for labour is higher than supply, underbidding of the workers when the supply is higher than demand (vol. XII, 29th lesson, "On the Relations of Labour and Capital", pp. 582–83).

In 1897, Walras indicates in this matter that it is necessary to aim at the suppression of strikes by means of "*rational State intervention*" for a more efficient functioning of the products and services markets (emphasis added, "L'économique appliquée et la défense des salaires", 1897c, vol. X, p. 254, English transl., 2005, p. 223). He observed that there are no strikes between entrepreneurs and capitalists, because the Stock exchange and the banks are markets that "have been organized somewhat better than the labour market, which is not organized at all" (*op. cit.*, p. 256, English transl., p. 225). Let us also recall that in the list of the three categories of markets from the best to the least organised, mentioned in the *Éléments d'économie politique pure*, the labour market does not appear. But will Walras suggest the setting up of *Bourses du travail* functioning by information and communication means, through a system of intermediaries to place workers without State intervention, as Gustave de Molinari so ardently wished?[10] Walras thinks in another direction, because for him the State must undertake the organisation of the labour market. Such a viewpoint could plunge us into great perplexity. However, it should be recalled that, according to our author, if free competition represents a "natural tendency" and constitutes within certain limits a "self-driven and self-regulating mechanism" of production of social wealth and transformation of services into products, in certain cases "one must help and control its running", which demands resorting to State intervention. From such a point of view, "there is reason for the State to intervene to organize it and to assure the conditions and circumstances for its working" (1880b, vol. X, p. 388; English transl., 2005, p. 339). Therefore, in the international context of the "Great Depression", between the years 1870 and 1890, Walras develops an approach in terms of organised free competition.

According to our author,

> The strikes we talked about take place between entrepreneurs and workers in industries where production should be restricted in order to maintain prices. The entrepreneurs want to maintain production because of the lower prices and the workers want the quantity of labour to be maintained without suffering a decrease in their wages. This will happen while in another industry, where production is growing, the prices of the products and the wages

---

[10] See G. de Molinari, *Les Bourses du travail* (Paris: Guillaumin, 1893) and his paper read at the Société d'économie politique during the meeting of 5 July 1893, "Des conditions aux quelles les Bourses du travail peuvent être utiles" (*Journal des économistes*, 5th series, vol. 15, 1893, pp. 117–24). Let us note that, in his writings, Walras never refers to the ideas of Molinari...a "master" for Pareto !

> increase unnecessarily. From whatever side they arise, these tendencies to counteract the establishment of economic equilibrium have to be suppressed. Not by articles of penal law (*Code pénal*), nor by cavalry patrols, but by organizing the products and services markets after organizing the enterprises (1897c, vol. X, p. 256, English transl.,2005, p. 225).

Before, in the same study, Walras specifies: "*to bring about or maintain equilibrium of production as far as wages are concerned labour must be diverted from enterprises where the wages tend to decrease to enterprises where the wages tend to increase*" (emphasis by L.W., *op cit.*, p. 255; English transl., 2005, p. 224).[11] However, he adds that the "increases or decreases in wages are just indications. These indications may be very slight, but we need them. All we have to do in practice is wait until they appear and then remove them at once by shifting labour from one point to another" (*op. cit.*, pp. 255–56; see also 1898c, vol. X, p. 429; English transl., 2005, pp. 225 and 375). Therefore, it would be possible to avoid strikes by means of these very slight changes in wages which act like signals. The State must facilitate the mobility of workers from one sector to another. The efficient running of the labour market requires that information circulates widely there. So Walras recommends the publication of *mercuriales*, of labour statistics which will highlight the areas and sectors where the entrepreneurs need manpower. The intervention of the State in this direction will be supported by the action of the "professional unions associations" (1897c, vol. X, p. 257; English transl., 2005, p. 226). On this subject, one can also point out the role of the technical schools which would undoubtedly make the transfers of workers easier (see *infra* on the relevancy of education).

Now, what about labour legislation and social insurance in the writings of Léon Walras?

14.5 Labour Legislation and Social Insurance

14.5.1 Need for Labour Legislation

Walras discusses labour legislation, and first of all the legislation in Switzerland. In this country, during summer 1875, a project of a federal law on the work in the factories was put under discussion in the press. This project will lead to the federal law of 23 March 1877 which constituted a big step in the field of the Swiss protection of workers. Solicited to comment on this project for the *Gazette des Tribunaux Suisses,* Walras delivers his reflections in an article published in February 1876. Basically, he is in favour of the project under discussion which contains protective measures for the work of women and children and gives a time limit for daily work: 11 h (10 h for Saturday and the day before holidays). However, according to him, this project gives a too-detailed legal intervention, and therefore too constraining on working

[11] Georges Sorel does not understand here how the State would proceed and he adds: "the State that Mr Walras dreams of is a rational and mathematical God" (1899, p. 123).

conditions, likely to harm Swiss industry and its presence in the foreign markets (1876a, vol. VII, pp. 228–29).

Twenty years later, in 1897, in "L'économique appliquée et la défense des salaires", Walras remarks that the questions concerning labour conditions in general (morality, hygiene, working hours) are not strictly speaking questions of applied economics, but rather of family and government's theories, fields which he himself did not explore. He also observes that these questions become a field for the French journalists trained in law school (*école du Droit*) and more or less close to the German 'socialists of the chair' (1897c, vol. X, p. 252; English transl., 2005, p. 222).

Undoubtedly after reading the series of reports submitted to the international congress of labour legislation (Brussels, 27–30 September 1897),[12] Walras notes that according to the statistics "only half" of the strikes succeed and that two-thirds of the conflicts were about wages and one-third about the conditions of work (hygiene, work of women and children, working hours in general).

In pure economics, the supply of daily work of the personal faculties' owners can vary with the prices of all the products and services. But for Walras, in the majority of cases this assumption cannot be carried out in practice and the economist "should not be fooled by his own abstractions". Walras estimates that in large- and medium-scale industry, the "quantity of daily work supplied and used is necessarily the same for all workers" and is established by the entrepreneurs in competition who aim at inexpensive products: that led to an unlimited increase in the working hours. Therefore, the State must fix some limits for the working day, including that of women and children[13] in factories: "A maximum should be imposed. Consequently, nothing is more natural than entrusting the State with this task, which will achieve it according to its objectives relating to morality, hygiene, etc." (1897c, vol. X, p. 253; English transl., 2005, p. 223). However, this limitation or this reduction of the working day should not be accompanied by a reduction of wages.[14]

Walras thinks that specific legislation is necessary on work conditions, but it should not be too constricting for the entrepreneurs. According to him, an "international agreement" would make it possible to solve several questions of working regulation, provided that the point of view of free trade will be considered.[15] Even here, Walras seeks a means to avoid the "social dumping"!

---

[12] L. Walras examined the possibility to make reading his article "L'économique appliquée et la défense des salaires" at the congress. See his letters to G. Maugin and Victor Brants dated 14 and 19 March 1897, respectively, in: *Correspondence*, II, l. 1304 and 1306, pp. 736 and 737–38.

[13] We will see below that, theoretically, Walras does not wish for women and children to work in factories.

[14] Walras's ideas arise in a context in which the daily work hours in France still remain very high. In the middle of the XIXth century, the daily work in the industry could reach 12 h and the situation was nearly the same during the Second Empire and the beginnings of the IIIrd République. The law of 2 November 1892 limited the daily work of women and children and then the laws of 1900, 1902, and 1904 gradually reduced daily work from 11 to 10 h. Later the struggle for daily work of 8 h began in France and will be successful only after the First World War, thanks to the 23 April 1919 law.

[15] On this topic, see 1897c, vol. X, p. 253 and note 2, English transl., 2005, p. 223.

In the context of the Universal Exhibition at Paris, a "Congrès international de la protection légale des travailleurs" is held (Musée Social, 25–28 July 1900). Paul Cauwès, as the president of the commission for organising this congress, asks Walras to join the "comité de patronage". Our author accepts without hesitation the proposal of the leader of the French "économie politique nationale", as "a decided supporter of the legal protection of workers and willing to protest at any time against the use of the word 'liberty' to conceal an unwarranted *laissez-faire*".[16] This international congress in Paris is important because it leads to the creation of the "International association for legal protection of the workers", of which the constituent assembly will be held in Bale in 1901. An International Labour Office will be formed for the publication of statistics, and the association will be organised in national sections.[17] It will play a decisive part in the adoption of an international standards of labour movement which will lead in 1919 to the birth of the International Labour Organization.

14.5.2 Controversy on Social Insurance

Walras declares himself opposed to public assistance, to the "provision by the State of free medicines, medical care,[18] bread, etc., etc., all provisions of private not public interest" ("Le problème fiscal", 1896d, vol. IX, p. 403, English transl., 2010, p. 331). According to him, we must expect much more of workers than of the State and it is almost necessary to be wary of the "State nurse" (*État nourrice*) (1897c, vol. X, pp. 258 and 261, English transl., 2005, p. 227). He criticises the aid and retirement funds imposed by the State on entrepreneurs (1895, vol. X, p. 180, English transl.,2005, p. 152) and he also confronts the social laws promoted by Bismarck, setting up in the German industry a compulsory workers insurance system with laws relating to health insurance (1883), accidents during work (1884), disability, and pension schemes (1889). On this point, his position agreed with that of French liberal economists who express themselves regularly in the meetings of the *Société d'économie politique de Paris*. In his "Notes d'humeur", Walras makes a copy of an extract which appeared in a parliamentary chronicle of Bern relating to the discussion of a project of law about health insurance, published in the *Gazette de Lausanne* (26 June 1897), in which one reads:

> Compulsory insurance conforms to the feudal org[anization] of corporations in the Middle Ages. But if we want to combine it with modern liberty of work, it denies its services to precisely those who should benefit from them in the front line. In fact, the workers who are unemployed or who cannot find long-term employment with the same person are excluded from insurance scheme[s] (2000, vol. XIII, p. 577).

---

[16] See L. Walras, letter to P.-L. Cauwès, 5 April 1900, in: *Correspondence*, III, l. 1449, p. 114.

[17] From 1901 to 1906, Paul Cauwès will be the first president of the Association nationale pour la protection légale des travailleurs.

[18] In France, in 1893, free medical assistance was established in favour of the indigent.

In France, compulsory insurance is introduced with the laws of 9 April 1898 on working accidents and of 5 April 1910 on the *"retraites ouvrières et paysannes"*. According to Walras, such initiatives cannot be useful. In particular, he criticises projects which aim at the setting up of an insurance system managed by the State. In this case, "the workers, having no incentive getting the premium back, will not be so alert, accidents will increase and the State will get into debt" (1897c, vol. X, p. 260, English transl., 2005, p. 228). He raises here the well-known problem today of *ex post* opportunism (moral hazard).

For Walras, insurance must involve individual initiative. The workers must be freely able to insure themselves as they wish, against unemployment, sickness, accidents, and old age. Therefore,

> [...] such a person, who insures himself, is superior to the man who gets himself insured by the State, as is also the man who educates himself and his children in comparison with the one who leaves this care to the State (*op. cit).*

But, among the free insurance systems, the workers must prefer mutual insurance, which is likely just like association to improve their condition. Therefore, Walras supports the principle of mutual aid associations to protect workers in the event of sickness, unemployment, and also mutual insurance companies for work-related accidents.[19] Thanks to this system,

> [...] workers will go to less dangerous industries than dangerous ones, but in the latter wages will be higher than in the former. Workers who feel strong and dexterous will enter the service of the more dangerous industries while taking out mutual insurance against accidents (*op cit.*, p. 260; English transl., 2005, p. 228).

So Walras's reformist position appears quite moderate, even if he indicated that he would just accept, for insurance as for cooperation, all the compromises in practice, even the "initiation" by the State. Finally, on the insurance topic, he abruptly questions the French radical politicians: "We certainly want the social army to pick up its stragglers. Our only request is that it does not slow down its pace to theirs, so as to prevent there being only stragglers left before long" (*op cit.*).

14.6 On Some Means to Maintain and Increase the Income of Workers

How to operate in order to maintain or increase the income of workers? Walras does not accept the setting of a minimum individual wage, either by the State through legislative means or by "certain private organisations" using threats and violence,[20]

---

[19] See the *Cours d'économie sociale*, 10th lesson, "On Good and Justice. On the Three Principles of Relations between Men" (vol. XII, p. 152). In the newspaper *Le Travail*, Walras praised the *Sécurité générale*, a private insurance company against work accidents, located in Paris (1867d).

[20] *Éléments d'économie politique pure*, "Price Fixing and Monopoly", vol. VIII, pp. 657–58, English transl., 2014, p. 440; "L'économique appliquée et la défense des salaires" (1897c), vol. X, p. 261, English transl., 2005, p. 229. Regarding these "private organisations", in the 1st edition of *Éléments*,

which would constitute an obstacle to the free formation of the price of the labour service. In several works[21] dealing with the "defense of wages", he considers solutions which would make it possible to maintain or increase the income of workers and which concerns their individual initiative. Three means appear important to him: limitation of the increase of worker population, worker education, and the cooperatives' development.

First of all, Walras warns against the effects of an increase in the labour supply resulting from too fast an increase of the worker population compared to that of the available capital. An increase in population must be preceded by an increase of capital. In the *Éléments d'économie politique pure*, he indicates: "we shall not go so far as to infer from this that Malthus brought to light a fundamental point in pure economics" (vol VIII, 36th lesson, p. 594, English transl., 1954, p. 388).

From this, he gives the following advice to the workers:

> No increase in the quantity of labour by an unwise increase in the population. To marry and to have a family only when they are able to provide for their subsistence [...] especially the workers must be careful and reserved in matters of marriage and family. They must know, and one could not repeat this to them too often, that there is no society, nor government which can be committed to maintaining in ease as many children as a proletarian and his wife can have (*Cours d'économie politique appliquée*, 29th lesson, vol. XII, pp. 585–86).

Moreover, Léon Walras thinks that with good reason the workers tend to be very hostile to competition with women and children (1897c, vol. X, p. 259; English transl., 2005, p. 227). Indeed, men must themselves provide for the subsistence of their family without putting their wives to work, who must care for their households, nor their children, who must be educated.[22] Our economist notes that even if the equality between men and women should be required in the name of justice, it does not follow that it must be expressed in "the situation where men and women do the same manual work or have the same intellectual profession" (*op cit.*, p. 258; English transl., 2005, p. 227).

Secondly, Léon Walras underlines the necessity for workers' education for more efficient employment in enterprises. It is advisable to make the utility and productivity of labour higher by means of general and specialised training, at the same time. This double education would have the advantage of making it possible for workers to more easily overcome the difficulties related to machinery and to benefit from its

Walras specifies at this point: "in the manner of the *Molly Maguires*" (*op. cit.*, p. 657). He alludes here to the violent actions carried out in Pennsylvania (United States), during the 1870s, by groups of coal miners of Irish origin, the "Molly Maguires". Their actions served as a pretext for a fierce repression of mine workers.

[21] "Défense des salaires" (1879b), vol. X, pp. 481–84; *Cours d'économie politique appliquée*, 29th lesson (vol. XII, pp. 585–86); "L'économique appliquée et la défense des salaires" (1897c), vol. X, pp. 258–61, English transl., 2005, pp. 228–29.

[22] Walras's refusal to consider women at work in workshops is already expressed in youthful writings ("Du matérialisme et du spiritualisme en économie politique et sociale", 1863c, vol. XIII, pp. 202–03).

advantages. Therefore, Walras was in favour of general and professional instruction in the form of public and free courses organised by the State, as exists in England.[23]

Thirdly, Walras is in favour of cooperation (1897c, vol. X, p. 261, English transl., 2005, p. 229). Indeed, after his move to Lausanne, he never repudiated his commitment to the Parisian cooperative movement. At the end of the *Cours d'économie politique appliquée*,[24] he regularly dedicates lessons to "popular cooperative associations" and, in several articles, expresses his support for different forms of cooperation. However, he seems to have lost hope in the development of cooperation in crafts or industry. On the other hand, he foresees the possibility of a rise in cooperation in the countryside with the shift to intensive agriculture. In 1907, he observes that "cooperation, which has rather failed in the cities, has found in the countryside the moral qualities it requires".[25] Already in 1874, he remarked: "Would it not be advantageous to recommend, above all, cooperative associations, whatever it might prove necessary, as a means of reconciling the needs of small-scale properties with those of medium or large-scale farming?"[26] This is all the more evident when one considers the perspective of land repurchase by the State. Thus, Walras can assert: "Free association has transformed industry, commerce and credit. It would have transformed agriculture had the social question been solved", 1898c, vol. X, p. 431, English transl., 2005, p. 377). In a single text, the conference "Défense des salaires", our author nevertheless expressed hope on the side of consumer cooperatives. He indeed indicated: "Seek in cooperative association and particularly in consumer cooperative association all the resources it offers for the fructification of very small savings" (1879b, vol. X, p. 484).

This perspective allows us to confront Walras's point of view with that of Charles Gide, on two occasions.

First, in a speech at the Congress of Consumer Cooperative Companies of France, held in Lyon in September 1886, Charles Gide opposes the revolutionary socialists who refuse to see in cooperative association the means of emancipation of the working class as a class. He challenges them:

> If you want to tell me that cooperation will not have the power to seize at once the 30 million workers who exist in France and raise them as on a shield all at once and in a single surge, – no, undoubtedly, it does not have this virtue. And if there is someone here who possesses the necessary secret to execute this Herculean task, let them say it, I do not know it! And moreover, I do not wish to know it.

On his copy of the speech, in the margin of this passage, Walras responds to this challenge: "Well, reforms in social and legal conditions do that!" Further on, Gide,

---

23 29th lesson, "On the Relations of Labour and Capital", vol. XII, p. 586; "Défense des salaires" (1879b), vol. X, pp. 482 and 484.

24 See section XII, "Association and Insurance", but also the 29th lesson of the *Cours d'économie politique appliquée*, vol. XII, p. 586.

25 "La paix par la justice sociale et le libre-échange" (1907a), vol. VII, p. 500.

26 "De l'influence de la communication des marchés sur la situation des populations agricoles" (1874b), vol. X, p. 242, English transl., 2005, p. 213.

recalling that cooperation is the opposite of individualism and "supposes solidarity", Walras notes in margin: "association, it is individualism".[27]

Then, in a speech at the International Congress of Consumer Cooperative Companies, held in September 1888, Charles Gide considers that the cooperative association of production is powerless to change the existing social order. To effectively fight producer associations such as trusts, cartels, and unions, he relies on the development of consumer cooperative companies. These, open to all classes, should develop a programme of conquest in three stages, with a view to establishing the "Cooperative Republic": first commerce, then manufacturing production, and finally agriculture (C. Gide, 1889). Walras cannot support this programme.[28] He points out to Gide:

> [This theory] seems to me to clash too directly with two fundamental principles: that of division of labour and that of initiative through personal responsibility. It results, in fact, in placing all economic production, agricultural, industrial, commercial, in the hands of the Boards of Directors elected by the consumers-capitalists, members of your consumer cooperative companies. That would be a huge task for them. Administration by councils leaves much to be desired even in specialised enterprises. What would it be like in universal enterprises?[29]

14.7 Conclusion

In his *Cours d'économie politique appliquée*, with an optimistic tone, Léon Walras asserts:

> Let them constitute, as they do, their *chambres syndicales*, their *sociétés* and *caisses de résistance* and they will manage to have for themselves, thanks to association, the same finance as the employers, and even a higher finance. One could say without exaggeration that it would be them who are the strongest. Undoubtedly, they will never force the entrepreneurs to work with losses; but they will force them to cut down to the normal interest of their capital (vol. XII, 29th lesson, p. 584).

However, Walras's ideas on the working of the labour market, social conflicts, labour legislation, insurances, cooperatives and land reform intended to solve the "social question", place him in quite a particular position in the French debates during the second half of the XIXth century. His proposals could not find a positive echo, neither among socialists of any tendency, nor among supporters of State intervention in economic life, nor among liberal economists, from the most moderate to the most extreme.

---

[27] C. Gide, 1886, p. 12. Brochure preserved in the Lausanne collection under the reference F. W. XI, G1.

[28] On Walras and Gide on cooperation, see R. Baranzini and S. Swaton, 2017.

[29] L. Walras, letter to C. Gide, 13 November 1889, in: *Correspondence*, II, l. 937, p. 373. Walras will write two short articles for the *Gazette de Lausanne* (14 December 1897 and 10 January 1898) to announce the free course given at the University of Lausanne by Charles Gide, from January 1898, on "Cooperation (the ideal and the practice)". The manuscripts and proofs of the announcement of 10 January 1898 are kept in the Lausanne collection under the reference F. W., V b, box 23.

Chapter 15
Towards the Repurchase of Land by the State and the Abolition of Taxes

15.1 Introduction

Among some contemporary philosophers, sociologists, and political scientists, the theme of hybrid forms between liberalism and socialism is always fascinating. Several research attempts to trace back the sources of ideas related to social liberalism and liberal socialism were made from the XIXth to the XXth century.[1] We will focus on Léon Walras's specific case. In *History of Economic Analysis*, Joseph A. Schumpeter observes that

> [...] unfortunately, Walras himself attached as much importance to his questionable philosophies about social justice, his land-nationalization scheme, his projects of monetary management, and other things that have nothing to do with his superb achievement in pure theory. They have cost him the goodwill of many a competent critic, and must, I imagine, try the patience of many of his readers (1954, pp. 827–28).

Consequently, for Schumpeter, the two volumes of *Études* are not of much importance and he ultimately concludes by asserting that "Walras is best described as a semi-socialist" (*op. cit.*, p. 888).

Léon Walras proclaims himself a "liberal socialist" because, greatly influenced by his father and in disagreement with French economists of the liberal school, he wishes to scientifically solve the "social question". This question would not be related to the relationship between capital and labour, as socialists believe (*Cours d'économie politique appliquée*, vol. XII, p. 584). We will begin by briefly tracing the stages of his claim to "liberal socialism" and also to "scientific socialism", which dates back to 1863. It can be noted immediately that he is neither the first, nor the last to use the formula of "liberal socialism"[2] in France during the XIXth century. As early as 1863, in a text he failed to publish, he declares himself "scientifically absolutely

[1] See notably in France M. Canto-Sperber and N. Urbinati, 2003 and S. Audier, 2006.

[2] Indeed, François Huet declares himself a "liberal socialist" in *Le régime social du christianisme* (1853), then in *La science de l'Esprit. Principes généraux de philosophie pure et appliquée* (1864), initially, in a perspective of reconciliation between Christianity and socialism. He supports the right

J.-P. Potier, *Léon Walras, Economist and Liberal Socialist*, Springer Studies in the History of Economic Thought, https://doi.org/10.1007/978-3-032-04670-3_15

socialist" and "politically as deeply, and sincerely liberal".[3] In 1867, he obtained permission to deliver six public lectures in Paris, which he immediately published in the newspaper *Le Travail* and later compiled into a volume under the title *Recherche de l'idéal social.* In these lectures, he again claims "scientific and liberal socialism" (1867–68, vol. IX, p. 147, English transl., 2010, p. 110) and also defines himself as a "democratic socialist" (*op. cit.,* p. 125, English transl., p. 94). He insists greatly on his socialist stance "from the scientific point of view" (1863a, vol. IX, p. 22, English transl., 2010, p. 14) and he uses the expression "scientific socialism" until the end of his life, which is commonly attributed to Karl Marx and Friedrich Engels. However, Marx and Engels rarely use this formula and very late, in the 1870s–1880s.[4] As for Walras, he makes more frequent use of it. In a "note d'humeur", probably written during the 1870s, he goes so far as to write: "I am not an economist. I am a socialist. But I know political economy better than economists".[5]

Insofar as, we will see later, he proposes a synthesis between socialism and liberalism and between individualism and communism, he claims to designate his theory under the name of "synthetism" and sometimes "synthetic socialism".[6] Finally, in

to assistance by the State, the right to an inheritance. For example, patrimonial goods given by nature like land, should return to all workers after the death of the owners. See J. Cunliffe and G. Erreygers (1999). Furthermore, the philosopher Charles Renouvier (1815–1903) claims a "liberal socialism" based on State intervention (public assistance, progressive taxation...), with associations and cooperatives. The socialist Alfred Naquet (1834–1916) also supports State interventionism, social legislation, progressive taxation in *Socialisme collectiviste et socialisme libéral* (1900).

[3] "Socialisme et libéralisme. Lettres à M. à Edmond Scherer", text refused by the newspaper *Le Temps* in 1863 and published only in 1866 and 1867, in three parts, in the journal *Le Travail* (1863a, p. 19, English transl., 2010, p. 12).

[4] See on this subject J. Grandjonc, 1989, pp. 233–36 and 251–52.

[5] On this document from the pen of L. Walras, the word "socialiste" is very legible, without erasure. However, the librarian of Lausanne University, A. Reymond, who transcribed the "Notes d'humeur" in 1922–23, made a curious transcription error by reading here the word "architecte" (in pencil and not in pen, in a space initially left blank), which was to trigger a chain of errors. On the problem of interpreting this "note d'humeur", see D. A. Walker, 1999a, 1999b, P. Bridel, 1999 and J.-P. Potier, 1999a.

[6] This is the case in "Théorie de la propriété" (1896c, vol. IX, p. 206) and in "Le problème fiscal" (1896d, vol. IX, p. 401, English transl., 2010, pp. 158 and 329). Let us note that the "integral socialism", "collectivism in economic matters" of his friend Georges Renard (successor of Benoît Malon as a manager of the *Revue socialiste* between 1894 and 1898), which seeks both the development of individuality and solidarity, also aims to be "synthetic" and "scientific" (see G. Renard, 1888, part III, "Current Socialism in France"; see also 1894, pp. 514–16). Walras considers that, in his 1888 study, Renard has "nicely formulated the doctrine of the reconciliation of *individualism* and *communism,* in matters of *politics* and *economics*" (emphasis by L. W., "Méthode de conciliation ou de synthèse", note 1 for his publication in the *Études d'économie sociale,* vol. IX, p. 151, note 1, English transl., 2010, p. 114, note 1). His perspective remains distant from that of Walras, and Renard nevertheless acknowledges:

> [...] and nowadays, among those who claim for the ideal its legitimate share in social matters, how many names would I not have to mention: Léon Walras, my colleague and friend, whose conclusions I do not accept entirely, but whose precision and clarity of approach I admire [...]." (1897, p. 141)

1909, during the jubilee ceremony of his "Fiftieth Anniversary as an Economist" at Lausanne University, Walras declares that he has finally succeeded in constructing a "scientific, liberal, and human (*humanitaire*) socialism" (1909c, vol. VII, p. 511). Obviously, Walras's "scientific socialism" is not "of the Marxian variety, but of the *petit-bourgeois* stamp" (W. Jaffé, 1971, p. 273). We will therefore outline the content of this "singular socialism",[7] in this chapter and in the next.

15.2 Preliminary Remarks

In his writings, Léon Walras often reminds us that, from a theoretical and economic standpoint, solving the "social question" involves addressing two problems. On one hand, it is about making the production of social wealth "as abundant as possible", and on the other hand, it is about making the distribution of this social wealth among people "as equitable as possible". This approach raises the problem of concordance (or harmony) between the principle of interest (usefulness), or economic efficiency, and that of equity or social justice.

15.2.1 The Method of Conciliation or Synthesis at Work

According to our author, contrary to what economists of the liberal school think, the individual exists only within the framework of society, which in turn exists independently of individuals. The individual and the State (or community) represent two natural "ideal types (*types idéaux*)", absolutely "equal", each having their own rights.[8] Furthermore, alongside the strictly scientific approach used in pure economics, which involves starting from "real types" to derive "ideal types" that will serve for the deduction of theorems, Walras uses a "method of conciliation or synthesis" in the field of social economics. He claims it recalls the "syncretic method" employed in the XVIth century by Pico della Mirandola and John Bessarion and their friends to merge the doctrines of Plato and Aristotle (1868c, vol. IX, p. 152, English transl., 2010, p. 115 and "Exposition et conciliation des doctrines sociales", 1872c, vol. XIII, p. 248). It should not be confused with superficial eclecticism (which adopts "common sense" as a criterion), as it can be found in philosophers such as Victor Cousin or his follower Théodore Jouffroy (the young Walras claimed allegiance to

On Renard as director of the *Revue socialiste*, see M. Rebérioux, 1987 and E. Jousse, 2017, pp. 213–23; see also Y. Billard, 1998 and J. Wright, 2012, pp. 28–38.

[7] On the characteristics of this socialism, see notably P. Dockès, 1994 and 1996, R. Baranzini, 2001b, and M. Herland, 2013.

[8] On the individual and the State in Walras, see P. Dockès, 1996, R. Arena, 2014, J. Lallement, 2014 and 2017. In fact, on one side, there are individual persons (individual, family, association of all kinds, of private law) and on the other side, collective persons (municipalities, the State, of public law).

the latter, then distanced himself—*cf.* Chap. 3, *Taxonomy of Sciences and Divisions of "Political and Social Economy": An Attempt at Reconstruction*).

For Walras, the method of conciliation or synthesis, or "synthetic method", has no place in mathematical, physical sciences, or pure economics. It is necessary when faced with entirely opposing doctrines, a priori irreconcilable. It involves conducting a critical analysis to assess their strengths and weaknesses and then "rejecting the wrong parts of the doctrines and synthetizing the true parts" (1868c, vol. IX, p. 152, English transl., 2010, p. 115). This method is fruitful in philosophy and social ethics. In philosophy, this is the case with materialism and spiritualism, empiricism and idealism. In social ethics, it is the case with liberalism and socialism, individualism and communism.[9] In 1868, Walras thus asserts: *"We will reconcile socialism and liberalism by introducing the distinction between science and politics. We will show that, in regard to scientific truth, socialism is right, and, in regard to political truth, liberalism is right*" (emphasis by L. W., *op. cit.*, p. 154, English transl., 2010, p. 116).

Indeed, according to him:

- on the scientific level, socialism is right against liberalism by asserting the importance of the social question and attempting to find solutions; but it is wrong concerning the political solutions proposed, that are authoritarian;
- on the political level, liberalism is right against socialism by defending liberty against authoritarian solutions; but it is wrong on the scientific level by underestimating the importance of the social question.

Walras extends his argument by adding: *"we will reconcile communism and individualism by introducing the distinction between social conditions and personal positions*" (*op. cit.*, p. 154, English transl., 2010, p. 116). In a note placed at the beginning of the study "Méthode de conciliation ou de synthèse" on the occasion of its publication in the *Revue socialiste* in 1896, he indicates regarding this conciliation: "I must confess that I took a good deal of it from the old Saint-Simonians with whom I kept company when I was young" (*op. cit.*, p. 151, note 1, English transl., 2010, p. 114, note 1). He does not cite any names, but it can be noted that this conciliation is indeed present among the Saint-Simonians and particularly those who had to part with Enfantin in November 1831. This is notably the case of Pierre Leroux[10] who, since his famous article "Économie politique" (1834), seeks a synthesis between individualism and socialism.[11]

---

[9] Let us note that É. Vacherot had established a parallelism between the empiricism-idealism opposition and the individualism-communism opposition (1863, vol. 3, p. 400).

[10] See M. Herland, 2013, p. 107.

[11] Pierre Leroux rejects individualism and socialism in the absolute sense. In a note of 1847, he specifies: "we are socialist, if by socialism one means the Doctrine that will not sacrifice any of the terms of the formula: *Liberty, Fraternity, Equality, Unity*, but which will reconcile them all" (emphasis by P. L., 1850, vol. 1, p. 376).

15.2.2 *The Theory of Justice from Auguste to Léon Walras*

Concerning the distinction between "social conditions" and "individual positions", Léon Walras borrows from his father a theory of justice, more precisely a theory of property and taxation. It is a theory of natural law constructed from a critical analysis of Thomas Hobbes's philosophy. In *De Cive*, Hobbes defends the right to private property of land. He refers to two maxims. The first maxim, the oldest, is expressed as follows: "*natura dedit omnia omnibus*" (nature has given all things to all). It establishes a collective natural right: no individual can be excluded from the benefits provided by nature, but without resolving the question of equality or inequality among men. The second maxim is as follows: "*natura dedit unicuique jus in omnia*" (nature has given an equal right to all things to each of us). It establishes an individual natural right: each individual would have an unlimited right over all things of nature, which would indeed lead to the war of all against all. Relying on the critical reading of Hobbes by a disciple of Pufendorf, Jean-Jacques Burlamaqui, Auguste Walras believes that Hobbes's error lies in considering the two formulas as equivalent.[12] However, from the old, very vague maxim, it is necessary to specify the right of the individual and that of the State, thus the question of property and community. What is the argument used by Auguste Walras on this subject? Far from Turgot's statements, which based the right of property on general utility,[13] he explains:

> The land considered as a useful and limited object [...], or the cultivable soil, is obviously an indestructible and inconsumable thing, a permanent and perpetual thing by its nature. Man, on the contrary, considered as an individual, is an ephemeral person, a mortal being who has only a short time to spend here below. As such, the individual cannot own the land. According to me, there must be a certain proportion, a certain analogy between the object and the subject of right, which seems to me obviously overlooked in the establishment of individual land property.[14]

---

[12] A. Walras, *Réfutation de la doctrine de Hobbes, sur le droit naturel de l'individu* (1835), vol. I, pp. 284–85.

[13] According to Turgot,

> [...] one must go back to the first rights of humanity; the earth was given to all men; they are all sons of the same father and none has been disinherited. The division of lands is a necessary consequence of the nature of society; particular inclinations necessarily lead to it and it is the path that Providence had traced to establish in societies this inequality of wealth [...]". ("Sur la géographie politique—(*Fragment*)" (1753–54), in: G. Schelle (ed.), 1913, vol. 1, p. 439).

[14] A. Walras, "De l'abolition de l'impôt, et de l'établissement de la Loi agraire, telle qu'elle peut être conçue et pratiquée au 19e siècle" (1831a), vol. I, p. 9; see also A. Walras, "La vérité sociale par un travailleur" (1848), vol. II, p. 46. This last reference is used by L. Walras in: *Cours d'économie sociale*, 30th lesson ("Moral Theory of Property"), vol. XII, p. 235.

In short, for Auguste Walras, "the land has never belonged to the first occupant; the land has always belonged to the human species".[15]

Several times, Léon Walras summarises his theory of justice in a motto borrowed from his father: "*Equality of conditions in the State; inequality of positions for the individual*", or "*Liberty for the individual, authority of the State. Equality of conditions, inequality of positions*".[16] The "personal positions" agree that individualism is right, while the "social conditions" agree that communism is right and the point is the synthesis.

For Walras, each human being possesses his own natural wealth, that is to say, his personal faculties (his human capital). The inequality of personal positions originates, in principle, from the efforts and merits of each individual, and any intervention by the State to reduce it is contrary to justice. To respect the "inequality of positions" (distributive justice), personal faculties, the service of labour that results from them, and wages belong by natural law to the individual.[17] On the other hand, men must possess in common what nature has given to all, the natural resources. To respect the "equality of [social] conditions" (commutative justice), that is to say, equality of opportunity among individuals, lands, land services (*rente*) that results from them, and rent (*fermages*) belong by natural law to humanity. All individuals ought to benefit equally of the resources provided by this natural capital. Indeed, "*the land does not belong to all the people of one generation; it belongs to humanity, that is to say, to all human generations* [...]. *In legal terms, humanity is the owner, and the present generation is the usufructuary of the land*" ("Théorie de la propriété", 1896c, vol. IX, p. 189, English transl., 2010, p. 145). However, the legitimate representative of humanity can only be the State.

For Walras, "if society were a conventional and free fact, the individuals contracting to establish it could decide to share the land in equal parts among themselves" (*op. cit.*). However, for our author, the idea of a social contract (from Hobbes to Rousseau) is absurd. Quite the contrary, society is a "natural fact" and the system of private land property, both agricultural and urban, constitutes a permanent violation of natural law, which historically appeared at the agricultural stage of humanity. In other words, "leaving the land in the hands of the landowners means perpetuating in society the indefinite enrichment of a parasitic class; putting the land into the State's hands means having the community benefit from the results of social progress" ("Le problème fiscal", 1896d, vol. IX, p. 411, English transl., 2010, p. 337). Very faithful to his father's ideas, Léon Walras insists on the fact that land has an "intrinsic value". But he also indicates that it is generally possible to distinguish in the value of a plot

[15] A. Walras, "Examen critique et réfutation du Livre de Mr. Thiers sur la Propriété" (1849a), vol. II, p. 344.

[16] See for example, *L'économie politique et la justice* (1860a), pp. 172 and 179; *Recherche de l'idéal social* (1867–68), 6th lesson, vol. IX, p. 140, English transl., 2010, p. 105; "Exposition et conciliation des doctrines sociales" (1872c), vol. XIII, p. 316; *Cours d'économie sociale*, vol. XII, p. 216; "Esquisse d'une doctrine économique et sociale" (1898c), vol. X, p. 413, English transl., 2005, pp. 361–62.

[17] This idea related to "self-property" dates back to John Locke (*Second Treatise of Civil Government, 1690*).

of land the "intrinsic value" and the value of the invested capital, thus distinguishing in the gross income the ground rent and the interest.[18] He thus opposes John Stuart Mill, who denies the possibility of such a distinction. Indeed, during his reading of the *Principles of Political Economy*, he highlights the following passage:

> If the land derived its productive power wholly from nature and not at all from industry, or *if there were any means of discriminating what is derived from each source,* it not only would not necessary, but it would be the height of injustice to let the gift of nature be engrossed by individuals ([1848] 1965, vol. 1, Book II, chap. II, § 5, p. 227).

In the margin of the underlined words in this passage in the French translation, Walras notes "*il existe* (it exists)".[19]

Finally, Walras's position on self-ownership and land property has not lost its relevance today as it can be usefully confronted with the theories of justice developed by the "left-libertarians" (Hillel Steiner, Peter Vallentyne, Michael Otsuka).[20]

If the attribution of property rights of "personal faculties" and of land is done by virtue of natural law, what about the property rights of enterprises, means of production (machines…), the service of "profit" and interests? For Walras, there is no theory of natural law for this wealth that has been produced by men. Enterprises belong either to individuals, or to the State or local communities. We will return to this later. It can be noted that the application of "equality of conditions" will leave aside the question of the distribution of "artificial capital"(or capital proper).

15.3 The Repurchase of Land by the State: The First Social Question

The repurchase of land by the State constitutes for Walras the practical solution to the "social question", or what he would call from the 1880s, only the "first" social question.

15.3.1 Opposition to Private Land Property and Ground Rent

During the XIXth century, the question of land as a natural resource and ground rent as "unearned income" was discussed by many authors. In *Qu'est-ce que la propriété ?*, Pierre-Joseph Proudhon delivered a famous invective on this subject: "To whom is the

[18] *Cours d'économie sociale*, 31st and 60th lessons, vol. XII, pp. 240 and 376–380; "Le cadastre et l'impôt foncier" (1873b), vol. IX, pp. 384–88, English transl., 2010, pp. 315–18. See also P. Dockès, 1996, pp. 113–16.

[19] Walras's annotations on his copy of the translation (2nd ed., 1861) of J. S. Mill's *Principles* are published and commented on by V. Bourdeau, 2006, pp. 103–04. The copy is kept at the Centre d'études interdisciplinaires Walras-Pareto de l'Université de Lausanne (ZAB 3189).

[20] See on this subject V. Bourdeau, 2006 and especially J.-S. Gharbi and P. Sekerler-Richardi, 2010.

rent of the land due? To the producer of the land, undoubtedly. Who made the land? God. In that case, owner, withdraw" ([1840] 1966, p 131). Many social reformers, particularly in England, given the superiority of large land property, were bringing solutions which put into question the statute of land private property and of rent:

1. The taxation of the increase in ground rent arising from natural causes and not from improvements introduced by the owners to increase the land's productive power (James Mill and John Stuart Mill).[21]
2. The confiscation of the ground rent through a "single tax" on land (Henry George's solution presented in his book *Progress and Poverty*, 1879).
3. The purchase of some lands by the State at market price in order to rent them to poor tenants or to agricultural cooperatives (J. S. Mill, 1870, pp. 691–93).
4. The systematic repurchase of land by the State, that is to say the "nationalisation of the land".[22]

And, in this option, several solutions are possible:

- Auguste Walras, in some unpublished papers during his lifetime, "De l'abolition de l'impôt, et de l'établissement de la Loi agraire, telle qu'elle peut être conçue et pratiquée au 19e siècle" (1831a) and "Théorie de la propriété" (1849d),[23] promoted a progressive repurchase of land by the State. Each year, the State would spend a part of the public expenses for the purchase of land, or the State could create transfer taxes (*droits de mutation*), or inheritance taxes paid only in land. In the long run, public expenses should be financed by ground rent, all taxes being eliminated.[24]
- Jean-Hippolyte Colins de Ham (1783–1859), a Belgian socialist, author of *Du Pacte social et de la liberté politique considérée comme complément moral de*

---

[21] J. Mill, [1821] 1826, chap. IV, section V, pp. 339–41; J. S. Mill, [1848] 1965, book V, chap. II, § 5 to 7 and III, § 2, vol. 2, pp. 819–24 and 825–26. However, James Mill also stated:

> [...] if a body of people were to emigrate into a new country, and land had not yet become private property, there would be this reason for considering the rent of land as a source peculiarly adapted to supply the exigencies of the government; that industry would not, by that means, sustain the smallest repression; and that the expense of the government would be defrayed without imposing any burden upon any individual (*op. cit.*, p. 338).

A. Walras finds these reflections "perfectly just" ("La vérité sociale par un travailleur" (1848), vol. II, pp. 74–75) and will point them out to his son (9 September 1860, in: *Correspondence*, vol. IV, p. 444). L. Walras is interested in this "ingenious and bold hypothesis, which clearly places the subject in the domain of natural law" ("Théorie mathématique du prix des terres", 1881b, p. 230, English transl., 2010 revised, p. 180; see also *Cours d'économie sociale*, 52nd lesson, vol. XII, pp. 334–35).

[22] Let us recall that in the XIXth century, the word "nationalise" has two meanings. The old and general sense, which comes from the French Revolution, is: "render national", extend public property at the expense of the private sphere. The modern sense, which appears from the 1840s, is: expropriate the capitalists' means of production (see J.-P. Machelon, 1985). As we will see later, the "nationalisation of land" for Walras refers to the first sense.

[23] This text forms two unpublished chapters of the *Théorie de la richesse sociale* (1849c).

[24] On the repurchase of land by A. Walras, see A. Diemer, 2012, pp. 444–50.

l'homme (anonymously, 1833) and *Qu'est-ce que la science sociale ?* (1851–54), wishes that the State acquires the land gradually thanks to the impossibility of inheritance from collateral relatives. Then, the State will rent out the land to workers, in return for a ground rent. This solution would free workers from the wage-system and provide the State with the means to cover its current expenses.
- James Bronterre O'Brien, in a series of articles published in 1846 in *The National Reformer*, explains that land, created by God, was given to all; therefore, the State must become the landowner which it will lease, allowing it to finance its current expenses and abolish ordinary taxes.[25]
- Hermann Heinrich Gossen, in his book *Entwickelung der Gesetze des menschlichen Verkehrs, und der daraus fliessenden Regeln für menschliches Handeln* (1854, see English transl., 1983 and French transl., by Walras, 1879a, 1995), argues that land private property prevents the individual from choosing the most profitable place for his activity and exploiting it as efficiently as possible. He revisits a plan outlined as early as 1843, consisting of the State repurchasing and renting out the land to farmers, which would eventually allow it to eliminate all taxes. The justification for State property of land does not come from a natural law.
- Alfred Russel Wallace (1823–1913), an English naturalist and biologist, author of *Land Nationalization. Its Necessity and Its Aims* (1882) and promoter of the "Land Nationalization Society" sees in the collective nature of land the means to ensure free access to land for all and to solve the problem of unemployment and poverty; each citizen could choose a plot among the free lands provided they occupy and develop it.[26]

In the first editions of the "Théorie mathématique du prix des terres et de leur rachat par l'État" (1881b and 1883), Léon Walras claims that "no socialist" defends the thesis he himself holds from his father, according to which land should be collective and ground rent the State's income. But on the occasion of the reprinting of this article in the *Études d'économie sociale*, he places the following note here: "I can now mention several socialists who have supported the right of the community to own the land: Colins, Rodbertus-Jagetzow, Alfred-R. Wallace, Henry George" (vol. IX, p. 229, note 2, English transl., 2010, p. 179). This list is debatable, given the exact positions of some of these authors (H. George, for example). Concerning Colins and Wallace, Walras will be informed of their works by the articles of a Belgian economist, a proponent of "rational socialism", Agathon de Potter.[27]

---

[25] On O' Brien, see E. Escarra, 1904, pp. 148–50.

[26] On the land's nationalisation for Wallace, see "Examen de la nationalisation du sol de M. Alfred Wallace", *La philosophie de l'avenir. Revue du socialisme rationnel*, 9th year, no. 99, October 1883, pp. 112–37 and D. Collard, 2009, pp. 611–17.

[27] The correspondence between Potter and Walras has unfortunately not been found in the Lausanne archives. On Colins, see A. de Potter, "Un nouveau partisan de la collectivité du sol", *La philosophie de l'avenir. Revue du socialisme rationnel*, 9th year, no. 102, January 1884, re-ed. in: P. Bridel, 1996, p. 219. It is a review of the *Théorie mathématique de la richesse sociale.*

15.3.2 Léon Walras's Solution

Influenced by his father, Léon Walras supports the option of the nationalisation of land.[28] But how does he envisage the allocation of land to the State concretely? In 1880, inspired by Gossen's theory (whose work he discovered two years earlier), he constructs a "mathematical theory of the price of land and its repurchase by the State". As the private appropriation of land was done from the perspective of the law in force, there is no question of brutally expropriating the landowners. Walras therefore cannot subscribe to the first demand of the *Manifesto of the Communist Party* by Karl Marx and Friedrich Engels, "expropriation of property in land and application of all rents to public purposes" ([1848] 1976, p. 505). The State would gradually and systematically repurchase the land, not below, but at market price, beginning with the most profitable agricultural and urban areas. However, being unable to purchase "cash", it must issue interest-bearing bonds. It will therefore borrow massively, and the landowners will be compensated by means of these bonds issued at the current interest rate, knowing that the State borrows more cheaply than individuals. With this radical reform, the class of landowners disappears, and the State becomes the collective landowner. What will it do with the land? It will not manage the land itself by creating public farms. Rather, it will lease the agricultural and urban land, through long-term leases (15, 20 years or more) to the highest bidder. This operation consists in selling the land service (*service de la rente*) that result from it against agricultural and urban rents. Part of the land would be rented out to consumers (construction of dwellings, gardens…) in the city or the countryside. But the largest part of the land would be leased to entrepreneurs in agriculture (farmers) or agricultural cooperatives,[29] and to industrial and commercial entrepreneurs (1881b, vol. IX, p. 304, English transl., 2005, p. 243).

In XIXth-century France, small-scale farming, with confusion in the same person between the landowner and the farming entrepreneur, predominated.[30] According to Walras, the repurchase of land by the State would allow the transition from extensive to intensive farming, using technical progress in large-scale farms,[31] hence the convergence of economic efficiency rules with the principles of social justice. Curiously, in his study "The Nationalisation of the Land" (1872), Marx uses the same efficiency argument to justify land nationalisation: large-scale farming using modern improvements ([1872] 1988 p. 132). To a French politician who would remind him of the attachment of French peasants to their property, Walras would observe:

---

[28] This expression appears in L. Walras's works. See for example, "Le problème fiscal" (1896d), vol. IX, p. 407, English transl., 2010, p. 334 and "Esquisse d'une doctrine économique et sociale" (1898c), vol. X, p. 422, English transl., 2005, p. 369.

[29] As we saw at the end of the previous chapter, Walras places his hopes in the rise of cooperation in agriculture.

[30] L. Walras laments that the sale of national assets during the Revolution was a missed opportunity to return the lands to the State (see *infra* Chap. 17, *Towards a Political Reform? Universal Suffrage and Professional Representation of Interests*).

[31] This preference for large-scale farming is reminiscent of physiocratic theses.

> I will grant you without any difficulty that peasants have an innate taste for landed property and that this property is for those who enjoy it a salutary stimulus, especially with the circumstance of the notable increase in value for ground rent in a progressive society. But the question is whether these advantages do not go against the rights of workers in public services, liberal professions, industry, commerce, even those in agriculture who are not owners.[32]

Indeed, for a certain number of years, agricultural rents and urban leases would not suffice to pay the interest on the bonds given to the former owners, and the State's debt would increase. In response to the objection, Walras refers to the new situation of agriculture with humanity's transition to the "industrial and commercial regime":

> [...] agriculture has to be undertaken with a very large investment of capital in order to nourish a much more numerous population. I believe that this evolution, which has as a consequence a further increase of rent without an increase in the rareté or value of agricultural products [...] has not yet been taken into account by the landowners. I believe, therefore, that if the State would buy up the land before this evolution just mentioned [...], it would amply find in the further increase [of rent] the means of amortizing the purchase price.[33]

The State would thus find itself in the position of a speculator on the rising price of land.[34] In a "progressive society", the price of land increases as well as land services and ground rents, and these increases will even accelerate over time.[35] At the same time, with the abundance of capital, the interest rate should decrease over time,[36] and thus the State would carry out successive conversions of the bonds. Walras hopes here that the Stock exchange accepts the bonds' State without problems ("La paix par la justice sociale et le libre-échange", 1907a, vol. VII, p. 500). Thanks to the increase in ground and urban rent, and thanks to the decrease in the interest rate, the amortisation of public debt would become effective in the long run.

In fact, Walras believes that once the debt is paid off, the amount of ground rent alone would allow for the financing of both current and investment expenses. The State would then have its own income, and it would become possible to eliminate

---

[32] L. Walras, letter to J.-B. Bienvenu-Martin, 17 May 1908, in: *Correspondence*, III, l. 1688, p. 359.

[33] "Un économiste inconnu: Hermann Heinrich Gossen" (1885a), vol. IX, p. 325, English transl., 2010, modified by us, p. 261. For Walras, "by a system of legislation and administration", the State could provoke or accelerate "economic progress", namely the increase of capital and population" (*op. cit.*, p. 305). Knut Wicksell (1898—see *infra*), a neo-Malthusian, could not accept State intervention to increase the population. See P. Dockès, 2004, p. 225.

[34] Walras notes on this subject:

> [...] it is one of the favourite methods of American billionaires to build railways by speculating on the increased value of adjacent lands. I find the profit they make thus excessive for individuals; but I would find it normal and legitimate if it were made by the State reconstituting its territorial wealth [...]. (letter to Paul Pic, 2 April 1902, in: *Correspondence*, III, l. 1525, p. 202).

[35] Walras indicates that rent increases can be set by arbitrators ("La paix par la justice sociale et le libre-échange", 1907a, vol. VII, p. 498).

[36] It should be noted that this double effect is already present in Auguste Walras. See, for example, *Théorie de la richesse sociale* (1849c), pp. 153–57.

all taxes on income and capital, thus achieving the "economic reconstruction of the State". At this stage, "social interest and social justice will then fully be satisfied, the social ideal will be realised" (1881b, vol. IX, p. 305, English transl., 2010 revised, p. 243).[37] Did Walras say anything about the duration of the process of land repurchase until its completion? Indeed, in 1909, during the jubilee ceremony, he spoke of "one hundred, one hundred fifty, or two hundred years",[38] further adding that Switzerland, rich in hydraulic and electric power, "could easily repurchase the land with the price of white coal (*houille blanche*)" (1909c, vol. VII, p. 514).[39] He was very sure of his convictions regarding the realisation of the social ideal. He declared even to Charles Gide: "I will only say to you, as far as I am concerned, that if I greatly love demonstration by reasoning, I also attach the greatest importance to confirmation by history."[40]

Can this evolution only be peaceful? Walras seems to admit as much in his various texts that discuss the question. But, in a passage of the "Théorie mathématique du prix des terres et de leur rachat par l'État", he observes:

> History teaches us that essential and radical changes in the organisation of society have almost never been achieved in an orderly and peaceful fashion [...]. Serfdom did not disappear, and the feudal society did not give up its place to the modern society, except through a violent revolution. It seems, more and more, that it would be the same with the transformation of individual land property into collective property, for, far from thinking of letting the State have possession of all the land anywhere, it is, more and more, everywhere deprived of the part of rent that have [*sic*] been reserved for it by a land tax.[41]

Concerning taxation now, we can recall that, for Walras, all systems of taxation are unjust, because the individuals do not benefit from public expenses in direct or increasing proportion to their income or capital. In fact, they all benefit equally from the public spending as members of society.[42] The worker, living exclusively from his

---

[37] In fact, we find here an old idea of Jean Bodin (*Les Six livres de la République*, Book I, chap. 1 and Book 6, chap. 2) and of J.-J. Rousseau (*Discours sur l'économie politique*), according to which the State must get its own income through its land fund.

[38] In a letter to Louise Renard dated 18 June 1906, Walras speaks of a

> [...] human (*humanitaire*) socialism which leads through the repurchase of land to the abolition of taxes, and through the abolition of taxes to absolute free trade, and to universal peace (of course, to be achieved only after a new period of several centuries)" (*Correspondence*, III, l. 1623, p. 301).

[39] See also the "Notes for 'Ruchonnet et le socialisme scientifique'" (1908a), vol. XIII, p. 651. In Switzerland, the "Frei-Land" (Free Land) association, led by H. George's disciples, had been advocating from the 1890s for the nationalisation of hydraulic forces (see M. Gitermann, 1910).

[40] L. Walras, letter to C. Gide, 29 December 1886, in: *Correspondence*, II, l. 759, p. 171.

[41] "Théorie mathématique du prix des terres et de leur rachat par l'État" (1881b), vol. IX, p. 305, English transl., 2010, p. 242. In his review of the *Études d'économie sociale*, A. de Potter quotes this passage to note that the appropriation of land could not be done in a peaceful manner ("Un nouveau partisan de la collectivité du sol", re-ed. in: P. Bridel, 1996, p. 222).

[42] "Note sur l'impôt progressif" (1876c), p. 479, "Le problème fiscal" (1896d), vol. IX, pp. 398–401; see also *Recherche de l'idéal social* (1867–68), 6th lesson, vol. IX, p. 141 *et seq.*, English transl.,

work, suffers the tax on wages and is prevented from saving, thus from becoming partially capitalist; he is reduced to the status of proletarian, which is almost equivalent to that of a serf or slave. Walras therefore rejects the principle of proportional or progressive taxation of income. However, while waiting for the land repurchase to be implemented or during the transitional period, Walras suggests a solution to avoid the intrusion of the State into the sphere of private interests: "An indirect tax on rent (*loyer*), or, rather, a direct tax on income evaluated according to rent received,[43] this would be the only tax that could pass as approximately proportional or progressive[44] without enormous material and moral disadvantages" (1896d, vol. IX, p. 410, English transl., 2010, p. 336).

But the only tax that finds favour in his eyes is that on ground rents, a position he defended in his youthful writings, in his communication to the congress on taxation in Lausanne (1860) and in his *Théorie critique de l'impôt* (1861e). Why? Because the principle of the land tax can be interpreted as a co-ownership of the State on the land (net, that is to say, after deduction of the capital associated with it). As long as the land repurchase cannot be realised, Walras accepts the land tax, by means of a percentage, the State would share the increase in value of ground rent with the landowners.[45] However, it is necessary beforehand to have a well-organised cadastre (land registry).

Through his teaching at the Law Faculty in Lausanne, Walras acknowledges not having succeeded in convincing the majority of his students about the advantages of land nationalisation, but he believes that some of them have rallied to it and "have remained supporters of the nationalisation of railways".[46] However, let us note that he convinced his colleague and friend, the philosopher Charles Secrétan (1815–1895).[47]

In fact, Walras does not realise that the trend of Western economies during the XIXth century contradicted his predictions. Certainly, he is not unaware of the decline in ground rents during the Great Depression (1873–95). Indeed, in 1885, he acknowledges the existence of "the present crisis of the world-wide levelling-out of ground rent" (which rises in America and falls in Europe), brought about by the development of transport means and the interconnection of markets, but for him, this crisis is only

2010, pp. 327–29 and 105 *et seq.* Walras rejects both the "benefit principle" and the "ability-to-pay principle".

[43] In France, from 1887 (Albert Dauphin project), parliamentary proposals for income tax based on "external signs", notably the amount of rent for housing, appear.

[44] This is the only text in which Walras accepts progressive taxation to relieve poor taxpayers (1896d, p. 402). Note that the Canton of Vaud is the first country to adopt progressive taxation from 1887. Jules Ferry then asks Walras to provide him with a 'dossier' or a bibliography on this subject (letter to L. Walras, 19 July 1887, in: *Correspondence*, II, l. 804, p. 216). The latter will send him official reports and press articles.

[45] "Le cadastre et l'impôt foncier" (1873b), vol. IX, pp. 378–87; "Le problème fiscal" (1896d), vol. IX, p. 413, English transl., 2010, pp. 311–18; "Esquisse d'une doctrine économique et sociale" (1898c), vol. X, pp. 424–25, English transl., 2005, pp. 371–72, "La paix par la justice sociale et le libre-échange" (1907a), vol. VII, pp. 495–96.

[46] L. Walras, letter to J.-B. Bienvenu-Martin, 17 May 1908, in: *Correspondence*, III, l. 1688, p. 360.

[47] "La question sociale, par Ch. Secrétan" (1886b), vol. IX, p. 207, note 1, English transl., 2010, p. 160, note 1. See on this subject C. Gide (1917).

conjunctural and in no way invalidates his theory: the new increase in value of rent that characterises the "industrial and commercial regime" will indeed occur after this agricultural crisis ("Un économiste inconnu, Hermann-Henri Gossen", 1885, p. 325, note 1, English transl., 2010, p. 261, note 1).[48]

15.3.3 Criticisms of the Walrasian Plan

The "plan" of Walras will be subject to criticism by several economists. We will examine the opinions of Charles Gide, Charles Rist, Knut Wicksell and Vilfredo Pareto.

Charles Gide, a Walras friend and a theorist of cooperation, expressed himself on several occasions regarding his plan. In 1883, in the article "De quelques nouvelles doctrines sur la propriété foncière (*Progress and Poverty*, by Henry George)", published in the *Journal des économistes*, he discusses the projects of taxing rent and nationalising land. First of all, he admits the Walrasian presupposition:

> The progressive increase in value of land is one of those propositions that reasoning *a priori* suffices to establish, in the absence of any observation of facts. A country cannot populate and enrich itself without the land becoming both more useful and rarer, and consequently acquiring a more considerable value (1883, p. 177).

Further on, he argues that in the Walras project, the State would never be able to balance the income from ground rents and the interest charges in the future and would have to borrow again or create new taxes. In addition, depending to climatic variations, reductions in rents would be asked of the State and democratic governments would have to yield.[49] Let us note that three pages earlier, Gide proposed to the socialists a solution he considers more economical for public finance:

> The State would propose to the owners to buy their lands *payable in cash and to be delivered after 99 years*. Or if one wishes to present this operation from another perspective, the State would propose to each owner to exchange his perpetual property title for a concession valid for 99 years, in return for compensation to be agreed amicably. There is every reason to believe that there are hardly any owners who would not consent to this deal, even at the price of very minimal compensation, for as a duration of 99 years is equivalent for each of us to perpetuity, the price received by the owner would be equivalent to a real gift and he would have no reason to be demanding. Assuming that the total value of land property in France is 100 billion, I imagine that under these conditions the State would not be obliged to disburse more than one billion to become the owner[50] or rather to ensure property to the society that

[48] See also his letters to C. Gide of 26 April 1885 and to the editor-in-chief of the *Journal des économistes* (G. de Molinari) of 29 April 1885, in: *Correspondence*, II, l. 646 and 647, pp. 43–45).

[49] About this argument, on the offprint of Gide's article (p. 25 [193]), Walras writes in the margin at this point: "perhaps, indeed, but what does that prove in matter of *Science*?" (emphasis by L. W., Lausanne collection, offprint kept under the reference F. W. XI, G1).

[50] On the offprint of Gide's article (p. 22 [190]), Walras notes in the margin: "Why spend a billion if you can have them for nothing by means of the surplus value, *which must result from the operation itself* ?" (emphasis by L. W.).

will live at the end of the XXth century. Indeed, 100 billion payable in 99 years is presently worth, according to annuity tables, 798 500 000 francs" (emphasis by C. G., 1883, p. 190, note 1).

The author then notes that collectivists could not rally to such a programme, as "it would postpone to a somewhat too distant deadline the realisation of their hopes".[51] He adds that one could reproach this project for "immorality", as it speculates on the improvidence of fathers stripping their descendants. Returning to the Walrasian project, Gide does not recommend attempting the experiment in France where there is an "army of agricultural landowners". He suggests rather trying it in England and also in the "new countries"[52] (United States, Canada, Australia, South America...) and in the colonies (Algeria) with grants of new land (Gide, 1883, pp. 95–97). The State could replace the system of perpetual concessions to immigrants with a system of temporary concessions, with a "concession price (*prix de ferme*)" determined by auction, allowing it to deriving an "incalculable" profit given the increase in value of land in new countries. At the end of his article, however, he points out a danger that would arise if a State succeeded in buying back the land, the enormous financial resources at government's disposal: "will it know how to make the best use of them?" (1883, p. 198).

In his "Notes d'humeur",[53] Walras expresses his dissatisfaction with the form of Gide's article:

> The theory of Gossen and of myself being the subject of the second part of this article, the title of my paper (which is only found in a note) should have been prominently displayed alongside the title of George's book. Then, since Gide largely appropriated my theory (he fully accepts it for new countries, that is to say, fully in principle), he should not have taken a mocking tone (vol. XIII, p. 539).

On the content, he will discuss Gide's arguments in his article "Le problème fiscal". First of all, he discusses Gide's proposal, reiterated by the author in similar terms in his *Principes d'économie politique* (5th ed., 1896). The cost of the project seems very expensive to him, amounting not to 798 million, but rather to about 8 billion francs (with an interest rate of 2.66% and not 5%, used by Gide). Walras considers his own plan more economical, because "the State repays its loans and pays for the land with the proceeds of the new increase of value", a surplus value made possible by the transformation of agriculture and a series of reforms concerning administration and economic policy. Even if Gide's plan is amendable and modifiable for application, it seems to him "materially a little expensive, and morally much too cheap" (1896d, p. 415, English transl., 2010, p. 341). Walras then discusses the recommendation of the experiment in new countries only. According to him, the experiment should concern old countries, which are not necessarily in decline, and in which owners are allowed to get richer and proletarians to get poorer. Moreover, as we have already

[51] On the offprint of Gide's article (p. 22 [190]), Walras notes in the margin at this point: "why these taunts addressed to people whose idea is going to be taken?".

[52] On the offprint of Gide's article (p. 27 [195]), at this point, Walras annotates: "ah! ah!".

[53] On the offprint of Gide's article (p. 30 [198]), Walras writes: "is it not much better to let the State live by begging and theft?".

seen in Chap. 2 (*From the theory of five stages to the "industrial and commercial regime"*), for Walras, the establishment of the "industrial and commercial regime" requires solving the social question and thus the establishment of this social reform (1896d, p. 416, English transl., 2010, p. 341).

Later, in his review of the *Études d'économie sociale* (1897), Charles Gide ironically notes that the solution given by Walras to the social question "seems to be the one that would be expected from a mathematical economist" (1897, p. 304). In reality, with his plan, the social question is not resolved "for the people". While Karl Marx directs his attacks against the capitalist, the latter "emerges unscathed from Mr. Walras's plan". Certainly, with the repurchase of land and natural monopolies, a brake can be put on great fortunes and "a sort of *aurea mediocritas* will be achieved for all" (1897, p. 305). Moreover, Gide declares himself unsatisfied with the elimination of taxes. First of all, on a moral level, it is detrimental to social solidarity, because for many people, the tax is the "only act of altruism" performed during their life. Then, in all countries, public expenses are far superior to the income that the State could derive from rent,[54] "even assuming expropriation is done without compensation, *a fortiori* if it is assumed to be done by fully reimbursing the price of the land" (1897, p. 306). Ultimately, the repurchase of the land will be done without compensation or not at all.

In 1909, the *Histoire des doctrines économiques depuis les physiocrates jusqu'à nos jours* by Charles Gide and Charles Rist was published. The latter was entrusted with writing the chapter on "the theory of rent and its applications". The "land nationalisation systems" seem utopian to him, because "such profound upheavals of land property are only possible in old countries at revolutionary times" (1909, p. 653). However, Rist presents the "most remarkable" systems of Gossen and Walras in a very balanced manner (1909, pp. 655–58). Walras is satisfied this time, as in his letter to Charles Gide on 29 October 1909, he indicates: "Your two chapters on the *Hedonists* and the *Theory of Rent* seem to me a justification of the 'land nationalisation' to which it will be difficult to resist" (*Correspondence*, III, l. 1775, pp. 436–37).

For his part, in his review of the *Études d'économie sociale*, written at the request of Eugen Böhm-Bawerk for the *Jahrbücher fur Nationalökonomie und Statistik*, Knut Wicksell also expresses serious doubts about the feasibility of the repurchase of land by the State project. According to him, land incomes depend on the gross yield of land (which cannot increase indefinitely), but above all on the density of the population and its concentration in cities. Should the State, therefore, to increase its land income, encourage these latter factors? Wicksell doubts that Walras, "too Malthusian", could really subscribe to such a perspective. In fact, even with a lower density and a better spatial distribution of the population, one could witness a decrease in land incomes in the long run (1898, p. 173). Moreover, the trend towards the gradual decline of

[54] Walras rejects this argument by stating that "the total amount of ground rent normally corresponds to the requirements of public services *when appropriately equipped*" (emphasis by L. W., "Esquisse d'une doctrine économique et sociale", 1898c, vol. X, p. 423, English transl., 2005, p. 370, a passage reprinted later in "La paix par la justice sociale et le libre-échange").

the interest rate envisaged by Walras risks being counteracted, given the weight of the State's issuance of bonds. Finally, his plan has the disadvantage of strengthening the consumption potential of the owner classes to the detriment of the workers who, in this social reform, have no role to play (1898, pp. 173–74).

Finally, in *Les systèmes socialistes* (1902–03), Vilfredo Pareto, through his criticism of land nationalization theories, implicitly targets Walras. According to him, there is no basis for asserting that the price of land would always rise. And, in the hypothesis where the State succeeds to become the single landowner, it would need to withstand collective pressure from all the tenants, because "*one cannot imagine how a government existing on the basis of universal suffrage could resist a vote by all of the farmers and tenants asking for a general reduction of ground rent*" (Pareto, 1903, vol. II, p. 311). So, we find again an objection from Charles Gide. Furthermore, the elimination of taxes is a utopian project, as the needs of the State are "infinite; the more they are satisfied, the more there are to be satisfied" (*op. cit.*, pp. 311–12).

Chapter 16
Public Services and Natural Monopolies: What Role for the State?

16.1 Introduction

For Léon Walras, the question of the "principle" of free competition, its applications, and its "exceptions" falls within the sphere of applied economics. He never claimed to have systematically clarified the areas where free competition should be the rule and the areas where it could not function. In a manuscript, he states on this subject:

> Even in my course at Lausanne University, I have not completely drawn the line of demarcation between collectivism and individualism in applied economics. Even more so, I have not done so in the works gathered under the title of *Études d'économie politique appliquée.* However, among these *Études*, one will find some that are apt to clearly establish the principles of the subject.[1]

He thus alludes to some works among which is his study on railways.

During the first two years of the *Cours d'économie politique appliquée* at the Faculty of Law in Lausanne, in 1870–71 and 1872–73, the professor did not dedicate a specific lesson to the areas where free competition could not function in his view. In 1874–75, he introduced for the first time a lesson entitled "Exceptions to the Free Competition Principle".[2] From 1878, and with a view to publishing the *Éléments d'économie politique appliquée*, he wished to remove it and create instead a new section of the course entirely devoted to the question of "Exceptions to the Free Competition Principle".[3] The main material would be provided by the study "L'État et les chemins de fer" (1875a) which the *Journal des économistes* refused to publish; however, the effective integration of this section was delayed until 1881, due to difficulties encountered in retrieving the manuscript lent to Jules Ferry. The author

[1] "Résumé d'une doctrine économique et sociale" (excerpt from the manuscript), in: vol. X, note 59, p. 506.

[2] This lesson, preserved in the course manuscript, is published in the appendix to section II (vol. XII, pp. 514–18).

[3] See Chap. 9.

J.-P. Potier, *Léon Walras, Economist and Liberal Socialist*, Springer Studies in the History of Economic Thought, https://doi.org/10.1007/978-3-032-04670-3_16

managed to have it published in 1897, in the *Revue du droit public et de la science politique*.[4] It can be said that the concern for "exceptions" is felt by Walras during the period of constructing the first edition of the *Éléments d'économie politique pure* (1874–77) and grew in the following decade.[5]

In 1881, Walras thus created a new section II of the *Cours* entirely devoted to the "Exceptions to the Free Competition Principle", comprising eight lessons, their material being provided almost exclusively by the study "L'État et les chemins de fer". Probably around the mid-1880s, he modified the text of the 29th lesson of the *Cours d'économie politique appliquée* ("On the Relations of Labour and Capital"). In the first draft of this lesson, during the 1870s, the "social question" on a practical (and not theoretical) level was placed exclusively in the field of "social economics" (with the proposal for the State to repurchase the land). In the new draft, the social question is placed partly in the field of social economics and partly in the field of applied economics: on the one hand, the State should repurchase the land and on the other hand, the great monopolies of mines, railways, issuing banks, etc., should be ended (see vol. XII, pp. 584–85 and note 35 p. 883). Subsequently, our author will always defend this vision of two social questions on a practical level.

For Walras, free competition is "generally possible" in terms of products and services of private interest which concern individuals aiming to satisfy their "personal positions", that is to say, the satisfaction of their individual wants. The principle of free competition should be understood as a principle of social interest, a *rule* allowing to achieve "within certain limits, the maximum utility". In certain situations, it cannot be applied and in the 22nd lesson of the *Éléments d'économie politique pure* (vol. VIII, pp. 335–36, English transl., 2014, pp. 249–50), Walras highlights the following three cases:

– When one is dealing with goods of social or public utility.

---

[4] The publication of the article (with an additional note and a brief bibliography of Walras) owes much to Léon Duguit, the leader of the "École du service public".

[5] At the end of the series of lessons "Exposition et conciliation des doctrines sociales" (1872c), in a passage borrowed from the study "Méthode de conciliation ou de synthèse" (1868c), not published at the time and whose original manuscript seems to have disappeared, Walras explains:

> [...] the solution to the social question is, if not entirely, at least for a good part, if not concerning production, at least regarding the distribution of social wealth among people in society, in the economic reconstitution of the State.

In this context, he sees the necessity of placing the lands in the hands of the State and does not refer to monopolies, just as in the 6th lesson of the *Recherche de l'idéal social* (1867–68, vol. IX, pp. 143–44, English transl., 2010, p. 107). However, for the publication of "Méthode de conciliation ou de synthèse" in 1896 in *Revue socialiste*, the following passage seems to have been added to the text: "we have allowed monopolies to be formed that are citadels from which capital exerts tyranny and despoliation on industry and credit". A dozen lines further, the passage cited above becomes: "From the economic point of view, the solution of the social question lies therefore in the reconstitution of the State, with respect to both the production and the distribution of social wealth among people of the society". (vol. IX, p. 172, English transl., 2010, p. 130). Most of these corrections appear on the manuscript of the "Exposition et conciliation des doctrines sociales", but they are undoubtedly much later.

- When competition cannot be *indefinite*. Free competition indeed supposes *free entry and free exit*, "the possibility of the flow of entrepreneurs towards enterprises where profits (*bénéfices*) are made and the turning away from enterprises in which entrepreneurs are making losses". The extreme case is the existence of *a natural and necessary monopoly*.
- Finally, it does not apply in matters of property because "free competition by highlighting the question of utility, leaves the question of justice completely aside".

16.2 Different "Exceptions" to Free Competition

In the *Cours d'économie politique appliquée* (vol. XII, p. 488), Walras notes that "artificial" monopolies can be created under the responsibility of the State (for example, a fiscal monopoly, such as that of tobacco) or under the protection of the State through compromises between the political and the business worlds. These monopolies are not exceptions to the free competition principle, but to its reality. It would therefore suffice to eliminate those distortions. On the other hand, there are situations of "moral monopoly" (public services) and situations of "natural and necessary monopolies". Let us recall the role that the State must play, according to our author.[6]

16.2.1 Moral Monopolies

The State must provide "services and products of public interest" which have a collective utility. These are sovereign functions, such as administration, maintaining public order (justice and police), national defence, public education (secondary and higher), the stimulation of sciences and arts, as well as the building of infrastructure works and means of communication.[7] The activities mentioned here are considered as "moral monopolies", because they are founded on natural law. And in this area, Walras will oppose the economists of the liberal school, such as Charles Dunoyer and Frédéric Bastiat, who are in favour of the privatisation of public services. Why are they "moral monopolies"?

- Firstly, because public services correspond to the satisfaction of identical and equal collective needs for all individuals. They therefore fall under the State, whose mission is to prepare the environment for the fulfilment of human destinies by establishing "general social conditions".

[6] See also on this question, P. Dockès, 1996, p. 195 *et seq*; J-P. Potier, 1998, pp. 387–89 and 1999, pp. 65–67; A. Béraud, 2011.

[7] Among the sovereign functions of the State, Walras adds that of "moderator" of the general price level by acting on the quantity of money (see his project of "gold money with regulating silver token"). On this question, see R. Baranzini, 2005.

- Secondly, because the utility of public services cannot be correctly perceived "in its entirety" by individuals (our author thus mentions the problem of the "free rider"). Conversely, the utility of public services can be "more or less judiciously" perceived by the State, and therefore these needs are perceived by "men as members of the community or the State". Walras indicates in this regard:

> One may quite well conceive the State as a consumer calculating the amount of services and products of exterior and interior security, justice, education, communication, etc., that it could consume if need be; comparing intensities of utility of units of both the same and different commodities; deciding how to spend its income to obtain the greatest possible effective utility, after evaluating the costs; and, finally, demanding a certain amount of services and products. Here ends the similarity, however. In general, there will only be a single consumer/demander for each service or product of public interest, the State (1875a, vol. X, p. 187, English transl., 2005, p. 164).

- But according to Walras, there are also goods and services whose social utility exceeds the utilities felt by individuals: today we would speak of externalities. A civil or criminal judgment does not simply serve the victim, but it also serves society as a whole. Similarly,

> […] the Museum of the Louvre contributes to the maintenance of the superiority of French art from which results the superiority of our luxury goods industries, thank to which France is sure to pay its imports by its exports ("The Fiscal Problem", 1896d, vol. IX, p. 399, English transl., 2010, p. 328).

Public services must be provided free of charge insofar as they are strictly collective needs. On the other hand, when enjoyment is partially unequal, when the aspect of "seeking a personal position" (thus the satisfaction of personal wants) is added to the aspect of "social conditions", gratuity is no longer at all evident.

16.2.2 Natural and Necessary Monopolies

Furthermore, the State must intervene in the case of certain "services and products of private interest" that have the character of "economic monopolies", more precisely "natural and necessary monopolies".[8] Walras indicates here:

> In the interests of society, and excluding exceptions founded on natural law, the *State* should undertake the production of *services or products or private interest that are not open to indefinite competition* at cost price, or should concede this production under a monopoly on its behalf to the lowest bidder on the selling price (emphasis by L. W., "L'économique

[8] It seems that John Stuart Mill is the first author to mention the question of natural monopolies. For him, "natural monopolies" or "practical monopolies" concern activities benefiting from economies of scale and which cannot be completely left to private initiative: gas lighting, water distribution, but also railways. J. S. Mill wishes for municipalities to take charge of the operation of gas and water (just like the "paving and cleaning of streets") and that the State, owner of the railway lines, cedes their operation under control to private companies (see J. S. Mill, [1848] 1965, vol. 1, book 1, chap. IX, § 3 and book 2, chap. XV, § 3, pp. 141–42 and 405, vol. 2, book 5, chap. XI, § 11, pp. 955–56).

appliquée et la défense des salaires", 1897c, vol. X, p. 248, English transl., 2005, revised by us, p. 218).

The State intervention is justified here by the "social interest", the economic efficiency. Walras refers to the exploitative quarries, mines, mineral water springs, gas,[9] but also to postal services.[10] Later, he will add to this list the "white coal (*houille blanche*)", that is to say, electricity produced by hydraulic power. These activities, described as "natural and necessary monopolies", are characterised by the existence of high fixed costs constituting a barrier to entry into the branch and by the presence of increasing returns to scale. The mechanism of inflow or outflow of entrepreneurs making profits or losses cannot persist sustainably. A municipality could not authorise an indefinite number of companies to lay water pipes in the streets. If there are several companies, the cut-throat competition between them would lead to their gradual elimination and a private monopoly itself would be established. The monopolist then charges a selling price higher than the cost in productive services achieving a "maximum profit (*bénéfice maximum*)" and uses a discriminatory price scale to the detriment of consumers. We will see later the possible modalities of State intervention in this area.

16.2.3 The Railways' Case

Finally, the State must intervene in activities pertaining to both "moral monopolies" (public services) and "economic monopolies" ("natural and necessary"): these are the means of communication: canals and railways.

Walras was particularly interested in the railways question, having worked at the *secrétariat* of the Compagnie du chemin de fer du Nord, between April 1862 and April 1865. He follows the recurring debates in France,[11] under the Second Empire, then under the Third Republic with the question of the legitimacy of the State's purchase of certain heavily indebted companies.[12] He does not share the view of the liberal economists, advocates of the construction and operation of railways

[9] Concerning water and gas, Walras quotes the *Principles* of J. S. Mill, in book 1, chap. IX ("L'État et les chemins de fer" (1875a, vol. X, pp. 197–98, English transl., 2005, p. 173). He had planned in the *Cours d'économie politique appliquée* a lesson "On the Monopoly of Mines and Mineral Waters", which he never wrote (see vol. XII, p. 513).

[10] *Cours d'économie politique appliquée*, former lesson "Exceptions to the Principle of Free Competition", vol. XII, p. 517; "L'économique appliquée et la défense des salaires" (1897c), vol. X, p. 249, English transl., 2005, p. 219.

[11] In France, the law of 11 June 1842, or "railway charter", establishes the initial legal framework wherein the State is responsible for the infrastructure (line layout, earthworks, engineering structures, stations...), while the private concessionary companies are responsible for the superstructures (track laying, rolling stock...). Alongside the six major companies (Nord, Est, Ouest, P.L.M., Midi, Orléans), there will exist a number of secondary and local interest companies.

[12] In 1878, from bankrupt companies in the South-West of the Loire, a small State network will be formed and later, in 1908, the State will repurchase the Ouest company.

by private companies. In his study "L'État et les chemins de fer", Walras uses the article "Chemins de fer" (1852), written by Michel Chevalier for the *Dictionnaire de l'économie politique* edited by Coquelin and Guillaumin. He describes Chevalier's entry as "still remarkable in many respects", although unfortunately the author unjustifiably rejects State intervention in railways' activities.[13] It should not be forgotten that Michel Chevalier was the technical advisor to the railway company founded by his friends, the Pereire brothers, and that he was always officially consulted by governments of the Second Empire on issues of operation and extension of railway networks.[14]

In "L'État et les chemins de fer" and in the *Cours d'économie politique appliquée*, Walras even very strongly opposes the defenders of private railway concession companies in France:

> Who could be cajoled into believing that nepotism and favouritism are unknown here? Who is unaware that their administration and operation is mediocre and mean-spirited? They underpay their employees, treat the public as an exploitable resource, stick to the highest rates even when it would certainly be in their interests to reduce them—in short, stingy and indifferent, they merely cream off a fruitful monopoly. At least they make a profit, it may be said! (1875a, vol. X, p. 212, English transl., 2005, p. 184; see also vol. XII, p. 511).[15]

According to Walras, railways represent both a "natural and necessary monopoly" and a "moral monopoly". Railway transport first provides a "service of private interest" (passengers and freight transport). Railway transport then offers a "service of public interest" with national defence and police, but also the transportation of participants to scientific conferences and industrial or artistic exhibitions (travellers "in society's interest"), as well as the distribution of the national press throughout the country.[16] Walras insists on this problem: "Indeed, one must be doubly blindfolded by the narrowest individualism and utilitarianism to deny that, irrespective of services rendered by the transport of goods, communication also serves another purpose, namely national unity." (1875a, vol. X, p. 196, English transl., 2005, p. 172). Moreover, it is essential to distinguish the question of the railway network from that of locomotion to show that, in both cases, we have a natural monopoly.

For the railway network, Léon Walras relies on the existence of increasing returns to scale and of barriers to entry, arguments that are still used today:

- the existence of multiple networks represents a waste of resources; a single track can serve the same movement of commodities and passengers as several tracks;

---

[13] "L'État et les chemins de fer" (1875a), vol. X, pp. 18–185, English transl., 2005, pp. 161–63. It should be noted, however, that M. Chevalier later changed his position on this subject. Indeed, in "Des moyens pour un État de refaire ses finances. La liberté du travail", published in *Journal des économistes* (1875, p. 30), he now explains that in most countries, private industry needs financing and interest guarantees from the State to ensure the costly communication works, such as railways.

[14] He participated, for example, in 1863, in the drafting of a voluminous "Enquête sur l'exploitation et la construction des chemins de fer", at the request of the Minister of Public Works.

[15] For a comparison between the views of L. Walras and W. S. Jevons, who writes at the same time on railways, see P. Sekerler-Richiardi, 2013.

[16] Once, Walras speaks in this regard of "mixed services", in "Le problème fiscal" (1896d), p. 400, note 1, English transl., 2010, p. 328, note 1).

- companies require public authority to expropriate land, and the State cannot allow an indefinite number of companies to expropriate.

However, concerning transportation, a difference exists between roads and canals on one hand, and railways on the other. Indeed, while roads and canals constitute natural monopolies, the traction that occurs there is the work of an indefinite number of operators. This is not the case with railways. Here, it is not possible to allow an indefinite number of operating companies to run on the track. And if only a few are allowed, the march towards monopoly will be found through the ruin of some for the benefit of one. According to Walras,

> It was at first thought that the liberty to use the tracks for the various entrepreneurs in the transport sector would be feasible, just as on roads and canals. It was soon realised, however, that on one hand entrepreneurs specializing in railway transport should license the track and therefore receive *toll* or rent. On the other hand, at the same time they should be receivers of *freight*, payment for the use of their engines and rolling stock (emphasis by L. W., 1875a, vol. X, p. 193, English transl., 2005, p. 169).

Walras is undoubtedly one of the first economists to be interested, on a theoretical level, in the distinction between network (infrastructure) and transportation, but he believes that in practice the two questions are not distinct from each other.

16.3 How to Organise Monopolies?

For Walras, concerning the "natural and necessary monopolies" on one hand, and railways on the other, the State would have the choice between several possible forms of organisation[17]:

- A private company is in charge of the monopoly with the authorisation or under supervision of the State.
- A private company holding a concession from the State, allotted after a bidding procedure: either by underbidding (*au rabais*) on the tariffs charged to customers, or by outbidding (*à l'enchère*) on the rent (*fermage*) to be paid to the State (1875a, vol. X, p. 213, English transl., 2005, p. 185; vol. XII, p. 512). In this case, the concessionary company must comply with a very precise specification drawn up by the State, indicating, for example, the maxima tariffs to be applied.
- A private company (or some companies) becomes "nationalised" and the exercise of the monopoly is ensured either directly by the State (through a *régie*—a public authority), or through a public company.[18]

[17] On these different solutions, see also "Esquisse d'une doctrine économique et sociale" (1898c), vol. X, pp. 427–28, English transl., 2005, pp. 373–74.

[18] This third option had already been considered by Auguste Walras: "the railways could well be executed by the State and, if so, the incomes from these new communication means would naturally fall into the coffers of the Public Treasury" ("Théorie de la propriété" (1849d), vol. II, p.183; see also "Examen critique et réfutation du Livre de Mr. Thiers sur la Propriété" (1849a), *op. cit.*, p. 231).

What are our author's preferences in this matter? Walras is not in favour of the first solution, as State supervision risks being ineffective. The second solution seems particularly appropriate to him for both natural monopolies and for railways. The third solution, consisting of the State's repurchase of mines, energy sources, railways, represents for him in 1875 a possible option (1875a, vol. X, pp. 213–14, English transl., 2005, pp. 185–86; vol. XII, p. 512). However, later in the years 1896–98, he considers this solution from a more favourable light,[19] given his openness towards "collectivism" (*cf. infra*).[20] Certainly, some authors might condemn nationalisations based on a critique of the public service. Walras's response here is scathing: "There where political minds are well formed, the press free and critical, public functions appropriately performed, magistrates incorruptible and brave officers, well-informed administrators and skilful engineers often do very important and extensive work for very modest remuneration" (*op. cit.*, p. 212, English transl., 2005, modified by us, p. 183).[21]

After a long critique of the pricing practices of railway concessionary companies in France, Walras believes that, as a general rule, the State should ensure that the equality between the selling price and the cost in productive services is respected as much as possible by the companies in charge of the monopoly. But in the case of railways, two different but advantageous modes are to be considered. Indeed:

> [...] the State could manage its monopoly in two quite distinct ways. It could regard the various lines as mutually independent and not intervene in their construction or working before they appeared ready to cover their costs. When a line began to yield regular profits it could then reduce its rates. Alternatively, the State could consider all the lines together

[19] See a note added in the *Études d'économie sociale* to the study "Théorie mathématique du prix des terres et de leur rachat par l'État" (1881b), vol. IX, p. 305 note 1, English transl., 2010, p. 243, note 1. In the supplementary "Note" to "L'État et les chemins de fer" (1897b), Walras proposes the repurchase of the six major railway companies and their operation, either by the State itself or by companies with concessions, followed by the creation of a network (p. 216, English transl., 2005, p. 187).

[20] For the anecdote, one of his mentors, Étienne Vacherot, in *La démocratie*, considers that for reasons of public utility the State should own mines and railways (1860, pp. 265 and 322–24).

[21] Walras' concerns deserve to be compared with those of Jules Dupuit, whose remarks are reported as follows during a session of the Société d'économie politique de Paris, held on 5 December 1861:

> [...] one has already been forced to revise several times concessions that were supposed to be secular, and hardly revised, new complaints arise sometimes for one thing, sometimes for another. The companies are monitored, controlled by an army of officials, so that it is permissible to ask whether an industry, which can only operate under such conditions, would not be better placed in the hands of the State. Mr Dupuit does not see what economic principle could be invoked against this solution which has been adopted in a neighbouring country [*Belgium*]. The large railway companies are small States, they have all the disadvantages: do they have all the advantages? It seems that there is in the State a better organisation, better controlled by the press and the public. (*Journal des économistes*, vol. 33, 2nd series, no. 23, January 1862, p. 134, re-ed. in: J. Dupuit, 2009, vol. I, p. 585).

According to Dupuit, the railways constitute a natural monopoly and the State can do better than the great companies: he demonstrated it with the postal service. For a comparison of Walras and Dupuit's analyses, see G. Numa, 2012 and 2013, pp. 163–83.

> as a single network, and rather than reducing the rates of the lines first built, it might build and run other lines at first unprofitable. Profits made by the former lines might serve to cover losses suffered by the latter; it would be enough for profits and losses to balance [...]. Anyway, operation will take place at cost price in some sense, both in the second and in the first mode. In the first mode, transport would be somewhat lower in price and completion of the railway network would be rather slower in the country in question. In the second mode, transport would be more expensive but completion of the network much quicker". (1875a, vol. X, pp. 208–09, English transl., 2005, p. 181; see also vol. XII, pp. 507–08).

Walras adds that if railways are considered as primarily providing a private service, the first method must be adopted, whereas if railways are considered primarily a public service, one should turn to the second method. But if one wants to accelerate the construction of the railway network, which generates externalities (here Walras notes the opening of markets and the stimulation of production that will result), one can imagine that "on all lines, the price of maximum profit would decrease constantly".[22]

16.4 The Sole Entrepreneur: Mimicking Competition

From the 1890s onwards, Walras becomes increasingly concerned with the multiplication of trusts and producer syndicates in Europe and the United States.[23] To the French jurist Henry Babled,[24] who questions him about his ideas on agreements and monopolies and the possible existence of anti-trust legislation in Switzerland, he replies that it is "perfectly demonstrated that free competition, in many cases, has a natural tendency to lead to monopolies", which justifies the intervention of the State and of the law (regulations).[25] On two copies preserved in the Lausanne collection of the *Études d'économie politique appliquée*, at the beginning of the second part (paragraphs 4 to 6) of the study "La Bourse, la spéculation et l'agiotage" (1880b), he indicates, no doubt with a view to a future second edition, "to say a word about the abuse of industrial and financial monopolies in one of these last three paragraphs"; moreover, in the margin of the passage of the "Esquisse d'une doctrine économique et sociale" dealing with the question, he advocates for the "regulation of industrial and financial monopolies".[26] Unfortunately, he never specifies what he means by this: is it a question of sanctioning cartels and/or vertical concentration operations?

---

[22] Concerning the railways, Jean-Jacques Laffont (1993) considers that Walras provided "the foundations of the French doctrine of public services, whose limits were only understood belatedly".

[23] See for example L. Walras, letter to A.-L. Lachenal, 23 December 1901, in: *Correspondence*, III, l. 1511, p. 185.

[24] Henry Babled is going to defend in Paris a Ph.D. thesis in law entitled *Les syndicats de producteurs et détenteurs de marchandises au double point de vue économique et pénal* (Paris: Arthur Rousseau, 1892).

[25] L. Walras, letter to H. Blabed, 7 February 1892, in: *Correspondence*, II, l. 1042, p. 478.

[26] See *Études d'économie politique appliquée*, 1898d, note 8, p. 497 and note 63, p. 507.

He does not explicitly comment on the American anti-trust legislation (the Sherman Act of 1890).[27]

In fact, since the first edition of the *Éléments d'économie politique pure*, Walras expressed the idea that monopolies were blameworthy in terms of economic efficiency and justice. The entrepreneur in a monopoly situation can make maximum profit by maintaining a margin between the selling price and the cost in productive services and discriminating selling prices. Is it possible for consumers to escape this scourge?

In the 4th edition of the *Eléments* (vol. VIII, 18th lesson, p. 284, English transl., 1954, p. 225), Walras explains that a "sole entrepreneur" (*entrepreneur unique*) can, just like so many entrepreneurs, reach production equilibrium *by mimicking competitive behaviour*, buying the services by outbidding and selling the products by underbidding and changing his production according to losses or profits. This behaviour is not possible for a sole private entrepreneur. Indeed, why would a private entrepreneur reduce his profits by increasing his production? Not out of fear of the entry of competitors, because for Walras, if there is a monopoly, it is because entry is impossible, either naturally or artificially. However, in the case of the collective entrepreneur, when a company is not only owned by the State but is managed, for example, in the form of a State company (a *régie*), it should operate *as in competition*, therefore with the outbidding and underbidding mechanism, varying its supply according to profits and losses aiming for zero profit insofar as the interest of individuals is targeted. It could just as well aim for the State income's maximisation, an expression of socialised interests.

However, the collective entrepreneur is neither the only nor the best solution. Allotting contracts to private agents allows to force, by introducing competition, the adjudicative company either to offer the lowest tariffs or to give up the highest rent (*fermage*) to the State. Thus, we find a fundamental choice between the interests of the individuals (solution 1) and the interests of society, i. e. of the State which represents it (solution 2).

In the years 1895–98, Walras reads Marx, takes an interest in Marxism, and carries out a critical reading of "Marxist collectivism".[28] However, he does not intend to

[27] He does not seem tempted by research on this question, although he had at his disposal, for example, the American institutional economist Richard T. Ely's book, *Monopolies and Trusts* (1900) sent by the author, which presented numerous classifications relating to monopolies. See the letter of R. T. Ely, 3 October and Walras's answer, 20 October 1901, in: *Correspondence*, III, l. 1497 and 1499, pp. 165–66 and 168.

[28] On an agenda, L. Walras notes on 23 October 1895 that he "has read Marx", without specifying the book (Antonelli collection of Montpellier, ANT 2715, Ms 8, fasc. 1/1). It is probably the French translation of Book I of *Capital*, which he would have then borrowed from a Lausanne library. Indeed, it was only on 9 December 1895 that this book was sent to him from Paris by the *Revue socialiste* (undoubtedly the J. Roy translation reissued by Oriol in 1884), as revealed by an unpublished letter of Valéry Hermay, administrative secretary of the *Revue socialiste* to L. Walras on 22 April 1896 (Lausanne collection, F. W., II, 9). Unfortunately, this copy has not been found in Walras's personal library (unlike Books II and III of *Capital*, Paris: Giard & Brière, 1900 and 1901–02). In the "Théorie de la propriété" (1896c, vol. IX, p. 197, note 1, English transl., 2010, p. 151, note 3), about "Marxist collectivism", Walras provides three bibliographical references (Marx is not

proceed in the manner of orthodox economists of the liberal school who think that "collectivism must be and remain absolutely impracticable" and who amuse themselves by "supposing the establishment of a universal direction of public subsistence, forming a special ministry and sitting in a monument in Paris, from where, through a vast system of call and reply tubes, it spread through the whole of France".[29] In reality, collectivism is possible, but under certain conditions, as we shall see. Along the way, our author rejects Marx's theory of value presented with a misinterpretation ("labour alone has value" and the value of commodities is "the value of quantities of labour they contain") and asserts that it leads to considering interests and ground rents as "extortions" committed to the detriment of workers.[30] A Marxist government that would want to eliminate these "extortions" would retain only the value of labour. Such a system makes it impossible to equalise supply and demand and to set the price of certain products, which would even have to be abandoned, such as bottles of Château-Laffitte or Château-Margaux! In his "Théorie de la propriété", Walras also observes:

> How, in the Marxist system, can the State as sole entrepreneur know beforehand which products should be placed on the list and which should be eliminated? To settle this point, it requires not only the elements of supply, which can be calculated if necessary, but also the elements of demand, which are to be found in the needs of the consumers, who cannot communicate them to the State for the reason that they may change from one moment to another. This uncertainty about the relation between supply and demand once production has taken place is not a problem in the system of the determination of prices in markets, because it has then only to be left to price variations to equilibrate supply and demand (1896c, vol. IX, p. 200, English transl., 2010, p. 153).

But if collectivists accept to take into account the different productive services and the equilibration of the economic system by the rise and fall of prices (outbidding and underbidding), then a possibility of agreement with them would become possible. For Walras, one can therefore imagine that all enterprises become collective; a State "sole entrepreneur" for the entire economy, a generalised collectivism seems conceivable to him.[31] In "L'économique appliquée et la défense des salaires", he will explain that.

> […] all enterprises could possibly be supposed collective, but they cannot all be supposed private. Collective production (*collectivisme de la production*) is materially possible[32] and

mentioned): an article by Karl Kautsky, "La répartition des produits dans l'État socialiste" (*Revue socialiste*, vol. IV, no. 19, July 1886), Georges Renard's book, *Études sur la France contemporaine* (Paris: A. Savine, 1888) part III on "Current Socialism in France" (probably referring to chapter IX, "The Future Society according to Collectivism", pp. 226–47) and an article by Émile Vandervelde, "Le collectivisme" (*La question sociale*, January–February 1896).

[29] A page removed by Walras from the manuscript of the "Théorie de la propriété" (1896c), vol. IX, p. 471.

[30] About this erroneous interpretation of the Marxian theory of value, see P. Dockès, 1996, p. 193 and vol. IX, p. 448, note 14.

[31] For this question, see P. Dockès, 1994 and 1996 (chap. 4) and R. Baranzini, 2001b.

[32] On the manuscript of this article, L. Walras had initially written: "the collectivism of production is perhaps the formula of the future. There is nothing contrary […]." (vol X, p. 481, note 18).

> would not, in itself, be contradictory to liberty, equality, order and justice. It is just a simple matter of social utility (1897c, vol. X, p. 251, English transl., 2005, p. 221).

At the end of the "Théorie de la propriété", he goes even further by stating: "I would not at all dislike declaring myself a collectivist, both in matters of production and *in matters of distribution of wealth*" (emphasis by us, 1896c, vol. IX, p. 206, English transl., 2010, p. 158).

If today many activities fall within the competence of the individuals and are subject to indefinite competition, what will happen tomorrow? Are not some, or even "perhaps all of them", destined to become collective monopolies due to progress of all kinds? Walras even proposes that an "important experiment" be organised to determine which activities would be more efficiently managed by the State-entrepreneur or by private agents. In sectors where industrial dynamism is important, private initiative would prevail, while in sectors where regularity and fidelity to tradition are important, State initiative would prevail. There should be no bias in this matter and "if there should really be such a bias then we should not adhere to exclusive individualism" (1897c, vol. X, p. 251, English transl., 2005, p. 221). But Walras will not return later to this "collectivist" perspective.

16.5 Conclusion

According to Walras, land property and "natural" or "artificial" monopolies represent a "feudalism", which explains, for example, in the United States, the "sources of the enormous fortunes of multimillionaires formed in a few years" ("Théorie de la propriété", 1896c, vol. IX, p. 205, English transl., 2010, p. 157). The resolution of these two social questions necessarily falls to collective initiative. ("Esquisse d'une doctrine économique et sociale", 1898c, vol. X, pp. 425–28, English transl., 2005, pp. 372–74). On their order of priority, Walras once encountered an objection from a supporter of the State's repurchase of land, Jean Converset,[33] who submitted a series of questions to him, "but would not it be advantageous to repurchase these monopolies before the land?" Unfortunately, Converset would not receive a response on this specific point.[34] A comprehensive plan would be necessary for the implementation of these reforms, and Walras had wished for the establishment of an association that would conduct a preliminary study, publishing a regular bulletin, but without success.[35]

---

[33] Jean Converset (1862–1924) is a commander of the French army, George's friend, son of Léon Walras.

[34] J. Converset, letter to L. Walras, 24 May 1909, in: *Correspondence*, III, l. 1749, p. 415. Neither the first (unpublished) response of Walras on 27 May 1909 (Lausanne collection, F. W., block I, box 2), nor the second response on 8 December 1909 mention this point (*op. cit.*, l. 1779, p. 441).

[35] L. Walras, letters to C.-E. Wickersheimer, 7 February 1897, in: *Correspondence*, II, l. 1295, p. 725 and letter to J. Converset, 8 December 1909, in: *Correspondence*, III, l. 1779, p. 441.

Chapter 17
Towards a Political Reform? Universal Suffrage and Professional Representation of Interests

17.1 Introduction

Of the four questions of "social science", Léon Walras claims to have tried to outline the industry and property problems, leaving to other researchers the task of constructing the theories of family and of government,[1] the latter referring to a science of politics, of rational government. But for him, the transition from the ideal to the real, the realisation of the Social Ideal falls within the realm of practice and politics. The scientist does not have to concern himself with it. Politicians must take charge of economic and social reforms, such as the "economic restoration of the State", which cannot be imposed authoritatively and must be implemented gradually, slowly, and patiently. Indeed,

> [...] the role of the statesman is to set a certain society on its way towards this ideal indicated by the scientist. The statesman must place himself at the point of view of the relative and seek compromises between the exigencies of science and the circumstances where he happens to be.[2]

In other words, "*reforms* must be made and not *revolutions*" and "every reform, before being carried out *politically*, must have been prepared and matured *scientifically*".[3] "Empirical" politics should therefore give way to "rational" politics.[4]

Already, the Revolution of 1789 had offered numerous examples of "empirical" politics. Walras regrets in the idealistic revolutionaries (apart from a few, such as

---

[1] "Esquisse d'une doctrine économique et sociale" (1898c), vol. X, p. 433, English transl., 2005, p. 378.

[2] *Op. cit.*, p. 410, English transl., 2005, p. 359. On this question, see P. Dockès, 1996, pp. 226–32.

[3] Emphasis by L. W., letter to Louise Renard, 25 October 1905, in: *Correspondence*, III, l. 1602, p. 280.

[4] L. Walras uses a picturesque expression on this subject: "we have to consult the sky and the compass; they [*the politicians*] have to be at the helm and direct the operation; in this way the ship will certainly advance in the direction of the port" ("Méthode de conciliation ou de synthèse", 1868c, vol. IX, p. 173, English transl., 2010, p. 131).

J.-P. Potier, *Léon Walras, Economist and Liberal Socialist*, Springer Studies in the History of Economic Thought, https://doi.org/10.1007/978-3-032-04670-3_17

Mirabeau), Constituants, Girondins, Montagnards, "the exclusive consideration of principles and the complete disregard for facts" (*Cours d'économie sociale*, 14th lesson, vol. XII, p. 169), visible notably in the "Declaration of the Rights of Man and of the Citizen" and in the successive constitutions which ignored traditions and circumstances.[5] He repeatedly highlights a major error that marks the French Revolution:

> Unfortunately, in relieving the feudal aristocracy of public functions, the land, the income from which had been payment for those functions, was, by negligence, not taken from them. There was an occasion to avoid this error, when the Revolution succeeded in taking over the possessions of the Crown, the Church, and the emigrated nobles. Unfortunately, there was a failure to retain them; the lands were sold for far less than their true worth. Because of this, existing as we are between a social order that has fallen apart and another that has yet to be reconstructed, we find that we are confronted with the social question ("Théorie de la propriété", 1896c, vol. IX, p. 191, English transl., 2010, p. 146).

According to Walras, the sale of national properties (*biens nationaux*) is a missed opportunity for the "economic restoration" of the French State with grave consequences.[6] Here is his indictment, as presented in the "Esquisse d'une doctrine économique et sociale":

> The sale of the *biens nationaux*, in particular, was a mistake whose repercussions are still felt nowadays. It created a privileged class, becoming conservative in consequence, on which Bonaparte leaned to put the throne and the altar back on their feet. Upon Bonaparte's fall this class was already strong enough to impose upon those of the *ancien régime* who came back the dubious and precarious transaction of a billion in compensation. Three times since the people of Paris have tried to retake and continue the '89 movement, always with insufficient preparation and by the violent and awkward means of revolution. Three times the above-mentioned class have stepped in to stop these people. In 1830 the moneyed bourgeoisie filched victory for them. In addition, in 1848 universal suffrage for landed farmers stole even their political freedom (1898c, vol. X, p. 436, English transl., 2005, p. 380).

In this chapter, we will focus on Léon Walras's viewpoint on the political system in France during the XIXth century, a country where, according to him, "official social science and empirical politics"[7] are unfortunately practised. Let us recall that throughout his life, he never supported a specific political party. He also observes: "I profess in politics the same scepticism as the politician in science. I do not believe in any party," adding further: "in politics, I am of the *honest* and *moderate* party (emphasis by L. W., "Notes d'humeur", 2000, vol. XIII, p. 514).

---

[5] Reference is made here to local and temporary circumstances. See also P. Dockès, 1996, pp. 161–63.

[6] He will advise Georges Renard's nephew, Georges Weulersse, to devote his Ph.D. thesis to the "history of the sale of the *biens nationaux*" (letter to G. Weulersse, 2 October 1897, in: *Correspondence*, II, l. 1327, p. 758).

[7] Walras deliberately refrained from publicly commenting on the Swiss political system. However, on certain occasions, he praises a country in which a "rational policy" is possible and where the two social questions can be resolved (see for example, "Notes for 'Ruchonnet et le socialism scientifique'", 1908a, vol. XIII, p. 651 and "Ruchonnet et le socialism scientifique", 1909c, vol. VII, p. 514).

Liberal in politics,[8] Walras nevertheless evolved over the course of his life concerning the question of the exercise of universal suffrage. Indeed, since his youth until the late 1870s, he was unreservedly in favour of the exercise of direct universal suffrage. But with the instability that characterises the Third Republic's governments, he loses confidence in this type of parliamentary democracy. He then wishes for a reform of the exercise of universal suffrage aimed at establishing a system of professional representation of interests. But is this an effective means to transition from an "empirical" policy to a "rational" policy capable of successfully implementing the social reforms desired by Walras?

17.2 Direct Universal Suffrage: Hopes and Lost Illusions

The defence of direct universal suffrage by Walras is attested in his writings between 1858 and 1879, thus during a period extending from the Second Empire to the early years of the Third Republic.[9] Our author obviously owes much to the views of his father, a convinced liberal and republican, on the Revolution of 1789 and the revolutions of 1830 and 1848.[10] Indeed, Auguste Walras joyfully witnesses the fall of the July Monarchy and later, from March 1848, he is a member of the "Association républicaine de Caen" and participates in the "Club des travailleurs", in which he wishes to give free lessons to workers.[11] The following year, the reaction forces him out of his position as an academy inspector in this city. In 1848, Léon Walras is only fourteen years old, but he already understands the political stakes of the revolution. Forty-eight years later, he will indicate: "I was then one of those young people whose heads and hearts the February Revolution had united in a movement upon which the *coup d'État* of December 1851 brutally fell".[12]

In the Preface of his novel *Francis Sauveur*, Léon Walras recalls the hopes raised by the Revolution of 1848 and attributes to it the emergence of a "principle that has become necessary and indispensable, but nevertheless now sacred, the *universal suffrage*". He adds shortly after:

> Nevertheless, however weak and powerless, and however justly engulfed the revolution of 1848 may have been, it deserves from us more regard than the mere respect owed to the dead, since from it, and it alone, we have inherited as a sacred legacy, the universal suffrage (1858b, p. IX).

---

[8] Walras firmly aligns himself with the "school of *liberal democracy*" (emphasis by L. W., "Le socialisme scientifique. Observations", 1868a, vol. VI, p. 269).

[9] However, it should be noted that Walras reserves the right to vote for men (see his vehement critique of women's suffrage in the "Notes d'humeur", 2000, vol. XIII, p. 612).

[10] On this question, see J. Lallement, 1990.

[11] See J.-M. Servet, 1997, pp. 13 and 15 and P.-H. Goutte, 2013, p. 52.

[12] L. Walras, letter to Juliette Adam, 9 December 1896, in: *Correspondence*, II, l. 1280, p. 711.

Further on, he observes: "No revolution can give to the people the equivalent of what it will cost them in blood and tears. Let those who are concerned with the future prepare for it through science and art" (*op. cit.*, p. XXXI).

Léon Walras appreciates Étienne Vacherot's book published in November 1859, *La Démocratie*, one of the "republican breviaries" under the Second Empire.[13] The author, who refused to swear allegiance to the power resulting from the *coup d'État* of 2 December 1851, notably declares: "there is an ideal type of perfection, a society, a State, a model government, by which every society, every State, every government must be judged and appreciated […]. Democracy is the only *true* form of politics" (emphasis by E. V., 1860, p. 2). Despite the reactions that slow the movement, modern European societies are inevitably moving towards democracy and civil and political liberties, through various, violent, or peaceful, paths. And democracy requires the application of direct universal suffrage (1860, pp. 19 and 353–55).

Walras, who participates with friends in discussion evenings on this book, wishes to devote an article to it in the *Journal des économistes*, particularly dealing with the "economic conditions of democracy"[14] and he even meets the author.[15] He will be shocked by the author's condemnation of the imperial regime. Indeed, on 6 January 1860, this book was the subject of a decision by the Paris correctional court. He was accused of attacking the imperial government, announcing the forthcoming advent in France and Europe of a democratic government, radically incompatible with monarchy, aristocracy, and the Catholic religion. The author was sentenced to one year in prison and a fine of 1000 F; the seized copies of the book were destroyed. On 29 February 1860, the Paris correctional chamber reduced Vacherot's prison sentence to three months.[16]

We have seen that, in the years 1865–68, Walras saw in the cooperative movement a school of democracy. He then considered that

> […] all members of a cooperative society, like those of a democratic society, must be regarded as strictly equal in rights within society, and that each of them, regardless of the amount of their share in the social fund, must have one vote, and only one, in the general assemblies.[17]

---

[13] See P.-H. Goutte, 2013, p. 52. L. Walras annotates his personal copy, kept at the Centre d'études interdisciplinaires Walras-Pareto de l'Université de Lausanne (ZAB 1319); see on this subject V. Bourdeau, 2004a, pp. 191–93 and 2023, pp. 148–57.

[14] A. Walras, letters to his son, 13, 21, and 23 November 1859, in: *Correspondence*, vol IV, pp. 368, 370–71 and 372–73. The "economic conditions of democracy" are the subject of the longest chapter (chapter VIII of book I) of *La Démocratie* by É. Vacherot. A. Walras considers that here appears the "weak side of the work" and that the author "gives too much importance to the principle of association". But as the book was seized, he advises his son against publishing an article about it in *Journal des économistes*.

[15] A. Walras, letter to his son, 23 May 1860, in: *Correspondence*, vol IV, p. 414.

[16] A second edition, "considerably augmented followed by the text of the judgments rendered in France against the book" is published in Brussels (A. Lacroix, Van Meenen et Cie, 1860).

[17] *Les Associations populaires de consommation, de production et de crédit*, 3rd lesson, vol. VI, p. 76; see also "Le mouvement d'association et la politique libérale" (1866a). See on this subject V. Bourdeau, 2004b, p. 29 *et seq.*

He would remain faithful to this idea throughout his life. In 1897, he still recalled the moral role of cooperative societies "of introducing democracy into the mechanism of production and opening access for everybody to business, the true school of political activity" ("L'économique appliquée et la défense des salaires", 1897c, vol. X, p. 261, English transl., 2005, p. 229).

After the Franco-Prussian war, the fall of the Empire and then the Paris Commune, the presidencies of Adolphe Thiers, then Marshal Mac-Mahon, bode nothing good for France in Walras's eyes. In June 1877, Mac-Mahon dissolved the Chamber with the support of the Senate, which was aligned with the monarchists. But the republicans remained the majority in the new Chamber and became the majority in the Senate two years later; Mac-Mahon then resigned, and the presidency went to Jules Grévy. In this new context, Walras noted that from two years,

> [...] there is a whole category of men who, until now quite different, are tempted for the first time to take an interest in public affairs: we mean those who, in these matters, are concerned above all with the regular accomplishment of social reforms ("De la culture et de l'enseignement des sciences morales et politiques", 1879c, vol. VII, p. 377).

However, he adds further on:

> The parliamentary government is an excellent mechanism when it functions in such a way as to alternately bring progressives or conservatives to power, depending on whether reforms need to be carried out or consolidated, but detestable when it results in incessant changes in legislation and perpetual government mobility. However, it cannot fail to produce this latter result wherever there are no studied and matured reforms ready to be implemented (*op. cit.*, p. 409).

Walras therefore places his hopes on the side of the moderate republicans, who thwarted the *coup d'État* plans of the monarchist parties "united under the clerical banner", and who will indeed carry out significant liberal reforms (press, trade unions, education...). In his letter (written as part of his efforts to obtain a university position in his native country) to Jules Ferry on 9 February 1879, the new Minister of Public Instruction, he hopes to see well-conceived reforms put in place:

> That soon some great reform well-prepared by science will be successfully completed by politics, the far-left will gradually disappear at the same time as the anti-constitutional right. There will be only the two parties necessary for any representative and parliamentary regime: that of the progressive republicans and that of the conservative republicans alternating in power depending on whether it is a question of carrying out reforms or consolidating accomplished reforms.[18]

But quite quickly, Walras loses his illusions about the "representative or parliamentary democracy", which unfortunately tends "to consider the public interest [...] as a number of coalitions of private interests that are enough to constitute an electoral majority". He adds that it would be illusory to rely on it to carry out the "preliminary

[18] L. Walras, letter to Jules Ferry, 9 February 1879, in: *Correspondence*, I, l. 429, p. 594.

studies", the "master plan" and the implementation of practical details for the State's repurchase of land.[19]

With ministerial instability from 1885 and the Boulangist threat, Walras's disappointment grows further. In the Preface to the *Théorie de la monnaie* (November 1886), he estimates that throughout the XIXth century, France has been shuttled between a "smug conservatism" that finds everything "wholly admirable", and a "muddled progressivism" that "turns everything upside down haphazardly" (1886a, vol. X, p. 60, English transl., 2005, p. 53). In his letter to Jules Ferry on 21 July 1887, he reveals that on the manuscript of this preface he had initially written "*radicalism*", then replaced it with "*progressivism*", "to avoid appearing to directly criticise the party that governs us in this country and of which I personally have no complaints".[20] However, in his lectures at the Academy of Lausanne, Walras is not afraid of words: "Between the Socialists and the Radicals who always want to move forward recklessly and the reactionaries who want to restore the past, the liberals or moderates, torn between the two, can achieve nothing".[21] According to him, this situation could even lead the country to the brink of revolution.[22]

A decade later, when the campaign for the revision of Alfred Dreyfus's trial is in full swing, Walras completes his pessimistic diagnosis of the political situation and social disintegration in France:

> Between narrow-minded conservatism and worrying socialism, militarism and clericalism find a role to play; the sword and the crosier are flourishing again [...]. One must have no experience in diagnosing social diseases to be mistaken about the present case. This is where the facts of monumental stupidity and the incredible lack of ethics that occur before our eyes come from. And it is the same with the antisemites as with the anarchists; they are a product of our morbid state.[23]

In fact, behind the conservative parties, one always finds the same classes opposing any change, because

> [...] since 1870, the bourgeoisie[24] and the united peasants, supported by what remains of the nobility and the clergy, oppose any move towards economic equality. No reforms and no science! Our social structure, built by Napoléon with materials from another age, threatens to collapse [...].[25]

[19] "Théorie mathématique du prix des terres et de leur rachat par l'État" (1881b), vol. IX, p. 306; see also "Un économiste inconnu: Hermann-Henri Gossen" (1885a), vol. IX, p. 325. English transl., 2010, pp. 244 and 261.

[20] Emphasis by L. W., letter to J. Ferry, 21 July 1887, in: *Correspondence*, II, l. 805, p. 217.

[21] *Cours d'économie sociale*, 14th lesson, marginal note, vol. XII, p. 815, note 80.

[22] In his last book, *La démocratie libérale* (1892), Étienne Vacherot will detail his grievances against Third Republic's parliamentarism, but by calling for the advent of a constitutional monarchy.

[23] L. Walras, letter to Maurice-Louis Vernes, 23 December 1898, in: *Correspondence*, III, l. 1384, pp. 54–55.

[24] According to Walras, the bourgeoisie was able to increase its fortune during the xix[th] century in "coal mines, railways, and other monopolies conceded without any serious care for the public interest, with industries protected at the expense of consumers" ("Le problème fiscal", 1896d, vol. IX, p. 420, English transl., 2010, p. 344).

[25] Primitive version of the "Esquisse" (1898c, vol. X, p. 509, note 77); in the published version, this passage is less precise. Similar remarks on the threat of ruin to the social organisation due to

Léon Walras thus condemns a system in which the State is the instrument of a particular social class or an alliance of classes, which compromises the progress towards the "industrial and commercial regime" and prevents the advent of social reforms.

17.3 Remedying the Defects of Universal Suffrage: The Professional Representation of Interests

On the first page of the Preface of *Francis Sauveur*, renamed "L'art et la démocratie", Walras pencilled the following annotation:

> My opinion on universal suffrage has changed following the distinction I have come to make between theory or social *science* and practice or *politics*. I still believe that universal suffrage is a *scientific* truth in the sense that it has its place in the social ideal provided it is rationally organised. But I also believe that its premature advent and its operation in a crude and brutal form will have been a *political* misfortune from which French democracy may well not recover.[26]

This annotation is not dated. William Jaffé estimates that it was added around 1882 (1956, p. 212), but without providing justifications. It is difficult to precisely date the change in Walras's viewpoint on the exercise of universal suffrage, but it probably occurred around the mid-1880s, even though he expresses it in his writings more in the 1890s.[27]

What are, according to our author, the major defects of the Third Republic's political system? During a period of crisis of parliamentarism in France and also in several European countries, he considers that it is necessary to get rid of, on the one hand, "our present-day deplorable universal suffrage" and on the other hand, our "deplorable parliamentarism" (1898c, vol. X, p. 434, English transl., 2005, p. 379). Regarding the second point, he undoubtedly targets ministerial instability and the predominance of parliamentary assemblies over executive and judicial bodies, which weaken the State.

How to remedy these defects? Walras believes he has found a solution to the first in the "system of the representation of interests". Indeed, he indicates:

> […] it seems to me that the fine works of the Belgian school on national representation and the system it calls the system of the *representation of interests*, and which I would prefer to call the system of *organic representation*, are perfectly in the desired direction (emphasis by L. W., *op. cit.*, p. 434).

Napoléon are found in the letter of L. Walras to Jules Ferry, 24 August 1888 (*Correspondence*, II, l. 845, pp. 264–65).

[26] Emphasis by L. W. Handwritten annotations on page VII on two copies of *Francis Sauveur*, kept in the Walras collection in Lyon under the reference FA I B: 07:01 and in the Walras collection in Lausanne under the reference VII, 24.

[27] In his letter to G. de Greef (*cf. infra*) of 27 November 1893, he declares: "I have been, for a long time already…, a staunch supporter of organic representation […]." (*Correspondence*, II, l. 1172, p. 600).

Who are the authors to whom Walras alludes? On the first manuscript of the "Esquisse d'une doctrine économique et sociale", he specified the names of the members of the "sociological school of Belgium" who defend this approach, "Prins, de Haulleville, de Greef" (1898c, vol. X, p. 508, note 72). Let us provide some details about these three authors.

Adolphe Prins (1845–1919), a jurist belonging to the Leplaysian sphere of influence, professor at the Brussels Free University, and general inspector of prisons, is best known for his works in criminal law and criminology. Nostalgic for the corporations of the Middle Ages, he published a book on *La démocratie et le régime parlementaire. Étude sur le régime corporatif et la représentation des intérêts* (1884, 2nd ed., 1886, with a preface by Émile de Laveleye).[28]

Prosper de Haulleville (1830–98), an ultra-conservative jurist, contributed to developing a Catholic press in Belgium. From 1888, he was professor at the Military School of Brussels, where he taught history, constitutional law, and philosophy of law. In 1891, he was appointed director of the Musées royaux des arts décoratifs et industriels. In 1894, he published an important article on "La représentation des intérêts" in the *Revue sociale et politique* of Brussels.

Guillaume de Greef (1842–1924), a jurist and sociologist, was a professor at the Brussels Free University until 1894, when he resigned after it refused the teaching of Élisée Reclus. He then became one of the founders of the New University and served as its rector. At the Institut des Hautes Études, he taught the history of philosophy. A socialist close to Hector Denis, he was influenced by A. Comte, A. Quételet, and H. Spencer.[29] He published a book on *La Constituante et le régime représentatif* (1892).[30]

Walras also became aware of French works on the professional representation of interests. Emerging during the 1880s, studies on this theme accelerated in the following decade in the context of Boulangism and the rise of trade unionism and worker agitation. A "note d'humeur" reveals that he was familiar with the works of Raoul de La Grasserie and Charles Benoist (2000, vol. XIII, pp. 606–07). Raoul de La Grasserie (1839–1914), a judge at the Rennes court,[31] was the author of articles on the theme of professional representation and a *Projet de constitution* (1896). Charles Benoist (1861–1936), an ultra-conservative (influenced by A. Comte and H. Spencer), journalist at the newspaper *Le Temps*, professor of constitutional history

[28] Later, he publishes *L'organisation de la liberté et le devoir social* (Brussels/Paris: Merzbach & Falk/F. Alcan, 1895 and *De l'esprit du gouvernement démocratique. Essai de science politique* (Brussels: Misch and Thron, 1905).

[29] He is especially known for his book *Le transformisme social. Essai sur le progrès et le regrès des sociétés* (Paris: F. Alcan, 1895).

[30] In 1893, thanks to a mutual friend, G. Renard, Walras is in correspondence with G. de Greef who sent him his book (see G. de Greef, letter to L. Walras of 24 November and the latter's response of 27 November 1893, in: *Correspondence*, II, l. 1171 and 1172, pp. 599–602.

[31] Raoul de la Grasserie is also the author of numerous works and brochures on birth rate, taxation, and legislative and administrative reforms. He is an associate member of the International Institute of Sociology of Brussels and is in contact with Guillaume de Greef.

at the École libre des sciences politiques,[32] authored eight articles published in the *Revue des Deux Mondes* in 1895–96, later included in his book entitled *La crise de l'État moderne. De l'organisation du suffrage universel* (1899).

All these intellectuals denounce the technical incompetence of representatives, the despotism of parties, the despotism of numbers, of majorities, the "individualistic" universal suffrage, and they advocate for an "organised" universal suffrage. Let us now provide some indications on the systems supported by these authors. In fact, three questions need to be resolved: the choice of the parliamentary assembly to exercise the professional representation of interests, the composition of the professional chamber, and the competencies of this chamber.

First of all, it is necessary to designate the parliamentary assembly that will exercise the professional representation of interests. Here, four possible modalities can be distinguished:

- the professional representation of interests established in a single chamber, which implies the disappearance of the Senate and the Chamber of Deputies in their current configurations; this is the ideal solution in the eyes of G. de Greef (1892, pp. 207 and 222);
- the professional representation of interests established in the Senate (G. Francolin, 1889; P. de Haulleville, 1894), with the Chamber of Deputies remaining elected by direct universal suffrage;
- the professional representation of interests established in the Chamber of Deputies (A. Prins, 1884; C. Benoist, 1895–96 and 1899)[33];
- the professional representation of interests established in a specific assembly, the National Professional Chamber, sitting alongside the Chamber of Deputies elected by universal suffrage and the Senate, which would participate in Congress for the election of the President of the Republic and the constitutional revisions (R. de La Grasserie, 1895).[34]

Next, it is necessary to determine the composition of the professional chamber. Should it be reserved solely for workers and denied to those who live on their income (owners, rentiers), as some socialists have proposed (G. Francolin, 1889), or should it be composed in such a way that the main (or even all) professions have representatives? In the latter case, what groupings should be considered? Several variations have been proposed on this subject.

For P. de Haulleville (1894), it would suffice to form a Senate from three major "classes": capitalists, workers, and "scientists", allowing for the representation of

[32] Deputy of the Seine from 1902 to 1919 (Republican Federation—centre-right), he is one of the authors of a project of *Code du travail* (1905). In 1928, he would rally to the royalism of *L'Action française*, led by Charles Maurras. On C. Benoist, see J.-P. Parrot (1974, pp. 52–55) and G. Pollet (2012, pp. 365–68).

[33] The Senate or "Chamber of Collective Lives" would be formed of members elected for 1/3 from municipal councils, for 1/3 from general councils and 1/3 from "constituted bodies" (academies, universities, chambers of commerce…).

[34] In his *Projet de constitution* (1896b), R. de La Grasserie replaces the Senate with the Council of State.

"Capital" (land, industry, commerce), "Labour" (land, industry, commerce), and "Intelligence" (lawyers, men of science, of letters, and artists). The aim is to put an end to the "class war" and ensure the pre-eminence of the "upper classes" in the face of the danger that the vote of the most numerous class constitutes.[35]

Concerning the sole chamber, G. de Greef (1892) envisions a representation of agriculture, industry, commerce, and private and public transport, but he adds the artistic, scientific, and legal professions.[36] Concerning agriculture, voters are the members of the cantonal assemblies (landowners, farmers, day workers). For industry, voters are the members of the industrial sections of enterprises with at least 400 employees (employers, employees, workers). For commerce, voters are the members of the local *chambres syndicales*.[37]

Concerning the dedicated chamber, R. de La Grasserie (1895) envisions an election at three levels: communal or cantonal professional councils, departmental professional councils, and a national professional chamber (composed of delegates from the departmental councils). Here, professional representation is based on employers' and workers' unions, providing a means to neutralise the class struggle.

In C. Benoist's view (1895–96 and 1899), the "organised universal suffrage" in the Chamber of Deputies takes the following form: by applying the electoral quotient, seats are first distributed among the departments in proportion to the registered voters, then seats are distributed within each department in proportion to the voters belonging to the different professional groups. For their composition, C. Benoist relies on the 1891 population census data. Allocating seats for the largest groups (agriculture, industry, commerce) does not pose too many problems. However, for the smaller groups (transport, public administration, liberal professions, and rentiers), it would be necessary either to aggregate groups or to consider seats at the level of several departments or a region.[38]

Finally, it is necessary to establish the responsibilities of the professional chamber. For G. de Greef (1892), the sole chamber must exercise the legislative function. According to R. de La Grasserie (1895), the national professional chamber, which brings its technical expertise, should be responsible for the initiative, preparation, presentation, and defence of laws before the Senate and the Chamber of Deputies,

---

[35] P. de Haulleville envisages 144 senators with the following distribution: Capital: 54, Labour: 54 and Intelligence: 36 (1894, pp. 433–34).

[36] The single professional chamber for Belgium would be composed of 296 representatives with the following distribution: Agriculture (60), Industry (54), Commerce (54), Science (46) and Law (42), Art (40).

[37] According to G. de Greef, members of local and central public administrations could be admitted to the national representation, but civil servants and military personnel would be excluded from eligibility because they depend too much on government to be fit to defend the country's interests.

[38] According to C. Benoist's calculations (1899, pp. 275–76), in a chamber of 500 deputies divided into seven groups, agriculture would have 225 representatives, industry 164, commerce 48, transport 17, public administration 8, liberal professions 13 and people living exclusively on their income (rentiers) 25. Intellectuals have no seat.

but not for voting on laws; each trade union section would be responsible for drafting the laws that specifically concern it.[39]

It is interesting to note that the professional representation of interests question also concerns the socialist Georges Renard. In *Le régime socialiste* (1898), he believes that the political organisation should be based on two assemblies: one territorial, the other professional. He indicates that in a socialist regime, each trade should be transformed into an electoral college (1898, pp. 102 and 108). However, in *Le socialisme à l'œuvre* (1907), his position on this subject has changed. Indeed, he now supports:

> The representation of interests and competencies, – an idea that the enemies of socialism have often used as a weapon, – could be organised alongside the legislative assemblies. Professional bodies, admitted to participate directly in the drawing up of laws, would bring their prejudices, their self-interested calculations; but they could play a very useful role if they had a consultative voice. It is true that for this, it would be unnecessary to grant them special representation; it would suffice to guarantee them the use of this right of initiative, whose importance we have acknowledged (1907, pp. 330–31).

Furthermore, corrections to the legislative power of assemblies can be made through the means of a referendum and popular initiative (1898, pp. 115–16; 1907, pp. 321–24).

In the second half of the 1890s, Léon Walras would advocate for a system of "organic representation", specifying: "The organic suffrage as I conceive it would always be *universal*, but it would no longer be *amorphous*" (emphasis by L. W., "Notes d'humeur" (2000), vol XIII, p. 606).[40] He shares the criticisms of the "amorphous" universal suffrage, which would have been engendered by "individualism". We can note here that the opposition "organic"/"amorphous" comes from Raoul de La Grasserie.[41] The expressions "organic universal suffrage" (as opposed to "inorganic") and "organic representation" also appear in the works of Charles Benoist.

However, Walras provides very few details on the political institutions he favours. Does he envisage a sole chamber, like the republicans of 1875 who were opposed to the Senate, or a dedicated chamber? He only speaks of "the Chamber". Regarding this body, he indicates in his "Notes d'humeur" that "the Chamber must represent society, not be its image, but its quintessence. Agriculture, industry, commerce, liberal professions, civil servants" (2000, vol XIII, p. 606). Here we find five categories among those indicated by Charles Benoist, whose articles he could have read in the *Revue des Deux Mondes* in 1896, because two are omitted: transport and… rentiers. However, it is unlikely that our author would accept Benoist's project, which would favour farmers. One might imagine he prefers the arrangements proposed by G. de Greef and R. de La Grasserie.

---

[39] For C. Benoist, the technical preparation of laws would be entrusted not to the professional chamber, but to the Council of State.

[40] The same sentence is found in a footnote deleted on the manuscript of the "Esquisse d'une doctrine économique et sociale" (1898c, vol. X, p. 508, note 74).

[41] See Raoul de La Grasserie, 1896a. In his library, Walras has the offprint of this study. Despite its title, it does not tackle the issue of the representation of interests.

According to Walras, in the system of "organic representation",

> [...] it would be necessary to combine the election of the Chamber by the bodies with the division of the Chamber into large permanent committees: finance, foreign affairs, public instruction, public works, etc., composed of specialists. If these committees proved too conservative, some progressive mechanism would need to be devised (*op. cit.*, p. 606).

A progressive element could be introduced, either within the Chamber (but here, no details are given), or through a referendum or popular initiative (*ibid.*). Regarding this second option, Walras refers to two institutions in use in Switzerland, which he will allude to in his "Notes for 'Ruchonnet et le socialisme scientifique'", "the *popular initiative* by which the people can demand from their representatives a legal reform they find urgent; and the referendum which allows them to reject a reform they deem premature".[42]

What is the justification for the professional representation of interests in the Chamber? In the "Esquisse d'une doctrine économique et sociale", Walras expresses himself on this subject as follows:

> Where all categories of producers have been meticulously determined by economics, let politics classify the voters in these categories and consent to represent them per category by well know and highly appreciated representatives elected by their peers according to their talents and honesty. This seems to me one of those great simple and rightful ideas founded upon both reason and experience. In the eyes of thoughtful persons these ideas bear their own mark of excellence (1898c, vol. X, p. 434, English transl., 2005, p. 379).

Thus, one could have the "government of the best (*gouvernement des meilleurs*)", the expression of the "aristocratic principle, understood in the good sense of the word" (the democratic principle now being qualified as a "false principle", "Notes d'humeur", 2000, vol. XIII, p. 607). Walras even thinks that through this political reform, "modern humanity will be stopped on the slope of decadence" (*op. cit.*, p. 607). And he wishes that in France the debate intensifies on the professional representation of interests. Having read, *Les lois sociales. Esquisse d'une sociologie* (1898) by Gabriel Tarde, he advises the author to look into this question.[43] However, it would still be necessary to "find an organisation of legislative and executive power" to rid oneself of parliamentarism, the second flaw mentioned earlier, but on this ground, our author will not pronounce.[44]

Walras thus advocates for the establishment of a corporative chamber exercising the legislative function, with the underlying idea that economic professional interests are dominant and determine all others. This choice of professional representation reveals a subtle influence of Saint-Simon's thought: scientific and especially professional competence, technicality would equate to the ability to legislate and to govern

---

[42] Emphasis by L. W., "Notes for 'Ruchonnet et le socialisme scientifique'" (1908a), vol. XIII, p. 652.

[43] L. Walras, letter to G. Tarde, 30 May 1898, in: *Correspondence*, III, l. 1357, pp. 23–24.

[44] He returns to this question in 1907. Indeed, at the end of the draft of a speech prepared in the event of receiving the Nobel Peace Prize, in which he wishes that France would take the initiative of a pacifist movement with the support of small nations (see *infra To conclude*), he adds: "but above all, abolition of parliamentarism". ("Notes d'humeur", vol. XIII, p. 621).

the State[45] and the corporate interests would converge towards the general interests of the country. Is this really the best tool to implement reforms such as the repurchase of lands? Our author does not provide us with convincing arguments on this matter, merely asserting: "If we want to achieve some socialist reforms, and if these reforms often consist of State intervention, is it not urgent first of all to establish a representation of the State less deplorable than the one we possess [...]".[46]

17.4 Conclusion

The "Esquisse d'une doctrine économique et sociale", placed at the end of the *Études d'économie politique appliquée* is the only text in which Walras *publicly* pronounces in favour of professional representation of interests. Among the authors of reviews of this book, only the philosopher Georges Palante[47] examines Walras's corporatist preferences and criticises them by noting that this electoral system "would lead to illiberal consequences by subordinating the individual too closely to his professional category". He adds that this categorisation of citizens "would take us back to the caste system and to a resurgence and generalisation of the bureaucratic spirit", with all its flaws (nepotism, favouritism, etc.). Ultimately, one would quickly regret the current universal suffrage with its imperfections (1899, p. 104).

Walras's reflections on the professional representation of interests appear during the period in which he declares himself in favour of the repurchase of mines, energy sources, railways by the State and is interested in Marxism and the possibility of establishing a "collectivism of production". One can therefore legitimately question this strange combination of progressivism and corporatism. Indeed, the political proposals would have a certain coherence if Walras clearly advocated the establishment of a professional "Chamber of Labour" excluding owners and rentiers, similar to some socialists of his time (G. Francolin, 1889).

It should be noted that in France, the professional representation of interests would make its way after the First World War. Indeed, in 1925 under the *Cartel des gauches*, the Conseil national économique (C.N.E.) was born, a consultative body composed of 47 titular members (1/3) and 94 substitute members (2/3), and structured into three major divisions: Population and consumption, labour (intellectual and education, direction, salaried, artisans), and capital.[48] This body, which

[45] Did Saint-Simon not write that it was necessary to "introduce the administrative mode in the direction of the general interests of society"? Certainly, he was not a supporter of universal suffrage.

[46] L. Walras, letter to G. de Greef, 27 November 1893, in: *Correspondence*, II, l. 1172, p. 600.

[47] Philosopher and sociologist, Georges Palante (1862–1925) advocates in his writings an individualism that aims to be aristocratic.

[48] See A. Chatriot, 2002.

functioned until 1940, was reformed in 1936 with notably the introduction of professional sections with a parity structure.[49] The C.N.E. project received the support of a sympathiser and a disciple of Walras: Charles Rist (1924, pp. 274–75) and Étienne Antonelli. According to the latter, S.F.I.O. deputy, an Economic Council must "prepare the evolution of political democracy towards the social democracy of tomorrow".[50] Conversely, Charles Gide is not in favour of the principle of professional representation, because.

> [...] it is better to have the government of incompetence, which is the current parliamentary regime, than the government of interests, which is that of the producers. It would leave the general interest no other guarantee than their rivalry, a weak chance as this would surely transform into a coalition" (1928, p. 1057).

However, he wishes to maintain the C.N.E. as a purely consultative body, as it could "serve as a lightning rod against the advent of a true government of professionals, whether it be that of Mussolini or even of the French fascists in the style of Georges Valois!"[51] (*ibid.*). But it was no longer the time of Léon Walras...

---

[49] After the Second World War, a Conseil économique will be recreated under the Fourth Republic, and then under the Fifth Republic a Conseil économique et social.

[50] É. Antonelli, "Pour la création d'un Conseil économique", *Le Peuple*, 27 June 1924, cited by A. Chatriot, 2002, p. 35.

[51] See G. Valois, *L'État syndical et la représentation corporative*, Paris: Librairie Valois, 1927.

General Conclusion

Our research enabled us to uncover many lesser-known or unknown facets of Léon Walras's work. Focusing exclusively on the field of pure economics and the theory of general equilibrium thus appears as a very reductive approach. In the intellectual context of the XIXth century, our author's contribution as a social reformer seeking a scientific solution to the "social question" cannot be underestimated.

In the preface to his book *Le Collectivisme*, denouncing the "hidden and unconscious collectivists", Paul Leroy-Beaulieu exclaims: "Who will deliver us from the conciliators, those floating and empty minded people who believe that twilight reconciles light and night? This mania for wanting to unite and merge opposites is the most characteristic sign of intellectual debility" (1884, p. VII). Feeling targeted by these attacks, Léon Walras notes with irony that the author of "a third version of the Bastiat's doctrine on value and property" is unaware that attempts at conciliation or synthesis have been proposed by "the greatest geniuses", in philosophy (Hegel and his dialectics), in science (Claude Bernard), in literature (Dante's *Divine Comedy* seeks to reconcile the Holy Roman Empire with the Papacy) and art (Raphael painted in the Vatican *The Dispute over the Holy Sacrament*—theology, opposite *The School of Athens*—philosophy).[1]

Georges Renard's judgement differs greatly from that of Paul Leroy-Beaulieu. In a review of the 1st edition of *Études d'économie politique appliquée*, published in *La Lanterne*[2] on 27 September 1898 and reprinted in the book entitled *Discussions sociales d'hier et de demain*, he states about his economist friend:

> A semi-collectivist, he wants to return land and basement's property to the nation; and as for enterprises necessary to satisfy general or particular needs, while admitting that they could all be collective, without this being contrary to liberty or justice, he believes it preferable that they be shared between individual initiative and the intervention or initiative of the State or the municipality (1909, p. 96).

[1] L. Walras, "Le problème fiscal", 1896d, vol. IX, p. 422, English transl., 2010, p. 346; see also a note from 1885 placed in the *Cours d'économie sociale*, 1996, p. 812.

[2] A newspaper edited by Alexandre Millerand.

J.-P. Potier, *Léon Walras, Economist and Liberal Socialist*, Springer Studies in the History of Economic Thought, https://doi.org/10.1007/978-3-032-04670-3

Upon rereading this commentary towards the end of his life, Walras reacts in the following manner in his "Notes d'humeur":

> Renard's expression towards me ("*semi-collectivist*") is perfectly accurate (p. 96). I am individualist for *personal faculties*, collectivist for *land*, semi-individualist or collectivist for *capital*. To abolish individual property of half the capital (saved) would be to abolish half of the savings and capital (emphasis by L. W., 2000, vol. XIII, p. 574–75).

In the second half of the 1890s, Léon Walras envisioned society of the future as follows:

> [...] in a rational society, we should imagine the mass of capital that does not belong to the State as being, in the hands of workers, in small fractions, in the form of shares and bonds of various firms, of bonds of cooperative enterprises, which adds to present well-being, assuring security for tomorrow, preparing for future retirement; all this thanks to private initiative, as it should be, without any interference from the State, except, if need be, to give disinterested and benevolent support (1896c, vol. IX, p. 205, English transl., 2010, p. 157).

He thus describes a commodity production ensured by small or medium-sized enterprises of various legal forms.[3] In this "rational society", "wealth would be both the consequence of and reward for their work and their savings, just as poverty would be the consequence and the punishment for laziness and dissipation" (1896d, vol. IX, p. 404, English transl., 2010, p. 331). The "inequality of positions" of individuals would be reduced to a minimum (absence of great fortunes, despite inheritance being unquestioned), class struggle would have disappeared and the State, as a landowner, would achieve the "equality of conditions" and take charge of moral and natural monopolies. Not hiding his belief in the inevitable long-term progress of man and society, Walras remained throughout his life convinced that "scientific and liberal socialism" will one day "reap its harvest". However, in our era of privatisation of agricultural land, natural resources, and public services on a global scale, his project regains significance within the context of reflections about the "commons".

As we have seen in a letter to Louise Renard dated 18 June 1906, Walras indicated that he had developed a form of socialism leading through the repurchase of land to the abolition of taxes, and through this to free trade and universal peace.[4] It is for this reason that in April 1905, he decided to compete for the newly founded Nobel Peace Prize, awarded by Norway. He probably believed that his candidacy was more worthy than that of the economist Frédéric Passy, laureate with Henry Dunant of the first Nobel Peace Prize in 1901. He sought the sponsorship for his candidacy from three non-economist colleagues at Lausanne University. In their letter addressed to the prize committee, Ernest Roguin (dean of the faculty of law), Maurice Millioud (professor of philosophy), and Alexandre Maurer (professor of German history and literature) first emphasised that "Mr. Walras devoted all his scientific activity to mathematical economic science, of which he was the principal founder". And further, they observed:

---

[3] One cannot help but think of Marx's "simple commodity production".

[4] L. Walras, letter to Louise Renard, 18 June 1906, in: *Correspondence*, III, l. 1623, p. 301.

> No doubt, for those who would only consider practical applications, the immediate results of Mr. Walras's work would not be the most apparent. But theoretical research is in some respects more important than practical activity: its scope is longer; its results are more lasting and more certain.[5]

Curiously, the candidate's contribution to the cause of peace is not mentioned in the letter (A. Sandmo, 2007, p. 219). However, the "notice" attached to this letter, largely prepared by the candidate, contains a plea in favour of international free trade as the most powerful means to establish and maintain the era of the "brotherhood of peoples". Walras's contribution to solving the social question (nationalisation of land and abolition of taxes and customs duties) is presented as the theoretical, scientific way to work towards the development of international free trade.[6]

But in 1905, Walras's application was received too late to be considered by the jury, and the prize was awarded to the Austrian pacifist Bertha von Suttner.[7] Walras then lucidly remarked to Louise Renard that, in fact, he "does not count on the Nobel Prize, which is awarded to efforts that are rather practical than scientific".[8] The 1906 Nobel Prize being awarded to the President of the United States, Theodore Roosevelt, for his role as an arbitrator in the conflict between Russia and Japan, Walras exclaimed to his friend Gustave Maugin, "Roosevelt has snatched the Nobel Prize from me".[9] Yet he did not become discouraged and renewed his application the following year, sending to the prize committee a text entitled "La paix par la justice sociale et le libre-échange" (1907a)—compiled from the 1905 "Notice" and excerpts of the "Théorie du libre échange" (1897a) and of the "Esquisse d'une doctrine économique et sociale" (1898c)—which was published in *Questions pratiques de législation ouvrière et d'économie sociale*, a Lyon-based journal directed by the jurist Paul Pic. He confided to Pic that this text was a "lottery ticket", which, if it won, would enable him to fund an elementary course in mathematical economics in Paris, Lyon, or Lausanne.[10] In his letter to the Nobel Prize committee, he expressed increasing astonishment that the question of peace was entrusted "almost exclusively, for the solution of the problem, to political and diplomatic action, while almost completely neglecting the scientific and economic path which could be so decisive".[11] However, in 1907 the prize was awarded to the French jurist Louis Renault and the Italian journalist Teodoro Moneta, both promoters of international arbitration and involved in pacifist organisations. In August 1909, a few months before his death, Walras was still trying to draw the Nobel committee's attention to him by sending his latest publications and documentation

---

[5] E. Roguin, M. Millioud, and A. Maurer, letter to the Nobel Peace Prize committee, 20 July 1905, in: *Correspondence*, III, l. 1595, p. 270.

[6] "Notice" attached to the letter of 20 July 1905 to the Nobel Peace Prize, in: *op. cit.*, pp. 271–72.

[7] On the examination of his file that year by the Nobel Prize committee, see A. Sandmo, 2007, pp. 222–24.

[8] L. Walras, letter to Louise Renard, 18 June 1906, in: *Correspondence*, III, l. 1623, p. 301.

[9] L. Walras, letter to G. Maugin, 5 April 1907, in: *op. cit.*, III, l. 1649, p. 325.

[10] L. Walras, letter to P. Pic, 21 August 1907, in: *Correspondence*, III, l. 1657, p. 331.

[11] L. Walras, letter to the Nobel Prize committee, 16 September 1907, in: *Correspondence*, III, l. 1662, pp. 334–35.

on his recent jubilee.[12] In his archives, we found a draft of a speech he would have delivered in the event of winning the Nobel Prize. Indeed, it is entitled "Lecture at Christiania. Peace or War".[13] It notably reads: "I have explained the system that will prepare and ensure peace and consisting of social justice, repurchase of the land and free trade. As for the system that will lead to war, it is the one we have at present [...]" ("Notes d'humeur", 2000, vol. XIII, p. 621). And Walras hopes that, in the face of the German threat, France "plays the leading role" by taking the initiative of a pacifist movement with the support of smaller nations such as Switzerland—all just seven years before the First World War.

---

[12] L. Walras, letter to the Nobel Prize committee, 10 August 1909, in: *Correspondence*, III, l. 1770, p. 433.

[13] Christiania is the former name of Oslo.

Bibliography

Alcouffe, A. (2013), « La première réception de Léon Walras chez les économistes allemands », in: A. Diemer and J.-P. Potier (Eds), *Léon Walras. Un siècle après (1910–2010)*, Brussels: Peter Lang, p. 169–189.

Alcouffe, A. and Belloc, B. (2000), « Équilibre général et équilibre général de concurrence pure et parfaite. G.-H. Bousquet et la tradition économique française », in: P. DOCKÈS, L. FROBERT, G. KLOTZ, J.-P. POTIER, A. TIRAN (Eds), *Les traditions économiques françaises, 1848–1939*, Paris: Éd. du C.N.R.S., p. 519–530.

Allisson, F. (2008), « Les premiers lecteurs de Walras en Russie (1890–1919) », *Les Cahiers OMI, Études d'économie walrassienne*, n°6, December, p. 57–75.

Allix, E. (1910), « J.-B. Say et les origines de l'industrialisme » [2nd part], *Revue d'économie politique*, vol. 24, n°5, p. 341–363.

Ampère, A.-M. (1834), *Essai sur la philosophie des sciences, ou Exposition analytique d'une classification naturelle de toutes les connaissances humaines* [1st part], Paris: Bachelier.

Ampère, A.-M. (1843), *Essai sur la philosophie des sciences, ou Exposition analytique d'une classification naturelle de toutes les connaissances humaines* [2nd part], Paris: Bachelier.

Antonelli, É. (1910), « Léon Walras », *Revue d'histoire des doctrines économiques et sociales*, vol. 3, n°2, p. 169–190.

Antonelli, É. (1914), *Principes d'économie pure. La théorie de l'échange sous le régime de la libre concurrence*, Paris: Marcel Rivière.

Antonelli, É. (1923), « Un économiste de 1830: Auguste Walras », *Revue d'histoire économique et sociale*, vol. XI, n°4, p. 516–538.

Antonelli, É. (1953), « Léon Walras et Carl Menger à travers leur correspondance », *Économie appliquée*, vol. VI, n° 2–3, April–September, p. 269–287.

Arena, R. (1991), « Joseph Garnier, 1813–1881. Libéral orthodoxe et théoricien éclectique », in: Y. Breton and M. Lutfalla, (Eds), *L'Économie politique en France au* xixe *siècle*, Paris: Economica, p. 111–139.

Arena, R. (2014), "Was Léon Walras a rational choice theorist?", in: J.-P. Potier (Ed), *Les Marmites de l'histoire. Mélanges en l'honneur de Pierre Dockès*, Paris: Éditions Classiques Garnier, p. 299–325.

Arena, R. and Ragni, L. (1994), « Libre concurrence et méthodologie walrasienne: une tentative de mise en relation », *Économies et sociétés-Cahiers de l'ISMEA*, vol. XXVIII, n° 10–11, Œconomia series, Histoire de la pensée économique, n°20–21, p. 161–182.

Astigarraga, J. and Zabalza, J. (2008), "The diffusion and reception of Walrasian ideas in Spain", *Les Cahiers OMI, Études d'économie walrassienne*, n°6, December, p. 35–56.

Audier, S. (2006), *Le socialisme libéral*, Paris: La Découverte, coll. Repères.

Aupetit, A. (1901), *Essai sur la théorie générale de la monnaie,* Ph.D. thesis, Faculty of Law, Paris University, Paris: Guillaumin.

J.-P. Potier, *Léon Walras, Economist and Liberal Socialist*, Springer Studies in the History of Economic Thought, https://doi.org/10.1007/978-3-032-04670-3

Backhouse, R. E. and Medema, S. G. (2014), "Walras in the age of Marshall: an analysis of English-language journals, 1890–1939", in: R. Baranzini and F. Allisson (Eds), *Economics and Other Branches. In the Shade of the Oak Tree. Essays in Honour of Pascal Bridel*, London: Pickering & Chatto, p. 69–86.

Baranzini, R. (1993), « Walras e l'inopportunità dell'opposizione tra economia positiva e economia normativa. Dal 1860 alla seconda edizione degli *Éléments* », *Economia Politica. Rivista di teoria e analisi*, vol. X, n° 3, December, p. 381–416.

Baranzini, R. (2001a), *Léon Walras e il fenomeno monetario (1860–1886). Contributo analitico ed epistemologico alla ricostruzione del modello monetario walrasiano*, Ph.D. thesis, École des Hautes Études Commerciales de l'Université de Lausanne.

Baranzini, R. (2001b), « Léon Walras: il singolare socialismo di un marginalista atipico », in: M. E. L. Guidi and L. Michelini (Eds), *Marginalismo e socialismo nell'Italia liberale, 1870–1925*, Milano: *Annali della Fondazione Feltrinelli*, p. 35–65.

Baranzini, R. (2005), *Léon Walras e la moneta senza velo*, Torino: U.T.E.T.

Baranzini, R. (2006), « Nature et statut épistémologique des lois économiques dans l'œuvre de Léon Walras », *Économies et sociétés-Cahiers de l'I.S.M.E.A.*, vol. XL, n° 12, Œconomia series, Histoire de la pensée économique, n°38, p. 1671–1691.

Baranzini, R. (2007), « Nature et statut épistémologique des lois économiques dans l'œuvre de Léon Walras », in: A. Berthoud, B. Delmas and T. Demals (Eds), *Y a-t-il des lois en économie ?*, Villeneuve d'Ascq : Presses Universitaires du Septentrion, p. 257–270.

Baranzini, R. (2011), « La concurrence et le tâtonnement à la lumière du réalisme walrassien. Une note sur les six premières sections des *Éléments* », in: R. Baranzini, A. Legris and L. Ragni (Eds), *Léon Walras et l'équilibre économique général. Recherches récentes*, Paris: Economica, p. 153–167.

Baranzini, R. (2014), « Pour une histoire de la théorie économique de Léon Walras », in: J.-P. Potier, (Ed), *Les Marmites de l'histoire. Mélanges en l'honneur de Pierre Dockès*, Paris: Éditions Classiques Garnier, p. 285–298.

Baranzini, R. (2016), "Marie-Esprit-Léon Walras (1834–1910)", in: G. Faccarello and H. D. Kurz, (Ed), *Handbook on the History of Economic Analysis*, vol. I, *Great Economists since Petty and Boisguilbert*, Cheltenham: Edward Elgar, p. 245–261.

Baranzini, R. and Tatti, E. (2002), « Léon Walras e il metodo matematico dell'economia pura: al di là della forma », *Economia politica. Rivista di teoria e analisi,* vol. XIX, n°1, April, p. 65–89.

Baranzini, R. and Bridel, P. (2005), « L' 'École de Lausanne', l'utilité marginale moyenne et l'idée de marché », in: Guy Bensimon (Ed), *Histoire des représentations du marché*, Paris: Michel Houdiard, p. 347–365.

Baranzini, R. and Swaton, S. (2017), "Persistent confusions about Walras's conception of 'social economy'", *History of Economic Ideas*, vol. XXV, n°1, p. 173–190.

Bartoli, H. (1990), « Chronique de la pensée économique en Italie », *Revue économique*, vol. 41, n° 6, november, p. 1087–1097.

Barucci, P. (1972), "The Spread of Marginalism in Italy, 1871–1890", *History of Political Economy*, vol. 4, n° 2, Fall, p. 512–532. Italian revised edition: « La diffusione del marginalismo, 1870–1890 », in: Massimo Finoia (Ed.), *Il pensiero economico italiano, 1850–1950*, Bologna: Cappelli, 1980, p. 67–91.

Baslé, M. (1991), « Paul Leroy-Beaulieu, 1843-1916. Un économiste français de la IIIe République commençante », in: Y. Breton and M. Lutfalla (Eds), *L'Économie politique en France au* xixe *siècle*, Paris: Economica, p. 203–246.

Bastiat, F. (1851), *Harmonies économiques*, 2nd ed., Paris: Guillaumin.

Baudrillart, H. (1860), *Des rapports de la morale et de l'économie politique. Cours professé au Collège de France*, Paris: Guillaumin.

Bee, M. (2011), « Les correspondances entre économie et philosophie dans les pensées de Léon Walras et de Charles Péguy », in: R. Baranzini, A. Legris and L. Ragni (Eds), *Léon Walras et l'équilibre économique général. Recherches récentes*, Paris: Economica, p. 79–98.

Bee, M. (2013), « 'Homo coenonicus': le caractère naturel de la division du travail et la nécessité du progrès industriel dans la théorie de l'histoire de Léon Walras », in: A. Diemer and J.-P. Potier (Eds.), Léon Walras. *Un siècle après (1910–2010)*, Brussels: Peter Lang, p. 87–106.

Benoist, C. (1895–96), « De l'organisation du suffrage universel », *Revue des Deux-Mondes*, 65th year, 4th period, vol. 130, 1st July 1895, p. 5–25 and 15 August 1895; p. 806–828, vol. 131, 15 October 1895, p. 825–844, vol. 132, 15 December 1895, p. 760–781 ; 66th year, vol. 134, 1st April 1896, p. 593–615, vol. 135, 1st June, p. 576–597, vol. 136, 1st August 1896, p. 520–543, vol. 138, 1st December 1896, p. 514–527.

Benoist, C. (1899), La crise de l'État moderne. De l'organisation du suffrage universel, Paris: Firmin-Didot et Cie.

Benvenuto Vialetto, A. and Ancona, G. (1969), « Boccardo Gerolamo », in: *Dizionario biografico degli italiani*, Roma: Treccani, vol. 11, p. 48–52.

BÉraud, A. (2011), « Walras et l'économie publique », *Œconomia-History, Methodology, Philosophy*, vol. 1, n°3, September, p. 351–392.

Bernard, C. (1865), *Introduction à l'étude de la méthode expérimentale*, Paris: Flammarion, coll. Champs, 1984.

Bernard, C. (1878), « Le problème de la physiologie générale », in: *La science expérimentale*, Paris: J.-B. Baillière, p. 99–148.

Berta, N. (2001), « Edgeworth, Walras et le tâtonnement: histoire d'un malentendu », *Économies et sociétés-Cahiers de l'I.S.M.E.A.*, vol. XXXV, n°11–12, Œconomia series, Histoire de la pensée économique, n°31, p. 1657–1675.

Berthoud, A. (1988), « Économie politique et morale chez Walras », *Économies et sociétés-Cahiers de l'ISMEA*, vol. XXII, n°3, Œconomia series, Histoire de la pensée économique, n°9, p. 65–93.

Bertrand, J. (1872), « Louis Poinsot. *Statique* de Poinsot, onzième édition. Paris: Gauthier-Villars », *Journal des savants*, July, p. 405–420.

Bertrand, J. (1883), « *Théorie mathématique de la richesse sociale*, par Léon Walras [...], *Recherches sur les principes mathématiques de la théorie des richesses* par Augustin Cournot », *Journal des savants*, September, p. 499–508.

Black, R. D. C. (1992), "Attempts by Jevons and Walras to publicise each other's work", *Revue européenne des sciences sociales. Cahiers Vilfredo Pareto*, vol. XXX, n° 92, p. 109–129.

Billard, Y. (1998), « Georges Renard, historien socialiste », *Jean Jaurès. Cahiers trimestriels*, n°148, July–September, p. 9–24.

Blanc, L. (1847), *Histoire de la Révolution française*, Paris: Langlois and Leclercq; Pagnerre; Perrotin, 2 vol.

Blanc, L. (1850), *Organisation du travail, 9e édition refondue et augmentée de chapitres nouveaux*, Paris: Au bureau du *Nouveau Monde*.

Block, M. (1890), *Les progrès de la science économique depuis Adam Smith. Révision des doctrines économiques*, Paris: Guillaumin, 2 vol.

Bonelli, F. (1969), « Bodio Luigi », in: *Dizionario biografico degli italiani*, Roma: Treccani, vol. 11, p. 103–107.

Borghini, G. (1999), « Alcune lettere inedite di Léon Walras ad Angelo Messedaglia », *Nuova Economia e Storia*, n°3, p. 239–555.

Boson, M. (1951), Léon Walras fondateur de la politique économique scientifique, Paris/Lausanne: L. G. D. J./Rouge.

Boson, M. (1963), *La pensée sociale et coopérative de Léon Walras*, Paris: Institut des études coopératives.

Bourdeau, V. (2004a), « Crédit et démocratie chez Léon Walras (1860–1874) », in: Roberto Baranzini, Arnaud Diemer and Claude Mouchot, (Eds), *Études walrassiennes*. Foreword by Jan Van Daal. Paris: L'Harmattan, p. 189–209.

Bourdeau, V. (2004b), « La «démocratie nouvelle»: représentation de l'homme économique en citoyen républicain chez Proudhon et Walras », *Corpus. Revue de philosophie*, n°47, p. 13–37.

Bourdeau, V. (2006), « Les républicains du 19e siècle étaient-ils des libertariens de gauche ? L'exemple d'Auguste et Léon Walras », *Raisons politiques. Études de pensée politique*, n°23, August, p. 93–108.

Bourdeau, V. (2023), *Le marché et le mérite. Léon Walras (1834–1910) et l'économie politique républicaine en France*, Rennes: Presses Universitaires de Rennes.

Bousquet, G.-H. (1924), « Vilfredo Pareto. Le développement et la signification historique de son œuvre », *Revue d'histoire économique et sociale*, vol. 12, p. 225–243 and p. 399–431.

Bousquet, G.-H. (1928), *Cours d'économie pure*, Paris: Marcel Rivière.

Bousquet, G.-H. (1948) « Gaëtan Pirou et l'École de Lausanne », in: *La vie et la pensée de Gaëtan Pirou*, Paris: Librairie du Recueil Sirey, p. 169–181.

Bousquet, G.-H. (Ed.) (1951), « Lettres de Léon et Aline Walras à Albert Aupetit », *Revue d'histoire économique et sociale*, vol. XXIX, n°2, p. 146–155.

Bouvier, É. (1901a), « La méthode mathématique en économie politique » *Revue d'économie politique*, vol. 15, n° 8–9, and n°12, p. 817–850 and p. 1029–1086, reprinted in: É. Bouvier, *La méthode mathématique en économie politique*, Paris: Librairie de la Société du recueil général des lois et des arrêts, 1901.

Bouvier, É. (1901b), « L'Économie politique mathématique. Quelques mots à propos du traité de M. Léon Walras », *Revue critique de législation et de jurisprudence*, vol. 30, December, p. 623–629.

Bratter, H. M. (1931), "Silver. Some fundamentals", *Journal of Political Economy*, vol. 39, n°3, June, p. 321–368.

Breton, Y. (1986), « Les économistes libéraux français et l'emploi des mathématiques en économie politique, 1800–1914 », *Économies et sociétés-Cahiers de l'ISMEA*, vol. XX, n°3, Œconomia series, Histoire de la pensée économique, n°5, p. 25–63.

Breton, Y. (1991), « Michel Chevalier, 1806–1879. Entre le saint-simonisme et le libéralisme », in: Y. Breton and M. Lutfalla, (Eds), *L'Économie politique en France au* xixe *siècle*, Paris: Economica, p. 247–275.

Breton, Y. (1992), « L'économie politique et les mathématiques en France. 1800–1940 », *Histoire et mesure*, vol. VII, n°1–2, p. 25–52.

Breton, Y. (1998a), "Hermann Laurent (1841–1908): in Search of a New Political Economy", in: W. J. Samuels, General Editor, *European Economists of the Early 20th Century*, vol. 1, *Studies of Neglected Thinkers of Belgium, France, The Netherlands and Scandinavia*, Cheltenham: Edward Elgar, p. 144–162.

Breton, Y. (1998b), "French Economists and Marginalism (1871–1918)", in: Gilbert Faccarello, (Ed), *Studies in the History of French Political Economy—From Bodin to Walras*, London: Routledge, p. 404–455.

Breton, Y. (2000), « Émile Bouvier (1862–1930) », in: L. Frobert, J.-P. Potier and A. Tiran (Eds), *Économistes en Lyonnais, en Dauphiné et en Forez—1750–1950*, Lyon: Éditions de l'Institut des Sciences de l'Homme, p. 22–34.

Breton, Y. (2010), « Les gouvernements et leurs attributions économiques chez Michel Chevalier (1806–1879). Rupture ou continuité avec Jean-Baptiste Say (1767–1832) ? », in: A. Tiran (Ed), *Jean-Baptiste Say. Influences, critiques et postérité*, Paris: Classiques Garnier, p. 305–334.

Breton, Y. and Klotz, G. (2009), « Aperçus biographiques et éditoriaux sur Jules Dupuit. Introduction générale aux œuvres économiques complètes de Jules Dupuit », in: Jules Dupuit, *Œuvres économiques complètes*, Y. Breton and G. Klotz (Eds), Paris: Economica, p. 1–34.

Bridel, P. (1987), « Léon Walras: théorie et politique économique », in: G. Busino and P. Bridel (Ed.), *L'école de Lausanne de Léon Walras à Pasquale Boninsegni*, Lausanne: Université de Lausanne, p. 13–28.

Bridel, P. (1988), « Quelques réflexions sur l'idée de 'main invisible' », *Revue européenne des sciences sociales. Cahiers Vilfredo Pareto*, vol. XXVI, n°82, p. 79–98.

Bridel, P., with the collaboration of Baranzini, R. (1996), *Le chêne et l'architecte. Un siècle de comptes rendus bibliographiques des* Éléments d'économie politique pure *de Léon Walras. Textes et commentaires,* Geneva: Droz.

Bridel, P. (1997), *Money and General Equilibrium Theory – From Walras to Pareto (1870–1923)*, Cheltenham: Edward Elgar.
Bridel, P. (1999), « Une note d'humeur de Léon Walras. Commentaire », *Économies et sociétés-Cahiers de l'ISMEA,* vol. XXXIII, n° 4, Œconomia series, Histoire de la pensée économique, n°28, p. 161–164.
Bridel, P. (2008), « Bortkiewicz et Walras. Notes sur une collaboration intellectuelle avortée », *Revue d'économie politique*, vol. 118, n°5, September–October, p. 711–742.
Bridel, P. (2011), "The normative origins of general equilibrium theory; or Walras's attempts at reconciling economic efficiency with social justice", in: Pascal Bridel (Ed), *General Equilibrium Analysis. A Century after Walras*, London: Routledge, p. 15–23.
Bridel, P., Dockès, P. and Potier, J.-P. (1996), « Introduction générale: l'enseignement de Léon Walras à Lausanne », in: *Cours*, vol. XII des *Œuvres économiques complètes*, Paris: Economica, p. 9–41.
Bridel, P. and Huck, E. (2002), "Yet another look at Léon Walras's theory of *tâtonnement*", *European Journal of the History of Economic Thought*, vol. 9, n° 4, Winter, p. 513–540.
Bridel, P. and Mornati, F. (2009), « De l'équilibre général comme 'branche de la métaphysique' Ou de l'opinion de Pareto sur le projet walrasien », *Revue économique*, vol. 60, n°4, July, p. 869–890.
Bruant, C. (2007), « Le Collège libre des sciences sociales, une université parallèle qui traverse le XXe siècle », *Les Études Sociales*, n°146, 2nd semester, p. 3–56.
Burlamaqui, J.-J. (1820), *Éléments du droit naturel;* et Pufendorf, *Devoirs de l'homme et du citoyen, tels qu'ils lui sont prescrits par la loi naturelle, traduits du latin par Barbeyrac [...],* new edition, Paris: Janet et Cotelle.
Busino, G. (1968), « Una fonte per la storia del pensiero economico in Italia: il carteggio di Léon Walras », *Rivista storica italiana*, April–June, p. 340–350, reprinted in: G. Busino, *Gli studi su Vilfredo Pareto oggi - Dall' agiografia alla critica (1923–1973)*, Roma: Bulzoni, 1974, p. 31–47.
Busino, G. (2005), « Un modello d'erudizione e d'acribia filologica. L'edizione delle opera economiche d'Auguste e Léon Walras », *Annali della Fondazione Luigi Einaudi*, vol. XXXIX, p. 3–38.
Camurri, R., (Ed) (1992), *La scienza moderata - Fedele Lampertico e l'Italia liberale*, Milano: Franco Angeli.
Canto-Sperber, M. and Urbinati, N. (collab.) (2003), *Le socialisme libéral. Une anthologie: Europe – États-Unis*, Paris: Esprit.
Carbonell, C.-O. (1976), *Histoire et historiens. Une mutation idéologique des historiens français, 1865–1885*, Toulouse: Privat.
Carnap, R. (1973), *Les fondements philosophiques de la physique*, Paris: A. Colin.
Cassani, C. (1985), « Cusumano Vito », in: *Dizionario biografico degli italiani*, Roma: Treccani, vol. 31, p. 526–529.
Castleton, E. (2014), « Proudhon, lecteur d'Auguste Walras. Annotations marginales sur Auguste Walras, *De la nature de la richesse et de l'origine de la valeur*, Paris, Furne, 1932 », *Économies et sociétés-Cahiers de l'ISMEA*, vol. XLVIII, n°6, Oeconomia series Histoire de la pensée économique, n°50, p. 901–938.
Cauwès, Paul (1878–79), *Précis du cours d'économie politique professé à la faculté de droit de Paris*, Paris: L. Larose, 2 vol.
Cauwès, P. (1893), *Cours d'économie politique*, 3rd edition, Paris: L. Larose & Forcel, 4 vol.
Chailley-bert, J. (1892), « L'enseignement de l'économie politique en France », *Journal des économistes*, 51st year, 5th series, vol. XII, n° 3, December, p. 340–366.
Chappey, J.-L. and Vincent, J. (2017), « Une chaire sans intitulé ? Les sciences morales et politiques au Collège de France (1795–1864) », in: W. Feuerhahn (Ed), *La politique des chaires au Collège de France*, Paris: Collège de France. Les Belles Lettres, p. 351–381.
CharlÉty, S. (1931), *Histoire du Saint-Simonisme (1825–1864)*, Paris: Hartmann, reed. Gonthier, 1965.
Chatriot, A. (2002), *La démocratie sociale à la française. L'expérience du Conseil national économique 1924–1940*, Paris: La Découverte.

Chevalier, M. (1852), « Chemins de fer », in: C. Coquelin and G.-U. Guillaumin, *Dictionnaire de l'économie politique*, Paris: Guillaumin, vol. 1, p. 337–362.

Chevalier, M. (1874), « Étude sur Adam Smith et l'origine de la science économique », *Journal des économistes*, 33rd year, 3rd series, 9th year, n° 97, January, p. 8–33.

Chevalier, M. (1875), « Des moyens pour un État de refaire ses finances. La liberté du travail », *Journal des économistes*, 34th year, 3rd series, 10th year, n°110, February, p. 27–56.

Chiecchi, S. (1971), « Luigi Cossa tra storia ed economia (Testimonianze del suo epistolario al Lampertico) », *Economia e storia*, vol. XVIII, fasc. 1, January–March, p. 77–93.

Chiecchi, S. (1976), « Stato moderno e società civile nella dottrina del Lampertico », *Economia e storia*, vol. XXIII, fasc. 2, April–June, reprinted in: R. Finzi (Ed), *Il ruolo dello Stato nel pensiero degli economisti*, Bologna: Il Mulino, 1977, p. 211–227.

ClÉment, A. (1852), « Introduction », in: C. Coquelin and G.-U. Guillaumin, *Dictionnaire de l'économie politique*, Paris: Guillaumin, vol. 1, p. IX–XXVII.

Clower, R. and Howitt, P. (1995), « Les fondements de l'économie », in: A. D'Autume and J. Cartelier (Eds), *L'Économie devient-elle une science dure?* Paris: Economica, p. 18–37.

Collard, D. (2009), "Alfred Russel Wallace and the political economists", *History of Political Economy*, vol. 41, n°4, Winter, p. 605–644.

Colson, C. (1901–1910), *Cours d'économie politique* Paris: Gauthier-Villars; definitive and enlarged edition, 1924–1933.

Commerçon, N. and Boureille, B. (2000), « Émile Levasseur ou le rapprochement de deux champs disciplinaires : l'économie et la géographie », in: P. Dockès, L. Frobert, G. Klotz, J.-P. Potier, A. Tiran (Eds), *Les traditions économiques françaises, 1848–1939*, Paris: Éd. du C.N.R.S., p. 139–153.

Coquelin, C. (1852a), « Concurrence », in: C. Coquelin and G.-U. Guillaumin, *Dictionnaire de l'économie politique*, Paris: Guillaumin, vol. 1, p. 448–455.

Coquelin, C. (1852b), « Économie politique », in: C. Coquelin and G.-U. Guillaumin, *Dictionnaire de l'économie politique*, Paris: Guillaumin, vol. 1, 643–666.

Cot, A.-L. and Lallement, J. (2006), « Éléments pour une histoire des théories de l'équilibre général de Walras à Arrow et Debreu », *Économies et Sociétés-Cahiers de l'I.S.M.E.A.*, vol. XL, n°12, Œconomia series, Histoire de la pensée économique, n°38, p. 1705–1752.

Courcelle-Seneuil, J.-G. (1867), *Traité théorique et pratique d'économie politique*, 2nd revised and enlarged edition, Paris: F. Amyot, 2 vol.

Courcelle-Seneuil, J.-G. (1872), « Étude sur le mandarinat français », *Journal des économistes*, vol. 38, 3rd series, 7th year, n° 84, December, p. 325–347.

Courcelle-Seneuil, J.-G. (1875), « Des obstacles que rencontre la diffusion des connaissances économiques », *Journal des économistes*, vol. 39, 3rd series, 10th year, 15 September, p. 309–323.

Cournot, A.-A. (1838), *Recherches sur les principes mathématiques de la théorie des richesses*, Introduction de Takashi Negishi, Paris: Dunod, 2001. English transl., *Researches into the Mathematical Principles of the Theory of Wealth*, N. T. Bacon (ed), London: Macmillan, 1897.

Cournot, A.-A. (1863), *Principes de la théorie des richesses*, Paris: Hachette.

Cousin, V. (1853), *Du Vrai, du Beau et du Bien*, 3rd edition entirely revised, Paris: Didier.

Creedy, John (1980), "The early use of Lagrange multipliers in Economics", *The Economic Journal*, vol. 90, June, p. 371–376.

Creedy, John (1986), Edgeworth and the Development of Neoclassical Economics, Oxford: Basil Blackwell.

Croce, B. (1899), *Materialismo storico ed economia marxistica*, 6th ed., 1941, Bari: Laterza, 1973.

Cunliffe, J. and Erreygers, G. (1999), "Moral philosophy and economics: the formation of François Huet's doctrine of property rights", *European Journal of History of Economic Thought*, vol. 6, n°4, Winter, p. 581–605.

Cusumano, V. (1872), « Il congresso degli economisti tedeschi in Eisenach », *Archivio giuridico*, vol. X, p. 222–228.

Cusumano, V. (1873–74), « Sulla condizione attuale degli studi economici in Germania », *Archivio giuridico*, vol. XI and XII, reprinted in: *Sulla condizione attuale degli studi economici in Germania. Studio*, Bologna: Tipi Fava e Garagnani, 1873.

Cusumano, V. (1874), « Lo Smithianismo, i Riformisti e i Socialisti cattedratici », *L'Economista d'Italia*, vol. VI, n° 43, 25 October, p. 554–556.

Cusumano, V. (1875), *Le scuole economiche della Germania in rapporto alla questione sociale - Studii*, Napoli: Giuseppe Marghieri.

Dal Pane, L. (1963), « Luigi Cossa », in: Massimo Finoia (Ed.), *Il pensiero economico italiano, 1850–1950*, Bologna: Cappelli, 1980, p. 293–308.

Debs, A. (2004), "'To be' or 'ought to be': the questions of empirical content and normative bias in Léon Walras's methodology", *Journal of the History of Economic Thought*, vol. 26, n°4, December, p. 479–492.

De Caro, G. (1980), « Sulla genesi dell'economia pura. Questione sociale e rivoluzione scientifica in Léon Walras », in: L. Walras, *Introduzione alla questione sociale*, Roma: Istituto della Enciclopedia Italiana, p. 1–92.

De Caro, G. (1989), « Sulla passività dell'imprenditore walrassiano », *Storia del pensiero economico*, new series, n° 17, p. 30–33.

De Caro, G. (1991), «Rileggere Walras », *Storia del pensiero economico*, new series, n° 21, p. 35–41.

De Caro, G. (1992), « Ambito e metodo dell'*Économie politique appliquée*. A proposito della nuova edizione degli *Études* walrasiani », *Storia del pensiero economico*, new series, n°24, p. 19–38.

De Coster, M. (1978), *L'analogie en sciences humaines*, Paris: P.U.F.

De Paoli, J. (2018), « Clément Colson et le développement de l'économie mathématique et de la statistique en France », *Revue d'histoire de la pensée économique*, n°6, p. 141–168.

De Paoli, J. (2020), *Science économique et pratique des ingénieurs économistes. L'exemple de Clément Colson*, Paris: Classiques Garnier.

De Vroey, M. (1998), "Is the tâtonnement hypothesis a good caricature of market forces ?", *Journal of Economic Methodology*, vol. 5, n° 2, December, p. 201–221.

De Vroey, M. (1999), "Transforming Walras into a Marshallian economist: A critical review of Donald Walker's *Walras's Market Models*", *Journal of the History of Economic Thought*, vol. 21, n° 4, December, p. 413–435.

De Vroey, M. (2003), "Perfect information *à la* Walras versus perfect information *à la* Marshall", *Journal of Economic Methodology*, vol. 10, n°4, p. 465–492.

DÉmier, F. (2005), « Louis Blanc face à l'économie de marché », in: Francis DÉmier, (Ed), *Louis Blanc. Un socialiste en république*, Paris: Creaphis, p. 133–150.

Desroche, Henri (1984), « Frédéric Le Play et les courants d'économie sociale au xixe siècle », *La Revue de l'économie sociale,* n° 2, October–December, p. 43–52.

Desroche, H. (1991), Histoires d'économies sociales - D'un Tiers État aux Tiers secteurs, 1791–1991, Paris: Syros.

Destutt de Tracy, A. (1817), *Éléments d'idéologie*, Paris: Courcier. Reprinted, Paris: Vrin, 1970.

Diemer, A. (2004), « Analyse épistémologique de l'œuvre de Walras à la lumière des travaux de Dupuit », in: R. Baranzini, A. Diemer and C. Mouchot (Eds), *Études walrassiennes*. Foreword by Jan Van Daal. Paris: L'Harmattan, p. 51–80.

Diemer, A. (2006), « Auguste Walras, les premiers pas de l'économie scientifique », *Économies et Sociétés-Cahiers de l'I.S.M.E.A.*, vol. XL, n°12, Œconomia series Histoire de la pensée économique, n° 38, p. 1753–1776.

Diemer, Arnaud (2010), « Auguste Walras et la critique de l'économie politique de J.-B. Say », in: A. Tiran, (Ed), *Jean-Baptiste Say. Influences, critiques et postérité*, Paris: Éditions Classiques Garnier, p. 501–542.

Diemer, A. (2012), « Comment concilier les droits de l'individu et les droits de la communauté? Les apports d'Auguste Walras », *Revue d'économie politique*, vol. 122, n°3, May-June, p. 437–465.

Diemer, A. (2013), « De la métaphysique à la théorie de la science. Retour sur le programme scientifique walrassien », in: A. Diemer and J.–P. Potier (Ed), *Léon Walras. Un siècle après (1910–2010)*, Brussels: Peter Lang, p. 59–85.

Diemer, A. and Guillemin, H. (2011), « De la 'connexion des sciences' à la science économique, le programme scientifique d'Auguste Walras », in: R. Baranzini, A. Legris and L. Ragni (Eds), *Léon Walras et l'équilibre économique général. Recherches récentes*, Paris: Economica, p. 21–42.

Dockès, P. (1992), "Léon Walras and the French 'intellectuals' (1896–1897)", in: S. Todd Lowry (Ed), *Perspectives in the History of Economic Thought*, vol. 8, Aldershot: Edward Elgar, p. 90–123.

Dockès, P. (1993), « Les idées socialistes de Léon Walras et leur réception au temps de l'Affaire Dreyfus (Péguy, Valéry et quelques autres) », in: *État et pouvoir (II)*, Actes du Colloque de Nice (17–19 september 1992) de l'Association Française des Historiens des Idées Politiques, Marseille: Presses Universitaires d'Aix-Marseille, p. 645–667.

Dockès, P. (1994), « 'La société n'est pas un pique-nique': le socialisme appliqué de Léon Walras », *Économies et sociétés-Cahiers de l'ISMEA*, vol. XXVIII, n° 10–11, Œconomia series, Histoire de la pensée économique, n° 20–21, p. 279–325.

Dockès, P. (1996), *La société n'est pas un pique-nique. Léon Walras et l'économie sociale. Le Vrai, le Juste, l'Utile*, Paris: Economica.

Dockès, P. (1999), « Ce qui est, ce qui devrait être, ce qui sera: Walras's economics as he saw it », *Revue européenne des sciences sociales. Cahiers Vilfredo Pareto*, vol. XXXVII, n°116, p. 13–36.

Dockès, P. (2004), « Léon Walras et le progrès économique », in: R. Baranzini, A. Diemer and C. Mouchot (Eds), *Études walrassiennes*. Foreword by Jan Van Daal. Paris: L'Harmattan, p. 211–231.

Dockès, P. (2005), « Léon Walras et la conciliation des vérités », Actes du 4e colloque de l'Association internationale Walras, *Les Cahiers du CERAS*, *Études d'économie walrassienne*, n°4, april, p. 169–188.

Dockès, P. (2006), « Léon Walras: la Vérité, l'Intérêt et la Justice réconciliés », *Économies et sociétés-Cahiers de l'I.S.M.E.A.*, vol. XL, n°12, Œconomia series, Histoire de la pensée économique, n°38, p. 1777–1812.

Dockès, P. (2011), « Lire Walras les autres. Une 'note d'humeur' », in: R. Baranzini, A. Legris and L. Ragni (Eds), *Léon Walras et l'équilibre économique général. Recherches récentes*, Paris: Economica, p. 1–17.

Dockès, P. (2014a), "Walras, Marx and the philosophy of history", in: Roberto Baranzini and François Allisson (Eds), *Economics and Other Branches. In the Shade of the Oak Tree. Essays in Honour of Pascal Bridel*, London: Pickering & Chatto, p. 39–52.

Dockès, P. (2014b), « La création du *Centre Auguste et Léon Walras* » [interview], *Économies et sociétés-Cahiers de l'I.S.M.E.A.*, vol. XLVIII, n°11–12, Œconomia series, Histoire de la pensée économique, n°51, p. 1748–1754.

Dockès, P. and Potier, J.-P. (2001), *La vie et l'œuvre économique de Léon Walras*, Paris: Economica.

Dockès, P. and Potier, J.-P. (2005), « Léon Walras et le statut de la concurrence: une étude à partir des *Éléments d'économie politique pure* », in: G. Bensimon (Ed), *Histoire des représentations du marché*, Paris: Michel Houdiard, p. 366–391.

Dockès, P. and Mouchot, C. (2009), « Lire Walras - Des fonds d'archives à l'édition et à la réinterprétation des *Œuvres économiques complètes* d'Auguste et Léon Walras », *Cahiers d'économie politique*, n°57, p. 197–210.

D'Orsi, A. (2000), (ed), "Achille Loria", *Quaderni di storia dell'Università di Torino*, n°3, Torino: Il Segnalibro.

Dos Santos Ferreira, R. (2011), « La filiation Cournot-Walras », in: R. Baranzini, A. Legris and L. Ragni (Eds), *Léon Walras et l'équilibre économique général. Recherches récentes*, Paris: Economica, p. 65–78.

Dos Santos Ferreira, R. (2014), "The case against market perfection: the two Bertrands' objections are one", in: R. Baranzini and F. Allisson (Ed), *Economics and Other Branches. In the Shade of the Oak Tree. Essays in Honour of Pascal Bridel*, London: Pickering & Chatto, p. 31–37.

Dos Santos Ferreira, R. and Ege, R. (2013), "General equilibrium as competitive equilibrium: the significance of Walras' achievement from a Cournotian viewpoint", *European Journal of the History of Economic Thought*, vol. 20, n°4, August, p. 625–645.

Du Bois-Reymond, E. (1878), « L'histoire de la civilisation et la science de la nature. [Conférences scientifiques de Cologne] », *Revue scientifique de la France et de l'étranger*, 2nd series, 7th year, n°29, 19 January, p. 669–686.

Du Mesnil-Marigny, J. (1859), *L'Économie politique devenue science exacte, ou les Libres échangistes et les protectionnistes conciliés*, Paris: Plon, 3rd ed., 1878.

Dumez, H. (1985), *L'économiste, la science et le pouvoir. Le cas Walras*, Paris: P.U.F.

Dupuit, J. (1844), « De la mesure de l'utilité des travaux publics », *Annales des Ponts et Chaussées*, 2nd series, vol. VIII, n°116, 2nd Semester, reprinted in: *Œuvres économiques complètes*, Y. Breton and G. Klotz (Eds), Paris: Economica, 2009, vol. 1, p. 203–241.

Dupuit, J. (1849), « De l'influence des péages sur l'utilité des voies de communication », *Annales des Ponts et Chaussées*, 2nd séries, vol. XVII, n°207, 1st Semester, reprinted in: *Œuvres économiques complètes*, Y. Breton and G. Klotz (Eds), Paris: Economica, 2009, vol. 1, p. 243–308.

Dupuit, J. (1853), « Voies de communication », in: C. Coquelin and G.-U. Guillaumin (Eds), *Dictionnaire de l'économie politique*, Paris: Guillaumin, vol. 2, p. 846–854, reprinted in: *Œuvres économiques complètes*, Y. Breton and G. Klotz (Eds), Paris: Economica, 2009, vol. 1, p. 431–452.

Dupuit, J. (1861), « Réponse à M. Dunoyer à propos de son rapport sur l'ouvrage intitulé *La Liberté commerciale*. À monsieur le Directeur du *Journal des économistes* », *Journal des économistes*, 2nd series, 9th year, vol. 31, n°17, July, p. 111–117, reprinted in: *Œuvres économiques complètes*, Y. Breton and G. Klotz (Eds), Paris: Economica, 2009, vol. 2, p. 539–547.

Durelle-Marc, Y.-A. (2011), « Pour une 'idée raisonnée de ce que doit être un bon système de finances': Paul Leroy-Beaulieu (1843–1916) ou la science des finances publiques à la fin du XIXe siècle », in: A. Stora-Lamarre, J.-L. Halperin, F. Audren (Eds), *La République et son droit (1870–1930)*, Besançon: Presses Universitaires de Franche-Comté, p. 165–183.

Edgeworth, F. Y. (1881), *Mathematical Psychics. An essay on the application of mathematics to the moral sciences*, London: P. Kegan.

Edgeworth, F. Y. (1891), « La théorie mathématique de l'offre et de la demande et le coût de production », *Revue d'économie politique*, vol. V, n°1, January, p. 10–28.

Escarra, É. (1904), *Nationalisation du sol et socialisme*, Ph.D. thesis, faculté de droit de l'Université de Paris, Paris: H. Jouve.

Etner, F. (2011), « Walras avait-il raison de critiquer Dupuit? », *Œconomia-History, Methodology, Philosophy*, vol. 1, n°4, December, p. 589–612.

Etner, F. and Silvant, C. (2017), *Histoire de la pensée économique en France. Depuis 1789*, Paris: Economica.

Faccarello, G. (2010), "Bold ideas. French liberal economists and the State: Say to Leroy-Beaulieu", *European Journal of the History of Economic Thought*, vol. 17, n°4, October, p. 719–758.

Faucci, R. (1975), « Francesco Ferrara fra politica ed economia (II) », *Giornale degli economisti e Annali di economia*, vol. XXXIV, new series, n° 9–10, September–October, p. 649–668.

Faucci, R. (1976–1977), « Revisione del marxismo e teoria economica della proprietà in Italia, 1880–1900: Achille Loria (e gli altri) », *Quaderni fiorentini per la storia del pensiero giuridico moderno*, n°5–6, p. 587–680.

Faucci, R. (1984), « Cossa Luigi », in: *Dizionario biografico degli italiani*, Roma: Treccani, vol. 30, p. 94–97.

Ferrara, F. (1874), « Il germanismo economico in Italia », *La nuova antologia*, vol. XXVI, n°8, august, reprinted in: *Opere complete*, vol. X, *Saggi, rassegne, memorie economiche e finanziarie*, Federico Caffè (Ed), Roma: Bancaria editrice, 1972, p. 555–591.

Ferraton, C. (2007), *Associations et coopératives. Une autre histoire économique*, Ramuville Saint-Ayne: Éditions Érès.

Filippi, I. (1984), « I socialisti della cattedra e Marx nella critica di Vito Cusumano », in: Piero Di Giovanni, (Ed), *Il marxismo e la cultura meridionale,* Palermo: Palumbo, p. 137–145.

Francolin, G. (1889), « Le Sénat professionnel », *La Revue socialiste*, vol. IX, n°52, 15 April, p. 462–463.

Frobert, L. (1997), « L'économie politique d'Étienne Antonelli (1879–1971) », *Revue économique*, vol. 48, n°6, November, p. 1529–1559.

Frobert, L. (2000), « Étienne Antonelli (1879–1971) », in: L. Frobert, J.-P. Potier and A. Tiran, (Eds), *Économistes en Lyonnais, en Dauphiné et en Forez - 1750–1950*, Lyon: Éditions de l'Institut des Sciences de l'Homme, p. 13–21.

Gharbi, J.-S. and Sekerler-Richardi, P. (2010), « Léon Walras, précurseur du libertarisme de gauche? », communication au 7e Colloque de l'Association Internationale Walras, « Léon Walras (1834–1910). Colloque du centenaire », Université Lumière-Lyon 2.

Garnier, J. (1845), « Organisation du travail, par M. Louis Blanc », *Journal des économistes*, vol. XI, n°44, July, p. 421–427.

Garnier, Joseph (1863), *Traité d'économie politique*, 5th ed., Paris: Guillaumin/Garnier.

Garnier, J. (1864), « Création d'une chaire d'économie politique à la faculté de droit de Paris », *Journal des économistes*, 2nd series, 11th year, vol. 44, n°130, October, p. 5–15.

Garnier, J. (1866a), « Chronique économique », *Journal des économistes*, 3rd series, 1st year, vol. 3, n° 9, September, p. 466–476.

Garnier, J. (1866b), « Chronique économique », *Journal des économistes*, 3rd series, 1st year, vol. 4, n°12, December, p. 503–508.

Garrigou-Lagrange, A. (1946), « Michel Chevalier et son cours au Collège de France », in: *Mélanges économiques dédiés à M. le professeur René Gonnard*, Paris: L.G.D.J., p. 137–147.

Garrouste, P. (1994), « Léon Walras et Carl Menger à propos de l'utilisation des mathématiques en économie politique », Économies et sociétés-Cahiers de l'ISMEA, vol. XXVIII, n°10–11, Œconomia series, Histoire de la pensée économique, n°20–21, p. 11–27.

Giddings, F. H. (1895), "Sociology and the Abstract Sciences. The Origin of the Social Feelings", *Annals of the American Academy of Political and Social Science*, vol. V, n°5, March, p. 94–101 [746–753].

Giddings, F. H. (1896), The Principles of Sociology. An Analysis of the Phenomena of Association and of Social Organization, New York: Macmillan, French transl., Principes de sociologie, Paris: V. Giard & E. Brière, 1897.

Giddings, F. H. (1897), *The Theory of Socialization: A Syllabus of Sociological Principles for the Use of College and University Classes, With References to the Third Edition of "The Principles of Sociology"*, New York: Macmillan.

Gide, C. (1883a), « De quelques nouvelles doctrines sur la propriété foncière (*Progress and Poverty*, by Henry George) », *Journal des économistes*, 4th series, vol. 22, 15 May, p. 169–199.

Gide, C. (1883b), « *Théorie mathématique de la richesse sociale* par Léon Walras », *Journal des économistes*, 4th series, vol. 23, 15 September, p. 444–448.

Gide, C. (1886), *Discours d'inauguration du congrès des Sociétés coopératives de consommation de France prononcé en séance solennelle au théâtre des Variétés de Lyon le 19 septembre 1886*, Paris: Joseph Kugelmann.

Gide, C. (1889), « De la coopération et des transformations qu'elle est appelée à réaliser dans l'ordre économique », *Revue d'économie politique*, vol. III, n° 5, May, p. 473–496.

Gide, C. (1890), "The economic schools and the teaching of political economy in France", *Political Science Quarterly*, vol. V, n°4, December, p. 603–635.

Gide, C. (1897), « Léon Walras. *Études d'économie sociale* », *Revue d'économie politique*, vol. 11, n°3, p. 301–307.

Gide, C. (1898), *Principes d'économie politique*, 6th edition revised and enlarged, Paris: L. Larose.

Gide, C. (1900), *L'enseignement des sciences sociales en France, enseignement supérieur*, Paris: F. Alcan.

Gide, C. (1907), "Economic Literature in France at the Beginning of the Twentieth Century", *The Economic Journal*, vol. XVII, June, p. 192–212.

Gide, C. (1917), « Secrétan économiste », *Revue de théologie et de philosophie*, new series, vol. 5, n°25, November–December, p. 253–264.

Gide, C. (1926), « Walras (Léon), *Éléments d'économie pure ou théorie de la richesse sociale* », *Revue d'économie politique*, vol. 40, n°2, March–April, p. 731.

Gide, C. (1928), « Le Conseil national économique », *Revue d'économie politique*, vol. 42, n°4, July–August, p. 1049–1059.

Gide, C. and Rist, C. (1909), *Histoire des doctrines économiques depuis les physiocrates jusqu'à nos jours*, Paris: L. Larose and L. Tenin; 2nd ed., 1913, 3rd ed., 1920, 4th ed., 1922, 5th ed., 1926, 6th ed., 1944.

Gioia, V. and Noto, S. (Eds) (2011), *Angelo Messedaglia e il suo tempo*, Macerata: Edizioni Università di Macerata.

Gitermann, M. (1910), « La révolution électrotechnique et la socialisation de la houille blanche (d'après quelques publications récentes) », *Les Annales de la régie directe*, 2nd year, n°10, August, p. 289–297.

Gloria, S. (2018), « Menger contre Walras », *Revue économique*, vol. 69, n°4, p. 593–613.

Goodwin, R. M. (1951), "Iteration, automatic, computers, and economic dynamics", *Metroeconomica*, 3, n° 1, April, p. 1–7.

Gossen, H. H. (1854), *Entwickelung der Gesetze des menschlichen Verkehrs, und der daraus fliessenden Regeln für menschliches Handeln*, Braunschweig: F. Vieweg & Sohn. English translation, *The Laws of Human Relations and the Rules of Human Action Derived Therefrom*, R. C. Blitz (Ed), with an introductory essay by N. Georgescu-Roegen, Cambridge, Mass.: The M.I.T. Press, 1983.

Goutte, P.-H. (2013), « Éditer les manuscrits philosophiques d'Auguste Walras », in: A. Diemer and J.-P. Potier (Eds), *Léon Walras. Un siècle après (1910–2010)*, Brussels: Peter Lang, p. 41–57.

Goutte, P.-H. and Servet, J.-M. (1990a), « Introduction aux œuvres économiques d'Auguste Walras: l'histoire des éditions », in: *Richesse, liberté et société, Œuvres économiques complètes*, vol. I, Paris: Economica, 1990, p. XLIX–CXX.

Goutte, P.-H. and Servet, J.-M. (1990b), « Auguste Walras de 1831 à 1848 », in: *Richesse, liberté et société, Œuvres économiques complètes*, vol. I, Paris: Economica, 1990, p. CXXI–CLXXII.

Gozzi, G. (1983), « Organizzazione degli interessi e razionalità amministrativa in Italia tra Otto e Novecento - Carlo Francesco Ferraris e la scienza dell'amministrazione », *Il pensiero politico*, vol. XVI, n°2, p. 215–240.

Gramsci, A. (1934), "Prison Notebook 22. Americanism and Fordism", in: Q. Hoare and G. Novell Smith (Eds), *Selections from the Prison Notebooks of Antonio Gramsci*, London: Lawrence & Wishart, 1971, p. 277–318.

Grandjonc, J. (1989), *Communisme/Kommunismus/Communism - Origine et développement international de la terminologie communautaire prémarxiste des utopistes aux néo-babouvistes, 1785–1842*, Trier: *Schriften aus dem Karl-Marx-Haus*, n° 39, 2 vol.

Greef, G. de (1892), *La Constituante et le régime représentatif*, Brussels: J. Lebègue.

Guesnerie, R. (2011), "On the modernity of Walras", in: P. Bridel (Ed), *General Equilibrium Analysis. A Century after Walras*, London: Routledge, p. 134–144.

Haulleville, P. de (1894), « La représentation des intérêts », *Revue sociale et politique* [Brussels], 4th year, n°6, p. 419–445.

Hauser, H. (1903), *L'enseignement des sciences sociales. État actuel de cet enseignement dans les divers pays du monde*, Paris: A. Chevalier-Maresq.

Hautcoeur, P.-C. (Ed) (2007), *Le marché financier français au* xixe *siècle*, vol. 1, *Récit*, Paris: Publications de la Sorbonne.

HÉbert, C. (1988), « Léon Walras et les associations populaires coopératives », *Revue d'économie politique*, vol. 98, n°2, March–April, p. 252–272.

HÉbert, C. and Potier, J.-P. (1987), "The surprising history of the *Mélanges d'économie politique et sociale,* a previously unpublished work by Léon Walras", *History of Economics Society Bulletin*, vol. IX, n° 1, Fall, p. 67–79.

HÉbert, C. and Potier, J.-P. (1990), « Introduction: Léon Walras et la coopération », in: L. Walras, *Les Associations populaires coopératives*, *OEC*, vol. VI, C. Hébert and J.-P. Potier (Eds), Paris: Economica, p. IX–XLIII.

Hebert, Robert F. (1987), "Isnard, Achylle Nicolas", in: *The New Palgrave. A Dictionary of Economics*, John Eatwell, Murray Milgate, Peter Newman (Eds), London: Macmillan, vol. 2, p. 1004–1005.

Henderson, J. M. and Quandt, R. E. (1958), *Microeconomic Theory*, New York: McGraw-Hill, 1958.

Herland, M. (1991), « Un monument de l'édition. Les œuvres économiques de MM. Walras », *Revue économique*, vol. 42, n°4, July, p. 765–771.

Herland, M. (1996), "Three French Socialist Economists: Leroux, Proudhon, Walras", *Journal of the History of Economic Thought*, vol. 18, n°1, Spring, p. 133–153.

Herland, M. (2000), « Léon Walras ou l'apothéose de l'économie politique et sociale », in: P. Dockès, L. Frobert, G. Klotz, J.-P. Potier and A. Tiran (Eds), *Les traditions économiques françaises, 1848–1939*, Paris: Éd. du C.N.R.S., p. 471–484.

Herland, M. (2013a), « Pourquoi Walras était plus libéral que socialiste ? », in: A. Diemer and J.-P. Potier (Eds), *Léon Walras. Un siècle après (1910–2010)*, Brussels: Peter Lang, p. 107–123.

Herland, M. (2013b), « Les Walras critiques de *La Justice* de Proudhon », *Économies et sociétés-Cahiers de l'ISMEA*, vol. XLVII, n°6, Oeconomia series, Histoire de la pensée économique, n°48, p. 827–852.

Hicks, J. R. (1934), "Léon Walras", *Econometrica*, vol. II, n°4, October, p. 338–348.

Hicks, J. R. (1976), "Some questions of time in economics", reprinted in: J. R. Hicks, *Money, Interest and Wages, Collected Essays on Economic Theory*, vol. II, Oxford: B. Blackwell, 1982, p. 282–300.

Hildenbrand, W. (1983), "Introduction" to *Mathematical Economics: Twenty Papers of Gérard Debreu*, Cambridge: Cambridge University Press, p. 1–29.

Huck, E. (1999), *Justice et "neutralité" de la concurrence au regard de la répartition des richesses dans l'oeuvre de Léon Walras*, Ph.D. thesis, Université Louis Pasteur, Strasbourg.

Hutchison, T. W. (1953), *A Review of Economic Doctrines, 1870–1929*, Oxford: Oxford University Press.

Ingrao, B. and Israel, G. (1987), La mano invisibile. L'equilibrio economico nella storia della scienza, Bari: Laterza; English transl., The Invisible Hand. Economic Equilibrium in the History of Science, Cambridge, Mass.: M.I.T. Press, 1990.

Isnard, A.-N. (1781), *Traité des richesses.* Contenant *l'analyse de l'usage des richesses en général & de leurs valeurs; les principes & les lois naturelles de la circulation des richesses, de leur distribution, du commerce, de la circulation des monnoies & de l'impôt* [...], London and Lausanne: Grasset, 2 vol, partial and bilingual edition, in: R. Van den Berg, *At the Origins of Mathematical Economics. The Economics of A. N. Isnard (1748–1803)*, London: Routledge, 2006, p. 68–197.

Jacoud, G. (2014), « Droit de propriété et économie politique dans l'analyse saint-simonienne », *Revue économique*, vol. 65, March, p. 299–315.

Jacoud, G. and Potier, J.-P. (2020), « Auguste and Léon Walras and Saint-Simonianism » *European Journal of the History of economic Thought*, vol. 27, n°3, June, p. 368–387.

Jaffé, W. (1935), "Unpublished papers and letters of Léon Walras", *Journal of Political Economy*, vol. 43, April, reprinted in: *William Jaffé's Essays on Walras*, D. A. Walker, (Ed) Cambridge: Cambridge U. Press, 1983, p. 17–35.

Jaffé, W. (1956), « Léon Walras et sa conception de l'économie politique », *Annales juridiques, politiques, économiques et sociales de la faculté de droit d'Alger*, 2nd year, n° 2, 1956, p. 207–221.

Jaffé, W. (1960), « Léon Walras et ses rapports avec les économistes américains », *Revue économique et sociale*, vol. 18, April, p. 133–140.

Jaffé, W. (1964), "New light on an old quarrel: Barone's unpublished review of Wicksteed's 'Essay on the Coordination of the Laws of Distribution' and related documents", *Cahiers Vilfredo Pareto*, n°3, p. 61–102, reprinted in: *William Jaffé's Essays on Walras*, D. A. Walker (Ed), Cambridge: Cambridge U. Press, 1983, p. 176–212.

JAFFÉ, W. (1965), "Biography and economic analysis", *Western Economic Journal*, vol. III, n°3, Summer, p. 223–232.

JAFFÉ, W. (1968), "Léon Walras", in: *International Encyclopedia of the Social Sciences*, D. L. Sills (Ed), New York: The Free Press, vol 16, reprinted in: *William Jaffé's Essays on Walras*, Donald A. Walker (Ed), Cambridge: Cambridge U. Press, 1983, p. 131–135.

JAFFÉ, W. (1969), "A. N. Isnard, progenitor of the Walrasian general equilibrium model", *History of Political Economy*, vol. 1, Spring, reprinted in: *William Jaffé's Essays on Walras*, D. A. Walker (Ed), Cambridge: Cambridge U. Press, 1983, p. 55–77.

JAFFÉ, W. (1971), "Reflections on the importance of Léon Walras", in: *P. Hennipman Festschrift*, 1971, A. Heertje et al. (Eds), reprinted in: *William Jaffé's Essays on Walras*, D. A. Walker (Ed), Cambridge: Cambridge U. Press, 1983, p. 269–287.

JAFFÉ, W. (1972), "Léon Walras's role in the 'Marginal Revolution' of the 1870s", *History of Political Economy*, vol. 4, Fall, p. 379–405, reprinted in: *William Jaffé's Essays on Walras*, D. A. Walker (Ed), Cambridge: Cambridge U. Press, 1983, p. 288–310.

JAFFÉ, W. (1976), "Menger, Jevons and Walras De-homogenized", *Economic Inquiry*, vol. 14, December, reprinted in: *William Jaffé's Essays on Walras*, D. A. Walker (Ed), Cambridge: Cambridge U. Press, 1983, p. 311–325.

JAFFÉ, W. (1977a), "A centenarian on a bicentenarian: Léon Walras's *Éléments* on Adam Smith's *Wealth of Nations*", *Canadian Journal of Economics*, vol. 10, February, reprinted in: *William Jaffé's Essays on Walras*, D. A. Walker (Ed), Cambridge: Cambridge U. Press, 1983, p. 93–107.

JAFFÉ, W. (1977b), "The Walras-Poincaré correspondence on the cardinal measurability of utility", *Canadian Journal of Economics*, vol. 10, May, reprinted in: *William Jaffé's Essays on Walras*, D. A. Walker (Ed), Cambridge: Cambridge U. Press, 1983, p. 300–307.

JAFFÉ, W. (1977c), "The birth of Léon Walras's *Éléments*", *History of Political Economy*, vol. 9, Summer, reprinted in: *William Jaffé's Essays on Walras*, D. A. Walker (Ed), Cambridge: Cambridge U. Press, 1983, p. 78–92.

JAFFÉ, W. (1977d), "The normative bias of the walrasian model: Walras versus Gossen", *Quarterly Journal of Economics*, vol. 91, August, reprinted in: *William Jaffé's Essays on Walras*, D. A. Walker (Ed), Cambridge: Cambridge U. Press, 1983, p. 326–342.

JAFFÉ, W. (1978), Review of Michio Morishima's *Walras's Economics: A Pure Theory of Capital and Money*, *The Economic Journal*, vol. 88, n°151, September, p. 574–576.

JAFFÉ, W. (1980), "Walras's economics as others see it", *Journal of Economic Literature*, vol. 18, n°2, June, reprinted in: *William Jaffé's Essays on Walras*, D. A. Walker (Ed), Cambridge: Cambridge U. Press, 1983, p. 343–370.

JAFFÉ, W. (1981), "Another look at Léon Walras's theory of *tâtonnement*", *History of Political Economy*, vol. 13, n°2, Summer, reprinted in: *William Jaffé's Essays on Walras*, D. A. Walker (Ed), Cambridge: Cambridge U. Press, 1983, p. 244–266.

JAMES, W. (1890), *The Principles of Psychology*, New York: Henry Holt, vol. 1.

Jevons, W. S. (1871), *The Theory of Political Economy*, London: Macmillan, 2[d] edition revised and enlarged, with new preface and appendices, 1879.

Jolink, A. (1991), *Liberté, Egalité, Rareté. The Evolutionary Economics of Léon Walras*, Rotterdam: Tinbergen Institute Research Series.

Jolink, A. (1993), "Review article. Economic equilibrium in the history of science: reviewing *The Invisible Hand*", *The Economic Journal*, vol. 103, n°420, September, p. 1303–1311.

Jolink, A. (1996), *The Evolutionist Economics of Léon Walras,* London: Routledge.

Jolink A. and Van Daal, J. (1989), "Léon Walras' latest book: *Mélanges d'économie politique et sociale*", *De Economist*, vol. 137, n° 3, p. 351–359.

Jousse, E. (2017), *Les hommes révoltés. Les origines intellectuelles du réformisme en France (1871–1917)*, Paris: Fayard.

Klotz, G. (1994), «Achylle Nicolas Isnard, précurseur de Léon Walras? », *Économies et sociétés-Cahiers de l'ISMEA*, vol. XXVIII, n°10–11, Œconomia series, Histoire de la pensée économique, n° 20–21, p. 29–52.

Kolm, S.-C. (1984), *Le libéralisme moderne*, Paris: P.U.F.

Koppl, R. (1992), "Price theory as physics: the Cartesian influence in Walras", *Methodus*, vol. 4, n°2, December, p. 17–28.

Koppl, R. (1995), "The Walras paradox", *Eastern Economic Journal*, vol. 21, n°1, p. 43-55.

Laffitte, P. (1886), « Matériaux pour servir à la biographie d'Auguste Comte », *La Revue occidentale philosophique, sociale et politique*, vol. 16, n°98, 1st trimester, p. 145–157.

Laffont, J.–J. (1993), « Walras et le service public », *Le Monde*, 21st December.

Laget, F. (2003), « Le droit subjectif de propriété chez Jean-Baptiste Say: un instrument de progrès », in: J.-P. Potier and A. Tiran (Eds), *Jean-Baptiste Say: nouveaux regards sur son œuvre*, Paris: Economica, p. 69–94.

La Grasserie, R. (1895), « De la représentation professionnelle », *Revue politique et parlementaire*, 2nd year, vol. V, n°11, August, p. 252–278.

La Grasserie, R. (1896a), « De la transformation du suffrage universel amorphe en suffrage universel organique », *Revue internationale de sociologie*, 4th year, n°4, April, p. 280–308.

La Grasserie, R. (1896b), *Projet de Constitution*, Paris: V. Giard & E. Brière.

Lallement, J. (1990), « Léon Walras et les idéaux de 1789 », *Économies et sociétés-Cahiers de l'ISMEA*, vol. XXIV, n°7–10, Œconomia series, Histoire de la pensée économique, n°13, p. 609–618.

Lallement, J. (1997), « L'économie pure de Walras est-elle normative ? », in: H. Brochier, R. Frydman, B. Gazier and J. Lallement (Eds), *L'Économie normative*, Paris: Economica, p. 73–88.

Lallement, J. (2000b), « Prix et équilibre selon Léon Walras », in: A. Beraud and G. Faccarello (Eds), *Nouvelle histoire de la pensée économique*, Paris: La Découverte, vol. 2, p. 449–497.

Lallement, J. (2004), « Walras et les mathématiques, un malentendu persistant », in: R. Baranzini, A. Diemer and C. Mouchot (Eds), *Études walrassiennes*. Foreword by Jan Van Daal. Paris: L'Harmattan, p. 81–104.

Lallement, J. (2014), "Walras between holism and individualism", in: R. Baranzini and F. Allisson (Eds), *Economics and Other Branches. In the Shade of the Oak Tree. Essays in Honour of Pascal Bridel*, London: Pickering & Chatto, p. 15–30.

Lallement, J. (2017), «Individu et société selon Walras », *Revue de philosophie économique*, vol. 18, n°1, p. 57–89.

Lampertico, F. (1875), « A Francesco Ferrara », *Giornale degli economisti,* 1st year, vol. II, n°8, November, p. 115–144.

Laplace, P.-S. (1796), *Exposition du système du monde*, reprinted Paris: Fayard, 1984.

Laurent, H. (1902), *Petit traité d'économie politique mathématique, rédigé conformément aux préceptes de l'École de Lausanne*, Paris: Charles Schmid.

Legris, A. and Ragni, L. (1999), « Recouvrement du champ de l'économie dans l'œuvre de Vilfredo Pareto : une mise en perspective du désaccord avec Léon Walras », *Revue européenne des sciences sociales. Cahiers Vilfredo Pareto,* vol. XXXVII, n°116, p. 325–346.

Lendjel, E. (1997), « Le 'biais empiriste' dans l'interprétation de Walker du tâtonnement walrassien », *Économies et sociétés-Cahiers de l'ISMEA*, vol. XXXI, n°10, October, Œconomia series, Histoire de la pensée économique, n°26, p. 47–84.

Lendjel, E. (1999), « Tâtonnement walrassien et marchandage parétien : une approche comparative », *Revue européenne des sciences sociales. Cahiers Vilfredo Pareto,* vol. XXXVII, n°116, p. 295–314.

Leroux, P. (1850), *Œuvres (1825–1850)*, Paris: Société typographique, vol. 1.

Leroy-Beaulieu, P. (1884), *Le Collectivisme. Examen critique du nouveau socialisme*, Paris: Guillaumin.

Leroy-Beaulieu, P. (1896), *Traité théorique et pratique d'économie politique*, Paris: Guillaumin, 4 vol.

Le Van-Lemesle, L. (1980a), « La promotion de l'économie politique en France au xixe siècle jusqu'à son introduction dans les facultés (1815–1881) », *Revue d'histoire moderne et contemporaine*, vol. XXVII, April–June, p. 270–294.

Le Van-Lemesle, L. (1980b), « La faculté de droit de Paris et l'introduction de l'économie politique dans son enseignement (1864–1878) », *Historical Reflexions-Réflexions historiques*, vol. 7, n°2 and 3, Summer-Fall, p. 327–336.

Le Van-Lemesle, L. (1983), « L'économie politique à la conquête d'une légitimité, 1896–1937 », *Actes de la recherche en sciences sociales*, n° 47–48, June, p. 113–117.

Le Van-Lemesle, L. (1991), « L'institutionnalisation de l'économie politique en France », in: Y. Breton and M. Lutfalla (Eds), *L'Économie politique en France au* xixe *siècle*, Paris: Economica, p. 355–388.

Le Van-Lemesle, L. (1992), « Étienne Antonelli (1879–1971). Un économiste moderniste aux origines de la sécurité sociale », in: A. Gueslin and P. Guillaume (Eds), *De la charité médiévale à la Sécurité sociale,* Paris: Éd. Ouvrières, p. 287–297.

Le Van-Lemesle, L. (1994a), « Antonelli, Étienne (1879–1971) », in: C. Fontanon and A. Grelon (Eds), *Les professeurs du Conservatoire National des Arts et Métiers. Dictionnaire biographique. 1794–1955*, Paris: INRP-CNAM, vol. 1, p. 108–116.

Le Van-Lemesle, L. (1994b), « Levasseur, Émile (1828–1911», in: C. Fontanon and A. Grelon (Eds), *Les professeurs du Conservatoire National des Arts et Métiers. Dictionnaire biographique. 1794–1955*, Paris: INRP-CNAM, vol. 2, p. 105–115.

Le Van-Lemesle, L. (2004), *Le Juste ou le Riche. L'enseignement de l'économie politique, 1815–1950*, Paris: Comité pour l'histoire économique de la France.

Levasseur, É. (1892), *La population française. Histoire de la population avant 1789 et démographie de la France comparée à celle des autres nations au XIX*[e] *siècle*, Paris: Arthur Rousseau, 3 vol.

Levasseur, É., Valette, C. and Wolowski, L. (1874), « Observations » [on Walras's « Principe d'une théorie mathématique de l'échange »], *Séances et travaux de l'Académie des sciences morales et politiques, Séances du 16 et 23 août 1873*, vol. 101, 33rd year, January, p. 117–120, reprinted in: *OEC*, vol. VII, C. Hébert and J.-P. Potier (Eds), Paris: Economica, 1987, p. 529–532.

Loveling, V. (1906): « Milan van Servië », *Groot Nederland*, vol. IV, reprinted in: Loveling Virginie, *Herinneringen [Bijeengebracht en ingeleid door Antonin van Elslander*], Hasselt: Uitgeverij Heideland, 1967, p. 144–155.

Lexis, W. (1881), « Zur mathematisch-ökonomischen Literatur », *Jahrbücher für Nationalökonomie und Statistik*, new series, vol. 3, august, p. 427–434; reprinted in: P. Bridel (Ed), *Le chêne et l'architecte. Un siècle de comptes rendus bibliographiques des* Éléments d'économie politique pure *de Léon Walras*, Geneva: Droz, 1996, p. 175–181.

Lhuillier, V. (1992), *Léon Walras, lecteur de Kant - Essai sur le statut épistémologique des* Études d'économie sociale, mémoire de D.E.A., GRESE, Université de Paris I.

Lhuillier, V. (2002), « Les trois premières *Tentatives d'application des mathématiques à l'économie politique* de Léon Walras et l'intégration progressive des choix subjectifs en économie pure », *Cahiers d'économie politique*, n°42, Spring, p. 29–48.

List, F. (1841), *National System of Political Economy*, translated from German by G. A. Matile, including the Notes of the French Translation by H. Richelot, with a Preliminary Essay and Notes by S. Colwell, Philadelphia: J. B. Lippincott and Co, 1856.

Lutfalla, M. (1991), « Louis Wolowski, 1810–1876 ou le libéralisme positif », in: Y. Breton and M. Lutfalla (Eds), *L'Économie politique en France au* xixe *siècle*, Paris: Economica, p. 185–201.

Luzzatti, L. (1874), « L'economia politica e le scuole germaniche », *La nuova antologia*, vol. XXVII, n°9, September, p. 174–192.

Machelon, J.-P. (1985), « L'idée de nationalisation en France de 1840 à 1914 », in: Bruguiere, Michel and al, *Administration et contrôle de l'économie - 1800–1914*, École pratique des hautes études – IVth section, Sciences historiques et philologiques, Geneva: Droz, p. 1–46.

Marchionatti, R. (1999), "The methodological foundations of pure and applied economics in Pareto. An anti-walrasian programme", *Revue européenne des sciences sociales. Cahiers Vilfredo Pareto*, vol. XXXVII, n°116, p. 277–294.

Marchionatti, R. (2007), "On the Application of Mathematics to Political Economy. The Edgeworth-Walras-Bortkiewicz Controversy, 1889–1891", *Cambridge Journal of Economics*, vol. 31, n°2, p. 291–307.

Markiewicz, P. (1994), « Wolowski, Louis (1810–1876) », in: C. Fontanon and A. Grelon (Eds), *Les professeurs du Conservatoire National des Arts et Métiers. Dictionnaire biographique. 1794–1955*, Paris: INRP-CNAM, vol. 2, p. 677–687.

Marx, K. (1872), "The nationalisation of the land", *The International Herald*, 15 June 1872, in: Marx-Engels, *Collected Works*, London: Lawrence & Wishart, vol. 23, 1988, p. 131–136.

Marx, K. and Engels, F. (1848), *Manifesto of the Communist Party*, in: Marx-Engels, *Collected Works*, London: Lawrence & Wishart, vol. 6, 1976, p. 477–519.

Ménard, C. (1990), "The Lausanne tradition: Walras and Pareto" and "Commentary" by Donald A. Walker, in: K. Hennings and W. J. Samuels (Eds), *Neoclassical Economic Theory, 1870 to 1930*, Boston: Kluwer, p. 95–136 and 137–150.

Meuwly, O. (2006), *Louis Ruchonnet. 1834–1893. Un homme d'État entre action et idéal*, Lausanne: Bibliothèque historique vaudoise.

Michel, G. (1899), *Léon Say - Sa vie, ses œuvres*, Paris: Calmann-Lévy.

Mill, J. (1821), *Elements of Political Economy*, 3rd ed. revised and corrected, London: Baldwin, Cradock and Joy, 1826, re-ed in: J. Mill, *Selected Economic Writings*, D. Winch (ed), Chicago: Chicago University Press, 1966, p. 203–366.

Mill, J. S. (1843), *A System of Logic Ratiocinative and Inductive,* London: J. W. Parker, 2 vol.

Mill, J. S. (1844), *Essays on Some Unsettled Questions of Political Economy*, London: John W. Parker.

Mill, J. S. (1st ed.1848, 7th ed., 1871), *Principles of Political Economy, with Some of Their Applications to Social Philosophy*, new edition J. M. Robson (Ed), *The Collected Works*, vol. II, Toronto/London: University of Toronto Press/Routledge and Kegan P., 1965, 2 tomes. French translation by H. Dussart and J.-G. Courcelle-Seneuil, *Principes d'économie politique avec quelques-unes de leurs applications à l'économie sociale*, Paris: Guillaumin, 1861, 3rd ed. revised on the 7th English ed., 1873, 2 vol.

Mill, J. S. (1870), "Land Tenure Reform", in: *Essays on Economics and Society*, J. M. Robson (Ed), *The Collected Works*, vol. V, Toronto/London: University of Toronto Press/Routledge and Kegan P., 1967, tome 2, p. 689–695.

Mill, J. S. (1873), *Autobiography*, with a Preface by J. J. Coss, New York: Columbia University Press, 1960.

Misaki, K. (2006), "The general equilibrium theory in Japanese economic thought: from Walras to Morishima", in: J. Backhaus and J. A. H. Maks (Eds), *From Walras to Pareto*, New York: Springer, p. 11–26.

Misaki, K. (2021), "Léon Walras and *The Wealth of Nations*: what did he really learn from Adam Smith ?", *European Journal of the History of Economic Thought*, vol. 28, n°3, June, p. 404–418.

Misaki, K. (2024), *Léon Walras's Economic Thought. The General Equilibrium Theory in Historical Perspective*, London/NewYork: Routledge.

Montet, C. (1982), « Le rôle de Charles Gide dans le développement de la pensée walrasienne en France », *Revue des études coopératives*, n°209–6, 4th trimester, p. 44–62.

Morini-Comby, J. (1953), « La carrière enseignante d'Étienne Antonelli », *Revue d'histoire économique et sociale*, vol. 31, n°4, p. 355–363.

Morishima, M. (1977), *Walras's Economics*, Cambridge: Cambridge U. Press.

Morishima, M. (1980), "W. Jaffé on Léon Walras: a comment", *Journal of Economic Literature*, vol. 18, n°2, June, p. 550–558.

Mornati, F. (1999a), *Pasquale Boninsegni e la Scuola di Losanna*, Torino : U.T.E.T.

Mornati, F. (1999b), « Le début des différends entre Pareto et Walras vus à travers leur correspondance et leurs ouvrages: 1891–1893 », *Revue européenne des sciences sociales. Cahiers Vilfredo Pareto*, vol. XXXVII, n°116, p. 261–275.

Mornati F. (2018–2020), *Vilfredo Pareto: An Intellectual Biography*, vol. I, *From Science to Liberty (1848–1891)*, 2018, vol. II, *The Illusions and Disillusions of Liberty (1891–1898)*, 2019, vol. III, *From Liberty to Science (1898–1923)*, 2020, London: Palgrave Macmillan.

Mouchot, C. (1988), « Histoire des différentes éditions des *Éléments d'économie politique pure* », Annex I, in: *OEC*, vol. VIII, C. Mouchot (Ed), Paris: Economica, p. 795–819.

Mouchot, C. (2004), « L'entrepreneur walrassien: modèle ou mythe ? », in: R. Baranzini, A. Diemer and C. Mouchot (Eds), *Études walrassiennes*. Foreword by Jan Van Daal. Paris: L'Harmattan, p. 169–177.

Mueller, T. M. (2017), "Can you put free will into an equation? The debate on determinism and mathematics at the end of the nineteenth century", *European Journal of the History of Economic Thought*, vol. 24, n°3, June, p. 441–464.

Nakakubo, K. (1999), "Half of Justice, Half of Utopia. Walras's Two Concepts of Justice and the Normative Bias of *Éléments*", *Revue Européenne des sciences Sociales. Cahiers Vilfredo Pareto*, vol. XXXVII, n°116, p. 37–50.

Nakakubo, K. (2000), "Walras as co-operator", in: P. Dockès, L. Frobert, G. Klotz, J.-P. Potier and A. Tiran (Eds), *Les traditions économiques françaises, 1848–1939*, Paris: Éd. du C.N.R.S., p. 485–502.

Negishi, T. (1989), "Walras and the General Equilibrium Theory", in: *History of economic theory*, chap. 7, Amsterdam: North Holland, reprinted in: *The Legacy of Léon Walras*, D. A. Walker (ed), Cheltenham: Edward Elgar, 2001, vol. 1, chap. 20, p. 363–399.

Northcott, C. H. (1948), "The Sociological Theories of Franklin Henry Giddings: Consciousness of Kind, Pluralistic Behavior, and Statistical Method", in: H. E. Barnes (Ed), *An Introduction to the History of Sociology*, Chicago: University of Chicago Press, p. 744–765.

Numa, G. (2012), "Dupuit and Walras on the natural monopoly in transport industries: what they really wrote and meant", *History of Political Economy*, vol. 44, n°1, Spring, p. 69–95.

Numa, G. (2013), *Réglementations et concurrence dans les chemins de fer français. 1823–1914*, Paris: Classiques Garnier.

Ott, A. (1890), « *Éléments d'économie politique pure*, par M. Léon Walras », *Journal des économistes*, 5th series, 49th year, January, p. 98–114.

Palante, G. (1899), « Léon Walras. *Études d'économie politique appliquée* », *Revue philosophique de la France et de l'étranger*, 24th year, vol. XLVIII, July, p. 102–104.

Palgrave, R. H. I. (1899), *Dictionary of Political Economy*, London: Macmillan, 3 vol.

Pareto, V. (1902), *L'Économie pure. Résumé du cours donné à l'École des Hautes Études Sociales de Paris,* Lausanne, chez l'auteur, reprinted in: V. Pareto, *Marxisme et économie pure, Œuvres complètes*, G. Busino (Ed), Geneva: Droz, vol. IX, 1966, p. 124–136.

Pareto, V. (1902–1903), *Les systèmes socialistes*, Paris: V. Giard & E. Brière, reprinted in: V. Pareto, *Œuvres complètes*, G. Busino (Ed), Geneva: Droz, vol. V, 1965.

Pareto, V. (1909), *Manuel d'économie politique*, translated on the Italian edition by Alfred Bonnet, Paris: V. Giard & E. Brière, reprinted in: V. Pareto, *Œuvres completes*, G. Busino (Ed), Geneva: Droz, vol. VII, 1981.

Pareto, V. (1910a), « L'œuvre scientifique de Léon Walras », *Gazette de Lausanne*, 112nd year, n°7, 8 January, p. 1, reprinted in: L. Walras, « Notice autobiographique » (1909a), Annex 6, vol. V, p. 42–43.

Pareto, V. (1910b), "Obituary. Walras", *The Economic Journal*, vol. 20, March, p. 137–140.

Pareto, V. (1982), *Écrits d'économie politique pure, Œuvres complètes*, G. Busino (Ed), Geneva: Droz, vol. XXVI.

Pareto, V. (1984), *Lettere a Maffeo Pantaleoni - 1890–1923*, G. De Rosa (Ed), Roma: Edizioni di storia e letteratura, reprinted in: *Œuvres complètes*, G. Busino (Ed), Geneva: Droz, vol. XXVIII-1 to 3.

Parisi Acquaviva D. (1978), « Congresso di economisti nel gennaio 1875 in Milano », *Rivista internazionale di scienze sociali*, vol. LXXXVI, n°3, p. 308–350.

Parodi, D. (1930), « La philosophie d'Étienne Vacherot », in: D. Parodi, *Du positivisme à l'idéalisme. Philosophies d'hier*, Paris: Vrin.

Parrot, J.-P. (1974), *La représentation des intérêts dans le mouvement des idées politiques*, Paris: P. U. F.

PÉguy, C. (1897), « Un économiste socialiste, M. Léon Walras », *La Revue socialiste*, n°146, 15 February, p. 174–186.

Pellanda, A. [1984), *Angelo Messedaglia. Tematiche economiche e indagini storiche*, Padova: Signum edizioni.

PÉnin, M. (1997), *Charles Gide, 1847–1932. L'esprit critique*, Paris: L'Harmattan.

Picory, C. (1989), « Orthodoxie libérale et hétérodoxie marginaliste : Clément Colson », *Revue économique*, vol. 40, n°4, July, p. 679–777.

Pietra, G. (1936–37), « Alcune lettere inedite di Léon Walras e di Angelo Messedaglia », *Atti del Reale Istituto Veneto di scienze, lettere ed arti*, 1936–37, vol. XCVI, Parte seconda (Scienze morali e lettere), Dispensa prima, p. 335–356.

Pirou, G. (1934), *Les théories de l'équilibre économique. Walras et Pareto. Conférences faites à l'E.P.H.E. en 1932–33 et 1933–34*, Paris: Domat-Montchrestien, 2nd ed., 1938, 3rd ed., 1946.

Pirou, G. (1945), « Nécrologie. Albert Aupetit », *Revue d'économie politique*, vol. 55, n°3–4, p. 97–98.

PoincarÉ, H. (1902), *La science et l'hypothèse*, English transl., *Science and Hypothesis*, New York: The Science Press, 1905.

Poinsot, L. (1842), Éléments de statique, suivis de quatre mémoires sur la composition des moments et des aires; sur le plan invariable du système du monde ; sur la nouvelle théorie générale de l'équilibre et du mouvement des systèmes ; et sur la théorie nouvelle de la rotation des corps, Paris: Bachelier (1st ed., 1803 ; 8th ed. revised and enlarged, 1842); Paris: Gauthier-Villars, 11th ed., 1872.

Pokorny D. (1978), "Smith and Walras: two theories of science", *Canadian Journal of Economics*, vol. XL, n°3, August, p. 387–403.

Pollet, G. (2012), « Les réseaux libéraux et la construction de l'État solidariste: entre libéralisme social et conservatisme politique », in: J.-L. Fournel, J. Guilhaumou and J.-P. Potier (Eds), *Libertés et libéralismes. Formation et circulation des concepts*, Lyon: ENS-Editions, 2012, p. 345–371.

Polsi, A. (1993), « Errera Alberto », in: *Dizionario biografico degli italiani*, Roma : Treccani, vol. 43, p. 246–249.

Potier, J.-P. (1986), *Lectures italiennes de Marx - Les conflits d'interprétation chez les économistes et les philosophes, 1883–1983,* Lyon: Presses universitaires de Lyon.

Potier, J.-P. (1988a), « Léon Walras, critique de l'enseignement de l'économie politique en France au xixe siècle », *Revue d'économie politique,* vol. 98, n° 2, March–April, p. 232–251.

Potier, J.-P. (1988b), « Léon Walras, critique de l'école libérale orthodoxe française », *Les Cahiers de l'Association Charles Gide pour l'étude de la pensée économique*, vol. 2, p. 165–190.

Potier, J.-P. (1989), « L'Assemblée Constituante et la question de la liberté du travail: un texte méconnu, la loi Le Chapelier », in: J.-M. Servet (Ed), *Idées économiques sous la Révolution (1789–1794),* Lyon: Presses universitaires de Lyon, p. 235–254.

Potier, J.-P. (1990), « Léon Walras et les débuts du journal *Le Travail* (1866–1867) », *Storia del pensiero economico - Bollettino di informazione*, new series, n°19, p. 41–59.

Potier, J.-P. (1994), « Classification des sciences et divisions de l' 'économie politique et sociale' dans l'œuvre de Léon Walras: une tentative de reconstruction », *Économies et sociétés-Cahiers de l'ISMEA*, vol. XXVIII, n°10–11, Œconomia series, Histoire de la pensée économique, n°20–21, p. 223–277.

Potier, J.-P. (1998a), « Léon Walras et l' 'école lombarde-vénitienne' à travers sa correspondance (1874–1886) », in: F. Michon (Ed), *L'Économie, une science pour l'homme et la société - Mélanges en l'honneur d'Henri Bartoli*, Paris: Publications de la Sorbonne, p. 117–145.

Potier, J.-P. (1998b), "Léon Walras and applied science—The significance of the free competition principle", in: G. Faccarello (Ed), *Studies in the History of French Political Economy. From Bodin to Walras,* London: Routledge, p. 369–403, reprinted in: *The Legacy of Léon Walras*, D. A. Walker (Ed), Cheltenham: Edward Elgar, volume II, 2001, p. 302–336.

Potier, J.-P. (1999a), « Une note d'humeur de Léon Walras – Commentaire », *Économies et sociétés-Cahiers de l'ISMEA*, vol. XXXIII, n°4, Œconomia series, Histoire de la pensée économique, n° 28, p. 165–172.

Potier, J.-P. (1999b), « L' 'économie politique appliquée' walrassienne: principe de la libre concurrence et intervention de l'État », *Revue européenne des sciences sociales. Cahiers Vilfredo Pareto,* vol. XXXVII, n°116, p. 51–72.

Potier, J.-P. (2000), « Quelques réflexions sur l'apport des 'Notes d'humeur' à la connaissance de Léon Walras », *Les Cahiers du CERAS, L'Économie walrasienne*, n° 1, June, p. 117–130.

Potier, J.-P. (2003), « Quelques remarques sur l'évolution des idées de Jean-Baptiste Say au sujet de la valeur et du prix », in: J.-P. Potier and A. Tiran (Eds), *Jean-Baptiste Say. Nouveaux regards sur son œuvre*, Paris: Economica, p. 283–301.

Potier, J.-P. (2005), « Léon Walras et la commission de la bibliothèque universitaire de Lausanne: les achats d'ouvrages d'économie politique dans les années 1870 », in: *Tables et index, Œuvres économiques complètes* d'Auguste and Léon Walras, vol. XIV, Paris: Economica, p. 355–375.

Potier, J.-P. (2006), « Léon Walras et les exceptions au principe de la libre concurrence », *Économies et sociétés-Cahiers de l'I.S.M.E.A.*, vol. XL, n° 12, Œconomia series, Histoire de la pensée économique, n°38, p. 1813–1826.

Potier, J.-P. (2011a), « Auguste Walras, le 'passeur' d'idées : de Jean-Baptiste Say à Léon Walras», in: R. Baranzini, A. Legris and L. Ragni (Eds), *Léon Walras et l'équilibre économique général. Recherches récentes*, Paris: Economica, p. 43–64.

Potier, J.-P. (2011b), « Marché du travail et législation sociale dans la pensée de Léon Walras », *Œconomia-History, Methodology, Philosophy*, vol. 1, n°3, September, p. 437–458.

Potier, J.-P. (2011c), « Le socialisme de Léon Walras », *L'Économie politique*, n°51, July, p. 33–48.

Potier, J.-P. (2012), « Léon Walras, un économiste socialiste libéral », in: J.-L. Fournel, J. Guilhaumou and J.-P. Potier (Eds), *Libertés et libéralismes. Formation et circulation des concepts*, Lyon: ENS-Éditions, p. 259–282.

Potier, J.-P. (2013), « Léon Walras, Paul Voituron et Constant Leirens à la rédaction du journal *Le Travail*: les polémiques sur la coopération dans les années 1866–1867 », in: A. Diemer and J.-P. Potier (Eds), *Léon Walras. Un siècle après (1910–2010)*, Brussels: Peter Lang, p. 277–299.

Potier, J.-P. (2014), « Espoirs et dangers du 'régime industriel et commercial' de l'humanité selon Léon Walras », *Innovations. Revue d'économie et de management de l'innovation*, n°45, p. 159–170.

Potier, J.-P. (2016), "The reception of the German Historical Schools among French economists (1857–1900)", in: J. L. Cardoso and M. Psalidopoulos (Eds), *The German Historical School and European Economic Thought*, London: Routledge, p. 22–41.

Potier, J.-P. (2018), "Charles Gide and marginalism in *Histoire des doctrines économiques*", in: J. L. Cardoso, H. D. Kurz and P. Steiner (Eds), *Economic Analyses in Historical Perspective. Festschrift in Honour of Gilbert Faccarello*, Abingdon: Routledge, p. 71–80.

Potier, J.-P. (2023), "Léon Walras: a trilogy of pure, applied and social economics », in: G. Faccarello and C. Silvant (Eds), *A History of Economic Thought in France,* vol. II, *The Long Nineteenth Century*, London: Routledge, 2023, p. 130–161.

Potier, J.-P. and Goutte, P.-H. (1992), « *Œuvres économiques complètes* d'Auguste et de Léon Walras: une nécessaire diversité des critères d'édition », *Revue européenne des sciences sociales. Cahiers Vilfredo Pareto*, vol. XXX, n° 92, p. 171–208.

Potier, J.-P. and Walker D. A. (Eds) (2004), *La correspondance entre Aline Walras et William Jaffé et autres documents*, Paris: Economica.

Prins, A. (1884), *La démocratie et le régime parlementaire. Étude sur le régime corporatif et la représentation des intérêts*, Brussels: C. Muquardt, 2d ed., with a preface by Émile de Laveleye, 1886.

Prochasson, C. (1985), « Sur l'environnement intellectuel de Georges Sorel: l'École des hautes études sociales (1899–1911) », *Cahiers Georges Sorel*, n°3, p. 16–38.

Proudhon, P.-J. (1840), *Qu'est-ce que la propriété ?*, Paris: Garnier-Flammarion, 1966.

Proudhon, P.-J. (1846), *Système des contradictions économiques, ou Philosophie de la misère*, Paris: Garnier.

Proudhon, P.-J. (1868), *De la Justice dans la Révolution et dans l'Église* (1st ed.,1858). New edition with notes and unpublished documents, in: *Œuvres complètes de P.-J. Proudhon* C. Bouglé and H. Moysset (Eds), Paris: Marcel Rivière, vol. VIII,1930–1935, 4 vol.

Ragni, L. (2011), « La méthode mathématique chez Walras et Cournot: comparaison et enjeux de discorde », *Cahiers d'économie politique*, n°60, p. 149–178.

Ragni, L. (2018), "Applying mathematics to economics according to Cournot and Walras", *European Journal of the History of Economic Thought*, vol. 25, n° 1, February, p. 73–105.

Rebérioux, M. (1987), « La *Revue socialiste* », *Cahiers Georges Sorel*, n°5, p. 15–38.

Rebeyrol, A. (1999), *La pensée économique de Walras*, Paris: Dunod.

Renard, G. (1888), *Études sur la France contemporaine*, Paris: Albert Savine.

Renard, G. (1894), « Notre programme », *La Revue socialiste*, vol. XIX, n°113, May, p. 513–519.

Renard, G. (1897), « La méthode d'étude de la question sociale », *La Revue socialiste*, vol. XXV, n°146, February, p. 129–144.

Renard, G. (1898), *Le régime socialiste. Principes de son organisation politique et économique*, Paris: F. Alcan.

Renard, G. (1907), *Le socialisme à l'œuvre. Ce qu'on a fait – Ce qu'on peut faire*, (in coll. with A. Berthod, G. Fréville, A. Landry, P. Mantoux, F. Simiand), Paris: Cornély.

Renard, G. (1909), *Discussions sociales d'hier et de demain*, Paris: Librairie scientifique et philosophique, A. Michel.

Reynaud, P.-L. (1953), « Préface », in: *Jean-Baptiste Say, Textes choisis*, Paris: Dalloz, p. 1–62.

Rist, C. (1904), « Économie optimiste et économie scientifique », *Revue de métaphysique et de morale*, vol. 12, n°4, p. 643–663.

Rist, C. (1907), « Économie optimiste et économie scientifique. II – Distribution des richesses », *Revue de métaphysique et de morale*, vol. 15, n°5, p. 596–619.

Rist, C. (1924), « La politique économique », in: Michel Augé-Laribé, Aimé Berthod, Émile Borel, *et alii*, *La politique républicaine*, Paris: Félix Alcan, p. 271–300.

Rod, É. (1910), « Sur un livre oublié [*Francis Sauveur*, by Léon Walras] », *La Revue hebdomadaire*, 19th year, n°7, 12 February, p. 141–158.

Roguin, E. (1923), *La science juridique pure*, Paris/Lausanne: L.G.D.J./F. Rouge, vol. 1.

Romani, R. (1988), « Romagnosi, Messedaglia, la 'scuola lombardo-veneta' e la costruzione di un sapere sociale », *Quaderni di storia dell' economia politica*, vol. VI, n°2, p. 105–145; reprinted with modifications in: R. Romani, *L'economia politica del Risorgimento italiano,* Torino: Bollati Boringhieri, 1994, p. 74–109.

Romani, R. (1994), « L'anglofilia degli economisti lombardo-veneti e il carattere nazionale », in: *L'economia politica del Risorgimento italiano,* Torino: Bollati Boringhieri, p. 201–241.

Ross, D. (1991), *The Origins of American Social Science*, Cambridge: Cambridge U. Press.

Rousseau, J.-J. (1754), *Discours sur l'origine et les fondements de l'inégalité parmi les hommes,* in: *Œuvres complètes,* Paris: Gallimard, 1959, vol. III.

Rueff, J. (1969), *Des sciences physiques aux sciences morales. Un essai de 1922 reconsidéré en 1969*, Paris: Payot.

Sabatier, M. (1868), « Les Chambres syndicales ouvrières », *Le Travail,* n°11, 31 May, in: *Les Associations populaires coopératives*, *OEC*, vol. VI, C. Hébert and J.-P. Potier (Eds), Paris: Economica, 1990, p. 355–363.

Salvat, C. (2004), « L'ambivalence de la référence physiocratique chez Walras », in: R. Baranzini, A. Diemer and C. Mouchot (Eds), *Études walrassiennes*. Préface de Jan Van Daal. Paris: L'Harmattan, p. 29–49.

Salvo, R. (1979), *Vito Cusumano dal liberismo al socialismo della cattedra*, Palermo: Quaderno dell'Istituto di storia dell'Università di Palermo annesso alla Facoltà di magistero.

Samuelson, P. A. (1941), "The stability of equilibrium: comparative statics and dynamics", *Econometrica*, vol. 9, n°2, April, p. 97–120.

Sandmo, A. (2007), "Retrospectives. Léon Walras and the Nobel Peace Prize", *Journal of Economic Perspectives*, vol. 21, n°4, Fall, p. 217–228.

Say, J.-B. (1st ed., 1803; 5th ed., 1826), *Traité d'économie politique. Édition variorum*, vol. 1 of *Œuvres complètes,* C. Mouchot, J.-P. Potier, J.-M. Servet, P. Steiner and A. Tiran (Eds), Paris: Economica, 2006, 2 tomes.

Say, J.-B. (2nd ed. 1821, 3rd ed. 1826), *Catéchisme d'économie politique*, in: *Catéchisme d'économie politique et opuscules divers*, vol. III of *Œuvres complètes*, P. Steiner and A. Tiran (Eds), Paris: Economica, 2020, p. 83–185.

Say, J.-B. (1st ed., 1828–29; 2nd ed., 1840), *Cours complet d'économie politique pratique – Édition variorum des deux éditions*, vol. II of *Œuvres complètes*, E. Blanc, P.-H. Goutte and J.-P. Potier (Eds), Paris: Economica, 2010, 2 tomes.

Say, J.-B. (1848), *Œuvres diverses*, Paris: Guillaumin.

Say, J.-B. (2024), *Notes et pièces diverses*, vol. VII of *Œuvres complètes*, E. Blanc, G. Jacoud and J.-P. Potier (Eds), Paris: Classiques Garnier, tome 1, *Manuscrits* ; tome 2, *Marginalia.*

Say, L. and Chailley-Bert, J. (Eds) (1891–92), *Nouveau dictionnaire d'économie politique*, Paris: Guillaumin, 2 vol.

Scaldaferri, R. (1992), « I modelli stranieri nel socialismo della cattedra italiano », in: R. Camurri (Ed), *La scienza moderata - Fedele Lampertico e l'Italia liberale*, Milano: Franco Angeli, p. 235–254.

Schumpeter, J. A. (1908), *Das Wesen und der Hauptinhalt der theoretischen Nationalökonomie*, Leipzig: Duncker & Humblot, Italian translation, *L'essenza e i principi dell'economia teorica*, Bari: Laterza, 1982.

Schumpeter, J. A. (1910), « Marie Esprit Léon Walras. 1834–1910 », *Zeitschrift für Volkswirtschaft, Sozialpolitik und Verwaltung*, vol. XIX, p. 397–402; English translation in: *Ten Great Economists. From Marx to Keynes*, London: Allen and Unwin, 1952, p. 74–79.

Schumpeter, J. A. (1954), *History of Economic Analysis*, New York: Oxford University Press.

Sekerler Richiardi, P. (2013), « Réformes sociales chez Jevons et Walras: la question du chemin de fer », in: A. Diemer and J.-P. Potier (Eds), *Léon Walras. Un siècle après (1910–2010)*, Brussels: Peter Lang, p. 257–276.

Servet, J.-M. (1997), « Introduction générale. Auguste Walras de 1848 à 1850 », in: *La vérité sociale, Œuvres économiques complètes*, vol. II, J. M. Servet and P. H. Goutte (Eds), Paris: Economica, p. 9–26.

Sherwood, S. (1897), "The Philosophical Basis of Economics: A Word to the Sociologists", *Annals of the American Academy of Political and Social Science*, vol. X, September, p. 58–92 [206–240].

Silvant, C. (2010), *L'école libérale française et l'intervention publique dans la deuxième moitié du xix*e *siècle*, Ph.D. thesis, Université de Paris Ouest Nanterre.

Smith, Adam (1st ed., 1776), *An Inquiry into the Nature and Causes of the Wealth of Nations.* General Editors R. H. Campbell and A. S. Skinner. Textual editor W. B. Todd (*The Glasgow Edition of the Works and Correspondence of Adam Smith*), Oxford: Oxford University Press, 1976, 2 vol.

Smith, V. L. (1987), "Auctions", in: *The New Palgrave. A Dictionary of Economics*, J. Eatwell, M. Milgate, P. Newman (Eds), London: Macmillan, vol. 1, p. 138–144.

Sorel, G. (1899), « *Études d'économie sociale* [...] par L. Walras », *L'Humanité nouvelle*, vol. 4, January, p. 123.

Soresina, M (2001), *Conoscere per ammistrare. Luigi Bodio. Statistico economico e pubblica amministrazione,* Milano: Franco Angeli.

Spencer, H. (1871), *The Classification of the Sciences to Which are Added Reasons for dissenting from the Philosophy of M. Comte*, 3rd ed., London: Williams and Norgate.

Spoto, L. (1984), « Il socialismo e gli economisti siciliani », in: P. Di Giovanni (Ed), *Il marxismo e la cultura meridionale,* Palermo: Palumbo, p. 229–250.

Steiner, P. (1994), « Pareto contre Walras: le problème de l'économie sociale », *Économies et sociétés-Cahiers de l'ISMEA*, vol. XXVIII, n°10–11, Œconomia series, Histoire de la pensée économique, n°20–21, p. 53–73.

Steiner, P. (1998), « Production, répartition, et passion de l'égalité: l'économie politique de Michel Chevalier », *Revue européenne des sciences sociales. Cahiers Vilfredo Pareto*, vol. XXXVI, n°110, p. 97–119.

Steiner, P. (2000), « Vilfredo Pareto et l'économie politique walrassienne », in: A. Béraud and G. Faccarello (Eds), *Nouvelle histoire de la pensée économique*, Paris: La Découverte, vol. 2, p. 498–523.

Taricone, F. (2015), « L'economista Michel Chevalier e il lievito dell'utopia », in: V. Gioia, S. Noto and A. Sanchez Hormigo (Ed), *Pensiero critico ed economia politica nel XIX secolo: da Saint-Simon a Proudhon*, Bologna: Il Mulino, p. 139–164.

Tatti, E. (2000a), « 'Etre' et 'devoir être' chez Léon Walras », in: P. Dockès, L. Frobert, G. Klotz, J.-P. Potier and A. Tiran (Eds), *Les traditions économiques françaises, 1848–1939*, Paris: Éd. du C.N.R.S., p. 417–428.

Tatti, E. (2000b), « La méthode de l'économie pure selon Léon Walras. Une analyse de ses fondements gnoséologiques », Master's thesis n°122, *Cahiers de recherches économiques*, École des H.E.C., Université de Lausanne.

Theocharis, R. D. (1993), *The Development of Mathematical Economics. The Years of Transition : From Cournot to Jevons*, London: Macmillan.

Tort, P. (1989), *La raison classificatoire. Quinze études*, Paris: Aubier.

Travagliante, P. (2003), La costruzione di un sapere sociale. Stato e questione sociale in Vito Cusumano, Milano: Franco Angeli.

Turgot, A.-R.-J. (circa 1851), « Plan du premier Discours sur la formation des gouvernements et le mélange des nations », in: *Œuvres de Turgot et documents le concernant,* G. Schelle (Ed), Paris: Félix Alcan, 1913, vol. 1, p. 277–298.

Turgot, A.-R.-J. (1753–54), « Sur la géographie politique – (*Fragment*) », in: *Œuvres de Turgot et documents le concernant,* G. Schelle (Ed), Paris: Félix Alcan, 1913, vol. 1, p. 436–441.

Turk, Michael H. (2012), "The mathematical turn in economics: Walras, the French mathematicians, and the road not taken", *Journal of the History of Economic Thought*, vol. 34, n°2, June, p. 149–167.

Vacherot, É. (1858), *La métaphysique et la science ou principes de métaphysique positive*, Paris: F. Chamerot, 2nd ed., 1863, 3 vol.

Vacherot, É. (1860), *La démocratie*, Paris: F. Chamerot.

Vacherot, É. (1892), *La démocratie libérale*, Paris: Calmann-Lévy.

ValÉry, P. (1896), « *Éléments d'économie politique pure*, par Léon Walras », *Revue générale de droit, de législation et de la jurisprudence en France et à l'étranger*, vol. 20, November–December, p. 574–576.

Van Daal, J. (1996), "From utilitarianism to hedonism: Gossen, Jevons and Walras", *Journal of the History of Economic Thought*, vol. 18, n°2, Autumn, p. 271–286.

Van Daal, J. (1999), « Léon Walras et le capitalisme », *Revue européenne des sciences sociales. Cahiers Vilfredo Pareto*, vol. XXXVII, n°116, p. 83–99.

Van Daal, J. (2005), "Introduction", in: Léon Walras, *Studies in Applied Economics*, London: Routledge, vol. I, p. XV–LXVII.

Van Daal, J. (2006), "Léon Walras's Economics: from Pure to Normative?", in: J. Backhaus and J. A. H. Maks, (Eds), *From Walras to Pareto*, New York: Springer, p. 51–67.

Van Daal, J. and Jolink, A. (1993), *The Equilibrium Economics of Léon Walras*, London: Routledge.

Van Daal, J. and Potier, J.-P. (1992), « Gossen et Walras: Léon Walras comme éditeur manqué de l'*Entwickelung* de Gossen », *Revue européenne des sciences sociales. Cahiers Vilfredo Pareto*, vol. XXX, n°92, p. 131–143.

Van Daal, J. and Walker, D. A. (2007), « Les œuvres économiques complètes d'Auguste et de Léon Walras », *Revue d'économie politique*, vol. 117, n°6, November–December, p. 891–919.

Van den Berg, R. (2006), At the Origins of Mathematical Economics. The Economics of A. N. Isnard (1748–1803), London: Routledge.

Varejão, M. (1997), Achille Loria. Saggio sulla fortuna di un positivista in Italia e all'estero, Milano: Unicopli.

Vinokur, A. (1986), "Political economy between faith and works: Saint-Simonism and the case of Michel Chevalier", *Économies et sociétés-Cahiers de l'ISMEA*, vol. XX, n°10, Œconomia series, Histoire de la pensée économique, n°6, p. 175–202.
Voituron, P. (1866 a), « Caractère du mouvement démocratique et social en Europe » [*unsigned article*], *Le Travail*, 1st year, n° 3, 30 September, col. 67–69.
Voituron, Paul (1866 b), « Le mouvement coopératif » [*unsigned article*], *Le Travailleur associé*, 1st year, n°4, 15 november, col. 99–104.
Voituron, P. (1867), « La définition des sociétés coopératives » [*unsigned article*], *Le Travailleur associé*, 2nd year, n°7, 15 July, col. 152–153.
Walker, D. A. (1984), "Is Walras's theory of general equilibrium a normative scheme?", *History of Political Economy*, vol. 16, n°3, Fall, p. 445–469.
Walker, D. A. (1986), "Walras's theory of the entrepreneur", *De Economist*, vol. 134, n°1, p. 1–24.
Walker, D. A. (1987), "Edgeworth versus Walras on the theory of tâtonnement", *Eastern Economic Journal*, vol. XIII, n°2, April–June, p. 155–165.
Walker, D. A. (1990), "Institutions and Participants in Walras's Model of Oral Pledges Markets", *Revue économique*, 41, n°4, July, p. 651–668.
Walker, D. A. (1996), *Walras's Market Models*, Cambridge: Cambridge U. Press.
Walker, D. A. (1997), *Advances in General Equilibrium Th*eory, Cheltenham: Edward Elgar.
Walker, D. A. (1999a), « Une note d'humeur de Léon Walras », *Économies et sociétés-Cahiers de l'ISMEA,* vol. XXXIII, n°4, Œconomia series, Histoire de la pensée économique, n°28, p. 151–160.
Walker, D. A. (1999b), « Une réponse à Jean-Pierre Potier », *Économies et sociétés-Cahiers de l'ISMEA,* vol. XXXIII, n°4, Œconomia series, Histoire de la pensée économique, n°28, p. 173–176.
Walker, D. A. (2000), « La relation entre la Bourse au xixe siècle et le modèle de Léon Walras d'un marché organisé », in: P. Dockès, L. Frobert, G. Klotz, J.-P. Potier and A. Tiran (Eds), *Les traditions économiques françaises - 1848–1939,* Paris: Éd. du C. N. R. S., p. 443–457.
Walker, D. A. (2001), "A factual account of the functioning of the nineteenth-century Paris Bourse", *European Journal of the History of Economic Thought*, vol. 8, n°2, Summer, p. 186–207.
Walker, D. A. (2004), « Les idées de Léon Walras sur la nature humaine », in: R. Baranzini, A. Diemer and C. Mouchot, (Eds), *Études walrassiennes.* Foreword by Jan Van Daal. Paris: L'Harmattan, p. 105–133.
Walker, D. A. (2006), *Walrasian Economics*, Cambridge: Cambridge U. Press.
Walker, D. A. (2019), "Paul A. Samuelson as historian of economic thought: an intimate memoir", in: R. Anderson, W. A. Barnett and R. A. Cord (Eds), *Paul Samuelson. Master of Modern Economics*, Basingstoke: Palgrave Macmillan, p. 137–170.
Walker, D. A. and Van Daal, J. (2014), "Translators' introduction", in: Léon Walras, *Elements of Theoretical Economics*, Cambridge: Cambridge University Press, p. IX–L.
Walras, A. (1831a), « De l'abolition de l'impôt, et de l'établissement de la Loi agraire, telle qu'elle peut être conçue et pratiquée au 19e siècle », in: *Richesse, liberté et société, Œuvres économiques complètes* (henceforth *OEC*), vol. I, P.-H. Goutte and J.-M. Servet (Eds), Paris: Economica, 1990, p. 7–20.
Walras, A. (1831b), *De la nature de la richesse, et de l'origine de la valeur*, Évreux: Ancelle fils, imprimeur-libraire, in: *Richesse, liberté et société*, *OEC*, vol. I, P.-H. Goutte and J.-M. Servet (Eds), Paris: Economica, 1990, p. 47–233.
Walras, A. (1833a), « De la connexité des connaissances humaines et des progrès scientifiques, en général; et, en particulier, de l'influence que l'étude de l'Économie politique est appelée à exercer sur l'avancement des sciences morales et historiques », *Recueil de la Société libre d'Agriculture, Sciences, Arts et Belles-Lettres du département de l'Eure*, tome 4, January, in: *Cours et pièces diverses*, *OEC*, vol. III, P.-H. Goutte and J.-M. Servet (Eds), Paris: Economica, 2005, p. 68–85.

Walras, A. (1833b), Cours d'économie politique. Évreux [16 December 1832–24 March 1833], in: *Cours et pièces diverses, OEC*, vol. III, P.-H. Goutte and J.-M. Servet (Eds), Paris: Economica, 2005, p. 86–513.

Walras, A. (1833c), « De la nature de la loi », *Recueil de la Société libre d'Agriculture, Sciences, Arts et Belles-Lettres du département de l'Eure*, tome 4, April, in: *Richesse, liberté et société, OEC*, vol. I, P.-H. Goutte and J.-M. Servet (Eds), Paris: Economica, 1990, p. 295–312.

Walras, A. (1835), *Réfutation de la doctrine de Hobbes, sur le droit naturel de l'individu*, Évreux: Ancelle fils, imprimeur-libraire, in: *Richesse, liberté et société, OEC*, vol. I, P.-H. Goutte and J.-M. Servet (Eds), Paris: Economica, 1990, p. 283–329.

Walras, A. (1836), « Études sur la richesse des nations, par Mr Louis Say », in: *Cours et pièces diverses, OEC*, vol. III, P.-H. Goutte and J.-M. Servet (Eds), Paris: Economica, 2005, p. 707–714.

Walras, A. (1837), Cours professé à l'Athénée royal de Paris [1836–June 1837], in: *Cours et pièces diverses, OEC*, vol. III, P.-H. Goutte and J.-M. Servet (Eds), Paris: Economica, 2005, p. 345–382.

Walras, A. (1840), « Objet de la philosophie »,12 f^{os}. Lyon. Université Lumière-Lyon 2, Fonds Walras. FA III A : 09 : 02.

Walras, A. (1841), « Programme de Philosophie. Résumé analytique de toutes les leçons de l'année scolaire 1840–1841 », 38 f^{os}. Lyon. Université Lumière-Lyon 2, Fonds Walras. FA III A : 09 : 03.

Walras, A. (1844), « Esquisse d'une théorie de la richesse », *Recueil des travaux de la Société libre d'Agriculture, Sciences, Arts et Belles-Lettres du département de l'Eure*, 2nd series, tome 4, 1843 [printed in July 1844], in: *Richesse, liberté et société, OEC*, vol. I, P.-H. Goutte and J.-M. Servet (Eds), Paris: Economica, 1990, p. 427–442.

Walras, A. (1848), « La vérité sociale par un travailleur », in: *La Vérité sociale, OEC*, vol. II, J.-M. Servet with the coll. of P.-H. Goutte, Paris: Economica, 1997, p. 35–105.

Walras, A. (1849a), « Examen critique et réfutation du Livre de Mr. Thiers sur la Propriété », in: *La Vérité sociale, OEC*, vol. II, J.-M. Servet with the coll. of P.-H. Goutte, Paris: Economica, 1997, p. 197–440.

Walras, A. (1849b), « Mémoire sur l'origine de la valeur d'échange ou Exposition critique et réfutation des opinions les plus accréditées, chez les économistes, sur cette question », *Séances et travaux de l'Académie des Sciences morales et politiques – Compte rendu par M. Ch. Vergé sous la direction de M. Mignet*, 2nd series, tome 6, in: *La Vérité sociale, OEC*, vol. II, J.-M. Servet with the coll. of P.-H. Goutte, Paris: Economica, 1997, p. 505–527.

Walras, A. (1849c), *Théorie de la richesse sociale ou Résumé des principes fondamentaux de l'économie politique*, Paris: Guillaumin, in: *La Vérité sociale, OEC*, vol. II, J.-M. Servet with the coll. of P.-H. Goutte, Paris: Economica, 1997, p. 113–170.

Walras, A. (1849d), « Théorie de la propriété », in: *La Vérité sociale, OEC*, vol. II, J.-M. Servet with the coll. of P.-H. Goutte, Paris: Economica, 1997, p. 177–189.

Walras, A. (1849e), « Un Chapitre de Mr Guizot annoté par un Travailleur. - De la Démocratie en France, par Mr Guizot. Chapitre quatrième. De la République sociale », in: *La Vérité sociale, OEC*, vol. II, J.-M. Servet with the coll. of P.-H. Goutte, Paris: Economica, 1997, p. 535–557.

Walras, A. (1859), « Notes sur Proudhon », in: *Cours et pièces diverses, OEC*, vol. III, P.-H. Goutte and J.-M. Servet (Eds), Paris: Economica, 2005, p. 607–656.

Walras, A. (avant 1863), « Il ne faut pas confondre l'idée de l'espace avec l'idée d'étendue », 19 f^{os} (+ f^{os} A et B). Lyon. Université Lumière-Lyon 2, Fonds Walras. FA III A : 13 : 01 :01.

Walras, A. (1863), « Cinq leçons sur le Vrai, le Bien, le Beau, la Science et la Classification des faits scientifiques », 24 f^{os}. Lyon. Université Lumière-Lyon 2, Fonds Walras. FA III A : 13 : 03.

Walras, A. (n. d.), « Vérité - Science & Art. Mais la question, telle que je viens de la poser, n'est elle-même qu'un cas particulier d'une question plus générale: quels sont les rapports qui existent entre l'idéal et le réel. » 6 f^{os}. Lyon. Université Lumière-Lyon 2, Fonds Walras. FA III A : 13 : 09.

Walras, A. (2005), *Correspondance, OEC*, vol. IV, C. Hébert (Ed), Paris: Economica.

Walras, L. (1853), Notes on *Éléments de Statique* by Louis Poinsot. 9 f^{os}. Bibliothèque cantonale et universitaire de Lausanne, Fonds Walras IS 1927 V/ 16/1–10 (former shelf mark: IV 15).

Walras, L. (1858a), *Philosophie de l'art. Première partie: Ontologie – Chapitre I. Synthèse du fait ontologique.* 2 cahiers (40 and 45 p.). Bibliothèque cantonale et universitaire de Lausanne, Fonds Walras IS 1927 V/15/01/01 (former shelf mark: Va 17).

Walras, L. (1858b), *Francis Sauveur,* Paris: E. Dentu.

Walras, L. (1859a), « Du sens esthétique; de l'art; et des opinions en matière d'art », in: *Œuvres diverses, OEC*, vol. XIII, P. Dockès, C. Mouchot and J.-P. Potier (Eds), Paris: Economica, 2000, p. 19–46.

Walras, L. (1859b), « Introduction à l'étude de la question sociale », in: *L'économie politique et la justice, OEC*, vol. V, P.-H. Goutte and J.-M. Servet (Eds), Paris: Economica, 2001, p. 77–143.

Walras, L. (1859–1861), « Critique de l'intelligence » [Notes on *La métaphysique et la science* by Étienne Vacherot]. 8 f^{os}. (16 p.). Bibliothèque cantonale et universitaire de Lausanne, Fonds Walras IS 1927 V/16/20 (former shelf mark: Vb 19).

Walras, L. (1860a), *L'économie politique et la justice. Examen critique et réfutation des doctrines économiques de M. P.-J. Proudhon, précédés d'une Introduction à l'étude de la question sociale,* Paris: Guillaumin, in: *L'économie politique et la justice, OEC*, vol. V, P.-H. Goutte and J.-M. Servet (Eds), Paris: Economica, 2001, p. 145–301.

Walras, L. (1860b), « Des rapports de la morale et de l'économie politique. Cours professé au Collège de France par M. H. Baudrillart », in: *Œuvres diverses, OEC*, vol. XIII, P. Dockès, C. Mouchot and J.-P. Potier (Eds), Paris: Economica, 2000, p. 163–164.

Walras, L. (1860c), « Paradoxes économiques. I. Que le sens commun n'est point le criterium de la science en général, ni en particulier celui de l'économie politique », *Journal des économistes.* 2nd series, tome 28, vol. 7, n°12, 15 Décember, in: *Mélanges d'économie politique et sociale, OEC*, vol. VII, C. Hébert and J.-P. Potier (Eds), Paris: Economica, 1987, p. 42–62.

Walras, L. (1860d), « Application des mathématiques à l'économie politique (1st attempt 1860) », in: *Théorie mathématique de la richesse sociale et autres écrits d'économie pure, OEC*, vol. XI, C. Mouchot (Ed), Paris: Economica, 1993, p. 329–339.

Walras, L. (1861a), « Des Réformes économiques », in: *Œuvres diverses, OEC*, vol. XIII, P. Dockès, C. Mouchot and J.-P. Potier (Eds), Paris: Economica, 2000, p. 55–65.

Walras, L. (1861b), « Paradoxes économiques. II. Que le point de vue économique est le point de vue social par excellence », in: *Œuvres diverses, OEC*, vol. XIII, P. Dockès, C. Mouchot and J.-P. Potier (Eds), Paris: Economica, 2000, p. 165–184.

Walras, L. (1861c), « Paradoxes économiques. II. De la richesse naturelle ou gratuite. – De la richesse sociale ou économique. – De la richesse intellectuelle », in: *Œuvres diverses, OEC*, vol. XIII, P. Dockès, C. Mouchot and J.-P. Potier (Eds), Paris: Economica, 2000, p. 47–54.

Walras, L. (1861d), « L'industrie moderne et l'économie politique », in: *Mélanges d'économie politique et sociale, OEC*, vol. VII, C. Hébert and J.-P. Potier (Eds), Paris: Economica, 1987, p. 135–152.

Walras, L. (1861e), *Théorie critique de l'impôt, précédée de Souvenirs du Congrès de Lausanne,* Paris: Guillaumin, in: *L'Économie politique et la justice, OEC*, vol. V, P.-H. Goutte and J.-M. Servet (Eds), Paris: Economica, 2001, p. 343–426.

Walras, L. (1861f), *De l'impôt dans le canton de Vaud. Mémoire auquel un quatrième accessit a été décerné à la suite du concours ouvert par le Conseil d'État du canton de Vaud sur les questions relatives à l'impôt*, Lausanne: Imprimerie de Louis Vincent, in: *L'économie politique et la justice, OEC*, vol. V, P.-H. Goutte and J.-M. Servet (Eds), Paris: Economica, 2001, p. 435–506.

Walras, L. (1863a), « Socialisme et libéralisme. Lettres à M. Éd. Schérer », *Le Travail*, vol. 1, n°4, 31 October 1866, n°6, 31 December 1866 and n°8, 28 February 1867, in: *Études d'économie sociale, OEC*, vol. IX, P. Dockès (Ed), Paris: Economica, 1990, p. 9–23.

Walras, L. (1863b), « *Principes de la théorie des richesses* de M. Cournot », *L'indépendant de la Moselle*, 13 July, in: *Mélanges d'économie politique et sociale, OEC*, vol. VII, C. Hébert and J.-P. Potier (Eds), Paris: Economica, 1987, p. 155–159.

Walras, L. (1863c), « Du matérialisme et du spiritualisme en économie politique et sociale », in: *Œuvres diverses, OEC*, vol. XIII, P. Dockès, C. Mouchot and J.-P. Potier (Eds), Paris: Economica, 2000, p. 185–217.

Walras, L. (1863d), « Recherche de l'idéal social en matière de propriété et d'impôt », in: *Œuvres diverses, OEC*, vol. XIII, P. Dockès, C. Mouchot and J.-P. Potier (Eds), Paris: Economica, 2000, p. 218–245.

Walras, L. (1864), « De l'enseignement de l'économie politique dans les facultés de droit », in: *Mélanges d'économie politique et sociale, OEC*, vol. VII, C. Hébert and J.-P. Potier (Eds), Paris: Economica, 1987, p. 349–358.

Walras, L. (1865), *Les associations populaires de consommation, de production et de crédit. Leçons publiques faites à Paris en janvier et février 1865*, Paris: E. Dentu, in: *Les associations populaires coopératives, OEC*, vol. VI, C. Hébert and J.-P. Potier (Eds), Paris: Economica, 1990, p. 15–89.

Walras, L. (1866a), « Le mouvement d'association et la politique libérale », *La Presse*, 2 April, in: *Les associations populaires coopératives, OEC*, vol. VI, C. Hébert and J.-P. Potier (Eds), Paris: Economica, 1990, p. 117–119.

Walras, L. (1866b), « Programme économique et politique », *Le Travail*, vol. 1, n°1, 31 July, in: *Les associations populaires coopératives, OEC*, vol. VI, C. Hébert and J.-P. Potier (Eds), Paris: Economica, 1990, p. 131–141.

Walras, L. (1866c), « Société coopérative immobilière. Type d'habitation à bon marché », *Le Travail*, vol. 1, n°2, 31 August, in: *Les associations populaires coopératives, OEC*, vol. VI, C. Hébert and J.-P. Potier (Eds), Paris: Economica, 1990, p. 143–151.

Walras, L. (1866d), « Société coopérative immobilière. Combinaison financière », *Le Travail*, vol. 1, n°3, 30 September, in: *Les associations populaires coopératives, OEC*, vol. VI, C. Hébert and J.-P. Potier (Eds), Paris: Economica, 1990, p. 151–157.

Walras, L. (1866e), « Des doctrines en matière d'association coopérative », *Le Travail*, vol. 1, n°6, 31 December, in: *Les associations populaires coopératives, OEC*, vol. VI, C. Hébert and J.-P. Potier (Eds), Paris: Economica, 1990, p. 171–176.

Walras, L. (1867a), « Discussion sur les coalitions et les grèves à la Société d'économie politique de Paris », *Le Travail*, vol. 1, n°10, 30 April, in: *Les associations populaires coopératives, OEC*, vol. VI, C. Hébert and J.-P. Potier (Eds), Paris: Economica, 1990, p. 209–212.

Walras, L. (1867b), Prospectus du journal *Le Travail*, in: *Les associations populaires coopératives, OEC*, vol. VI, C. Hébert and J.-P. Potier (Eds), Paris: Economica, 1990, p. 399–401.

Walras, L. (1867c), « La discussion du Corps législatif sur les sociétés à capital variable », *Le Travail*, vol. 1, n°12, 30 June, in: *Les associations populaires coopératives, OEC*, vol. VI, C. Hébert and J.-P. Potier (Eds), Paris: Economica, 1990, p. 217–229.

Walras, L. (1867d), « La sécurité générale », *Le Travail*, vol. 2, n°6, 31 December, in: *Les associations populaires coopératives, OEC*, vol. VI, C. Hébert and J.-P. Potier (Eds), Paris: Economica, 1990, p. 271–274.

Walras, L. (1867–68), *Recherche de l'idéal social. Leçons publiques faites à Paris. Première série (1867–68). Théorie générale de la société,* Paris: Guillaumin/Agence générale de Librairie des auteurs et compositeurs, in: *Études d'économie sociale, OEC*, vol. IX, P. Dockès (Ed), Paris: Economica, 1990, p. 25–173.

Walras, L. (1868a), « Le socialisme scientifique. Observations », *Le Travail*, vol. 2, n°7, 31 January, in: *Les associations populaires coopératives, OEC*, vol. VI, C. Hébert and J.-P. Potier (Eds), Paris: Economica, 1990, p. 259–269.

Walras, L. (1868b), « De la spéculation. Étude d'économie financière », *Le Travail*, vol. 2, n°10 et 12, 30 April et 30 June, in: *Œuvres diverses, OEC*, vol. XIII, P. Dockès, C. Mouchot and J.-P. Potier (Eds), Paris: Economica, 2000, p. 343–356.

Walras, L. (1868c), « Méthode de conciliation ou de synthèse », *Revue socialiste*, vol. 23, n°136, 15 April 1896. in: *Études d'économie sociale, OEC*, vol. IX, P. Dockès (Ed), Paris: Economica, 1990, p. 151–173.

Walras, L. (1870a), « Application des mathématiques à l'économie politique. (2nd attempt 1869–1870) », in: *Théorie mathématique de la richesse sociale et autres écrits d'économie pure, OEC*, vol. XI, C. Mouchot (Ed), Paris: Economica, 1993, p. 341–359.

Walras, L. (1870b), « Capitaux et revenus », in: *Théorie mathématique de la richesse sociale et autres écrits d'économie pure, OEC*, vol. XI, C. Mouchot (Ed), Paris: Economica, 1993, p. 361–378.

Walras, L. (1870c), « Programme d'un cours d'Éc[onomie] pol[itique]. Saint-Aubin-sur-Mer, 1870 », in: *Cours, OEC*, vol. XII, P. Dockès, J.- P. Potier, P. Bridel (Eds), Paris: Economica, 1996, p. 30–34.

Walras, L. (1871a), « Des billets de banque en Suisse », *Bibliothèque universelle et Revue suisse*, new period, tome 41, vol. 76, n°163, July, in: *Œuvres diverses, OEC*, vol. XIII, P. Dockès, C. Mouchot and J.-P. Potier (Eds), Paris: Economica, 2000, p. 369–384.

Walras, L. (1871b), « Application des mathématiques à l'économie politique (1871) 3rd attempt (*la bonne*, v. p. 15) », in: *Théorie mathématique de la richesse sociale et autres écrits d'économie pure, OEC*, vol. XI, C. Mouchot (Ed), Paris: Economica, 1993, p. 385–409.

Walras, L. (1872a), « Discours d'installation en qualité de Professeur ordinaire d'économie politique à l'Académie de Lausanne prononcé dans la séance académique du 20 octobre 1871 », in: *Séances académiques du 23 octobre 1870, du 31 octobre 1870 et du 20 octobre 1871. Discours d'installation*, Lausanne: Imprimerie S. Genton, in: *Mélanges d'économie politique et sociale, OEC*, vol. VII, C. Hébert and J.-P. Potier (Eds), Paris: Economica, 1987, p. 359–376.

Walras, L. (1872b), « Système des phénomènes économiques. Nature de la richesse. Leçons publiques faites à l'Hôtel de Ville de Genève », in: *Théorie mathématique de la richesse sociale et autres écrits d'économie pure, OEC*, vol. XI, C. Mouchot (Ed), Paris: Economica, 1993, p. 411–473.

Walras, L. (1872c), « Exposition et conciliation des doctrines sociales », in: *Œuvres diverses, OEC*, vol. XIII, P. Dockès, C. Mouchot and J.-P. Potier (Eds), Paris: Economica, 2000, p. 247–324.

Walras, L. (1873a), « Sur la théorie mathématique de l'échange. Lettre à M. Paul Piccard, 25 octobre 1873 », *Bulletin de la Société vaudoise des sciences naturelles*, vol. 12, n°70, November, in: *Théorie mathématique de la richesse sociale et autres écrits d'économie pure, OEC*, vol. XI, C. Mouchot (Ed), Paris: Economica, 1993, p. 317–21.

Walras, L. (1873b), « Le cadastre et l'impôt foncier », *Bibliothèque Universelle et Revue Suisse*, tome 48, vol. 78, n°189 et 192, November and December, in: *Études d'économie sociale, OEC*, vol. IX, P. Dockès (Ed), Paris: Economica, 1990, p. 361–389.

Walras, L. (1874a), « Principe d'une théorie mathématique de l'échange », *Séances et travaux de l'Académie des sciences morales et politiques, Séances du 16 et 23 août 1873*, vol. 101, n°1, january. Other publication : *Journal des économistes.* 3rd series, tome 34, vol. 9, n°100, April, in: *Mélanges d'économie politique et sociale, OEC*, vol. VII, C. Hébert and J.-P. Potier (Eds), Paris: Economica, 1987, p. 261–281.

Walras, L. (1874b), « De l'influence de la communication des marchés sur la situation des populations agricoles », *Journal de la Société vaudoise d'utilité publique*, n°5 et 6, May and June, in: *Études d'économie politique appliquée, OEC*, vol. X, J.-P. Potier (Ed), Paris: Economica, 1992, p. 221–243.

Walras, L. (1874c), « Correspondance entre M. Jevons, Professeur à Manchester et M. Walras, Professeur à Lausanne », *Journal des économistes.* 3rd series, tome 34, vol. 9, n°102, 15 June, in: *Mélanges d'économie politique et sociale, OEC*, vol. VII, C. Hébert and J.-P. Potier (Eds), Paris: Economica, 1987, p. 281–287.

Walras, L. (1874d), *Éléments d'économie politique pure, ou Théorie de la richesse sociale.* First part, 1st ed. Lausanne/ Paris/ Basel: Corbaz/ Guillaumin/ Georg, in: *Éléments d'économie politique pure, OEC*, vol. VIII, C. Mouchot (Ed), Paris: Economica, 1988.

Walras, L. (1874e), « *L'Italia industriale* et de *Le Nuove Istituzioni economiche nel secolo* xix de Alberto Errera », *Journal des économistes.* 3rd series, tome 36, vol. 9, n°107, November, in: *Œuvres diverses, OEC*, vol. XIII, P. Dockès, C. Mouchot and J.-P. Potier (Eds), Paris: Economica, 2000, p. 483–488.

Walras, L. (1875a), « L'État et les chemins de fer », *Revue du droit public et de la science politique en France et à l'étranger*, vol. 7, n°3, May–June et vol. 8, n°1, July–August 1897, in: *Études d'économie politique appliquée, OEC*, vol. X, J.-P. Potier (Ed), Paris: Economica, 1992, p. 183–214.

Walras, L. (1875b), « *Biblioteca dell'Economista* », *Journal des économistes,* 3rd series, tome 40, vol. 10, n°118, October, in: *Théorie mathématique de la richesse sociale et autres écrits d'économie pure, OEC*, vol. XI, C. Mouchot (Ed), Paris: Economica, 1993, Annexe I, p. 607–608.

Walras, L. (1876a), « La loi fédérale sur le travail dans les fabriques », *Gazette des tribunaux suisses*, vol. 2, n°5, 10 February, in: *Mélanges d'économie politique et sociale, OEC*, vol. VII, C. Hébert and J.-P. Potier (Eds), Paris: Economica, 1987, p. 219–229.

Walras, L. (1876b), « Une branche nouvelle de la mathématique. De l'application des mathématiques à l'économie politique », in: *Mélanges d'économie politique et sociale, OEC*, vol. VII, C. Hébert and J.-P. Potier (Eds), Paris: Economica, 1987, p. 291–329.

Walras, L. (1876c), « Note sur l'impôt progressif », in: *Études d'économie sociale, OEC*, vol. IX, P. Dockès (Ed), Paris: Economica, 1990, p. 479–482.

Walras, L. (1877), *Éléments d'économie politique pure, ou Théorie de la richesse sociale.* Second part, 1st ed. Lausanne/ Paris/ Basel: Corbaz/ Guillaumin/ Georg, in: *Éléments d'économie politique pure, OEC*, vol. VIII, C. Mouchot (Ed), Paris: Economica, 1988.

Walras, L. (1878a), « Discours de M. Du Bois-Reymond sur l'histoire de la civilisation et la science de la nature - L'américanisme », *Gazette de Lausanne*, 23 February, in: *Œuvres diverses, OEC*, vol. XIII, P. Dockès, C. Mouchot and J.-P. Potier (Eds), Paris: Economica, 2000, p. 491–497.

Walras, L. (1878b), en collaboration avec W. S. Jevons, « Bibliographie des ouvrages relatifs à l'application des mathématiques à l'économie politique », *Journal des économistes.* 4th series, tome 4, vol. 1, n°12, 15 December, in: *Théorie mathématique de la richesse sociale et autres écrits d'économie pure, OEC*, vol. XI, C. Mouchot (Ed), Paris: Economica, 1993, Annex II, p. 609–622.

Walras, L. (1879a), Translation of *Entwickelung der Gesetze des menschlichen Verkehrs, und der daraus fliessenden Regeln für menschliches Handeln* by H. H. Gossen, with the collaboration of C. Secrétan, *Exposition des lois de l'échange et des règles de l'industrie qui s'en déduisent*, J. Van Daal, A. Jolink, J.-P. Potier and J.-M. Servet (Eds), Paris: Economica, 1995.

Walras, L. (1879b), « Défense des salaires » [conference], in: *Études d'économie politique appliquée, OEC*, vol. X, J.-P. Potier (Ed), Paris: Economica, 1992, note 27, p. 481–484.

Walras, L. (1879c), « De la culture et de l'enseignement des sciences morales et politiques », *Bibliothèque Universelle et Revue Suisse.* 3rd period, tome 3, vol. 84, n°7 et 8, July and August, in: *Mélanges d'économie politique et sociale, OEC*, vol. VII, C. Hébert and J.-P. Potier (Eds), Paris: Economica, 1987, p. 377–418.

Walras, L. (1879d), « Note sur l'organisation de l'enseignement de l'économie politique et sociale à l'École pratique des Hautes Études », in: *Mélanges d'économie politique et sociale, OEC*, vol. VII, C. Hébert and J.-P. Potier (Eds), Paris: Economica, 1987, p. 419–423.

Walras, L. (1879e), « De l'émission des billets de banque », *Gazette de Lausanne*, 2 and 3 December 1879, in: *Œuvres diverses, OEC*, vol. XIII, P. Dockès, C. Mouchot and J.-P. Potier (Eds), Paris: Economica, 2000, p. 385–390.

Walras, L. (1880a), Translation of *The Theory of Political Economy* by W. S. Jevons, 2nd edition, 1879, *La Théorie de l'économie politique, traduite par Léon Walras.* Critical edition by N. Chaigneau and J.-P. Potier, Paris: Editions Classiques Garnier, 2022.

Walras, L. (1880b), « La Bourse, la spéculation et l'agiotage », *Bibliothèque Universelle et Revue Suisse.* 3rd period, tomes 5 et 6, vol. 85, n°3 et 4, March and April, in: *Études d'économie politique appliquée, OEC*, vol. X, J.-P. Potier (Ed), Paris: Economica, 1992, p. 365–401.

Walras, L. (1880c), « De la propriété intellectuelle », *Gazette de Lausanne*, 10, 11 et 12 june, in: *Études d'économie sociale, OEC*, vol. IX, P. Dockès (Ed), Paris: Economica, 1990, p. 213–226.

Walras, L. (1880d), « De l'enseignement de l'économie politique en France », in: *Mélanges d'économie politique et sociale, OEC*, vol. VII, C. Hébert and J.-P. Potier (Eds), Paris: Economica, 1987, p. 424–442.

Walras, L. (1880e), « Théorie mathématique du billet de banque », *Bulletin de la Société vaudoise des sciences naturelles.* 2nd series, vol. 16, n°83, May, in: *Études d'économie politique appliquée, OEC*, vol. X, J.-P. Potier (Ed), Paris: Economica, 1992, p. 311–342.

Walras, L. (1881a), « Théorie mathématique du bimétallisme », *Journal des économistes,* 4th series, tome 14, vol. 4, n°5, May, in: *Théorie mathématique de la richesse sociale et autres écrits d'économie pure, OEC*, vol. XI, C. Mouchot (Ed), Paris: Economica, 1993, p. 137–155.

Walras, L. (1881b), « Théorie mathématique du prix des terres et de leur rachat par l'État », *Bulletin de la Société vaudoise des sciences naturelles.* 2nd series, vol. 17, n°85, June, in: *Études d'économie sociale, OEC*, vol. IX, P. Dockès (Ed), Paris: Economica, 1990, p. 229–309.

Walras, L. (1883), *Théorie mathématique de la richesse sociale* (7 memoirs). Lausanne/ Paris/ Roma/ Leipzig: Corbaz/ Guillaumin/ Loescher/ Duncker und Humblot, in: *Théorie mathématique de la richesse sociale et autres écrits d'économie pure, OEC*, vol. XI, C. Mouchot (Ed), Paris: Economica, 1993, p. 23–278.

Walras, L. (1884), « Monnaie d'or avec billon d'argent régulateur. Principes proposés à la conférence monétaire internationale pour la prorogation de l'Union Latine », *Revue de droit international et de législation comparée*, vol. 16, n°6, 1st December, in: *Études d'économie politique appliquée, OEC*, vol. X, J.-P. Potier (Ed), Paris: Economica, 1992, p. 5–18.

Walras, L. (1885a), « Un économiste inconnu, Hermann-Henri Gossen », *Journal des économistes.* 4th series, tome 30, vol. 8, n°4, April, in: *Études d'économie sociale, OEC*, vol. IX, P. Dockès (Ed), Paris: Economica, 1990, p. 311–330.

Walras, L. (1885b), « *Primi Elementi di Economia politica* et *Primi Elementi di Scienza delle Finanze* de Luigi Cossa », *Bibliothèque Universelle et Revue Suisse*, tome 27, vol. 90, n°8, August, in: *Œuvres diverses, OEC*, vol. XIII, P. Dockès, C. Mouchot and J.-P. Potier (Eds), Paris: Economica, 2000, p. 499–500.

Walras, L. (1886a), *Théorie de la monnaie.* Lausanne/Paris/Roma/Leipzig: Corbaz/Larose et Forcel/ Löscher/Dunker und Humblot, in: *Études d'économie politique appliquée, OEC*, vol. X, J.-P. Potier (Ed), Paris: Economica, 1992, p. 57–145.

Walras, L. (1886b), « La question sociale, par Ch. Secrétan », *Gazette de Lausanne*, 22 July, in: *Études d'économie sociale, OEC*, vol. IX, P. Dockès (Ed), Paris: Economica, 1990, p. 207–211.

Walras, L. (1889a), « Théorème de l'utilité maxima des capitaux neufs », *Revue d'économie politique*, vol. 3, n°3, May–June, in: *Théorie mathématique de la richesse sociale et autres écrits d'économie pure, OEC*, vol. XI, C. Mouchot (Ed), Paris: Economica, 1993, p. 517–522.

Walras, L. (1889b], « Des fonctions et de leur représentation géométrique. Théorie mathématique de la chute des corps », in: *Éléments d'économie politique pure ou théorie de la richesse sociale.* Lausanne: Rouge, re-ed. in: *Mélanges d'économie politique et sociale, OEC*, vol. VII, C. Hébert and J.-P. Potier (Eds), Paris: Economica, 1987, p. 236–260.

Walras, L. (1889c), *Éléments d'économie politique pure, ou théorie de la richesse sociale.* 2nd ed. Lausanne/ Paris/ Leipzig: Rouge/ Guillaumin/ Duncker und Humblot, in: *Éléments d'économie politique pure, OEC*, vol. VIII, C. Mouchot (Ed), Paris: Economica, 1988. English translation, *Elements of Theoretical Economics, or The Theory of Social Wealth* [second–third edition], D. A. Walker and J. van Daal (Eds), Cambridge : Cambridge University Press, 2014.

Walras, L. (1890), « Observations sur le principe de la théorie du prix de MM. Auspitz et Lieben », *Revue d'économie politique*, vol. 4, n°3, May–June, Appendice II, in: *Éléments d'économie politique pure, OEC*, vol. VIII, C. Mouchot (Ed), Paris: Economica, 1988, p. 711–714.

Walras, L. (1891), « De l'échange de plusieurs marchandises entre elles », *Mémoires et Compte Rendu des Travaux de la Société des Ingénieurs Civils.* 5e série, vol. 44, n°1, January, in: *Théorie mathématique de la richesse sociale et autres écrits d'économie pure, OEC*, vol. XI, C. Mouchot (Ed), Paris: Economica, 1993, p. 523–538.

Walras, L. (1892), « Théorie géométrique de la détermination des prix. De l'échange de produits et services entre eux. De l'échange d'épargnes contre capitaux neufs », *Recueil Inaugural de l'Université de Lausanne, Travaux des Facultés*, Lausanne: Imprimerie Ch. Viret-Genton, in: *Éléments d'économie politique pure, OEC*, vol. VIII, C. Mouchot (Ed), Paris: Economica, 1988, p. 693–710.

Walras, L. (1893), « Université de Lausanne [Entrefilet Pareto] », *Gazette de Lausanne*, 15 April, in: *Cours, OEC*, vol. XII, P. Dockès, J.- P. Potier, P. Bridel (Eds), Paris, Economica, 1996, p. 37–40.

Walras, L. (1895), « Le péril bimétalliste », *Revue socialiste*, vol. 22, n°127, 15 July, in: *Études d'économie politique appliquée, OEC*, vol. X, J.-P. Potier (Ed), Paris: Economica, 1992, p. 167–180.

Walras, L. (1896a), *Éléments d'économie politique pure, ou Théorie de la richesse sociale.* 3e éd. Lausanne/ Paris/Leipzig: Rouge/Guillaumin/ Duncker und Humblot, in: *Éléments d'économie politique pure, OEC*, vol. VIII, C. Mouchot (Ed), Paris: Economica, 1988. English translation, *Elements of Theoretical Economics, or The Theory of Social Wealth* [second–third edition], D. A. Walker and J. van Daal (Eds), Cambridge : Cambridge University Press, 2014.

Walras, L. (1896b), « Note sur la réfutation de la théorie anglaise du fermage de M. Wicksteed », *Recueil publié par la faculté de droit de l'Université de Lausanne à l'occasion de l'exposition nationale suisse*, Lausanne: Viret-Genton, in: *Éléments d'économie politique pure, OEC*, vol. VIII, C. Mouchot (Ed), Paris: Economica, 1988, p. 715–722.

Walras, L. (1896c), « Théorie de la propriété », *Revue socialiste*, vol. 23 et 24, n°138 et 139, 15 June and 15 July, in: *Études d'économie sociale, OEC*, vol. IX, P. Dockès (Ed), Paris: Economica, 1990, p. 177–212.

Walras, L. (1896d), « Le problème fiscal », *Revue socialiste*, vol. 24, n°142 et 143, 15 October and 15 November, in: *Études d'économie sociale, OEC*, vol. IX, P. Dockès (Ed), Paris: Economica, 1990, p. 391–424.

Walras, L. (1896e), *Études d'économie sociale (Théorie de la répartition de la richesse sociale)*, 1st ed. Lausanne/ Paris: Rouge/ Pichon, in: *Études d'économie sociale, OEC*, vol. IX, P. Dockès (Ed), Paris: Economica, 1990. English translation, *Studies in Social Economics.* J. van Daal and D. A. Walker (Eds), Abingdon: Routledge, 2010.

Walras, L. (1897a), « Théorie du libre-échange », *Revue d'économie politique*, vol. 11, n°7, July, in: *Études d'économie politique appliquée, OEC*, vol. X, J.-P. Potier (Ed), Paris: Economica, 1992, p. 263–279.

Walras, L. (1897b), «Note » [at the end of the article « L'État et les chemins de fer »], *Revue du droit public et de la science politique en France et à l'étranger*, vol. 8, n°1, July–August 1897, in: *Études d'économie politique appliquée, OEC*, vol. X, J.-P. Potier (Ed), Paris: Economica, 1992, p. 215–218.

Walras, L. (1897c), « L'économique appliquée et la défense des salaires », *Revue d'économie politique*, vol. 11, n°12, December, in: *Études d'économie politique appliquée, OEC*, vol. X, J.-P. Potier (Ed), Paris: Economica, 1992, p. 245–261.

Walras, L. (1898a), « À l'Université [Réclame Charles Gide] », *Gazette de Lausanne*, 10 January, p. 3.

Walras, L. (1898b), « Théorie du crédit », *Revue d'économie politique*, vol. 12, n°2, february, in: *Études d'économie politique appliquée, OEC*, vol. X, J.-P. Potier (Ed), Paris: Economica, 1992, p. 283–307.

Walras, L. (1898c), « Esquisse d'une doctrine économique et sociale », in: *Études d'économie politique appliquée, OEC*, vol. X, J.-P. Potier (Ed), Paris: Economica, 1992, p. 405–441.

Walras, L. (1898d), *Études d'économie politique appliquée (Théorie de la production de la richesse sociale)*, 1st ed. Lausanne/ Paris: Rouge/ Pichon, in: *Études d'économie politique appliquée, OEC*, vol. X, J.-P. Potier (Ed), Paris: Economica, 1992. English translation, *Studies in Applied Economics. Theory of the Production of Social Wealth*, J. van Daal (Ed), Abingdon : Routledge, 2005, 2 vols.

Walras, L. (1899), « Équations de la circulation », *Bulletin de la Société vaudoise des sciences naturelles.* 2nd series, vol. 35, n°132, June, in: *Théorie mathématique de la richesse sociale et autres écrits d'économie pure, OEC*, vol. XI, C. Mouchot (Ed), Paris: Economica, 1993, p. 563–588.

Walras, L. (1900), *Éléments d'économie politique pure, ou Théorie de la richesse sociale.* 4th ed. Lausanne/ Paris: Rouge/ Pichon, in: *Éléments d'économie politique pure, OEC*, vol. VIII, C. Mouchot (Ed), Paris: Economica, 1988. English translation *Elements of Theoretical Economics, or The Theory of Social Wealth* [definitive edition], W. Jaffé (Ed), London : George Allen & Unwin, 1954.

Walras, L. (1902), « Entrevue avec M. Léon Say en 1883 », in: *Les associations populaires coopératives, OEC*, vol. VI, C. Hébert and J.-P. Potier (Eds), Paris: Economica, 1990, p. 3–8.

Walras, L. (1905), « Cournot et l'économique mathématique », *Gazette de Lausanne*, 13 July, in: *Mélanges d'économie politique et sociale, OEC*, vol. VII, C. Hébert and J.-P. Potier (Eds), Paris: Economica, 1987, p. 461–466.

Walras, L. (1907a), « La paix par la justice sociale et le libre-échange », *Questions pratiques de législation ouvrière et d'économie sociale*, vol. 8, n°6, 7–8 et 9–10, June, July–August and September–October, in: *Mélanges d'économie politique et sociale, OEC*, vol. VII, C. Hébert and J.-P. Potier (Eds), Paris: Economica, 1987, p. 467–503.

Walras, L. (1907–1908), Notes on « Masse et rareté », in: *Théorie mathématique de la richesse sociale et autres écrits d'économie pure, OEC*, vol. XI, C. Mouchot (Ed), Paris: Economica, 1993, Annex III, p. 623–650.

Walras, L. (1908a), Notes for « Ruchonnet et le socialisme scientifique », in: *Œuvres diverses, OEC*, vol. XIII, P. Dockès, C. Mouchot and J.-P. Potier (Eds), Paris: Economica, 2000, p. 649–652.

Walras, L. (1908b), « Un initiateur en économie politique, A. A. Walras », *Revue du Mois*, tome VI, vol. 3, n°32, 10 August, in: *Correspondance OEC*, vol. IV, C. Hébert (Ed), Paris: Economica, 2004, p.30–47.

Walras, L. (1909a), « Notice autobiographique », in: *L'économie politique et la justice*, vol. V des *OEC*, edited by P.-H. Goutte and J.-M. Servet, Paris: Economica, 2001, p. 11–27.

Walras, L. (1909b), « Économique et mécanique », *Bulletin de la Société vaudoise des sciences naturelles*. 5e série, vol. 45, n°166, June, in: *Mélanges d'économie politique et sociale, OEC*, vol. VII, C. Hébert and J.-P. Potier (Eds), Paris: Economica, 1987, p. 330–341.

Walras, L. (1909c), « Ruchonnet et le socialisme scientifique », *Gazette de Lausanne*, 11 June, in: *Mélanges d'économie politique et sociale, OEC*, vol. VII, C. Hébert and J.-P. Potier (Eds), Paris: Economica, 1987, p. 504–514.

Walras, L. (1910), « Doctrines économiques », *Gazette de Lausanne*, 6 january, in: *Mélanges d'économie politique et sociale, OEC*, vol. VII, C. Hébert and J.-P. Potier (Eds), Paris: Economica, 1987, p. 515–517.

Walras, L. (1965), *Correspondence of Léon Walras and Related Papers*, William JAFFÉ (Ed), Amsterdam: North Holland, vol. I (1857–1883), vol. II (1884–1897), vol. III (1898–1909)

Walras, L. (1996), *Cours (Cours d'économie sociale, Cours d'économie politique appliquée,* Matériaux sur le *Cours d'économie politique pure), OEC*, vol. XII, P. Dockès, J.- P. Potier, P. Bridel (Eds), Paris, Economica.

Walras, L. (2000), « Notes d'humeur », in: *Œuvres diverses, OEC*, vol. XIII, P. Dockès, C. Mouchot and J.-P. Potier (Eds), Paris: Economica, p. 501–622.

Walras, A. and L. (2005), *Tables et index, OEC*, vol XIV, R. Baranzini, C. Mouchot and J.-P. Potier (Eds), Paris: Economica.

Wicksell, K. (1898), "Léon Walras, *Études d'économie sociale*", *Jahrbücher für National-ökonomie und Statistik*, vol. 15, 3rd series, January, English translation in: *Selected Essays in Economics*, B. Sandelin (ed), London: Routledge, vol. II, p. 171–174.

Wolfelsperger, A. (1972), « Introduction au Catéchisme de Jean-Baptiste Say», in: J.-B. Say, *Catéchisme d'économie politique*, Paris: Mame, p. 5–29.

Wright, J. (2012), « Réformisme et historiographie révolutionnaire. Georges Renard et Eugène Fournière, historiens du XIXe siècle », *Mil neuf cent*, n°30, p. 21–38.

Zouboulakis, M. (2000), « Éclectisme théorique et libéralisme pragmatique dans l'œuvre de Clément Colson », in: P. DOCKÈS, L. FROBERT, G. KLOTZ, J.-P. POTIER, A. TIRAN (Eds), *Les traditions économiques françaises, 1848–1939*, Paris: Éd. du C.N.R.S., p. 581–593.

Zylberberg, A. (1988), « L'économie mathématique chez les actuaires français au temps de Walras (1870–1914) », *Économies et sociétés-Cahiers de l'ISMEA*, vol. XXII, n°3, Œconomia series, Histoire de la pensée économique, n°9, p. 35–63.

Zylberberg, A. (1990), *L'Économie mathématique en France. 1870–1914*, Paris: Economica.

Zylberberg, A. (1994), « Les premiers disciples français de Léon Walras », *Économies et sociétés-Cahiers de l'ISMEA*, vol. XXVIII, n°10–11, Œconomia series, Histoire de la pensée économique, n°20–21, p. 75–85.

Université de Lausanne. Jubilé Walras (1909), Lausanne: Imprimeries réunies.

Université de Lausanne. Jubilé du Professeur V. Pareto. 1917, *Œuvres complètes*, G. Busino (ed), Geneva: Droz, vol. XX, 1975.

Author Index

J.-P. Potier, *Léon Walras, Economist and Liberal Socialist*, Springer Studies in the History of Economic Thought, https://doi.org/10.1007/978-3-032-04670-3

Subject Index

J.-P. Potier, *Léon Walras, Economist and Liberal Socialist*, Springer Studies in the History of Economic Thought, https://doi.org/10.1007/978-3-032-04670-3

MIX
Papier aus verantwortungsvollen Quellen
Paper from responsible sources
FSC® C105338

If you have any concerns about our products,
you can contact us on
ProductSafety@springernature.com

In case Publisher is established outside the EU,
the EU authorized representative is:
Springer Nature Customer Service Center GmbH
Europaplatz 3, 69115 Heidelberg, Germany

Printed by Libri Plureos GmbH
in Hamburg, Germany